Mitsubishi Eclipse & Eagle Talon Automotive Repair Manual

by Alan Ahlstrand
and John H Haynes
Member of the Guild of Motoring Writers

Models covered:

All Mitsubishi Eclipse models - 1995 through 2005
All Eagle Talon models - 1995 through 1998

(6Q9 - 68031)   ᴬ

Haynes Publishing Group
Sparkford Nr Yeovil
Somerset BA22 7JJ England

Haynes North America, Inc
861 Lawrence Drive
Newbury Park
California 91320 USA

About this manual

Its purpose

The purpose of this manual is to help you get the best value from your vehicle. It can do so in several ways. It can help you decide what work must be done, even if you choose to have it done by a dealer service department or a repair shop; it provides information and procedures for routine maintenance and servicing; and it offers diagnostic and repair procedures to follow when trouble occurs.

We hope you use the manual to tackle the work yourself. For many simpler jobs, doing it yourself may be quicker than arranging an appointment to get the vehicle into a shop and making the trips to leave it and pick it up. More importantly, a lot of money can be saved by avoiding the expense the shop must pass on to you to cover its labor and overhead costs. An added benefit is the sense of satisfaction and accomplishment that you feel after doing the job yourself.

Using the manual

The manual is divided into Chapters. Each Chapter is divided into numbered Sections, which are headed in bold type between horizontal lines. Each Section consists of consecutively numbered paragraphs.

At the beginning of each numbered Section you will be referred to any illustrations which apply to the procedures in that Section. The reference numbers used in illustration captions pinpoint the pertinent Section and the Step within that Section. That is, illustration 3.2 means the illustration refers to Section 3 and Step (or paragraph) 2 within that Section.

Procedures, once described in the text, are not normally repeated. When it's necessary to refer to another Chapter, the reference will be given as Chapter and Section number. Cross references given without use of the word "Chapter" apply to Sections and/or paragraphs in the same Chapter. For example, "see Section 8" means in the same Chapter.

References to the left or right side of the vehicle assume you are sitting in the driver's seat, facing forward.

Even though we have prepared this manual with extreme care, neither the publisher nor the author can accept responsibility for any errors in, or omissions from, the information given.

NOTE

A **Note** provides information necessary to properly complete a procedure or information which will make the procedure easier to understand.

CAUTION

A **Caution** provides a special procedure or special steps which must be taken while completing the procedure where the Caution is found. Not heeding a Caution can result in damage to the assembly being worked on.

WARNING

A **Warning** provides a special procedure or special steps which must be taken while completing the procedure where the Warning is found. Not heeding a Warning can result in personal injury.

Acknowledgements

We are grateful to the Chrysler Corporation for providing technical information and certain illustrations.

© Haynes North America, Inc. 2002, 2008
With permission from J.H. Haynes & Co. Ltd.

A book in the Haynes Automotive Repair Manual Series

Printed in the U.S.A.

ISBN 13: 978-1-56392-707-2
ISBN 10: 1-56392-707-1

Library of Congress Control Number: 2008920977

Contents

Haynes author, mechanic and photographer with 2001 Mitsubishi Eclipse Spyder

Introduction to the
Mitsubishi Eclipse and Eagle Talon

These models are available in two-door liftback and convertible body styles.

The transversely mounted engines used in these models come in inline four-cylinder and V6 designs. All are equipped with electronic fuel injection. Some models are turbocharged.

The engine drives the front wheels through either a five-speed manual or an automatic transaxle via independent drive-axles. Some models use a transfer case and driveshaft to send power to a rear differential and then to the rear wheels, with independent driveaxles to provide four-wheel drive (4WD).

Independent suspension, featuring coil spring/strut damper units, is used on all four wheels. The power-assisted rack-and-pinion steering unit is mounted behind the engine.

The brakes are disc at the front wheels and disc or drum at the rear, with power assist standard.

Vehicle identification numbers

Modifications are a continuing and unpublicized process in vehicle manufacturing. Since spare parts lists and manuals are compiled on a numerical basis, the individual vehicle numbers are necessary to correctly identify the component required.

Vehicle Identification Number (VIN)

This very important identification number is stamped on a plate attached to the dashboard inside the windshield on the driver's side of the vehicle **(see illustration)**. The VIN also appears on the Vehicle Certificate of Title and Registration. It contains information such as where and when the vehicle was manufactured, the model year and the body style.

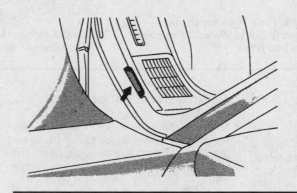

The Vehicle Identification Number (VIN) is important for identifying the vehicle and engine type - it is on the front of the dash, visible from outside the vehicle, looking through the windshield on the driver's side

The type of engine installed in the vehicle is indicated by the eighth digit of the VIN. A Y indicates a 2.0L DOHC non-turbo four-cylinder engine, an F indicates a 2.0L DOHC turbo four-cylinder engine, a G indicates a 2.4L SOHC non-turbo four-cylinder engine, and an H indicates a 3.0L SOHC V6 engine.

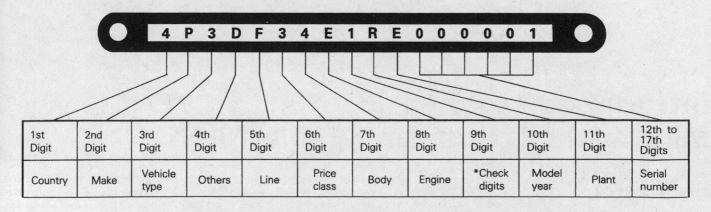

1st Digit	2nd Digit	3rd Digit	4th Digit	5th Digit	6th Digit	7th Digit	8th Digit	9th Digit	10th Digit	11th Digit	12th to 17th Digits
Country	Make	Vehicle type	Others	Line	Price class	Body	Engine	*Check digits	Model year	Plant	Serial number

This chart shows the information conveyed by the VIN. Check Digits are used by the factory to verify the correct VIN. The eighth digit identifies the engine - see the text for further explanation.

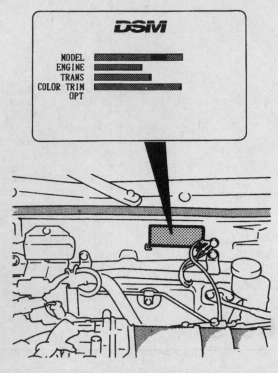

The Vehicle Identification Code Plate is on the engine compartment firewall - it is particularly useful in identifying paint and trim colors and types

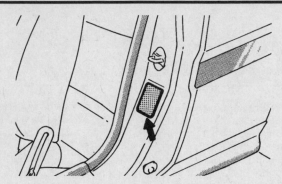

The Vehicle Certification Label is visible in the door jamb, after opening the driver's side door

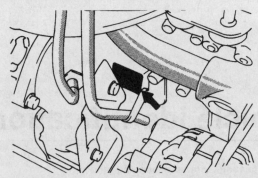

The engine model number is stamped onto a pad on the front side of the engine - see the text for an explanation of the number

Vehicle Identification Code Plate

The Vehicle identification code plate is riveted to the engine compartment firewall **(see illustration)**. The plate lists the model code, engine model, transaxle model and body code. Also listed is the paint and trim code.

Vehicle Certification Label

The Vehicle Certification Label is attached to the driver's side door pillar **(see illustration)**. Information on this label includes the name of the manufacturer, the month and year of production, the Gross Vehicle Weight Rating (GVWR), the Gross Axle Weight Rating (GAWR) and the certification statement.

Engine model number

The engine model number is stamped onto a machined pad on the front (radiator) side of the engine block **(see illustration)**. 2.0L DOHC non-turbo engines are designated by the model number 420A. 2.0L DOHC turbo engines are designated by the model number 4G63. 2.4L SOHC engines are designated by the model number 4G64. V6 engines are designated by the model number 6G72.

Buying parts

Replacement parts are available from many sources, which generally fall into one of two categories - authorized dealer parts departments and independent retail auto parts stores. Our advice concerning these parts is as follows:

Retail auto parts stores: Good auto parts stores will stock frequently needed components which wear out relatively fast, such as clutch components, exhaust systems, brake parts, tune-up parts, etc. These stores often supply new or reconditioned parts on

an exchange basis, which can save a considerable amount of money. Discount auto parts stores are often very good places to buy materials and parts needed for general vehicle maintenance such as oil, grease, filters, spark plugs, belts, touch-up paint, bulbs, etc. They also usually sell tools and general accessories, have convenient hours, charge lower prices and can often be found not far from home.

Authorized dealer parts department: This is the best source for parts which are

unique to the vehicle and not generally available elsewhere (such as major engine parts, transmission parts, trim pieces, etc.).

Warranty information: If the vehicle is still covered under warranty, be sure that any replacement parts purchased - regardless of the source - do not invalidate the warranty!

To be sure of obtaining the correct parts, have engine and chassis numbers available and, if possible, take the old parts along for positive identification.

Maintenance techniques, tools and working facilities

Maintenance techniques

There are a number of techniques involved in maintenance and repair that will be referred to throughout this manual. Application of these techniques will enable the home mechanic to be more efficient, better organized and capable of performing the various tasks properly, which will ensure that the repair job is thorough and complete.

Fasteners

Fasteners are nuts, bolts, studs and screws used to hold two or more parts together. There are a few things to keep in mind when working with fasteners. Almost all of them use a locking device of some type, either a lockwasher, locknut, locking tab or thread adhesive. All threaded fasteners should be clean and straight, with undamaged threads and undamaged corners on the hex head where the wrench fits. Develop the habit of replacing all damaged nuts and bolts with new ones. Special locknuts with nylon or fiber inserts can only be used once. If they are removed, they lose their locking ability and must be replaced with new ones.

Rusted nuts and bolts should be treated with a penetrating fluid to ease removal and prevent breakage. Some mechanics use turpentine in a spout-type oil can, which works quite well. After applying the rust penetrant, let it work for a few minutes before trying to loosen the nut or bolt. Badly rusted fasteners may have to be chiseled or sawed off or removed with a special nut breaker, available at tool stores.

If a bolt or stud breaks off in an assembly, it can be drilled and removed with a special tool commonly available for this purpose. Most automotive machine shops can perform

this task, as well as other repair procedures, such as the repair of threaded holes that have been stripped out.

Flat washers and lockwashers, when removed from an assembly, should always

be replaced exactly as removed. Replace any damaged washers with new ones. Never use a lockwasher on any soft metal surface (such as aluminum), thin sheet metal or plastic.

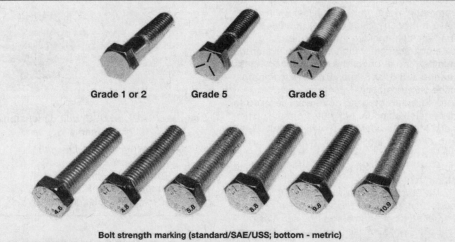

Grade 1 or 2   Grade 5   Grade 8

Bolt strength marking (standard/SAE/USS; bottom - metric)

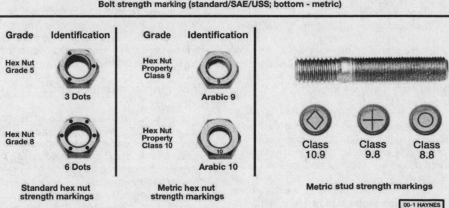

Grade	Identification	Grade	Identification
Hex Nut Grade 5	3 Dots	Hex Nut Property Class 9	Arabic 9
Hex Nut Grade 8	6 Dots	Hex Nut Property Class 10	Arabic 10

Standard hex nut strength markings

Metric hex nut strength markings

Class 10.9   Class 9.8   Class 8.8

Metric stud strength markings

00-1 HAYNES

Fastener sizes

For a number of reasons, automobile manufacturers are making wider and wider use of metric fasteners. Therefore, it is important to be able to tell the difference between standard (sometimes called U.S. or SAE) and metric hardware, since they cannot be interchanged.

All bolts, whether standard or metric, are sized according to diameter, thread pitch and length. For example, a standard 1/2 - 13 x 1 bolt is 1/2 inch in diameter, has 13 threads per inch and is 1 inch long. An M12 - 1.75 x 25 metric bolt is 12 mm in diameter, has a thread pitch of 1.75 mm (the distance between threads) and is 25 mm long. The two bolts are nearly identical, and easily confused, but they are not interchangeable.

In addition to the differences in diameter, thread pitch and length, metric and standard bolts can also be distinguished by examining the bolt heads. To begin with, the distance across the flats on a standard bolt head is measured in inches, while the same dimension on a metric bolt is sized in millimeters (the same is true for nuts). As a result, a standard wrench should not be used on a metric bolt and a metric wrench should not be used on a standard bolt. Also, most standard bolts have slashes radiating out from the center of the head to denote the grade or strength of the bolt, which is an indication of the amount of torque that can be applied to it. The greater the number of slashes, the greater the strength of the bolt. Grades 0 through 5 are commonly used on automobiles. Metric bolts have a property class (grade) number, rather than a slash, molded into their heads to indicate bolt strength. In this case, the higher the number, the stronger the bolt. Property class numbers 8.8, 9.8 and 10.9 are commonly used on automobiles.

Strength markings can also be used to distinguish standard hex nuts from metric hex nuts. Many standard nuts have dots stamped into one side, while metric nuts are marked with a number. The greater the number of dots, or the higher the number, the greater the strength of the nut.

Metric studs are also marked on their ends according to property class (grade). Larger studs are numbered (the same as metric bolts), while smaller studs carry a geometric code to denote grade.

It should be noted that many fasteners, especially Grades 0 through 2, have no distinguishing marks on them. When such is the case, the only way to determine whether it is standard or metric is to measure the thread pitch or compare it to a known fastener of the same size.

Standard fasteners are often referred to as SAE, as opposed to metric. However, it should be noted that SAE technically refers to a non-metric fine thread fastener only. Coarse thread non-metric fasteners are referred to as USS sizes.

Since fasteners of the same size (both standard and metric) may have different strength ratings, be sure to reinstall any bolts, studs or nuts removed from your vehicle in their original locations. Also, when replacing a fastener with a new one, make sure that the new one has a strength rating equal to or greater than the original.

Metric thread sizes	Ft-lbs	Nm
M-6	6 to 9	9 to 12
M-8	14 to 21	19 to 28
M-10	28 to 40	38 to 54
M-12	50 to 71	68 to 96
M-14	80 to 140	109 to 154

Pipe thread sizes	Ft-lbs	Nm
1/8	5 to 8	7 to 10
1/4	12 to 18	17 to 24
3/8	22 to 33	30 to 44
1/2	25 to 35	34 to 47

U.S. thread sizes	Ft-lbs	Nm
1/4 - 20	6 to 9	9 to 12
5/16 - 18	12 to 18	17 to 24
5/16 - 24	14 to 20	19 to 27
3/8 - 16	22 to 32	30 to 43
3/8 - 24	27 to 38	37 to 51
7/16 - 14	40 to 55	55 to 74
7/16 - 20	40 to 60	55 to 81
1/2 - 13	55 to 80	75 to 108

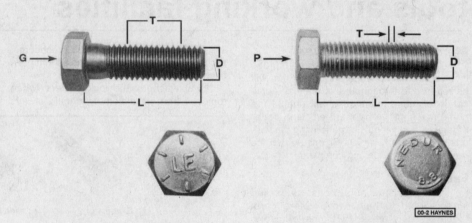

Standard (SAE and USS) bolt dimensions/grade marks

G   Grade marks (bolt strength)
L   Length (in inches)
T   Thread pitch (number of threads per inch)
D   Nominal diameter (in inches)

Metric bolt dimensions/grade marks

P   Property class (bolt strength)
L   Length (in millimeters)
T   Thread pitch (distance between threads in millimeters)
D   Diameter

Tightening sequences and procedures

Most threaded fasteners should be tightened to a specific torque value (torque is the twisting force applied to a threaded component such as a nut or bolt). Overtightening the fastener can weaken it and cause it to break, while undertightening can cause it to eventually come loose. Bolts, screws and studs, depending on the material they are made of and their thread diameters, have specific torque values, many of which are noted in the Specifications at the beginning of each Chapter. Be sure to follow the torque recommendations closely. For fasteners not assigned a specific torque, a general torque value chart is presented here as a guide. These torque values are for dry (unlubricated) fasteners threaded into steel or cast iron (not aluminum). As was previously mentioned, the size and grade of a fastener determine the amount of torque that can safely be applied to it. The figures listed here are approximate for Grade 2 and Grade 3 fasteners. Higher grades can tolerate higher torque values.

Fasteners laid out in a pattern, such as cylinder head bolts, oil pan bolts, differential

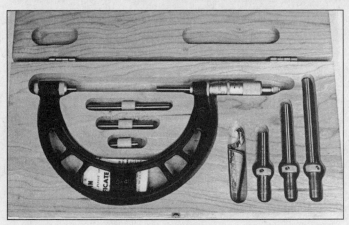
Micrometer set

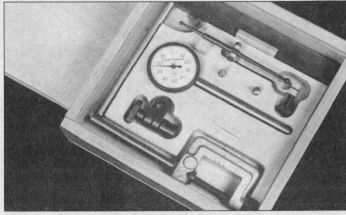
Dial indicator set

cover bolts, etc., must be loosened or tightened in sequence to avoid warping the component. This sequence will normally be shown in the appropriate Chapter. If a specific pattern is not given, the following procedures can be used to prevent warping.

Initially, the bolts or nuts should be assembled finger-tight only. Next, they should be tightened one full turn each, in a crisscross or diagonal pattern. After each one has been tightened one full turn, return to the first one and tighten them all one-half turn, following the same pattern. Finally, tighten each of them one-quarter turn at a time until each fastener has been tightened to the proper torque. To loosen and remove the fasteners, the procedure would be reversed.

Component disassembly

Component disassembly should be done with care and purpose to help ensure that the parts go back together properly. Always keep track of the sequence in which parts are removed. Make note of special characteristics or marks on parts that can be installed more than one way, such as a grooved thrust washer on a shaft. It is a good idea to lay the disassembled parts out on a clean surface in the order that they were removed. It may also be helpful to make sketches or take instant photos of components before removal.

When removing fasteners from a component, keep track of their locations. Sometimes threading a bolt back in a part, or putting the washers and nut back on a stud, can prevent mix-ups later. If nuts and bolts cannot be returned to their original locations, they should be kept in a compartmented box or a series of small boxes. A cupcake or muffin tin is ideal for this purpose, since each cavity can hold the bolts and nuts from a particular area (i.e. oil pan bolts, valve cover bolts, engine mount bolts, etc.). A pan of this type is especially helpful when working on assemblies with very small parts, such as the carburetor, alternator, valve train or interior dash and trim pieces. The cavities can be marked with paint or tape to identify the contents.

Whenever wiring looms, harnesses or connectors are separated, it is a good idea to identify the two halves with numbered pieces of masking tape so they can be easily reconnected.

Gasket sealing surfaces

Throughout any vehicle, gaskets are used to seal the mating surfaces between two parts and keep lubricants, fluids, vacuum or pressure contained in an assembly.

Many times these gaskets are coated with a liquid or paste-type gasket sealing compound before assembly. Age, heat and pressure can sometimes cause the two parts to stick together so tightly that they are very difficult to separate. Often, the assembly can be loosened by striking it with a soft-face hammer near the mating surfaces. A regular hammer can be used if a block of wood is placed between the hammer and the part. Do not hammer on cast parts or parts that could be easily damaged. With any particularly stubborn part, always recheck to make sure that every fastener has been removed.

Avoid using a screwdriver or bar to pry apart an assembly, as they can easily mar the gasket sealing surfaces of the parts, which must remain smooth. If prying is absolutely necessary, use an old broom handle, but keep in mind that extra clean up will be necessary if the wood splinters.

After the parts are separated, the old gasket must be carefully scraped off and the gasket surfaces cleaned. Stubborn gasket material can be soaked with rust penetrant or treated with a special chemical to soften it so it can be easily scraped off. A scraper can be fashioned from a piece of copper tubing by flattening and sharpening one end. Copper is recommended because it is usually softer than the surfaces to be scraped, which reduces the chance of gouging the part. Some gaskets can be removed with a wire brush, but regardless of the method used, the mating surfaces must be left clean and smooth. If for some reason the gasket surface is gouged, then a gasket sealer thick enough to fill scratches will have to be used during reassembly of the components. For most applications, a non-drying (or semi-drying) gasket sealer should be used.

Hose removal tips

Warning: *If the vehicle is equipped with air conditioning, do not disconnect any of the A/C hoses without first having the system depressurized by a dealer service department or a service station.*

Hose removal precautions closely parallel gasket removal precautions. Avoid scratching or gouging the surface that the hose mates against or the connection may leak. This is especially true for radiator hoses. Because of various chemical reactions, the rubber in hoses can bond itself to the metal spigot that the hose fits over. To remove a hose, first loosen the hose clamps that secure it to the spigot. Then, with slip-joint pliers, grab the hose at the clamp and rotate it around the spigot. Work it back and forth until it is completely free, then pull it off. Silicone or other lubricants will ease removal if they can be applied between the hose and the outside of the spigot. Apply the same lubricant to the inside of the hose and the outside of the spigot to simplify installation.

As a last resort (and if the hose is to be replaced with a new one anyway), the rubber can be slit with a knife and the hose peeled from the spigot. If this must be done, be careful that the metal connection is not damaged.

If a hose clamp is broken or damaged, do not reuse it. Wire-type clamps usually weaken with age, so it is a good idea to replace them with screw-type clamps whenever a hose is removed.

Tools

A selection of good tools is a basic requirement for anyone who plans to maintain and repair his or her own vehicle. For the owner who has few tools, the initial investment might seem high, but when compared to the spiraling costs of professional auto maintenance and repair, it is a wise one.

To help the owner decide which tools are needed to perform the tasks detailed in this manual, the following tool lists are offered: *Maintenance and minor repair, Repair/overhaul* and *Special.*

The newcomer to practical mechanics

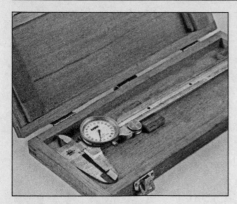

Dial caliper

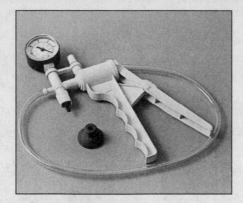

Hand-operated vacuum pump

Timing light

Compression gauge with spark plug
hole adapter

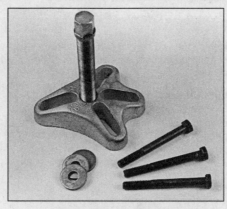

Damper/steering wheel puller

General purpose puller

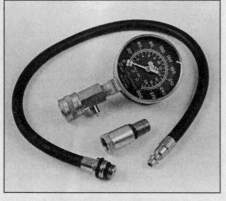

Hydraulic lifter removal tool

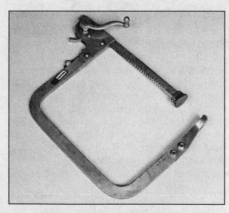

Valve spring compressor

Valve spring compressor

Ridge reamer

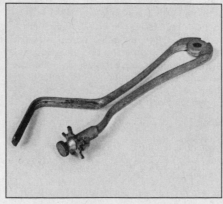

Piston ring groove cleaning tool

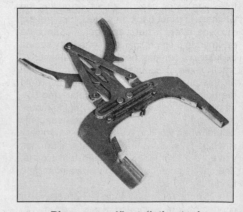

Ring removal/installation tool

Ring compressor

Cylinder hone

Brake hold-down spring tool

Torque angle gauge

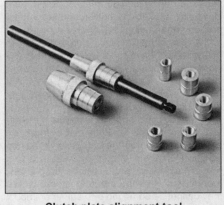

Clutch plate alignment tool

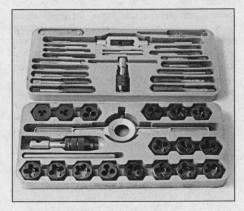

Tap and die set

should start off with the *maintenance and minor repair* tool kit, which is adequate for the simpler jobs performed on a vehicle. Then, as confidence and experience grow, the owner can tackle more difficult tasks, buying additional tools as they are needed. Eventually the basic kit will be expanded into the *repair and overhaul* tool set. Over a period of time, the experienced do-it-yourselfer will assemble a tool set complete enough for most repair and overhaul procedures and will add tools from the special category when it is felt that the expense is justified by the frequency of use.

Maintenance and minor repair tool kit

The tools in this list should be considered the minimum required for performance of routine maintenance, servicing and minor repair work. We recommend the purchase of combination wrenches (box-end and open-end combined in one wrench). While more expensive than open end wrenches, they offer the advantages of both types of wrench.

Combination wrench set (1/4-inch to 1 inch or 6 mm to 19 mm)
Adjustable wrench, 8 inch
Spark plug wrench with rubber insert
Spark plug gap adjusting tool
Feeler gauge set
Brake bleeder wrench
Standard screwdriver (5/16-inch x 6 inch)
Phillips screwdriver (No. 2 x 6 inch)

Combination pliers - 6 inch
Hacksaw and assortment of blades
Tire pressure gauge
Grease gun
Oil can
Fine emery cloth
Wire brush
Battery post and cable cleaning tool
Oil filter wrench
Funnel (medium size)
Safety goggles
Jackstands (2)
Drain pan

Note: *If basic tune-ups are going to be part of routine maintenance, it will be necessary to purchase a good quality stroboscopic timing light and combination tachometer/dwell meter. Although they are included in the list of special tools, it is mentioned here because they are absolutely necessary for tuning most vehicles properly.*

Repair and overhaul tool set

These tools are essential for anyone who plans to perform major repairs and are in addition to those in the maintenance and minor repair tool kit. Included is a comprehensive set of sockets which, though expensive, are invaluable because of their versatility, especially when various extensions and drives are available. We recommend the 1/2-inch drive over the 3/8-inch drive. Although the larger drive is bulky and more expensive, it has the capacity of accepting a very wide range of

large sockets. Ideally, however, the mechanic should have a 3/8-inch drive set and a 1/2-inch drive set.

Socket set(s)
Reversible ratchet
Extension - 10 inch
Universal joint
Torque wrench (same size drive as sockets)
Ball peen hammer - 8 ounce
Soft-face hammer (plastic/rubber)
Standard screwdriver (1/4-inch x 6 inch)
Standard screwdriver (stubby - 5/16-inch)
Phillips screwdriver (No. 3 x 8 inch)
Phillips screwdriver (stubby - No. 2)
Pliers - vise grip
Pliers - lineman's
Pliers - needle nose
Pliers - snap-ring (internal and external)
Cold chisel - 1/2-inch
Scribe
Scraper (made from flattened copper tubing)
Centerpunch
Pin punches (1/16, 1/8, 3/16-inch)
Steel rule/straightedge - 12 inch
Allen wrench set (1/8 to 3/8-inch or 4 mm to 10 mm)
A selection of files
Wire brush (large)
Jackstands (second set)
Jack (scissor or hydraulic type)

Note: *Another tool which is often useful is an electric drill with a chuck capacity of 3/8-inch and a set of good quality drill bits.*

Special tools

The tools in this list include those which are not used regularly, are expensive to buy, or which need to be used in accordance with their manufacturer's instructions. Unless these tools will be used frequently, it is not very economical to purchase many of them. A consideration would be to split the cost and use between yourself and a friend or friends. In addition, most of these tools can be obtained from a tool rental shop on a temporary basis.

This list primarily contains only those tools and instruments widely available to the public, and not those special tools produced by the vehicle manufacturer for distribution to dealer service departments. Occasionally, references to the manufacturer's special tools are included in the text of this manual. Generally, an alternative method of doing the job without the special tool is offered. However, sometimes there is no alternative to their use. Where this is the case, and the tool cannot be purchased or borrowed, the work should be turned over to the dealer service department or an automotive repair shop.

> *Valve spring compressor*
> *Piston ring groove cleaning tool*
> *Piston ring compressor*
> *Piston ring installation tool*
> *Cylinder compression gauge*
> *Cylinder ridge reamer*
> *Cylinder surfacing hone*
> *Cylinder bore gauge*
> *Micrometers and/or dial calipers*
> *Hydraulic lifter removal tool*
> *Balljoint separator*
> *Universal-type puller*
> *Impact screwdriver*
> *Dial indicator set*
> *Stroboscopic timing light (inductive pick-up)*
> *Hand operated vacuum/pressure pump*
> *Tachometer/dwell meter*
> *Universal electrical multimeter*
> *Cable hoist*
> *Brake spring removal and installation tools*
> *Floor jack*

Buying tools

For the do-it-yourselfer who is just starting to get involved in vehicle maintenance and repair, there are a number of options available when purchasing tools. If maintenance and minor repair is the extent of the work to be done, the purchase of individual tools is satisfactory. If, on the other hand, extensive work is planned, it would be a good idea to purchase a modest tool set from one of the large retail chain stores. A set can usually be bought at a substantial savings over the individual tool prices, and they often come with a tool box. As additional tools are needed, add-on sets,

individual tools and a larger tool box can be purchased to expand the tool selection. Building a tool set gradually allows the cost of the tools to be spread over a longer period of time and gives the mechanic the freedom to choose only those tools that will actually be used.

Tool stores will often be the only source of some of the special tools that are needed, but regardless of where tools are bought, try to avoid cheap ones, especially when buying screwdrivers and sockets, because they won't last very long. The expense involved in replacing cheap tools will eventually be greater than the initial cost of quality tools.

Care and maintenance of tools

Good tools are expensive, so it makes sense to treat them with respect. Keep them clean and in usable condition and store them properly when not in use. Always wipe off any dirt, grease or metal chips before putting them away. Never leave tools lying around in the work area. Upon completion of a job, always check closely under the hood for tools that may have been left there so they won't get lost during a test drive.

Some tools, such as screwdrivers, pliers, wrenches and sockets, can be hung on a panel mounted on the garage or workshop wall, while others should be kept in a tool box or tray. Measuring instruments, gauges, meters, etc. must be carefully stored where they cannot be damaged by weather or impact from other tools.

When tools are used with care and stored properly, they will last a very long time. Even with the best of care, though, tools will wear out if used frequently. When a tool is damaged or worn out, replace it. Subsequent jobs will be safer and more enjoyable if you do.

How to repair damaged threads

Sometimes, the internal threads of a nut or bolt hole can become stripped, usually from overtightening. Stripping threads is an all-too-common occurrence, especially when working with aluminum parts, because aluminum is so soft that it easily strips out.

Usually, external or internal threads are only partially stripped. After they've been cleaned up with a tap or die, they'll still work. Sometimes, however, threads are badly damaged. When this happens, you've got three choices:

1) *Drill and tap the hole to the next suitable oversize and install a larger diameter bolt, screw or stud.*
2) *Drill and tap the hole to accept a threaded plug, then drill and tap the plug to the original screw size. You can also buy a plug already threaded to the original size. Then you simply drill a hole to the specified size, then run the threaded*

plug into the hole with a bolt and jam nut. Once the plug is fully seated, remove the jam nut and bolt.
3) *The third method uses a patented thread repair kit like Heli-Coil or Slimsert. These easy-to-use kits are designed to repair damaged threads in straight-through holes and blind holes. Both are available as kits which can handle a variety of sizes and thread patterns. Drill the hole, then tap it with the special included tap. Install the Heli-Coil and the hole is back to its original diameter and thread pitch.*

Regardless of which method you use, be sure to proceed calmly and carefully. A little impatience or carelessness during one of these relatively simple procedures can ruin your whole day's work and cost you a bundle if you wreck an expensive part.

Working facilities

Not to be overlooked when discussing tools is the workshop. If anything more than routine maintenance is to be carried out, some sort of suitable work area is essential.

It is understood, and appreciated, that many home mechanics do not have a good workshop or garage available, and end up removing an engine or doing major repairs outside. It is recommended, however, that the overhaul or repair be completed under the cover of a roof.

A clean, flat workbench or table of comfortable working height is an absolute necessity. The workbench should be equipped with a vise that has a jaw opening of at least four inches.

As mentioned previously, some clean, dry storage space is also required for tools, as well as the lubricants, fluids, cleaning solvents, etc. which soon become necessary.

Sometimes waste oil and fluids, drained from the engine or cooling system during normal maintenance or repairs, present a disposal problem. To avoid pouring them on the ground or into a sewage system, pour the used fluids into large containers, seal them with caps and take them to an authorized disposal site or recycling center. Plastic jugs, such as old antifreeze containers, are ideal for this purpose.

Always keep a supply of old newspapers and clean rags available. Old towels are excellent for mopping up spills. Many mechanics use rolls of paper towels for most work because they are readily available and disposable. To help keep the area under the vehicle clean, a large cardboard box can be cut open and flattened to protect the garage or shop floor.

Whenever working over a painted surface, such as when leaning over a fender to service something under the hood, always cover it with an old blanket or bedspread to protect the finish. Vinyl covered pads, made especially for this purpose, are available at auto parts stores.

Jacking and towing

Jacking

Warning: *The jack supplied with the vehicle should only be used for changing a tire or placing jackstands under the frame. Never work under the vehicle or start the engine while this jack is being used as the only means of support.*

The vehicle should be on level ground. Place the shift lever in Park, if you have an automatic, or Reverse if you have a manual transaxle. Block the wheel diagonally opposite the wheel being changed. Set the parking brake.

Remove the spare tire and jack from stowage. Remove the wheel cover and trim ring (if so equipped) with the tapered end of the lug nut wrench by inserting and twisting the handle and then prying against the back of the wheel cover. Loosen, but do not remove, the lug nuts (one-half turn is sufficient).

Place the scissors-type jack under the side of the vehicle and adjust the jack height until it fits between the notches in the vertical rocker panel flange nearest the wheel to be changed. There is a front and rear jacking point on each side of the vehicle **(see illustration)**.

Turn the jack handle clockwise until the tire clears the ground. Remove the lug nuts and pull the wheel off. Replace it with the spare.

Install the lug nuts with the beveled edges facing in. Tighten them snugly. Don't attempt to tighten them completely until the vehicle is lowered or it could slip off the jack. Turn the jack handle counterclockwise to lower the vehicle. Remove the jack and tighten the lug nuts in a criss-cross pattern.

Install the cover (and trim ring, if used) and be sure it's snapped into place all the way around.

Stow the tire, jack and wrench. Unblock the wheels.

Towing

Two-wheel drive models should be towed with the front (drive) wheels off the ground. If a professional tow vehicle is not available, place the front wheels on an approved towing dolly. The ignition key must be in the OFF (not LOCK) position, since the steering lock mechanism isn't strong enough to hold the front wheels straight while towing.

Four-wheel drive vehicles must be towed with all four wheels off the ground; this is a job

Jacking points

for a professional.

Equipment specifically designed for towing should be used. It should be attached to the frame members of the vehicle; not the bumpers or brackets.

Safety is a major consideration when towing and all applicable state and local laws must be obeyed. A safety chain system must be used at all times. Remember that power steering and power brakes will not work with the engine off.

Booster battery (jump) starting

Observe these precautions when using a booster battery to start a vehicle:

a) *Before connecting the booster battery, make sure the ignition switch is in the Off position.*

b) *Turn off the lights, heater and other electrical loads.*

c) *Your eyes should be shielded. Safety goggles are a good idea.*

d) *Make sure the booster battery is the same voltage as the dead one in the vehicle.*

e) *The two vehicles MUST NOT TOUCH each other!*

f) *Make sure the transaxle is in Neutral (manual) or Park (automatic).*

g) *If the booster battery is not a maintenance-free type, remove the vent caps and lay a cloth over the vent holes.*

Connect the red jumper cable to the positive (+) terminals of each battery **(see illustration)**.

Connect one end of the black jumper cable to the negative (-) terminal of the booster battery. The other end of this cable should be connected to a good ground on the vehicle to be started, such as a bolt or bracket on the body.

Start the engine using the booster battery, then, with the engine running at idle speed, disconnect the jumper cables in the reverse order of connection.

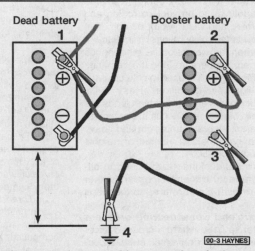

Make the booster battery cable connections in the numerical order shown (note that the negative cable of the booster battery is NOT attached to the negative terminal of the dead battery)

Automotive chemicals and lubricants

A number of automotive chemicals and lubricants are available for use during vehicle maintenance and repair. They include a wide variety of products ranging from cleaning solvents and degreasers to lubricants and protective sprays for rubber, plastic and vinyl.

Cleaners

Carburetor cleaner and choke cleaner is a strong solvent for gum, varnish and carbon. Most carburetor cleaners leave a dry-type lubricant film which will not harden or gum up. Because of this film it is not recommended for use on electrical components.

Brake system cleaner is used to remove brake dust, grease and brake fluid from the brake system, where clean surfaces are absolutely necessary. It leaves no residue and often eliminates brake squeal caused by contaminants.

Electrical cleaner removes oxidation, corrosion and carbon deposits from electrical contacts, restoring full current flow. It can also be used to clean spark plugs, carburetor jets, voltage regulators and other parts where an oil-free surface is desired.

Demoisturants remove water and moisture from electrical components such as alternators, voltage regulators, electrical connectors and fuse blocks. They are non-conductive and non-corrosive.

Degreasers are heavy-duty solvents used to remove grease from the outside of the engine and from chassis components. They can be sprayed or brushed on and, depending on the type, are rinsed off either with water or solvent.

Lubricants

Motor oil is the lubricant formulated for use in engines. It normally contains a wide variety of additives to prevent corrosion and reduce foaming and wear. Motor oil comes in various weights (viscosity ratings) from 0 to 50. The recommended weight of the oil depends on the season, temperature and the demands on the engine. Light oil is used in cold climates and under light load conditions. Heavy oil is used in hot climates and where high loads are encountered. Multi-viscosity oils are designed to have characteristics of both light and heavy oils and are available in a number of weights from 5W-20 to 20W-50.

Gear oil is designed to be used in differentials, manual transmissions and other areas where high-temperature lubrication is required.

Chassis and wheel bearing grease is a heavy grease used where increased loads and friction are encountered, such as for wheel bearings, balljoints, tie-rod ends and universal joints.

High-temperature wheel bearing grease is designed to withstand the extreme temperatures encountered by wheel bearings in disc brake equipped vehicles. It usually contains molybdenum disulfide (moly), which is a dry-type lubricant.

White grease is a heavy grease for metal-to-metal applications where water is a problem. White grease stays soft under both low and high temperatures (usually from -100 to +190-degrees F), and will not wash off or dilute in the presence of water.

Assembly lube is a special extreme pressure lubricant, usually containing moly, used to lubricate high-load parts (such as main and rod bearings and cam lobes) for initial start-up of a new engine. The assembly lube lubricates the parts without being squeezed out or washed away until the engine oiling system begins to function.

Silicone lubricants are used to protect rubber, plastic, vinyl and nylon parts.

Graphite lubricants are used where oils cannot be used due to contamination problems, such as in locks. The dry graphite will lubricate metal parts while remaining uncontaminated by dirt, water, oil or acids. It is electrically conductive and will not foul electrical contacts in locks such as the ignition switch.

Moly penetrants loosen and lubricate frozen, rusted and corroded fasteners and prevent future rusting or freezing.

Heat-sink grease is a special electrically non-conductive grease that is used for mounting electronic ignition modules where it is essential that heat is transferred away from the module.

Sealants

RTV sealant is one of the most widely used gasket compounds. Made from silicone, RTV is air curing, it seals, bonds, waterproofs, fills surface irregularities, remains flexible, doesn't shrink, is relatively easy to remove, and is used as a supplementary sealer with almost all low and medium temperature gaskets.

Anaerobic sealant is much like RTV in that it can be used either to seal gaskets or to form gaskets by itself. It remains flexible, is solvent resistant and fills surface imperfections. The difference between an anaerobic sealant and an RTV-type sealant is in the curing. RTV cures when exposed to air, while an anaerobic sealant cures only in the absence of air. This means that an anaerobic sealant cures only after the assembly of parts, sealing them together.

Thread and pipe sealant is used for sealing hydraulic and pneumatic fittings and vacuum lines. It is usually made from a Teflon compound, and comes in a spray, a paint-on liquid and as a wrap-around tape.

Chemicals

Anti-seize compound prevents seizing, galling, cold welding, rust and corrosion in fasteners. High-temperature ant-seize, usually made with copper and graphite lubricants, is used for exhaust system and exhaust manifold bolts.

Anaerobic locking compounds are used to keep fasteners from vibrating or working loose and cure only after installation, in the absence of air. Medium strength locking compound is used for small nuts, bolts and screws that may be removed later. High-strength locking compound is for large nuts, bolts and studs which aren't removed on a regular basis.

Oil additives range from viscosity index improvers to chemical treatments that claim to reduce internal engine friction. It should be noted that most oil manufacturers caution against using additives with their oils.

Gas additives perform several functions, depending on their chemical makeup. They usually contain solvents that help dissolve gum and varnish that build up on carburetor, fuel injection and intake parts. They also serve to break down carbon deposits that form on the inside surfaces of the combustion chambers. Some additives contain upper cylinder lubricants for valves and piston rings, and others contain chemicals to remove condensation from the gas tank.

Miscellaneous

Brake fluid is specially formulated hydraulic fluid that can withstand the heat and pressure encountered in brake systems. Care must be taken so this fluid does not come in contact with painted surfaces or plastics. An opened container should always be resealed to prevent contamination by water or dirt.

Weatherstrip adhesive is used to bond weatherstripping around doors, windows and trunk lids. It is sometimes used to attach trim pieces.

Undercoating is a petroleum-based, tar-like substance that is designed to protect metal surfaces on the underside of the vehicle from corrosion. It also acts as a sound-deadening agent by insulating the bottom of the vehicle.

Waxes and polishes are used to help protect painted and plated surfaces from the weather. Different types of paint may require the use of different types of wax and polish. Some polishes utilize a chemical or abrasive cleaner to help remove the top layer of oxidized (dull) paint on older vehicles. In recent years many non-wax polishes that contain a wide variety of chemicals such as polymers and silicones have been introduced. These non-wax polishes are usually easier to apply and last longer than conventional waxes and polishes.

Conversion factors

Length (distance)
Inches (in)	X	25.4	= Millimeters (mm)	X 0.0394	= Inches (in)
Feet (ft)	X	0.305	= Meters (m)	X 3.281	= Feet (ft)
Miles	X	1.609	= Kilometers (km)	X 0.621	= Miles

Volume (capacity)
Cubic inches (cu in; in³)	X	16.387	= Cubic centimeters (cc; cm³)	X 0.061	= Cubic inches (cu in; in³)
Imperial pints (Imp pt)	X	0.568	= Liters (l)	X 1.76	= Imperial pints (Imp pt)
Imperial quarts (Imp qt)	X	1.137	= Liters (l)	X 0.88	= Imperial quarts (Imp qt)
Imperial quarts (Imp qt)	X	1.201	= US quarts (US qt)	X 0.833	= Imperial quarts (Imp qt)
US quarts (US qt)	X	0.946	= Liters (l)	X 1.057	= US quarts (US qt)
Imperial gallons (Imp gal)	X	4.546	= Liters (l)	X 0.22	= Imperial gallons (Imp gal)
Imperial gallons (Imp gal)	X	1.201	= US gallons (US gal)	X 0.833	= Imperial gallons (Imp gal)
US gallons (US gal)	X	3.785	= Liters (l)	X 0.264	= US gallons (US gal)

Mass (weight)
Ounces (oz)	X	28.35	= Grams (g)	X 0.035	= Ounces (oz)
Pounds (lb)	X	0.454	= Kilograms (kg)	X 2.205	= Pounds (lb)

Force
Ounces-force (ozf; oz)	X	0.278	= Newtons (N)	X 3.6	= Ounces-force (ozf; oz)
Pounds-force (lbf; lb)	X	4.448	= Newtons (N)	X 0.225	= Pounds-force (lbf; lb)
Newtons (N)	X	0.1	= Kilograms-force (kgf; kg)	X 9.81	= Newtons (N)

Pressure
Pounds-force per square inch (psi; lbf/in²; lb/in²)	X	0.070	= Kilograms-force per square centimeter (kgf/cm²; kg/cm²)	X 14.223	= Pounds-force per square inch (psi; lbf/in²; lb/in²)
Pounds-force per square inch (psi; lbf/in²; lb/in²)	X	0.068	= Atmospheres (atm)	X 14.696	= Pounds-force per square inch (psi; lbf/in²; lb/in²)
Pounds-force per square inch (psi; lbf/in²; lb/in²)	X	0.069	= Bars	X 14.5	= Pounds-force per square inch (psi; lbf/in²; lb/in²)
Pounds-force per square inch (psi; lbf/in²; lb/in²)	X	6.895	= Kilopascals (kPa)	X 0.145	= Pounds-force per square inch (psi; lbf/in²; lb/in²)
Kilopascals (kPa)	X	0.01	= Kilograms-force per square centimeter (kgf/cm²; kg/cm²)	X 98.1	= Kilopascals (kPa)

Torque (moment of force)
Pounds-force inches (lbf in; lb in)	X	1.152	= Kilograms-force centimeter (kgf cm; kg cm)	X 0.868	= Pounds-force inches (lbf in; lb in)
Pounds-force inches (lbf in; lb in)	X	0.113	= Newton meters (Nm)	X 8.85	= Pounds-force inches (lbf in; lb in)
Pounds-force inches (lbf in; lb in)	X	0.083	= Pounds-force feet (lbf ft; lb ft)	X 12	= Pounds-force inches (lbf in; lb in)
Pounds-force feet (lbf ft; lb ft)	X	0.138	= Kilograms-force meters (kgf m; kg m)	X 7.233	= Pounds-force feet (lbf ft; lb ft)
Pounds-force feet (lbf ft; lb ft)	X	1.356	= Newton meters (Nm)	X 0.738	= Pounds-force feet (lbf ft; lb ft)
Newton meters (Nm)	X	0.102	= Kilograms-force meters (kgf m; kg m)	X 9.804	= Newton meters (Nm)

Vacuum
Inches mercury (in. Hg)	X	3.377	= Kilopascals (kPa)	X 0.2961	= Inches mercury
Inches mercury (in. Hg)	X	25.4	= Millimeters mercury (mm Hg)	X 0.0394	= Inches mercury

Power
Horsepower (hp)	X	745.7	= Watts (W)	X 0.0013	= Horsepower (hp)

Velocity (speed)
Miles per hour (miles/hr; mph)	X	1.609	= Kilometers per hour (km/hr; kph)	X 0.621	= Miles per hour (miles/hr; mph)

Fuel consumption*
Miles per gallon, Imperial (mpg)	X	0.354	= Kilometers per liter (km/l)	X 2.825	= Miles per gallon, Imperial (mpg)
Miles per gallon, US (mpg)	X	0.425	= Kilometers per liter (km/l)	X 2.352	= Miles per gallon, US (mpg)

Temperature
Degrees Fahrenheit = (°C x 1.8) + 32   Degrees Celsius (Degrees Centigrade; °C) = (°F - 32) x 0.56

*It is common practice to convert from miles per gallon (mpg) to liters/100 kilometers (l/100km), where mpg (Imperial) x l/100 km = 282 and mpg (US) x l/100 km = 235

Safety first!

Regardless of how enthusiastic you may be about getting on with the job at hand, take the time to ensure that your safety is not jeopardized. A moment's lack of attention can result in an accident, as can failure to observe certain simple safety precautions. The possibility of an accident will always exist, and the following points should not be considered a comprehensive list of all dangers. Rather, they are intended to make you aware of the risks and to encourage a safety conscious approach to all work you carry out on your vehicle.

Essential DOs and DON'Ts

DON'T rely on a jack when working under the vehicle. Always use approved jackstands to support the weight of the vehicle and place them under the recommended lift or support points.

DON'T attempt to loosen extremely tight fasteners (i.e. wheel lug nuts) while the vehicle is on a jack - it may fall.

DON'T start the engine without first making sure that the transmission is in Neutral (or Park where applicable) and the parking brake is set.

DON'T remove the radiator cap from a hot cooling system - let it cool or cover it with a cloth and release the pressure gradually.

DON'T attempt to drain the engine oil until you are sure it has cooled to the point that it will not burn you.

DON'T touch any part of the engine or exhaust system until it has cooled sufficiently to avoid burns.

DON'T siphon toxic liquids such as gasoline, antifreeze and brake fluid by mouth, or allow them to remain on your skin.

DON'T inhale brake lining dust - it is potentially hazardous (see *Asbestos* below).

DON'T allow spilled oil or grease to remain on the floor - wipe it up before someone slips on it.

DON'T use loose fitting wrenches or other tools which may slip and cause injury.

DON'T push on wrenches when loosening or tightening nuts or bolts. Always try to pull the wrench toward you. If the situation calls for pushing the wrench away, push with an open hand to avoid scraped knuckles if the wrench should slip.

DON'T attempt to lift a heavy component alone - get someone to help you.

DON'T *rush or take unsafe shortcuts to finish a job.*

DON'T allow children or animals in or around the vehicle while you are working on it.

DO wear eye protection when using power tools such as a drill, sander, bench grinder, etc. and when working under a vehicle.

DO keep loose clothing and long hair well out of the way of moving parts.

DO make sure that any hoist used has a safe working load rating adequate for the job.

DO get someone to check on you periodically when working alone on a vehicle.

DO carry out work in a logical sequence and make sure that everything is correctly assembled and tightened.

DO keep chemicals and fluids tightly capped and out of the reach of children and pets.

DO remember that your vehicle's safety affects that of yourself and others. If in doubt on any point, get professional advice.

Steering, suspension and brakes

These systems are essential to driving safety, so make sure you have a qualified shop or individual check your work. Also, compressed suspension springs can cause injury if released suddenly - be sure to use a spring compressor.

Airbags

Airbags are explosive devices that can **CAUSE** injury if they deploy while you're working on the vehicle. Follow the manufacturer's instructions to disable the airbag whenever you're working in the vicinity of airbag components.

Asbestos

Certain friction, insulating, sealing, and other products - such as brake linings, brake bands, clutch linings, torque converters, gaskets, etc. - may contain asbestos or other hazardous friction material. Extreme care must be taken to avoid inhalation of dust from such products, since it is hazardous to health. If in doubt, assume that they do contain asbestos.

Fire

Remember at all times that gasoline is highly flammable. Never smoke or have any kind of open flame around when working on a vehicle. But the risk does not end there. A spark caused by an electrical short circuit, by two metal surfaces contacting each other, or even by static electricity built up in your body under certain conditions, can ignite gasoline vapors, which in a confined space are highly explosive. Do not, under any circumstances, use gasoline for cleaning parts. Use an approved safety solvent.

Always disconnect the battery ground (-) cable at the battery before working on any part of the fuel system or electrical system. Never risk spilling fuel on a hot engine or exhaust component. It is strongly recommended that a fire extinguisher suitable for use on fuel and electrical fires be kept handy in the garage or workshop at all times. Never try to extinguish a fuel or electrical fire with water.

Fumes

Certain fumes are highly toxic and can quickly cause unconsciousness and even death if inhaled to any extent. Gasoline vapor falls into this category, as do the vapors from some cleaning solvents. Any draining or pouring of such volatile fluids should be done in a well ventilated area.

When using cleaning fluids and solvents, read the instructions on the container carefully. Never use materials from unmarked containers.

Never run the engine in an enclosed space, such as a garage. Exhaust fumes contain carbon monoxide, which is extremely poisonous. If you need to run the engine, always do so in the open air, or at least have the rear of the vehicle outside the work area.

The battery

Never create a spark or allow a bare light bulb near a battery. They normally give off a certain amount of hydrogen gas, which is highly explosive.

Always disconnect the battery ground (-) cable at the battery before working on the fuel or electrical systems.

If possible, loosen the filler caps or cover when charging the battery from an external source (this does not apply to sealed or maintenance-free batteries). Do not charge at an excessive rate or the battery may burst.

Take care when adding water to a non maintenance-free battery and when carrying a battery. The electrolyte, even when diluted, is very corrosive and should not be allowed to contact clothing or skin.

Always wear eye protection when cleaning the battery to prevent the caustic deposits from entering your eyes.

Household current

When using an electric power tool, inspection light, etc., which operates on household current, always make sure that the tool is correctly connected to its plug and that, where necessary, it is properly grounded. Do not use such items in damp conditions and, again, do not create a spark or apply excessive heat in the vicinity of fuel or fuel vapor.

Secondary ignition system voltage

A severe electric shock can result from touching certain parts of the ignition system (such as the spark plug wires) when the engine is running or being cranked, particularly if components are damp or the insulation is defective. In the case of an electronic ignition system, the secondary system voltage is much higher and could prove fatal.

Hydrofluoric acid

This extremely corrosive acid is formed when certain types of synthetic rubber, found in some O-rings, oil seals, fuel hoses, etc. are exposed to temperatures above 750-degrees F (400-degrees C). The rubber changes into a charred or sticky substance containing the acid. *Once formed, the acid remains dangerous for years. If it gets onto the skin, it may be necessary to amputate the limb concerned.*

When dealing with a vehicle which has suffered a fire, or with components salvaged from such a vehicle, wear protective gloves and discard them after use.

DECIMALS to MILLIMETERS

Decimal	mm	Decimal	mm
0.001	0.0254	0.500	12.7000
0.002	0.0508	0.510	12.9540
0.003	0.0762	0.520	13.2080
0.004	0.1016	0.530	13.4620
0.005	0.1270	0.540	13.7160
0.006	0.1524	0.550	13.9700
0.007	0.1778	0.560	14.2240
0.008	0.2032	0.570	14.4780
0.009	0.2286	0.580	14.7320
		0.590	14.9860
0.010	0.2540		
0.020	0.5080		
0.030	0.7620		
0.040	1.0160	0.600	15.2400
0.050	1.2700	0.610	15.4940
0.060	1.5240	0.620	15.7480
0.070	1.7780	0.630	16.0020
0.080	2.0320	0.640	16.2560
0.090	2.2860	0.650	16.5100
		0.660	16.7640
0.100	2.5400	0.670	17.0180
0.110	2.7940	0.680	17.2720
0.120	3.0480	0.690	17.5260
0.130	3.3020		
0.140	3.5560		
0.150	3.8100		
0.160	4.0640	0.700	17.7800
0.170	4.3180	0.710	18.0340
0.180	4.5720	0.720	18.2880
0.190	4.8260	0.730	18.5420
		0.740	18.7960
0.200	5.0800	0.750	19.0500
0.210	5.3340	0.760	19.3040
0.220	5.5880	0.770	19.5580
0.230	5.8420	0.780	19.8120
0.240	6.0960	0.790	20.0660
0.250	6.3500		
0.260	6.6040		
0.270	6.8580	0.800	20.3200
0.280	7.1120	0.810	20.5740
0.290	7.3660	0.820	21.8280
		0.830	21.0820
0.300	7.6200	0.840	21.3360
0.310	7.8740	0.850	21.5900
0.320	8.1280	0.860	21.8440
0.330	8.3820	0.870	22.0980
0.340	8.6360	0.880	22.3520
0.350	8.8900	0.890	22.6060
0.360	9.1440		
0.370	9.3980		
0.380	9.6520		
0.390	9.9060	0.900	22.8600
0.400	10.1600	0.910	23.1140
0.410	10.4140	0.920	23.3680
0.420	10.6680	0.930	23.6220
0.430	10.9220	0.940	23.8760
0.440	11.1760	0.950	24.1300
0.450	11.4300	0.960	24.3840
0.460	11.6840	0.970	24.6380
0.470	11.9380	0.980	24.8920
0.480	12.1920	0.990	25.1460
0.490	12.4460	1.000	25.4000

FRACTIONS to DECIMALS to MILLIMETERS

Fraction	Decimal	mm	Fraction	Decimal	mm
1/64	0.0156	0.3969	33/64	0.5156	13.0969
1/32	0.0312	0.7938	17/32	0.5312	13.4938
3/64	0.0469	1.1906	35/64	0.5469	13.8906
1/16	0.0625	1.5875	9/16	0.5625	14.2875
5/64	0.0781	1.9844	37/64	0.5781	14.6844
3/32	0.0938	2.3812	19/32	0.5938	15.0812
7/64	0.1094	2.7781	39/64	0.6094	15.4781
1/8	0.1250	3.1750	5/8	0.6250	15.8750
9/64	0.1406	3.5719	41/64	0.6406	16.2719
5/32	0.1562	3.9688	21/32	0.6562	16.6688
11/64	0.1719	4.3656	43/64	0.6719	17.0656
3/16	0.1875	4.7625	11/16	0.6875	17.4625
13/64	0.2031	5.1594	45/64	0.7031	17.8594
7/32	0.2188	5.5562	23/32	0.7188	18.2562
15/64	0.2344	5.9531	47/64	0.7344	18.6531
1/4	0.2500	6.3500	3/4	0.7500	19.0500
17/64	0.2656	6.7469	49/64	0.7656	19.4469
9/32	0.2812	7.1438	25/32	0.7812	19.8438
19/64	0.2969	7.5406	51/64	0.7969	20.2406
5/16	0.3125	7.9375	13/16	0.8125	20.6375
21/64	0.3281	8.3344	53/64	0.8281	21.0344
11/32	0.3438	8.7312	27/32	0.8438	21.4312
23/64	0.3594	9.1281	55/64	0.8594	21.8281
3/8	0.3750	9.5250	7/8	0.8750	22.2250
25/64	0.3906	9.9219	57/64	0.8906	22.6219
13/32	0.4062	10.3188	29/32	0.9062	23.0188
27/64	0.4219	10.7156	59/64	0.9219	23.4156
7/16	0.4375	11.1125	15/16	0.9375	23.8125
29/64	0.4531	11.5094	61/64	0.9531	24.2094
15/32	0.4688	11.9062	31/32	0.9688	24.6062
31/64	0.4844	12.3031	63/64	0.9844	25.0031
1/2	0.5000	12.7000	1	1.0000	25.4000

Troubleshooting

Contents

This section provides an easy reference guide to the more common problems which may occur during the operation of your vehicle. These problems and their possible causes are grouped under headings denoting various components or systems, such as Engine, Cooling system, etc. They also refer you to the chapter and/or section which deals with the problem.

Remember that successful troubleshooting is not a mysterious "black art" practiced only by professional mechanics. It is simply the result of the right knowledge combined with an intelligent, systematic approach to the problem. Always work by a process of elimination, starting with the simplest solution and working through to the most complex - and never overlook the obvious. Anyone can run the gas tank dry or leave the lights on overnight, so don't assume that you are exempt from such oversights.

Finally, always establish a clear idea of why a problem has occurred and take steps to ensure that it doesn't happen again. If the electrical system fails because of a poor connection, check the other connections in the system to make sure that they don't fail as well. If a particular fuse continues to blow, find out why - don't just replace one fuse after another. Remember, failure of a small component can often be indicative of potential failure or incorrect functioning of a more important component or system.

Engine

1 Engine will not rotate when attempting to start

1   Battery terminal connections loose or corroded (Chapter 1).
2   Battery discharged or faulty (Chapter 1).
3   Automatic transmission not completely engaged in Park (Chapter 7) or clutch not completely depressed (Chapter 8).
4   Broken, loose or disconnected wiring in the starting circuit (Chapters 5 and 12).
5   Starter motor pinion jammed in flywheel ring gear (Chapter 5).
6   Starter solenoid faulty (Chapter 5).
7   Starter motor faulty (Chapter 5).
8   Ignition switch faulty (Chapter 12).
9   Starter pinion or flywheel teeth worn or broken (Chapter 5).

2 Engine rotates but will not start

1   Fuel tank empty.
2   Battery discharged (engine rotates slowly) (Chapter 5).
3   Battery terminal connections loose or corroded (Chapter 1).
4   Leaking fuel injector(s), faulty fuel pump, pressure regulator, etc. (Chapter 4).
5   Fuel not reaching fuel rail (Chapter 4).
6   Ignition components damp or damaged (Chapter 5).

7   Worn, faulty or incorrectly gapped spark plugs (Chapter 1).
8   Broken, loose or disconnected wiring in the starting circuit (Chapter 5).
9   Loose distributor or crank angle sensor is changing ignition timing (Chapter 5 or 6).
10   Broken, loose or disconnected wires at the ignition coil or faulty coil (Chapter 5).

3 Engine hard to start when cold

1   Battery discharged or low (Chapter 1).
2   Malfunctioning fuel system (Chapter 4).
3   Injector(s) leaking (Chapter 4).
4   Distributor rotor carbon tracked (V6 models) (Chapter 5).

4 Engine hard to start when hot

1   Air filter clogged (Chapter 1).
2   Fuel not reaching the fuel injection system (Chapter 4).
3   Corroded battery connections, especially ground (Chapter 1).

5 Starter motor noisy or excessively rough in engagement

1   Pinion or flywheel gear teeth worn or broken (Chapter 5).
2   Starter motor mounting bolts loose or missing (Chapter 5).

6 Engine starts but stops immediately

1   Loose or faulty electrical connections at distributor (or crank angle sensor), coil or alternator (Chapter 5).
2   Insufficient fuel reaching the fuel injector(s) (Chapters 1 and 4).
3   Vacuum leak at the gasket between the intake manifold and throttle body or between the intake manifold and engine (Chapters 2 and 4).

7 Oil puddle under engine

1   Oil pan gasket and/or oil pan drain bolt washer leaking (Chapter 2).
2   Oil pressure sending unit leaking (Chapter 2).
3   Cylinder head (valve) covers leaking (Chapter 2).
4   Engine oil seals leaking (Chapter 2).

8 Engine lopes while idling or idles erratically

1   Vacuum leakage. Check the mounting bolts/nuts at the throttle body and the air duct

between the airflow meter and the throttle body for tightness, ensuring there's no possibility of air leaking at the gasket surface, at duct connections or through rips in the duct. Make sure that all vacuum hoses are connected properly and in good condition. Use a stethoscope of a length of fuel hose held against your ear to listen for vacuum leaks while the engine is running. A hissing sound will be heard. Especially check the throttle body and intake manifold gasket areas and also the points where the fuel injectors enter the engine (the O-rings sometimes harden and allow vacuum leaks).
2   Leaking EGR valve (Chapter 6).
3   Spark plug(s) fouled, spark plug wires damaged or shorted, distributor cap/rotor (V6) damaged or carbon tracked (Chapter 1).
4   Air filter clogged (Chapter 1).
5   Fuel pump not delivering sufficient fuel to the fuel injection system (Chapter 4).
6   Leaking head gasket (Chapter 2).
7   Timing belt and/or pulleys worn (Chapter 2).
8   Camshaft lobes worn (Chapter 2).

9 Engine misses at idle speed

1   Spark plugs worn or not gapped properly (Chapter 1).
2   Spark plug(s) fouled, spark plug wires damaged or shorted, distributor cap/rotor damaged or carbon tracked (Chapter 1).
3   Vacuum leaks (Section 8 of *Troubleshooting*; also *Vacuum gauge checks* in Chapter 2E).
4   Uneven or low compression (Chapter 2).

10 Engine misses throughout driving speed range

1   Fuel filter clogged and/or impurities in the fuel system (Chapter 1).
2   Low fuel output at the injector(s) - first try cleaning the injectors - (Chapter 4).
3   Faulty or incorrectly gapped spark plugs (Chapter 1).
4   Cracked distributor cap, disconnected distributor wires or damaged distributor components (V6 models) (Chapters 1 and 5).
5   Leaking spark plug wires (Chapters 1 or 5).
6   Faulty emission system components (Chapter 6).
7   Low or uneven cylinder compression pressures (Chapter 2).
8   Weak or faulty ignition system (Chapter 5).
9   Vacuum leaks (Section 8 of *Troubleshooting*; also *Vacuum gauge checks* in Chapter 2E).

11 Engine stumbles on acceleration

1   Spark plugs fouled (Chapter 1).

2 Fuel injection system component faulty (Chapter 4).
3 Fuel filter clogged (Chapters 1 and 4).
4 Ignition system malfunctioning (Chapter 5).
5 *Vacuum leaks (Section 8 of Troubleshooting; also Vacuum gauge checks in Chapter 2E).*

12 Engine surges while holding accelerator steady

1 *Vacuum leaks (Section 8 of Troubleshooting; also Vacuum gauge checks in Chapter 2E).*
2 Fuel pump faulty (Chapter 4).
3 Loose fuel injector wire harness connectors (Chapter 4).
4 Defective computer (PCM) or information sensor (Chapter 6).

13 Engine stalls

1 Idle speed incorrect (Chapter 1).
2 Fuel filter clogged and/or water and impurities in the fuel system (Chapters 1 and 4).
3 Distributor components damp or damaged (Chapter 5).
4 Faulty emissions system components (Chapter 6).
5 Faulty or incorrectly gapped spark plugs (Chapter 1).
6 Faulty spark plug wires (Chapter 1).
7 *Vacuum leaks (Section 8 of Troubleshooting; also Vacuum gauge checks in Chapter 2E).*

14 Engine lacks power

1 Excessive play in distributor shaft (V6 models) (Chapter 5).
2 Worn rotor, distributor cap or wires (V6 models) (Chapters 1 and 5).
3 Faulty or incorrectly gapped spark plugs (Chapter 1).
4 Fuel injection system out of adjustment or excessively worn (Chapter 4).
5 Faulty coil (Chapter 5).
6 Brakes binding (Chapter 9).
7 Automatic transaxle fluid level incorrect (Chapter 1).
8 Clutch slipping (Chapter 8).
9 Fuel filter clogged and/or impurities in the fuel system (Chapters 1 and 4).
10 Emission control system not functioning properly (Chapter 6).
11 Low or uneven cylinder compression pressures (Chapter 2).
12 Obstructed exhaust system (Chapter 4).
13 *Vacuum leaks (Section 8 of Troubleshooting; also Vacuum gauge checks in Chapter 2E).*

15 Engine backfires

1 Emission control system not functioning properly (Chapter 6).
2 Ignition system malfunctioning (Chapter 5).
3 Faulty secondary ignition system (cracked spark plug insulator, faulty plug wires, V6 distributor cap and/or rotor) (Chapters 1 and 5).
4 Fuel injection system malfunctioning (Chapter 4).
5 *Vacuum leaks (Section 8 of Troubleshooting; also Vacuum gauge checks in Chapter 2E).*
6 Damaged or worn lash adjuster and/or valves sticking (Chapter 2).

16 Pinging or knocking engine sounds during acceleration or uphill

1 Incorrect grade of fuel.
2 Ignition system malfunctioning (Chapter 5).
3 Fuel injection system faulty (Chapter 4).
4 Improper or damaged spark plugs or wires (Chapter 1).
5 Worn or damaged distributor components (V6 models) (Chapter 5).
6 EGR valve not functioning (Chapter 6).
7 *Vacuum leaks (Section 8 of Troubleshooting; also Vacuum gauge checks in Chapter 2E).*

17 Engine runs with oil pressure light on

1 Low oil level (Chapter 1).
2 Short in wiring circuit (Chapter 12).
3 Faulty oil pressure sender (Chapter 2).
4 Worn engine bearings and/or oil pump (Chapter 2).

18 Engine diesels (continues to run) after switching off

Leaking fuel injector(s).

Engine electrical system

19 Battery will not hold a charge

1 Alternator drivebelt defective or not adjusted properly (Chapter 1).
2 Battery electrolyte level low (Chapter 1).
3 Battery terminals loose or corroded (Chapter 1).
4 Alternator not charging properly (Chapter 5).
5 Loose, broken or faulty wiring in the charging circuit (Chapter 5).

6 Short in vehicle wiring (Chapter 12).
7 Internally defective battery (Chapters 1 and 5).

20 Alternator light fails to go out

1 Faulty alternator or charging circuit (Chapter 5).
2 Alternator drivebelt defective or out of adjustment (Chapter 1).
3 Alternator voltage regulator inoperative (Chapter 5).

21 Alternator light fails to come on when key is turned on

1 Warning light bulb defective (Chapter 12).
2 Fault in the printed circuit, dash wiring or bulb holder (Chapter 12).

Fuel system

22 Excessive fuel consumption

1 Dirty or clogged air filter element or engine in need of tune-up (Chapter 1).
2 Ignition system malfunctioning (Chapter 5).
3 Emissions system not functioning properly (Chapter 6).
4 Fuel injection internal parts excessively worn or damaged (Chapter 4).
5 Low tire pressure or incorrect tire size (Chapter 1).

23 Fuel leakage and/or fuel odor

1 Leaking fuel feed or return line (Chapters 1 and 4).
2 Tank overfilled.
3 Evaporative canister filter clogged (Chapters 1 and 6).
4 Fuel injector internal parts excessively worn (Chapter 4).

Cooling system

24 Overheating

1 Insufficient coolant in system (Chapter 1).
2 Water pump faulty (Chapter 3).
3 Radiator core blocked or grille restricted (Chapter 3).
4 Thermostat faulty (Chapter 3).
5 Electric coolant fan blades broken or cracked (Chapter 3).
6 Radiator cap not maintaining proper pressure (Chapter 3).

25 Overcooling

1 Faulty thermostat (Chapter 3).
2 Inaccurate temperature gauge sending unit (Chapter 3)

26 External coolant leakage

1 Deteriorated/damaged hoses; loose clamps (Chapters 1 and 3).
2 Water pump defective (Chapter 3).
3 Leakage from radiator core or coolant reservoir bottle (Chapter 3).
4 Engine drain or water jacket core plugs leaking (Chapter 2).

27 Internal coolant leakage

1 Leaking cylinder head gasket (Chapter 2).
2 Cracked or leaking cylinder sleeve or cylinder head (Chapter 2).

28 Coolant loss

1 Too much coolant in system (Chapter 1).
2 Coolant boiling away because of overheating (Chapter 3).
3 Internal or external leakage (Chapter 3).
4 Faulty radiator cap (Chapter 3).

29 Poor coolant circulation

1 Inoperative water pump (Chapter 3).
2 Restriction in cooling system (Chapters 1 and 3).
3 Water pump drivebelt defective/out of adjustment (Chapter 1).
4 Thermostat sticking (Chapter 3).

Clutch

30 Clutch release system problems

Malfunctions in the hydraulic clutch release system can cause a variety of problems. Listed here are problems with their most common causes:

Pedal travels to floor - no pressure or very little resistance
a) Master or release cylinder faulty (Chapter 8)
b) Hose/pipe burst or leaking (Chapter 8)
c) Connections leaking (Chapter 8)
d) No fluid in reservoir (Chapter 1)
e) If fluid in reservoir rises as pedal is depressed, master cylinder center valve seal is faulty (Chapter 8)

f) If there is fluid on the dust seal at the master cylinder, the piston primary seal is leaking (Chapter 8)
g) Broken release bearing or fork (Chapter 8)

Fluid in the area of the master cylinder dust cover and on the pedal
Rear seal failure in the master cylinder (Chapter 8)

Fluid on the release cylinder
Release cylinder piston seal faulty (Chapter 8)

Pedal feels spongy when depressed
Air in system. Bleed the system (see Chapter 8)

31 Unable to select gears

1 Faulty transaxle (Chapter 7).
2 Faulty clutch disc (Chapter 8).
3 Release lever and bearing not assembled properly (Chapter 8).
4 Faulty pressure plate (Chapter 8).
5 Pressure plate-to-flywheel bolts loose (Chapter 8).

32 Clutch slips (engine speed increases with no increase in vehicle speed)

1 Clutch plate worn (Chapter 8).
2 Clutch plate is oil soaked by leaking rear main seal (Chapter 8).
3 Clutch plate not seated. It may take 30 or 40 normal starts for a new one to seat.
4 Warped pressure plate or flywheel (Chapter 8).
5 Weak diaphragm spring (Chapter 8).
6 Clutch plate overheated. Allow to cool.

33 Grabbing (chattering) as clutch is engaged

1 Oil on clutch plate lining, burned or glazed facings (Chapter 8).
2 Worn or loose engine or transaxle mounts (Chapters 2 and 7).
3 Worn splines on clutch plate hub (Chapter 8).
4 Warped pressure plate or flywheel (Chapter 8).
5 Burned or smeared resin on flywheel or pressure plate (Chapter 8).

34 Transaxle rattling (clicking)

1 Release lever loose (Chapter 8).
2 Clutch plate damper spring failure (Chapter 8).
3 Low engine idle speed (Chapter 4).

35 Noise in clutch area

1 Fork shaft improperly installed (Chapter 8).
2 Faulty bearing (Chapter 8).

36 Clutch pedal stays on floor

1 Faulty or damaged clutch master or slave cylinder (Chapter 8).
2 Broken release bearing or fork (Chapter 8).

37 High pedal effort

1 Pedal mechanism binding (Chapter 8).
2 Pressure plate faulty (Chapter 8).
3 Incorrect size master or release cylinder (Chapter 8).

Manual transaxle

38 Knocking noise at low speeds

1 Worn driveaxle constant velocity (CV) joints (Chapter 8).
2 Worn side gear shaft counterbore in differential case (Chapter 7A).*

39 Noise most pronounced when turning

Differential gear noise (Chapter 7A).*

40 Clunk on acceleration or deceleration

1 Loose engine or transaxle mounts (Chapters 2 and 7A).
2 Worn differential pinion shaft in case.*
3 Worn side gear shaft counterbore in differential case (Chapter 7A).*
4 Worn or damaged driveaxle inboard CV joints (Chapter 8).

41 Clicking noise in turns

Worn or damaged outboard CV joint (Chapter 8).

42 Vibration

1 Rough wheel bearing (Chapter 10).
2 Damaged driveaxle or driveshaft (Chapter 8).
3 Out of round tires (Chapter 1).
4 Tire out of balance (Chapters 1 and 10).
5 Worn CV joint (Chapter 8).

43 Noisy in neutral with engine running

1 Damaged input gear bearing (Chapter 7A).*
2 Damaged clutch release bearing (Chapter 8).

44 Noisy in one particular gear

1 Damaged or worn constant mesh gears (Chapter 7A).*
2 Damaged or worn synchronizers (Chapter 7A).*
3 Bent reverse fork (Chapter 7A).*
4 Damaged fourth speed gear or output gear (Chapter 7A).*
5 Worn or damaged reverse idler gear or idler bushing (Chapter 7A).*

45 Noisy in all gears

1 Insufficient lubricant (Chapter 7A).
2 Damaged or worn bearings (Chapter 7A).*
3 Worn or damaged input gear shaft and/or output gear shaft (Chapter 7A).*

46 Slips out of gear

1 Worn or improperly adjusted linkage (Chapter 7A).
2 Transaxle loose on engine (Chapter 7A).
3 Shift linkage does not work freely, binds (Chapter 7A).
4 Input gear bearing retainer broken or loose (Chapter 7A).*
5 Dirt between clutch cover and engine housing (Chapter 7A).
6 Worn shift fork (Chapter 7A).*

47 Leaks lubricant

1 Side gear shaft seals worn (Chapter 7).
2 Excessive amount of lubricant in transaxle (Chapters 1 and 7A).
3 Loose or broken input gear shaft bearing retainer (Chapter 7A).*
4 Input gear bearing retainer O-ring and/or lip seal damaged (Chapter 7A).*

48 Locked in gear

Lock pin or interlock pin missing (Chapter 7A).*

Although the corrective action necessary to remedy the symptoms described is beyond the scope of the home mechanic, the above information should be helpful in isolating the cause of the condition so that the owner can communicate clearly with a professional mechanic.

Automatic transaxle

Note: *Due to the complexity of the automatic transaxle, it is difficult for the home mechanic to properly diagnose and service this component. For problems other than the following, the vehicle should be taken to a dealer or transmission shop.*

49 Fluid leakage

1 Automatic transmission fluid is a deep red color. Fluid leaks should not be confused with engine oil, which can easily be blown onto the transaxle by air flow.
2 To pinpoint a leak, first remove all built-up dirt and grime from the transaxle housing with degreasing agents and/or steam cleaning. Then drive the vehicle at low speeds so air flow will not blow the leak far from its source. Raise the vehicle and determine where the leak is coming from. Common areas of leakage are:
a) **Pan** *(Chapters 1 and 7)*
b) **Dipstick tube** *(Chapters 1 and 7)*
c) **Transaxle oil lines** *(Chapter 7)*
d) **Speed sensor** *(Chapter 7)*

50 Transaxle fluid brown or has a burned smell

Transaxle fluid burned (Chapter 1).

51 General shift mechanism problems

1 Chapter 7, Part B, deals with checking and adjusting the shift linkage on automatic transaxles. Common problems which may be attributed to poorly adjusted linkage are:
a) *Engine starting in gears other than Park or Neutral.*
b) *Indicator on shifter pointing to a gear other than the one actually being used.*
c) *Vehicle moves when in Park.*
2 Refer to Chapter 7B for the shift linkage adjustment procedure.

52 Transaxle will not downshift with accelerator pedal pressed to the floor

Throttle valve cable out of adjustment (Chapter 7B).

53 Engine will start in gears other than Park or Neutral

Neutral start switch malfunctioning (Chapter 7B).

54 Transaxle slips, shifts roughly, is noisy or has no drive in forward or reverse gears

There are many probable causes for the above problems, but the home mechanic should be concerned with only one possibility - fluid level. Before taking the vehicle to a repair shop, check the level and condition of the fluid as described in Chapter 1. Correct the fluid level as necessary or change the fluid and filter if needed. If the problem persists, have a professional diagnose the cause.

Driveaxles

55 Clicking noise in turns

Worn or damaged front outboard CV joint (Chapter 8).

56 Shudder or vibration during acceleration

1 Excessive toe-in (Chapter 10).
2 Incorrect spring heights (Chapter 10).
3 Worn or damaged inboard or outboard CV joints (Chapter 8).
4 Sticking inboard CV joint assembly (Chapter 8).

57 Vibration at highway speeds

1 Out of balance front wheels and/or tires (Chapters 1 and 10).
2 Out of round front tires (Chapters 1 and 10).
3 Worn CV joint(s) (Chapter 8).

Transfer case (4WD models)

58 Transfer case noisy

Insufficient or incorrect grade of lubricant. Drain and refill (Chapter 1).

59 Lubricant leaks from or output shaft seal

1 Transfer case is overfilled. Drain to proper level (Chapter 1).
2 Vent is clogged or jammed closed. Clear or replace the vent.
3 Driveshaft seal is incorrectly installed or damaged. Replace the seal and check surfaces for nicks and scoring (Chapter 8).

Driveshaft (4WD models)

60 Oil leak at seal end of driveshaft

Defective transfer case oil seal. Check the splined yoke for burrs or a rough condition which may be damaging the seal. Burrs can be removed with crocus cloth or a fine whetstone.

61 Knock or clunk when the transmission is under initial load (just after transmission is put in gear)

1 Loose or disconnected rear suspension components. Check all mounting bolts, nuts and bushings (See Chapter 10).
2 Loose driveshaft bolts. Inspect all mounting bolts and nuts and tighten them to the specified torque.
3 Worn or damaged universal joint bearings. Check as described in Chapter 8.

62 Metallic grinding sound consistent with vehicle speed

Pronounced wear in the universal joint bearings. Check as described in Chapter 8.

63 Vibration

Note: *Before assuming that the driveshaft is at fault, make sure the tires are perfectly balanced and perform the following test.*
1 Install a tachometer inside the vehicle and note the engine speed as the vehicle is driven. Drive the vehicle and note the engine speed at which the vibration (roughness) is most pronounced. Now shift the transaxle to a different gear and bring the engine speed to the same point.
2 If the vibration occurs at the same engine speed (rpm) regardless of which gear the transaxle is in, the driveshaft is NOT at fault since the driveshaft speed varies.
3 If the vibration decreases or is eliminated when the transaxle is in a different gear at the same engine speed, refer to the following probable causes.
4 Bent or dented driveshaft. Inspect or replace as necessary (See Chapter 8).
5 Undercoating or build-up dirt, etc. on the driveshaft. Clean the shaft thoroughly and recheck.
6 Worn universal joint bearings. Remove and inspect (Chapter 8).
7 Driveshaft and/or companion flange out of balance. Check for missing weights on the shaft. Remove the driveshaft (Chapter 8) and reinstall 180-degrees from original position, then retest. Have the driveshaft professionally balanced.

Rear axle (4WD models)

64 Noise

1 Road noise. No corrective procedures available.
2 Tire noise. Inspect the tires and check tire pressures (Chapter 1).
3 Rear axle bearings worn or damaged (Chapter 8 and 10).

65 Vibration

See probable causes under Driveshaft. Proceed under the guidelines listed for driveshaft. If the problem persists, check the axle bearings by raising the vehicle and spinning the rear wheels by hand. Listen for evidence of rough (noisy) bearings. Remove and inspect (Chapter 8).

66 Oil leakage

1 Pinion seal damaged (See Chapter 8).
2 Driveaxle output seals damaged (See Chapter 8).

Brakes

Note: *Before assuming that a brake problem exists, make sure that:*
a) *The tires are in good condition and properly inflated (Chapter 1).*
b) *The front end alignment is correct (Chapter 10).*
c) *The vehicle is not loaded with weight in an unequal manner.*

67 Vehicle pulls to one side during braking

1 Incorrect tire pressures (Chapter 1).
2 Front end out of line (have the front end aligned).
3 Front, or rear, tires not matched to one another.
4 Restricted brake lines or hoses (Chapter 9).
5 Malfunctioning caliper assembly (Chapter 9).
6 Loose suspension parts (Chapter 10).
7 Loose calipers (Chapter 9).
8 Excessive wear of brake pad on one side.

68 Noise (high-pitched squeal when the brakes are applied)

Front disc brake pads worn out. The noise comes from the wear sensor rubbing against the disc (does not apply to all vehicles). Replace pads with new ones immediately (Chapter 9).

69 Brake roughness or chatter (pedal pulsates)

1 Excessive lateral runout (Chapter 9).
2 Uneven pad wear (Chapter 9).
3 Defective disc (Chapter 9).

70 Excessive brake pedal effort required to stop vehicle

1 Malfunctioning power brake booster (Chapter 9).
2 Partial system failure (Chapter 9).
3 Excessively worn pads (Chapter 9).
4 Piston in caliper stuck or sluggish (Chapter 9).
5 Brake pads contaminated with oil or grease (Chapter 9).
6 New pads installed and not yet seated. It will take a while for the new material to seat against the disc.

71 Excessive brake pedal travel

1 Partial brake system failure (Chapter 9).
2 Insufficient fluid in master cylinder (Chapters 1 and 9).
3 Air trapped in system (Chapters 1 and 9).

72 Dragging brakes

1 Incorrect adjustment of brake light switch (Chapter 9).
2 Master cylinder pistons not returning correctly (Chapter 9).
3 Restricted brakes lines or hoses (Chapters 1 and 9).
4 Incorrect parking brake adjustment (Chapter 9).

73 Grabbing or uneven braking action

1 Malfunction of proportioning valve (Chapter 9).
2 Malfunction of power brake booster unit (Chapter 9).
3 Binding brake pedal mechanism (Chapter 9).

74 Brake pedal feels spongy when depressed

1 Air in hydraulic lines (Chapter 9).
2 Master cylinder mounting bolts loose (Chapter 9).
3 Master cylinder defective (Chapter 9).

75 Brake pedal travels to the floor with little resistance

1 Little or no fluid in the master cylinder

reservoir caused by leaking caliper piston(s) (Chapter 9).
2   Loose, damaged or disconnected brake lines (Chapter 9).

76   Parking brake does not hold

Parking brake linkage improperly adjusted (Chapters 1 and 9).

Suspension and steering systems

Note: *Before attempting to diagnose the suspension and steering systems, perform the following preliminary checks:*

a) *Tires for wrong pressure and uneven wear.*
b) *Steering universal joints from the column to the rack-and-pinion for loose connectors or wear.*
c) *Front and rear suspension and the rack and pinion assembly for loose or damaged parts.*
d) *Out-of-round or out-of-balance tires, bent rims and loose and/or rough wheel bearings.*

77   Vehicle pulls to one side

1   Mismatched or uneven tires (Chapter 10).
2   Broken or sagging springs (Chapter 10).
3   Wheel alignment (Chapter 10).
4   Front brake dragging (Chapter 9).

78   Abnormal or excessive tire wear

1   Wheel alignment (Chapter 10).
2   Sagging or broken springs (Chapter 10).
3   Tire out of balance (Chapter 10).
4   Worn strut damper (Chapter 10).
5   Overloaded vehicle.
6   Tires not rotated regularly.

79   Wheel makes a thumping noise

1   Blister or bump on tire (Chapter 10).
2   Improper strut damper action (Chapter 10).

80   Shimmy, shake or vibration

1   Tire or wheel out-of-balance or out-of-round (Chapter 10).
2   Loose or worn front hub or wheel bearings (Chapters 1, 8 and 10).
3   Worn tie-rod ends (Chapter 10).
4   Worn lower balljoints (Chapters 1 and 10).

5   Excessive wheel runout (Chapter 10).
6   Blister or bump on tire (Chapter 10).

81   Hard steering

1   Lack of lubrication at balljoints, tie-rod ends and rack and pinion assembly (Chapter 10).
2   Front wheel alignment (Chapter 10).
3   Low tire pressure(s) (Chapters 1 and 10).

82   Poor returnability of steering to center

1   Lack of lubrication at balljoints and tie-rod ends (Chapter 10).
2   Binding in balljoints (Chapter 10).
3   Binding in steering column (Chapter 10).
4   Lack of lubricant in steering gear assembly (Chapter 10).
5   Front wheel alignment (Chapter 10).

83   Abnormal noise at the front end

1   Lack of lubrication at balljoints and tie-rod ends (Chapters 1 and 10).
2   Damaged strut mounting (Chapter 10).
3   Worn control arm bushings or tie-rod ends (Chapter 10).
4   Loose stabilizer bar (Chapter 10).
5   Loose wheel nuts (Chapters 1 and 10).
6   Loose suspension bolts (Chapter 10)

84   Wander or poor steering stability

1   Mismatched or uneven tires (Chapter 10).
2   Lack of lubrication at balljoints and tie-rod ends (Chapters 1 and 10).
3   Worn strut assemblies (Chapter 10).
4   Loose stabilizer bar (Chapter 10).
5   Broken or sagging springs (Chapter 10).
6   Wheels out of alignment (Chapter 10).

85   Erratic steering when braking

1   Front hub bearings worn (Chapter 10).
2   Broken or sagging springs (Chapter 10).
3   Leaking wheel cylinder or caliper (Chapter 10).
4   Warped rotor (Chapter 9).

86   Excessive pitching and/or rolling around corners or during braking

1   Loose stabilizer bar (Chapter 10).
2   Worn strut dampers or mountings (Chapter 10).
3   Broken or sagging springs (Chapter 10).
4   Overloaded vehicle.

87   Suspension bottoms

1   Overloaded vehicle.
2   Worn strut dampers (Chapter 10).
3   Incorrect, broken or sagging springs (Chapter 10).

88   Cupped tires

1   Front wheel or rear wheel alignment (Chapter 10).
2   Worn strut dampers (Chapter 10).
3   Wheel bearings worn (Chapter 10).
4   Excessive tire or wheel runout (Chapter 10).
5   Worn balljoints (Chapter 10).

89   Excessive tire wear on outside edge

1   Inflation pressures incorrect (Chapter 1).
2   Excessive speed in turns.
3   Front end alignment incorrect (excessive toe-in). Have professionally aligned.
4   Suspension arm bent or twisted (Chapter 10).

90   Excessive tire wear on inside edge

1   Inflation pressures incorrect (Chapter 1).
2   Front end alignment incorrect (toe-out). Have professionally aligned.
3   Loose or damaged steering or suspension components (Chapter 10).

91   Tire tread worn in one place

1   Tires out of balance.
2   Damaged or buckled wheel. Inspect and replace if necessary.
3   Defective tire (Chapter 1).

92   Excessive play or looseness in steering system

1   Front hub bearing(s) worn (Chapter 10).
2   Tie-rod end loose (Chapter 10).
3   Steering gear loose (Chapter 10).
4   Worn or loose steering intermediate shaft (Chapter 10).

93   Rattling or clicking noise in steering gear

1   Steering gear loose (Chapter 10).
2   Steering gear defective.

Chapter 1
Tune-up and routine maintenance

Contents

Specifications

Recommended lubricants and fluids

Note: *Listed here are manufacturer recommendations at the time this manual was written. Manufacturers occasionally upgrade their fluid and lubricant specifications, so check with your local auto parts store for current recommendations.*

Engine oil type	API grade "certified for gasoline engines"
Viscosity	See accompanying chart
Automatic transaxle fluid type	MOPAR ATF or equivalent automatic transmission fluid
Manual transaxle lubricant type	
2.0L non-turbo	MOPAR MS9417 or equivalent manual transmission fluid
All others	API GL-4 SAE 75W-90 or 75W-85W gear lubricant
Transfer case lubricant type (4WD models)	API GL-4 SAE 75W-90 or 75W-85W hypoid gear lubricant
Rear differential lubricant type (4WD models)	
Above 10-degrees F	API GL-5 SAE 90, 85W-90 or 80W-90 gear lubricant
Between minus 30-degrees F and 10-degrees F	API GL-5 SAE 80 or 80W-90 gear lubricant
Below minus 30-degrees F	API GL-5 SAE 75W
Brake and clutch fluid type	DOT 3 or DOT 4 brake fluid
Power steering system fluid	DEXRON II automatic transmission fluid
Engine oil (including filter)	4.5 qts

Capacities*

Coolant
2.0L four-cylinder engines (turbo and non-turbo)	7.4 qts
2.4L four-cylinder engine	7.4 qts
3.0L V6 engine	8.5 qts

Non-turbo

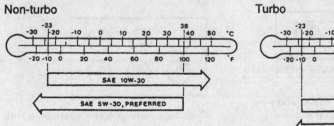

Turbo

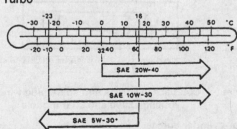

Engine oil viscosity chart - for best fuel economy and cold starting, select the lowest SAE viscosity grade for the expected temperature range

Capacities* (continued)

Automatic transaxle (dry fill**)
2.0L four-cylinder non-turbo engine	9.1 quarts
2.0L four-cylinder turbo engine	7.1 quarts
2.4L four-cylinder engine	
1996 through 1999 models...	6.4 quarts
2000 and later models	8.1 quarts
3.0L V6 engine	8.8 quarts

Manual transaxle
2.0L four-cylinder non-turbo engine	2.1 qts
2.0L four-cylinder turbo engine	2.4 qts
2.4L four-cylinder engine..	2.3 qts
3.0L V6 engine	3.0 qts
Transfer case (4WD models)...	0.5 qts
Rear axle (4WD models)	0.85 qts

*All capacities approximate. Add as necessary to bring to appropriate level.

**Since this is a dry-fill specification, the amount required during a routine fluid change will be substantially less. The best way to determine the amount of fluid to add during a routine fluid change is to measure the amount drained. Begin the refill procedure by initially adding 1/3 of the amount drained. Then, with the engine running, add 1/2-pint at a time (cycling the shifter through each gear position between additions) until the level is correct on the dipstick. It is important to not overfill the transaxle.*

Ignition system

Spark plug type and gap
2.0L four-cylinder non-turbo engine	
Type...	Champion RN9YC, RNYC5 or equivalent
Gap	
RNYC	0.033 to 0.038 inch
RNYC5	0.048 to 0.053 inch
2.0L four-cylinder turbo engine	
Type...	NGK BPR6EKN or equivalent
Gap	0.028 to 0.031 inch
2.4L four-cylinder engine	
Type...	Champion RC10YC4 or equivalent
Gap	0.039 to 0.043 inch
3.0L V6 engine	
1995 through 2001	
Type...	Champion RC8PYP4 or equivalent
Gap (non adjustable)	
Standard	0.039 to 0.043 inch
Limit	0.051 inch
2002 to 2003	
GT Models	
Type	Denso PK16PR11 or equivalent
Gap (non adjustable)	
Standard...	0.039 to 0.043 inch
Limit...	0.051 inch
GTS Models	
Type	Denso SK20PR-B8 or equivalent
Gap (non adjustable)	
Standard...	0.028 to 0.031 inch
Limit...	0.039 inch
2004 to 2005	
GT Models	
Type	NGKFR5EI or equivalent
Gap (do not adjust)	

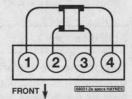

Cylinder numbering and spark plug wire routing (2.0L four-cylinder non-turbo engine)

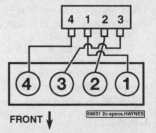

Cylinder numbering and spark plug wire routing (2.0L four-cylinder turbo engine)

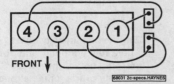

Coil pack locations and spark plug wire routing - 1999 and earlier models

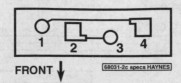

Coil pack locations and spark plug wire routing - 2000 and later models

2.4L four-cylinder engine

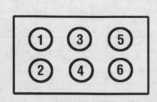

Cylinder numbering and spark plug wire terminal locations - V6 models

GTS Models
    Type .... NGK FR6EI or equivalent
    Gap (do not adjust)
Spark plug wire resistance limit
    2.0L four-cylinder non-turbo engine .... 8000 ohms
    All other engines .... 22,000 ohms
Engine firing order
    2.0L four-cylinder and 2.4L four-cylinder engines 1-3-4-2
    3.0L V6 engine 1-2-3-4-5-6

Cooling system
Thermostat rating
    2.0L four-cylinder non-turbo engine
        Starts to open .... 195-degrees F
        Fully open .... 216-degrees F
    2.0L four-cylinder turbo engine
        Starts to open .... 180-degrees F
        Fully open .... 203-degrees F
    2.4L four-cylinder and 3.0L V6engines
        Starts to open .... 190+/-3 degrees F
        Fully open .... 212-degrees F

Clutch
Pedal height
    2.0L four-cylinder engines... 7 to 7-1/8 inches
    2.4L four-cylinder and 3.0L V6 engines .... 6-1/2 inches
Pedal freeplay... 1/4 to 1/2 inch

Brakes
Disc brake pad lining thickness (minimum) .... 3/32 inch
Drum brake shoe lining thickness (minimum)............................. 3/64 inch
Parking brake adjustment
    Vehicles with rear drum brakes.. 3 to 5 clicks
    Vehicles with rear disc brakes.. 5 to 7 clicks

Suspension and steering
Steering wheel freeplay limit... 1-3/16 inch

Torque specifications
Ft-lbs (unless otherwise indicated)

Note: *One foot-pound (ft-lb) of torque is equivalent to 12 inch-pounds (in-lbs) of torque. Torque values below approximately 15 ft-lbs are expressed in inch-pounds, since most foot-pound torque wrenches are not accurate at these smaller values.*

Automatic transaxle
    Pan bolts
        2.0L four-cylinder non-turbo, 1998 and 1999 2.4L four-cylinder .... 168 inch-lbs
        2.0L four-cylinder turbo... 96 inch-lbs
    Drain plugs (2.0L four-cylinder turbo, 2000 and later
    2.4L four-cylinder and all V6 engines)
        Upper plug.. 29
        Lower plug.. 23 to 25
    Fluid filter (2000 and later 2.4L, all 3.0L) .... 3/4 turn or 87 to 113 inch-lbs
Manual transaxle drain and filler plugs
    2.0L four-cylinder non-turbo.. 22
    2.0L four-cylinder turbo, 2.4L, 3.0L 24
Transfer case (4WD models) drain and filler plugs 24
Differential (4WD models) drain and filler plugs .... Not specified
Spark plugs
    2.0L four-cylinder non-turbo.. 20
    2.0L four-cylinder turbo 18
    2.4L four-cylinder, 3.0L V6 .... 14 to 22
Engine oil pan drain plug
    2.0L four-cylinder non-turbo.. 25
    2.0L four-cylinder turbo 29
    2.4L four-cylinder, 3.0L V6 .... 25 to 33
Wheel lug nuts... 87 to 101

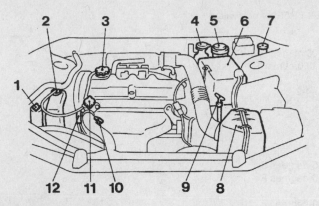

Engine compartment components (typical 2.0L non-turbo model)

1	Power steering fluid reservoir	7	Clutch fluid reservoir
2	Coolant reservoir	8	Air filter housing
3	Engine oil filler cap	9	Automatic transaxle fluid level dipstick
4	Windshield washer fluid reservoir	10	Engine oil dipstick
5	Brake fluid reservoir	11	Radiator cap
6	Battery	12	Drivebelt

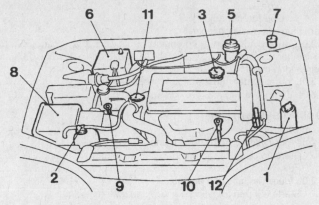

Engine compartment components (typical 2.0L turbo model)

1	Power steering fluid reservoir	8	Air filter housing
2	Coolant reservoir	9	Automatic transaxle fluid level dipstick
3	Engine oil filler cap	10	Engine oil dipstick
5	Brake fluid reservoir	11	Radiator cap
6	Battery	12	Drivebelt
7	Clutch fluid reservoir		

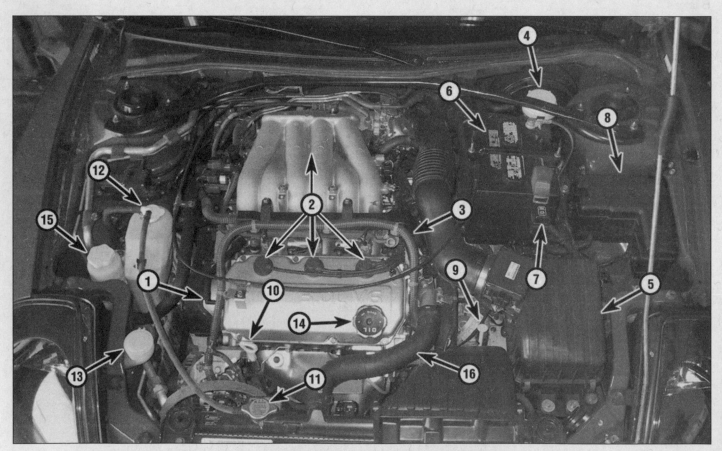

Engine compartment components (typical 3.0L V6 model)

1	PCV valve	6	Battery	12	Coolant reservoir
2	Spark plug locations (rear three plugs hidden by intake plenum)	7	Fusible link	13	Windshield washer fluid reservoir
3	Distributor	8	Fuse/relay/fusible link box	14	Engine oil filler cap
4	Brake fluid reservoir	9	Automatic transaxle fluid dipstick	15	Power steering fluid reservoir
5	Air filter housing	10	Engine oil dipstick	16	Radiator hose
		11	Radiator cap		

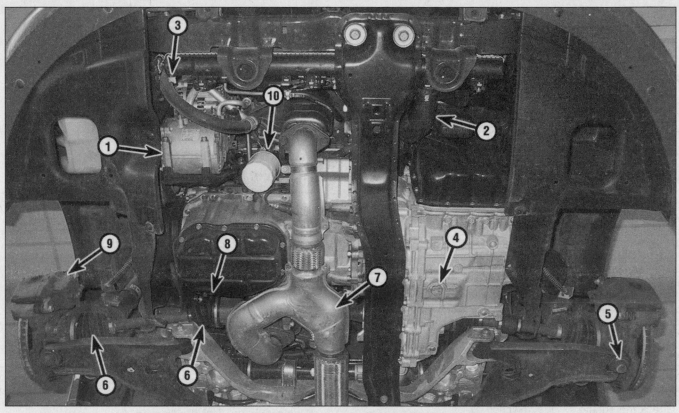

Engine compartment underside components (3.0L model shown, others similar)

1 Air conditioning compressor	3 Radiator drain fitting	5 Suspension balljoint	8 Engine oil drain plug
2 Lower radiator hose	4 Automatic transaxle drain plug	6 Driveaxle boot	9 Brake caliper
		7 Exhaust pipe	10 Engine oil filter

Typical rear underside components (3.0L model shown, others similar)

1   Muffler
2   Exhaust pipe
3   Stabilizer bar
4   Shock absorber assembly
5   Suspension trailing arm
6   Suspension lateral arm
7   Suspension compression arm

1 Mitsubishi Elipse/Eagle Talon Maintenance schedule

The maintenance intervals in this manual are provided with the assumption that you, not the dealer, will be doing the work. These are the minimum maintenance intervals recommended by the factory for vehicles that are driven daily. If you wish to keep your vehicle in peak condition at all times, you may wish to perform some of these procedures even more often. Because frequent maintenance enhances the efficiency, performance and resale value of your car, we encourage you to do so. If you drive in dusty areas, tow a trailer, idle or drive at low speeds for extended periods or drive for short distances (less than four miles) in below-freezing temperatures, shorter intervals are also recommended.

When your vehicle is new, it should be serviced by a factory authorized dealer service department to protect the factory warranty. In many cases, the initial maintenance check is done at no cost to the owner.

Every 250 miles or weekly, whichever comes first

Check the engine oil level (Section 4)
Check the engine coolant level (Section 4)
Check the windshield washer fluid level (Section 4)
Check the brake fluid level (Section 4)
Check the tires and tire pressures (Section 5)

Every 3000 miles or 3 months, whichever comes first

All items listed above plus:
Check the power steering fluid level (Section 6)
Check the automatic transaxle fluid level (Section 7)
Change the engine oil and oil filter (Section 8)

Every 6000 miles or 6 months, whichever comes first

All items listed above plus:
Inspect the seat belts (Section 9)
Inspect and replace if necessary the windshield wiper blades (Section 10)
Check and adjust, if necessary, the clutch pedal height and freeplay (Section 11)
Check and service the battery (Section 12)
Check and adjust or replace if necessary the engine drivebelts (Section 13)
Inspect and replace if necessary the underhood hoses (Section 14)
Check the cooling system (Section 15)
Rotate the tires (Section 16)

Every 15,000 miles or 12 months, whichever comes first

Inspect the fuel system (Section 17)
Inspect the brake system (Section 18)*
Check the manual transaxle lubricant level (Section 19)
Check the transfer case lubricant level (4WD models) (Section 20)
Check the rear axle lubricant level (4WD models) (Section 21)

Every 30,000 miles or 24 months, whichever comes first

All items listed above plus:
Inspect the exhaust system (Section 22)
Replace the air filter (Section 23)*
Replace the spark plugs (except platinum plugs) (Section 24)*
Check and replace if necessary the PCV valve (Section 25)
Service the cooling system (drain, flush and refill) (Section 26)
Change the automatic transaxle fluid and filter (Section 27)
Change the manual transaxle lubricant (Section 28)
Change the transfer case lubricant (4WD models) (Section 29)
Change the rear differential lubricant (4WD models) (Section 30)
Inspect the suspension and steering components (Section 31)

Every 60,000 miles or 48 months, whichever comes first

Replace the spark plugs (platinum plugs) (Section 24)
Inspect and replace if necessary the distributor cap and rotor (V6 engines only) and spark plug wires (Section 32)
Replace the fuel filter (Section 33)
Inspect the evaporative emissions control system (Section 34)
Replace the timing belt (Chapter 2)

* If your vehicle tows a trailer frequently, is operated at idle for extended periods, is operated at low speeds and/or is used for short trips at freezing temperatures, replace the spark plugs at 15,000-mile/12-month intervals and check the brakes more frequently. If your vehicle is driven in sandy, dusty or salty areas, check the brakes and air filter more frequently than indicated.

2   Introduction

This Chapter is designed to help the home mechanic maintain the Eagle Talon and Mitsubishi Eclipse for peak performance, economy, safety and long life.

In Section 1 is a master maintenance schedule, followed by sections dealing specifically with each item on the schedule. Visual checks, adjustments, component replacement and other helpful items are included. Refer to the accompanying illustrations of the engine compartment and the underside of the vehicle for the location of various components.

Servicing your vehicle in accordance with the mileage/time maintenance schedule and the following Sections will provide it with a planned maintenance program that should result in a long and reliable service life. This is a comprehensive plan, so maintaining some items but not others at the specified service intervals will not produce the same results.

As you service your vehicle, you will discover that many of the procedures can and should be grouped together because of the nature of the particular procedure you're performing or because of the close proximity of two otherwise unrelated components to one another.

For example, if the vehicle is raised for any reason, you should inspect the exhaust, suspension, steering and fuel systems while you're under the vehicle. When you're rotating the tires, it makes good sense to check the brakes and wheel bearings since the wheels are already removed.

Finally, let's suppose you have to borrow or rent a torque wrench. Even if you only need to tighten the spark plugs, you might as well check the torque of as many critical fasteners as time allows.

The first step of this maintenance program is to prepare yourself before the actual work begins. Read through all sections pertinent to the procedures you're planning to do, then make a list of and gather together all the parts and tools you will need to do the job. If it looks as if you might run into problems during a particular segment of some procedure, seek advice from your local parts person or dealer service department.

Owner's Manual and VECI label information

Your vehicle Owner's Manual was written for your year and model and contains very specific information on component locations, specifications, fuse ratings, part numbers, etc. The Owner's Manual is an important resource for the do-it-yourselfer to have; if one was not supplied with your vehicle, it can generally be ordered from a dealer parts department.

Among other important information, the Vehicle Emissions Control Information (VECI) label contains specifications and procedures for tune-up adjustments (if applicable) and spark plugs (see Chapter 6 for more information on the VECI label). The information on

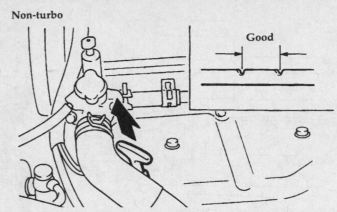

4.2a The 2.0L four-cylinder non-turbo engine oil dipstick is located on the front of the engine, toward the passenger side

this label is the *exact* maintenance data recommended by the manufacturer. This data often varies by intended operating altitude, local emissions regulations, month of manufacture, etc.

This Chapter contains procedural details, safety information and more ambitious maintenance intervals than you might find in manufacturer's literature. However, you may also find procedures or specifications in your Owner's Manual or VECI label that differ with what's printed here. In these cases, the Owner's manual or VECI label can be considered correct, since it is specific to your particular vehicle.

3   Tune-up general information

The term tune-up is used in this manual to represent a combination of individual operations rather than one specific procedure.

If, from the time the vehicle is new, the routine maintenance schedule is followed closely and frequent checks are made of fluid levels and high wear items, as suggested throughout this manual, the engine will be kept in relatively good running condition and the need for additional work will be minimized.

More likely than not, however, there will be times when the engine is running poorly due to lack of regular maintenance. This is even more likely if a used vehicle, which has not received regular and frequent maintenance checks, is purchased. In such cases, an engine tune-up will be needed outside of the regular routine maintenance intervals.

The first step in any tune-up or engine diagnosis to help correct a poor running engine would be a cylinder compression check. A check of the engine compression and vacuum (see Chapter 2) will give valuable information regarding the overall performance of many internal components and should be used as a basis for tune-up and repair procedures. If, for instance, a compression check indicates serious internal engine wear, a conventional tune-up will not help the running condition of the engine and would be a waste of time and money.

The following series of operations are those most often needed to bring a generally poor running engine back into a proper state of tune.

Minor tune-up

Check all engine-related fluids (Section 4)
Clean, inspect and test the battery (Section 12)
Check and adjust the drivebelts (Section 13)
Replace the spark plugs (Section 24)
Inspect the distributor cap and rotor (V6 engine only) (Section 32)
Inspect the spark plug wires and, if equipped, coil wire (Section 32)
Check the air filter (Section 23)
Check the cooling system (Section 15)
Check all underhood hoses (Section 14)

Major tune-up

All items listed under Minor tune-up, plus . . .
Check the charging system (Chapter 5)
Check the fuel system (Section 17)
Replace the air filter (Section 23)
Replace the distributor cap and rotor (3.0L engine only) (Section 32)
Replace the spark plug wires (Section 32)

4   Fluid level checks (every 250 miles or weekly)

1   Fluids are an essential part of the lubrication, cooling, brake, clutch and other systems. Because these fluids gradually become depleted and/or contaminated during normal operation of the vehicle, they must be periodically replenished. See *Recommended lubricants and fluids* and *Capacities* at the beginning of this Chapter before adding fluid to any of the following components. **Note:** *The vehicle must be on level ground before fluid levels can be checked.*

Engine oil

Refer to illustrations 4.2a, 4.2b, 4.2c, 4.4 and 4.6

2   The engine oil level is checked with a dipstick located in the engine compartment **(see illustrations)**. The dipstick extends

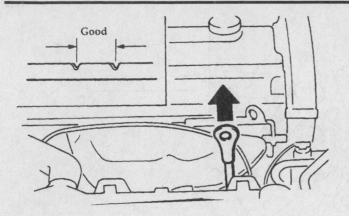

4.2b The 2.0L four-cylinder turbo and 1998 and 1999 2.4L four-cylinder engine oil dipstick is located on the front of the engine, toward the driver's side; the 2000 and later 2.4L engine oil dipstick is located on the rear of the engine, toward the passenger side

4.2c The 3.0L V6 engine oil dipstick is located on the front of the engine, toward the passenger side

through a metal tube from which it protrudes down into the engine oil pan.

3   The oil level should be checked before the vehicle has been driven, or about 5 minutes after the engine has been shut off. If the oil is checked immediately after driving the vehicle, some of the oil will remain in the upper engine components, producing an inaccurate reading on the dipstick.

4   Pull the dipstick from the tube and wipe all the oil from the end with a clean rag or paper towel. Insert the clean dipstick all the way back into its metal tube and pull it out again. Observe the oil at the end of the dipstick. At its highest point, the level should be between the two notches **(see illustration)**.

5   It takes one quart of oil to raise the level from the L notch to the F notch on the dipstick. Do not allow the level to drop below the L mark or oil starvation may cause engine damage. Conversely, overfilling the engine (adding oil above the F mark) may cause oil-fouled spark plugs, oil leaks or oil seal failures.

6   Remove the threaded cap from the valve cover to add oil **(see illustration)**. Use a funnel to prevent spills. After adding the oil, install the filler cap hand tight. Start the engine and look carefully for any small leaks around the oil filter or drain plug. Stop the engine and check the oil level again after it has had sufficient time to drain from the upper block and cylinder head galleys.

7   Checking the oil level is an important preventive maintenance step. A continually dropping oil level indicates oil leakage through damaged seals, from loose connections, or past worn rings or valve guides. If the oil looks milky in color or has water droplets in it, a cylinder head gasket may be blown. The engine should be checked immediately. The condition of the oil should also be checked. Each time you check the oil level, slide your thumb and index finger up the dipstick before wiping off the oil. If you see small dirt or metal particles clinging to the dipstick, the oil should be changed (see Section 8).

Engine coolant

Refer to illustration 4.8

Warning: *Do not allow antifreeze to come in contact with your skin or painted surfaces of the vehicle. Flush contaminated areas immediately with plenty of water. Don't store new coolant or leave old coolant lying around where it's accessible to children or pets - they're attracted by its sweet smell. Ingestion of even a small amount of coolant can be fatal! Wipe up garage floor and drip pan spills immediately. Keep antifreeze containers covered and repair cooling system leaks as soon as they're noticed.*

8   All vehicles covered by this manual are equipped with a pressurized coolant recovery system. A white coolant reservoir located in the right (passenger side) front corner of the engine compartment is connected by a hose to the base of the coolant filler cap **(see illustration)**. If the coolant heats up during engine operation, coolant can escape through a pressurized filler cap, then through a connecting

4.4 The oil filler cap is located on the valve cover - always make sure the area around the opening is clean before unscrewing the cap to prevent dirt from contaminating the engine

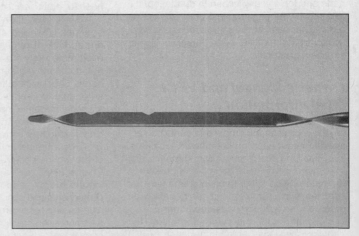

4.6 The oil level should be at or near the upper notch on the dipstick - if it isn't, add enough oil to bring the level to near the upper notch (it takes one quart of oil to raise the level from the lower to the upper notch)

4.8 The coolant reservoir is located in the right front corner of the engine compartment - keep the level between the FULL and LOW lines

4.14a On 2.0L four-cylinder non-turbo models, the windshield washer fluid reservoir is located at the left rear corner of the engine compartment - fluid can be added after flipping up the cap

hose into the reservoir. As the engine cools, the coolant is automatically drawn back into the cooling system to maintain the correct level.

9   The coolant level should be checked regularly. It must be between the FULL and LOW lines on the reservoir. The level will vary with the temperature of the engine. When the engine is cold, the coolant level should be at or slightly above the LOW mark on the tank. Once the engine has warmed up, the level should be at or near the FULL mark. If it isn't, allow the fluid in the tank to cool, then remove the cap from the reservoir and add coolant to bring the level up to the FULL mark. Use only ethylene glycol type coolant and water in the mixture ratio recommended by your owner's manual. Do not use supplemental inhibitors or additives. If only a small amount of coolant is required to bring the system up to the proper level, water can be used. However, repeated additions of water will dilute the recommended antifreeze and water solution. In order to maintain the proper ratio of antifreeze and water, it is advisable to top up the coolant

level with the correct mixture. Refer to your owner's manual for the recommended ratio.

10   If the coolant level drops within a short time after replenishment, there may be a leak in the system. Inspect the radiator, hoses, engine coolant filler cap, drain plugs, air bleeder plugs and water pump. If no leak is evident, have the radiator cap pressure tested by your dealer. **Warning:** *Never remove the radiator cap or the coolant recovery reservoir cap when the engine is running or has just been shut down, because the cooling system is hot. Escaping steam and scalding liquid could cause serious injury.*

11   If it is necessary to open the radiator cap, wait until the system has cooled completely, then wrap a thick cloth around the cap and turn it to the first stop. If any steam escapes, wait until the system has cooled further, then remove the cap.

12   When checking the coolant level, always note its condition. It should be relatively clear. If it is brown or rust colored, the system should be drained, flushed and refilled. Even

if the coolant appears to be normal, the corrosion inhibitors wear out with use, so it must be replaced at the specified intervals.

13   Do not allow antifreeze to come in contact with your skin or painted surfaces of the vehicle. Flush contacted areas immediately with plenty of water.

Washer fluid

Refer to illustrations 4.14a, 4.14b and 4.14c

14   Fluid for the windshield washer system is stored in a plastic reservoir. On 2.0L non-turbo four-cylinder models, the reservoir for the front washers is located at the left rear corner of the engine compartment, while the reservoir for the rear washer (if equipped) is located in the luggage compartment **(see illustrations)**. On 2.0 turbo models, the reservoir for both front and rear wipers is located in the luggage compartment **(see illustration 4.14b)**. On 2.4L and 3.0 models, the reservoir for both front and rear washers is located in the right front corner of the engine compartment **(see illustration)**. In milder climates,

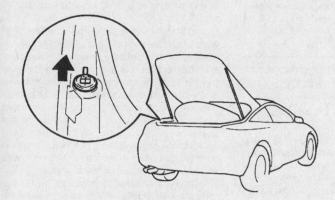

4.14b The reservoir in the rear compartment on the left side contains fluid for the rear washer (2.0L four-cylinder non-turbo models) and both front and rear washers (2.0L four-cylinder turbo models)

4.14c On 2.4L four-cylinder and 3.0L V6 models, the reservoir for front and rear washers is at the front of the engine compartment on the passenger side

4.16 The brake fluid and clutch (if equipped) fluid level should be kept between the MIN and MAX marks on the translucent plastic reservoir(s) - unscrew the cap to add fluid

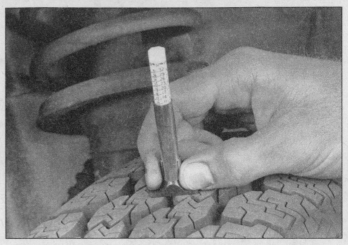

5.2 Use a tire tread depth indicator to monitor tire wear - they are available at auto parts stores and service stations and cost very little

plain water can be used to top up the reservoir, but the reservoir should be kept no more than two-thirds full to allow for expansion should the water freeze. In colder climates, the use of a specially designed windshield washer fluid, available at your dealer and any auto parts store, will help lower the freezing point of the fluid. Mix the solution with water in accordance with the manufacturer's directions on the container. Do not use regular antifreeze. It will damage the vehicle's paint.

Brake and clutch fluid

Refer to illustration 4.16

15   The brake master cylinder is mounted on the front of the power booster unit in the engine compartment. The clutch master cylinder used on manual transaxles is mounted on the firewall next to it. On some models, the brake reservoir is mounted directly on top of the master cylinder. On others, it's mounted separately from the master cylinder and connected to it by a hose.

16   To check the fluid level of the brake master cylinder or clutch reservoir, simply look at the MAX and MIN marks on the translucent plastic reservoir. The level inside should be visible and should be between the MAX and MIN lines, but close to the MAX line **(see illustration)**.

17   If the level is low for either reservoir, wipe the top of the reservoir cover with a clean rag to prevent contamination of the brake or clutch system before lifting the cover.

18   Add only the specified brake fluid to the brake or clutch reservoir (refer to *Recommended lubricants and fluids* at the front of this Chapter or to your owner's manual). Mixing different types of brake fluid can damage the system. **Warning:** *Use caution when filling either reservoir - brake fluid can harm your eyes and damage painted surfaces. Do not use brake fluid that has been opened for more than one year or has been left open. Brake fluid absorbs moisture from the air. Excess*

moisture can cause a dangerous loss of braking.

19   While the reservoir cap is removed, inspect the master cylinder reservoir for contamination. If deposits, dirt particles or water droplets are present, the system should be drained and refilled (see Chapter 8 or Chapter 9).

20   After filling the reservoir to the proper level, make sure the lid is properly seated to prevent fluid leakage and/or system pressure loss.

21   The brake fluid in the master cylinder will drop slightly as the brake pads at each wheel wear down during normal operation. If the master cylinder requires repeated replenishing to keep it at the proper level, this is an indication of leakage in the brake system, which should be corrected immediately. Check all brake lines and connections, along with the wheel cylinders and booster (see Section 18 for more information).

22   If, upon checking the master cylinder fluid level, you discover one or both reservoirs empty or nearly empty, the clutch or brake system should be bled (see Chapter 8 or Chapter 9).

---

5   Tire and tire pressure checks (every 250 miles or weekly)

Refer to illustrations 5.2, 5.3, 5.4a, 5.4b and 5.8

1   Periodic inspection of the tires may spare you from the inconvenience of being stranded with a flat tire. It can also provide you with vital information regarding possible problems in the steering and suspension systems before major damage occurs.

2   Normal tread wear can be monitored with a simple, inexpensive device known as a tread depth indicator **(see illustration)**. When the tread depth reaches the specified minimum, replace the tire(s).

3   Note any abnormal tread wear **(see illustration)**. Tread pattern irregularities such as cupping, flat spots and more wear on one side than the other are indications of front end alignment and/or balance problems. If any of these conditions are noted, take the vehicle to a tire shop or service station to correct the problem.

4   Look closely for cuts, punctures and embedded nails or tacks. Sometimes a tire will hold its air pressure for a short time or leak down very slowly even after a nail has embedded itself into the tread. If a slow leak persists, check the valve stem core to make sure it is tight **(see illustration)**. Examine the tread for an object that may have embedded itself into the tire or for a "plug" that may have begun to leak (radial tire punctures are repaired with a plug that is installed in a puncture). If a puncture is suspected, it can be easily verified by spraying a solution of soapy water onto the puncture area **(see illustration)**. The soapy solution will bubble if there is a leak. Unless the puncture is inordinately large, a tire shop or gas station can usually repair the punctured tire.

5   Carefully inspect the inner sidewall of each tire for evidence of brake fluid leakage. If you see any, inspect the brakes immediately.

6   Correct tire air pressure adds miles to the life span of the tires, improves mileage and enhances overall ride quality. Tire pressure cannot be accurately estimated by looking at a tire, particularly if it is a radial. A tire pressure gauge is therefore essential. Keep an accurate gauge in the glove box. The pressure gauges fitted to the nozzles of air hoses at gas stations are often inaccurate.

7   Always check tire pressure when the tires are cold. "Cold," in this case, means the vehicle has not been driven over a mile in the three hours preceding a tire pressure check. A pressure rise of four to eight pounds is not uncommon once the tires are warm.

8   Unscrew the valve stem cap protruding from the wheel or hubcap and push the

UNDERINFLATION

CUPPING

Cupping may be caused by:
- Underinflation and/or mechanical irregularities such as out-of-balance condition of wheel and/or tire, and bent or damaged wheel.
- Loose or worn steering tie-rod or steering idler arm.
- Loose, damaged or worn front suspension parts.

OVERINFLATION

INCORRECT TOE-IN OR EXTREME CAMBER

FEATHERING DUE TO MISALIGNMENT

5.3 This chart will help you determine the condition of the tires, the probable cause(s) of abnormal wear and the corrective action necessary

gauge firmly onto the valve **(see illustration)**. Note the reading on the gauge and compare this figure to the recommended tire pressure shown on the tire placard on the left door. Be sure to reinstall the valve cap to keep dirt and moisture out of the valve stem mechanism. Check all four tires and, if necessary, add enough air to bring them up to the recommended pressure levels.

9   Don't forget to keep the spare tire inflated to the specified pressure (consult your owner's manual). Note that the air pressure specified for the compact spare is significantly higher than the pressure of the regular tires.

6   Power steering fluid level check (every 3000 miles or 3 months)

Refer to illustration 6.4

1   Unlike manual steering, the power steering system relies on fluid which may, over a period of time, require replenishing.

2   The fluid reservoir for the power steering pump is located on the inner fender panel at the left (driver) side of the engine compartment on 2.0 turbo models and at the right (passenger) side on all others.

3   For the check, the front wheels should be pointed forward and the engine should be off.

4   Look through the translucent plastic reservoir and note the fluid level. It should be

5.4a If a tire loses air on a steady basis, check the valve stem core first to make sure it's snug (special inexpensive wrenches are commonly available at auto parts stores)

5.4b If the valve stem core is tight, raise the corner of the vehicle with the low tire and spray a soapy water solution onto the tread as the tire is turned slowly - leaks will cause small bubbles to appear

5.8 To extend the life of the tires, check the air pressure at least once a week with an accurate gauge (don't forget the spare!)

6.4 The power steering fluid reservoir is in the engine compartment on the passenger side (all except 2.0L four-cylinder turbo models) or the driver's side (2.0L turbo models)

7.4 The automatic transaxle fluid dipstick is in the engine compartment on the driver's side (2.0L four-cylinder non-turbo models, all 2000 and later models), the passenger side (2.0L turbo models), or the front (1998 and 1999 2.4L engine models)

kept between the MIN and MAX marks on the reservoir **(see illustration)**.

5   If additional fluid is required, use a clean rag to wipe off the area around the cap. This will help prevent any foreign matter from entering the reservoir.

6   Twist off the cap and pour the specified type directly into the reservoir, using a funnel to prevent spills.

7   If the reservoir requires frequent fluid additions, all power steering hoses, hose connections, the power steering pump and the rack-and-pinion assembly should be carefully checked for leaks.

7   Automatic transaxle fluid level check (every 3000 miles or 3 months)

Refer to illustrations 7.4 and 7.6

1   The level of the automatic transaxle fluid should be carefully maintained. Low fluid level can lead to slipping or loss of drive, while overfilling can cause foaming, loss of fluid and transaxle damage.

2   For greatest accuracy, the transaxle fluid level should be checked when the transaxle is hot (at its normal operating temperature). If the vehicle has just been driven over 10 miles (15 miles in a frigid climate) and the fluid temperature is 160 to 175-degrees F, the transaxle is hot. **Caution:** *If the vehicle has just been driven for a long time at high speed or in city traffic in hot weather, or if it has been pulling a trailer, an accurate fluid level reading cannot be obtained. Allow the fluid to cool down for about 30 minutes.*

3   If the vehicle has not just been driven, park the vehicle on level ground, set the parking brake and start the engine. While the engine is idling, depress the brake pedal and move the selector lever through all the gear ranges, beginning in Park. If you're working on a 2.0L non-turbo model, move the selector

lever back to Park. If you're working on any other model, move the selector lever back to Neutral.

4   With the engine still idling, remove the dipstick from its tube in the engine compartment **(see illustration)**. On 2.0L four-cylinder non-turbo models, it's on the left (driver's) side behind the air cleaner. On 2.0L turbo, 2.4L four-cylinder and V6 models, it's at the left front of the engine compartment.

5   Wipe the fluid from the dipstick with a clean rag and reinsert it back into the filler tube until the cap seats.

6   Pull the dipstick out again and note the fluid level **(see illustration)**.

a) If you're working on a 2.0L non-turbo model, the level should be above the WARM mark (in the HOT range) if the transaxle is fully warmed up, or between the WARM and ADD marks if the vehicle had been operated between one and 15 minutes.

b) If you're working on a 2.0L turbo, 2.4L or 3.0L engine model, the fluid level should be within the HOT range on the dipstick.

7   If the level is below the specified range, add the specified automatic transmission fluid through the dipstick tube with a funnel. Add just enough of the recommended fluid to

fill the transaxle to the proper level. It takes about one pint to raise the level from the low mark to the high mark when the fluid is hot, so add the fluid a little at a time and keep checking the level until it is correct.

8   The condition of the fluid should also be checked along with the level. If the fluid at the end of the dipstick is black or a dark reddish brown color, or if it emits a burned smell, the fluid should be changed (see Section 27). If you are in doubt about the condition of the fluid, purchase some new fluid and compare the two for color and smell.

8   Engine oil and oil filter change (every 3000 miles or 3 months)

Refer to illustrations 8.2, 8.7, 8.13 and 8.15

1   Frequent oil changes are the best preventive maintenance the home mechanic can give the engine, because aging oil becomes diluted and contaminated, which leads to premature engine wear.

2   Make sure that you have all the necessary tools before you begin this procedure **(see illustration)**. You should also have plenty of rags or newspapers handy for mopping up any spills.

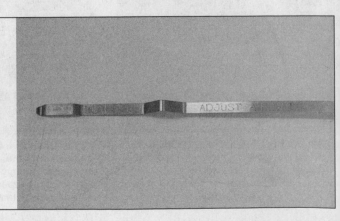

7.6 Check the fluid with the transaxle at normal operating temperature - the level should be kept in the HOT range with the transaxle at normal operating temperature

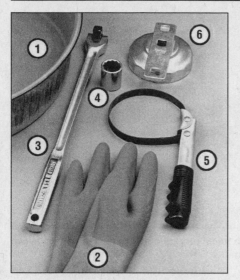

8.2 These tools are required when changing the engine oil and filter

1   **Drain pan** - It should be fairly shallow in depth, but wide to prevent spills
2   **Rubber gloves** - When removing the drain plug and filter, you will get oil on your hands (the gloves will prevent burns)
3   **Breaker bar** - Sometimes the oil drain plug is tight, and a long breaker bar is needed to loosen it
4   **Socket** - To be used with the breaker bar or a ratchet (must be the correct size to fit the drain plug - six-point preferred)
5   **Filter wrench** - This is a metal band-type wrench, which requires clearance around the filter to be effective
6   **Filter wrench** - This type fits on the bottom of the filter and can be turned with a ratchet or breaker bar (different-size wrenches are available for different types of filters)

3   Access to the underside of the vehicle is greatly improved if the vehicle can be lifted on a hoist, driven onto ramps or supported by jackstands. **Warning:** Do not work under a vehicle which is supported only by a bumper, hydraulic or scissors-type jack.
4   If this is your first oil change, get under the vehicle and familiarize yourself with the location of the oil drain plug. The engine and exhaust components will be warm during the actual work, so try to anticipate any potential problems before the engine and accessories are hot.
5   Park the vehicle on a level spot. Start the engine and allow it to reach its normal operating temperature (the needle on the temperature gauge should be at least above the bottom mark). Warm oil and sludge will flow out more easily. Turn off the engine when it's warmed up. Remove the filler cap in the valve cover.
6   Raise the vehicle and support it on jackstands. **Warning:** To avoid personal injury,

8.7 Use a proper-size box-end wrench or socket to remove the oil drain plug and avoid rounding it off

never get beneath the vehicle when it is supported by only by a jack. The jack provided with your vehicle is designed solely for raising the vehicle to remove and replace the wheels. Always use jackstands to support the vehicle when it becomes necessary to place your body underneath the vehicle.
7   Being careful not to touch the hot exhaust components, place the drain pan under the drain plug in the bottom of the pan and remove the plug and gasket **(see illustration)**. You may want to wear gloves while unscrewing the plug the final few turns if the engine is really hot.
8   Allow the old oil to drain into the pan. It may be necessary to move the pan farther under the engine as the oil flow slows to a trickle. Inspect the old oil for the presence of metal shavings and chips.
9   After all the oil has drained, wipe off the drain plug with a clean rag. Even minute metal particles clinging to the plug would immediately contaminate the new oil.
10   Place a new gasket on the drain plug. **Note:** The gasket is directional. The side with the fold faces toward the oil pan. The smooth side faces away from the oil pan. Clean the area around the drain plug opening, reinstall the plug and tighten it securely, but do not strip the threads.
11   Move the drain pan into position under the oil filter.
12   Remove all tools, rags, etc. from under the vehicle, being careful not to spill the oil in the drain pan, then lower the vehicle.
13   Loosen the oil filter **(see illustration)** by turning it counterclockwise with the filter wrench. Any standard filter wrench will work. Sometimes the oil filter is screwed on so tightly that it cannot be loosened. If this situation occurs, punch a metal bar or long screwdriver directly through the side of the canister and use it as a T-bar to turn the filter. Be prepared for oil to spurt out of the canister as it is punctured. Once the filter is loose, use your hands to unscrew it from the block. Just as the filter is detached from the block, imme-

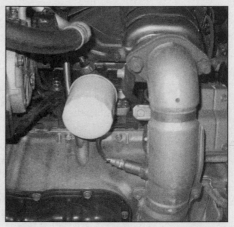

8.13 Since the oil filter is on very tight, you'll need a special wrench for removal - DO NOT use the wrench to tighten the new filter

diately tilt the open end up to prevent the oil inside the filter from spilling out. **Warning:** The engine exhaust manifold will still be hot, so be careful.
14   With a clean rag, wipe off the mounting surface on the block. If a residue of old oil is allowed to remain, it will smoke when the block is heated up. It will also prevent the new filter from seating properly. Also make sure that the none of the old gasket remains stuck to the mounting surface. It can be removed with a scraper if necessary.
15   Compare the old filter with the new one to make sure they are the same type. Smear some engine oil on the rubber gasket of the new filter and screw it into place **(see illustration)**. Because overtightening the filter will damage the gasket, do not use a filter wrench to tighten the filter. Tighten it by hand until the gasket contacts the seating surface. Then seat the filter by giving it an additional 3/4-turn.
16   Add new oil to the engine through the oil filler cap in the valve cover. Use a spout or funnel to prevent oil from spilling onto the top

8.15 Lubricate the oil filter gasket with clean engine oil before installing the filter on the engine

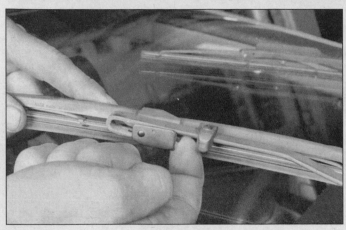

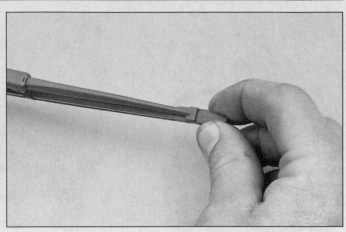

10.6 Depress the release lever (finger is on it here) and slide the wiper assembly down the wiper arm and out of the hook in the end of the arm

10.7 Squeeze the two metal prongs of the blade element to allow it to slide out of the assembly - you may need pliers

of the engine. Pour three quarts of fresh oil into the engine. Wait a few minutes to allow the oil to drain into the pan, then check the level on the oil dipstick (see Section 4 if necessary). If the oil level is at or near the F mark, install the filler cap hand tight, start the engine and allow the new oil to circulate.

17   Allow the engine to run for about a minute. While the engine is running, look under the vehicle and check for leaks at the oil pan drain plug and around the oil filter. If either is leaking, stop the engine and tighten the plug or filter slightly.

18   Wait a few minutes to allow the oil to trickle down into the pan, then recheck the level on the dipstick and, if necessary, add enough oil to bring the level to the upper mark.

19   During the first few trips after an oil change, make it a point to check frequently for leaks and proper oil level.

20   The old oil drained from the engine cannot be reused in its present state and should be discarded. Oil reclamation centers, auto repair shops and gas stations will normally accept the oil, which can be refined and used again. After the oil has cooled, it can be drained into a suitable container (capped plastic jugs, topped bottles, milk cartons, etc.) for transport to one of these disposal sites.

9   Seat belt check (every 6000 miles or 6 months)

1   Check seat belts, buckles, latch plates and guide loops for obvious damage and signs of wear.

2   Where the seat belt receptacle bolts to the floor of the vehicle, check that the bolts are secure.

3   See if the seat belt Warning light comes on when the key is turned to the Run or Start position. A buzzer or chime should also sound.

10   Windshield wiper blade inspection and replacement (every 6000 miles or 6 months)

Refer to illustrations 10.6 and 10.7

1   The wiper and blade assembly should be inspected periodically for damage, loose components and cracked or worn blade elements.

2   Road film can build up on the wiper blades and affect their efficiency, so they

should be washed regularly with a mild detergent solution.

3   The action of the wiping mechanism can loosen bolts, nuts and fasteners, so they should be checked and tightened, as necessary, at the same time the wiper blades are checked.

4   If the wiper blade elements are cracked, worn or warped, or no longer clean adequately, they should be replaced with new ones.

5   Lift the arm assembly away from the glass for clearance.

6   Press the release lever and slide the blade assembly out of the hook in the end of the wiper arm **(see illustration)**.

7   If necessary, use needle-nose pliers to squeeze the two metal prongs at the end of the element, then slide the element out of the frame **(see illustration)**.

8   Slide the new element into the frame and make sure the prongs snap out behind the last clip of the blade assembly.

9 Installation is the reverse of the removal steps.

11   Clutch pedal height and freeplay - check and adjustment (every 6000 miles or 6 months)

Refer to illustration 11.1, 11.2, 11.3 and 11.4

1   Measure the clutch pedal height (the distance from the top of the clutch pedal to the floor) **(see illustration)**. The distance should be as listed in this Chapter's Specifications.

2   If the pedal height is not correct, reach under the dash and loosen the locknut until the adjusting bolt (non-cruise control) or clutch switch (cruise control) turns freely. Turn the adjusting bolt or the switch to achieve the specified pedal height **(see illustration)**.

3   Press down lightly on the clutch pedal and, with a small steel ruler, measure the distance that it moves freely before the clutch

11.1 Clutch pedal height is measured from the floor to the top of the pedal pad

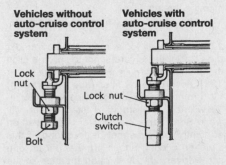

11.2 To adjust clutch pedal height, loosen the locknut and turn the bolt or clutch switch until the height is correct, then tighten the locknut

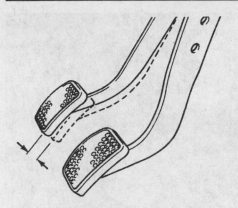

11.3 To determine the clutch pedal freeplay, depress the pedal, stop the moment clutch resistance is felt, then measure the distance

11.4 Adjust clutch pedal freeplay by loosening the locknut, rotating the pushrod until the freeplay is correct, then tightening the locknut

12.1 Tools and materials required for battery maintenance

resistance is felt **(see illustration)**. The freeplay should be within the limits listed in this Chapter's Specifications. If it isn't, it must be adjusted.

4   To adjust the freeplay, reach up under the dash, loosen the locknut and adjust the clutch pedal pushrod until the freeplay is correct, then tighten the locknut securely **(see illustration)**.

Terminal end corrosion or damage.

Insulation cracks.

Chafed insulation or exposed wires.

Burned or melted insulation.

12.5 Typical battery cable problems

12 Battery check, maintenance and charging (every 6000 miles or 6 months)

Refer to illustrations 12.1, 12.5, 12.6a, 12.6b, 12.7a and 12.7b
Warning: *Certain precautions must be followed when checking and servicing the battery. Hydrogen gas, which is highly flammable, is always present in the battery cells, so keep lighted tobacco and all other open flames and sparks away from the battery. The electrolyte inside the battery is actually dilute sulfuric acid, which will cause injury if splashed on your skin or in your eyes. It will also ruin clothes and painted surfaces. When removing the battery cables, always detach the negative cable first and hook it up last!*

Check and maintenance

1   A routine preventive maintenance program for the battery in your vehicle is the only way to ensure quick and reliable starts. But before performing any battery maintenance, make sure that you have the proper equipment necessary to work safely around the battery **(see illustration)**.

2   There are also several precautions that should be taken whenever battery maintenance is performed. Before servicing the battery, always turn the engine and all accessories off and disconnect the cable from the negative terminal of the battery.

3   The battery produces hydrogen gas, which is both flammable and explosive. Never create a spark, smoke or light a match around the battery. Always charge the battery in a ventilated area.

1   *Face shield/safety goggles - When removing corrosion with a brush, the acidic particles can easily fly up into your eyes*

2   *Baking soda - A solution of baking soda and water can be used to neutralize corrosion*

3   *Petroleum jelly - A layer of this on the battery posts will help prevent corrosion*

4   *Battery post/cable cleaner - This wire-brush cleaning tool will remove all traces of corrosion from the battery posts and cable clamps*

5   *Treated felt washers - Placing one of these on each post, directly under the cable clamps, will help prevent corrosion*

6   *Puller - Sometimes the cable clamps are very difficult to pull off the posts, even after the nut/bolt has been completely loosened. This tool pulls the clamp straight up and off the post without damage*

7   *Battery post/cable cleaner - Here is another cleaning tool which is a slightly different version of Number 4 above, but it does the same thing*

8   *Rubber gloves - Be sure to wear these; remember, that's acid inside the battery!*

4   Electrolyte contains poisonous and corrosive sulfuric acid. Do not allow it to get in your eyes, on your skin on your clothes. Never ingest it. Wear protective safety glasses when working near the battery. Keep children away from the battery.

5   Note the external condition of the battery. If the positive terminal and cable clamp on your vehicle's battery is equipped with a rubber protector, make sure that it's not torn or damaged. It should completely cover the terminal. Look for any corroded or loose connections, cracks in the case or cover or loose hold-down clamps. Also check the entire length of each cable for cracks and frayed conductors **(see illustration)**.

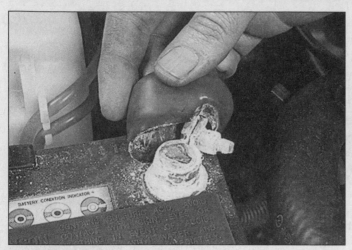

12.6a Battery terminal corrosion usually appears as light, fluffy powder

12.6b Removing the cable from a battery post with a wrench - sometimes special battery pliers are required for this procedure if corrosion has caused deterioration of the nut hex (always remove the ground cable first and hook it up last!)

6   If corrosion, which looks like white, fluffy deposits **(see illustration)** is evident, particularly around the terminals, the battery should be removed for cleaning. Loosen the cable clamp bolts with a wrench, being careful to remove the ground cable first, and slide them off the terminals **(see illustration)**. Then disconnect the hold-down clamp bolt and nut, remove the clamp and lift the battery from the engine compartment.

7   Clean the cable clamps thoroughly with a battery brush or a terminal cleaner and a solution of warm water and baking soda **(see illustration)**. Wash the terminals and the top of the battery case with the same solution but make sure that the solution doesn't get into the battery. When cleaning the cables, terminals and battery top, wear safety goggles and rubber gloves to prevent any solution from coming in contact with your eyes or hands. Wear old clothes too - even diluted, sulfuric acid splashed onto clothes will burn holes in them. If the terminals have been extensively corroded, clean them up with a terminal cleaner **(see illustration)**. Thoroughly wash all cleaned areas with plain water.

8   Make sure that the battery tray is in good condition and the hold-down clamp bolts are tight. If the battery is removed from the tray, make sure no parts remain in the bottom of the tray when the battery is reinstalled. When reinstalling the hold-down clamp bolts, do not overtighten them.

9   Information on removing and installing the battery can be found in Chapter 5. Information on jump starting can be found at the front of this manual. For more detailed battery checking procedures, refer to the *Haynes Automotive Electrical Manual*.

Cleaning

10   Corrosion on the hold-down components, battery case and surrounding areas can be removed with a solution of water and baking soda. Thoroughly rinse all cleaned areas with plain water.

11   Any metal parts of the vehicle damaged by corrosion should be covered with a zinc-based primer, then painted.

Charging

Warning: *When batteries are being charged, hydrogen gas, which is very explosive and flammable, is produced. Do not smoke or allow open flames near a charging or a recently charged battery. Wear eye protection when near the battery during charging. Also, make sure the charger is unplugged before connecting or disconnecting the battery from the charger.*

12   Slow-rate charging is the best way to restore a battery that's discharged to the point where it will not start the engine. It's also a good way to maintain the battery charge in a vehicle that's only driven a few miles between starts. Maintaining the battery charge is particularly important in the winter when the battery must work harder to start the engine and electrical accessories that drain the battery are in greater use.

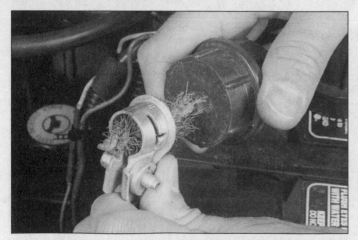

12.7a When cleaning the cable clamps, all corrosion must be removed (the inside of the clamp is tapered to match the taper on the post, so don't remove too much material)

12.7b Regardless of the type of tool used on the battery posts, a clean, shiny surface should be the result

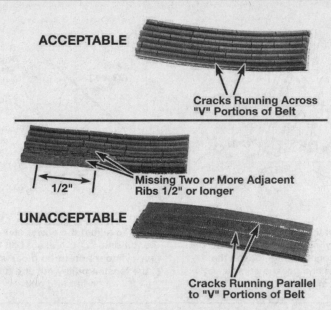

ACCEPTABLE

Cracks Running Across
"V" Portions of Belt

1/2"

Missing Two or More Adjacent
Ribs 1/2" or longer

UNACCEPTABLE

Cracks Running Parallel
to "V" Portions of Belt

13.3 Check ribbed belts for signs of wear like these - if they look worn, replace them as a set

13 It's best to use a one or two-amp battery charger (sometimes called a "trickle" charger). They are the safest and put the least strain on the battery. They are also the least expensive. For a faster charge, you can use a higher amperage charger, but don't use one rated more than 1/10th the amp/hour rating of the battery. Rapid boost chargers that claim to restore the power of the battery in one to two hours are hardest on the battery and can damage batteries not in good condition; this type of charging should only be used in emergency situations.

14 The average time necessary to charge a battery should be listed in the instructions that come with the charger. As a general rule, a trickle charger will charge a battery in 12 to 16 hours.

15 Remove all the cell caps (if equipped) and cover the holes with a clean cloth to prevent spattering electrolyte. Disconnect the negative battery cable and hook the battery charger leads to the battery posts (positive to positive, negative to negative), then plug in the charger. Make sure it is set at 12 volts if it has a selector switch.

16 If you're using a charger with a rate higher than two amps, check the battery regularly during charging to make sure it doesn't overheat. If you're using a trickle charger, you can safely let the battery charge overnight after you've checked it regularly for the first couple of hours.

17 If the battery has removable cell caps, measure the specific gravity with a hydrometer every hour during the last few hours of the charging cycle. Hydrometers are available inexpensively from auto parts stores - follow the instructions that come with the hydrometer. Consider the battery charged when there's no change in the specific gravity reading for two hours and the electrolyte in the cells is gassing (bubbling) freely. The specific gravity reading from each cell should be very close to the others. If not, the battery probably has a bad cell(s).

18 Some batteries with sealed tops have built-in hydrometers on the top that indicate the state of charge by the color displayed in the hydrometer window. Normally, a bright-colored hydrometer indicates a full charge and a dark hydrometer indicates the battery still needs charging. Check the battery manufacturer's instructions to be sure you know what the colors mean.

19 If the battery has a sealed top and no built-in hydrometer, you can hook up a digital voltmeter across the battery terminals to check the charge. A fully charged battery should read 12.6 volts or higher.

20 Further information on the battery and jump starting can be found in Chapter 5 and at the front of this manual.

13 Drivebelt check, adjustment and replacement (every 6000 miles or 6 months)

Refer to illustrations 13.3 and 13.4

Check

1 Drivebelts are located at the front of the engine and play an important role in the overall operation of the engine and its components. Due to their function and material make up, the belts are prone to wear and should be periodically inspected.

2 The drivebelts drive the alternator, power steering pump and air conditioning compressor (if equipped), as well as the water pump on 2.0L four-cylinder turbo and 2.4L four-cylinder engine models. The water pump on 2.0L four-cylinder non-turbo and V6 models is driven by the timing belt.

3 With the engine off, open the hood and locate the drivebelts at the left end of the engine. With a flashlight, check each belt for separation of the adhesive rubber on both sides of the core, core separation from the belt side and a severed core. On V-ribbed belts, also check for separation of the ribs from the adhesive rubber, cracking or separation of the ribs, and torn or worn ribs or cracks in the inner ridges of the ribs. On all belts, also check for fraying and glazing, which gives the belt a shiny appearance. Both sides of the belt should be inspected, which means you will have to twist the belt to check the underside **(see illustration)**.

Adjustment

4 To check the tension of the drivebelts, push firmly on the belt with your thumb at a distance halfway between the pulleys and note how far the belt moves (deflects) **(see illustration)**. As a rule of thumb, the belt should deflect 1/4-inch if the distance from pulley center to pulley center is between 7 and 11 inches; the belt should deflect 1/2-inch if the distance from pulley center to pulley center is between 12 and 16 inches.

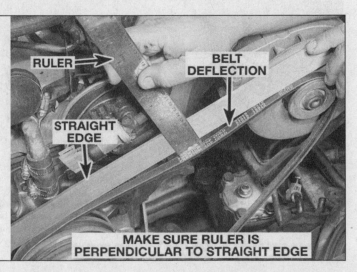
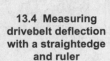

13.4 Measuring drivebelt deflection with a straightedge and ruler

RULER

BELT DEFLECTION

STRAIGHT EDGE

MAKE SURE RULER IS PERPENDICULAR TO STRAIGHT EDGE

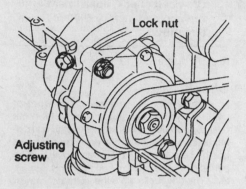

13.5 To adjust the 2.0L four-cylinder non-turbo alternator belt, loosen the alternator pivot bolt and locknut and turn the adjusting screw

13.6 To adjust the power steering belt on 2.0L four-cylinder non-turbo models without air conditioning, loosen the mounting bolts and pry the pump away from the engine

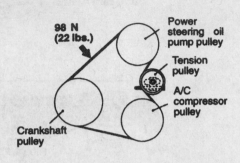

13.7 To adjust the power steering/air conditioning compressor belt on 2.0L four-cylinder non-turbo models, loosen the tension pulley nut and turn the adjusting bolt

2.0L four-cylinder non-turbo models

Refer to illustrations 13.5, 13.6 and 13.7

5   To adjust the alternator belt, remove the under cover side panel for access. Loosen the alternator pivot bolt and locknut, turn the adjusting bolt to set belt tension and tighten the nuts (**see illustration**).

6   To adjust the power steering belt on vehicles without air conditioning, loosen the power steering pump mounting bolts (**see illustration**). Carefully pry the pump away from the engine to tighten the belt, then tighten the bolts.

7   To adjust the power steering/air conditioning compressor belt on models so equipped, loosen the tensioner pulley nut (**see illustration**). Turn the adjusting bolt to set belt tension and tighten the pulley nut.

2.0L four-cylinder turbo models

Refer to illustrations 13.8, 13.9 and 13.10

8   To adjust the alternator belt, Loosen the alternator pivot bolt and adjuster lockbolt,

turn the adjuster bolt to set belt tension, and tighten the pivot nut and adjuster lockbolt (**see illustration**).

9   To adjust the power steering belt, loosen the power steering pump mounting bolts (**see illustration**). Carefully pry the pump away from the engine to tighten the belt, then tighten the bolts. Rotate the crankshaft one full turn clockwise, then recheck the belt tension and readjust it if necessary.

10   To adjust the air conditioning compressor belt, loosen the tensioner lockbolt (**see illustration**). Turn the adjusting bolt to set belt tension and tighten the pulley nut.

2.4L four-cylinder engine models

11   To adjust the alternator belt, loosen the alternator pivot bolt and adjuster lockbolt, turn the adjuster bolt to set belt tension, and tighten the pivot nut and adjuster lockbolt.

12   To adjust the power steering belt (and the air conditioning compressor belt on models so equipped), loosen the tensioner pulley nut (located behind the tensioner pulley). Turn

the tensioner adjusting bolt to set tension, then tighten the pulley nut.

V6 engine models

Refer to illustrations 13.13 and 13.14

13   To adjust the alternator and air conditioning compressor belt, loosen the tensioner pulley nut, then retighten it to 11 ft-lbs. Turn the tensioner adjusting bolt to set belt tension, then tighten the tensioner pulley nut securely (**see illustration**).

14   To adjust the power steering belt, loosen the tensioner locknut and bolt (**see illustration**). Turn the adjuster bolt to set belt tension, then tighten the locknut and bolt.

Replacement

Refer to illustration 13.17

15   To replace a belt, follow the above procedures for drivebelt adjustment to loosen the belt, but, when it's sufficiently loose, slip the belt off the crankshaft pulley and remove it. Since some belts may be installed outside

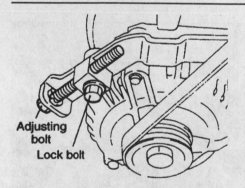

13.8 To adjust the 2.0L four-cylinder turbo alternator belt, loosen the pivot bolt and adjuster lockbolt and turn the adjusting bolt

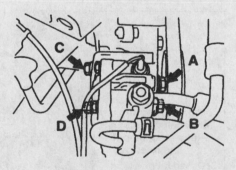

13.9 To adjust the 2.0L four-cylinder turbo power steering belt, loosen the power steering pump mounting bolts and pry the pump away from the engine

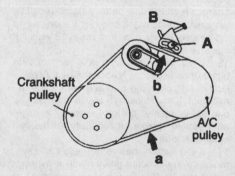

13.10 To adjust the 2.0L four-cylinder turbo air conditioning compressor belt, loosen the tensioner lockbolt (A) and turn the adjusting bolt (B)

13.13 Loosen the tensioner pulley nut (upper arrow), retighten it to 11 ft-lbs and turn the tensioner adjusting bolt (lower arrow) (V6 alternator/AC compressor belt) (straightedge and ruler show checking drivebelt tension)

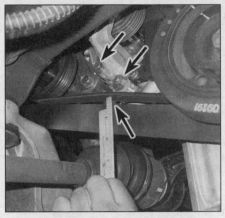

13.14 Loosen the tensioner locknut and pivot bolt (upper arrows) and turn the adjuster bolt (hidden, lower arrow) (V6 power steering belt) (straightedge and ruler show checking drivebelt tension)

of the belt you're trying to remove, you may have to remove other belts before you can get to the belt you're removing. Because of this and because belts tend to wear out more or less together, it is a good idea to replace all belts at the same time. Mark each belt and its appropriate pulley groove so the replacement belts can be installed in their proper positions.

16   Take the old belts to the parts store in order to make a direct comparison for length, width and design.

17   After replacing a V-ribbed drivebelt, make sure that it fits properly in the pulley or ribbed grooves in the pulleys **(see illustration)**. It is essential that the belt be properly centered.

18   Adjust the belt(s) in accordance with the procedure outlined above.

14   Underhood hose check and replacement (every 6000 miles or 6 months)

Warning: *Replacement of air conditioning hoses must be left to a dealer service department or air conditioning shop that has the equipment to depressurize the system safely. Never remove air conditioning components or hoses until the system has been depressurized.*

General

1   High temperatures in the engine compartment can cause the deterioration of the rubber and plastic hoses used for engine, accessory and emission systems operation. Periodic inspection should be made for cracks, loose clamps, material hardening and leaks.

2   Information specific to the cooling system hoses can be found in Section 15.

3   Some, but not all, hoses are secured to the fittings with clamps. Where clamps are used, check to be sure they haven't lost their tension, allowing the hose to leak. If clamps aren't used, make sure the hose has not

expanded and/or hardened where it slips over the fitting, allowing it to leak.

Vacuum hoses

4   It's quite common for vacuum hoses, especially those in the emissions system, to be color coded or identified by colored stripes molded into them. Various systems require hoses with different wall thicknesses, collapse resistance and temperature resistance. When replacing hoses, be sure the new ones are made of the same material.

5   Often the only effective way to check a hose is to remove it completely from the vehicle. If more than one hose is removed, be sure to label the hoses and fittings to ensure correct installation.

6   When checking vacuum hoses, be sure to include any plastic T-fittings in the check. Inspect the fittings for cracks and the hose where it fits over the fitting for distortion, which could cause leakage.

7   A small piece of vacuum hose (1/4-inch inside diameter) can be used as a stethoscope to detect vacuum leaks. Hold one end of the hose to your ear and probe around vacuum hoses and fittings, listening for the "hissing" sound characteristic of a vacuum leak. **Warning:** *When probing with the vacuum hose stethoscope, be very careful not to come into contact with moving engine components such as the drivebelts, cooling fan, etc.*

Fuel hose

Warning: *Gasoline is extremely flammable, so take extra precautions when you work on*

any part of the fuel system. Don't smoke or allow open flames or bare light bulbs near the work area, and don't work in a garage where a gas-type appliance (such as a water heater or a clothes dryer) is present. Since gasoline is carcinogenic, wear latex gloves when there's a possibility of being exposed to fuel, and, if you spill any fuel on your skin, rinse it off immediately with soap and water. Mop up any spills immediately and do not store fuel-soaked rags where they could ignite. The fuel system is under constant pressure, so, if any fuel lines are to be disconnected, the fuel pressure in the system must be relieved first (see Chapter 4 for more information). When you perform any kind of work on the fuel system, wear safety glasses and have a Class B type fire extinguisher on hand.*

8   Check all rubber fuel lines for deterioration and chafing. Check especially for cracks in areas where the hose bends and just before fittings, such as where a hose attaches to the fuel filter.

9   When replacing a hose, use only hose that is specifically designed for your fuel-injection system.

Metal lines

10   Sections of metal line are often used for fuel line between the fuel pump and fuel rail. Check carefully to be sure the line has not been bent or crimped and that cracks have not started in the line.

11   If a section of metal fuel line must be replaced, only seamless steel tubing should be used, since copper and aluminum tubing don't have the strength necessary to withstand normal engine vibration.

12   Check the metal brake lines where they enter the master cylinder and brake proportioning unit (if used) for cracks in the lines or loose fittings. Any sign of brake fluid leakage calls for an immediate thorough inspection of the brake system.

15   Cooling system check (every 6000 miles or 6 months)

Refer to illustration 15.4

1   Many major engine failures can be attributed to a faulty cooling system. If the vehicle is equipped with an automatic transaxle, the cooling system also cools the transaxle fluid and thus plays an important role in prolonging transaxle life.

2   The cooling system should be checked with the engine cold. Do this before the vehicle is driven for the day or after the engine

13.17 When installing a V-ribbed belt, make sure it is centered - it must not overlap either edge of the pulley

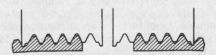

CORRECT   WRONG   WRONG

Check for a chafed area that could fail prematurely.

Check for a soft area indicating the hose has deteriorated inside.

Overtightening the clamp on a hardened hose will damage the hose and cause a leak.

Check each hose for swelling and oil-soaked ends. Cracks and breaks can be located by squeezing the hose

15.4 Hoses, like drivebelts, have a habit of failing at the worst possible time - to prevent the inconvenience of a blown radiator or heater hose, inspect them carefully, as shown here

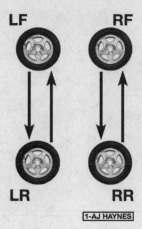

16.2a The recommended four-tire rotation pattern for directional radial tires

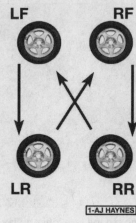

16.2b The recommended four-tire rotation pattern for non-directional radial tires

has been shut off for at least three hours.

3   Remove the radiator cap by turning it to the left until it reaches a stop. If you hear a hissing sound (indicating there is still pressure in the system), wait until it stops. Now press down on the cap with the palm of your hand and continue turning to the left until the cap can be removed. Thoroughly clean the cap, inside and out, with clean water. Also clean the filler neck on the radiator. All traces of corrosion should be removed. The coolant inside the radiator should be relatively transparent. If it's rust colored, the system should be drained and refilled (see Section 26). If the coolant level isn't up to the top, add additional antifreeze/coolant mixture (see Section 4).

4   Carefully check the large upper and lower radiator hoses along with the smaller diameter heater hoses which run from the engine to the firewall. Inspect each hose along its entire length, replacing any hose which is cracked, swollen or shows signs of deterioration. Cracks may become more apparent if the hose is squeezed **(see illustration)**. Regardless of condition, it's a good idea to replace

hoses with new ones every two years.

5   Make sure that all hose connections are tight. A leak in the cooling system will usually show up as white or rust colored deposits on the areas adjoining the leak. If wire-type clamps are used at the ends of the hoses, it may be a good idea to replace them with more secure screw-type clamps.

6   Use compressed air or a soft brush to remove bugs, leaves, etc. from the front of the radiator or air conditioning condenser. Be careful not to damage the delicate cooling fins or cut yourself on them.

7   Every other inspection, or at the first indication of cooling system problems, have the cap and system pressure tested. If you don't have a pressure tester, most gas stations and repair shops will do this for a minimal charge.

16   Tire rotation (every 6000 miles or 6 months)

Refer to illustrations 16.2a and 16.2b

1   The tires should be rotated at the specified intervals and whenever uneven wear is noticed. Since the vehicle will be raised and the tires removed anyway, check the brakes (see Section 18) at this time.

2   Radial tires must be rotated in a specific pattern **(see illustrations)**. Note: *Most vehicles are sold with non-directional radial tires, but some replacement performance tires are available that are directional and have a different rotation pattern. Directional tires have an arrow on the sidewall indicating the direction they must turn when mounted on the vehicle.*

3   Refer to the information in *Jacking and towing* at the front of this manual for the proper procedures to follow when raising the vehicle and changing a tire. If the brakes are to be checked, do not apply the parking brake as stated. Make sure the tires are blocked to prevent the vehicle from rolling.

4   Preferably, the entire vehicle should be raised at the same time. This can be done on a hoist or by jacking up each corner and then lowering the vehicle onto jackstands placed

under the frame rails. Always use four jackstands and make sure the vehicle is firmly supported.

5   After rotation, check and adjust the tire pressures as necessary and be sure to check the lug nut tightness.

6   For further information on the wheels and tires, refer to Chapter 10.

17   Fuel system check (every 15,000 miles or 12 months)

Refer to illustration 17.5

Warning: *Gasoline is extremely flammable, so take extra precautions when you work on any part of the fuel system. Don't smoke or allow open flames or bare light bulbs near the work area, and don't work in a garage where a gas-type appliance (such as a water heater or a clothes dryer) is present. Since gasoline is carcinogenic, wear latex gloves when there's a possibility of being exposed to fuel, and, if you spill any fuel on your skin, rinse it off immediately with soap and water. Mop up any spills immediately and do not store fuel-soaked rags where they could ignite. The fuel system is under constant pressure, so, if any fuel lines are to be disconnected, the fuel pressure in the system must be relieved first (see Chapter 4 for more information). When you perform any kind of work on the fuel system, wear safety glasses and have a Class B type fire extinguisher on hand.*

1   If you smell gasoline while driving or after the vehicle has been sitting in the sun, inspect the fuel system immediately.

2   Remove the gas filler cap and inspect it for damage and corrosion. The gasket should have an unbroken sealing imprint. If the gasket is damaged or corroded, remove it and install a new one.

3   Inspect the fuel feed and return lines for cracks. Make sure that the threaded flare-nut-type connectors which secure the metal fuel lines to the fuel injection system and the banjo bolts which secure the banjo fittings to the in-line fuel filter are tight.

17.5 Inspect the fuel filler hose for cracks and make sure the clamps (arrow) are tight on all hoses in the system

18.7a You will find an inspection hole like this in each caliper (arrow) - placing a ruler across the hole should enable you to determine the thickness of remaining pad material for both inner and outer pads

18.7b If the outer pad's thickness is hard to see through the inspection hole, look up at the pad from above the caliper

4   Since some components of the fuel system - the fuel tank and part of the fuel feed and return lines, for example - are underneath the vehicle, they can be inspected more easily with the vehicle raised on a hoist. If that's not possible, raise the vehicle and support it securely on jackstands.

5   With the vehicle raised and safely supported, inspect the fuel tank and filler neck for punctures, cracks and other damage **(see illustration)**. The connection between the filler neck and the tank is particularly critical. Sometimes, a rubber filler neck will leak because of loose clamps or deteriorated rubber. These are problems a home mechanic can usually rectify. **Warning:** *Do not, under any circumstances, try to repair a fuel tank (except rubber components). A welding torch or any open flame can easily cause fuel vapors inside the tank to explode.*

6   Carefully check all rubber hoses and metal lines leading away from the fuel tank. Check for loose connections, deteriorated hoses, crimped lines and other damage. Carefully inspect the lines from the tank to the fuel injection system. Repair or replace damaged sections as necessary (see Chapter 4).

18   Brake check (every 15,000 miles or 12 months)

Refer to illustrations 18.7a, 18.7b and 18.13
Warning: *Dust produced by lining wear and deposited on brake components is hazardous to your health. DO NOT blow it out with compressed air and DO NOT inhale it! DO NOT use gasoline or solvents to remove the dust. Brake system cleaner should be used to flush the dust into a drain pan. After the brake components are wiped with a damp rag, dispose of the contaminated rag(s) and brake cleaner in a covered and labeled container. Try to use non-asbestos replacement parts whenever possible.*
Note: *For detailed photographs of the brake system, refer to Chapter 9.*
1   In addition to the specified intervals, the

brakes should be inspected every time the wheels are removed or whenever a defect is suspected.

2   Any of the following symptoms could indicate a potential brake system defect: The vehicle pulls to one side when the brake pedal is depressed; the brakes make squealing or dragging noises when applied; brake travel is excessive; the pedal pulsates; brake fluid leaks, usually onto the inside of the tire or wheel.

3   These models are equipped with disc brakes on the front wheels and either disc or drum brakes at the rear. The front disc brake pads have built-in wear indicators which should make a high-pitched squealing or scraping noise when they are worn to the replacement point. When you hear this noise, replace the pads immediately or expensive damage to the discs can result.

4   Loosen the wheel lug nuts.

5   Raise the vehicle and place it securely on jackstands.

6   Remove the wheels (see *Jacking and towing* at the front of this book, or your owner's manual, if necessary).

Disc brake pad/caliper check

7   There are two pads - an outer and an inner - in each caliper. The pads are visible through an inspection hole in each caliper **(see illustrations)**.

8   Check the pad thickness by looking at each end of the caliper and through the inspection hole in the caliper body. If the lining material is less than the thickness listed in this Chapter's Specifications, replace the pads. **Note:** *Keep in mind that the lining material is riveted or bonded to a metal backing plate and the metal portion is not included in this measurement.*

9   If it is difficult to determine the exact thickness of the remaining pad material by the above method, or if you are at all concerned about the condition of the pads, remove the caliper(s), then remove the pads for further

inspection (see Chapter 9).

10   Once the pads have been removed, clean them with brake cleaner and re-measure them.

11   Measure the disc thickness with a micrometer to make sure that it still has service life remaining. If any disc is thinner than the specified minimum thickness, replace it (see Chapter 9). Even if the disc has service life remaining, check its condition. Look for scoring, gouging and burned spots. If these conditions exist, remove the disc and have it resurfaced (see Chapter 9).

Drum brake check

12   Refer to Chapter 9 for the rear brake shoe, drum and wheel cylinder checking procedures.

Brake hose and line check

13   Before installing the wheels, check all brake lines and hoses for damage, wear, deformation, cracks, corrosion, leakage, bends and twists, particularly in the vicinity of the rubber hoses at the calipers **(see illustration)**. Check the clamps for tightness and

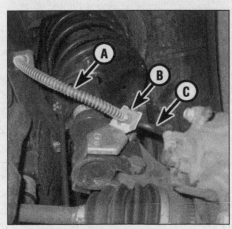

18.13 Inspect the flexible brake hoses (A) at each caliper, the connections at the caliper (B) and where the flexible line joins the steel line (C)

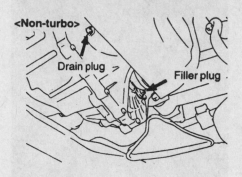

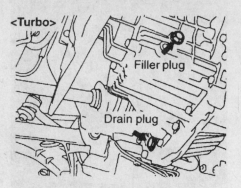

19.1a Remove the fill plug from the transaxle and use your finger to make sure the lubricant level is even with the bottom of the plug hole - here are the 2.0L four-cylinder non-turbo fill and drain plugs . . .

19.1b . . . and the 2.0L turbo fill and drain plugs (2.4L four cylinder and V6 similar)

the connections for leakage. Make sure that all hoses and lines are clear of sharp edges, moving parts and the exhaust system. If any of the above conditions are noted, repair, reroute or replace the lines and/or fittings as necessary (see Chapter 9).

Brake booster check

14   Sit in the driver's seat and perform the following sequence of tests.
15   With the brake fully depressed, start the engine - the pedal should move down a little when the engine starts.
16   With the engine running, depress the brake pedal several times - the travel distance should not change.
17   Depress the brake, stop the engine and hold the pedal in for about 30 seconds - the pedal should neither sink nor rise.
18   Restart the engine, run it for about a minute and turn it off. Then firmly depress the brake several times - the pedal travel should decrease with each application.
19   If your brakes do not operate as described, the brake booster has failed. Refer to Chapter 9 for the replacement procedure.

Parking brake check

20   Slowly pull up on the parking brake and count the number of clicks you hear until the handle is up as far as it will go. The adjustment is correct if you hear the number of clicks listed in this Chapter's Specifications. If you hear more or fewer clicks, it's time to adjust the parking brake (see Chapter 9).
21   An alternative method of checking the parking brake is to park the vehicle on a steep hill with the parking brake set and the transmission in Neutral (be sure to stay in the vehicle for this check!). If the parking brake cannot prevent the vehicle from rolling, it is in need of adjustment (see Chapter 9).

19   Manual transaxle lubricant level check (every 15,000 miles or 12 months)

Refer to illustrations 19.1a and 19.1b

1   The manual transaxle does not have a dipstick. To check the fluid level, raise the vehicle and support it securely on jackstands. On the lower front or side of the transaxle housing, you will see a threaded plug **(see illustrations)**. Unscrew and remove it. If the

lubricant level is correct, it should be up to the lower edge of the hole.
2   If the transaxle needs more lubricant (if the level is not up to the hole), use a syringe or pump to add more of the specified lubricant (see this Chapter's Specifications). Stop filling the transaxle when the lubricant begins to run out the hole.
3   Install the plug and tighten it securely. Drive the vehicle a short distance, then check for leaks.

20   Transfer case lubricant level check (4WD models only) (every 15,000 miles or 12 months)

Refer to illustration 20.1

1   Raise the vehicle and support it securely on jackstands. On the side of the transfer case housing, you will see a plug **(see illustration)**. Unscrew and remove it. If the lubricant level is correct, it should be up to the lower edge of the hole.
2   If the transfer case needs more lubricant (if the level is not up to the hole), use a syringe or pump to add more. Stop filling the transaxle when the lubricant begins to run out the hole.
3   Install the plug and tighten it securely. Drive the vehicle a short distance, then check for leaks.

21   Rear differential lubricant level check (4WD models only) (every 15,000 miles or 12 months)

Refer to illustration 21.1

1   To check the fluid level, raise the vehicle and support it securely on jackstands. On the rear differential cover, you will see a plug **(see illustration)**. Remove it. If the lubricant level is correct, it should be up to the lower edge of the hole.
2   If the differential needs more lubricant (if the level is not up to the hole), use a syringe

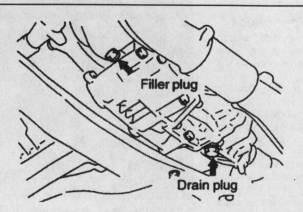

20.1 Remove the transfer case filler plug (arrow) and make sure the lubricant level is even with the bottom of the plug hole

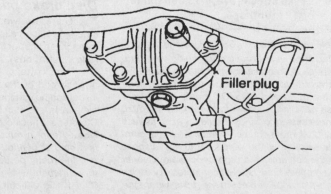

21.1 Rear differential filler plug location (arrow) (4WD models) - the lubricant level must be even with the bottom of the plug hole

22.2a Inspect for rustout or for signs of damage or leakage at the front pipe, exhaust hangers and the catalytic converter

22.2b At the rear of the vehicle, inspect the muffler, the rear pipe flange and the tailpipe

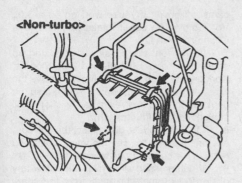

23.2a Here are the 2.0L four-cylinder non-turbo air filter cover clips

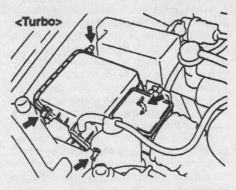

23.2b Here are the 2.0L four-cylinder turbo air filter cover clips

23.2c Here are the 2.4L four-cylinder and V6 air filter cover clips (arrows - one clip hidden)

or a gear oil pump to add more. Stop filling the differential housing when the lubricant begins to run out the hole.

3   Install the plug and tighten it securely. Drive the vehicle a short distance, then check for leaks.

22 Exhaust system check (every 30,000 miles or 24 months)

Refer to illustrations 22.2a and 22.2b

1   With the engine cold (at least three hours after the vehicle has been driven), check the complete exhaust system from its starting point at the engine to the end of the tailpipe. This should be done on a hoist where unrestricted access is available.

2   Check the pipes and connections for evidence of leaks, severe corrosion or damage. Make sure that all brackets and hangers are in good condition and tight **(see illustrations)**.

3   At the same time, inspect the underside of the body for holes, corrosion, open seams, etc. which may allow exhaust gases to enter the passenger compartment. Seal all body openings with silicone or body putty.

4   Rattles and other noises can often be traced to the exhaust system, especially the mounts and hangers. Try to move the pipes, muffler and catalytic converter. If the components can come in contact with the body or suspension parts, secure the exhaust system with new mounts.

5   Check the running condition of the engine by inspecting inside the end of the tailpipe. The exhaust deposits here are an indication of engine state-of-tune. If the pipe is black and sooty or coated with white deposits, the engine is in need of a tune-up, including a thorough fuel system inspection.

23 Air filter replacement (every 30,000 miles or 24 months)

Refer to illustrations 23.2a, 23.2b, 23.2c and 23.3

1   The air filter is located inside a housing in the engine compartment.

2   Detach the spring clips **(see illustrations)**.

3   Detach the cover and remove the air filter element **(see illustration)**.

4   Inspect the outer surface of the filter element. If it is dirty, replace it. If it is only moderately dusty, it can be reused by blowing it clean from the back to the front surface with compressed air. Because it is a pleated paper type filter, it cannot be washed or oiled. If it cannot be cleaned satisfactorily with compressed air, discard and replace it.

5   Installation is the reverse of removal.

23.3 Lift the element out of the housing

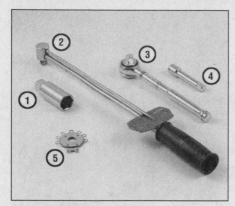

24.1 Tools required for changing spark plugs

1   **Spark plug socket** - *This will have special padding inside to protect the spark plug's porcelain insulator*
2   **Torque wrench** - *Although not mandatory, using this tool is the best way to ensure the plugs are tightened properly*
3   **Ratchet** - *Standard hand tool to fit the spark plug socket*
4   **Extension** - *A longer one is usually necessary on 2.0L (DOHC) models, since the spark plugs are set deeply into the cylinder head*
5   **Spark plug gap gauge** - *This gauge for checking the gap comes in a variety of styles. Make sure the gap for your engine is included*

24   Spark plug check and replacement (every 30,000 miles or 24 months)

Refer to illustrations 24.1, 24.4a, 24.4b, 24.7, 24.10, 24.12a and 24.12b
Caution: *The center electrode on iridium spark plugs is very small with a fine needle-like point, and this gap cannot be adjusted. Do not insert a flat feeler gauge as this point may be broken off, or the iridium coating could be scraped off.*

1   Spark plug replacement requires a spark plug socket which fits onto a ratchet wrench. This socket is lined with a rubber grommet to protect the porcelain insulator of the spark plug and to hold the plug while you insert it into the spark plug hole. You will also need a wire-type feeler gauge to check and adjust the spark plug gap and a torque wrench to tighten the new plugs to the specified torque **(see illustration)**.
2   If you are replacing the plugs, purchase the new plugs, adjust them to the proper gap and then replace each plug one at a time. **Note:** *When buying new spark plugs, it's essential that you obtain the correct plugs for your specific vehicle. This information can be found in the Specifications Section at the beginning of this Chapter, on the Vehicle Emissions Control Information (VECI) label located on the underside of the hood or in the own-*

24.4a Spark plug manufacturers recommend using a wire-type gauge when checking the gap - if the wire does not slide between the electrodes with a slight drag, adjustment is required

er's manual. If these sources specify different plugs, purchase the spark plug type specified on the VECI label because that information is provided specifically for your engine.
3   Inspect each of the new plugs for defects. If there are any signs of cracks in the porcelain insulator of a plug, don't use it.
4   Check the electrode gaps of the new plugs. Check the gap by inserting the wire gauge of the proper thickness between the electrodes at the tip of the plug **(see illustration)**. The gap between the electrodes should be identical to that listed in this Chapter's Specifications or on the VECI label. If the gap is incorrect, use the notched adjuster on the feeler gauge body to bend the curved side electrode slightly **(see illustration)**.
5   If the side electrode is not exactly over the center electrode, use the notched adjuster to align them. **Caution:** *If the gap of a new plug must be adjusted, bend only the base of the side electrode - do not touch the tip.*

Removal

6   On turbo models, remove the screws and detach the spark plug cover from the

24.7 When removing the spark plug wires, pull only on the boot and twist it back-and-forth

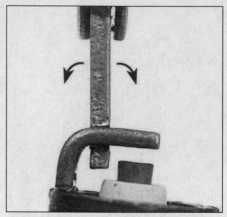

24.4b To change the gap, bend the side electrode only, as indicated by the arrows, and be very careful not to crack or chip the porcelain insulator surrounding the center electrode

camshaft cover. If you're working on a 3.0L V6, remove the upper intake manifold (see Chapter 2, Part D).
7   To prevent the possibility of mixing up spark plug wires on 2.0L and 3.0L models, work on one spark plug at a time. Remove the wire and boot from one spark plug. Grasp the boot, not the cable, give it a half twist and pull straight up **(see illustration)**.
8   On 2.4L models, disconnect the coil connector. Remove the coil mounting bolts and remove the coil/plug wire assembly.
9   If compressed air is available, blow any dirt or foreign material away from the spark plug area before proceeding.
10   Remove the spark plug **(see illustration)**.
11   Whether you are replacing the plugs at this time or intend to re-use the old plugs, compare each old spark plug with those shown in the color photos on the inside back cover of this manual to determine the overall running condition of the engine.

Installation

12   Prior to installation, apply a coat of anti-

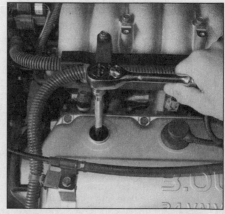

24.10 Use a socket wrench with a long extension to unscrew the spark plugs

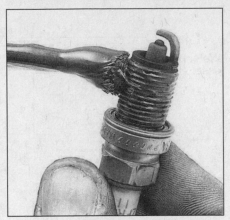

24.12a Apply a coat of anti-seize compound to the spark plug threads

24.12b A length of snug-fitting rubber hose will save time and prevent damaged threads when installing the spark plugs

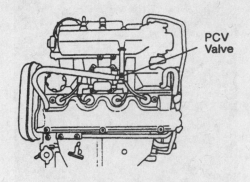

25.2a Here's the 2.0L four-cylinder non-turbo PCV valve . . .

seize compound to the spark plug threads (**see illustration**). It's often difficult to insert spark plugs into their holes without cross-threading them. To avoid this possibility, fit a short piece of rubber hose over the end of the spark plug (**see illustration**). The flexible hose acts as a universal joint to help align the plug with the plug hole. Should the plug begin to cross-thread, the hose will slip on the spark plug, preventing thread damage. Tighten the plug to the torque listed in this Chapter's Specifications.

13   Attach the plug wire to the new spark plug, again using a twisting motion on the boot until it is firmly seated on the end of the spark plug.

14   Follow the above procedure for the remaining spark plugs, replacing them one at a time to prevent mixing up the spark plug wires.

25   Positive Crankcase Ventilation (PCV) valve and hose check and replacement (every 30,000 miles or 24 months)

Refer to illustrations 25.2a, 25.2b and 25.2c

1   The PCV valve and hose are located in the valve cover.

2   Disconnect the hose, unscrew the PCV valve from the cover, then reconnect the hose (**see illustrations**).

3   With the engine idling at normal operating temperature, place your finger over the valve opening. If there's no vacuum at the valve, check for a plugged hose or valve. Replace any plugged or deteriorated hoses.

4   Turn off the engine and insert a small rod into the valve from the threaded side and make sure the plunger inside the valve moves. If the valve doesn't move, replace it with a new one.

5   When purchasing a replacement PCV valve, make sure it's for your particular vehicle and engine size. Compare the old valve with the new one to make sure they're the same.

26   Cooling system servicing (draining, flushing and refilling) (every 30,000 miles or 24 months)

Warning: *Do not allow engine coolant (antifreeze) to come in contact with your skin or painted surfaces of the vehicle, since it will irritate your skin or damage the paint. Rinse off spills immediately with plenty of water. Do not store new coolant or leave old coolant lying around where it accessible to children or pets, because they are attracted by its sweet smell. Antifreeze is highly toxic if ingested. Never leave antifreeze lying around in an open container or in puddles on the floor; children and pets are attracted by its sweet smell and may drink it. Check with local authorities about disposing of used antifreeze. Many communities have collection centers which will see that antifreeze is disposed of safely.*

1   Periodically, the cooling system should be drained, flushed and refilled to replenish the antifreeze mixture and prevent formation of rust and corrosion, which can impair the performance of the cooling system and cause engine damage. When the cooling system is serviced, all hoses and the radiator cap should be checked and replaced if necessary.

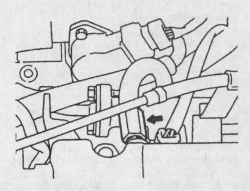

25.2b . . . the 2.0L four-cylinder turbo PCV valve (2.4L similar) . . .

Draining

Refer to illustrations 26.4, 26.5a, 26.5b and 26.5c

2   Apply the parking brake and block the wheels. If the vehicle has just been driven, wait several hours to allow the engine to cool down before beginning this procedure.

3   Once the engine is completely cool,

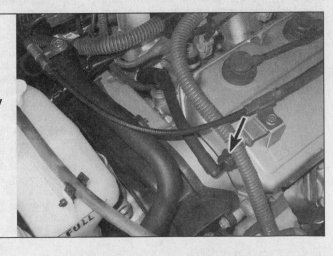

25.2c . . . and the V6 PCV valve (2.4L four-cylinder similar)

26.4 The drain fitting (arrow) is located at the lower corner of the radiator - turn it counterclockwise to loosen it

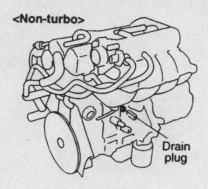

26.5a Here's the 2.0L four-cylinder non-turbo engine block drain . . .

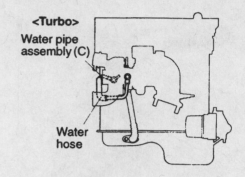

26.5b . . . the 2.0L turbo engine block drain . . .

remove the radiator cap and inspect it, as described in Section 15.

4   Move a large container under the radiator drain to catch the coolant. Open the drain fitting (a pair of pliers may be required to turn it) **(see illustration)**.

5   After the coolant stops flowing out of the radiator, move the container under the engine drain plug (all except 2.0 turbo engines) or the coolant tube on the side of the engine (2.0L four-cylinder turbo) **(see illustrations)**. Remove the plug(s) (all except 2.0L four-cylinder turbo) or disconnect the hose from the tube (2.0L four-cylinder turbo). Allow the coolant to drain from the block. **Note:** *Frequently, the coolant will not drain from the block after the plug or hose is removed. This is due to a built-up rust layer. Insert a Phillips screwdriver to break the rust barrier.*

6   While the coolant is draining, check the condition of the radiator hoses, heater hoses and clamps (refer to Section 15 if necessary).

7   Replace any damaged clamps or hoses (see Chapter 3).

Flushing

8   Once the system is completely drained, flush the radiator with fresh water from a garden hose until water runs clear at the drain. The flushing action of the water will remove sediments from the radiator but will not remove rust and scale from the engine and cooling tube surfaces.

9   These deposits can be removed by the chemical action of a cleaner. Follow the procedure outlined in the manufacturer's instructions. If the radiator is severely corroded, damaged or leaking, it should be removed (see Chapter 3) and taken to a radiator repair shop.

10   Remove the overflow hose from the coolant recovery reservoir. Drain the reservoir and flush it with clean water, then reconnect the hose.

Refilling

11   Close and tighten the radiator and block drains. If you're working on a 2.0L four-cylinder turbo model, connect the hose to the

metal tube.

12   Place the heater temperature control in the maximum heat position.

13   Slowly add new coolant (a 50/50 mixture of water and antifreeze) to the radiator until it's full. Add coolant to the reservoir up to the lower mark.

14   Leave the radiator cap off and run the engine in a well-ventilated area until the thermostat opens (coolant will begin flowing through the radiator and the upper radiator hose will become hot).

15   Turn the engine off and let it cool. Add more coolant mixture to bring the level back up to the lip on the radiator filler neck.

16   Squeeze the upper radiator hose to expel air, then add more coolant mixture, if necessary. Replace the radiator cap.

17   Start the engine, allow it to reach normal operating temperature and check for leaks.

27   Automatic transaxle fluid and filter change (every 30,000 miles or 24 months)

1   At the specified time intervals, the automatic transaxle fluid should be drained and replaced.

2   Before beginning work, purchase the specified transmission fluid (see *Recommended fluids and lubricants* at the front of this Chapter).

3   Other tools necessary for this job include jackstands to support the vehicle in a raised position, a wrench, a drain pan capable of holding at least eight pints, newspapers and clean rags.

4   The fluid should be drained immediately after the vehicle has been driven. Hot fluid is more effective than cold fluid at removing built up sediment. **Warning:** *Fluid temperature can exceed 350-degrees F in a hot transaxle. Wear protective gloves and make sure the fluid cannot spill on you!*

5   After the vehicle has been driven to warm up the fluid, raise it and place it on jackstands for access to drain the fluid.

26.5c . . . and the 3.0L engine block drain

6   Move the necessary equipment under the vehicle, being careful not to touch any of the hot exhaust components.

2.0L four-cylinder non-turbo models

Refer to illustration 27.7

7   With the drain pan in place, loosen the pan bolts, but don't remove them yet **(see illustration)**. Tap the pan with a rubber mallet to separate it from the transaxle and allow the fluid to drain. Once the fluid has drained, remove the bolts and lower the pan. **Warning:** *There is hot fluid in the pan that often splashes out, so position yourself out of the way!*

8   Remove the filter retaining bolt(s) and lower the filter from the transaxle. Be careful when lowering the filter as it contains residual fluid.

9   Place the new filter in position and install the bolt(s). Tighten the bolts to the torque listed in the Specifications Section at the beginning of this Chapter.

10   Carefully clean the gasket surfaces of the fluid pan, removing all traces of old gasket material. Noting the location, remove the magnets, wash the pan in clean solvent and dry it with compressed air. Be sure to clean and reinstall the magnets.

11   Install a new gasket, place the fluid pan

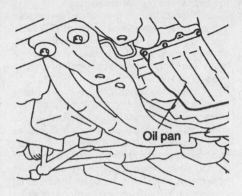

27.7 On 2.0L four-cylinder non-turbo models, loosen the pan bolts and remove the pan partway, then remove it the rest of the way after the fluid has drained

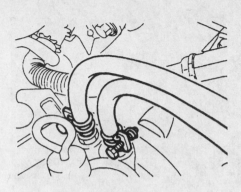

27.17 On 2.0L four-cylinder turbo and 1998 and 1999 2.4L four-cylinder models, disconnect the fluid cooler hose at the radiator . . .

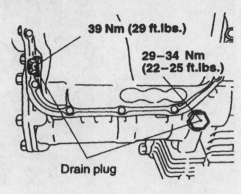

27.19 . . . and remove both transaxle drain plugs

in position and install the bolts in their original positions. Tighten the bolts to the torque listed in this Chapter's Specifications.

12   Lower the vehicle.

13   With the engine off, add new fluid to the transaxle through the dipstick tube (see *Recommended fluids and lubricants* for the recommended fluid type and capacity). Use a funnel to prevent spills. It is best to add a little fluid at a time. Allow the fluid time to drain into the pan.

14   Start the engine and let it idle for one minute. Shift the selector into all positions from P through L, then shift into P and apply the parking brake.

15   With the engine idling, check the fluid level. Add fluid up to 1/8-inch below the Add mark on the dipstick.

16   Operate the vehicle to bring transmission temperature up to normal, then recheck the level on the dipstick. It should be within the Hot range.

2.0L four-cylinder turbo models, 1998 and 1999 2.4L engine models

Refer to illustrations 27.17 and 27.19

17   If you're working on a 1998 or later 2.0 turbo model, locate the oil cooler hoses on top of the transaxle (see illustration). Disconnect the transaxle end of the hose that runs to the rear of the vehicle and point it into the drain pan. Cap off the fitting on the transaxle to keep out dirt. Be prepared for fluid to be expelled from the hose with considerable force.

18   Have an assistant start the engine and let it idle in neutral while you watch the hose. Let the engine run until the fluid stops coming out, then shut the engine off immediately (but in any case, don't let the engine run longer than one minute).

19   Remove the drain plugs from the transaxle and drain the fluid (see illustration).

20   Unbolt the oil pan from the transaxle. Clean the oil pan, replace the filter and reinstall the oil pan as described in Steps 8 through 11 above.

21   Reinstall the drain plugs and lower the vehicle.

22   With the engine off, add new fluid to the transaxle through the dipstick tube (see *Recommended fluids and lubricants* for the recommended fluid type and capacity). Use a funnel to prevent spills. It is best to add a little fluid at a time. Allow the fluid time to drain into the transaxle.

23   Repeat Step 18 above to pump more fluid into the pan, then drain a small amount from one of the drain plugs and check it for contamination (it should be red, not brown, and should not have a burned smell). If it's contaminated, add more fluid, then repeat Step 18 and this Step again.

24   Uncap the transaxle hose fitting and reconnect the hose. Install the drain plug.

25   Start the engine and let it idle for one to two minutes. Shift the selector into all positions from P through L, then shift into P and apply the parking brake.

26   With the engine idling, check the fluid level. It should be up to the Cold mark on the dipstick. Add fluid slowly to bring the level up if necessary.

27   Operate the vehicle to bring transmission temperature up to normal, then recheck the level on the dipstick. It should be within the Hot range.

2000 and later 2.4L four-cylinder, all V6 engine models

Refer to illustrations 27.28 and 27.30

28   If you're working on one of these models, locate the oil cooler hose that connects to the metal tube at the radiator (see illustration). Disconnect the hose from the tube and point it into the drain pan. Cap off the fitting on the transaxle to keep out dirt. Be prepared for the fluid to be expelled from the hose with considerable force.

29   Have an assistant start the engine and let it idle in neutral while you watch the hose. Let the engine run until the fluid stops coming out, then shut the engine off immediately (but in any case, don't let the engine run longer than one minute).

30   Remove the drain plug from the transaxle and drain the fluid (see illustration).

31   With the engine off, add new fluid to the transaxle through the dipstick tube (see *Recommended fluids and lubricants* for the rec-

27.28 On 2000 and later 2.4L four-cylinder models and all V6 models, disconnect the fluid cooler hose at the radiator . . .

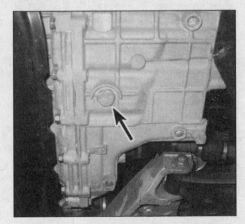

27.30 . . . and remove the transaxle drain plug

31.10 Flex the inner and outer driveaxle boots by hand to check for cracks and/ or leaking grease

ommended fluid type and capacity). Use a funnel to prevent spills. It is best to add a little fluid at a time. Allow the fluid time to drain into the transaxle.

32   Repeat Step 29 above to pump more fluid into the pan, then drain a small amount from the drain plugs and check it for contamination (it should be red, not brown, and should not have a burned smell). If it's contaminated, add more fluid, then repeat Step 29 and this Step again.

33   Reconnect the fluid hose to the fitting at the radiator. Install and tighten the drain plug(s).

34   Start the engine and let it idle for one to two minutes. Shift the selector into all positions from P through L, then shift into P and apply the parking brake.

35   With the engine idling, check the fluid level. It should be up to the Cold mark on the dipstick. Add fluid slowly to bring the level up if necessary.

36   Operate the vehicle to bring transmission temperature up to normal, then recheck the level on the dipstick. It should be within the Hot range.

37   These models may be equipped with an external oil filter that resembles an engine oil filter. If so, unscrew it from the transmission, using an oil filter wrench. Coat the gasket of the new filter with a thin film of transmission fluid, then screw it on until the gasket contacts the mating surface and tighten an additional 3/4-turn.

38   Repeat Step 36 to recheck the transmission fluid level and add some if necessary.

28   Manual transaxle lubricant change (every 30,000 miles or 24 months)

1   Remove the transaxle filler plug, then unscrew and remove the drain plug and drain the fluid (see Section 19).

2   Reinstall the drain plug and tighten it securely.

3   Add new fluid until it begins to run out of the filler hole (see Section 19). See *Recom-*

mended lubricants and fluids for the specified lubricant type.

29   Transfer case lubricant change (4WD models only) (every 30,000 miles or 24 months)

1   Remove the transfer case filler plug, then remove the drain plug and drain the fluid (see Section 20).

2   Reinstall the drain plug securely.

3   Add new fluid until it begins to run out of the filler hole (see Section 20). See *Recommended lubricants and fluids* for the specified lubricant type.

30   Rear differential lubricant change (4WD models only) (every 30,000 miles or 24 months)

1   Remove the differential filler plug, then unscrew and remove the drain plug and drain the fluid (see Section 21).

2   Reinstall the drain plug securely.

3   Add new fluid until it begins to run out of the filler hole (see Section 21). See *Recommended lubricants and fluids* for the specified lubricant type.

31   Steering, suspension and driveaxle boot check (every 30,000 miles or 24 months)

Note: *For detailed illustrations of the steering and suspension components, refer to Chapter 10.*

With the wheels on the ground

1   With the vehicle stopped and the front wheels pointed straight ahead, rock the steering wheel gently back and forth. If freeplay is excessive, a front wheel bearing, intermediate shaft U-joint, control arm balljoint or tie-rod end is worn or the steering gear is out of adjustment or broken. Refer to Chapter 10 for

the appropriate repair procedure.

2   Other symptoms, such as excessive vehicle body movement over rough roads, swaying (leaning) around corners and binding as the steering wheel is turned, may indicate faulty steering and/or suspension components.

3   Check the shock absorbers by pushing down and releasing the vehicle several times at each corner. If the vehicle does not come back to a level position within one or two bounces, the shocks/struts are worn and must be replaced. When bouncing the vehicle up and down, listen for squeaks and noises from the suspension components. Additional information on suspension components can be found in Chapter 10.

Under the vehicle

Refer to illustration 31.10

4   Raise the vehicle with a floor jack and support it securely on jackstands. See *Jacking and towing* at the front of this book for the proper jacking points.

5   Check the tires for irregular wear patterns and proper inflation. See Section 5 in this Chapter for information regarding tire wear and Chapter 10 for the wheel bearing replacement procedures.

6   Inspect the universal joint between the steering shaft and the steering gear housing. Check the rack-and-pinion housing for fluid leakage or oozing. Make sure the dust seals and boots are not damaged and that the boot clamps are not loose. Check the steering linkage for looseness or damage. Check the tie-rod ends for excessive play. Look for loose bolts, broken or disconnected parts and deteriorated rubber bushings on all suspension and steering components. While an assistant turns the steering wheel from side to side, check the steering components for free movement, chafing and binding. If the steering components do not seem to be reacting with the movement of the steering wheel, try to determine where the slack is located.

7   Check each front wheel's balljoint for wear by grasping the wheel securely and moving it in-and-out to ensure there is no play. If any balljoint does have play, replace it. See Chapter 10 for the front balljoint replacement procedure.

8   Inspect the balljoint boots for damage and leaking grease. Replace the balljoints with new ones if they are damaged (see Chapter 10).

9   The driveaxle boots are very important because they prevent dirt, water and foreign material from entering and damaging the constant velocity (CV) joints. Oil and grease can cause the boot material to deteriorate prematurely, so it's a good idea to wash the boots with soap and water.

10   Inspect the boots for tears and cracks as well as loose clamps **(see illustration)**. If there is any evidence of cracks or leaking lubricant, they must be replaced as described in Chapter 8.

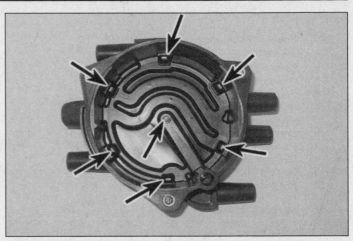

32.10a Remove the wires from the distributor cap one at a time, by pulling on the boots

32.10b Check the distributor cap for carbon tracking and worn or burned contacts (if in doubt about its condition, install a new one)

32 Spark plug wire, distributor cap and rotor check and replacement (every 60,000 miles or 48 months)

Note: *Only 3.0L V6 engines require a distributor cap and rotor check. All other engines are equipped with a direct ignition system that does not use a distributor.*

All engines

1   Begin this procedure by making a visual check of the spark plug wires while the engine is running. In a darkened garage (make sure there is ventilation) start the engine and observe each plug wire. Be careful not to come into contact with any moving engine parts. If there is a break in the wire, you will see arcing or a small spark at the damaged area. If arcing is noticed, make a note to obtain new wires, then allow the engine to cool and check the distributor cap and rotor (if equipped).

2   The spark plug wires should be inspected one at a time to prevent mixing up the order, which is essential for proper engine operation. Each original plug wire should be numbered to help identify its location. If the number is

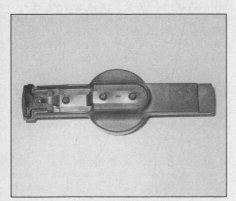

32.11 The V6 engine ignition rotor should be checked for wear and corrosion (if in doubt about its condition, buy a new one)

illegible, a piece of tape can be marked with the correct number and wrapped around the plug wire.

3   Remove the ignition coils and spark plug wires (See Section 24).

4   Check inside the boot for corrosion, which will look like a white crusty powder.

5   Push the wire and boot back onto the end of the spark plug. It should fit tightly onto the end of the plug. If it doesn't, remove the wire and use pliers to carefully crimp the metal connector inside the wire boot until the fit is snug.

6   Using a clean rag, wipe the entire length of the wire to remove built-up dirt and grease. Once the wire is clean, check for burns, cracks and other damage. Do not bend the wire sharply, because the conductor might break.

7   Disconnect the wire from the distributor or coil pack. Again, pull only on the rubber boot. Check for corrosion and a tight fit. Replace the wire in the distributor.

8   Inspect the remaining spark plug wires, making sure that each one is securely fastened at the distributor or coil pack and spark plug when the check is complete.

9   If new spark plug wires are required, purchase a set for your specific engine model. Pre-cut wire sets with the boots already installed are available. Remove and replace the wires one at a time to avoid mix-ups in the firing order.

V6 engines only

Refer to illustrations 32.10a, 32.10b and 32.11

10   Disconnect the plug wires from the distributor cap **(see illustration)**. Detach the distributor cap by removing the cap retaining screws. Look inside it for cracks, carbon tracks and worn, burned or loose contacts **(see illustration)**.

11   Pull the rotor off the distributor shaft and examine it for cracks and carbon tracks **(see illustration)**. Replace the cap and rotor if any damage or defects are noted.

12   It is common practice to install a new cap and rotor whenever new spark plug wires are installed, but if you wish to continue using the old cap, check the resistance between the spark plug wires and the cap first. If the indicated resistance is more than the maximum value listed in this Chapter's Specifications, replace the cap and/or wires.

13   When installing a new cap, remove the wires from the old cap one at a time and attach them to the new cap in the exact same location - do not simultaneously remove all the wires from the old cap or firing order mix-ups may occur.

33 Fuel filter replacement (every 60,000 miles or 48 months)

Warning: *Gasoline is extremely flammable, so take extra precautions when you work on any part of the fuel system. Don't smoke or allow open flames or bare light bulbs near the work area, and don't work in a garage where a gas-type appliance (such as a water heater or a clothes dryer) is present. Since gasoline is carcinogenic, wear latex gloves when there's a possibility of being exposed to fuel, and, if you spill any fuel on your skin, rinse it off immediately with soap and water. Mop up any spills immediately and do not store fuel-soaked rags where they could ignite. The fuel system is under constant pressure, so, if any fuel lines are to be disconnected, the fuel pressure in the system must be relieved first (see Chapter 4 for more information). When you perform any kind of work on the fuel system, wear safety glasses and have a Class B type fire extinguisher on hand.*

2.0L four-cylinder models

Refer to illustration 33.1

1   Relieve the fuel system pressure (see Chapter 4). The fuel filter is mounted in the line between the fuel tank and the fuel rail in the engine compartment **(see illustration)**.

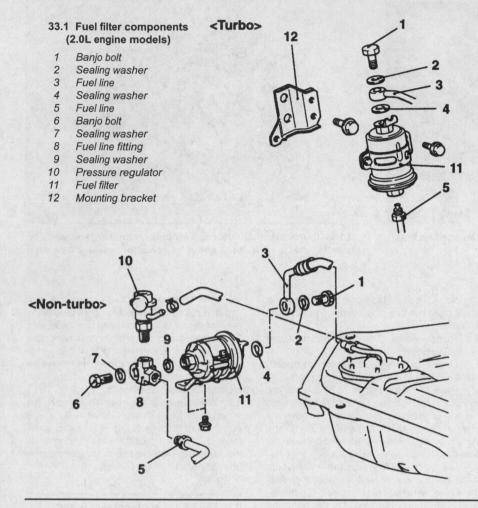

33.1 Fuel filter components
(2.0L engine models)

1   Banjo bolt
2   Sealing washer
3   Fuel line
4   Sealing washer
5   Fuel line
6   Banjo bolt
7   Sealing washer
8   Fuel line fitting
9   Sealing washer
10 Pressure regulator
11 Fuel filter
12 Mounting bracket

<Turbo>

<Non-turbo>

34.2 Check the evaporative emission (charcoal) canister for damage and the hose connections for cracks and damage

2   If necessary for access to the lower fuel filter fitting, raise the vehicle and support it securely on jackstands.

3   If you're working on a turbo model, remove the battery (see Chapter 5) and the air cleaner intake hose.

4   Using a back-up wrench to steady the filter, unscrew the banjo bolt at the top fuel fitting, removing the bolt and the two copper sealing washers, which are often called "crush" washers.

5   Remove the two bolts securing the filter bracket to the body.

6   If you're working on a non-turbo model, disconnect the banjo bolt at the lower end of the filter as described in Step 4.

7   If you're working on a turbo model, again secure the filter with a back-up wrench and use a flare-nut wrench to unscrew the flare-nut fitting at the bottom of the filter.

8   Remove the clamp bolt and detach the filter from the bracket. Install the new filter in the bracket, making sure it faces the same way as the old filter.

9   On turbo models, thread the lower flare-nut fitting into the filter by hand. **Note:** *This is done first to allow you to move the filter, as necessary, to align the threads when screwing in the flare-nut fitting; this is often more difficult with the filter bracket attached to the vehicle.* Steadying the filter with a back-up wrench, tighten the lower flare-nut fitting securely.

10 Install and tighten the two bolts that secure the filter bracket to the vehicle.

11 Install the upper banjo bolt (using a new sealing washer on each side of the hose fit-

ting) and, using a back-up wrench, tighten the bolt securely. If you're working on a non-turbo model, install the lower banjo bolt in the same way.

12 Run the engine and check for fuel leaks.

2.4L four-cylinder and V6 engine models

13 The fuel filter on these models is part of the fuel pump module, mounted inside the fuel tank. See Chapter 4 for replacement procedures.

34   Evaporative emissions control system check (every 30,000 miles or 24 months)

Refer to illustration 34.2

1   The function of the evaporative emissions control system is to draw fuel vapors from the gas tank and fuel system, store them in a charcoal canister and then burn them during normal engine operation.

2   The most common symptom of a fault in the evaporative emissions system is a strong fuel odor in the engine compartment. If a fuel odor is detected, inspect the charcoal canister, located in the engine compartment or at the rear of the vehicle, depending on model. Check the canister and all hoses for damage and deterioration **(see illustration)**.

3   The evaporative emissions control system is explained in more detail in Chapter 6.

Chapter 2 Part A
2.0L four-cylinder non-turbo engine

Contents

Specifications

General
Firing order	1-3-4-2
Cylinder numbers (drivebelt end-to-transaxle end)	1-2-3-4

Camshaft
Camshaft endplay	0.006 inch
Lobe lift	
Intake	0.324 inch
Exhaust	0.276 inch
Camshaft journal diameter	1.0217 to 1.0224 inches
Camshaft bearing bore diameter	1.024 to 1.025 inches
Camshaft bearing oil clearance	0.0027 to 0.0028 inch

Cylinder head
Warpage limit	0.004 inch

Intake and exhaust manifolds
Warpage limit (all engines)	
Standard	0.006 inch
Service limit	0.008 inch

Timing belt
Timing belt deflection	Tension automatically adjusted

FRONT ↓   68031-2a specs HAYNES

Cylinder numbering and spark
plug wire routing

Oil pump

Clearances

Rotor-to-straightedge clearance limit	0.004 inch
Cover warpage limit	0.003 inch
Rotor thickness limit	0.301 inch
Outer rotor diameter limit	3.148 inches
Outer rotor clearance limit	0.015 inch
Inner to outer rotor clearance limit	0.008 inch
Pressure relief spring free length	2.39 inches

Engine mounts

Roll stopper height	1.69 +/-0.12 inches

Torque specifications*   **Ft-lbs** (unless otherwise noted)

Note: *One foot-pound (ft-lb) of torque is equivalent to 12 inch-pounds (in-lbs) of torque. Torque values below approximately 15 ft-lbs are expressed in inch-pounds, since most foot-pound torque wrenches are not accurate at these smaller values.*

Camshaft bearing cap bolts	
Outside bearing cap bolts	21
Inside bearing cap bolts	107 inch-lbs
Camshaft sprocket bolt	75
Crankshaft pulley bolt	105
Cylinder head bolts	
Step 1	Long bolts to 25
Step 2	Short bolts to 20
Step 3	Long bolts to 50
Step 4	Short bolts to 20 again
Step 5	Long bolts to 50 again
Step 6	Short bolts to 20 a third time
Step 7	Long bolts 1/4-turn further
Step 8	Short bolts 1/4-turn further
Exhaust manifold-to-engine nuts/bolts	17
Flywheel or driveplate bolts	Not specified
Intake manifold-to-engine nuts/bolts	17
Intake manifold stay bolts	17
Oil pan bolts/nuts	107 in-lbs
Oil pick-up tube and screen mounting bolts	21
Oil pump bolts	17
Oil pump rotor cover screws	108 inch-lbs
Oil pump relief valve plug	39
Timing belt front cover bolts	
Lower bolt	21
Upper bolt	107 inch-lbs
Timing belt rear cover bolts	85 inch-lbs
Timing belt tensioner bolt(s)	
Plunger-type	23
Bracket-type	20
Valve cover bolts	
Step 1	40 inch-lbs
Step 2	80 inch-lbs
Step 3	107 inch-lbs

Refer to Part E for additional torque specifications

1   General information

This Part of Chapter 2 is devoted to in-vehicle engine repair procedures. Information concerning engine removal and installation and engine block and cylinder head overhaul can be found in Part E of this Chapter.

The following repair procedures are based on the assumption that the engine is installed in the vehicle. If the engine has been removed from the vehicle and mounted on a stand, many of the steps outlined in this Part of Chapter 2 will not apply.

The Specifications included in this Part of Chapter 2 apply only to the procedures contained in this Part. Part E of Chapter 2 contains the Specifications necessary for cylinder head and engine block rebuilding.

This Part of Chapter 2 covers the 2.0L Double Overhead Camshaft (DOHC) non-turbo engine.

2   Repair operations possible with the engine in the vehicle

Many major repair operations can be accomplished without removing the engine from the vehicle.

Clean the engine compartment and the exterior of the engine with some type of degreaser before any work is done. It will make the job easier and help keep dirt out of the internal areas of the engine.

Depending on the components involved, it may be helpful to remove the hood to improve access to the engine as repairs are performed (refer to Chapter 11 if necessary). Cover the fenders to prevent damage to the paint. Special pads are available, but an old bedspread or blanket will also work.

If vacuum, exhaust, oil or coolant leaks develop, indicating a need for gasket or seal replacement, the repairs can generally be made with the engine in the vehicle. The intake and exhaust manifold gaskets, oil pan gasket, crankshaft oil seals and cylinder head gasket are all accessible with the engine in place.

Exterior engine components, such as the intake and exhaust manifolds, the oil pan, the oil pump, the water pump, the starter motor, the alternator, the distributor and the fuel system components can be removed for repair with the engine in place.

Since the camshaft(s) and cylinder head can be removed without pulling the engine, valve component servicing can also be accomplished with the engine in the vehicle. Replacement of the timing belt(s) and sprockets is also possible with the engine in the vehicle.

In extreme cases caused by a lack of necessary equipment, repair or replacement of piston rings, pistons, connecting rods and rod bearings is possible with the engine in the vehicle. However, this practice is not recommended because of the cleaning and preparation work that must be done to the components involved.

3 Top Dead Center (TDC) for number one piston - locating

Refer to illustration 3.7

1 Top Dead Center (TDC) is the highest point in the cylinder that each piston reaches as it travels up-and-down when the crankshaft turns. Each piston reaches TDC on the compression stroke and again on the exhaust stroke, but TDC generally refers to piston position on the compression stroke.

2 Positioning the piston(s) at TDC is an essential part of many procedures such as rocker arm removal, camshaft and timing belt/sprocket removal and crankshaft/cam-shaft position sensor removal.

3 Before beginning this procedure, be sure to place the transmission in Neutral and apply the parking brake or block the rear wheels. Also, disable the ignition system by disconnecting the electrical connector at the ignition coil pack (see Chapter 5). Remove the spark plugs (see Chapter 1).

4 In order to bring any piston to TDC, the crankshaft must be turned using one of the methods outlined below. When looking at the drivebelt end of the engine, normal crankshaft rotation is clockwise.

a) *The preferred method is to turn the crankshaft with a ratchet and an extension inserted into the drivebelt end of the crankshaft.*

b) *A remote starter switch, which may save some time, can also be used. These switches are available inexpensively from auto parts stores. Follow the instructions included with the switch. Once the piston is close to TDC, use a socket and ratchet as described in the previous paragraph.*

c) *If an assistant is available to turn the ignition switch to the Start position in short bursts, you can get the piston close to TDC without a remote starter switch. Make sure your assistant is out of the vehicle, away from the ignition switch, then use a socket and ratchet as described in Paragraph a) to complete the procedure.*

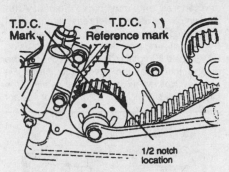

3.7 Align the mark on the crankshaft sprocket with the TDC mark on the front of the engine; turn it 1/2-notch BTDC when installing the timing belt

5 Install a compression pressure gauge in the number one spark plug hole (see Chapter 2E). It should be a gauge with a screw-in fitting and a hose at least six inches long.

6 Remove the timing belt cover (see Section 5).

7 Rotate the crankshaft using one of the methods described above while observing the compression gauge. When TDC for the compression stroke of number one cylinder is reached, compression pressure will show on the gauge as the crankshaft sprocket mark is beginning to line up with the reference mark on the front of the engine (see illustration).

8 After the number one piston has been

positioned at TDC on the compression stroke, TDC for any of the remaining pistons can be located by turning the crankshaft and following the firing order. Make a mark on the crankshaft sprocket exactly 180-degrees opposite the notch. Rotate the crankshaft 180-degrees clockwise from the number-one-cylinder TDC position: this is the number-three-cylinder TDC position. Then rotate the crankshaft clockwise another 180-degrees, back to where the notch is aligned with the T mark on the pulley: this is the number-four-cylinder TDC position. Finally, rotate the crankshaft another 180-degrees clockwise: this is the number-two-cylinder TDC position.

4 Valve cover - removal and installation

Refer to illustrations 4.3, 4.5 and 4.6

1 Remove the spark plug wires and ignition coil pack (see Chapter 1). Use numbered pieces of tape to label the wires so they can be returned to their original locations on reassembly.

2 Clearly label and disconnect any emission hoses and cables which connect to, or cross over, the valve cover.

3 Remove the valve cover bolts (see illustration) and lift the cover off. If the cover sticks to the cylinder head, tap on it with a soft-face hammer or place a block of wood against the cover and tap on the wood with a hammer.

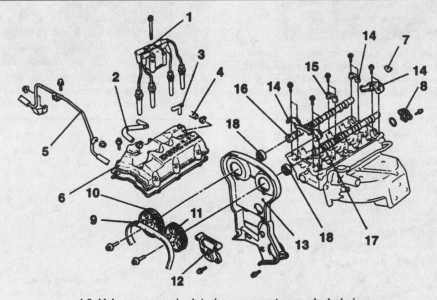

4.3 Valve cover and related components - exploded view

1	Ignition coil pack	10	Intake camshaft sprocket
2	PCV hose	11	Exhaust camshaft sprocket
3	Breather hose	12	Bracket
4	Air hose	13	Rear timing belt cover
5	Evaporative emission tube and hoses	14	Outside camshaft bearing cap
6	Valve cover	15	Camshaft bearing caps
7	Semicircular seal	16	Intake camshaft
8	Camshaft position sensor	17	Exhaust camshaft
9	Timing belt	18	Camshaft oil seals

Caution: *If you have to pry between the valve cover and the cylinder head, be extremely careful not to gouge or nick the gasket surfaces of either part. A leak could develop after reassembly.*

4   Thoroughly clean the valve cover and remove all traces of old gasket material. Gasket removal solvents are available from auto parts stores and may prove helpful. After cleaning the surfaces, degrease them with a rag soaked in lacquer thinner or acetone.

5   Install a new gasket on the cover, using RTV to hold it in place. Place the cover on the engine and install the cover bolts. **Note:** *Be sure to install a new semi-circular seal into the cylinder head. Apply a small amount of sealant to the bottom of the seal and, after it has been installed, to the top of the seal, at the seal-to-valve cover joints* **(see illustration).**

6   Tighten the bolts in sequence, in the three stages listed in this Chapter's Specifications **(see illustration).**

7   The remaining steps are the reverse of removal. When finished, run the engine and check for oil leaks.

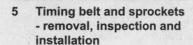

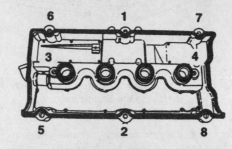

4.5 Apply silicone sealant to the bottom of the semi-circular seal, then apply sealant to the top of the seal, overlapping its edges

4.6 Tighten the valve cover bolts in the sequence shown, in the three stages listed in this Chapter's Specifications

5   Timing belt and sprockets - removal, inspection and installation

Removal

> ** ★★ CAUTION ★★**
> The timing system is complex. Severe engine damage will occur if you make any mistakes. Do not attempt this procedure unless you are highly experienced with this type of repair. If you are at all unsure of your abilities, consult an expert. Double-check all your work and be sure everything is correct before you attempt to start the engine.

Refer to illustrations 5.6a, 5.6b, 5.8, 5.9a, 5.9b and 5.12

Caution: *Do not try to turn the crankshaft with the camshaft sprocket bolt and do not rotate the crankshaft counterclockwise. Also, don't turn the crankshaft or camshaft after the timing belt has been removed.*

1   Position the number one piston at Top Dead Center (see Section 3).

2   Disconnect the battery cable from the negative battery terminal.

3   Set the parking brake and block the rear wheels. Raise the front of the vehicle and support it securely on jackstands.

4   Loosen the alternator and power steering belts, them remove them from their pulleys (see Chapter 1).

5   Remove the power steering pump and bracket (see Chapter 10).

6   Remove the crankshaft pulley bolt, then remove the pulley with a three-jaw puller **(see illustrations).**

7   Remove the left engine mount and bracket (see Section 16). **Note:** *Make sure the engine is supported with a piece of wood and a floor jack placed under the oil pan. The wood will prevent the floor jack from denting or damaging the oil pan.*

8   Remove the timing belt cover **(see illustration).**

9   Check the timing belt alignment marks on the crankshaft and camshaft sprockets to make sure no. 1 cylinder is at TDC compression **(see illustrations).**

10   Make a mark on the timing belt in the direction of rotation so it may be reinstalled in the same direction in the event the timing belt is reused. Unbolt the timing belt tensioner and remove the belt from the sprockets.

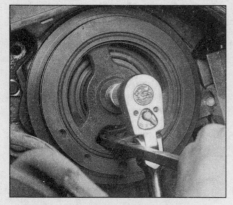

5.6a Insert a large screwdriver or bar through the opening in the crankshaft pulley and wedge it against the engine block, then loosen the bolt with a socket and breaker bar

5.6b Remove the crankshaft pulley with a 3-jaw puller (use the proper insert to keep from damaging the crankshaft threads)

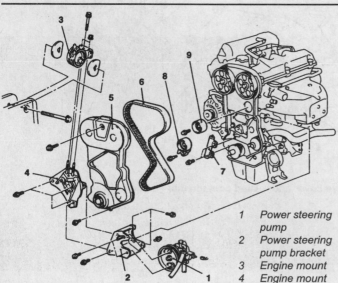

5.8 Timing belt and related components - exploded view

1	Power steering pump	6	Timing belt
2	Power steering pump bracket	7	Timing belt tensioner
3	Engine mount	8	Tensioner pulley
4	Engine mount bracket	9	Idler pulley
5	Timing belt front cover		

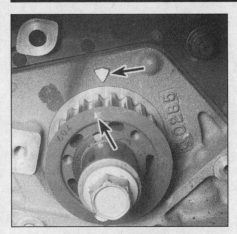

5.9a Rotate the crankshaft clockwise to 1/2-tooth BTDC (arrows)

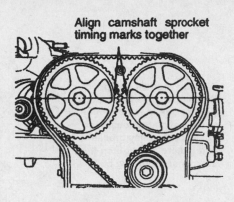

5.9b Align the camshaft sprocket marks (arrows) with each other and with the cylinder head top surface

5.12 Use this special tool or an equivalent pin wrench to hold the camshaft sprockets while you loosen the bolts

11   Remove the tensioner pulley (if installed) and idler pulley **(see illustration 5.8)**.

12   If you plan to replace or remove the camshaft(s) or camshaft oil seal(s), remove the camshaft sprocket(s). Hold the camshaft sprocket with the special tool or equivalent and remove the camshaft sprocket bolt **(see illustration)**. Slide the sprocket off the camshaft. The camshaft oil seals can be pried out of the cylinder head with a screwdriver - wrap the screwdriver tip with tape to prevent damage. Drive in the new seal(s) with a hammer and socket.

Inspection

Refer to illustration 5.14

13   Rotate the tensioner and idler pulleys by hand and move them side-to-side to detect roughness and excess play. Visually inspect the sprockets for any signs of damage and wear. Replace parts as necessary. Also, replace the pulley if there is a lubricant leak.

14   Inspect the timing belts for cracks, separation, wear, missing teeth and oil contamination. Replace the belt if it's in questionable condition **(see illustration)**.

15   Check the automatic tensioner for leaks or any obvious damage to the body. Also, check the rod end for wear or damage. Replace if necessary.

Installation

** CAUTION **
Before starting the engine, carefully rotate the crankshaft by hand through at least two full revolutions (use a socket and breaker bar on the crankshaft pulley center bolt). If you feel any resistance, STOP! There is something wrong - most likely, valves are contacting the pistons. You must find the problem before proceeding. Check your work and see if any updated repair information is available.

Refer to illustrations 5.18, 5.20 and 5.25

16   Reinstall the timing belt sprockets, if they were removed. Tighten the camshaft sprocket

bolts to the values listed in this Chapter's Specifications.

17   Align the timing marks located on the camshaft and crankshaft sprockets **(see illustrations 5.9a and 5.9b)**. Position the crankshaft mark at TDC initially, then move it to 1/2-tooth BTDC.

18   On models equipped with plunger-type tensioners, prepare the automatic tensioner for installation. Place the tensioner in a vise that is equipped with soft jaws (or put a shop rag over the jaws to prevent damage to the tensioner). If the rod is easily retracted, replace it with a new unit. The tensioner should have a fair amount of strength or resistance. **Caution:** *Be sure the tensioner is in a level position when it is in the vise. Also, place a washer over the plug on the bottom of the tensioner to prevent the vise from contacting the plug.* Once the tensioner is compressed place a small allen wrench, or something similar, through the hole to keep the rod retracted for reassembly on the engine **(see illustration)**.

19   On models equipped with plunger-type tensioners, install the tensioner pulley and tighten the center bolt finger tight. On models with pulley-type tensioners, bolt the tensioner and bracket assembly back onto the front of the engine.

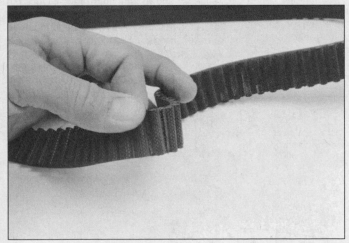

5.14 Carefully inspect the timing belt - bending it backwards will often make damage or wear more apparent

5.18 On models equipped with plunger-type tensioners, place the tensioner in a vise with the hole (arrow) facing up, compress the piston and insert an Allen wrench or drill bit into the hole to lock the tensioner

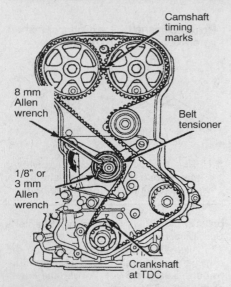

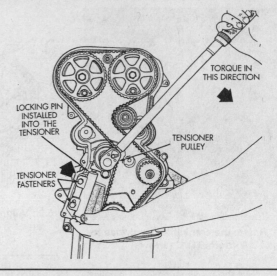

5.25 On models equipped with plunger-type tensioners, apply torque in the direction shown, slide the tensioner against the pulley bracket, hold it there and tighten the tensioner mounting bolts

5.20 Some later models have a spring-loaded tensioner pulley and bracket assembly bolted to the front of the engine. Before installing the belt, move the tensioner away from the belt with an 8mm Allen wrench and lock it in place with a small Allen wrench

20   On some later models, the timing belt tensioner and pulley are a single unit attached to a bracket and bolted to the front of the engine. Use an 8mm Allen wrench to rotate the tensioner pulley counterclockwise, then lock it in place, against spring tension, with a 3mm Allen wrench **(see illustration)**.

21   Recheck the alignment of the camshaft and crankshaft sprocket timing marks (see Step 17).

22   On models equipped with plunger-type tensioners, install the timing belt in the following sequence:

a) *Install the timing belt around the crankshaft sprocket and hold the timing belt to the tensioner pulley with your left hand.*

b) *Pulling the belt with your right hand, install it around the water pump sprocket.*

c) *Install the belt around the idler pulley.*

d) *Install the belt around the camshaft sprockets, then around the tensioner pulley.*

23   On models equipped with plunger-type tensioners, install the tensioner on the engine and tighten its bolts loosely. Don't remove the Allen wrench from the tensioner yet.

24   Turn the crankshaft clockwise to move the number 1 cylinder to TDC, taking up slack in the timing belt.

25   On models equipped with plunger-type tensioners, have an assistant place a torque wrench on the center bolt of the tensioner pulley and apply 21 ft-lbs of torque in a clockwise direction. With the torque applied to the tensioner pulley, move the tensioner up against the tensioner pulley bracket and tighten the tensioner bolts to the torque listed in this Chapter's Specifications **(see illustration)**. Remove the torque wrench.

26   Pull the Allen wrench or drill bit from the tensioner. On models with pulley/tensioner assemblies, the tensioning is factory pre-set and will be correct. On models with plunger-type tensioners, the timing belt tension is correct when the pin can be withdrawn and reinserted easily. Verify that the timing marks on the camshaft sprocket(s) and crankshaft sprocket are still aligned at TDC.

27   Using the bolt in the center of the crankshaft sprocket, turn the crankshaft clockwise two complete revolutions. **Caution:** *If you feel resistance while turning the crankshaft, STOP - the valves may be hitting the pistons from incorrect valve timing. Stop and re-check the valve timing.* **Note:** *The camshaft and crankshaft sprocket marks will align every two revolutions of the crankshaft.* Recheck the alignment of the timing marks **(see illustrations 5.9a and 5.9b)**. If the marks do not align properly, loosen the tensioner, slip the belt off the camshaft sprocket(s), realign the marks, reinstall the belt, and check the alignment again.

28   On models with plunger-type tensioners, after crankshaft rotation, recheck the timing belt tension by inserting the retaining pin back into the tensioner. If the retaining pin cannot be inserted and withdrawn freely, readjust the timing belt tension and repeat Steps 23 through 26.

29   The remaining installation steps are the reverse of removal. Tighten the crankshaft pulley bolt to the torque listed in this Chapter's Specifications.

30   Start the engine and road test the vehicle.

6   Camshafts, rocker arms and hydraulic valve lash adjusters - removal, inspection and installation

Camshaft removal

Refer to illustrations 6.2 and 6.3

1   Remove the timing belt and camshaft sprockets (see Section 5).

2   The camshaft bearing caps are identified with their numbered locations in the cylinder head **(see illustration)**.

3   Remove the outside bearing caps at each end of the camshafts first. Remove the remaining camshaft bearing caps, loosening the bolts a little at a time to prevent distorting the camshafts by loosening the caps in the sequence shown **(see illustration)**. Once the bearing caps have all been loosened enough for removal, they may still be difficult to remove. Using the bearing cap bolts for extra leverage, move the cap back and forth to loosen the cap from the cylinder head. If they are still difficult to remove you can tap them

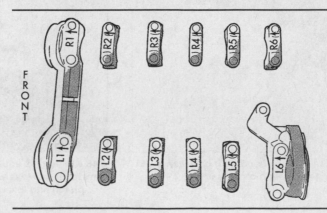

6.2 Camshaft bearing cap location numbers - they must be reinstalled in their original locations

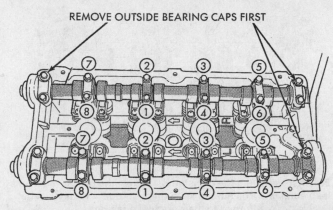

REMOVE OUTSIDE BEARING CAPS FIRST

6.3 Remove the outside camshaft bearing caps first, then loosen the remaining cap bolts in the sequence shown, 1/4 turn at a time, until they can be unscrewed by hand

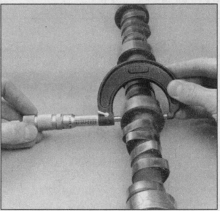

6.7 Measure the camshaft journal diameters with a micrometer and compare the measurements to those listed in this Chapter's Specifications

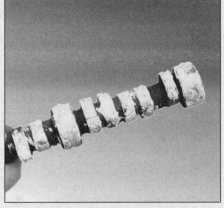

6.15 Prior to installing the camshaft, lubricate the bearing journals, thrust surfaces and lobes with assembly lube or clean engine oil

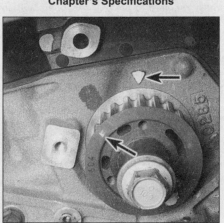

6.16 Rotate the crankshaft timing sprocket counterclockwise three teeth BTDC (arrows)

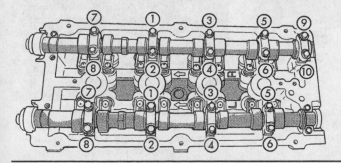

6.17 Tighten the bearing caps (not including the outside bearing caps) in the sequence shown

gently with a soft face mallet so they can be lifted off. **Caution:** *Store them in order so they can be returned to their original locations, with the same side facing forward.*

4   Carefully lift the camshafts out of the cylinder head. Mark the camshafts INTAKE and EXHAUST. They are not interchangeable.

5   Remove the front seal from each camshaft. **Note:** *Now is a good time to inspect the rocker arms and lash adjusters (see below).*

Camshaft inspection

Refer to illustration 6.7

6   Thoroughly clean the camshaft(s) and the gasket surface. Visually inspect the camshaft for wear and/or damage to the lobe surfaces, bearing journals and seal contact surfaces. Visually inspect the camshaft bear-

ing surfaces in the cylinder head and bearing caps for scoring and other damage.

7   Measure the camshaft bearing journal diameters **(see illustration)**. Measure the inside diameter of the camshaft bearing surfaces in the cylinder head, using a telescoping gauge (temporarily install the bearing caps). Subtract the journal measurement from the bearing measurement to obtain the camshaft bearing oil clearance. Compare this clearance with the value listed in this Chapter's Specifications. Replace worn components as required.

8   Replace the camshaft if it fails any of the above inspections. **Note:** *If the lobes are worn, replace the rocker arms and lash adjusters along with the camshaft.* Cylinder head replacement may be necessary if the camshaft bearing surfaces in the head are damaged or excessively worn.

9   Clean and inspect the cylinder head as described in Part E of this Chapter.

Camshaft endplay measurement

10   Lubricate the camshaft(s) and cylinder head bearing journals with clean engine oil.

11   Place the camshaft in its respective place in the cylinder head. **Note:** *Do not install the rocker arms for this check.* Install the rear bearing cap and tighten the bolts to the torque listed in this Chapter's Specifications.

12   Install a dial indicator set up on the cylinder head and place the indicator tip on the camshaft at the sprocket end.

13   Using a screwdriver, carefully pry the camshaft fully to the rear (toward the camshaft position sensor) until it stops. Zero the dial indicator and pry the camshaft fully to the front (toward the dial indicator end). The amount of indicator travel is the camshaft endplay. Compare the endplay measurement with the tolerance given in this Chapter's Specifications. If the endplay is excessive, check the camshaft and cylinder head bearing journals for wear and replace as necessary.

Camshaft installation

Refer to illustrations 6.15, 6.16, 6.17 and 6.18

14   If removed, install the valve lash adjusters and rocker arms (see Section 6).

15   Clean the camshaft and bearing journals and caps. Liberally coat the journals, lobes and thrust portions of the camshaft with assembly lube or engine oil **(see illustration)**.

16   Carefully install the camshafts in the cylinder head in their correct locations. Temporarily install the camshaft sprockets and rotate the camshafts so their timing marks align **(see illustration 5.9a)**. Make sure the crankshaft is positioned with the crankshaft sprocket timing mark at three teeth BTDC **(see illustration)**. **Caution:** *If the pistons are at TDC when tightening the camshaft bearing caps, damage to the engine may occur.*

17   Install the bearing caps, except for the No. 1 and No. 6 (left side) end caps **(see illustration)**. Tighten the bolts in 3 progressive steps in the sequence shown to the torque listed in this Chapter's Specifications.

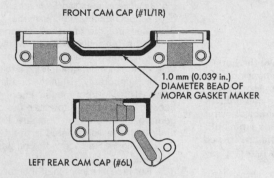

FRONT CAM CAP (#1L/1R)

1.0 mm (0.039 in.)
DIAMETER BEAD OF
MOPAR GASKET MAKER

LEFT REAR CAM CAP (#6L)

6.18 Apply a small bead of anaerobic sealant to the no. 1 and left side no. 6 bearing caps as shown

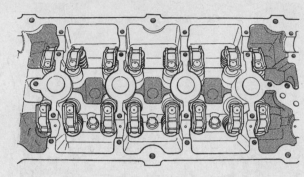

6.23 After removing the camshafts, remove the rocker arms and lash adjusters - be sure to keep them in order so they can be returned to their original positions

18   Apply a small bead of anaerobic sealant (approximately 1/8 inch) to the No. 1 and No. 6 (left side) bearing caps **(see illustration)**. Install the bearing caps and tighten the bolts to the torque listed in this Chapter's Specifications.

19   Install new camshaft oil seals (see Section 8).

20   Install the timing belt, covers and related components (see Section 5).

21   Run the engine while checking for oil leaks.

Rocker arm and lash adjuster removal

Refer to illustration 6.23

22   Remove both camshafts as described above.

23   Once the camshafts have been removed, the rocker arms (a.k.a. cam followers) can be lifted off **(see illustration)**. **Caution:** *Each rocker arm and valve lash adjuster must be placed back in its original location, so mark them or place them in a marked container (such as an egg carton or cupcake tray) so they won't get mixed up.*

24   Remove the rocker arms and hydraulic valve lash adjusters from the cylinder head.

Rocker arm and lash adjuster inspection

Refer to illustration 6.25

25   Visually check the rocker arm tip, roller and lash adjuster pocket for wear **(see illustration)**. Replace them if evidence of wear or damage is found.

26   Inspect each adjuster carefully for signs of wear and damage, particularly on the ball tip that contacts the rocker arm. Since the lash adjusters frequently become clogged, we recommend replacing them if you're concerned about their condition or if the engine is exhibiting valve "tapping" noises.

Rocker arm and lash adjuster installation

27   Prior to installation, the lash adjusters must be partially full of engine oil - indicated by little or no plunger action when the adjuster is depressed. If there's excessive

plunger travel, place the rocker arm assembly into clean engine oil and pump the plunger until the plunger travel is eliminated. **Note:** *If the plunger still travels within the rocker arm when full of oil it's defective and the rocker arm assembly must be replaced.*

28   Install the hydraulic lash adjusters and rocker arms back in their proper locations on the cylinder head.

29   Install the camshafts as described above.

30   When re-starting the engine after replacing the rocker arm/lash adjusters, the adjusters will normally make "tapping" noises. After warm-up, slowly raise the speed of the engine from idle to 3,000 rpm and back to idle over a one minute period. If the adjuster(s) do not become silent, replace the defective lash adjuster assembly.

7   Valve springs, retainers and seals - replacement

Refer to illustrations 7.4, 7.7, 7.8, 7.13 and 7.15

Note: *Broken valve springs and defective valve stem seals can be replaced without removing the cylinder heads. Two special tools and a compressed air source are nor-*

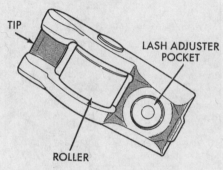

TIP

LASH ADJUSTER POCKET

ROLLER

6.25 Check the tip, roller and lash adjuster pocket for wear and damage

mally required to perform this operation, so read through this Section carefully and rent or buy the tools before attempting the job.

1   Remove the valve cover (see Section 4).

2   Remove the spark plug from the cylinder which has the defective component. If all of the valve stem seals are being replaced, all of the spark plugs should be removed.

3   Turn the crankshaft until the piston in the affected cylinder is at Top Dead Center on the compression stroke (see Chapter 2E). If you're replacing all of the valve stem seals, begin with cylinder number one and work on

7.4 This is what the air hose adapter that threads into the spark plug hole looks like - they're commonly available from auto parts stores

7.7 Use needle-nose pliers (shown) or a small magnet to remove the valve spring keepers - be careful not to drop them down into the engine!

7.8 Remove the valve guide seal with a pair of pliers

7.13 Gently tap the new seal into place with a hammer and a deep socket

7.15 Apply a small dab of grease to each keeper before installation to hold it in place on the valve stem until the spring is released

the valves for one cylinder at a time. Move from cylinder-to-cylinder following the firing order sequence (see this Chapter's Specifications).

4   Thread an adapter into the spark plug hole **(see illustration)** and connect an air hose from a compressed air source to it. Most auto parts stores can supply the air hose adapter. **Note:** *Many cylinder compression gauges utilize a screw-in fitting that may work with your air hose quick-disconnect fitting.*

5   Remove the camshaft and rocker arms (see Section 6).

6   Apply compressed air to the cylinder. **Warning:** *The piston may be forced down by compressed air, causing the crankshaft to turn suddenly. If the wrench used when positioning the number one piston at TDC is still attached to the crankshaft bolt, it could cause damage or injury when the crankshaft moves.*

7   Stuff clean shop rags into the cylinder head holes above and below the valves to prevent parts and tools from falling into the engine, then use a valve spring compressor to compress the spring. Remove the keepers with small needle-nose pliers or a magnet **(see illustration).**

8   Remove the spring retainer and valve spring, then remove the valve guide seal/

spring seat assembly **(see illustration). Caution:** *If air pressure fails to hold the valve in the closed position during this operation, the valve face and/or seat is probably damaged. If so, the cylinder head will have to be removed for additional repair operations.*

9   Wrap a rubber band or tape around the top of the valve stem so the valve won't fall into the combustion chamber, then release the air pressure.

10   Inspect the valve stem for damage. Rotate the valve in the guide and check the end for eccentric movement, which would indicate that the valve is bent and needs to be replaced.

11   Move the valve up-and-down in the guide and make sure it doesn't bind. If the valve stem binds, either the valve is bent or the guide is damaged. In either case, the head will have to be removed for repair.

12   Pull up on the valve stem to close the valve, reapply air pressure to the cylinder to retain the valve in the closed position, then remove the tape or rubber band from the valve stem.

13   Lubricate the valve stem with engine oil and install a new valve guide seal/spring seat assembly. Tap into place with deep socket **(see illustration).**

14   Install the spring in position over the valve.

15   Install the valve spring retainer. Compress the valve spring and carefully position the keepers in the groove. Apply a small dab of grease to the inside of each keeper to hold it in place if necessary **(see illustration).**

16   Remove the pressure from the spring tool and make sure the keepers are seated.

17   Disconnect the air hose and remove the adapter from the spark plug hole.

18   Install the rocker arms and camshafts (see Section 6).

19   Install the spark plug(s) and connect the wire(s).

20   Install the valve cover (see Section 4).

21   Start and run the engine, then check for oil leaks and unusual sounds coming from the valve cover area.

8   Crankshaft front oil seal - replacement

Refer to illustrations 8.2, 8.3, 8.5 and 8.6
Caution: *Do not rotate the camshaft(s) or crankshaft when the timing belt is removed or damage to the engine may occur.*

1   Remove the timing belt (see Section 5).

2   Remove the crankshaft timing belt sprocket from the crankshaft with a bolt-type gear puller **(see illustration).** Remove the Woodruff key from the crankshaft keyway.

3   Wrap the tip of a small screwdriver with tape. Working from below the right inner fender, use the screwdriver to carefully pry the seal out of its bore **(see illustration).** Take care to prevent damaging the oil pump assembly, the crankshaft and the seal bore.

4   Thoroughly clean and inspect the seal bore and sealing surface on the crankshaft. Minor imperfections can be removed with emery cloth. If there is a groove worn in the crankshaft sealing surface (from contact with the seal), installing a new seal will probably not stop the leak.

8.2 Attach a bolt-type gear puller to the crankshaft sprocket and remove the sprocket from the crankshaft

8.3 Carefully pry the crankshaft front oil seal from its bore with a small screwdriver

5   Lubricate the new seal with engine oil and using a hammer and the appropriate size socket, drive the seal into the bore until it's flush with the oil pump housing. **(see illustration)**.

6   Install the Woodruff key and the crankshaft timing belt sprocket with the word FRONT facing out onto the crankshaft **(see illustration)**.

7   The remaining installation steps are the reverse of removal. Tighten the crankshaft pulley bolt to the torque listed in this Chapter's Specifications.

8   Start the engine and check for oil leaks.

9   Intake manifold - removal and installation

Warning: *Allow the engine to cool completely before beginning this procedure.*

Removal

Refer to illustrations 9.5 and 9.8

1   Relieve the fuel system pressure (see Chapter 4).

2   Disconnect the negative battery cable (see Chapter 5).

3   Drain the cooling system and remove the coolant reservoir (see Chapters 1 and 3).

4   Remove the air cleaner intake hose (see Chapter 4).

5   Clearly label and disconnect all vacuum hoses, electrical wires, brackets and emission hoses which run to the fuel injection system, throttle body and intake manifold **(see illustration)**.

6   Disconnect the throttle cable from the throttle body and remove the cable retaining clips (see Chapter 4).

7   Remove the throttle body (see Chapter 4).

8   Remove the intake manifold stays and the engine hanger **(see illustration)**. Be sure to disconnect any electrical connections that are fastened to the support bracket before trying to move the parts out of the way.

9   Unbolt the manifold plenum (upper manifold) from the lower manifold. Lift off the plenum and gasket.

10   Remove the fuel rail and injector assembly (see Chapter 4).

11   Unbolt the intake manifold and remove it from the engine. If it sticks, lightly tap the manifold with a soft-face hammer or carefully pry it from the head. **Caution:** *Do not pry between gasket sealing surfaces or tap on any fuel injector boss.*

Inspection

12   Remove intake manifold gasket by carefully scraping all traces of gasket material from both the cylinder head and the intake manifold. **Caution:** *The cylinder head and intake manifold are made of aluminum and are easily nicked or gouged. Don't damage the gasket surfaces or a leak may result after the work is complete. Gasket removal sol-*

8.5 Lubricate the new front crankshaft seal with engine oil and drive it into the bore with a hammer and socket until it's flush with the oil pump housing

8.6 Position the crankshaft sprocket with the word FRONT (arrow) facing out and install it onto the crankshaft

vents are available from auto parts stores and may prove helpful.

13   Using a straightedge and feeler gauge, check the intake manifold mating surface for warpage. Check the intake manifold surface on the cylinder head also. If the warpage on any surface exceeds the limits listed in this Chapter's Specifications, the intake manifold and/or cylinder head must be replaced or resurfaced by an automotive machine shop.

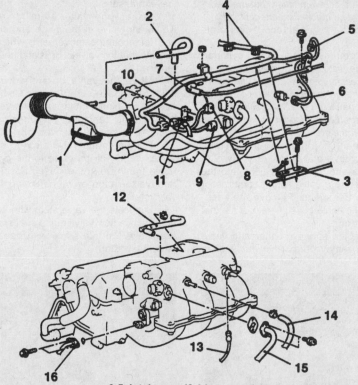

9.5 Intake manifold connections

1	Air cleaner intake hose	9	AIS motor connector
2	Breather hose	10	Control wiring harness
3	Throttle cable connection	11	Alternator connector
4	Retaining clips	12	PCV hose
5	MAP sensor connector	13	Vacuum hose
6	Charge temperature sensor connector	14	Brake booster vacuum hose
7	Vacuum hose	15	EGR pipe
8	Throttle position sensor connector	16	High pressure fuel hose

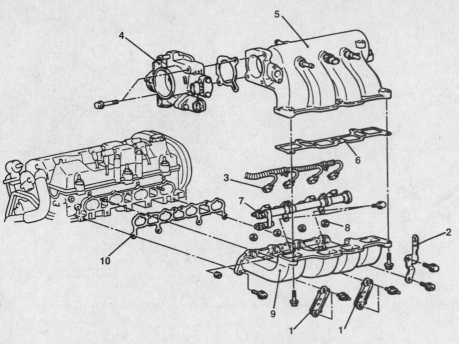

9.8 Intake manifold - exploded view

1	Intake manifold stay	6	Plenum gasket
2	Engine hanger	7	Fuel rail
3	Fuel injector connector	8	O-ring
4	Throttle body	9	Intake manifold
5	Intake manifold plenum	10	Intake manifold gasket

Installation

14 Install the intake manifold, using a new gasket or O-rings as applicable. Tighten the bolts in stages, working from the center outward, to the torque listed in this Chapter's Specifications.

15 The remaining installation steps are the reverse of removal. Refer to Chapter 1 for coolant filling procedures.

10 Exhaust manifold - removal and installation

Refer to illustration 10.3

Warning: *Allow the engine to cool completely before beginning this procedure.*

Removal

1 Disconnect the battery cable from the negative terminal of the battery.

2 Drain the cooling system (see Chapter 1).

3 Remove the air cleaner intake hose **(see illustration)**.

4 Disconnect the air hose and control wiring harness **(see illustration 10.3)**.

5 Pull out the engine oil dipstick and lay it aside.

6 Disconnect the hoses from the coolant tube and unbolt the tube from the engine.

7 Remove the bolts that secure the upper and lower heat shields to the exhaust manifold. Separate the heat shields and take them off.

8 Remove any brackets that may be bolted to the exhaust manifold.

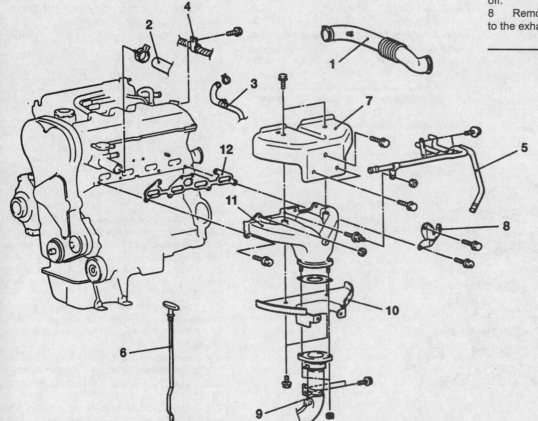

10.3 Exhaust manifold - exploded view

1   *Air cleaner intake hose*
2   *Radiator upper hose*
3   *Air hose*
4   *Control wiring harness retainer*
5   *Coolant pipes*
6   *Dipstick*
7   *Heat shield*
8   *Engine hanger*
9   *Exhaust pipe*
10 *Heat shield*
11 *Exhaust manifold*
12 *Gasket*

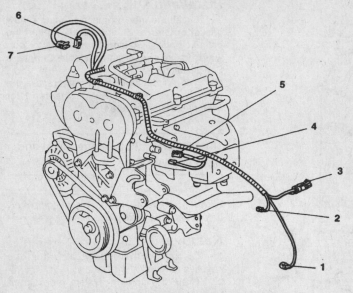

11.6a Wiring harness connections (1 of 2)

1   Air conditioning compressor connector
2   Power steering pressure switch connector
3   Oxygen sensor connector
4   Coolant temperature gauge sending unit connector
5   Coolant temperature sensor connector
6   MAP sensor connector
7   Intake air temperature sensor connector

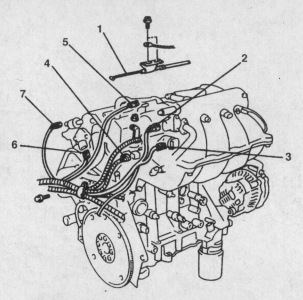

11.6b Wiring harness connections (2 of 2)

1   Throttle cable
2   Throttle position sensor connector
3   Idle air control motor connector
4   Fuel injector harness connector
5   Ignition coil connector
6   Camshaft position sensor connector
7   EGR solenoid connector

9   Apply penetrating oil to the threads and remove the exhaust manifold mounting nuts, brackets and emission components.
10   Slip the manifold off the studs and remove it from the engine compartment.

Installation

11   Clean and inspect the exhaust manifold studs, replacing any that show thread damage.
12   Using a scraper, remove all traces of gasket material from the mating surfaces and

inspect them for wear and cracks. **Caution:** *When removing gasket material from any surface, especially aluminum, be very careful not to scratch or gouge the gasket surface. Any damage to the surface may cause a leak after reassembly. Gasket removal solvents are available from auto parts stores and may prove helpful.*
13   Place a new gasket over the studs, install the manifold and tighten the nuts in several stages, working from the center out, to the torque listed in this Chapter's Specifications.

14   Reinstall the remaining parts in the reverse order of removal.
15   Refer to Chapter 1 and refill the cooling system.
16   Run the engine and check for exhaust leaks.

11   Cylinder head - removal and installation

Warning: *Allow the engine to cool completely before following this procedure.*

Removal

Refer to illustrations 11.6a, 11.6b, 11.7, 11.10 and 11.13

1   Position the number one piston at Top Dead Center (see Chapter 2C).
2   Disconnect the negative battery cable (see Chapter 5).
3   Drain the cooling system, drain the engine oil and remove the spark plugs (see Chapter 1).
4   Remove the air cleaner housing (see Chapter 4).
5   Relieve the fuel system pressure (see Chapter 4).
6   Label and disconnect the wires that connect to components on the cylinder head or cross over the cylinder head **(see illustrations)**.
7   At the flywheel end of the engine, disconnect the heater hose and the small coolant hose **(see illustration)**. Disconnect the upper

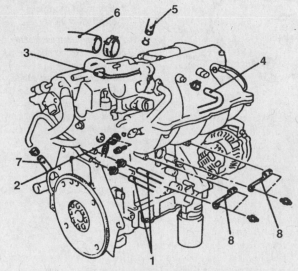

11.7 Hose connections

1   Heater hoses
2   High pressure fuel hose
3   Purge air hose
4   Brake booster vacuum hose
5   Coolant overflow tube
6   Radiator upper hose
7   Coolant hose
8   Intake manifold stay

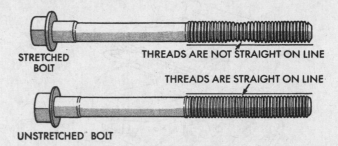

11.13 Lay a precision straightedge along the bolt threads; if any threads don't contact the straightedge, replace the bolt

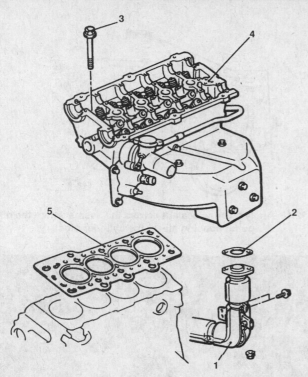

11.10 Cylinder head and gasket

1	*Exhaust pipe*	4	*Cylinder head*
2	*Exhaust pipe gasket*	5	*Head gasket*
3	*Cylinder head bolt*		

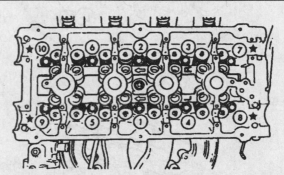

★ Location of 110 mm (4.330 in.) short bolts.

11.16 Cylinder head bolt tightening sequence (asterisks indicate locations of short bolts)

radiator hose and coolant overflow hose from the top of the engine. **Note:** *Make alignment marks on the radiator hose and its clamp so the clamp can be positioned properly during installation.*

8   Remove the intake manifold stays **(see illustration 11.7)**. The manifold can be left in place if you're removing the head just for gasket replacement. If you need to remove the intake manifold, refer to Section 9.

9   Remove the camshafts (see Section 6).

10   Disconnect the exhaust pipe from the manifold **(see illustration)**.

11   Loosen the cylinder head bolts, 1/4-turn at a time, in the *reverse* order of the tightening sequence **(see illustration 11.16)** until they can be removed by hand. **Note:** *Mark the locations of the different length bolts so they can be reinstalled in their original locations.*

12   Carefully lift the cylinder head straight up and place the head on wood blocks to prevent damage to the sealing surfaces. If the head sticks to the engine block, dislodge it by placing a wood block against the head casting and tapping the wood with a hammer or by prying the head with a prybar placed carefully on a casting protrusion. **Note:** *Cylinder head disassembly and inspection procedures are covered in Chapter 2, Part E. It's also a good idea to have the head checked for warpage, even if you're just replacing the gasket.*

13   Remove all traces of old gasket material from the block and head. **Caution:** *The cylinder head is aluminum, so be very care-ful not to gouge the sealing surfaces.* Special gasket removal solvents that soften gaskets and make removal much easier are available at auto parts stores. When working on the block, place clean shop rags into the cylinders to help keep out debris. Use a vacuum cleaner to remove any contamination from the engine. Use a tap of the correct size to chase the threads in the engine block. Clean and inspect all threaded fasteners for damage. Inspect the cylinder head bolt threads for "necking," where the diameter of threads narrow due to bolt stretching **(see illustration)**. If any cylinder head bolt exhibits damage or necking, it must be replaced. **Note:** *If further disassembly of the cylinder head is required, refer to Part E of this Chapter.*

14   Refer to Part E of this Chapter for cleaning and inspection of the cylinder head.

Installation
Refer to illustration 11.16

15   Place a new gasket and the cylinder head in position on the engine block.

16   Apply clean engine oil to the cylinder head bolt threads and install them back in their original locations **(see illustration)**.

17   Tighten the cylinder head bolts in the sequence shown **(see illustration 11.16)** progressing in 3 stages to the torque listed in this Chapter's Specifications. **Note:** *The center bolts and outer bolts have different torque settings.* After the third pass, tighten the bolts in the proper sequence, an addi-

tional 90-degrees (1/4-turn) more. **Note:** *A torque wrench is not required for the 1/4-turn procedure. Before performing the final pass, mark the bolts in relation to the cylinder head and place another mark 90-degrees clockwise from the starting mark. Tightening less than 90-degrees will allow the bolts to loosen. If you accidentally tighten more than 90-degrees, unscrew all of the head bolts and start the procedure over.*

18   Install the rocker arms, hydraulic valve lash adjusters and camshafts (see Section 9).

19   Install the timing belt (see Section 5). After installation, slowly rotate the crankshaft by hand clockwise through two complete revolutions. Recheck the camshaft timing marks.

20   Reinstall the remaining components in the reverse order of removal.

21   Be sure to refill the cooling system and engine oil and check all fluid levels (see Chapter 1 if necessary).

22   Start the engine and run it until normal operating temperature is reached. Check for leaks and proper operation.

12   Oil pan - removal and installation

Refer to illustrations 12.6 and 12.10

Removal

1   Disconnect the battery cable from the negative battery terminal.

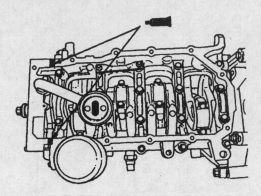

12.10 Apply silicone sealant across the seams where the oil pump housing meets the cylinder block

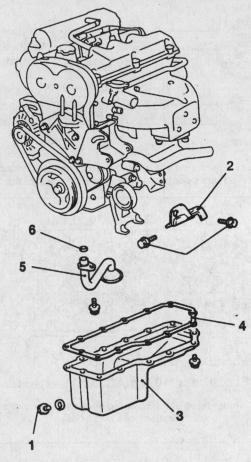

12.6 Oil pan details

1	Drain plug	3	Oil pan	5	Oil pick-up
2	Support plate	4	Gasket		tube
				6	O-ring

13.4 Remove the oil pump mounting bolts (arrows) and separate the pump from the cylinder block

2   Raise the vehicle and support it securely on jackstands.

3   Drain the engine oil (see Chapter 1).

4   Remove the splash pan under the drivebelt end of the engine, then remove the engine oil dipstick.

5   Disconnect the exhaust pipe from the manifold and let the exhaust hang loosely under the car.

6   Remove the support plate **(see illustration)**.

7   Remove the bolts and lower the oil pan from the vehicle. If the pan is stuck, tap it with a soft-face hammer or place a block of wood against the pan and tap the wood with a hammer. **Caution:** *If you're wedging something between the oil pan and the engine block to separate the two, be extremely careful not to gouge or nick the gasket surface of either part; an oil leak could result.*

8   Remove the oil pump pickup tube and screen assembly and clean both the tube and screen thoroughly. Install the pick-up tube and screen with a new gasket.

9   Thoroughly clean the oil pan and sealing surfaces on the block and pan. Use a scraper to remove all traces of old gasket mate-

rial. Gasket removal solvents are available at auto parts stores and may prove helpful. Check the oil pan sealing surface for distortion. Straighten or replace as necessary. After cleaning and straightening (if necessary), wipe the gasket surfaces of the pan and block clean with a rag soaked in lacquer thinner or acetone.

Installation

10   Apply a bead of RTV sealant to the oil pan flange and smear small dabs of sealant across the seams where the oil pump housing meets the cylinder block **(see illustration)**. **Note:** *When applying the sealant, lay the bead in the center of the oil pan rail, except for the bolt holes, where you'll need to go around the inside edge of the bolt holes. If you apply the RTV to the outside of the bolt holes, an oil leak at the bolt-hole area will result.*

11   Place the oil pan into position and install the bolts finger tight. Working side-to-side from the center out, tighten the bolts to the torque listed in this Chapter's Specifications.

12   Reinstall the remaining parts in the reverse order of removal.

13   Refill the crankcase with the proper

quantity and grade of oil and run the engine, checking for leaks. Road test the vehicle and check for leaks again.

13 Oil pump - removal, inspection and installation

Removal

Refer to illustrations 13.4, 13.5a, 13.5b, 13.5c, 13.7 and 13.8

1   Remove the timing belt, crankshaft sprocket and rear timing belt cover (see Section 5).

2   Remove the crankshaft sprocket (see Section 8).

3   Remove the oil pan, then unbolt the oil pickup tube and screen from the bottom of the pump housing (see Section 12).

4   If you're planning to remove the relief valve, loosen the cap now while the pump is still bolted to the engine **(see illustration)**. Unbolt the oil pump and take it off the engine.

5   Unscrew the mounting screws and remove the rotor assembly cover from the oil pump housing. Withdraw the inner and outer

13.5a Remove the rotor cover screws (arrows) . . .

13.5b . . . and lift off the rotor cover

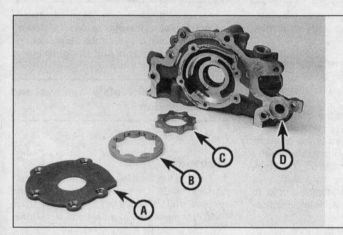

13.5c Oil pump details

A   Rotor cover
B   Outer rotor
C   Inner rotor
D   Oil pump body

**13.7 Remove the discharge port O-ring -
coat the new O-ring with clean
engine oil on installation**

rotors from the body **(see illustrations)**.**Caution:** *Be very careful with these components. Close tolerances are critical in creating the correct oil pressure. Any nicks or other damage will require replacement of the complete pump assembly.*

6   Using a hammer and brass drift, carefully remove the crankshaft front seal from the oil pump housing and discard it.

7   Remove the O-ring seal from the oil pump discharge port and discard it **(see illustration)**.

8   Disassemble the relief valve, noting which way the relief valve piston is installed. Unscrew the cap bolt and remove the bolt, washer, spring and relief valve **(see illustration)**.

Inspection

Refer to illustrations 13.12a through 13.12e

9   Clean all components including the block surfaces and oil pan with solvent, then inspect all surfaces for excessive wear and/or damage.

10   Inspect the oil pressure relief valve pis-

ton sliding surface and valve spring for damage. If either the spring or the valve is damaged, they must be replaced as a set.

11   Measure the relief valve spring free length and compare it with the dimension given in this Chapter's Specifications. Replace the spring if it's out of tolerance by more than 1/8 of an inch.

12   Check the oil pump rotor dimensions

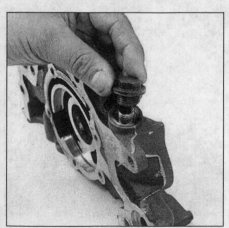

**13.8 Unscrew the relief valve cap and
dump out the spring and piston**

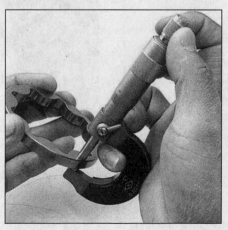

**13.12a Measure the outer rotor thickness
at four locations equally spaced**

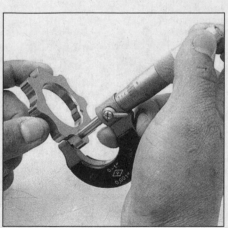

**13.12b Measure the inner rotor thickness
at four locations equally spaced**

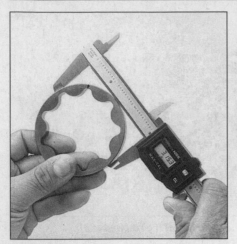

13.12c Measure the outer rotor diameter at four locations equally spaced

13.12d Use a flat feeler gauge to measure the outer rotor-to-oil pump body clearance

13.12e With the rotors installed, lay a precision straightedge across the cover surface and measure the clearance between the rotors and straightedge

and clearances with a micrometer or vernier calipers and a feeler gauge **(see illustrations)** and compare the results to the tolerances given in this Chapter's Specifications. Replace both rotors if any dimension is out of tolerance.

Installation

Refer to illustration 13.16

13   Lubricate the relief valve piston, piston bore and spring with clean engine oil. Install the relief valve piston into the bore with the grooved end going in first followed by the spring and cap bolt. Tighten the cap bolt to the torque listed in this Chapter's Specifications. **Note:** *If the relief valve piston is installed incorrectly, serious engine damage could occur.*

14   Lubricate the oil pump rotor recess in the housing and the inner and outer rotors with clean engine oil and install both rotors in the body. If the inner rotor has a chamfer, install it so the chamfer is facing the rotor cover. Next,

fill the rotor cavity with clean engine oil and install the cover. Tighten the cover screws to the torque listed in this Chapter's Specifications.

15   Install a new O-ring in the oil discharge passage.

16   Apply anaerobic sealant to the oil pump body sealing surface **(see illustration)**, and position the pump assembly on the block aligning the inner rotor and crankshaft drive flats. Tighten the oil pump attaching bolts to the torque listed in this Chapter's Specifications.

17   Install all components removed for access.

18   Install a new oil filter (see Chapter 1). Lower the vehicle.

19   Fill the crankcase with the proper quantity and grade of oil (see *Recommended lubricants and fluids* Section in Chapter 1).

20   Connect the negative battery cable.

21   After the sealant has cured per the manufacturer's directions, start the engine and check for leaks.

14   Flywheel/driveplate - removal and installation

Refer to illustrations 14.3 and 14.5

Removal

1   Raise the vehicle and support it securely on jackstands, then refer to Chapter 7 and remove the transaxle and All Wheel Drive (AWD) components (if equipped). If it's leaking, now would be a very good time to replace the transaxle front seal (on automatic transaxles, the torque converter must be removed to gain access to this seal).

2   Remove the pressure plate and clutch disc (manual transaxle equipped vehicles) (see Chapter 8). Now is a good time to check/replace the clutch components and the pilot bearing.

3   The bolt holes are either staggered or symmetrical on the flywheel/driveplate bolt

13.16 Apply a coat of anaerobic sealant to the pump housing sealing surface as shown

14.3 Match-mark the position of the driveplate or flywheel to the crankshaft and, using an appropriate tool to hold the driveplate, remove the bolts

14.5 Remove the driveplate or flywheel from the crankshaft

15.3 Very carefully pry the crankshaft rear main seal out of its bore - DO NOT nick or scratch the sealing surfaces on the bore or crankshaft

15.5 Don't put any lubricant on this seal - with the words THIS SIDE OUT facing away from the engine, tap it in only until it's flush with the block - any more will cause an oil leak

pattern. To ensure correct alignment during reinstallation, mark the position of the flywheel/driveplate to the crankshaft before removal **(see illustration)**.

4   Remove the bolts that secure the flywheel/driveplate to the crankshaft. If the crankshaft turns, wedge a screwdriver in the ring gear teeth to jam the flywheel.

5   Remove the flywheel/driveplate from the crankshaft **(see illustration)**. Since the flywheel is fairly heavy, be sure to support it while removing the last bolt.

6   Clean the flywheel to remove grease and oil. Inspect the surface for cracks, rivet grooves, burned areas and score marks. Light scoring can be removed with emery cloth. Check for cracked and broken ring gear teeth. Lay the flywheel on a flat surface and use a straightedge to check for warpage. **Note:** *Flywheels can be re-surfaced by a machine shop. Also, starter ring gears are available separately and can be installed by an automotive machine shop.*

7   Clean and inspect the mating surfaces of the flywheel/driveplate and the crankshaft. If the crankshaft rear seal is leaking, replace it before reinstalling the flywheel/driveplate (see Section 14).

Installation

8   Position the flywheel/driveplate against the crankshaft. If the bolt holes aren't staggered, align the previously applied match marks. Before installing the bolts, apply thread locking compound to the threads.

9   Wedge a screwdriver in the ring gear teeth to keep the flywheel/driveplate from turning as you tighten the bolts to the torque listed in this Chapter's Specifications.

10   The remainder of installation is the reverse of the removal procedure.

15   Rear main oil seal - replacement

Refer to illustrations 15.3 and 15.5

1   The one-piece rear main oil seal is pressed into a bore machined into the rear

main bearing cap and engine block.

2   Remove the transaxle, clutch (manual transaxle models) and driveplate (see Chapters 7 and 8 and Section 14).

3   **Note:** *Observe that the oil seal is installed flush with the outer surface of the block.* Pry out the old seal with a 3/16-inch flat blade screwdriver **(see illustration). Caution:** *To prevent an oil leak, be very careful not to scratch or otherwise damage the crankshaft sealing surface or the seal bore in the engine block.*

4   Clean the crankshaft and seal bore in the block thoroughly and de-grease the areas by wiping them with a rag soaked in lacquer thinner or acetone. DO NOT lubricate the lip or outer diameter of the new seal - it must be installed as it comes from the manufacturer - DRY.

5   Position the new seal onto the crankshaft. **Note:** *When installing the new seal, if so marked, the words THIS SIDE OUT on the seal must face out, toward the rear of the engine.* Using an appropriate size driver and pilot tool, drive the seal into the cylinder block until it is flush with the outer surface of the block. If the seal is driven in past flush, there will be an oil leak. Check that the seal is flush **(see illustration)**.

6   The remaining installation steps are the reverse of removal.

16   Engine mounts - check and replacement

1   Engine mounts seldom require attention, but broken or deteriorated mounts should be replaced immediately or the added strain placed on the driveline components may cause damage or wear.

Check

Refer to illustration 16.2

2   Before jacking up the engine, measure the distance from the crossmember to the

front roll stopper's through-bolt **(see illustration)**. If it's not within the range listed in this Chapter's Specifications, replace the roll stopper as described below. During the rest of the check, the engine must be raised slightly to remove the weight from the mounts.

3   Raise the vehicle and support it securely on jackstands, then position a jack under the engine oil pan. Place a large block of wood between the jack head and the oil pan to prevent oil pan damage, then carefully raise the engine just enough to take the weight off the mounts. **Warning:** *DO NOT place any part of your body under the engine when it's supported only by a jack!*

4   Check the mounts to see if the rubber is cracked, hardened or separated from the metal backing. Sometimes the rubber will split right down the center.

5   Check for relative movement between the mount plates and the engine or frame (use a large screwdriver or pry bar to attempt to move the mounts). If movement is noted, lower the engine and tighten the mount fasteners.

6   Rubber preservative may be applied to the mounts to slow deterioration.

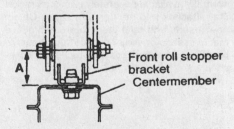

16.2 If the roll stopper height (A) is not within Specifications with the engine's weight on the roll stopper, replace it

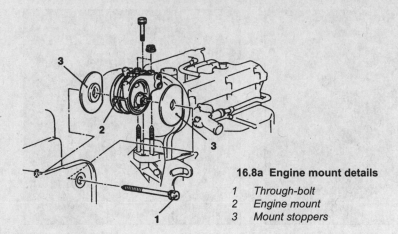

16.8a Engine mount details

1   Through-bolt
2   Engine mount
3   Mount stoppers

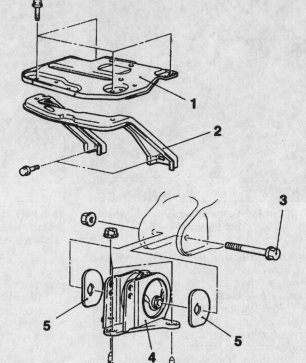

16.8b Transaxle mount details

1	Battery bracket	4	Transaxle mount
2	Battery bracket brace	5	Mount stoppers
3	Through bolt		

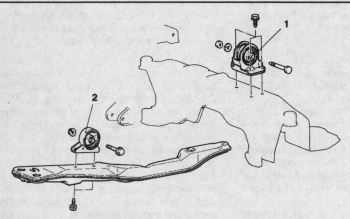

16.8c Engine roll stopper details

1   Rear roll stopper   2   Front roll stopper

Replacement

Refer to illustrations 16.8a, 16.8b, 16.8c, 16.10a and 16.10b

7   Disconnect the battery cable from the negative battery terminal, then raise the vehicle and support it securely on jackstands (if not already done). **Caution:** *Do not disconnect more than one mount at a time, except during engine/transaxle removal.*

8   Remove the fasteners and detach the mount from the frame and engine **(see illustrations)**.

9   The rubber portion of the mounts are normally available separately from the bracket that attaches it to the frame or block. Obtain new inserts and take them to an automotive machine shop or dealer service department to be pressed into the existing bracket, if necessary.

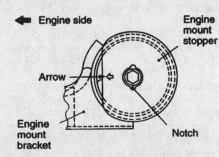

16.10a Position the engine mount stopper arrows in the direction shown to align the notches correctly

16.10b Position the transaxle mount stopper arrows in the direction shown to align the notches correctly

10   Installation is the reverse of removal. Install the engine mount and transaxle mount stoppers with the arrow marks pointing in the proper direction **(see illustrations)**. Use thread locking compound on the mount bolts and be sure to tighten them securely.

Chapter 2 Part B
2.0L four-cylinder turbo engine

Contents

Specifications

General
Firing order	1-3-4-2
Cylinder numbers (drivebelt end-to-transaxle end)	1-2-3-4

Camshaft
Lobe height	
Standard	1.3744 inches
Service limit	1.3547 inches
Camshaft journal diameter	1.022 inches

Cylinder head
Warpage limit	
Standard	0.002 inch
Service limit	0.008 inch

Intake and exhaust manifolds
Warpage limit (all engines)	
Standard	0.006 inch
Service limit	0.008 inch

Timing belt
Timing belt deflection	Tension automatically adjusted
Balance shaft belt deflection	1/4-inch
Projection of tensioner rod	0.150 to 0.177 inch
Tensioner rod movement @ 22 to 44 lbs pressure	0.040 inch or less

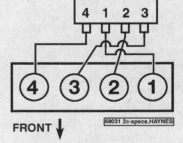

Cylinder numbering and spark plug wire routing

Oil pump

Side clearance
    Drive gear.. 0.0031 to 0.0055 inch
    Driven gear... 0.0051 to 0.0071 inch

Engine mounts

Roll stopper height.. 1.69 +/-0.12 inches

Torque specifications*   Ft-lbs (unless otherwise noted)

Note: *One foot-pound (ft-lb) of torque is equivalent to 12 inch-pounds (in-lbs) of torque. Torque values below approximately 15 ft-lbs are expressed in inch-pounds, since most foot-pound torque wrenches are not accurate at these smaller values.*

Balance shaft sprocket bolt 33
Balance shaft belt tensioner bolt .... 168 inch-lbs
Camshaft bearing cap bolts.. 168 inch-lbs
Camshaft sprocket bolts... 65
Crankshaft pulley bolts... 18
Crankshaft sprocket bolt... 80 to 94
Cylinder head bolts
    Step 1 58
    Step 2 .... Loosen completely
    Step 3 15
    Step 4 .... Tighten 1/4-turn
    Step 5 .... Tighten 1/4-turn further
Engine hanger-to-exhaust manifold bolts 17
Exhaust manifold bolts/nuts... 17
Exhaust pipe-to-exhaust manifold bolts/nuts.................................... 33
Flywheel or driveplate bolts... 94 to 101
Front case bolts.. 17
Front case plug... 17
Intake manifold-to-engine nuts/bolts
    Nuts... 26
    Bolt (including engine hanger) 26
    Bolts (not including engine hanger)... 168 inch-lbs
Oil cooler bolt... 28 to 33
Oil filter bracket bolts... 132 to 192 inch-lbs
Oil pan bolts/nuts... 168 inch-lbs
Oil pick-up tube and screen mounting bolts .... 61 inch-lbs
Oil pump sprocket nut... 40
Oil pressure sending unit.. 84 inch-lbs
Oil pressure switch .... 84 inch-lbs
Oil pan baffle plate bolts.. 72 inch-lbs
Oil pump cover screws .... 84 inch-lbs
Oil pump cover bolts... 132 to 156 inch-lbs
Oil pump driven gear bolt... 26
Oil pump relief valve plug 33
Rear main oil seal retainer bolts.. 96 inch-lbs
Timing belt front cover bolts
    Without washer .... 86 to 104 inch-lbs
    With washer .... 78 inch-lbs
Timing belt tensioner mounting bolts... 17
Water pump pulley bolts... 78 inch-lbs
Timing belt tensioner pulley bolt/nut 35
Valve cover bolts
    Cover-to-cylinder head bolts .... 30 inch-lbs
    Center cover bolts.. 26 inch-lbs

Refer to Part E for additional torque specifications

3.4 To rotate the crankshaft by hand, insert a 1/2-inch drive extension and breaker bar into this square hole in the crankshaft pulley bolt

1   General information

This Part of Chapter 2 is devoted to in-vehicle engine repair procedures. Information concerning engine removal and installation and engine block and cylinder head overhaul can be found in Part E of this Chapter.

The following repair procedures are based on the assumption that the engine is installed in the vehicle. If the engine has been removed from the vehicle and mounted on a stand, many of the steps outlined in this Part of Chapter 2 will not apply.

The Specifications included in this Part of Chapter 2 apply only to the procedures contained in this Part. Part E of Chapter 2 contains the Specifications necessary for cylinder head and engine block rebuilding.

This Part of Chapter 2 covers the 2.0L Double Overhead Camshaft (DOHC) turbo engine.

2   Repair operations possible with the engine in the vehicle

Many major repair operations can be accomplished without removing the engine from the vehicle.

Clean the engine compartment and the exterior of the engine with some type of degreaser before any work is done. It will make the job easier and help keep dirt out of the internal areas of the engine.

Depending on the components involved, it may be helpful to remove the hood to improve access to the engine as repairs are performed (refer to Chapter 11 if necessary). Cover the fenders to prevent damage to the paint. Special pads are available, but an old bedspread or blanket will also work.

If vacuum, exhaust, oil or coolant leaks develop, indicating a need for gasket or seal replacement, the repairs can generally be made with the engine in the vehicle. The

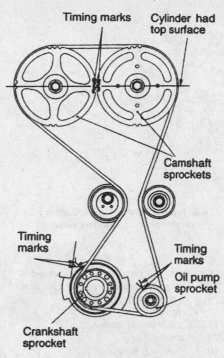

3.6 Timing marks

intake and exhaust manifold gaskets, oil pan gasket, crankshaft oil seals and cylinder head gasket are all accessible with the engine in place.

Exterior engine components, such as the turbocharger, intake and exhaust manifolds, the oil pan, the oil pump, the water pump, the starter motor, the alternator and the fuel system components can be removed for repair with the engine in place.

Since the camshafts and cylinder head can be removed without pulling the engine, valve component servicing can also be accomplished with the engine in the vehicle. Replacement of the timing belts and sprockets is also possible with the engine in the vehicle.

In extreme cases caused by a lack of necessary equipment, repair or replacement of piston rings, pistons, connecting rods and rod bearings is possible with the engine in the vehicle. However, this practice is not recommended because of the cleaning and preparation work that must be done to the components involved.

3   Top Dead Center (TDC) for number one piston - locating

Refer to illustrations 3.4 and 3.6

1   Top Dead Center (TDC) is the highest point in the cylinder that each piston reaches as it travels up-and-down when the crankshaft turns. Each piston reaches TDC on the compression stroke and again on the exhaust stroke, but TDC generally refers to piston position on the compression stroke.

2   Positioning the piston(s) at TDC is an essential part of many procedures such as rocker arm removal, camshaft and timing belt/sprocket removal and distributor or crankshaft/camshaft position sensor removal.

3   Before beginning this procedure, be sure to place the transmission in Neutral and apply the parking brake or block the rear wheels. Also, disable the ignition system by detaching the electrical connector at the ignition coil pack (see Chapter 5). Remove the spark plugs (see Chapter 1).

4   In order to bring any piston to TDC, the crankshaft must be turned using one of the methods outlined below. When looking at the drivebelt end of the engine, normal crankshaft rotation is clockwise.

a)   *The preferred method is to turn the crankshaft with a ratchet and an extension inserted into the drivebelt end of the crankshaft (see illustration).*

b)   *A remote starter switch, which may save some time, can also be used. These switches are available inexpensively from auto parts stores. Follow the instructions included with the switch. Once the piston is close to TDC, use a socket and ratchet as described in the previous paragraph.*

c)   *If an assistant is available to turn the ignition switch to the Start position in short bursts, you can get the piston close to TDC without a remote starter switch. Make sure your assistant is out of the vehicle, away from the ignition switch, then use a socket and ratchet as described in Paragraph a) to complete the procedure.*

5   Remove the timing belt upper cover (see Section 5). If there are no timing marks on the crankshaft pulley and lower timing belt cover, remove the timing belt lower cover.

6   Turn the crankshaft (see Paragraph 3 above) until the timing marks on the camshaft sprockets are aligned with each other and with the upper surface of the cylinder head, and the crankshaft pulley timing marks are aligned (see illustration). If the crankshaft pulley timing marks are aligned, but the camshaft sprocket timing marks are not, the number one piston is at TDC on the exhaust stroke, not the compression stroke. Go to Step 7.

7   To get the piston to TDC on the compression stroke, turn the crankshaft one complete turn (360-degrees) clockwise. The camshaft sprocket marks should now be aligned. When the crankshaft pulley marks and the camshaft sprocket marks are aligned, the number one piston is at TDC on the compression stroke.

8   After the number one piston has been positioned at TDC on the compression stroke, TDC for any of the remaining pistons can be located by turning the crankshaft and following the firing order. Make a mark on the crankshaft pulley exactly 180-degrees opposite the notch. Rotate the crankshaft 180-degrees clockwise from the number-one-cylinder TDC position: this is the number-three-cylinder TDC position. Then rotate the crankshaft clock-

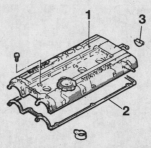

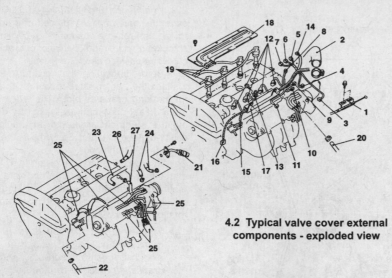

4.2 Typical valve cover external components - exploded view

4.4 Valve cover details

1	Valve cover	3	Semi-circular
2	Gasket		seal

1   Throttle cable
2   Air hose
3   Idle air control motor connector
4   Knock sensor connector
5   Oxygen sensor connector
6   Coolant temperature gauge sending unit connector
7   Coolant temperature sensor connector
8   Ignition power transistor connector
9   Throttle position sensor connector
10 Capacitor connector
11 Manifold differential pressure sensor connector
12 Fuel injector connectors
13 Ignition coil connector

14 Camshaft position sensor connector
15 Crankshaft position sensor connector
16 Air conditioning compressor connector
17 Control wiring harness
18 Center cover
19 Spark plug wires
20 Brake booster vacuum hose
21 High pressure fuel hose
22 Fuel return hose
23 Bypass valve hose
24 Coolant hoses
25 Vacuum hoses
26 Breather hose
27 PCV hose

of the seal, at the seal-to-valve cover joints. Also apply a small dab of sealant to each of the corners at the front end of the cylinder head **(see illustration)**.
7   Tighten the bolts to the torque listed in this Chapter's Specifications. The remaining steps are the reverse of removal. When finished, run the engine and check for oil leaks.

5   Timing belt, balance shaft belt and sprockets - removal, inspection and installation

Removal

> ** ** CAUTION ** **
> The timing system is complex. Severe engine damage will occur if you make any mistakes. Do not attempt this procedure unless you are highly experienced with this type of repair. If you are at all unsure of your abilities, consult an expert. Double-check all your work and be sure everything is correct before you attempt to start the engine.

Caution: *Do not try to turn the crankshaft with the camshaft sprocket bolts and do not rotate the crankshaft counterclockwise. Also, don't turn the crankshaft or camshafts after the timing belt has been removed.*
Note: *Special tools are required for this procedure. Read all Steps thoroughly before proceeding.*
1   Position the number one piston at Top

---

wise another 180-degrees, back to where the notch is aligned with the T mark on the pulley: this is the number-four-cylinder TDC position. Finally, rotate the crankshaft another 180-degrees clockwise: this is the number-two-cylinder TDC position.

4   Valve cover - removal and installation

Refer to illustrations 4.2, 4.4 and 4.6
1   Disconnect the battery cable from the negative battery terminal. Remove the upper timing belt cover (see Section 5).
2   Detach the spark plug wires and cable brackets from the valve cover (see Chapter 1). Remove the center cover **(see illustration)** and disconnect the wires from the spark plugs (see Chapter 1). Use numbered pieces of tape to label the wires so they can be returned to their original locations on reassembly.
3   Clearly label and disconnect any emission hoses and cables which connect to, or cross over, the valve cover.
4   Remove the valve cover bolts and lift the cover off **(see illustration)**. If the cover sticks to the cylinder head, tap on it with a soft-face hammer or place a block of wood against the cover and tap on the wood with a hammer.

Caution: *If you have to pry between the valve cover and the cylinder head, be extremely careful not to gouge or nick the gasket surfaces of either part. A leak could develop after reassembly.*
5   Thoroughly clean the valve cover and remove all traces of old gasket material. Gasket removal solvents are available from auto parts stores and may prove helpful. After cleaning the surfaces, degrease them with a rag soaked in lacquer thinner or acetone.
6   Install a new gasket on the cover, using RTV to hold it in place. Place the cover on the engine and install the cover bolts. **Note:** *Be sure to install a new semi-circular seal* **(see illustration 4.4)** *into the cylinder head. Apply a small amount of sealant to the bottom of the seal and, after it has been installed, to the top*

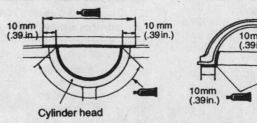

4.6 Apply sealant to the darkened areas around the semi-circular seal and the corners of the valve cover gasket

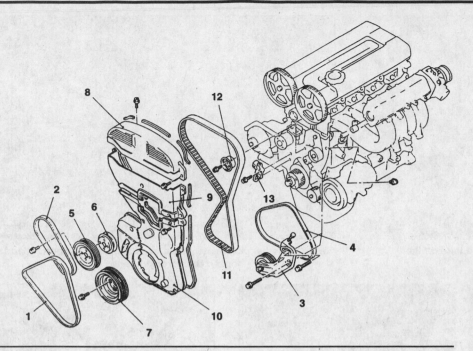

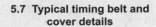

5.7 Typical timing belt and cover details

1   *Alternator belt*
2   *Power steering pump belt*
3   *Tensioner pulley bracket*
4   *Air conditioning compressor belt*
5   *Water pump pulley*
6   *Water pump pulley (for power steering pump)*
7   *Crankshaft pulley*
8   *Timing belt upper cover*
9   *Timing belt center cover*
10 *Timing belt lower cover*
11 *Timing belt*
12 *Tensioner pulley*
13 *Tensioner*

5.9 Remove the four bolts that attach the pulleys to the crankshaft (arrows)

Dead Center (see Section 3).

2   Disconnect the battery cable from the negative battery terminal.

3   Set the parking brake and block the rear wheels. Raise the front of the vehicle and support it securely on jackstands.

4   Remove the left engine mount and bracket (see Section 18). **Note:** *Make sure the engine is supported with a piece of wood and a floor jack placed under the oil pan. The wood will prevent the floor jack from denting or damaging the oil pan.*

5   Remove the splash pan from beneath the drivebelt end of the engine.

Main timing belt

Refer to illustrations 5.7, 5.9, 5.10, 5.11, 5.13, 5.14a, 5.14b, 5.15a and 5.15b

6   Remove the clamp and bracket for the power steering pressure hose (if equipped) and the clamp for the air conditioning hose, if equipped.

7   Remove the drivebelts (see Chapter 1) and the tensioner pulley bracket (**see illustration**).

8   Remove the water pump pulleys. **Note:** *The smaller of the two pulleys runs the power steering pump.*

9   Loosen the large crankshaft sprocket bolt in the center of the crankshaft pulley. It might be very tight, so, to break it loose, wrap a rag around the pulley and attach a chain wrench. Slip a 1/2-inch drive extension through the hole in the inner fender and into the sprocket bolt head (**see illustration 3.4**). Turn the extension with a breaker bar. If you are unable to loosen the bolt due to the chain wrench slipping, you can prevent the crankshaft from turning by having an assistant wedge a flat-blade screwdriver in the flywheel/driveplate ring gear teeth. To do this, you must first remove the flywheel/driveplate cover. Next, remove the bolts and remove the crankshaft pulley (**see illustration**).

10 Remove the retaining bolts from the upper and lower timing belt covers and remove the covers and gaskets (**see illustration 5.7 and the accompanying illustration**).

11 Check that the timing marks are aligned (**see illustration 3.6**). Make a mark on the timing belt in the direction of rotation (**see illustration**) so it may be reinstalled in the same direction in the event the timing belt is reused.

5.10 Remove the bolt at the side (arrow) and two at the top and lift off the upper cover

5.11 Mark an arrow on the belt so it can be reinstalled in the proper direction if you reuse it - also, note the locations of the timing marks (circle) and camshaft sprocket dowels (arrows)

5.13 Remove the bolts (arrows) and take off the automatic tensioner

5.14a Hold the camshafts with a wrench on the hex portion and loosen the sprocket bolts . . .

5.14b . . . if a sprocket bolt is very tight, brace the wrench with a wooden block to protect the cylinder head when the bolt breaks loose

5.15a Unscrew the plug from the cylinder block and insert a Phillips screwdriver to keep the balance shaft from turning

5.15b Unscrew the oil pump sprocket nut (arrow) with a socket and breaker bar and remove the sprocket

12   Loosen the tensioner pulley center bolt and push the pulley toward the water pump to create slack in the timing belt, then remove the timing belt. **Caution:** *Be sure that the timing marks are correctly aligned before removing the timing belt* **(see illustration 3.6).**
13   Unbolt and remove the tensioner **(see illustration).**

14   If you plan to replace or remove the camshaft(s) or camshaft oil seal(s), remove the camshaft sprocket(s). Using an adjustable wrench or an open-end wrench, hold the camshaft at the hexagon and remove the camshaft sprocket bolt **(see illustration)**. If the sprocket bolt cannot be loosened easily, place a block of wood between the head and the wrench **(see illustration)** to prevent damage to the head so more force can be used on the camshaft sprocket bolt. Remove the bolt and slide the sprocket off the camshaft.
15   If it's necessary to remove the balance shaft sprocket or oil pump, remove the plug on the side of the engine block and insert a Phillips screwdriver to prevent the shaft from turning **(see illustration)**. Remove the oil pump sprocket nut with a socket and a breaker bar and remove the oil pump sprocket **(see illustration).**

Balance shaft belt

Refer to illustrations 5.16a and 5.16b
16   If you're planning to install the same belt, mark the direction of rotation on the belt **(see illustration)**. If you're planning to remove the

balance shaft sprocket, loosen the bolt before you remove the belt. Be sure the alignment marks are positioned correctly before removing the belt **(see illustration)**. Remove the bolt from the center of the tensioner pulley, remove the pulley, then remove the belt. To remove the crankshaft sprocket, pull it off - it may be necessary to use a bolt-type puller.

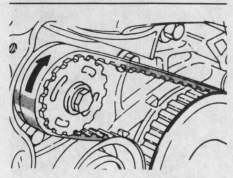

5.16a Mark the balancer belt with a directional arrow so it can be reinstalled in the correct direction if you reuse it

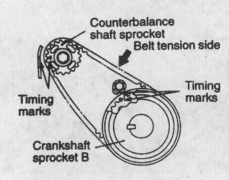

5.16b Counterbalancer timing marks

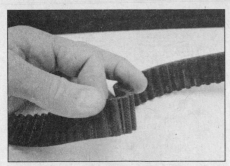

5.18 Carefully inspect the timing belt - bending it backwards will often make wear or damage more apparent

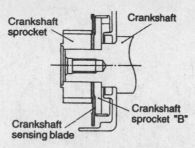

5.20 Make sure the crankshaft sensing blade faces in the proper direction

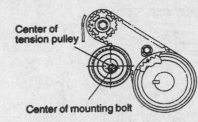

5.23a Position the center of the tensioner pulley above and to the left of the mounting bolt

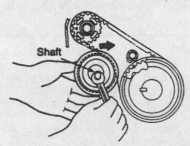

5.23b Push the pulley in the direction shown (arrow), hold it there to keep the other side of the belt tight and tighten the pulley bolt without letting the pulley shaft turn . . .

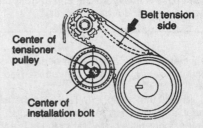

5.23c . . . after tightening the bolt, push on the other side of the belt to check belt tension

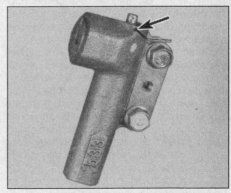

5.25 Compress the rod into the tensioner, then slide a pin into the hole (arrow) to keep it there

Inspection

Refer to illustration 5.18

17   Rotate the tensioner pulleys by hand and move them side-to-side to detect roughness and excess play. Visually inspect the sprockets for any signs of damage and wear. Replace parts as necessary. Also, replace the pulley if there is a lubricant leak.

18   Inspect the timing belts for cracks, separation, wear, missing teeth and oil contamination. Replace the belt if it's in questionable condition (see illustration).

19   Check the automatic tensioner for leaks or any obvious damage to the body. Also, check the rod end for wear or damage. Press the rod end against a metal surface, such as a vise, with 22 to 44 lbs force and measure the rod movement. If it's more than 1/32-inch, replace the tensioner.

Installation

> ** CAUTION **
>
> Before starting the engine, carefully rotate the crankshaft by hand through at least two full revolutions (use a socket and breaker bar on the crankshaft pulley center bolt). If you feel any resistance, STOP! There is something wrong - most likely, valves are contacting the pistons. You must find the problem before proceeding. Check your work and see if any updated repair information is available.

Refer to illustration 5.20

20   Reinstall the timing belt sprockets, if they were removed. Tighten the bolts to the values listed in this Chapter's Specifications. Note: *Be sure to properly install the crankshaft sensing blade so it faces the proper direction* (see illustration).

Balance shaft belt

Refer to illustrations 5.23a, 5.23b and 5.23c

21   Install the balance shaft belt. Be sure the timing mark on the crankshaft sprocket and the balance shaft sprocket are aligned properly (see illustration 5.16b). Install the tensioner and bolt, but don't tighten the bolt completely at this time.

22   After installing the balance shaft belt, make sure the tension side has no slack.

23   Make sure the tension sprocket for the balance shaft belt has the center located just to the left side of the mounting bolt with the pulley directed to the front of the engine (see illustration). Lift the tensioner up with one finger to tighten the belt (see illustration) and tighten the tensioner bolt and the balance shaft bolt to the torque listed in this Chapter's Specifications. Note: *After tightening the bolt, use your index finger and press firmly on the timing belt. The belt deflection should be 1/4-inch* (see illustration).

Timing belt

Refer to illustrations 5.25, 5.31a, 5.31b and 5.35

24   Align the timing marks located on the camshaft, crankshaft and oil pump sprockets (see illustration 3.6). When aligning the oil pump sprocket marks, it is critical that the balance shaft has the weighted portion at the bottom of the shaft (it is possible to align the marks with the balance shaft weight at the top; if you do this accidentally, severe engine vibration will result). Before installing the timing belt, slightly rock the oil pump sprocket by hand and watch carefully that the sprocket has the tendency to remain stationary (return to approximately the marks-aligned position) when the sprocket is rotated. This means the sprocket is CORRECTLY timed. If the sprocket has the tendency to rotate clockwise when spun lightly, the shaft is INCORRECTLY timed. If there is any doubt about whether or not the balance shaft is in the correct posi-

tion, insert a screwdriver through the hole in the left side of the cylinder block (see illustration 5.15a). Make sure the screwdriver extends approximately 2-1/2 inches into the hole and also make sure the sprocket cannot be rotated with the screwdriver in place; now you can be sure the timing is correct.

25   Prepare the automatic tensioner for installation. Place the tensioner in a vise that is equipped with soft jaws (or put a shop rag over the jaws to prevent damage to the tensioner). If the rod is easily retracted, replace it with a new unit. The tensioner should have a fair amount of strength or resistance. Caution: *Be sure the tensioner is in a level position when it is in the vise. Also, place a washer over the plug on the bottom of the tensioner to prevent the vise from contacting the plug.* Once the tensioner is compressed, place a small Allen wrench, or something similar, through the hole to keep the rod retracted for reassembly on the engine (see illustration).

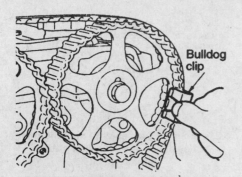

5.31a Use a heavy spring clip to hold the belt on the sprocket

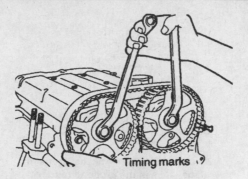

5.31b Use two wrenches to align the sprocket timing marks with the top of the cylinder head

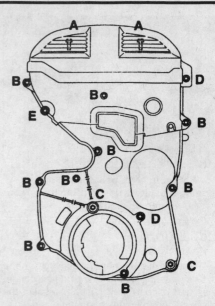

5.35 Timing belt cover bolt lengths and locations

A	16 mm	D	25 mm
B	18 mm		(flange bolt)
C	25 mm	E	45 mm
	(with washer)		

26   Install the automatic tensioner onto the engine, keeping it in the compressed position.

27   Install the tensioner pulley onto the tensioner arm. Position the two small holes in the tensioner pulley hub just to the left of the center bolt. Tighten the center bolt finger tight. Don't remove the Allen wrench from the tensioner yet.

28   Turn the two camshaft sprockets until the dowel pins are located at the top and the timing marks are facing each other and aligned with the upper surface of the cylinder head **(see illustration 3.6)**. Note: *When the exhaust camshaft is released, it will tend to rotate one tooth in the counterclockwise direction. This shift must be taken into account when installing the timing belt onto the sprockets. Also, the camshaft sprockets are identical and are provided with two timing marks. When the sprocket is mounted on the exhaust camshaft, use the timing mark on the right with the dowel pin hole on the top. On the intake camshaft sprocket, use the one on the left with the dowel pin hole on the top.*

29   Align the crankshaft sprocket timing mark and the oil pump sprocket timing mark with their pointers **(see illustration 3.6)**.

30   Remove the plug on the side of the block and insert a Phillips screwdriver or a long punch through the hole **(see illustration 5.15a)**. If the tool CAN be inserted into the hole as deep as 2 1/2-inches or more, the timing marks are aligned correctly. If the tool CANNOT be inserted more than 1-inch, the oil pump sprocket must be reset. When it's positioned properly, reinstall the screwdriver and keep it there until the timing belt is installed.

31   Install the timing belt in the following sequence:

a) *Install the timing belt around the intake camshaft sprocket and clip it in place with a spring clip* **(see illustration)**. *These are available at office supply stores.*

b) *Use two wrenches to hold the camshaft sprocket timing marks in alignment* **(see illustration)**, *install the timing belt on the exhaust camshaft sprocket and clip it in place with another butterfly clip.*

c) *Install the belt around the idler pulley.*

d) *Install the timing belt around the oil pump sprocket, making sure the timing marks stay aligned* **(see illustration 3.6)**.

e) *Install the timing belt around the tensioner pulley.*

f) *Remove the clips from the camshaft sprockets and timing belt.*

g) *Gently raise the tensioner pulley so the belt does not sag, then temporarily tighten the center bolt.*

32   Adjust the timing belt tension in the following sequence:

a) *Turn the crankshaft 1/4 turn counterclockwise, then clockwise to move the number 1 cylinder to TDC.*

b) *Loosen the tensioner center bolt and attach Mitsubishi special tool no. MD998752 (or equivalent) to a torque wrench.* **Note:** *The torque wrench must be capable of measuring small increments between 0 and 30 in-lbs. Apply between 23 and 25 in-lbs. to the tensioner.*

c) *While holding tension on the timing belt tensioner, tighten the center bolt to the torque listed in this Chapter's Specifications.*

d) *Screw Mitsubishi special tool no. MD998738 (or equivalent) into the engine left support bracket until its end makes contact with the tensioner arm. Continue to screw the tool into the pulley and when tension is relieved from the automatic tensioner, remove the Allen wrench, or whatever was used to keep the tensioner retracted, that was inserted into the tensioner. An alternate method would be to pry the tensioner pulley towards the front of the vehicle (don't pry against the belt) until the automatic tensioner is compressed, then remove the Allen wrench.*

e) *Remove the special tool, if used.*

f) *Rotate the crankshaft six complete turns and wait 15 minutes for the tensioner plunger to extend fully.* **Caution:** *If you feel resistance while turning the crankshaft, the valves may be hitting the pistons from incorrect valve timing. Stop and re-check the valve timing.* **Note:** *The*

camshaft, crankshaft and front balance shaft sprocket marks will align every two revolutions of the crankshaft; however, since the front (oil pump) sprocket turns at 2/3 crankshaft speed, its marks will only align every six crankshaft revolutions. Measure how far the tensioner plunger protrudes from the tensioner body (the distance between the tensioner arm and the automatic tensioner body). It should be between 5/32 and 3/16-inch (3.8 to 4.5 mm). Also check that all timing marks are still aligned.

33   If the tensioner protrusion is not as specified, repeat the belt adjustment procedure.

34   Install the timing covers.

35   Reinstall the remaining parts in the reverse order of removal. Note that the timing belt cover bolts come in different lengths **(see illustration)**.

36   Start the engine, check the ignition timing (see Chapter 5) and road test the vehicle.

6   Camshafts, rocker arms and lash adjusters - removal, inspection and installation

Camshafts

Removal

1   Remove the valve cover (see Section 4), timing belt and camshaft sprockets (see Section 5).

2   Remove the camshaft position sensor (see Chapter 6).

3   Remove the camshaft bearing caps, loosening the bolts a little at a time to prevent

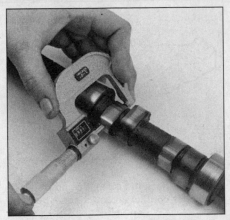

6.5 Measure the camshaft lobe heights with a micrometer

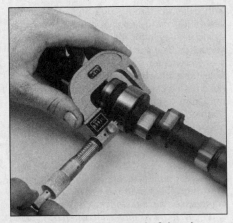

6.6 Measure the camshaft bearing journal diameters

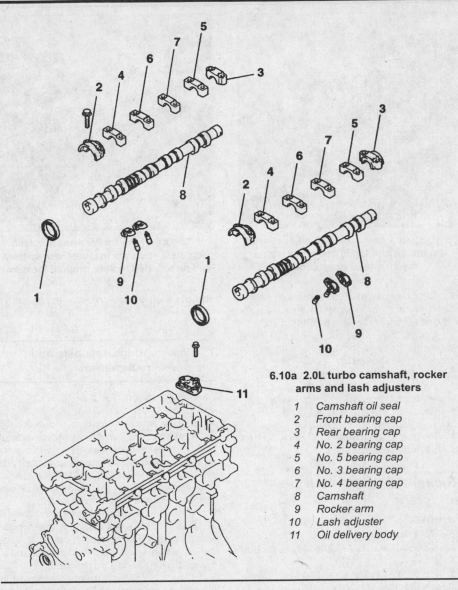

6.10a 2.0L turbo camshaft, rocker arms and lash adjusters

1   Camshaft oil seal
2   Front bearing cap
3   Rear bearing cap
4   No. 2 bearing cap
5   No. 5 bearing cap
6   No. 3 bearing cap
7   No. 4 bearing cap
8   Camshaft
9   Rocker arm
10 Lash adjuster
11 Oil delivery body

distorting the camshafts by loosening the caps from the ends of the shaft towards the center. Once the bearing caps have all been loosened enough for removal, they may still be difficult to remove. Using the bearing cap bolts for extra leverage, move the cap back and forth to loosen the cap from the cylinder head. If they are still difficult to remove you can tap them gently with a soft face hammer so they can be lifted off. **Caution:** *Store the caps in order so they can be returned to their original locations, with the same side facing forward. It's a good idea to mark them so there's no possibility of making a mistake.* Carefully lift the camshafts out of the cylinder head.

Inspection

Refer to illustrations 6.5 and 6.6

4   Remove the seal(s) from the camshaft(s) and thoroughly clean the camshaft(s) and the gasket surface. Visually inspect the camshaft for wear and/or damage to the lobe surfaces, bearing journals and seal contact surfaces. Visually inspect the camshaft bearing surfaces in the cylinder head for scoring and other damage.
5   Measure the camshaft lobe heights **(see illustration)** and compare them to this Chapter's Specifications.

6   Measure the camshaft bearing journal diameters **(see illustration)**. Compare this measurement with this Chapter's Specifications.
7   Replace the camshaft if it fails any of the above inspections. **Note:** *If the lobes are worn, replace the rocker arms along with the camshaft. Cylinder head replacement may be necessary if the camshaft bearing surfaces in the head are damaged or excessively worn.*

Installation

Refer to illustrations 6.10a, 6.10b and 6.11
8   Very carefully clean the camshaft and bearing journals/caps. Liberally coat the journals, lobes and thrust portions of the camshaft with assembly lube or engine oil.
9   Carefully install the camshaft(s) in the cylinder head.
10   Install the lash adjusters and rocker arms if they were removed. Next install the camshaft and camshaft bearing caps **(see illustration)**. Make sure the camshaft with the slit to drive the cam angle sensor at the rear of the shaft **(see illustration)** is placed on the

intake side of the head. Tighten the bearing cap bolts a little at a time, working from the center journals outward, doing one camshaft at a time, until the torque listed in this Chapter's Specifications is reached. **Note:** *Bearing cap numbers 2 through 5 are the same shape. Check the markings on the caps to identify the correct journal number and intake/exhaust position.*

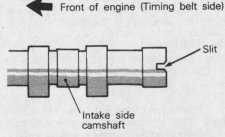

Front of engine (Timing belt side)

Slit

Intake side camshaft

6.10b The intake camshaft has a slit to drive the camshaft position sensor

6.11 Coat a new camshaft oil seal with engine oil and tap it into place with a hammer and deep socket

6.18 Lift off the rocker arms and lash adjusters - be sure to label them so they can be returned to their original locations

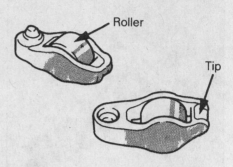

6.19 Check the roller, tip and lash-adjuster contact areas for score marks and pitting

11   Coat new camshaft oil seals with engine oil and press them into place with a hammer and deep socket **(see illustration)**.
12   Install the camshaft sprocket(s) and tighten the bolts to the torque listed in this Chapter's Specifications.
13   Install the timing belt (see Section 5).
14   Reinstall the camshaft/crankshaft angle sensor (see Chapter 6).
15   Reinstall the valve cover and run the engine while checking for oil leaks.
16   Reinstall the remaining parts in the reverse order of removal.

Rocker arms and lash adjusters

Removal
Refer to illustration 6.18
17   Remove the camshafts as described above.
18   Lift off the rocker arms and lash adjusters **(see illustration)**.

Inspection
Refer to illustration 6.19
19   Visually check the rocker arms for wear **(see illustration)**. Replace them if evidence of wear or damage is found.
20   Inspect each lash adjuster carefully for signs of wear and damage, particularly on the ball tip that contacts the rocker arm. Since the lash adjusters frequently become clogged, we recommend replacing them if you're concerned about their condition or if the engine is exhibiting valve "tapping" noises.

Installation
21   When reinstalling used parts, make sure they go back into their original locations.
22   The remainder of installation is the reverse of the removal steps.
23   When re-starting the engine after replacing the lash adjusters, the adjusters will normally make "tapping" noises. After warm-up, raise the speed of the engine from idle to 3,000 rpm for one minute. If the adjuster(s)

do not become silent, replace the defective ones.

7   Valve springs, retainers and seals - replacement

Refer to illustrations 7.4, 7.7, 7.8, 7.13 and 7.15
Note: *Broken valve springs and defective valve stem seals can be replaced without removing the cylinder head. Two special tools and a compressed air source are normally required to perform this operation, so read through this Section carefully and rent or buy the tools before attempting the job.*
1   Remove the valve cover (see Section 4).
2   Remove the spark plug from the cylinder which has the defective component. If all of the valve stem seals are being replaced, all of the spark plugs should be removed.
3   Turn the crankshaft until the piston in the affected cylinder is at Top Dead Center on the compression stroke (Section 3). If you're replacing all of the valve stem seals, begin

7.4 This is what the air hose adapter that threads into the spark plug hole looks like - they're commonly available from auto parts stores

with cylinder number one and work on the valves for one cylinder at a time. Move from cylinder-to-cylinder following the firing order sequence (see this Chapter's Specifications).
4   Thread an adapter into the spark plug hole **(see illustration)** and connect an air hose from a compressed air source to it. Most auto parts stores can supply the air hose adapter. **Note:** *Many cylinder compression gauges utilize a screw-in fitting that may work with your air hose quick-disconnect fitting.*
5   Remove the camshafts and rocker arms (see Section 6).
6   Apply compressed air to the cylinder. **Warning:** *The piston may be forced down by compressed air, causing the crankshaft to turn suddenly. If the wrench used when positioning the number one piston at TDC is still attached to the crankshaft bolt, it could cause damage or injury when the crankshaft moves.*
7   Stuff clean shop rags into the cylinder head holes above and below the valves to prevent parts and tools from falling into the engine, then use a valve spring compressor to compress the spring. Remove the keepers with small needle-nose pliers or a magnet **(see illustration)**.
8   Remove the spring retainer and valve

7.7 Use needle-nose pliers (shown) or a small magnet to remove the valve spring keepers - be careful not to drop them down into the engine!

7.8 Remove the valve stem seal with a pair of pliers

7.13 Gently tap the new seal into place with a hammer and a deep socket

7.15 Apply a small dab of grease to each keeper before installation to hold it in place on the valve stem until the spring is released

spring, then remove the valve guide seal/spring seat assembly **(see illustration)**. **Note:** *If air pressure fails to hold the valve in the closed position during this operation, the valve face and/or seat is probably damaged. If so, the cylinder head will have to be removed for additional repair operations.*

9   Wrap a rubber band or tape around the top of the valve stem so the valve won't fall into the combustion chamber, then release the air pressure.

10   Inspect the valve stem for damage. Rotate the valve in the guide and check the end for eccentric movement, which would indicate that the valve is bent and needs to be replaced.

11   Move the valve up-and-down in the guide and make sure it doesn't bind. If the valve stem binds, either the valve is bent or the guide is damaged. In either case, the head will have to be removed for repair.

12   Pull up on the valve stem to close the valve, reapply air pressure to the cylinder to retain the valve in the closed position, then remove the tape or rubber band from the valve stem.

13   Lubricate the valve stem with engine oil and install a new valve guide seal/spring seat assembly. Tap it into place with a deep socket **(see illustration)**.

14   Install the spring in position over the valve.

15   Install the valve spring retainer. Compress the valve spring and carefully position the keepers in the groove. Apply a small dab of grease to the inside of each keeper to hold it in place if necessary **(see illustration)**.

16   Remove the pressure from the spring tool and make sure the keepers are seated.

17   Disconnect the air hose and remove the adapter from the spark plug hole.

18   Install the rocker arms and camshafts (see Section 6).

19   Install the valve cover (see Section 4).

20   The remainder of installation is the reverse of the removal steps.

21   Start and run the engine, then check for oil leaks and unusual sounds coming from the valve cover area.

8.2 Crankshaft sprocket and oil seal details

1   Sprocket
2   Woodruff key
3   Oil seal

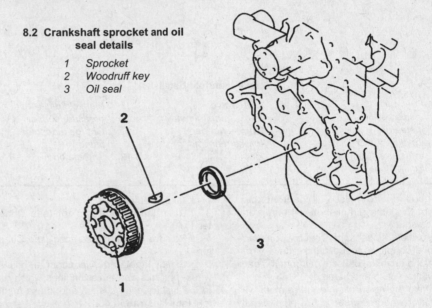

8   Crankshaft front oil seal - replacement

Refer to illustrations 8.2 and 8.4

1   Remove the timing belt and the crankshaft sprockets (see Section 5).

2   Wrap the tip of a small screwdriver with tape. Working from below the left inner fender, use the screwdriver to pry the seal out of its bore **(see illustration)**. Take care to prevent damaging the crankshaft and the seal bore.

3   Thoroughly clean and inspect the seal bore and sealing surface on the crankshaft. Minor imperfections can be removed with emery cloth. If there is a groove worn in the crankshaft sealing surface (from contact with the seal), installing a new seal will probably not stop the leak. Such wear normally indicates the internal engine components are also worn. Consider overhauling the engine.

4   Lubricate the new seal with engine oil and drive the seal into place with a hammer and socket **(see illustration)**.

5   Another method of replacement is used if the front cover has been removed (see Section 8) and you can drive the seal out from the back side of the cover. If the cover is removed,

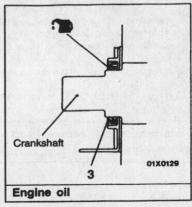

Crankshaft

01X0129

Engine oil

8.4 Install the oil seal so it's flush with the front case

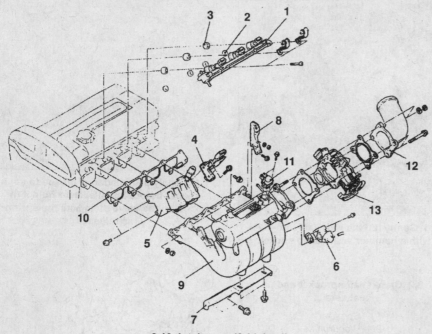

9.10 Intake manifold details

1 Fuel rail	6 EGR valve	11 Manifold differential
2 Insulator	7 Intake manifold stay	pressure sensor
3 Insulator	8 Engine hanger	12 Charge air cooler
4 Ignition power	9 Intake manifold	fitting
transistor	10 Gasket	13 Throttle body
5 Ignition coil		

9.11 CAREFULLY scrape all traces of gasket off the intake manifold mating surfaces

it's a good idea to replace all the front cover seals at this time (crankshaft, oil pump and balance shaft).

6   Position the seal and front cover assembly on a couple of wood blocks on a workbench and drive the old seal out from the back side with a punch and hammer.

7   Drive the new seal into the retainer with a block of wood or a section of pipe slightly smaller in diameter than the outside diameter of the seal.

8   Lubricate the lip of the new seal with clean engine oil. Position a new front case gasket on the engine block.

9   Slowly and carefully push the seal onto the crankshaft. The seal lip is stiff, so work it onto the crankshaft with a smooth object such as the end of an extension as you push the retainer against the cylinder block.

10   Install the front case bolts (see Section 13).

11   The remaining steps are the reverse of removal.

12   Run the engine and check for oil leaks.

9   Intake manifold - removal and installation

Removal

Refer to illustration 9.10

1   Relieve the fuel system pressure (see Chapter 4)

2   Remove the battery and ignition coil

pack (see Chapter 5).

3   Drain the cooling system (see Chapter 1).

4   Remove the air intake hose (see Chapter 4).

5   Clearly label and disconnect all hoses, wires, brackets and emission lines which run to the fuel injection system and intake manifold **(see illustration 4.2)**.

6   Remove the fuel rail, fuel injector and pressure regulator (see Chapter 4).

7   Remove the ignition coil and the ignition power transistor unit (see Chapter 5).

8   Remove the charge air cooler fitting and throttle body (see Chapter 4).

9   Remove the intake manifold stay and engine hanger. Be sure to disconnect any electrical connections that are fastened to the support stay before trying to move the parts out of the way.

10   Unbolt the intake manifold and remove it from the engine. If it sticks, tap the manifold with a soft-face hammer or carefully pry it from the head **(see illustration)**. **Caution:** *Do not pry between gasket sealing surfaces.*

Installation

Refer to illustration 9.11

11   Carefully scrape all traces of gasket material off both the cylinder head and the intake manifold **(see illustration)**. **Caution:** *The cylinder head and intake manifold are made of aluminum and are easily nicked or gouged. Don't damage the gasket surfaces or a leak may result after the work is complete.*

Gasket removal solvents are available from auto parts stores and may prove helpful.

12   After cleaning, check the intake manifold mating surface for warpage. Lay a precision straightedge across the surface along the top and bottom edges, as well as corner-to-corner. Measure any gap between the straightedge and manifold with a feeler gauge. The manufacturer doesn't list a warpage limit for this surface, but if it's more than about 0.002-inch, have the manifold resurfaced by a machine sop.

13   Install the manifold, using a new gasket. Tighten the nuts in several stages, working from the center out, until the torque listed in this Chapter's Specifications is reached.

14   Reinstall the remaining parts in the reverse order of removal.

15   Adjust the accelerator cable (see Chapter 4).

16   Add coolant, run the engine and check for leaks and proper operation.

10   Exhaust manifold - removal and installation

Refer to illustration 10.7
Warning: *Allow the engine to cool completely before beginning this procedure.*

Removal

1   Disconnect the battery cable from the negative terminal of the battery.

2   Set the parking brake and block the rear wheels. Raise the vehicle and support it securely on jackstands.

3   Drain the cooling system and engine oil (see Chapter 1). Remove the dipstick tube from the engine block.

4   If the vehicle is equipped with air conditioning, remove the condenser fan (see Chapter 3).

5   Remove the front oxygen sensor from the manifold (see Chapter 6).

6   Remove the air cleaner and its intake hose (see Chapter 4).

10.7 2.0L turbo exhaust manifold and turbocharger details

1   Condenser fan (air conditioning equipped vehicles)
2   Front oxygen sensor
3   Engine oil dipstick tube
4   Air cleaner
5   Air hose
6   Coolant hose
7   Coolant hose
8   Oil line
9   Heat shield
10 Heat shield
11 Engine hanger
12 Front exhaust pipe
13 Bolts
14 Nut
15 Coned disc spring
16 Exhaust manifold
17 Gasket
18 Sealing ring
19 Gasket

Cylinder block

O-ring

11   Cylinder head - removal and installation

Caution: *Allow the engine to cool completely before following this procedure or the cylinder head may be warped.*

Removal

Refer to illustration 11.10

1   Position the number one piston at Top Dead Center (see Section 3).
2   Disconnect the battery cable from the negative battery terminal.
3   Drain the cooling system and remove the spark plugs (see Chapter 1).
4   Remove the ignition system components (see Chapter 5).
5   Remove the valve cover (see Section 4).
6   Remove the timing belt (see Section 5).
7   Remove the intake manifold (see Section 9).
8   Remove the exhaust manifold (see Section 10).
9   Loosen the cylinder head bolts, 1/4-turn at a time, in the reverse of the tightening sequence **(see illustration 11.13)** until they can be removed by hand.
10 Carefully lift the cylinder head **(see illustration)** straight up and place the head on wood blocks to prevent damage to the sealing surfaces. If the head sticks to the engine block, dislodge it by placing a block of wood against the head casting and tapping the

---

7   Disconnect the coolant hoses and the oil line from the turbocharger **(see illustration)**.
8   Remove the upper and lower heat shields.
9   Unbolt the engine hanger from the engine **(see illustration 10.7)**.
10 Working from under the vehicle, remove the nuts that secure the exhaust system to the bottom of the turbocharger. Apply penetrating oil to the threads to make removal easier.
11 Remove any brackets that may be bolted to the exhaust manifold.
12 Apply penetrating oil to the threads and remove the exhaust manifold mounting nuts, brackets and emission components.
13 Slip the manifold off the studs and remove it from the engine compartment.
14 If necessary, remove the turbocharger from the manifold (see Chapter 6).

Installation

15 Clean and inspect the exhaust manifold studs, replacing any that show thread damage.
16 Using a scraper, remove all traces of gasket material from the mating surfaces and inspect them for wear and cracks. **Caution:** *When removing gasket material from any surface, especially aluminum, be very careful not to scratch or gouge the gasket surface. Any damage to the surface may cause a leak after reassembly. Gasket removal solvents are available from auto parts stores and may prove helpful.*
17 Place a new gasket over the studs, install the manifold and tighten the nuts in several stages, working from the center out, to the torque listed in this Chapter's Specifications.

18 Reinstall the remaining parts in the reverse order of removal.
19 Run the engine and check for exhaust leaks.

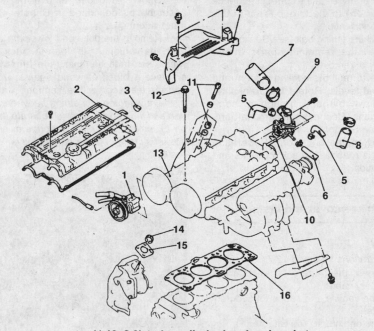

11.10 2.0L turbo cylinder head and gasket

1	Power steering pump	7	Radiator upper hose	12	Cylinder head bolts
2	Valve cover	8	Radiator lower hose	13	Cylinder head
3	Semi-circular seal	9	Thermostat case	14	Sealing ring
4	Heat shield	10	O-ring	15	Gasket
5	Coolant hose	11	Turbocharger bolts and nut	16	Head gasket
6	Coolant hose				

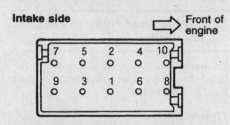

Intake side   Front of engine

Exhaust side

11.13 Cylinder head bolt TIGHTENING sequence

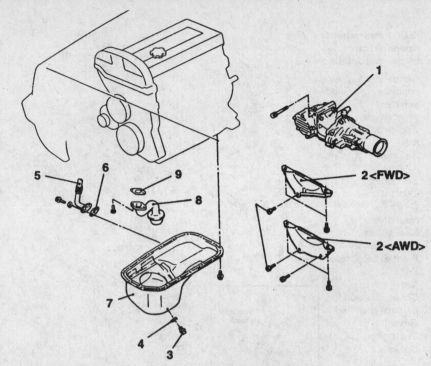

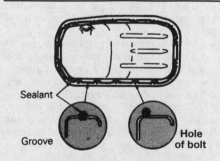

12.6 Oil pan and related components

1	Transfer unit (4WD models)	3	Oil pan drain plug	7	Oil pan
2	Transaxle bell housing cover	4	Gasket	8	Oil pick-up tube
		5	Oil return line	9	Gasket
		6	Gasket		

wood with a hammer or by prying the head with a prybar placed carefully on a casting protrusion or in an exhaust port. **Note:** *Cylinder head disassembly and inspection procedures are covered in Chapter 2, Part E. It's a good idea to have the head checked for warpage, even if you're just replacing the gasket.*

11   Remove all traces of old gasket material from the block and head. Do not allow anything to fall into the engine. Clean and inspect all threaded fasteners and be sure the threaded holes in the block are clean and dry.

Installation

Refer to illustration 11.13

12   Place a new gasket and the cylinder head in position on the engine block with the identification mark "4G63K" on the end of the gasket upwards.

13   The cylinder head bolts should be tightened in several stages in the correct sequence **(see illustration)** to the torque listed in this Chapter's Specifications.

14   Reinstall the timing belt (see Section 5).

15   Reinstall the remaining parts in the reverse order of removal.

16   Be sure to refill the cooling system and check all fluid levels. Rotate the crankshaft clockwise slowly by hand through six complete revolutions. Recheck the camshaft timing marks (see Section 5).

17   Run the engine until normal operating temperature is reached. Check for leaks and proper operation.

12   Oil pan - removal and installation

Removal

Refer to illustrations 12.6 and 12.7

1   Disconnect the battery cable from the negative battery cable.

2   Raise the vehicle and support it securely on jackstands.

3   Drain the engine oil (see Chapter 1).

4   Remove the splash pan under the drivebelt end of the engine, then remove the dipstick and drain the engine oil (see Chapter 1). Unbolt the oil return pipe from the side of the oil pan.

5   Disconnect the exhaust pipe from the manifold and let the exhaust hang loosely under the car.

6   On 4WD models, remove the transfer assembly as described in Chapter 8 **(see illustration).**

7   Remove the bolts and lower the oil pan from the vehicle. If the pan is stuck, tap it with a soft-face hammer **(see illustration)** or place a block of wood against the pan and tap the wood with a hammer. **Caution:** *If you're wedging something between the oil pan and the engine block to separate the two, be extremely careful not to gouge or nick the gasket surface of either part; an oil leak could result.*

12.7 If the pan is stuck, tap it with a soft-face hammer or place a block of wood against the pan and tap the wood with a hammer

8   Remove the oil pump pickup tube and screen assembly and clean both the tube and screen thoroughly. Install the pick-up tube and screen with a new gasket.

9   Thoroughly clean the oil pan and sealing surfaces on the block and pan. Use a scraper to remove all traces of old gasket material. Gasket removal solvents are available at auto parts stores and may prove helpful. Check the oil pan sealing surface for distortion. Straighten or replace as necessary. After cleaning and straightening (if necessary), wipe the gasket surfaces of the pan and block clean with a rag soaked in lacquer thinner or acetone.

12.10 Apply a 4 mm bead of RTV sealant to the oil pan flange - be sure to apply the sealant on the inside edge of the bolt holes

Sealant

Groove

Hole of bolt

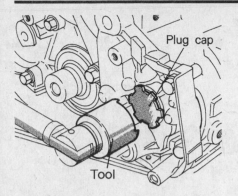

13.3 Remove the plug cap with either the special tool shown or a large pair of locking pliers

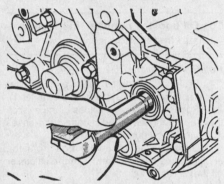

13.5 Unscrew and remove the oil pump driven gear bolt

Installation

Refer to illustration 12.10

10 Apply a 4 mm bead of RTV sealant to the oil pan flange **(see illustration). Note:** *When applying the sealant, lay the bead in the center of the oil pan rail, except for the bolt holes, where you'll need to go around the inside edge of the bolt holes, as shown in the inset to the illustration. If you apply the RTV to the outside of the bolt holes, an oil leak at the bolt-hole area will result.*

11 Place the oil pan into position and install the bolts finger tight. Working side-to-side from the center out, tighten the bolts to the torque listed in this Chapter's Specifications.

12 Reinstall the remaining parts in the reverse order of removal.

13 Refill the crankcase with the proper quantity and grade of oil and run the engine, checking for leaks. Road test the vehicle and check for leaks again.

13 Front case - removal and installation

Removal

Refer to illustrations 13.3, 13.5 and 13.6

1 Remove the timing belt, sprockets and all tensioners (see Section 5).

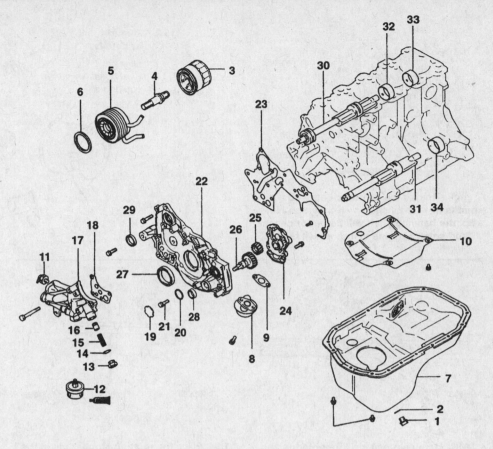

13.6 2.0 turbo engine front case and oil pump - exploded view

1	Oil pan drain plug	12	Oil pressure gauge	23	Gasket
2	Gasket		sending unit	24	Oil pump cover
3	Oil filter	13	Relief valve plug	25	Oil pump driven gear
4	Oil cooler bolt	14	Gasket	26	Oil pump drive gear
5	Oil cooler	15	Relief valve spring	27	Crankshaft front oil seal
6	Oil seal	16	Relief valve plunger	28	Oil pump oil seal
7	Oil pan	17	Oil filter bracket	29	Balance shaft oil seal
8	Oil pick-up tube	18	Gasket	30	Right balance shaft
9	Gasket	19	Plug	31	Left balance shaft
10	Oil pan baffle	20	O-ring	32	Balance shaft bearing
11	Oil pressure switch	21	Bolt	33	Balance shaft bearing
		22	Front case	34	Balance shaft bearing

2 Remove the oil pan and oil pump pick-up tube and screen (see Section 12).

3 Unscrew the plug cap with either a special tool **(see illustration)**, available at most auto parts stores, or strike it squarely on the face of the plug with a hammer two or three times to break it loose, and the plug can be removed with a standard wrench or pliers.

4 Remove the bolt from the side of the block and insert a Phillips screwdriver or a small punch to keep the balance shaft from turning **(see illustration 5.15a)**.

5 Remove the bolt securing the oil pump driven gear to the balance shaft **(see illustration)**.

6 Remove the bolts and the front case from the engine block **(see illustration)**. If the case is difficult to remove, use a screwdriver or prybar placed against a casting protrusion. Be sure not to pry against gasket surfaces.

Caution: *The bolts are of different lengths, so be sure to label them so they can be placed back in their original locations.*

Installation

7 Make sure all gasket surfaces are clean and free of all old gasket material.

8 Be sure to replace the crankshaft, balance shaft and oil pump seals, located in the front case, before reassembly (see Section 8). Lubricate all seal lips before reassembly.

9 Place the new gasket in position.

10 When placing the front case back on the engine be **VERY** careful not to damage the new seals, since you're lining up more than one seal at a time - try to keep the case parallel to the front of the engine at all times.

11 The remainder of installation is the reverse of the removal steps.

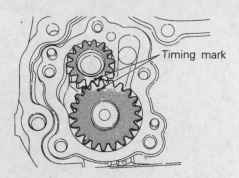

14.9a Install the oil pump gears so the marks line up as shown - if they don't line up, the balance shaft will be out of phase and severe engine vibration will result

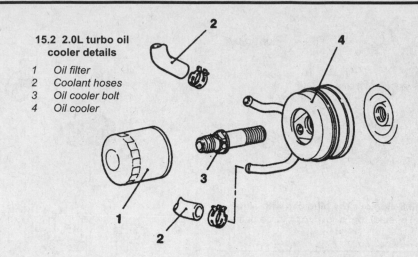

15.2 2.0L turbo oil cooler details

1   Oil filter
2   Coolant hoses
3   Oil cooler bolt
4   Oil cooler

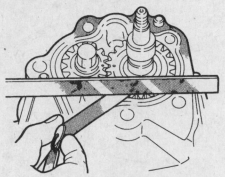

14.9b Using a precision straightedge and a feeler gauge, check the clearance of the gears to the top of the pump housing (side clearance)

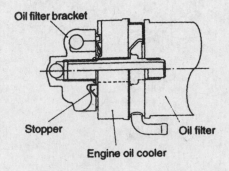

15.4 Place the rotation stopper pin in the slot in the oil filter bracket

14 Oil pump - removal, inspection and installation

Removal

1   Remove the timing belt, balance shaft belt and crankshaft sprocket (see Section 5).
2   Unbolt the oil pickup tube and screen from the bottom of the pump housing **(see illustration 12.6)**.
3   Remove the oil pan (see Section 12).
4   Remove the front case (see Section 13).
5   Remove the screws that attach the oil pump cover to the back side of the case **(see illustration 13.6)**.
6   Remove the pressure relief valve plug, spring and plunger.

Inspection

Refer to illustrations 14.9a and 14.9b

7   Clean all parts thoroughly and remove all traces of old gasket material from the sealing surfaces. Visually inspect the gears for chips, score marks or possible overheating conditions (a bluish discoloration of the gears). If any of these conditions are found, replace the gears.
8   Also inspect the front case housing where the gears ride to look for similar wear indications, scoring, galling or evidence of an overheat condition. If any of these are found in the pump housing area, the front case will have to be replaced.
9   Install the oil pump outer and inner gears so the marks line up as shown **(see illustration)** and measure the side clearance of each rotor **(see illustration)**. Compare the clearances to the values listed in this Chapter's Specifications. Measure the free length of the pressure regulator spring and compare the measurement to this Chapter's Specifications. Replace parts as necessary. Pack the pump cavity with petroleum jelly and install the cover. Tighten the bolts to the torque listed in this Chapter's Specifications. **Caution:** *You must line up the oil pump gear marks on reassembly. If you don't, the balance shaft will be out of phase and severe engine vibration will result.*

Installation

10   Install the pressure regulator valve components and tighten the plug securely.
11   Install the pump cover, making sure to install the bolts in their proper locations, according to length **(see illustration 13.6)**. Tighten the bolts to the torque listed in this Chapter's Specifications.
12   Reinstall the remaining parts in the reverse order of removal.
13   Add oil, start the engine and check for oil pressure and leaks.

15 Oil cooler - removal, inspection and installation

Refer to illustrations 15.2 and 15.4

1   Drain the engine oil, remove the oil filter and drain the cooling system (see Chapter 1).
2   Squeeze the coolant hose clamps, slide them up the hoses and disconnect the hoses from the fittings **(see illustration)**.
3   Unscrew the oil cooler bolt from the engine with a deep socket. Take the oil cooler off the oil filter bracket.
4   Installation is the reverse of the removal steps. Insert the rotation stopper pin on the oil cooler into the slot in the oil filter bracket **(see illustration)**. Tighten the oil cooler bolt to the torque listed in this Chapter's Specifications.
5   Refill the engine oil and coolant (see Chapter 1).

16 Flywheel/driveplate - removal and installation

Refer to illustrations 16.3 and 16.4

Removal

1   Raise the vehicle and support it securely on jackstands, then refer to Chapter 7 and remove the transaxle (and transfer case if equipped). If it's leaking, now would be a very good time to replace the transaxle front seal (on automatic transaxle equipped models, the torque converter must be removed to gain access to this seal).
2   Remove the pressure plate and clutch disc (manual transaxle equipped vehicles) (see Chapter 8). Now is a good time to check/replace the clutch components and the pilot bearing.
3   The bolt holes are either staggered or symmetrical on the flywheel/driveplate bolt pattern. To ensure correct alignment during reinstallation, mark the position of the flywheel/driveplate to the crankshaft before removal **(see illustration)**.
4   Remove the bolts that secure the fly-

16.3 Mark the relationship of the flywheel/driveplate to the crankshaft hub to ensure correct alignment during installation

16.4 2.0L turbo flywheel and driveplate details

1   Flywheel bolt
2   Flywheel (manual transaxle
3   Crankshaft bushing (automatic transaxle)
4   Drive plate bolt
5   Adapter plate (automatic transaxle)
6   Drive plate (automatic transaxle)
7   Crankshaft rear oil seal

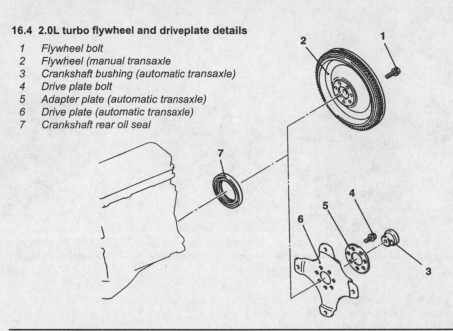

wheel/driveplate to the crankshaft (**see illustration**). If the crankshaft turns, wedge a screwdriver in the ring gear teeth to jam the flywheel.

5   Remove the flywheel/driveplate from the crankshaft. Since the flywheel is fairly heavy, be sure to support it while removing the last bolt.

6   Clean the flywheel to remove grease and oil. Inspect the surface for cracks, rivet grooves, burned areas and score marks. Light scoring can be removed with emery cloth. Check for cracked and broken ring gear teeth. Lay the flywheel on a flat surface and use a straightedge to check for warpage. **Note:** *Flywheels can be re-surfaced by a machine shop. Also, starter ring gears are available separately and can be installed by an automotive machine shop.*

7   Clean and inspect the mating surfaces of the flywheel/driveplate and the crankshaft. If the crankshaft rear seal is leaking, replace it before reinstalling the flywheel/driveplate (see Section 17).

Installation

8   Position the flywheel/driveplate against the crankshaft. If the bolt holes aren't staggered, align the previously applied match marks. Before installing the bolts, apply thread locking compound to the threads.

9   Wedge a screwdriver in the ring gear teeth to keep the flywheel/driveplate from turning as you tighten the bolts to the torque listed in this Chapter's Specifications.

10   The remainder of installation is the reverse of the removal procedure.

17   Rear main oil seal - replacement

Refer to illustrations 17.2a, 17.2b, 17.5 and 17.6

1   The transaxle must be removed from the vehicle for this procedure (see Chapter 7).

2   The seal can be replaced without remov-

ing the oil pan or seal retainer. However, this method is not recommended because the lip of the seal is quite stiff and it's possible to cock the seal in the retainer bore or damage it during installation. If you want to take the chance, pry out the old seal (**see illustration**). Apply a film of clean oil to the crankshaft seal journal and the lip of the new seal and carefully tap the new seal into place (**see illustration**). The lip is stiff, so carefully work it onto the seal journal of the crankshaft with a smooth object like the rounded end of a socket extension as you tap the seal into place. Don't rush it or you may damage the seal.

3   The following method is recommended but requires removal of the oil pan (see Section 12) and the seal retainer.

4   After the oil pan has been removed, remove the bolts, detach the seal retainer and peel off all the old gasket material.

5   Position the seal and retainer assembly on a couple of wood blocks on a workbench

17.2a The quick (but not recommended) way to replace the rear main oil seal is to simply pry the old one out

17.2b Lubricate the crankshaft journal and the lip of the new seal with engine oil and tap the new seal into place - the seal lip is stiff and can be easily damaged during installation if you're not careful

17.5 If the seal housing is removed, support the housing on two wood blocks and drive out the old seal with a punch or screwdriver and hammer

17.6 Drive the new seal into the housing with a block of wood or a section of pipe, if you don't have one large enough - make sure you don't cock the seal in the bore

and drive the old seal out from the back side with a punch and hammer **(see illustration)**.

6   Drive the new seal into the retainer with a block of wood **(see illustration)** or a section of pipe slightly smaller in diameter than the outside diameter of the seal.

7   Lubricate the crankshaft seal journal and the lip of the new seal with clean engine oil. Position a new gasket on the engine block.

8   Slowly and carefully push the seal onto the crankshaft. The seal lip is stiff, so work it onto the crankshaft with a smooth object such as the rounded end of a socket extension as you push the retainer against the block.

9   Install and tighten the retainer bolts to the torque listed in this Chapter's Specifications. The bottom sealing flange of the retainer must not extend below the bottom sealing flange (oil pan rail) of the block.

10   The remaining steps are the reverse of removal.

11   Run the engine and check for oil leaks.

18   Engine mounts - check and replacement

1   Engine mounts seldom require attention, but broken or deteriorated mounts should be replaced immediately or the added strain placed on the driveline components may cause damage or wear.

Check
Refer to illustration 18.2

2   Before jacking up the engine, measure the distance from the crossmember to the front roll stopper's through-bolt **(see illustration)**. If it's not within the range listed in this Chapter's Specifications, replace the roll stopper as described below. During the rest of the check, the engine must be raised slightly to remove the weight from the mounts.

3   Raise the vehicle and support it securely on jackstands, then position a jack under the engine oil pan. Place a large block of wood between the jack head and the oil pan to prevent oil pan damage, then carefully raise the engine just enough to take the weight off the mounts. **Warning:** *DO NOT place any part of your body under the engine when it's supported only by a jack!*

4   Check the mounts to see if the rubber is cracked, hardened or separated from the metal backing. Sometimes the rubber will split right down the center.

5   Check for relative movement between the mount plates and the engine or frame (use a large screwdriver or pry bar to attempt to move the mounts). If movement is noted, lower the engine and tighten the mount fasteners.

6   Rubber preservative may be applied to the mounts to slow deterioration.

Replacement
Refer to illustrations 18.8a, 18.8b, 18.8c, 18.10a and 18.10b

7   Disconnect the battery cable from the negative battery terminal, then raise the vehicle and support it securely on jackstands (if not already done). **Caution:** *Do not disconnect more than one mount at a time, except during engine/transaxle removal.*

8   Remove the fasteners and detach the mount from the frame and engine **(see illustrations)**.

9   The rubber portion of the mounts are normally available separately from the bracket that attaches it to the frame or block. Obtain

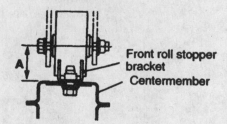

18.2 If the roll stopper clearance (A) is not within Specifications with the engine's weight on the roll stopper, replace it

Front roll stopper
bracket
Centermember

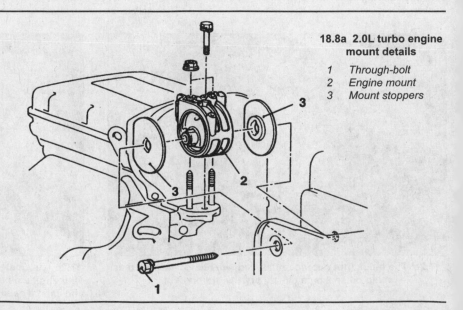

18.8a 2.0L turbo engine mount details

1   *Through-bolt*
2   *Engine mount*
3   *Mount stoppers*

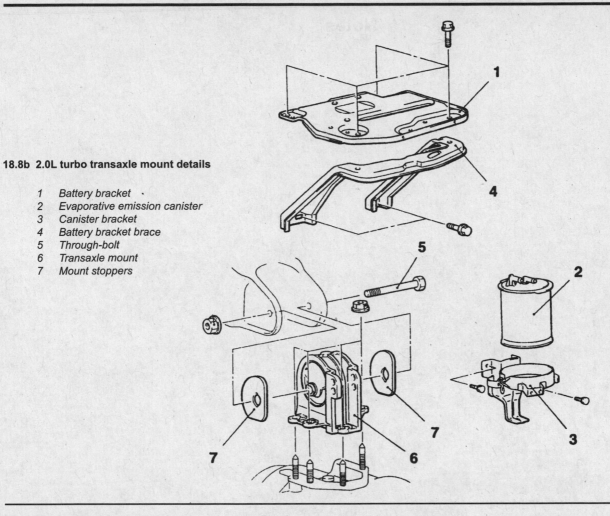

18.8b 2.0L turbo transaxle mount details

1   Battery bracket
2   Evaporative emission canister
3   Canister bracket
4   Battery bracket brace
5   Through-bolt
6   Transaxle mount
7   Mount stoppers

new inserts and take them to an automotive machine shop or dealer service department to be pressed into the existing bracket, if necessary.

10   Installation is the reverse of removal.

Install the engine mount and transaxle mount stoppers with the arrow marks pointing in the proper direction **(see illustrations)**. Use thread locking compound on the mount bolts and be sure to tighten them securely.

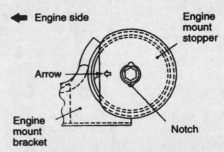

18.10a Position the engine mount stopper arrows in the direction shown to align the notches correctly

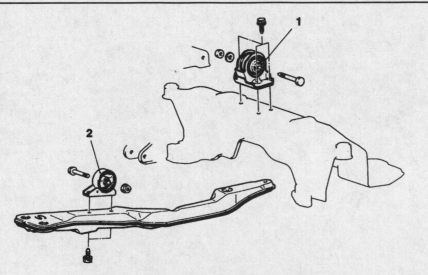

18.8c 2.0L turbo engine roll stopper details

1   Rear roll stopper   2   Front roll stopper

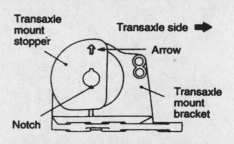

18.10b Position the transaxle mount stopper arrows in the direction shown to align the notches correctly

Notes

Chapter 2 Part C
2.4L four-cylinder engine

Contents

Specifications

General

Firing order	1-3-4-2
Cylinder numbers (drivebelt end-to-transaxle end)	1-2-3-4

Camshaft

Lobe height

1999 and earlier models

Intake

Standard	1.4720 inches
Service limit	1.4524 inches

Exhaust

Standard	1.4752 inches
Service limit	1.4555 inches

2000 and later models

Intake

Standard	1.472 inches
Service limit	1.452 inches

Exhaust

Manual transaxle

Standard	1.462 inches
Service limit	1.453 inches

Automatic transaxle

Standard	1.450 inches
Service limit	1.430 inches
Camshaft journal diameter	1.77 inches

Cylinder head

Warpage limit

Standard	0.002 inch
Service limit	0.008 inch
Resurfacing limit (combined head and block)	0.008 inch

Timing belt

Timing belt deflection	Tension automatically adjusted
Balance shaft belt deflection	1/4-inch
Projection of tensioner rod	0.47
Tensioner rod movement @ 22 to 44 lbs pressure	0.040 inch or less

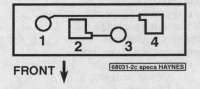

Coil pack locations and spark plug wire routing - 1999 and earlier models

Coil pack locations and spark plug wire routing - 2000 and later models

Oil pump

Side clearance

Drive gear..	0.0031 to 0.0055 inch
Driven gear...	0.0024 to 0.0047 inch

Torque specifications*   Ft-lbs (unless otherwise noted)

Note: *One foot-pound (ft-lb) of torque is equivalent to 12 inch-pounds (in-lbs) of torque. Torque values below approximately 15 ft-lbs are expressed in inch-pounds, since most foot-pound torque wrenches are not accurate at these smaller values.*

Balance shaft sprocket bolt	33
Balance shaft belt tensioner bolt	168 inch-lbs
Camshaft sprocket bolt...	65
Crankshaft pulley bolts	18
Crankshaft sprocket bolt	
1995 through 2001 models	87
2002 through 2004 models	119
2005 models..	123
Cylinder head bolts**	
Step 1	58
Step 2	Loosen completely
Step 3	15
Step 4	Tighten 1/4-turn
Step 5	Tighten 1/4-turn further
Exhaust manifold bolts/nuts	
M8 nuts..	20
M10 nuts..	22
Exhaust pipe-to-exhaust manifold bolts/nuts...................	33
Flywheel or driveplate bolts	98
Front case bolts...	17
Front case plug..	17
Intake manifold-to-engine nuts/bolts	
1999 and earlier	13
2000 and later	14
Intake manifold stay	
1999 and earlier	22
2000 and later	
M8	13
M10..	22
Oil filter bracket bolts..	168 inch-lbs
Oil pan bolts/nuts..	60 inch-lbs
Oil pick-up tube and screen mounting bolts	168 inch-lbs
Oil pump sprocket nut	
1999 and earlier	40
2000 and later	22 to 30
Oil pressure switch	
1999 and earlier	84 inch-lbs
2000 and later	86 to 104 inch-lbs
Oil pump cover screws	
1999 and earlier	84 inch-lbs
2000 and later	70 to 104 inch-lbs
Oil pump cover bolts...	144 inch-lbs
Oil pump driven gear bolt	27
Oil pump relief valve plug	33
Rocker arm shaft bolt	23
Timing belt front cover bolts	
6 mm shaft diameter	
Without washer	86 to 104 in-lbs
With washer..	78 inch-lbs
8 mm shaft diameter	113 to 127 inch-lbs
Timing belt tensioner arm bolt	
1999 and earlier	15
2000 and later	13 to 19
Timing belt tensioner mounting bolts.................................	17
Water pump pulley bolts	96 inch-lbs
Timing belt idler pulley bolt	
1999 and earlier	26
2000 and later	29 to 37
Valve cover bolts	30 inch-lbs

Refer to Part E for additional torque specifications.
**Apply engine oil to the threads.*

1 General information

This Part of Chapter 2 is devoted to in-vehicle engine repair procedures. Information concerning engine removal and installation and engine block and cylinder head overhaul can be found in Part E of this Chapter.

The following repair procedures are based on the assumption that the engine is installed in the vehicle. If the engine has been removed from the vehicle and mounted on a stand, many of the steps outlined in this Part of Chapter 2 will not apply.

The Specifications included in this Part of Chapter 2 apply only to the procedures contained in this Part. Part E of Chapter 2 contains the Specifications necessary for cylinder head and engine block rebuilding.

This Part of Chapter 2 covers the 2.4L Single Overhead Camshaft (SOHC) four cylinder engine. **Note:** *On 1999 and earlier models, the engine is mounted with its timing belt end toward the driver's side of the vehicle. On 2000 and later models, the timing belt end is toward the passenger side of the vehicle. On all 2.4L models, the intake side is toward the rear of the vehicle and the exhaust side is toward the front. This means that following the standard practice of considering the timing belt end to be the front of the engine, the intake ports and rocker arms are on the left side of the cylinder head on 1999 and earlier models, and on the right side of the cylinder head on 2000 and later models. However, except for this change, the basic design of the engine is the same for all model years.*

2 Repair operations possible with the engine in the vehicle

Many major repair operations can be accomplished without removing the engine from the vehicle.

Clean the engine compartment and the exterior of the engine with some type of degreaser before any work is done. It will make the job easier and help keep dirt out of the internal areas of the engine.

Depending on the components involved, it may be helpful to remove the hood to improve access to the engine as repairs are performed (refer to Chapter 11 if necessary). Cover the fenders to prevent damage to the paint. Special pads are available, but an old bedspread or blanket will also work.

If vacuum, exhaust, oil or coolant leaks develop, indicating a need for gasket or seal replacement, the repairs can generally be made with the engine in the vehicle. The intake and exhaust manifold gaskets, oil pan gasket, crankshaft oil seals and cylinder head gasket are all accessible with the engine in place.

Exterior engine components, such as the intake and exhaust manifolds, the oil pan, the oil pump, the water pump, the starter motor, the alternator and the fuel system components can be removed for repair with the engine in place.

Since the camshaft and cylinder head can be removed without pulling the engine, valve component servicing can also be accomplished with the engine in the vehicle. Replacement of the timing belts and sprockets is also possible with the engine in the vehicle.

In extreme cases caused by a lack of necessary equipment, repair or replacement of piston rings, pistons, connecting rods and rod bearings is possible with the engine in the vehicle. However, this practice is not recommended because of the cleaning and preparation work that must be done to the components involved.

3 Top Dead Center (TDC) for number one piston - locating

1   Top Dead Center (TDC) is the highest point in the cylinder that each piston reaches as it travels up-and-down when the crankshaft turns. Each piston reaches TDC on the compression stroke and again on the exhaust stroke, but TDC generally refers to piston position on the compression stroke.

2   Positioning the piston(s) at TDC is an essential part of many procedures such as rocker arm removal, camshaft and timing belt/sprocket removal and camshaft position sensor removal.

3   Before beginning this procedure, be sure to place the transmission in Neutral and apply the parking brake or block the rear wheels. Also, disable the ignition system by detaching the electrical connector at the ignition coil pack (see Chapter 5). Remove the spark plugs (see Chapter 1).

4   In order to bring any piston to TDC, the crankshaft must be turned using one of the methods outlined below. When looking at the drivebelt end of the engine, normal crankshaft rotation is clockwise.

 a) The preferred method is to turn the crankshaft with a ratchet and extension inserted into the drivebelt end of the crankshaft **(see illustration 3.4 in Chapter 2B).**

 b) A remote starter switch, which may save some time, can also be used. These switches are available inexpensively from auto parts stores. Follow the instructions included with the switch. Once the piston is close to TDC, use a socket and ratchet as described in the previous paragraph.

 c) If an assistant is available to turn the ignition switch to the Start position in short bursts, you can get the piston close to TDC without a remote starter switch. Make sure your assistant is out of the vehicle, away from the ignition switch, then use a socket and ratchet as described in Paragraph a) to complete the procedure.

5   Remove the timing belt upper cover (see Section 5).

6   Turn the crankshaft until the timing mark on the camshaft sprocket is aligned with the camshaft TDC mark, and the crankshaft pulley timing marks are aligned **(see illustration 3.6 in Chapter 2B)**. If the crankshaft pulley timing marks are aligned, but the camshaft sprocket timing marks are not, the number one piston is at TDC on the exhaust stroke, not the compression stroke. Go to Step 7.

7   To get the piston to TDC on the compression stroke, turn the crankshaft one complete turn (360-degrees) clockwise. The camshaft sprocket marks should now be aligned. When the crankshaft pulley marks and the camshaft sprocket marks are aligned, the number one piston is at TDC on the compression stroke.

8   After the number one piston has been positioned at TDC on the compression stroke, TDC for any of the remaining pistons can be located by turning the crankshaft and following the firing order. Make a mark on the crankshaft pulley exactly 180-degrees opposite the notch. Rotate the crankshaft 180-degrees clockwise from the number-one-cylinder TDC position: this is the number-three-cylinder TDC position. Then rotate the crankshaft clockwise another 180-degrees, back to where the notch is aligned with the T mark on the pulley: this is the number-four-cylinder TDC position. Finally, rotate the crankshaft another 180-degrees clockwise: this is the number-two-cylinder TDC position.

4 Valve cover - removal and installation

Removal

1   Disconnect the battery cable from the negative battery terminal. Remove the upper timing belt cover (see Section 5).

2   Disconnect the spark plug wires (see Chapter 1). Use numbered pieces of tape to label the wires so they can be returned to their original locations on reassembly.

3   Clearly label and disconnect any emission hoses and cables which connect to, or cross over, the valve cover. Disconnect the throttle cable from its attachment at the valve cover.

4   Remove the valve cover bolts and lift the cover off. If the cover sticks to the cylinder head, tap on it with a soft-face hammer or place a block of wood against the cover and tap on the wood with a hammer. **Caution:** *If you have to pry between the valve cover and the cylinder head, be extremely careful not to gouge or nick the gasket surfaces of either part. A leak could develop after reassembly.*

5   Remove the valve cover gasket and spark plug tube seals. Thoroughly clean the valve cover and remove all traces of old gasket material. Gasket removal solvents are available from auto parts stores and may prove helpful. After cleaning the surfaces, degrease them with a rag soaked in lacquer thinner or acetone.

Installation

Refer to illustrations 4.6 and 4.7

6   Install the new spark plug tube seals (see illustration).

7   Install a new gasket on the cover, using RTV sealant to hold it in place (see illustration). Place the cover on the engine and install the cover bolts.

8   Place the cover on the engine and install the cover bolts. Tighten the bolts in three stages to the torque listed in this Chapter's Specifications using a criss-cross pattern, starting in the middle of the cover and working outwards.

9   The remaining installation steps are the reverse of removal. When finished, run the engine and check for oil leaks.

Spark plug tube replacement

Refer to illustration 4.13

10   Remove the valve cover (see Steps 1 through 5).

11   Grasp the spark plug tube with locking pliers, carefully twist it back and forth and remove the tube from the cylinder head.

12   Clean the locking agent from the tube end and the socket in the cylinder head with solvent, then wipe dry.

13   Apply an approximately 1/8-inch wide strip of Loctite sealant no. 271 or equivalent around the lower end of the tube and install the tube into the cylinder head. Carefully tap the tube into the receptacle with a soft face mallet or wood block. Tap the tube in until it's fully seated in the cylinder head (see illustration).

14   Allow the Loctite to cure according to manufacturer's instructions.

15   Install the valve cover (see Steps 6 through 9).

---

5   Timing belt, balance shaft belt and sprockets - removal, inspection and installation

Removal

**** CAUTION ****
The timing system is complex. Severe engine damage will occur if you make any mistakes. Do not attempt this procedure unless you are highly experienced with this type of repair. If you are at all unsure of your abilities, consult an expert. Double-check all your work and be sure everything is correct before you attempt to start the engine.

Caution: *Do not try to turn the crankshaft with the camshaft sprocket bolts and do not rotate the crankshaft counterclockwise. Also, don't turn the crankshaft or camshafts after the timing belt has been removed.*

1   Position the number one piston at Top Dead Center (see Section 3).

2   Disconnect the battery cable from the

4.6 Install new spark plug tube seals and make sure they seat properly in the valve cover

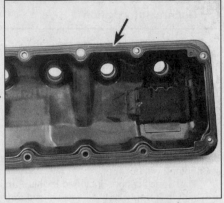

4.7 Apply a light coat of RTV sealant onto the cover sealing surfaces and install the new gasket (arrow)

4.13 Apply a small amount of Loctite 271 to the bottom of each spark plug tube and tap it in until it's fully seated

negative battery terminal.

3   Set the parking brake and block the rear wheels. Raise the front of the vehicle and support it securely on jackstands.

4   Remove the left engine mount and bracket (see Section 18). **Note:** *Make sure the engine is supported with a piece of wood and a floor jack placed under the oil pan. The wood will prevent the floor jack from denting or damaging the oil pan.*

5   Remove the splash pan from beneath the drivebelt end of the engine (if equipped).

Main timing belt

Refer to illustration 5.9

6   Remove the clamp and bracket for the power steering pressure hose (if equipped) and the clamp for the air conditioning hose, if equipped.

7   Remove the drivebelts (see Chapter 1) and on 1999 and earlier models, the tensioner pulley bracket.

8   Remove the water pump pulley(s). **Note:** *On 1999 and earlier models, the smaller of the two pulleys runs the power steering pump.*

9   Loosen the large crankshaft sprocket bolt in the center of the crankshaft pulley. It might be very tight, so, to break it loose, wrap a rag around the pulley and attach a chain wrench. Slip a 1/2-inch drive extension through the hole in the inner fender and into the sprocket bolt head. Turn the extension with a breaker

5.9 Remove the four bolts that attach the pulleys to the crankshaft (arrows)

bar. If you are unable to loosen the bolt due to the chain wrench slipping, you can prevent the crankshaft from turning by having an assistant wedge a flat-blade screwdriver in the flywheel/driveplate ring gear teeth. To do this, you must first remove the flywheel/driveplate cover. Next, remove the bolts and remove the crankshaft pulley (see illustration).

10   Remove the retaining bolts from the upper and lower timing belt covers and remove the covers and gaskets.

11   Make a mark on the timing belt in the direction of rotation so it may be reinstalled in

the same direction in the event the timing belt is reused.

12   Loosen the tensioner pulley center bolt and push the pulley toward the water pump to create slack in the timing belt, then remove the timing belt. **Caution:** *Be sure that the timing marks are correctly aligned before removing the timing belt*. The camshaft sprocket timing mark should be in the 12 o'clock position, so it aligns with the timing mark on the valve cover. The crankshaft sprocket timing marks and oil pump sprocket timing marks are the same as for the 2.0L turbo engine **(see illustration 3.6 in Chapter 2B)**.

13   Unbolt and remove the tensioner **(see illustration 5.13 in Chapter 2B)**.

14   If you plan to replace or remove the camshaft or camshaft oil seal, remove the camshaft sprocket. Hold the sprocket with the special tool or equivalent and loosen the camshaft sprocket bolt **(see illustration 5.12 in Chapter 2A)**. Remove the bolt and slide the sprocket off the camshaft.

15   If it's necessary to remove the balance shaft sprocket or oil pump, remove the plug on the side of the engine block and insert a Phillips screwdriver to prevent the shaft from turning **(see illustration 5.15a in Chapter 2B)**. Remove the oil pump sprocket nut with a socket and a breaker bar and remove the oil pump sprocket **(see illustration 5.15b in Chapter 2B)**.

Balance shaft belt

16   If you're planning to install the same belt, mark the direction of rotation on the belt **(see illustration 5.16a in Chapter 2B)**. If you're planning to remove the balance shaft sprocket, loosen the bolt before you remove the belt. Be sure the alignment marks are positioned correctly before removing the belt **(see illustration 5.16b in Chapter 2B)**. Remove the bolt from the center of the tensioner pulley, remove the pulley, then remove the belt. To remove the crankshaft sprocket, pull it off - it may be necessary to use a bolt-type puller.

Inspection

17   Rotate the tensioner pulleys by hand and move them side-to-side to detect roughness and excess play. Visually inspect the sprockets for any signs of damage and wear. Replace parts as necessary. Also, replace the pulley if there is a lubricant leak.

18   Inspect the timing belts for cracks, separation, wear, missing teeth and oil contamination. Replace the belt if it's in questionable condition **(see illustration 5.18 in Chapter 2B)**.

19   Check the automatic tensioner for leaks or any obvious damage to the body. The rod should protrude 1/2-inch from the body when the tensioner is not compressed. Replace the tensioner if the amount of protrusion is incorrect, or if the rod end is worn or damaged. Press the rod end against a metal surface, such as a vise, with 22 to 44 lbs force and measure the rod movement. If it's more than 1/32-inch, replace the tensioner.

Installation

** CAUTION **
Before starting the engine, carefully rotate the crankshaft by hand through at least two full revolutions (use a socket and breaker bar on the crankshaft pulley center bolt). If you feel any resistance, STOP! There is something wrong - most likely, valves are contacting the pistons. You must find the problem before proceeding. Check your work and see if any updated repair information is available.

20   Reinstall the timing belt sprockets, if they were removed. Tighten the bolts to the values listed in this Chapter's Specifications. **Note:** *Degrease the crankshaft sensing blade and install it after the crankshaft inner sprocket, with its offset side facing toward the engine.*

Balance shaft belt

21   Install the balance shaft belt. Be sure the timing mark on the crankshaft sprocket and the balance shaft sprocket are aligned properly **(see illustration 5.16b in Chapter 2B)**. Install the tensioner and bolt, but don't tighten the bolt completely at this time.

22   After installing the balance shaft belt, make sure the tension side has no slack.

23   Make sure the tension sprocket for the balance shaft belt has the center located just to the left side of the mounting bolt with the pulley directed to the front of the engine **(see illustration 5.23a in Chapter 2B)**. Lift the tensioner up with one finger to tighten the belt **(see illustration 5.23b in Chapter 2B)** and tighten the tensioner bolt and the balance shaft bolt to the torque listed in this Chapter's Specifications. **Note:** *After tightening the bolt, use your index finger and press firmly on the timing belt. The belt deflection should be 1/4-inch* **(see illustration 5.23c in Chapter 2B)**.

Main timing belt

24   Place the single timing mark on the camshaft sprocket in the 12 o'clock position so it aligns with the mark on the valve cover. Align the crankshaft and oil pump sprocket timing marks **(see illustration 3.6 in Chapter 2B)**. When aligning the oil pump sprocket marks, it is critical that the balance shaft has the weighted portion at the bottom of the shaft (it is possible to align the marks with the balance shaft weight at the top; if you do this accidentally, severe engine vibration will result). Before installing the timing belt, slightly rock the oil pump sprocket by hand and watch carefully that the sprocket has the tendency to remain stationary (return to approximately the marks-aligned position) when the sprocket is rotated. This means the sprocket is CORRECTLY timed. If the sprocket has the tendency to rotate clockwise when spun lightly, the shaft is INCORRECTLY timed. If there is any doubt about whether or not the

balance shaft is in the correct position, insert a screwdriver through the hole in the left side of the cylinder block **(see illustration 5.15a in Chapter 2B)**. Make sure the screwdriver extends approximately 2-1/2 inches into the hole and also make sure the sprocket cannot be rotated with the screwdriver in place; now you can be sure the timing is correct. If the screwdriver can only be inserted about one inch into the hole, the timing is not correct.

25   Prepare the automatic tensioner for installation. Place the tensioner in a vise that is equipped with soft jaws (or put a shop rag over the jaws to prevent damage to the tensioner). If the rod is easily retracted, replace it with a new unit. The tensioner should have a fair amount of strength or resistance. **Caution:** *Be sure the tensioner is in a level position when it is in the vise. Also, place a washer over the plug on the bottom of the tensioner to prevent the vise from contacting the plug*. Once the tensioner is compressed place a small Allen wrench, or something similar, through the holes in the tensioner and rod to keep the rod retracted for reassembly on the engine **(see illustration 5.25 in Chapter 2B)**.

26   Install the automatic tensioner onto the engine, keeping it in the compressed position (that is, leave the pin in the holes for now).

27   Install the tensioner pulley onto the tensioner arm. Position the two small holes in the tensioner pulley hub horizontally below the center bolt. Tighten the center bolt finger tight. Don't remove the pin from the automatic tensioner yet.

28   Make sure the timing marks on the camshaft, oil pump sprocket and crankshaft sprocket are still correctly aligned.

29   Remove the plug on the side of the block and insert a Phillips screwdriver or a long punch through the hole **(see illustration 5.15a in Chapter 2B)**. If the tool CAN be inserted into the hole as deep as 2 1/2-inches or more, the timing marks are aligned correctly. If the tool CANNOT be inserted more than 1-inch, the oil pump sprocket must be reset. When it's positioned properly, reinstall the screwdriver and keep it there until the timing belt is installed.

30   Install the timing belt in the following sequence:

a) *Around the crankshaft sprocket*
b) *Around the idler pulley*
c) *Around the camshaft sprocket*
d) *Around the tensioner pulley*
e) *Gently raise the tensioner pulley so the belt does not sag, then temporarily tighten the center bolt.*
f) *Remove the screwdriver from the engine block hole and install the plug.*

31   Adjust the timing belt tension in the following sequence:

a) *Turn the crankshaft 1/4 turn counterclockwise, then clockwise to move the number 1 cylinder to TDC.*
b) *Loosen the tensioner center bolt and attach Mitsubishi special tool no.*

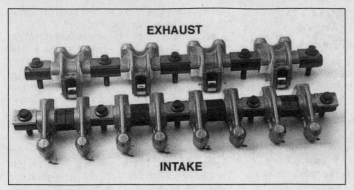

6.6 2.4L engine rocker arms and shaft assemblies

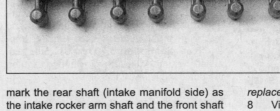

6.8 Rocker arm/ valve lash adjuster assembly (intake rocker arm shown)

1   *Hydraulic valve lash adjuster*
2   *Rocker shaft bore*
3   *Roller*

6.13 Intake rocker arm spacer locations (arrows)

MD998752 (or equivalent) to a torque wrench. **Note:** *The torque wrench must be capable of measuring small increments between 0 and 40 inch-lbs. Apply 30 inch-lbs. to the tensioner.*
c)   *While holding tension on the timing belt tensioner, tighten the center bolt to the torque listed in this Chapter's Specifications.*
d)   *Remove the special tool, if used.*
e)   *Rotate the crankshaft two complete turns and wait 15 minutes while the tensioner extends fully.* **Caution:** *If you feel resistance while turning the crankshaft, the valves may be hitting the pistons from incorrect valve timing. Stop and re-check the valve timing.*
f)   *Pull on the pin in the tensioner. It should move freely. If not, repeat the installation procedure.*
g)   *If the pin does move freely, pull it out and measure how far the tensioner plunger protrudes from the tensioner body (the distance between the tensioner arm and the automatic tensioner body). It should be between 5/32 and 3/16-inch (3.8 to 4.5 mm). Also check that all timing marks are still aligned.*

32   If the tensioner protrusion is not as specified, repeat the belt adjustment procedure.
33   Install the timing covers.
34   Reinstall the remaining parts in the reverse order of removal. Note that the timing belt cover bolts come in different lengths; make sure they're reinstalled in the correct holes.
35   Start the engine, check the ignition timing (see Chapter 5) and road test the vehicle.

6   Rocker arms and lash adjusters - removal, inspection and installation

Removal

Refer to illustration 6.6

1   Position the number one piston at Top Dead Center (see Section 3).
2   Disconnect the negative battery cable from the battery.
3   Remove the valve cover (see Section 4).
4   Prior to removing the rocker arm shafts,

mark the rear shaft (intake manifold side) as the intake rocker arm shaft and the front shaft (exhaust manifold side) as the exhaust. **Caution:** *Do not interchange the rocker arms onto a different shaft as this could lead to premature wear.*
5   Loosen the rocker arm shaft bolts 1/4-turn at a time each, until the valve spring pressure is relieved, in the *reverse* order of the tightening sequence **(see illustration 6.15)**. Completely loosen the bolts, but do not remove them, since leaving them in place will prevent the assembly from falling apart when it is lifted off the cylinder head.
6   Lift the rocker arms and shaft assemblies from the cylinder head and set them on the workbench **(see illustration)**. **Note:** *The hydraulic valve lash adjusters may become dislodged from the rocker arms during shaft removal. If required, secure the adjusters in place using electrical tape.*
7   Disassemble the rocker arm shaft components. **Caution:** *Before disassembly, mark the rocker arm shafts, rocker arms, shaft retainers and plastic shaft spacers (intake only) so all the parts can be reassembled in their original locations. To keep the rocker arms and related parts in order, it's a good idea to remove them and put them onto two lengths of wire (such as unbent coat hangers) in the same order as they're removed, marking each wire (which simulates the rocker shaft) as to whether it's the intake or exhaust.*

Inspection

Refer to illustration 6.8

Note: *The valve lash adjuster is an integral part of each rocker arm and cannot be*

replaced separately.
8   Visually check the rocker arms for wear **(see illustration)**. Replace them if evidence of wear or damage is found.
9   Inspect each lash adjuster carefully for signs of wear and damage, particularly on the surface that contacts the valve tip. Since the lash adjusters frequently become clogged, we recommend replacing the rocker arm/lash adjuster assembly if you're concerned about their condition or if the engine is exhibiting valve "tapping" noises.
10   Check all the rocker shaft components. Look for worn or scored shafts, etc. and replace any parts found to be damaged or worn excessively.

Installation

Refer to illustrations 6.13, 6.14 and 6.15

11   Prior to installation, the lash adjusters must be partially full of engine oil - indicated by little or no plunger action when the adjuster is depressed. If there's excessive plunger travel, place the rocker arm assembly into clean engine oil and pump the plunger until the plunger travel is eliminated. **Note:** *If the plunger still travels within the rocker arm when full of oil it's defective and the rocker arm assembly must be replaced.*
12   When assembling the rocker arms on the shaft assembly, make sure they're reinstalled in their original locations.
13   On the intake rocker arm shaft, make sure the plastic spacers are installed on the shaft in the correct locations **(see illustration)**.
14   Install the rocker arm assemblies with the notch in each rocker arm shaft located at the timing belt end of the engine and facing

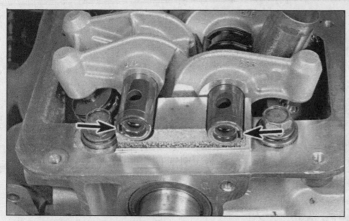

6.14 Both rocker arm shafts must be installed with the notches (arrows) facing outward (directly away from each other) and at the timing belt end of the engine

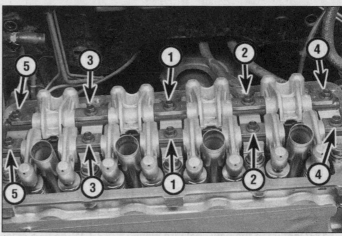

6.15 2.4L engine rocker arm shaft bolt tightening sequence

outward (away from each other) (**see illustration**).

15 Tighten the rocker arm bolts in the sequence shown (**see illustration**) using 3 steps to reach the torque listed in this Chapter's Specifications.

16 The remaining installation steps are the reverse of removal. Run the engine and check for oil leaks and proper operation.

17 When re-starting the engine after replacing the rocker arm/lash adjusters, the adjusters will normally make "tapping" noises. After warm-up, slowly raise the speed of the engine from idle to 3,000 rpm and back to idle over a one minute period. If the adjuster(s) do not become silent, replace the defective rocker arm/lash adjuster assembly.

7 Valve springs, retainers and seals - replacement

Refer to illustrations 7.4, 7.7, 7.8, 7.13 and 7.15

Note: *Broken valve springs and defective valve stem seals can be replaced without*

removing the cylinder head. Two special tools and a compressed air source are normally required to perform this operation, so read through this Section carefully and rent or buy the tools before attempting the job.

1 Remove the spark plugs (see Chapter 1).

2 Remove the valve cover (see Section 4).

3 Turn the crankshaft until the piston in the affected cylinder is at Top Dead Center on the compression stroke (see Section 3). If you're replacing all of the valve stem seals, begin with cylinder number one and work on the valves for one cylinder at a time. Move from cylinder-to-cylinder following the firing order sequence (see this Chapter's Specifications).

4 Thread an adapter into the spark plug hole (**see illustration**) and connect an air hose from a compressed air source to it. Most auto parts stores can supply the air hose adapter. **Note:** *Many cylinder compression gauges utilize a screw-in fitting that may work with your air hose quick-disconnect fitting.*

5 Remove the rocker arms (see Section 6).

6 Apply compressed air to the cylinder.

Warning: *The piston may be forced down by compressed air, causing the crankshaft to turn suddenly. If the wrench used when positioning the number one piston at TDC is still attached to the crankshaft bolt, it could cause damage or injury when the crankshaft moves.*

7 Stuff clean shop rags into the cylinder head holes above and below the valves to prevent parts and tools from falling into the engine, then use a valve spring compressor to compress the spring. Remove the keepers with small needle-nose pliers or a magnet (**see illustration**).

8 Remove the spring retainer and valve spring, then remove the valve guide seal/spring seat assembly (**see illustration**). **Note:** *If air pressure fails to hold the valve in the closed position during this operation, the valve face and/or seat is probably damaged. If so, the cylinder head will have to be removed for additional repair operations.*

9 Wrap a rubber band or tape around the top of the valve stem so the valve won't fall into the combustion chamber, then release the air pressure.

10 Inspect the valve stem for damage. Rotate the valve in the guide and check the

7.4 This is what the air hose adapter that threads into the spark plug hole looks like - they're commonly available from auto parts stores

7.7 Use needle-nose pliers (shown) or a small magnet to remove the valve spring keepers - be careful not to drop them down into the engine!

7.8 Remove the valve stem seal with a pair of pliers

7.13 Gently tap the new seal into place with a hammer and a deep socket

7.15 Apply a small dab of grease to each keeper before installation to hold it in place on the valve stem until the spring is released

end for eccentric movement, which would indicate that the valve is bent and needs to be replaced.

11   Move the valve up-and-down in the guide and make sure it doesn't bind. If the valve stem binds, either the valve is bent or the guide is damaged. In either case, the head will have to be removed for repair.

12   Pull up on the valve stem to close the valve, reapply air pressure to the cylinder to retain the valve in the closed position, then remove the tape or rubber band from the valve stem.

13   Lubricate the valve stem with engine oil and install a new valve guide seal/spring seat assembly. Tap it into place with a deep socket **(see illustration)**.

14   Install the spring in position over the valve.

15   Install the valve spring retainer. Compress the valve spring and carefully position the keepers in the groove. Apply a small dab of grease to the inside of each keeper to hold it in place if necessary **(see illustration)**.

16   Remove the pressure from the spring tool and make sure the keepers are seated.

17   Disconnect the air hose and remove the adapter from the spark plug hole.

18   Install the rocker arms (see Section 6).
19   Install the valve cover (see Section 4).
20   The remainder of installation is the reverse of the removal steps.
21   Start and run the engine, then check for oil leaks and unusual sounds coming from the valve cover area.

---

8   Camshaft - removal, inspection and installation

Removal

1   On 1999 and earlier models, remove the battery (see Chapter 5). On 2000 and later models, remove the air cleaner (see Chapter 4).
2   Remove the valve cover (see Section 4).
3   Remove the timing belt sprocket from the camshaft (see Section 5).
4   Remove the rocker arms and lash adjusters (see Section 6).
5   Remove the camshaft position sensor (see Chapter 6).

6   Carefully withdraw the camshaft from the opening in the cylinder head opposite the timing belt end. **Caution:** *Don't damage the camshaft lobes or bearing journals during removal and installation through the opening in the cylinder head.*
7   Remove the camshaft front seal from the cylinder head (see Section 9).

Inspection

Refer to illustration 8.9

8   Thoroughly clean the camshaft. Visually inspect the camshaft for wear and/or damage to the lobe surfaces, bearing journals and seal contact surfaces. Visually inspect the camshaft bearing surfaces in the cylinder head for scoring and other damage.
9   Measure the camshaft bearing journal diameters **(see illustration)**. Measure the inside diameter of the camshaft bearing surfaces in the cylinder head, using a telescoping gauge. Subtract the journal measurement from the bearing measurement to obtain the camshaft bearing oil clearance. Compare this clearance with the value listed in this Chapter's Specifications. Replace worn components as required.
10   Replace the camshaft if it fails any of the above inspections. **Note:** *If the lobes are worn, replace the rocker arms and lash adjusters along with the camshaft.* Cylinder head replacement may be necessary if the camshaft bearing surfaces in the head are damaged or excessively worn.
11   Clean and inspect the cylinder head as described in Part E of this Chapter.

Camshaft endplay measurement

Refer to illustration 8.14

12   Lubricate the camshaft and cylinder head bearing journals with clean engine oil.
13   Carefully insert the camshaft into the cylinder head and install the camshaft position sensor. Tighten the bolts to the torque listed in this Chapter's Specifications.
14   Install a dial indicator set up on the cylinder head and place the indicator tip on the camshaft at the sprocket end **(see illustration)**.

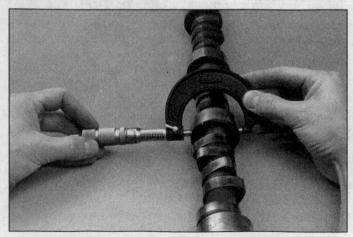

8.9 Measure the camshaft bearing journal diameters

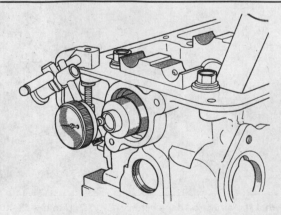

8.14 Measure the camshaft end play with a dial indicator positioned on the sprocket end of the camshaft as shown

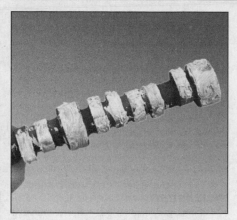

8.16 Prior to installing the camshaft, lubricate the bearing journals, thrust surfaces and lobes with assembly lube or clean engine oil

9.5 Carefully pry the camshaft seal out of the bore - DO NOT nick or scratch the camshaft or seal bore

9.7a Using a hammer and socket, gently tap the new seal into place with the spring side facing inward

15   Using a screwdriver, carefully pry the camshaft fully to the rear (toward the camshaft position sensor) until it stops. Zero the dial indicator and pry the camshaft fully to the front (toward the dial indicator end). The amount of indicator travel is the camshaft endplay. Compare the endplay measurement with the tolerance given in this Chapter's Specification Section. If the endplay is excessive, check the camshaft and cylinder head bearing journals for wear and replace as necessary.

Installation

Refer to illustration 8.16

16   Very carefully clean the camshaft and bearing journals. Liberally coat the journals, lobes and thrust portions of the camshaft with assembly lube or clean engine oil **(see illustration)**.
17   Carefully install the camshaft in the cylinder head.
18   Install a new camshaft oil seal (see Section 9).
19   The remainder of installation is the reverse of the removal steps.
20   Run the engine while checking for oil leaks.

9   Camshaft oil seal - replacement

Refer to illustrations 9.5, 9.7a, 9.7b and 9.9
Caution: *Do not rotate the camshaft(s) or crankshaft when the timing belt is removed or damage to the engine may occur.*
1   Remove the timing belt (see Section 5).
2   Rotate the crankshaft counterclockwise until the crankshaft sprocket is three teeth BTDC. This will prevent engine damage if the camshaft sprocket is inadvertently rotated during sprocket bolt removal.
3   While holding the camshaft sprocket, remove the camshaft sprocket bolt. Then, using two large screwdrivers, lever the sprocket off the camshaft. **Note:** *To hold the camshaft/sprocket while loosening the bolt, a strap-type damper/pulley holder tool is recommended and is available at most auto parts stores. If the strap wrench is unavailable, remove the valve cover to access the wrenching flats on the camshaft.*
4   Remove the bolts securing the rear timing belt cover to the engine block and cylinder head. Remove the rear cover.
5   Carefully pry out the camshaft oil seal using a small screwdriver **(see illustration)**.

Don't scratch the bore or damage the camshaft in the process (if the camshaft is damaged, the new seal will end up leaking).
6   Clean the bore and coat the outer edge of the new seal with engine oil or multi-purpose grease. Also lubricate the seal lip.
7   Using a socket with an outside diameter slightly smaller than the outside diameter of the seal and a hammer **(see illustration)**, carefully drive the new seal into the cylinder head until it's flush with the face of the cylinder head. If a socket isn't available, a short section of pipe will also work. **Note:** *If engine location makes it difficult to use a hammer to install the camshaft seal, fabricate a seal installation tool from a piece of pipe cut to the appropriate length, a bolt and a large washer* **(see illustration)**. *Place the section of pipe over the seal and thread the bolt into the camshaft. The seal can now be pressed into the bore by tightening the bolt.*
8   Install the rear timing belt cover.
9   Install the camshaft sprocket, aligning the pin in the camshaft with the hole in the sprocket **(see illustration)**. Use an appropriate tool to hold the camshaft sprocket while tightening the sprocket bolt to the torque listed in this Chapter's Specifications.

9.7b If space is limited and you can't use a hammer and socket to install the seal, a seal installer can be made from a section of pipe (of appropriate diameter), a bolt and washer. Place the pipe over the seal and press it into place by tightening the bolt

9.9 When installing the camshaft sprocket, make sure the pin in the camshaft is aligned with the hole in the sprocket (arrows)

10   Reinstall the timing belt (see Section 5).
11   Run the engine and check for oil leaks.

10   Crankshaft front oil seal - replacement

1   Remove the timing belt and the crankshaft sprockets (see Section 5).
2   Wrap the tip of a small screwdriver with tape. Working from below the left inner fender, use the screwdriver to pry the seal out of its bore. Take care to prevent damaging the crankshaft and the seal bore.
3   Thoroughly clean and inspect the seal bore and sealing surface on the crankshaft. Minor imperfections can be removed with emery cloth. If there is a groove worn in the crankshaft sealing surface (from contact with the seal), installing a new seal will probably not stop the leak. Such wear normally indicates the internal engine components are also worn. Consider overhauling the engine.
4   Lubricate the new seal with engine oil and drive the seal into place with a hammer and socket.
5   Another method of replacement is used if the front case has been removed (see Section 14) and you can drive the seal out from the back side of the cover. If the cover is removed, it's a good idea to replace all the front cover seals at this time (crankshaft, oil pump and balance shaft).
6   Position the seal and front cover assembly on a couple of wood blocks on a workbench and drive the old seal out from the back side with a punch and hammer.
7   Drive the new seal into the retainer with a block of wood or a section of pipe slightly smaller in diameter than the outside diameter of the seal.
8   Lubricate the lip of the new seal with clean engine oil. Position a new front case gasket on the engine block.
9   Slowly and carefully push the seal onto the crankshaft. The seal lip is stiff, so work it onto the crankshaft with a smooth object such as the end of an extension as you push the retainer against the cylinder block.
10   Install the front case bolts (see Section 15).
11   The remaining steps are the reverse of removal.
12   Run the engine and check for oil leaks.

11   Intake manifold - removal and installation

Removal

1   Relieve the fuel system pressure (see Chapter 4)
2   Remove the battery and ignition coil pack (see Chapter 5).
3   Drain the cooling system (see Chapter 1).
4   Remove the air intake hose (see Chapter 4).
5   Clearly label and disconnect all coolant tube, hoses, wires, brackets and emission lines which run to the fuel injection system and intake manifold.
6   Remove the fuel rail, fuel injector and pressure regulator (see Chapter 4).
7   Remove the intake manifold stay and engine hanger. Be sure to disconnect any electrical connections that are fastened to the support stay before trying to move the parts out of the way.
8   Remove the intake manifold nuts and bolts, then remove the manifold from the engine. If it sticks, tap the manifold with a soft-face hammer or carefully pry it from the head. **Caution:** *Do not pry between gasket sealing surfaces.*

Installation

9   Carefully scrape all traces of gasket material off both the cylinder head and the intake manifold. **Caution:** *The cylinder head and intake manifold are made of aluminum and are easily nicked or gouged. Don't damage the gasket surfaces or a leak may result after the work is complete. Gasket removal solvents are available from auto parts stores and may prove helpful.*
10   After cleaning, check the intake manifold mating surface for warpage. Lay a precision straightedge across the surface along the top and bottom edges, as well as corner-to-corner. Measure any gap between the straightedge and manifold with a feeler gauge. The manufacturer doesn't list a warpage limit for this surface, but if it's more than about 0.002-inch, have the manifold resurfaced by a machine sop.
11   Install the manifold, using a new gasket. Tighten the nuts in several stages, working from the center out, until the torque listed in this Chapter's Specifications is reached.
12   Reinstall the remaining parts in the reverse order of removal.
13   Adjust the accelerator cable (see Chapter 4).
14   Add coolant, run the engine and check for leaks and proper operation.

12   Exhaust manifold - removal and installation

Warning: *Allow the engine to cool completely before beginning this procedure.*

Removal

1   Disconnect the battery cable from the negative terminal of the battery.
2   Set the parking brake and block the rear wheels. Raise the vehicle and support it securely on jackstands.
3   Drain the cooling system and engine oil (see Chapter 1). Remove the dipstick tube from the engine block.
4   If necessary for access on vehicles equipped with air conditioning, remove the condenser fan (see Chapter 3).
5   Disconnect the oxygen sensor electrical connector (see Chapter 6).
6   Remove the heat shield.

7   Working from below the vehicle, remove the nuts that secure the exhaust system to the manifold.
8   Remove the manifold bolts, noting the location of the engine hanger. Apply penetrating oil to the threads to make removal easier.
9   Remove any brackets that may be bolted to the exhaust manifold.
10   Apply penetrating oil to the threads and remove the exhaust manifold mounting nuts, brackets and emission components.
11   Slip the manifold off the studs and remove it from the engine compartment.

Installation

12   Clean and inspect the exhaust manifold studs, replacing any that show thread damage.
13   Using a scraper, remove all traces of gasket material from the mating surfaces and inspect them for wear and cracks. **Caution:** *When removing gasket material from any surface, especially aluminum, be very careful not to scratch or gouge the gasket surface. Any damage to the surface may cause a leak after reassembly. Gasket removal solvents are available from auto parts stores and may prove helpful.*
14   Place a new gasket over the studs, install the manifold and tighten the nuts in several stages, working from the center out, to the torque listed in this Chapter's Specifications.
15   Reinstall the remaining parts in the reverse order of removal.
16   Run the engine and check for exhaust leaks.

13   Cylinder head - removal and installation

Caution: *Allow the engine to cool completely before following this procedure or the cylinder head may be warped.*

Removal

Refer to illustrations 13.10 and 13.11

1   Position the number one piston at Top Dead Center (see Section 3).
2   Disconnect the battery cable from the negative battery terminal.
3   Drain the cooling system and remove the spark plugs (see Chapter 1).
4   Remove the ignition system components (see Chapter 5).
5   Remove the valve cover (see Section 4).
6   Remove the timing belt (see Section 5).
7   Remove the intake manifold (see Section 10).
8   Remove the exhaust manifold (see Section 11).
9   Loosen the cylinder head bolts, 1/4-turn at a time, in the reverse of the tightening sequence **(see illustrations 13.13a and 13.13b)** until they can be removed by hand.
10   Carefully lift the cylinder head **(see illustration)** straight up and place the head on

13.10 Carefully lift the cylinder head straight up and place the head on wood blocks to prevent damage to the sealing surfaces

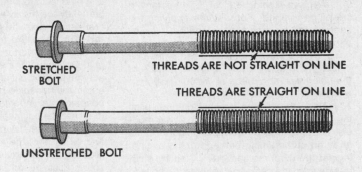

13.11 Lay a precision straightedge along the bolt threads; if any threads don't contact the straightedge, replace the bolt

wood blocks to prevent damage to the sealing surfaces. If the head sticks to the engine block, dislodge it by placing a block of wood against the head casting and tapping the wood with a hammer or by prying the head with a prybar placed carefully on a casting protrusion or in an exhaust port. **Note**: *Cylinder head disassembly and inspection procedures are covered in Chapter 2, Part E. It's a good idea to have the head checked for warpage, even if you're just replacing the gasket.*

11 Remove all traces of old gasket material from the block and head. Do not allow anything to fall into the engine. Clean and inspect all threaded fasteners and be sure the threaded holes in the block are clean and dry. If any of the bolts are stretched along the threads (indicated by necking of the bolt), replace them **(see illustration)**.

Installation

Refer to illustrations 13.13a and 13.13b

12 Place a new gasket and the cylinder head in position on the engine block.
13 The cylinder head bolts should be tightened in several stages in the correct sequence **(see illustrations)** to the torque listed in this Chapter's Specifications.

14 Reinstall the timing belt (see Section 5).
15 Reinstall the remaining parts in the reverse order of removal.
16 Be sure to refill the cooling system and check all fluid levels. Rotate the crankshaft clockwise slowly by hand through two complete revolutions. Recheck the camshaft timing marks (see Section 5).
17 Run the engine until normal operating temperature is reached. Check for leaks and proper operation. Shut off the engine. Remove the valve cover and retorque the cylinder head bolts, unless the gasket manufacturer states otherwise.

14 Oil pan - removal and installation

Removal

1 Disconnect the battery cable from the negative battery cable.
2 Raise the vehicle and support it securely on jackstands.
3 Drain the engine oil (see Chapter 1).
4 Remove the splash pan under the drivebelt end of the engine, then remove the dipstick and drain the engine oil (see Chapter 1).

5 Disconnect the exhaust pipe from the manifold and let the exhaust hang loosely under the car.
6 Remove the bolts and lower the oil pan from the vehicle. If the pan is stuck, tap it with a soft-face hammer or place a block of wood against the pan and tap the wood with a hammer. **Caution:** *If you're wedging something between the oil pan and the engine block to separate the two, be extremely careful not to gouge or nick the gasket surface of either part; an oil leak could result.*
7 Remove the oil pump pickup tube and screen assembly and clean both the tube and screen thoroughly. Install the pick-up tube and screen with a new gasket.
8 Thoroughly clean the oil pan and sealing surfaces on the block and pan. Use a scraper to remove all traces of old gasket material. Gasket removal solvents are available at auto parts stores and may prove helpful. Check the oil pan sealing surface for distortion. Straighten or replace as necessary. After cleaning and straightening (if necessary), wipe the gasket surfaces of the pan and block clean with a rag soaked in lacquer thinner or acetone.

13.13a Head bolt TIGHTENING sequence (1999 and earlier models)

13.13b Head bolt TIGHTENING sequence (2000 and later models)

Installation

9   Apply a 4 mm bead of RTV sealant to the oil pan flange. **Note:** *When applying the sealant, lay the bead in the center of the oil pan rail, except for the bolt holes, where you'll need to go around the inside edge of the bolt holes. If you apply the RTV to the outside of the bolt holes, an oil leak at the bolt-hole area will result.*

10   Place the oil pan into position and install the bolts finger tight. On 2000 and later models, note the location of the two shorter bolts (they go at the timing belt end of the engine, toward the oil pump sprocket). Working side-to-side from the center out, tighten the bolts to the torque listed in this Chapter's Specifications.

11   Reinstall the remaining parts in the reverse order of removal.

12   Refill the crankcase with the proper quantity and grade of oil and run the engine, checking for leaks. Road test the vehicle and check for leaks again.

15   Front case - removal and installation

This procedure is the same as for the 2.0L turbo engine. See Chapter 2B for procedures.

16   Oil pump - removal, inspection and installation

This procedure is the same as for the 2.0L turbo engine. See Chapter 2B for procedures.

17   Flywheel/driveplate - removal and installation

Removal

1   Raise the vehicle and support it securely on jackstands, then refer to Chapter 7 and remove the transaxle. If it's leaking, now would be a very good time to replace the transaxle front seal (on automatic transaxle equipped models, the torque converter must be removed to gain access to this seal).

2   Remove the pressure plate and clutch disc (manual transaxle equipped vehicles) (see Chapter 8). Now is a good time to check/replace the clutch components and the pilot bearing.

3   The bolt holes are either staggered or symmetrical on the flywheel/driveplate bolt pattern. To ensure correct alignment during reinstallation, mark the position of the flywheel/driveplate to the crankshaft before removal.

4   Remove the bolts that secure the flywheel/driveplate to the crankshaft. If the

crankshaft turns, wedge a screwdriver in the ring gear teeth to jam the flywheel.

5   Remove the flywheel/driveplate from the crankshaft **(see illustration 16.5 in Chapter 2D)**. Since the flywheel is fairly heavy, be sure to support it while removing the last bolt. On manual transaxle models, there's an adapter plate on either side of the flywheel. On automatic transaxle models, there's a single adapter plate, mounted behind the driveplate (between the bolt heads and the driveplate).

6   Clean the flywheel to remove grease and oil. Inspect the surface for cracks, rivet grooves, burned areas and score marks. Light scoring can be removed with emery cloth. Check for cracked and broken ring gear teeth. Lay the flywheel on a flat surface and use a straightedge to check for warpage. **Note:** *Flywheels can be re-surfaced by a machine shop. Also, starter ring gears are available separately and can be installed by an automotive machine shop.*

7   Clean and inspect the mating surfaces of the flywheel/driveplate and the crankshaft. If the crankshaft rear seal is leaking, replace it before reinstalling the flywheel/driveplate (see Section 18).

Installation

8   Position the flywheel/driveplate against the crankshaft. If the bolt holes aren't staggered, align the previously applied match marks. Before installing the bolts, apply thread locking compound to the threads.

9   Wedge a screwdriver in the ring gear teeth to keep the flywheel/driveplate from turning as you tighten the bolts to the torque listed in this Chapter's Specifications.

10   The remainder of installation is the reverse of the removal procedure.

18   Rear main oil seal - replacement

1   The one-piece rear main oil seal is pressed into a bore machined into the rear main bearing cap and engine block.

2   Remove the transaxle, clutch (manual transaxle models) and flywheel/driveplate (see Chapters 7 and 8 and Section 17).

3   Remove the oil pan (see Section 14).

4   **Note:** *Observe that the oil seal is installed flush with the outer surface of the block.* Pry out the old seal with a flat blade screwdriver. **Caution:** *To prevent an oil leak, be very careful not to scratch or otherwise damage the crankshaft sealing surface or the seal bore in the engine block.*

5   Clean the crankshaft and seal bore in the block thoroughly and de-grease the areas by wiping them with a rag soaked in lacquer thinner or acetone.

6   Smear a film of oil onto the inner diameter of the new seal and position it onto the crankshaft. **Note:** *When installing the new seal, if so marked, the words THIS SIDE OUT*

on the seal must face out, toward the rear of the engine. Using an appropriate size driver and pilot tool, drive the seal into the cylinder block until it is flush with the outer surface of the block. If the seal is driven in past flush, there will be an oil leak.

7   The remaining installation steps are the reverse of removal.

19   Engine mounts - check and replacement

1   Engine mounts seldom require attention, but broken or deteriorated mounts should be replaced immediately or the added strain placed on the driveline components may cause damage or wear.

Check

2   Raise the vehicle and support it securely on jackstands, then position a jack under the engine oil pan. Place a large block of wood between the jack head and the oil pan to prevent oil pan damage, then carefully raise the engine just enough to take the weight off the mounts. **Warning:** *DO NOT place any part of your body under the engine when it's supported only by a jack!*

3   Check the mounts to see if the rubber is cracked, hardened or separated from the metal backing. Sometimes the rubber will split right down the center.

4   Check for relative movement between the mount plates and the engine or frame (use a large screwdriver or pry bar to attempt to move the mounts). If movement is noted, lower the engine and tighten the mount fasteners.

5   Rubber preservative may be applied to the mounts to slow deterioration.

Replacement

6   Disconnect the battery cable from the negative battery terminal, then raise the vehicle and support it securely on jackstands (if not already done). **Caution:** *Do not disconnect more than one mount at a time, except during engine/transaxle removal.*

7   Remove the fasteners and detach the mount from the frame and engine.

8   The rubber portion of the mounts are normally available separately from the bracket that attaches it to the frame or block. Obtain new inserts and take them to an automotive machine shop or dealer service department to be pressed into the existing bracket, if necessary.

9   Installation is the reverse of removal. Install the engine mount and transaxle mount stoppers with the arrow marks pointing in the proper direction **(see illustrations 18.10a and 18.10b in Chapter 2B)**. Use thread locking compound on the mount bolts and be sure to tighten them securely.

Chapter 2 Part D
V6 engine

Contents

Specifications

General
Bore	3.59 inches
Stroke	2.99 inches
Displacement	181 cubic inches (2.97 liters)
Firing order	1-2-3-4-5-6

Camshaft
Journal diameter	1.8 inches
Lobe height	
Intake	
Standard	1.485 inches
Service limit	1.465 inches
Exhaust	
Standard	1.465 inches
Service limit	1.433 inches

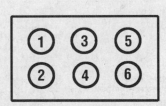 

Cylinder numbering and spark plug wire terminal locations

FRONT OF VEHICLE

Cylinder head
Gasket surface warpage limit	0.007 inch
Surface grinding limit (total of head and block)	0.007 inch

Oil pump
Inner rotor-to-outer rotor lobe clearance	0.003 to 0.007 inch
Outer rotor-to-housing clearance	
Standard	0.004 to 0.007 inch
Service limit	0.013 inch
Rotor-to-cover clearance (side clearance)	0.002 to 0.003 inch

Torque specifications
Ft-lbs (unless otherwise indicated)

Note: *One foot-pound (ft-lb) of torque is equivalent to 12 inch-pounds (in-lbs) of torque. Torque values below approximately 15 ft-lbs are expressed in inch-pounds, since most foot-pound torque wrenches are not accurate at these smaller values.*

Camshaft sprocket bolt	65
Camshaft thrust case bolts	113 inch-lbs
Crankshaft damper/pulley bolt	134
Crankshaft rear main seal retainer bolts	95 inch-lbs
Cylinder head bolts	
First stage	80
Second stage	Loosen completely
Third stage	80
EGR tube to intake manifold plenum bolts	156 inch-lbs
EGR tube to exhaust manifold flare nut	44

Torque specifications (continued)

Ft-lbs (unless otherwise indicated)

Engine mounting nuts/bolts
Dynamic damper to engine mount	44 inch-lbs
Engine mount bracket to engine bolts	33
Engine mount stay to mount bolt	26
Engine mount to chassis through-bolt	60
Engine mount to bracket nuts/bolts	64
Roll stopper through-bolts	34
Roll stopper to crossmember bolts	34
Transaxle mount to bracket nuts	42
Transaxle mount to chassis through-bolt	60

Exhaust manifold-to-cylinder head nuts 33
Exhaust manifold-to-exhaust pipe nuts 26
Exhaust manifold heat shield bolts ..... 120 inch-lbs
Flywheel/driveplate-to-crankshaft bolts 55

Intake manifold
Upper intake manifold bolts/nuts	156 inch-lbs

Lower intake manifold nuts
Step 1	Rear nuts 56 inch-lbs
Step 2	Front nuts 16
Step 3	Rear nuts 16
Step 4	Front nuts 16 (again)
Step 5	Rear nuts 16 (again)

Oil filter adapter bolts 17

Oil pan bolts
Lower pan to upper pan	95 inch-lbs
Baffle to upper pan	95 inch-lbs
Upper pan to cylinder block	52 inch-lbs
Upper pan to transaxle	26

Oil pump
Attaching bolts
M8 bolts	122 inch-lbs
M10 bolts	30
Cover screws	87 inch-lbs
Pick-up tube bolts	14
Relief valve cap bolt	33

Rocker arm shaft bolts 23

Timing belt
Cover bolts
M6 bolts	95 inch-lbs
M8 bolts	122 inch-lbs
Tensioner arm assembly bolt	33
Tensioner pulley bolt	35
Tensioner mounting bolts	17

Valve cover bolts ..... 31 inch-lbs

*Refer to Part C for additional torque specifications.

**Tighten slightly with the engine jacked up, then tighten fully with the vehicle level and the weight of the engine resting on the mount.

1   General information

This Part of Chapter 2 is devoted to in-vehicle engine repair procedures. Information concerning engine removal and installation and engine block and cylinder head overhaul can be found in Part E of this Chapter.

The following repair procedures are based on the assumption that the engine is installed in the vehicle. If the engine has been removed from the vehicle and mounted on a stand, many of the steps outlined in this Part of Chapter 2 will not apply.

The Specifications included in this Part of Chapter 2 apply only to the procedures contained in this Part. Part E of Chapter 2 contains the Specifications necessary for cylinder head and engine block rebuilding. This Part of Chapter 2 covers V6 engines.

2   Repair operations possible with the engine in the vehicle

Many major repair operations can be accomplished without removing the engine from the vehicle.

Clean the engine compartment and the exterior of the engine with some type of degreaser before any work is performed. It will make the job easier and help keep dirt out of the internal areas of the engine.

Depending on the components involved, it may be helpful to remove the hood to improve access to the engine as repairs are performed (refer to Chapter 11 if necessary). Cover the fenders to prevent damage to the paint. Special pads are available, but an old bedspread or blanket will also work.

If vacuum, exhaust, oil or coolant leaks develop, indicating a need for gasket or seal replacement, the repairs can generally be made with the engine in the vehicle. The intake and exhaust manifold gaskets, oil pan gasket, camshaft and crankshaft oil seals and cylinder head gasket are all accessible with the engine in place.

Exterior engine components, such as the intake and exhaust manifolds, the oil pan, the oil pump, the water pump, the starter motor, the alternator, the distributor and the fuel system components can be removed for repair with the engine in place.

Since the camshafts and cylinder head can be removed without pulling the engine, valve component servicing can also be accomplished with the engine in the vehicle. Replacement of the timing belt and sprockets is also possible with the engine in the vehicle.

4.6 Valve cover mounting bolts (arrows)

4.7 Remove and replace the seal from each spark plug tube

In extreme cases caused by a lack of necessary equipment, repair or replacement of piston rings, pistons, connecting rods and rod bearings is possible with the engine in the vehicle. However, this practice is not recommended because of the cleaning and preparation work that must be done to the components involved.

3 Top Dead Center (TDC) for number one piston - locating

Note: *The crankshaft timing marks on these engines aren't visible until the timing belt covers have been removed.*

1   Top Dead Center (TDC) is the highest point in the cylinder that each piston reaches as it travels up-and-down when the crankshaft rotates. Each piston reaches TDC on the compression stroke and again on the exhaust stroke, but TDC generally refers to piston position on the compression stroke.
2   Positioning the piston(s) at TDC is an essential part of many procedures such as rocker arm removal, camshaft and timing belt/ sprocket removal and distributor removal.
3   Before beginning this procedure, be sure to place the transmission in Neutral and apply the parking brake or block the rear wheels. Also, disable the ignition system by detaching the electrical connector at the ignition coil pack (see Chapter 5). Remove all accessible spark plugs (see Chapter 1). **Note:** *On these engines, the spark plugs for cylinders 1, 3 and 5 are located under the upper intake manifold and are not easily accessible. Unless they must be removed for the procedure you are performing, leave them installed.*
4   Remove the splash shield from under the timing belt end of the engine.
5   In order to bring any piston to TDC, the crankshaft must be turned using one of the methods outlined below. When looking at the drivebelt end of the engine, normal crankshaft rotation is clockwise.
   a) *The preferred method is to turn the crankshaft with a ratchet and socket on the crankshaft pulley bolt.*

   b) *A remote starter switch, which may save some time, can also be used. These switches are available inexpensively from auto parts stores. Follow the instructions included with the switch. Once the piston is close to TDC, use a socket and ratchet as described in the previous paragraph.*
   c) *If an assistant is available to turn the ignition switch to the Start position in short bursts, you can get the piston close to TDC without a remote starter switch. Make sure your assistant is out of the vehicle, away from the ignition switch, then use a socket and ratchet as described in Paragraph a) to complete the procedure.*

6   **Note:** *The following steps assume that the upper intake manifold is installed, making the number one spark plug inaccessible.*
7   Remove the upper left timing belt cover (see Section 7).
8   Install a compression gauge (screw-in type with a hose) in the number 6 cylinder spark plug hole. Place the gauge dial where you can see it while turning the crankshaft damper/pulley bolt. **Note:** *The number 6 cylinder is located at the rear (transaxle) end of the left cylinder bank (refer to this Chapter's Specifications if necessary).*
9   Rotate the crankshaft clockwise until you see compression building up on the gauge, indicating you are on the compression stroke.
10   Look at the camshaft timing mark for the left camshaft **(see illustration 7.11a)**. If the number 6 piston is near TDC, the camshaft timing mark should be approximately 60-degrees counterclockwise of the timing mark on the rear timing belt cover.
11   Turn the crankshaft clockwise (see Step 3 above) until the timing mark on the left camshaft sprocket is aligned with the timing mark on the rear timing belt cover **(see illustration 7.11a)**. The number one piston is now at TDC on the compression stroke. **Note:** *If you turn the crankshaft too far, it will be necessary to rotate the crankshaft clockwise approximately 1-3/4 turns to approach the compression stroke again.* **Caution:** *Don't turn the crankshaft counterclockwise or the timing belt may jump a tooth on the sprockets.*

12   After the number one piston has been positioned at TDC on the compression stroke, TDC for any of the remaining pistons can be located by turning the crankshaft exactly 120-degrees from that position, following the spark plug firing order (1-2-3-4-5-6); that is, the first 120-degree rotation from number one piston TDC will bring the number 2 cylinder piston to TDC on its compression stroke, another 120-degree rotation will bring the number 3 cylinder piston to TDC on its compression stroke, etc.

4 Valve cover - removal and installation

Removal
Refer to illustrations 4.6 and 4.7
1   Disconnect the negative battery cable from the battery (see Chapter 5, Section 1).
2   Remove the air cleaner assembly (see Chapter 4).
3   If removing the rear valve cover (near the firewall), remove the upper intake manifold (see Section 5).
4   Clearly label then remove the spark plug wires from the valve cover (see Chapter 1 if necessary).
5   Clearly label and disconnect any emission hoses and electrical cables which connect to, or cross over, the valve cover.
6   Remove the valve cover bolts and lift off the cover **(see illustration)**. If the cover sticks to the cylinder head, tap on it with a soft-face hammer or place a wood block against the cover and tap on the wood with a hammer. **Caution:** *If you have to pry between the valve cover and the cylinder head, be extremely careful not to gouge or nick the gasket surfaces of either part. A leak could develop after reassembly.*
7   Remove the spark plug tube seals. Even if they look OK, they should be replaced **(see illustration)**.
8   Thoroughly clean the valve cover and remove all traces of old gasket material. Gasket removal solvents are available from auto parts stores and may prove helpful. After

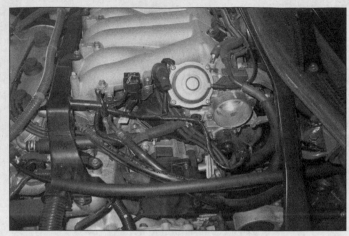

5.3a Disconnect the hoses and electrical connectors at the timing belt end of the engine . . .

5.3b . . . at the distributor end . . .

cleaning the surfaces, degrease them with a rag soaked in lacquer thinner or acetone.

Installation

9   Install the new spark plug seals onto the tubes.

5.3c . . . at the rear near the motor mount . . .

10   Install a new gasket on the cover, using anaerobic RTV sealant to hold it in place.
11   Tighten the valve cover bolts in 3 steps to the torque listed in this Chapter's Specifications using a criss-cross pattern starting in the middle of the cover and working outwards.
12   The remaining installation steps are the reverse of removal. When complete, run the engine and check for oil leaks.

Spark plug tube replacement

13   Remove the applicable valve cover (see above).
14   Grasp the spark plug tube gently with locking pliers, carefully twist back and forth and remove the tube from the cylinder head.
15   Clean the locking agent from the tube and the recess in the cylinder head with solvent, and dry thoroughly.
16   Apply a small amount of Loctite No. 271, or equivalent, around the lower end of the tube and install the tube into the cylinder head. Carefully tap the tube into the recess with a wood block and mallet until it's fully seated in the cylinder head.

5   Intake manifold - removal and installation

Upper intake manifold
Removal
Refer to illustrations 5.3a, 5.3b, 5.3c, 5.3d, 5.5, 5.6 and 5.7
1   Disconnect the negative battery cable from the ground stud on the left shock tower (see Chapter 5, Section 1).
2   Remove the air filter inlet duct from the throttle body (see Chapter 4 if necessary).
3   Clearly label and disconnect all hoses, wires, brackets and emission lines which attach to the intake manifold **(see illustrations)**.
4   Disconnect the accelerator cable and cruise control cable (if applicable) from the throttle body (see Chapter 4 if necessary).
5   Remove the bolts securing the upper intake manifold to the right and left side support brackets **(see illustration)**.
6   Remove the EGR tube **(see illustration)**.
7   Loosen the upper intake manifold bolts and nuts in a criss-cross pattern 1/4-turn at a time until they can be removed by hand **(see**

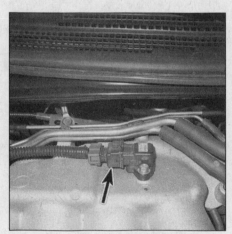

5.3d . . . and at the rear near the manifold differential pressure sensor; also disconnect the sensor (arrow)

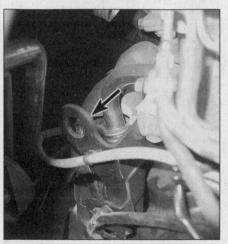

5.5 Remove the intake manifold stays at the front (shown) and rear

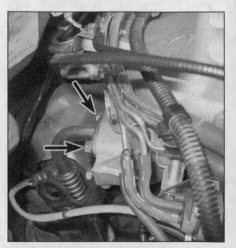

5.6 Unbolt the EGR tube (arrows) and remove it from the manifold

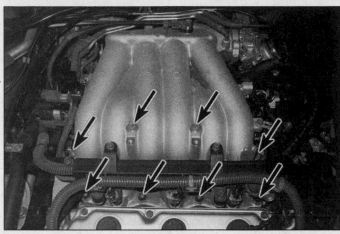

5.7 Remove the upper intake manifold bolts and nuts (nuts partially hidden)

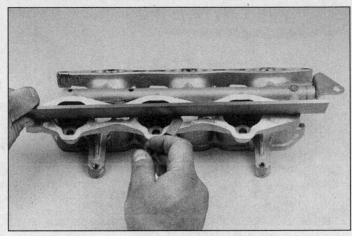

5.22 Check the lower intake manifold gasket surface for warpage

illustration). Remove the upper intake manifold, and induction control valve assembly (if applicable) from the engine. If it sticks, tap the manifold with a soft-face hammer or carefully pry it from the lower intake manifold. **Caution:** *Do not pry between the gasket sealing surfaces.*

8   To minimize the chance of gasket debris or other contamination from getting into the engine, place clean rags into the lower intake manifold passages.

9   Remove all traces of gasket material from both the upper and lower intake manifold by carefully scraping them using a suitable gasket scraper. **Caution:** *The intake manifold components are made of aluminum and are easily nicked or gouged. Do not damage the gasket surfaces or a leak may result after the work is complete. Gasket removal solvents are available from auto parts stores and may prove helpful.*

10   Using a precision straightedge and feeler gauge, check the upper and lower intake manifold mating surfaces for warpage **(see illustration 5.22)**. If the warpage on any surface exceeds the limits listed in this Chapter's Specifications, the discrepant intake manifold must be replaced or resurfaced by an automotive machine shop.

Installation

11   Remove the rags from the lower intake manifold. Use a shop vacuum to remove any contamination that may be present.

12   Install the upper intake manifold, and induction control valve assembly (if applicable), using a new gasket. Tighten the bolts in 3 stages, working from the center out, to the torque listed in this Chapter's Specifications.

13   Install the EGR tube using new gaskets. Tighten the bolts to the torque listed in this Chapter's Specifications.

14   The remaining installation steps are the reverse of removal.

Lower intake manifold

Removal

Refer to illustration 5.22

15   Perform the fuel pressure relief procedure (see Chapter 4).

16   Remove the upper intake manifold (see above).

17   Remove the fuel rail and injector assembly (see Chapter 4).

18   Loosen the intake manifold nuts in the *reverse* order of the tightening sequence **(see illustration 5.24 and this Chapter's Specifications)**, 1/4 turn at a time until they can be removed by hand. Remove the washers.

19   Remove the lower intake manifold from the engine. If it sticks, tap the manifold with a soft-face hammer or carefully pry it from the heads. **Caution:** *Do not pry between gasket sealing surfaces.*

20   To minimize the chance of gasket debris or other contamination from getting into the engine, place clean rags into the cylinder head intake passages.

21   Remove all traces of gasket material from the upper and lower intake manifold and cylinder heads by carefully scraping them using a suitable gasket scraper. **Caution:** *The intake manifold components and cylinder heads are made of aluminum and are easily nicked or gouged. Do not damage the gasket surfaces or a leak may result after the work is complete. Gasket removal solvents are available from auto parts stores and may prove helpful.*

22   Using a precision straightedge and feeler gauge, check the upper and lower intake manifold gasket surfaces for warpage **(see illustration)**. Check the gasket surface on the cylinder head also. If the warpage on any surface exceeds the limits listed in this Chapter's Specifications, the discrepant component must be replaced or resurfaced by an automotive machine shop.

Installation

Refer to illustration 5.24

23   Remove the rags from the cylinder head intake passages. Use a shop vacuum to remove any contamination that may be present.

24   Install the lower intake manifold, using a new gaskets. Tighten the nuts **(see illustration)** in five stages, following the sequence

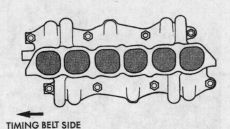

TIMING BELT SIDE

5.24 Tighten the lower intake manifold nuts in sequence (see this Chapter's Specifications)

listed in this Chapter's Specifications, to the final torque.

25   Install the fuel rail (see Chapter 4).

26   Install the upper intake manifold, using a new gasket. Tighten the bolts in three stages, working from the center out, to the torque listed in this Chapter's Specifications.

27   Install the EGR tube using new gaskets. Tighten the bolts to the torque listed in this Chapter's Specifications.

28   The remaining installation steps are the reverse of removal.

6   Exhaust manifold - removal and installation

Warning: *Allow the engine to cool completely before beginning this procedure.*
Note: *This procedure can be used to remove one or both of the exhaust manifolds as required.*

Removal

Refer to illustrations 6.4, 6.6a, 6.6b, 6.6c, 6.8 and 6.9

1   Disconnect the negative battery cable from the battery, then remove the battery and the battery tray (see Chapter 5).

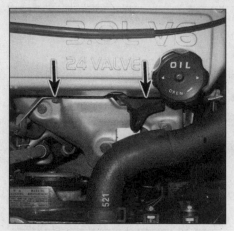

6.4 Remove the dipstick tube bolt (left)
and upper heat shield (right)
(front manifold)

6.6a Remove the lower heat shield from
the rear exhaust manifold . . .

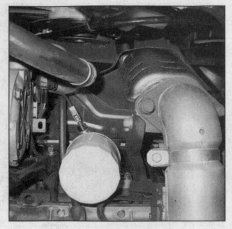

6.6b . . . and from the front
exhaust manifold . . .

6.6c . . . unbolt the upper heat shield
(arrows) and slide it along the oxygen
sensor wiring harness (disconnect the
harness to remove the heat
shield completely)

2　Remove the air cleaner (see Chapter 4).
3　Remove the strut tower crossbar (see Chapter 10).
4　Remove the engine oil dipstick and dipstick tube **(see illustration)**. Remove the automatic transmission dipstick and dipstick tube (if equipped).

5　If you're working on a 2000 California or any 2001 model, disconnect the electrical connector for the upstream oxygen sensor.
6　Remove the EGR tube from the rear manifold **(see illustration 5.6)**. Remove the exhaust manifold heat shield(s) **(see illustration 6.4 and the accompanying illustrations)**.
7　To make removal easier, apply penetrating oil to the exhaust manifold and manifold-to-pipe fasteners.
8　Detach the exhaust system from the manifold **(see illustration)**. **Note:** *It may be necessary to remove, or partially remove, the exhaust system to facilitate rear manifold removal* (see Chapter 4 if necessary).
9　Unscrew the mounting nuts, remove the exhaust manifold and gasket **(see illustration)**.
10　Using a wire brush, clean the exhaust manifold studs, replacing any that show thread damage.
11　Using a scraper, remove all traces of gasket material from the exhaust manifold, cylinder head, and exhaust pipe mating surfaces and inspect them for wear and cracks. **Caution:** *When removing gasket material from any surface, especially aluminum, be very careful not to scratch or gouge the gasket sur-*

face. Any damage to the surface may cause a leak after reassembly. Gasket removal solvents are available from auto parts stores and may prove helpful.
12　Using a precision straightedge and feeler gauge, check the exhaust manifold gasket surfaces for warpage. Check the surface on the cylinder head also. If the warpage on any surface exceeds the limits listed in this Chapter's Specifications, the exhaust manifold and/or cylinder head must be replaced or resurfaced by an automotive machine shop.

Installation

13　Install the new exhaust gasket(s) onto the cylinder head.
14　Apply Loctite No. 271 to the exhaust manifold mounting stud threads.
15　Install the manifold, washers and nuts. Tighten the nuts in three stages, working from the center out, to the torque listed in this Chapter's Specifications.
16　The remaining installation steps are the reverse of removal. Install a new gasket(s) between the exhaust manifold and exhaust pipe(s). Tighten the nuts to the torque listed in this Chapter's Specifications.
17　Run the engine and check for exhaust leaks.

6.8 Remove the nuts from the exhaust manifold-to-exhaust
system connection (arrows; front manifold shown)

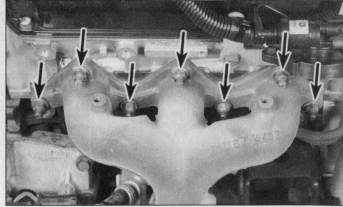

6.9 Exhaust manifold mounting nuts (arrows) (front manifold
shown, heat shield removed)

7.4a To keep the crankshaft from turning, insert a large screwdriver or bar through the opening in the damper/pulley and wedge it against the engine block, then loosen the bolt with a socket and breaker bar

7 Timing belt - removal, inspection and installation

Caution: *If the timing belt failed with the engine operating, damage to the valves may have occurred. Perform an engine compression check after belt replacement to determine if any valve damage is present.*

Removal

> ## ** CAUTION **
> The timing system is complex. Severe engine damage will occur if you make any mistakes. Do not attempt this procedure unless you are highly experienced with this type of repair. If you are at all unsure of your abilities, consult an expert. Double-check all your work and be sure everything is correct before you attempt to start the engine.

Refer to illustrations 7.4a, 7.4b, 7.6, 7.7, 7.9, 7.11a, 7.11b, 7.12 and 7.13
Caution: *Do not turn the crankshaft or camshafts after the timing belt has been removed,*

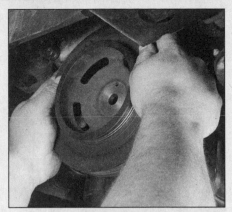

7.4b Remove the damper/pulley from the crankshaft

as this will damage the valves from contact with the pistons. Do not try to turn the crankshaft with the camshaft sprocket bolt(s) and do not rotate the crankshaft counterclockwise as viewed from the timing belt end of the engine.
Note: *In order to perform this procedure, a special tool is required to properly tension the timing belt. The manufacturer's tool number is "MD 998767" and it may be available from a dealership parts department or directly from Miller Special Tools (phone no. 800-801-5420).*

1 Position the number one piston at Top Dead Center (see Section 3).
2 Disconnect the negative battery cable from the battery (see Chapter 5).
3 Remove the drivebelts (see Chapter 1).
4 Loosen the large bolt in the center of the crankshaft damper/pulley. Since it might be very tight, to break it loose insert a large screwdriver or bar through the opening in the pulley to keep the crankshaft stationary, then loosen the bolt with a socket and breaker bar. Remove the bolt, washer and damper/pulley from the crankshaft **(see illustrations)**.
5 After removing the crankshaft pulley, reinstall the crankshaft bolt using an appropriate spacer (this will enable you to turn the crankshaft later).
6 Remove the upper-left timing belt cover **(see illustration)**.
7 Remove the lower timing belt cover **(see illustration)**.

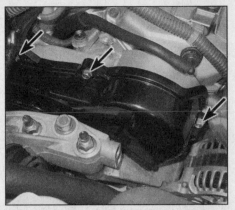

7.6 Timing belt upper left (front cylinder bank) cover bolt locations

7.7 Remove the bolts (arrows) that attach the timing belt lower cover to the engine

8 Detach the power steering pump bracket from the engine (see Chapter 10 if necessary).
9 Remove the upper-right timing belt cover **(see illustration)**.
10 Remove the right (passenger side) engine mount and the mounting bracket from the engine (see Section 18). **Note:** *Make sure the engine is supported with a floor jack placed under the oil pan. Place a wood block on the jack head to prevent the floor jack from denting or damaging the oil pan.*
11 Make sure the timing marks on the crankshaft sprocket and camshaft sprockets align

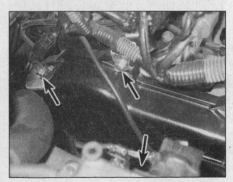

7.9 Timing belt upper right (rear cylinder bank) cover locations

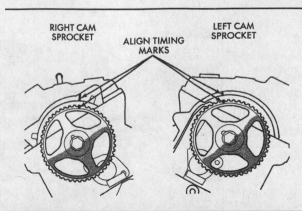

RIGHT CAM SPROCKET   ALIGN TIMING MARKS   LEFT CAM SPROCKET

7.11a Verify that the camshaft sprocket timing marks are aligned with their respective marks on the rear timing belt covers

7.11b Crankshaft timing belt sprocket and oil pump housing timing marks (arrows)

7.12 Paint an arrow on the timing belt in the direction of rotation (clockwise) so it may be reinstalled in the same direction

7.13 Timing belt tensioner mounting bolts (arrows)

7.18 Carefully inspect the timing belt for damage or wear - bending it backwards will often make defects more apparent

with their respective marks before removing the timing belt **(see illustrations)**.

12   If you plan to reuse the timing belt, paint an arrow on it to indicate the direction of rotation (clockwise) **(see illustration)**.

13   Loosen the timing belt tensioner mounting bolts and then remove the tensioner **(see illustration)**. **Note:** *The tensioner piston will extend when the assembly is removed.*

14   Carefully slip the timing belt off the sprockets and set it aside. If you plan to reuse the timing belt, place it in a plastic bag - do not allow the belt to come in contact with any type of oil or water as this will greatly shorten belt life.

Inspection

Refer to illustration 7.18

15   With the timing belt covers removed, now is a good time to inspect the front crankshaft and camshaft seals for leakage. If leakage is evident, replace the seals (see Sections 8 and 9, respectively).

16   Inspect the water pump for evidence of leakage (usually indicated by a trail of wet or dried coolant). Check the pulley for excessive radial play and bearing roughness. Replace if necessary (see Chapter 3).

17   Rotate the tensioner pulley and idler pulley by hand and move them side-to-side to detect bearing roughness and/or excessive

play. Visually inspect all timing belt sprockets for any signs of damage or wear. Replace as necessary.

18   Inspect the timing belt for cracks, separation, wear, missing teeth and oil contamination **(see illustration)**. Replace the belt if it's in questionable condition or the engine mileage is close to that referenced in the *Maintenance Schedule* (see Chapter 1).

19   Check the timing belt tensioner unit for leaks or any other obvious damage, replace if necessary.

Installation

> **** CAUTION ****
> Before starting the engine, carefully rotate the crankshaft by hand through at least two full revolutions (use a socket and breaker bar on the crankshaft pulley center bolt). If you feel any resistance, STOP! There is something wrong - most likely, valves are contacting the pistons. You must find the problem before proceeding. Check your work and see if any updated repair information is available.

Refer to illustrations 7.22, 7.24, 7.25 and 7.27

20   Confirm that the timing marks on both camshaft sprockets are aligned with their

respective marks on the rear timing belt covers **(see illustration 7.11a)**. Reposition the camshafts if required. **Caution:** *If it is necessary to rotate the camshafts to align the timing marks, first rotate the crankshaft slightly counterclockwise (three notches on the sprocket) to ensure the valves do not contact the pistons.*

21   Position the crankshaft sprocket with the timing marks aligned **(see illustration 7.11b)**.

22   Install the timing belt as follows; first place the belt onto the right camshaft sprocket (the one towards the rear of the vehicle) and clamp it to the sprocket. While maintaining tension on the belt, wrap it under the water pump pulley and place it onto the left sprocket camshaft sprocket. Secure the timing belt to the left camshaft sprocket **(see illustration)**. Continue to wrap the timing belt over the idler pulley, around the crankshaft sprocket and finishing with the tensioner pulley. Remove the clamps from the camshaft sprockets.

23   Make sure the timing belt is tight between the left camshaft sprocket and the crankshaft sprocket, all the slack is at the tensioner pulley and all the timing marks are aligned.

24   Before installation, the timing belt tensioner piston must be compressed into the tensioner housing. Place the tensioner in a vise so the surface with the pin hole is facing up. Slowly compress the tensioner using the vise, then install an appropriate size Allen wrench or drill bit through the body and into the piston to retain the piston in this position

7.22 Binder clips (arrows) can be used to retain the timing belt in position on the camshaft sprockets during installation

7.24 Compress the timing belt tensioner in a soft-jawed vise until the holes in the housing and piston align, then slip an Allen wrench (arrow) or drill bit through the holes to keep the piston in position

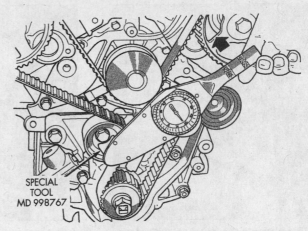

7.25 Using special tool MD 998767 attached to a torque wrench, apply 39 in-lbs of torque (in a counterclockwise direction) to the tensioner pulley, then move the tensioner unit up against the tensioner pulley bracket and tighten the tensioner mounting bolts to the torque listed in this Chapter's Specifications

(see illustration). Remove the tensioner from the vise.
25 Using the special tool "MD 998767" engaged in the tensioner pulley, have an assistant apply 39 inch-lbs of torque in a counterclockwise direction (see illustration).
26 With the torque applied to the tensioner pulley, install the tensioner assembly. Move the tensioner up against the tensioner pulley bracket and tighten the mounting bolts to the torque listed in this Chapter's Specifications. Remove the torque wrench and special tool from the tensioner pulley.
27 Remove the Allen wrench or drill bit retaining the piston from the tensioner. The timing belt tension is correct when the tensioner piston retaining pin (Allen wrench or drill bit) can be withdrawn and reinserted easily (see illustration). Verify that the timing marks on the camshaft sprockets and crankshaft sprocket are still aligned with their respective timing marks (see illustrations 7.11a and 7.11b).

28 Using the bolt in the center of the crankshaft sprocket, slowly turn the crankshaft clockwise two complete revolutions. **Caution:** *If you feel strong resistance while turning the crankshaft - STOP, the valves may be hitting the pistons from incorrect valve timing. Stop and re-check the valve timing.* **Note:** *The camshafts and crankshaft sprocket marks will align every two revolutions of the crankshaft.* Recheck the alignment of the timing marks (see illustrations 7.11a and 7.11b). If the marks do not align properly, remove the timing belt tensioner, slip the belt off the camshaft sprockets, realign the marks, reinstall the belt and tensioner, then check the alignment again.
29 After crankshaft rotation, recheck the timing belt tension by inserting the tensioner piston retaining pin (Allen wrench or drill bit) back into the tensioner. If the retaining pin cannot be inserted and withdrawn freely, readjust the timing belt tension and repeat Steps 24 through 29.

30 The remaining installation steps are the reverse of removal. Tighten the crankshaft damper/pulley bolt to the torque listed in this Chapter's Specifications.

8 Crankshaft front oil seal - replacement

Refer to illustrations 8.2, 8.3 and 8.5
Caution: *Do not rotate the camshafts or crankshaft when the timing belt is removed or damage to the engine may occur.*
1 Remove the timing belt (see Section 7).
2 Remove the crankshaft timing belt sprocket using a gear puller. Remove the Woodruff key from the crankshaft keyway (see illustration).
3 Wrap the tip of a small screwdriver with vinyl tape. Carefully use the screwdriver to pry the seal out of its bore (see illustration). Take care to prevent damaging the oil pump

7.27 If the timing belt tension is set correctly, the tensioner piston retaining pin (arrow) (an Allen wrench in this case) can be removed and installed easily

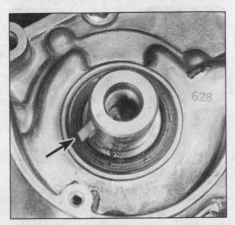

8.2 After removing the timing belt sprocket, remove the Woodruff key (arrow) from the crankshaft

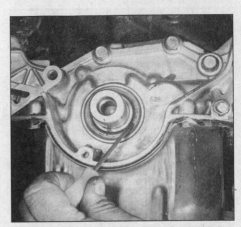

8.3 Using a hooked tool or screwdriver, carefully pry the crankshaft front seal out of its bore - DO NOT nick or scratch the crankshaft or seal bore

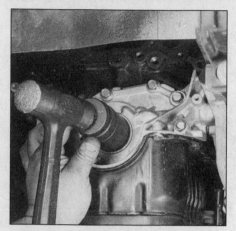

8.5 Lubricate the new seal with clean engine oil and drive it into place using a hammer and socket

9.3 Pad the sprocket with an old piece of timing belt and hold it with a chain wrench while removing the sprocket bolt

9.4 Using a hooked tool or screwdriver, carefully pry the camshaft seal out of the bore - DO NOT nick or scratch the camshaft or seal bore

assembly, the crankshaft and the seal bore.

4   Thoroughly clean and inspect the seal bore and sealing surface on the crankshaft. Minor imperfections can be removed with fine emery cloth. If there is a groove worn in the crankshaft sealing surface (from contact with the seal), installing a new seal will probably not stop the leak.

5   Lubricate the new seal with engine oil. Using a hammer and the appropriate size socket, drive the seal into the bore until it's flush with the oil pump housing (**see illustration**).

6   Install the Woodruff key into the slot in the crankshaft. Place the crankshaft timing belt sprocket onto the crankshaft with the timing belt retaining lip facing inward (toward the engine).

7   The remaining installation steps are the reverse of removal. Tighten the crankshaft pulley bolt to the torque listed in this Chapter's Specifications.

8   Start the engine and check for oil leaks.

---

9   Camshaft oil seal - replacement

Refer to illustrations 9.3, 9.4, 9.6a and 9.6b
Caution: *Do not rotate the camshafts or crankshaft when the timing belt is removed or damage to the engine may occur.*

1   Remove the timing belt (see Section 7).

2   Rotate the crankshaft counterclockwise until the crankshaft sprocket is three notches BTDC. This will prevent engine damage if the camshaft sprocket is inadvertently rotated during removal.

3   While keeping the camshaft from rotating, remove the camshaft sprocket bolt. Then using two large screwdrivers, lever the sprocket off the camshaft. **Note:** *A strap-type damper/pulley holder tool is available at most auto parts stores and is recommended for this procedure. However, if you are not going to reuse the old timing belt, you can wrap a piece of it around the sprocket and use a chain wrench to hold the sprocket in place as shown* (**see illustration**).

4   Carefully pry out the camshaft oil seal using a small hooked tool or screwdriver (**see illustration**). Don't scratch the bore or damage the camshaft in the process (if the camshaft is damaged, the new seal will end up leaking).

5   Clean the bore and coat the outer edge of the new seal with engine oil or multi-purpose grease. Also lubricate the seal lip.

6   Using a socket with an outside diameter slightly smaller than the outside diameter of the seal and a hammer (**see illustration**), carefully drive the new seal into the cylinder head until it's flush with the face of the cylinder head. If a socket isn't available, a short section of pipe will also work. **Note:** *If engine location makes it difficult to use a hammer to install the camshaft seal, fabricate a seal installation tool from a piece of pipe cut to the appropriate length, a bolt and a large washer* (**see illustration**). *Place the section of pipe over the seal and thread the bolt into the camshaft. The seal can now be pressed into the bore by tightening the bolt.*

7   Install the camshaft sprocket, aligning the pin in the camshaft with the hole in the

sprocket. Using an appropriate tool to hold the camshaft sprocket, tighten the camshaft sprocket bolt to the torque listed in this Chapter's Specifications.

8   Install the timing belt (see Section 7).

9   Run the engine and check for oil leaks.

---

10   Rocker arm and hydraulic valve lash adjuster assembly - removal, inspection and installation

Removal

1   Disconnect the negative battery cable from the battery.

2   Position the number one piston at Top Dead Center (see Section 3).

3   Remove the valve cover(s) as required (see Section 4).

4   Prior to removing the rocker arm shafts, identify each rocker arm and shaft as to its proper location (cylinder number and intake or exhaust). **Caution:** *Do not interchange the rocker arms onto a different shaft or shaft*

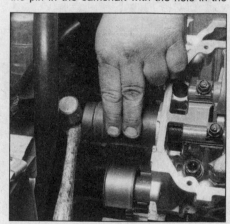

9.6a Using a hammer and the appropriate size socket, drive the camshaft seal into the bore until it is flush with the cylinder head

9.6b If the space is too confined to tap the seal into place, fabricate a tool using a bolt, washer and section of pipe. Place the section of pipe over the seal and thread the bolt into the camshaft to press the seal into the bore

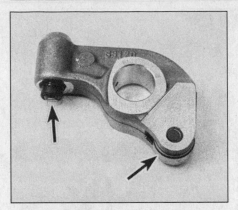

10.8 Visually inspect the hydraulic lash adjuster and roller (arrows) for damage and excessive play - check the rocker arm shaft bore for score marks or excessive wear

assemblies onto a different location as this could lead to premature wear.

5   Loosen the rocker arm shaft bolts 1/4-turn at a time, until they can be loosened by hand, in the *reverse* order of the tightening sequence **(see illustration 10.17)**. Completely loosen the bolts, but do not remove them, leaving them in place will prevent the assembly from falling apart when it is lifted off the cylinder head.

6   Lift the rocker arms and shaft assemblies from the cylinder head and set them on the workbench. **Note:** *The hydraulic valve lash adjusters may become dislodged from the rocker arms during shaft removal. If required, secure the adjusters in place with vinyl tape.*

7   Disassemble the rocker arm shaft components paying close attention to their positions. **Note:** *To keep the rocker arms and related parts in order, it's a good idea to remove them and put them onto two lengths of wire (such as unbent coat hangers) in the same order as they're removed, marking each wire (which simulates the rocker shaft) as to which end would be the front of the engine.*

Inspection

Refer to illustration 10.8

Note: *The valve lash adjuster is an integral part of each rocker arm and cannot be replaced separately. If defective, both must be replaced.*

8   Visually check the rocker arms for excessive wear or damage **(see illustration)**. Replace them if evidence of wear or damage is found.

9   Inspect each lash adjuster carefully for signs of wear and damage, particularly on the surface that contacts the valve tip. Use a small diameter wire to check the oil holes for restrictions.

10   Since the lash adjusters frequently become clogged, we recommend replacing the rocker arm/lash adjuster assembly if you're concerned about their condition or if the engine is exhibiting valve "tapping" noises.

11   Inspect all rocker arm shaft components. Look for cracks, worn or scored surfaces or other damage. Replace any parts found to be damaged or worn excessively.

Installation

Refer to illustrations 10.14 and 10.17

12   Prior to installation, the lash adjusters must be partially full of engine oil - indicated by little or no plunger action when the adjuster is depressed. If there's excessive plunger travel, place the rocker arm assembly into clean engine oil and pump the plunger until the plunger travel is eliminated. **Note:** *If the plunger still travels within the rocker arm when full of oil, it's defective and the rocker arm assembly must be replaced.*

13   Install the rocker arms (and springs - intake shafts only) onto the shafts, making sure they are reinstalled in their original locations.

14   On the intake rocker arm shafts, make sure that the springs are installed on the shaft in the correct locations **(see illustration)**.

15   On the right (rear) cylinder head, install the rocker arm assemblies with the flat at the

end of each rocker arm shaft located at the timing belt end of the engine and positioned toward their respective valves.

16   On the left (front) cylinder head, install the rocker arm assemblies with the flat at the end of each rocker arm shaft located at the transaxle end of the engine and positioned toward their respective valves.

17   Tighten the rocker arm shaft bolts in sequence shown **(see illustration)** in three steps to the torque listed in this Chapter's Specifications.

18   The remaining installation steps are the reverse of removal. Run the engine and check for oil leaks and proper operation.

19   When re-starting the engine after replacing the rocker arm/lash adjusters, the adjusters will normally make "tapping" noises due to air in the lubrication system. To bleed air from the lash adjusters, start the engine and allow it to reach operating temperature, slowly raise the speed of the engine from idle to 3,000 rpm and back to idle over a one minute period. If, after several attempts, the adjuster(s) do not become silent, replace the defective rocker arm/lash adjuster assembly.

11   Camshafts - removal, inspection and installation

Note: *The camshaft(s) cannot be removed with the cylinder head(s) installed on the engine.*

Removal

Refer to illustration 11.5

1   Remove the rocker arm shaft assemblies (see Section 10).

2   If you are removing the camshaft in the right (rear) cylinder head, remove the distributor (see Chapter 5).

3   Remove the cylinder head (see Section 13).

4   On the right cylinder head, carefully withdraw the camshaft from the distributor opening in the rear of the cylinder head. **Caution:** *Do not damage the camshaft lobes or bear-*

10.14 The intake rocker arm shaft springs (arrows) must be installed as shown

10.17 Rocker arm shaft bolt TIGHTENING sequence

11.5 On the left (front) cylinder head, remove the thrust cover and carefully withdraw the camshaft

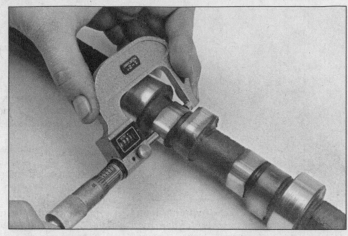

11.10 Check the camshaft lobes for wear with a micrometer

ing journals during removal. **Note:** *If you are removing both camshafts, identify each one as it is removed from the cylinder head so that it may be installed back in it's original location.*

5   On the left (front) cylinder head, remove the thrust case from the rear of the cylinder head and withdraw the camshaft **(see illustration)**. **Caution:** *Do not damage the camshaft lobes or bearing journals during removal.*

6   Remove the camshaft seal(s) from the cylinder head(s) (see Section 9 if necessary).

Inspection

Refer to illustration 11.10

7   Using a suitable scraper, remove all traces of gasket material from all gasket surfaces. **Caution:** *When removing gasket material from any surface, especially aluminum, be very careful not to scratch or gouge the gasket surface. Any damage to the surface may a leak after reassembly. Gasket removal solvents are available from auto parts stores and may prove helpful.*

8   Thoroughly clean the camshaft(s) with a rag soaked in lacquer thinner or acetone. Visually inspect the camshaft(s) for wear and/or damage to the lobe surfaces, bearing journals and seal contact surfaces. Visually inspect the camshaft bearing surfaces in the cylinder head(s) for scoring and other damage. Cylinder head replacement may be necessary if the camshaft bearing surfaces in the head are damaged or excessively worn.

9   Replace any component that fails the above inspections.

10   Using a micrometer, check the camshaft lobes for excessive wear by measuring the center of the lobe (the area the rocker arm roller rides on) and comparing it with the edges of the lobes (the area the rocker arm roller does not ride on) **(see illustration)**. If any wear is indicated, check the corresponding rocker arm, replace the camshaft and rocker arms if necessary.

Camshaft endplay measurement

Refer to illustration 11.13

11   Lubricate the camshaft(s) and cylinder head bearing journals with clean engine oil.

12   Carefully insert the camshaft into the cylinder head and install the thrust case or distributor as applicable. Tighten the bolts to the torque listed in this Chapter's Specifications.

13   Install a dial indicator set up on the cyl-

inder head and place the indicator tip on the camshaft at the sprocket end **(see illustration)**.

14   Using a screwdriver, carefully pry the camshaft to the rear of the cylinder head until it stops. Zero the dial indicator and pry the camshaft forward. The amount of indicator travel is the camshaft endplay. Compare the endplay measurement with the tolerance listed in this Chapter's Specifications. If the endplay is excessive, check the camshaft and cylinder head thrust bearing surfaces for wear and replace components as necessary.

Installation

Refer to illustration 11.15

15   Very carefully clean the camshaft and bearing journals. Liberally coat the bearing journals, lobes and thrust bearing surfaces of the camshaft with engine assembly lube or engine oil **(see illustration)**.

16   Carefully insert the camshaft into the cylinder head. On the left side cylinder head, install the thrust case, using a new O-ring, and tighten the bolts to the torque listed in this Chapter's Specifications.

17   Install a new camshaft oil seal in the cyl-

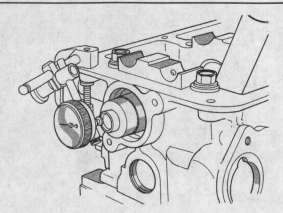

11.13 Measure the camshaft endplay with a dial indicator positioned on the sprocket end of the camshaft as shown

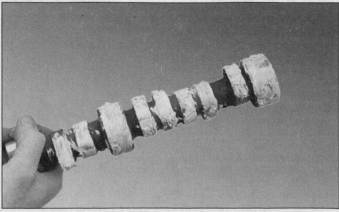

11.15 Prior to installing the camshaft, lubricate the bearing journals, thrust surfaces and lobes with engine assembly lube or clean engine oil

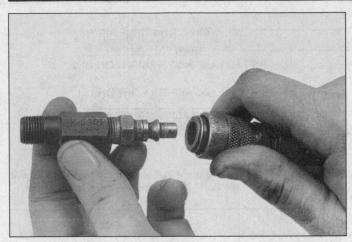

12.5 This is what the air hose adapter that threads into the spark plug hole looks like - they're readily available from auto parts stores

12.7 Use a small magnet (shown) or needle-nose pliers to remove the valve spring keepers - be careful not to drop them down into the engine!

inder head (see Section 9).

18   Inspect the cylinder head bolts and install the cylinder head(s) (see Section 12). Torque the cylinder head bolts as described in Section 13.

19   If removed, install the distributor using a new O-ring (see Chapter 5). Tighten the mounting nuts to the torque listed in the Chapter 5 Specifications.

20   The remaining installation steps are the reverse of removal. Start the engine and check for leaks and proper operation.

12   Valve springs, retainers and seals - replacement

Refer to illustrations 12.5, 12.7, 12.8, 12.13 and 12.15

Note: *Broken valve springs and defective valve stem seals can be replaced without removing the cylinder heads. Two special tools and a compressed air source are normally required to perform this operation, so read through this Section carefully and rent or buy the tools before beginning the job.*

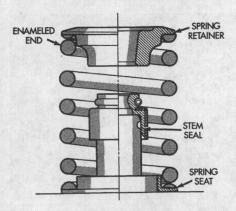

12.8 Cut-away view of the valve seal and spring components

1   Remove the appropriate valve cover (see Section 4).

2   Remove the rocker arm assemblies (see Section 10).

3   Remove the spark plugs from the cylinder head you're working on (see Chapter 1 if necessary).

4   Turn the crankshaft until the piston in the affected cylinder is at Top Dead Center on the compression stroke (see Section 3). If you're replacing all of the valve stem seals, begin with cylinder number one and work on the valves for one cylinder at a time. Move from cylinder-to-cylinder following the firing order sequence (see this Chapter's Specifications).

5   Thread an adapter into the spark plug hole **(see illustration)** and connect an air hose from a compressed air source to it. Most auto parts stores can supply the air hose adapter. **Note:** *Many cylinder compression gauges utilize a screw-in fitting that may work with your air hose quick-disconnect fitting.*

6   Apply compressed air to the cylinder. **Warning:** *The piston may be forced down by compressed air, causing the crankshaft to turn suddenly. If the wrench used when positioning the number one piston at TDC is still attached to the crankshaft pulley bolt, it could cause damage or injury when the crankshaft moves.*

7   Stuff clean shop rags into the cylinder head holes above and below the valves to prevent parts and tools from falling into the engine, then use a valve spring compressor tool to compress the spring. Remove the keepers with small needle-nose pliers or a magnet **(see illustration)**.

8   Remove the spring retainer and valve spring. Next, using pliers, remove the valve guide seal and lift off the spring seat **(see illustration). Caution:** *If air pressure fails to hold the valve in the closed position during this operation, the valve face and/or seat is probably damaged. If so, the cylinder head will have to be removed for additional repair operations.*

9   Wrap a rubber band or tape around the top of the valve stem so the valve won't fall into the combustion chamber, then release the air pressure.

10   Inspect the valve stem for damage. Rotate the valve in the guide and check the end for eccentric movement, which would indicate that the valve is bent.

11   Move the valve up-and-down in the guide and make sure it doesn't bind. If the valve stem binds, either the valve is bent or the guide is damaged. In either case, the head will have to be removed for repair.

12   Pull up on the valve stem to close the valve, reapply air pressure to the cylinder to retain the valve in the closed position, then remove the tape or rubber band from the valve stem.

13   Install the valve spring seat. Lubricate the valve stem with clean engine oil and place the new valve guide seal. Tap it into place with a deep socket **(see illustration)**.

14   Install the spring in position over the valve.

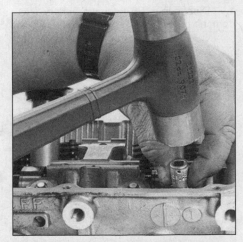

12.13 Gently tap the new seal onto the valve guide with a hammer and deep socket

12.15 Apply a small dab of grease to each keeper before installation to hold it in place on the valve stem until the spring is released

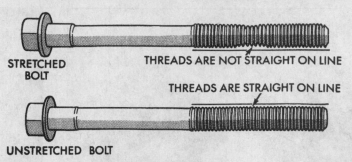

13.16 Place a precision straightedge along the cylinder head bolt thread profile - if any of the threads don't touch the straightedge, the bolt is stretched and must be replaced

15   Install the valve spring retainer. Compress the valve spring and carefully position the keepers in the groove. Apply a small dab of grease to the inside of each keeper to hold it in place if necessary **(see illustration)**.

16   Remove the pressure from the spring tool and make sure the keepers are seated.

17   Disconnect the air hose and remove the adapter from the spark plug hole. Repeat the procedure for any other defective valves.

18   Install the rocker arm assemblies (see Section 10).

19   Install the spark plug and connect the wire(s).

20   Install the valve cover (see Section 4).

21   Start and run the engine, then check for oil leaks and unusual sounds coming from the valve cover area.

13 Cylinder head - removal and installation

Caution: *Allow the engine to cool completely before beginning this procedure.*

Removal

Refer to illustrations 13.16, 13.17a and 13.17b

1   Disconnect the negative battery cable from the battery.

2   Position the number one piston at Top Dead Center (see Section 3).

3   Remove the timing belt (see Section 7).

4   Remove camshaft sprocket(s) (see Section 11).

5   Remove the alternator and bracket (see Chapter 5).

6   Remove the upper and lower intake manifolds (see Section 5).

7   Drain the cooling system, remove the spark plugs and spark plug wires (see Chapter 1). **Note:** *Leave the plug wires attached to the distributor cap.*

8   If you are removing the right (rear) cylinder head, remove the distributor (see Chapter 5).

9   Remove the thermostat housing from the rear of the cylinder heads (see Chapter 3).

10   Remove rocker arm shaft assemblies (see Section 10).

11   Remove the exhaust manifold(s) (see Section 6).

12   Clearly label and disconnect any hoses, lines, brackets or electrical connections that may interfere with cylinder head removal.

13   Loosen the cylinder head bolts, 1/4-turn at a time, in the *reverse* order of the tightening sequence **(see illustration 13.22)** until they can be removed by hand.

14   Carefully lift the cylinder head straight up and place it on wood blocks to prevent damage to the sealing surfaces. If the head sticks to the engine block, dislodge it by placing a

wood block against the head casting and tapping the wood with a hammer or by prying the head with a prybar placed carefully on a casting protrusion. **Note:** *If further disassembly of the cylinder head is required, refer to Part E of this Chapter.*

15   Remove all traces of old gasket material from the block and head. Special gasket removal solvents that soften gaskets and make removal much easier are available at auto parts stores. **Caution:** *The cylinder head is aluminum, be very careful not to gouge the sealing surfaces.* When working on the block, place clean shop rags into the cylinders to help keep out debris. Use a vacuum to remove any contamination from the engine. Use a tap of the correct size to chase the threads in the engine block. Clean and inspect all threaded fasteners for damage.

16   Inspect the cylinder head bolt threads for "necking," where the diameter of threads narrow due to bolt stretching **(see illustration)**. If any cylinder head bolt exhibits damage or necking, it must be replaced.

17   Using a precision straightedge and feeler gauge, check all gasket surfaces for warpage **(see illustrations)**. If the warpage on any surface exceeds the limits listed in this Chapter's Specifications, the discrepant component must be replaced or resurfaced by an automotive machine shop.

18   Refer to Part E of this Chapter for cleaning and inspection of the cylinder head.

13.17a Checking the cylinder head-to-engine block gasket surface for warpage

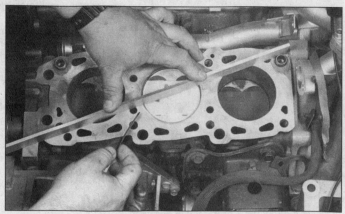

13.17b Checking the engine block head gasket surface for warpage

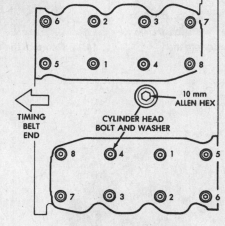

13.20 When installing the head gasket onto the block, make sure all passages in the block align with the holes in the gasket

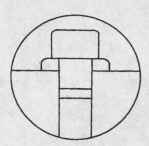

13.21 Install the head bolt washers with the chamfered side facing up

Installation

Refer to illustrations 13.20, 13.21 and 13.22

19   Install the camshaft(s) if removed (see Section 11).

20   Place a new gasket on the engine block **(see illustration)**. Use no sealer unless indicated by the gasket manufacturer. Note any directions printed on the gasket such as "Front" or "This side up." Place the cylinder head(s) in position on the engine block.

21   Install the washers onto the cylinder head bolts as shown **(see illustration)**. Apply clean engine oil to the cylinder head bolt threads and install them into the cylinder head.

22   Tighten the cylinder head bolts in the sequence shown **(see illustration)** progressing in three stages to the torque listed in this Chapter's Specifications.

23   The remaining installation steps are the reverse of removal.

24   Refill the cooling system and check all fluid levels (see Chapter 1 if necessary).

25   Start the engine and let it run until normal operating temperature is reached. Check for leaks and proper operation.

---

14   Oil pan - removal and installation

Removal

Refer to illustrations 14.5, 14.8, 14.9a, 14.9b, 14.11, 14.12a and 14.12b

1   Disconnect the negative battery cable

13.22 Cylinder head bolt TIGHTENING sequence

14.5 Engine oil dipstick tube mounting bolt (arrow) - exhaust manifold heat shield removed for clarity

from the battery.

2   Raise the vehicle and support it securely on jackstands.

3   Remove the accessory drivebelt splash shield.

4   Drain the engine oil (see Chapter 1).

5   Remove the dipstick tube **(see illustration)**.

6   Remove the starter motor (see Chapter 5).

7   Remove the front exhaust pipe (see Chapter 4).

8   Remove the mounting bolts and separate the lower sump from the main oil pan **(see illustration)**. If the sump is stuck, tap it with a soft-face hammer or place a wood block against the pan and tap the wood block with a hammer. **Caution:** *If you're wedging something between the sump and main oil pan to separate them, be extremely careful not to gouge or nick the gasket surface of either part; an oil leak could result.*

9   Remove the mounting bolts and separate the main oil pan from the engine block

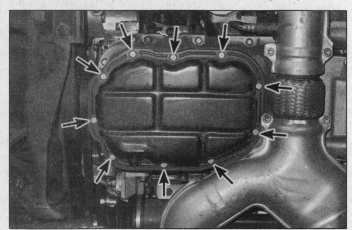

14.8 Unbolt the oil pan lower sump from the main oil pan

14.9a Here are some of the upper oil pan bolts (arrows); tighten them in the sequence shown during installation

14.9b Some of the upper oil pan bolts thread into the transaxle (arrows)

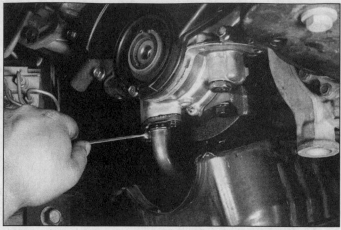

14.11 Remove the oil pump pick-up tube from the pump body

14.12a Thoroughly clean the oil pan and engine block gasket surfaces with a scraper to remove all traces of old gasket material

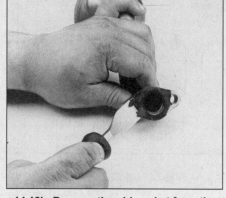

14.12b Remove the old gasket from the oil pump pick-up tube

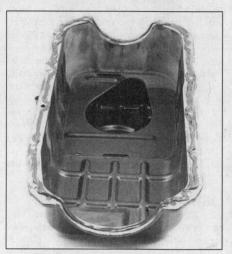

14.15 Apply a 1/8-inch bead of RTV sealant to the oil pan sealing surface as shown - stay on the inside of the bolt holes

and transaxle **(see illustrations)**. If it's stuck, screw a pair of bolts into the removal holes, located next to the two rear bolt holes. Tighten the bolts evenly to break the gasket seal, then remove the oil pan from the vehicle.

10   Unbolt the lower oil pan baffle from the main oil pan and take it out.

11   Remove the oil pump pickup tube and screen assembly from the engine **(see illustration)**.

12   Thoroughly clean all gasket sealing surfaces. Use a scraper to remove all traces of old gasket material **(see illustrations)**. Gasket removal solvents are available at auto parts stores and may prove helpful. Check the oil pan sealing surface for distortion. Straighten or replace as necessary. After cleaning and straightening (if necessary), wipe the gasket surfaces of the pan and block clean with a rag soaked in lacquer thinner or acetone.

Installation

Refer to illustration 14.15

13   If you removed the lower baffle from the main oil pan, install it and tighten its bolts to the torque listed in this Chapter's Specifications.

14   Install the oil pump pick-up tube, using a new gasket. Tighten the bolts to the torque listed in this Chapter's Specifications.

15   Apply a 1/8-inch bead of RTV sealant to the oil pan as shown **(see illustration)**. Also apply a light coating of RTV sealant to the underside of the oil pan bolt heads.

16   Place the oil pan into position under the engine block and install the bolts finger-tight. **Caution:** *The holes for the two bolts closest to the transaxle are cut away on the transaxle side, which makes it possible to insert them at an angle (leaning towards the transaxle). Be sure NOT to do this; instead, insert the bolts straight up.* Working from the center and proceeding outward in a criss-cross pattern, tighten the oil pan bolts to the torque listed in this Chapter's Specifications.

17   Apply sealant to the gasket surface of the sump. Place the sump into position under the oil pan and install the bolts finger-tight. Working from the center and proceeding outward in a criss-cross pattern, tighten the sump bolts to the torque listed in this Chapter's Specifications.

18   The remaining installation steps are the reverse of removal.

19   Lower the vehicle and fill the crankcase with the proper quantity and grade of engine oil (see *Recommended lubricants and fluids* at the beginning of Chapter 1) and run the engine, checking for leaks. Road test the vehicle and check for leaks again.

15   Oil pump - removal, inspection and installation

Removal

Refer to illustrations 15.7, 15.8, 15.9 and 15.10

1   Disconnect the negative battery cable from the battery.

2   Raise the vehicle and support it securely on jackstands.

3   Remove the drivebelts (see Chapter 1).

4   Remove the timing belt (see Section 7), crankshaft sprocket and Woodruff key (see Section 8).

5   Remove the oil pan (see Section 14).

6   If equipped, remove the air conditioning

15.7 Remove the oil pump mounting bolts (arrows) and detach the pump from the engine - bolt (A) also secures the air conditioning compressor bracket (if equipped)

15.8 The oil filter passage O-ring seals (arrows) may remain attached to the engine block

15.9 Remove the rotor cover mounting screws (arrows)

15.10 The alignment mark has worn off the inner rotor on this oil pump; in this case we'll use a permanent marker to match-mark the rotors for reinstallation - oil pressure relief cap bolt (A)

compressor bracket from the engine and position it out of the way.

7   Remove the bolts and detach the oil pump from the engine **(see illustration)**. **Caution:** *If the pump doesn't come off by hand, tap it gently with a soft-faced hammer or pry on a casting boss.*

8   Remove the oil filter passage O-ring seals and discard them. They may stick to the engine block as shown **(see illustration)** or remain in the oil pump housing.

9   Remove the oil pump rotor cover **(see illustration)**.

10   New rotors are manufactured with arrows on them which are aligned at installation. If both arrows are not clearly visible **(see illustration)**, use a permanent marker to match-mark the rotors so they can be installed back in their original position. Remove the inner and outer rotor from the body. **Caution:** *Be very careful with these components. Close tolerances are critical in creating the correct oil pressure. Any nicks or other damage will require replacement of the complete pump assembly.*

11   Using a hammer and drift, carefully and evenly drive the crankshaft front seal from the

oil pump housing and discard it.

12   Disassemble the oil pressure relief valve assembly, taking note of the way the relief valve piston is installed. Unscrew the cap bolt and remove the bolt, washer, spring and relief valve **(see illustration 15.10)**.

13   Thoroughly clean all gasket sealing surfaces. Use a scraper to remove all traces of old gasket material. Gasket removal solvents are available at auto parts stores and may prove helpful. Check the oil pan sealing surface for distortion. Straighten or replace as necessary. After removing the residual gasket material, wipe the gasket surfaces of the oil pan and block clean with a rag soaked in lacquer thinner or acetone.

Inspection

Refer to illustrations 15.16a, 15.16b, 15.16c and 15.16d

14   Clean all oil pump components with solvent and inspect them for excessive wear and/or damage. Replace as required. **Note:** *If either rotor is damaged, they must be replaced as a set.*

15   Inspect the oil pressure relief valve pis-

ton sliding surface and valve spring for damage. **Note:** *If either the spring or the valve is damaged, they must be replaced as a set.*

16   Install the rotors into the pump housing with the match-marks aligned **(see illustration)**. Check the oil pump rotor clearances using a precision straightedge and feeler

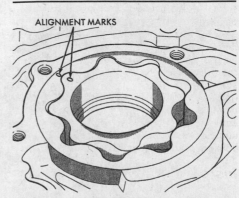

15.16a Install the rotors into the oil pump body with the match marks aligned

15.16b Use a feeler gauge to measure the inner rotor-to-outer rotor lobe clearance

15.16c Measuring the outer rotor-to-pump body clearance

15.16d Place a precision straightedge over the rotors and measure the clearance between the rotors and the straightedge to determine the rotor-to-cover clearance

gauges **(see illustrations)**. Compare the results to the tolerances listed in this Chapter's Specifications. Replace both rotors if any clearance is out of tolerance.

Installation

Refer to illustration 15.19

17   Lubricate the relief valve piston, piston bore and spring with clean engine oil. Install the relief valve piston into the bore maintaining original orientation followed by the spring and cap bolt. Tighten the cap bolt to the torque listed in this Chapter's Specifications. **Caution:** *If the relief valve piston is installed incorrectly, serious engine damage could occur.*

18   Lubricate the oil pump rotor recess in the housing and the inner and outer rotors with clean engine oil. Install the rotors into the pump housing with the match-marks aligned **(see illustration 15.16a)**. Next, fill the rotor cavity with clean engine oil and install the cover. Tighten the cover screws to the torque listed in this Chapter's Specifications.

19   Install new O-ring seals in the oil pump passages located on the pump body **(see illustration)**. If necessary, apply a light coating of grease on the O-rings to hold them in place.

20   Install the new crankshaft front seal into the oil pump housing (see Section 8).

21   Apply a 1/8 inch bead of anaerobic sealant to the oil pump body sealing surface, and position the pump assembly on the block aligning the inner rotor and crankshaft drive flats. Install the mounting bolts.

22   If equipped, install the air conditioning bracket onto the engine (one bolt secures both the air conditioning bracket and the oil pump housing).

23   Tighten the oil pump attaching bolts **(see illustration 15.7)** to the torque listed in this Chapter's Specifications.

24   Install the Woodruff key, crankshaft timing belt sprocket (see Section 8) and timing belt (see Section 7).

25   Install the oil pan (see Section 14).

26   If applicable, install a new oil filter (see Chapter 1).

27   The remaining installation steps are the reverse of removal.

28   Lower the vehicle and fill the crankcase with the proper quantity and grade of oil (see *Recommended lubricants and fluids* in Chapter 1).

29   Connect the negative battery cable to the battery.

30   After the sealant has cured per the manufacturer's directions, start the engine and check for leaks.

16   Flywheel/driveplate - removal and installation

Removal

Refer to illustration 16.5

1   Raise the vehicle and support it securely on jackstands.

2   Remove the transaxle assembly (see Chapter 7).

3   To ensure correct alignment during reinstallation, match-mark the backing plate and driveplate to the crankshaft before removal.

4   Remove the bolts securing the driveplate to the crankshaft. A tool is available at most auto parts stores to hold the driveplate while loosening the bolts, if the tool is not available, wedge a screwdriver in the ring gear teeth to jam the driveplate.

5   If you're working on a manual transaxle model, remove the two adapter plates that go under the bolts heads. If you're working on an automatic transaxle model, remove the single adapter plate. Remove the flywheel/driveplate from the crankshaft **(see illustration)**.

15.19 Install new O-ring seals on the oil filter passages (arrows)

16.5 Remove the flywheel/driveplate from the crankshaft

17.3 Carefully pry the crankshaft seal out of the bore - DO NOT nick or scratch the crankshaft or seal bore

17.6 With the seal retainer supported on wood blocks, use a hammer and drift to drive the seal out of the retainer

6   Clean the driveplate to remove any grease and oil. Inspect it for cracks, distortion and missing or excessively worn ring gear teeth. Replace if necessary.

7   Clean and inspect the mating surfaces of the driveplate and the crankshaft. Check the crankshaft rear main seal for leakage; if leakage is evident, replace it before reinstalling the driveplate (see Section 16).

Installation

8   Position the flywheel/driveplate and adapter plate(s) on the crankshaft. Align the previously applied match marks. Before installing the bolts, apply thread locking compound to the threads.

9   Hold the flywheel/driveplate with the special holding tool, or wedge a screwdriver in the ring gear teeth to keep the flywheel/driveplate from turning as you tighten the bolts to the torque listed in this Chapter's Specifications.

10   The remaining installation steps are the reverse of removal.

17   Rear main oil seal - replacement

Refer to illustrations 17.3, 17.6 and 17.12

1   The crankshaft rear main oil seal is pressed into a retainer and bolted to the rear of the engine block.

2   Remove the driveplate (see Section 16).

3   The crankshaft rear main oil seal can be renewed without removing the oil pan or seal retainer. However, this method is NOT recommended because the lip of the seal is quite stiff and it's possible to cock the seal in the retainer bore or damage it during installation. If you want to take the chance, carefully and evenly pry out the old seal using a 3/16 flat blade screwdriver - do not damage the crankshaft sealing surface **(see illustration)**. Apply a light coating of clean engine oil to the crankshaft seal journal and the lip of the new seal, then carefully tap the new seal into place using a hammer and socket. The seal lip is stiff, so carefully work it onto the seal journal

of the crankshaft with a smooth object like the rounded end of a socket extension as you tap the seal into place **(see illustration 17.12)**. Don't force it or you may damage the seal.

4   The following method is recommended and requires removal of the oil pan (see Section 14).

5   Remove the mounting bolts from the crankshaft rear seal retainer and separate the retainer from the engine block.

6   Using a hammer and drift, carefully drive the old seal out of the retainer and discard it **(see illustration)**.

7   Thoroughly clean all gasket sealing surfaces. Use a scraper to remove all traces of old gasket material. Gasket removal solvents are available at auto parts stores and may prove helpful. Check the oil pan sealing surface for distortion. Straighten or replace as necessary. After removing the residual gasket material, wipe the gasket surfaces clean using a rag soaked in lacquer thinner or acetone.

8   Thoroughly clean and inspect the seal bore and sealing surface on the crankshaft. Minor imperfections can be removed with fine emery cloth. If there is a groove worn in the crankshaft sealing surface (from contact with the seal), installing a new seal will probably not stop the leak.

9   Install the new seal into the retainer using a socket (or block of wood) and a hammer. Drive it in until it's flush with the retainer.

10   Apply a 1/8 inch bead of RTV sealant to the retainer gasket sealing surface.

11   Lubricate the lip of the new seal and the crankshaft sealing surface with a light coat of clean engine oil.

12   Place the seal retainer in position on the engine block and install the mounting bolts. The seal lip is stiff, so carefully work it onto the seal journal of the crankshaft with a smooth object like the rounded end of a socket extension as you tap the seal into place **(see illustration)**. Don't force it or you may damage the seal. Tighten the bolts to the torque listed in this Chapter's Specifications.

13   Install the oil pan (see Section 14).

17.12 Using a rounded object like a socket extension, carefully work the seal onto the crankshaft

14   The remaining installation steps are the reverse of removal.

18   Engine mounts - check and replacement

1   Engine mounts seldom require attention, but broken or deteriorated mounts should be replaced immediately or the added strain placed on the driveline components may cause damage or wear.

Check

2   During the check, the engine must be raised slightly to relieve the weight from the mounts.

3   Raise the vehicle and support it securely on jackstands, then position a jack under the engine oil pan. Place a large wood block between the jack head and the oil pan to prevent oil pan damage, then carefully raise the engine just enough to take the weight off the mounts. **Warning:** *DO NOT place any part of your body under the engine when it's supported only by a jack!*

18.9a 3.0L V6 front engine mount (arrow)

18.9b 3.0L V6 transaxle mount

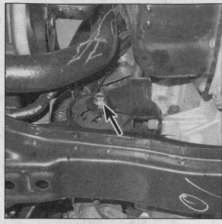

18.9c 3.0L V6 front roll stopper

4   Inspect the mounts to see if the rubber is cracked, hardened or separated from the metal backing. Sometimes the rubber will split right down the center.

5   Check for relative movement between the mount plates and the engine or frame (use a large screwdriver or pry bar to attempt to move the mounts). If movement is noted, lower the engine and tighten the mount fasteners.

6   Rubber preservative may be applied to the mounts to slow deterioration.

Replacement
Refer to illustrations 18.9a, 18.9b, 18.9c, 18.9d, 18.10a and 18.10b

7   Disconnect the negative battery cable from the ground stud on the left shock tower

(see Chapter 5, Section 1). Raise the vehicle and support it securely on jackstands.

8   Place a floor jack under the engine (with a wood block between the jack head and oil pan) and raise the engine slightly to relieve the weight from the mount to be replaced.

9   Remove the fasteners and detach the mount from the frame and engine **(see illustrations). Caution:** *Do not disconnect more than one mount at a time, except during engine/transaxle removal.*

10   Installation is the reverse of removal. Install the engine mount and transaxle mount stoppers with the arrow marks pointing in the proper direction **(see Illustrations)**. Install the front roll stopper with the small hole in its bracket toward the front of the vehicle. Use thread locking compound on the mount bolts and be sure to tighten them securely

18.9d 3.0L V6 rear roll stopper

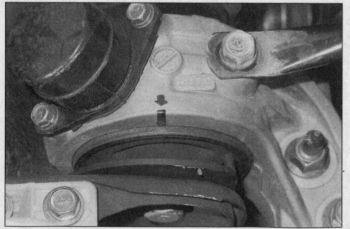

18.10a Position the engine mount stopper arrows in the direction shown to align the notches correctly

18.10b Position the transaxle mount stopper arrows in the direction shown to align the notches correctly

Chapter 2 Part E
General engine overhaul procedures

Contents

Specifications

General

Cylinder compression pressure (at 250 to 400 rpm)
- 2.0L non-turbo engine
  - Standard .... 170 to 225 psi
  - Service limit 100
  - Difference between cylinders .... 25 percent maximum
- 2.0L turbo engine
  - Standard .... 178 psi
  - Service limit .... 133 psi
  - Difference between cylinders .... 14 psi maximum
- 2.4L engine
  - Standard .... 185 psi
  - Service limit .... 139 psi
  - Difference between cylinders .... 14 psi maximum
- 3.0L engine
  - Standard .... 119 psi
  - Service limit .... 83 psi
  - Difference between cylinders .... 14 psi maximum

Oil pressure (2.4L and 3.0L engines)
- At idle .... 4 psi minimum
- At 3500 rpm .... 43 to 100

Cylinder head
Warpage limit .... 0.007 inch

Valves and related components
Face angle
- 2.0L non-turbo engine .... 44.5 to 45-degrees
- 2.0L turbo, 2.4L, 3.0L V6 engines .... 45.0 to 45.5-degrees
Seat angle 45-degrees
Seat width .... 0.035 to 0.051 inch
Valve length
- 2.0L non-turbo engine
  - Intake .... 4.389 to 4.409 inches
  - Exhaust .... 4.314 to 4.334 inches
- 2.0L turbo engine .... Not specified
- 2.4L four-cylinder, 3.0L V6 engines
  - Intake
    - Standard .... 4.421 inches
    - Service limit .... 4.402 inches

Valves and related components (continued)

2.4L four-cylinder, 3.0L V6 engines (continued)

   Exhaust

      Standard .... 4.493 inches

      Service limit .... 4.473 inches

Valve margin width limit

   2.0L non-turbo engine

      Intake

         Standard .... 0.050 to 0.063 inch

         Service limit .... 0.041 inch

      Exhaust

         Standard .... 0.038 to 0.050 inch

         Service limit .... 0.037 inch

   2.0L turbo engine

      Intake

         Standard .... 0.039 inch

         Service limit .... 0.019 inch

      Exhaust

         Standard .... 0.059 inch

         Service limit .... 0.039 inch

   2.4L engine

      Intake

         Standard .... 0.039 inch

         Service limit .... 0.019 inch

      Exhaust

         Standard .... 0.047 inch

         Service limit .... 0.027 inch

   3.0L engine

      Intake

         Standard .... 0.040 inch

         Service limit .... 0.020 inch

      Exhaust

         Standard .... 0.050 inch

         Service limit .... 0.030 inch

Valve stem diameter

   2.0L non-turbo engine

      Intake .... 0.233 to 0.234 inch

      Exhaust .... 0.232 to 0.233 inch

   2.0L turbo and 2.4L engines

      Intake .... 0.260 inch

      Exhaust .... 0.259 inch

   3.0L V6 engine (intake and exhaust) .... 0.24 inch

Valve stem-to-guide clearance

   2.0L non-turbo engine

      Intake

         Standard .... 0.0019 to 0.0026 inch

         Service limit .... 0.003 inch

      Exhaust

         Standard .... 0.0029 to 0.0037 inch

         Service limit .... 0.004 inch

   2.0L turbo engine

      Intake

         Standard .... 0.0008 to 0.0020 inch

         Service limit .... 0.004 inch

      Exhaust

         Standard .... 0.0020 to 0.0035 inch

         Service limit .... 0.006 inch

   2.4L four-cylinder and 3.0L V6 engines

      Intake

         Standard .... 0.0008 to 0.0019 inch

         Service limit .... 0.003 inch

      Exhaust

         Standard .... 0.0012 to 0.0027 inch

         Service limit .... 0.005 inch

Valve spring

   Out-of-square limit

      2.0L non-turbo engine .... 0.059 inch

      2.0L turbo, 2.4L four-cylinder and 3.0L V6 engines 4-degrees

Free length (intake and exhaust)
  2.0L non-turbo engine.. 1.811 inches
  2.0L turbo engine
    Standard... 1.85 inches
    Service limit... 1.81 inches
  2.4L four-cylinder and 3.0L V6 engines
    Standard... 2.00 inches
    Service limit... 1.97 inches
Installed height
  2.0L non-turbo engine.. 1.496 inches
  2.0L turbo engine... 1.57 inches
  2.4L four-cylinder and 3.0L V6 engines .... 1.74 inches
Load
  2.0L non-turbo engine.. 55 to 60 lbs at installed height
  2.0L turbo engine... 40 lbs at installed height
  2.4L four-cylinder and 3.0L V6 engines .... 44.2 lbs at installed height

Crankshaft and connecting rods

2.0L non-turbo engine
  Connecting rod journal
    Diameter .... 2.0075 to 2.0081 inches
    Out-of-round limit.. 0.0001 inch
    Taper limit .... 0.0001 inch
  Connecting rod bearing oil clearance
    Standard... 0.0010 to 0.0023 inch
    Service limit... 0.003 inch
  Connecting rod endplay (side clearance)
    Standard... 0.0051 to 0.0150 inch
    Service limit... 0.015 inch
  Crankshaft main bearing journal
    Diameter .... 2.0469 to 2.0475 inches
    Out-of-round limit.. 0.0001 inch
    Taper limit .... 0.0001 inch
  Crankshaft endplay .... 0.0035 to 0.0094 inch
  Crankshaft main bearing oil clearance... 0.0009 to 0.0024 inch
2.0L turbo engine
  Connecting rod journal
    Diameter .... 1.771 inches
    Out-of-round limit.. Not specified
    Taper limit .... Not specified
  Connecting rod bearing oil clearance
    Standard... 0.0008 to 0.0020 inch
    Service limit... 0.004 inch
  Connecting rod endplay (side clearance)
    Standard... 0.0039 to 0.0098 inch
    Service limit... 0.015 inch
  Crankshaft main bearing journal
    Diameter .... 2.244 inches
    Out-of-round limit.. Not specified
    Taper limit .... Not specified
  Crankshaft endplay .... 0.0020 to 0.0071 inch
  Crankshaft main bearing oil clearance
    Standard... 0.0008 to 0.0016 inch
    Limit.. 0.004 inch
2.4L engine
  Connecting rod journal
    Diameter .... 1.771 inches
    Out-of-round limit.. Not specified
    Taper limit .... Not specified
  Connecting rod bearing oil clearance
    Standard... 0.0008 to 0.0019 inch
    Service limit... 0.003 inch
  Connecting rod endplay (side clearance)
    Standard... 0.0039 to 0.0098 inch
    Service limit... 0.015 inch
  Crankshaft main bearing journal
    Diameter .... 2.244 inches
    Out-of-round limit.. Not specified
    Taper limit .... Not specified

Crankshaft and connecting rods (continued)

2.4L engine (continued)
  Crankshaft endplay
    Standard .... 0.002 to 0.009 inch
    Service limit .... 0.015 inch
  Crankshaft main bearing oil clearance
    Standard .... 0.0008 to 0.0015 inch
    Limit .... 0.003 inch

3.0L V6 engine
  Connecting rod journal
    Diameter .... 1.968 inches
    Out-of-round limit .... Not specified
    Taper limit .... Not specified
  Connecting rod bearing oil clearance
    Standard .... 0.0008 to 0.0019 inch
    Service limit .... 0.003 inch
  Connecting rod endplay (side clearance)
    Standard .... 0.0039 to 0.0098 inch
    Service limit .... 0.02 inch
  Crankshaft main bearing journal
    Diameter .... 2.362 inches
    Out-of-round limit .... Not specified
    Taper limit .... Not specified
  Crankshaft endplay
    Standard .... 0.002 to 0.009 inch
    Service limit .... 0.015 inch
  Crankshaft main bearing oil clearance
    Standard .... 0.0008 to 0.0015 inch
    Limit .... 0.003 inch

Engine block

Cylinder bore diameter
  2.0L non-turbo engine .... 3.4446 to 3.4452 inches
  2.0L turbo engine .... 3.346 inches
  2.4L engine .... 3.405 inches
  3.0L V6 engine .... 3.586 inches
Stroke
  2.0L non-turbo engine .... 3.267 inches
  2.0L turbo engine .... 3.46 inches
  2.4L engine .... 3.94 inches
  3.0L V6 engine .... 2.99 inches
Out-of-round and cylinder taper limits
  2.0L non-turbo engine (limit) .... 0.002 inch
  2.0L turbo engine (standard) .... 0.0004 inch
  2.4L four-cylinder and 3.0L V6 engines (standard) .... 0.0003 inch
Block deck surface flatness (gasket surface)
  2.0L non-turbo engine .... Not specified
  2.0L turbo, 2.4L four-cylinder, 3.0L V6 engines
    Standard .... 0.002 inch
    Service limit .... 0.004 inch
Main bearing cap bolt length limit (2.0L turbo and 2.4L engines) .... 2.79 inches

Pistons and rings

Piston diameter*
  2.0L non-turbo engine .... 3.4434 to 3.4441 inches
  2.0L engine .... 3.334 inches
  2.4L four-cylinder engine .... 3.405 inches
  3.0L V6 engine .... 3.586 inches

  Measured 11/16-inch up from the bottom of the piston skirt.

Piston-to-bore clearance
  2.0L non-turbo engine .... 0.0005 to 0.0017 inch
  2.0L turbo engine .... 0.0012 to 0.0020 inch
  2.4L four-cylinder and 3.0L V6 engines .... 0.0008 to 0.0015 inch
Piston ring side clearance
  2.0L non-turbo engine
    Compression rings (top and second)
      Standard .... 0.0010 to 0.0026 inch
      Service limit .... 0.004 inch

2.0L turbo engine
  Number 1 (top) compression ring
    Standard .... 0.0016 to 0.0031 inch
    Service limit .... 0.004 inch
  Number 2 compression ring
    Standard .... 0.0008 to 0.0024 inch
    Service limit .... 0.004 inch
2.4L engine
  Compression rings (top and second)
    Standard .... 0.0012 to 0.0027 inch
    Service limit .... 0.003 inch
3.0L V6 engine
  Number 1 (top) compression ring
    Standard .... 0.0012 to 0.0027 inch
    Service limit .... 0.003 inch
  Number 2 compression ring
    Standard .... 0.0008 to 0.0023 inch
    Service limit .... 0.003 inch
Piston ring end gap
  2.0L non-turbo engine
    Number 1 (top) compression ring
      Standard .... 0.009 to 0.020
      Service limit .... 0.031 inch
    Number 2 compression ring
      Standard .... 0.019 to 0.031 inch
      Service limit .... 0.039 inch
    Oil ring
      Standard .... 0.009 to 0.026 inch
      Service limit .... 0.039 inch
  2.0L turbo and 2.4L engines
    Number 1 compression ring
      Standard .... 0.0098 to 0.0138 inch
      Service limit .... 0.031 inch
    Number 2 compression ring
      Standard .... 0.0157 to 0.0217 inch
      Service limit .... 0.031 inch
    Oil ring
      Standard .... 0.0039 to 0.0157 inch
      Service limit .... 0.039 inch
  3.0L engine
    Number 1 compression ring
      Standard .... 0.012 to 0.017 inch
      Service limit .... 0.031 inch
    Number 2 compression ring
      Standard .... 0.018 to 0.023 inch
      Service limit .... 0.031 inch
    Oil ring
      Standard .... 0.008 to 0.023 inch
      Service limit .... 0.039 inch

Torque specifications*
                                                          Ft-lbs (unless otherwise indicated)

Note: *One foot-pound (ft-lb) of torque is equivalent to 12 inch-pounds (in-lbs) of torque. Torque values below approximately 15 ft-lbs are expressed in inch-pounds, since most foot-pound torque wrenches are not accurate at these smaller values.*

Main bearing cap bolts
  2.0L non-turbo engine
    Step 1 .... Outer bolts finger-tight
    Step 2 .... Cap bolts to 55 ft-lbs
    Step 3 .... Outer bolts to 21 ft-lbs
  2.0L turbo engine
    Step 1 18
    Step 2 .... 90-degrees further
  2.4L engine
    1999 and earlier
      Step 1 .... 168 in-lbs
      Step 2 .... 90-degrees further
    2000 and later
      Step 1 18
      Step 2 .... 90-degrees further
  3.0L V6 engine .... 65 to 73

Torque specifications* (continued)

	Ft-lbs (unless otherwise indicated)
Connecting rod cap nuts	
2.0L non-turbo engine	
Step 1	20
Step 2	90-degrees further
2.0L turbo and 2.4L engines	
Step 1	174 inch-lbs
Step 2	90-degrees further
3.0L V6 engine	37 to 39

Refer to Part A, B, C or D for additional torque specifications.

1 General information

Included in this portion of Chapter 2 are the general overhaul procedures for the cylinder head and internal engine components.

The information ranges from advice concerning preparation for an overhaul and the purchase of replacement parts to detailed, step-by-step procedures covering removal and installation of internal engine components and the inspection of parts.

The following Sections have been written based on the assumption that the engine has been removed from the vehicle. For information concerning in-vehicle engine repair, as well as removal and installation of the external components necessary for the overhaul, see Parts A through D of this Chapter. For information on determining models and engine numbers, refer to the *Vehicle Identification Numbers* at the front of this manual.

The Specifications included in this Part are only those necessary for the inspection and overhaul procedures which follow. Refer to Parts A through D for additional Specifications.

2 Engine overhaul - general information

Refer to illustration 2.4

It's not always easy to determine when, or if, an engine should be completely overhauled, as a number of factors must be considered.

High mileage is not necessarily an indication that an overhaul is needed, while low mileage doesn't preclude the need for an overhaul. Frequency of servicing is probably the most important consideration. An engine that's had regular and frequent oil and filter changes, as well as other required maintenance, will most likely give many thousands of miles of reliable service. Conversely, a neglected engine may require an overhaul very early in its life.

Excessive oil consumption is an indication that piston rings, valve seals and/or valve guides are in need of attention. Make sure that oil leaks aren't responsible before deciding that the rings and/or guides are bad. Perform a compression check to determine the extent of the work required (see Section 3).

Check the oil pressure with a gauge installed in place of the oil pressure sending unit **(see illustration)** and compare it to the Specifications in this Chapter. If it's extremely low, the bearings and/or oil pump are probably worn out.

Loss of power, rough running, knocking or metallic engine noises, excessive valve train noise and high fuel consumption rates may also point to the need for an overhaul, especially if they're all present at the same time. If a complete tune-up doesn't remedy the situation, major mechanical work is the only solution.

An engine overhaul involves restoring the internal parts to the specifications of a new engine. During an overhaul, the piston rings are replaced and the cylinder walls are reconditioned (rebored and/or honed). If a rebore is done by an automotive machine shop, new oversize pistons will also be installed. The main bearings, connecting rod bearings and camshaft bearings are generally replaced with new ones and, if necessary, the crankshaft may be reground to restore the journals. Generally, the valves are serviced as well, since they're usually in less-than-perfect condition at this point. While the engine is being overhauled, other components, such as the distributor, starter and alternator, can be rebuilt as well. The end result should be a like-new engine that will give many trouble free miles. **Note:** *Critical cooling system components such as the hoses, drivebelts, thermostat and water pump MUST be replaced with new parts when an engine is overhauled. The radiator should be checked carefully to ensure that it isn't clogged or leaking (see*

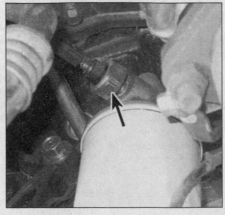

2.4 The oil pressure can be checked by removing the sending unit (arrow) and installing a pressure gauge in the threaded hole (3.0L V6 shown)

Chapter 3). Also, we don't recommend overhauling the oil pump - always install a new one when an engine is rebuilt.

Before beginning the engine overhaul, read through the entire procedure to familiarize yourself with the scope and requirements of the job. Overhauling an engine isn't difficult, but it is time consuming. Plan on the vehicle being tied up for a minimum of two weeks, especially if parts must be taken to an automotive machine shop for repair or reconditioning. Check on availability of parts and make sure that any necessary special tools and equipment are obtained in advance. Most work can be done with typical hand tools, although a number of precision measuring tools are required for inspecting parts to determine if they must be replaced. Often an automotive machine shop will handle the inspection of parts and offer advice concerning reconditioning and replacement. **Note:** *Always wait until the engine has been completely disassembled and all components, especially the engine block, have been inspected before deciding what service and repair operations must be performed by an automotive machine shop. Since the block's condition will be the major factor to consider when determining whether to overhaul the original engine or buy a rebuilt one, never purchase parts or have machine work done on other components until the block has been thoroughly inspected. As a general rule, time is the primary cost of an overhaul, so it doesn't pay to install worn or substandard parts.*

As a final note, to ensure maximum life and minimum trouble from a rebuilt engine, everything must be assembled with care in a spotlessly clean environment.

3 Cylinder compression check

1   A compression check will tell you what mechanical condition the upper end (pistons, rings, valves, head gaskets) of your engine is in. Specifically, it can tell you if the compression is down due to leakage caused by worn piston rings, defective valves and seats or a blown head gasket. **Note:** *The engine must be at normal operating temperature and the battery must be fully charged for this check. Also, the choke valve must be all the way open to get an accurate compression reading (if the engine's warm, the choke should be open).*

2   Begin by cleaning the area around the

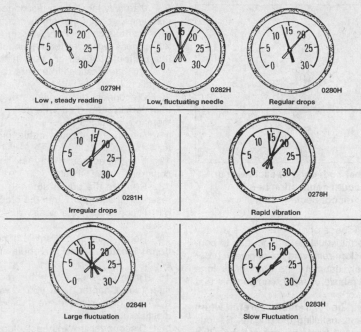

Low , steady reading   Low, fluctuating needle   Regular drops

Irregular drops   Rapid vibration

Large fluctuation   Slow Fluctuation

4.6 Typical vacuum gauge diagnostic readings

spark plugs before you remove them (compressed air should be used, if available). The idea is to prevent dirt from getting into the cylinders as the compression check is being done.

3   Remove all of the spark plugs from the engine (see Chapter 1).

4   Block the throttle wide open.

5   Disconnect the primary (low voltage) wires from the ignition coils (four-cylinder engines) or distributor (3.0L V6 engine) (see Chapter 5). Also disable the fuel system (see Chapter 4, Section 2).

6   Install the compression gauge in the number one spark plug hole.

7   Crank the engine over at least seven compression strokes and watch the gauge. The compression should build up quickly in a healthy engine. Low compression on the first stroke, followed by gradually increasing pressure on successive strokes, indicates worn piston rings. A low compression reading on the first stroke, which doesn't build up during successive strokes, indicates leaking valves or a blown head gasket (a cracked head could also be the cause). Deposits on the undersides of the valve heads can also cause low compression. Record the highest gauge reading obtained.

8   Repeat the procedure for the remaining cylinders and compare the results to the Specifications in this Chapter.

9   Add some engine oil (about three squirts from a plunger-type oil can) to each cylinder, through the spark plug hole, and repeat the test.

10   If the compression increases after the oil is added, the piston rings are definitely worn. If the compression doesn't increase significantly, the leakage is occurring at the valves or head gasket. Leakage past the valves may be caused by burned valve seats and/or faces or warped, cracked or bent valves.

11   If two adjacent cylinders have equally low compression, there's a strong possibility that the head gasket between them is blown. The appearance of coolant in the combustion chambers or the crankcase would verify this condition.

12   If one cylinder is 20 percent lower than the others, and the engine has a slightly rough idle, a worn exhaust lobe on the camshaft could be the cause.

13   If the compression is unusually high, the combustion chambers are probably coated with carbon deposits. If that's the case, the cylinder head should be removed and decarbonized.

14   If compression is way down or varies greatly between cylinders, it would be a good idea to have a leak-down test performed by an automotive repair shop. This test will pinpoint exactly where the leakage is occurring and how severe it is.

15   **Caution:** *After performing this procedure, be sure to unblock the throttle before starting the engine.*

4   Vacuum gauge diagnostic checks

Refer to illustration 4.6

A vacuum gauge provides valuable information about what is going on in the engine at a low-cost. You can check for worn rings or cylinder walls, leaking head or intake manifold gaskets, incorrect carburetor adjustments, restricted exhaust, stuck or burned valves, weak valve springs, improper ignition or valve timing and ignition problems.

Unfortunately, vacuum gauge readings are easy to misinterpret, so they should be used in conjunction with other tests to confirm the diagnosis.

Both the absolute readings and the rate of needle movement are important for accurate interpretation. Most gauges measure vacuum in inches of mercury (in-Hg). The following references to vacuum assume the diagnosis is being performed at sea level. As elevation increases (or atmospheric pressure decreases), the reading will decrease. For every 1,000 foot increase in elevation above approximately 2000 feet, the gauge readings will decrease about one inch of mercury.

Connect the vacuum gauge directly to intake manifold vacuum, not to ported (throttle-body) vacuum. Be sure no hoses are left disconnected during the test or false readings will result.

Before you begin the test, allow the engine to warm up completely. Block the wheels and set the parking brake. With the transmission in neutral (or Park, on automatics), start the engine and allow it to run at normal idle speed. **Warning:** *Carefully inspect the fan blades for cracks or damage before starting the engine. Keep your hands and the vacuum tester clear of the fan and do not stand in front of the vehicle or in line with the fan when the engine is running.*

Read the vacuum gauge; an average, healthy engine should normally produce about 17 to 22 inches of vacuum with a fairly steady needle **(see illustration)**. Refer to the following vacuum gauge readings and what they indicate about the engines condition:

1   A low steady reading usually indicates a leaking gasket between the intake manifold and throttle body, a leaky vacuum hose, late ignition timing or incorrect camshaft timing. Check ignition timing with a timing light and eliminate all other possible causes, utilizing the tests provided in this Chapter before you remove the timing belt cover to check the timing marks.

2   If the reading is three to eight inches below normal and it fluctuates at that low reading, suspect an intake-manifold gasket leak at an intake port or a faulty injector.

3   If the needle has regular drops of about two to four inches at a steady rate the valves are probably leaking. Perform a compression or leak-down test to confirm this.

4   An irregular drop or down-flick of the needle can be caused by a sticking valve or an ignition misfire. Perform a compression or leak-down test and read the spark plugs.

5   A rapid vibration of about four in-Hg at idle combined with exhaust smoke indicates worn valve guides. Perform a leak-down test to confirm this. If the rapid vibration occurs with an increase in engine speed, check for a leaking intake manifold gasket or head gasket, weak valve springs, burned valves or ignition misfire.

6   A slight fluctuation, say one inch up and down, may mean ignition problems. Check all the usual tune-up items and, if necessary, run the engine on an ignition analyzer.

7   If there is a large fluctuation, perform a

compression or leak-down test to look for a weak or dead cylinder or a blown head gasket.

8   If the needle moves slowly through a wide range, check for a clogged PCV system, incorrect idle fuel mixture, carburetor/throttle body or intake manifold gasket leaks.

9   Check for a slow return after revving the engine by quickly snapping the throttle open until the engine reaches about 2,500 rpm and let it shut. Normally the reading should drop to near zero, rise above normal idle reading (about 5 in-Hg over) and then return to the previous idle reading. If the vacuum returns slowly and doesn't peak when the throttle is snapped shut, the rings may be worn. If there is a long delay, look for a restricted exhaust system (often the muffler or catalytic converter). An easy way to check this is to temporarily disconnect the exhaust ahead of the suspected part and repeat the test.

5   Engine removal - methods and precautions

If you've decided that an engine must be removed for overhaul or major repair work, several preliminary steps should be taken.

Locating a suitable place to work is extremely important. Adequate work space, along with storage space for the vehicle, will be needed. If a shop or garage isn't available, at the very least a flat, level, clean work surface made of concrete or asphalt is required.

Cleaning the engine compartment and engine before beginning the removal procedure will help keep tools clean and organized.

An engine hoist or A-frame will also be necessary. Make sure the equipment is rated in excess of the combined weight of the engine and accessories. Safety is of primary importance, considering the potential hazards involved in lifting the engine out of the vehicle.

If the engine is being removed by a novice, a helper should be available. Advice and aid from someone more experienced would also be helpful. There are many instances when one person cannot simultaneously perform all of the operations required when lifting the engine out of the vehicle.

Plan the operation ahead of time. Arrange for or obtain all of the tools and equipment you'll need prior to beginning the job. Some of the equipment necessary to perform engine removal and installation safely and with relative ease are (in addition to an engine hoist) a heavy duty floor jack, complete sets of wrenches and sockets as described in the front of this manual, wooden blocks and plenty of rags and cleaning solvent for mopping up spilled oil, coolant and gasoline. If the hoist must be rented, make sure that you arrange for it in advance and perform all of the operations possible without it beforehand. This will save you money and time.

Plan for the vehicle to be out of use for quite a while. A machine shop will be required to perform some of the work which the do-it-yourselfer can't accomplish without special

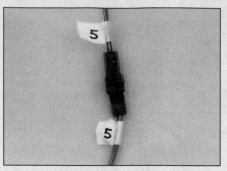

6.9 Label both ends of each wire or vacuum connection before disconnecting them

equipment. These shops often have a busy schedule, so it would be a good idea to consult them before removing the engine in order to accurately estimate the amount of time required to rebuild or repair components that may need work.

Always be extremely careful when removing and installing the engine. Serious injury can result from careless actions. Plan ahead, take your time and a job of this nature, although major, can be accomplished successfully.

6   Engine - removal and installation

Refer to illustration 6.9
Note: *Read through the entire Section before beginning this procedure. The transaxle is removed from the vehicle, then the engine is removed separately.*
Warning: *These models have airbags. Always disable the airbag system and wait two minutes before working in the vicinity of any airbag system components to avoid the possibility of accidental deployment of the airbags, which could cause personal injury (see Chapter 12).*

Removal

1   If the vehicle is equipped with air conditioning, have the system discharged by a dealer service department or a service station.
2   Place protective covers on the front fenders and cowl. Special protective covers are available, but an old bedspread or blanket will also work.
3   Remove the hood (see Chapter 11).
4   Relieve the fuel system pressure (see Chapter 4).
5   Disconnect and remove the battery (see Chapter 5).
6   Remove the air cleaner assembly (see Chapter 4). On vehicles equipped with a turbocharger, remove the turbocharger intake hose (see Chapter 4).
7   Drain the cooling system (see Chapter 1) and remove the radiator and the coolant reservoir (see Chapter 3). **Note:** *On vehicles equipped with an automatic transaxle, remove the fluid cooler hoses from the radiator.*
8   Remove the transaxle (see Chapter 7).

9   Carefully label, then disconnect all vacuum lines, coolant and emissions hoses and wire harness connectors. Masking tape and felt-tip pens work well for marking items **(see illustration)**. If necessary, take instant photos or sketch the locations to ensure correct reinstallation.
10   Disconnect the fuel lines from the fuel injection system (see Chapter 4) and cap them to prevent leakage.
11   Detach the throttle cable (see Chapter 4).
12   If equipped, remove the air conditioning compressor (see Chapter 3).
13   Remove the power steering pump and reservoir (if equipped) from the brackets without disconnecting the hoses and set them aside.
14   Remove the splash shield (if not already done) located at the drivebelt end of the engine.
15   Drain the engine oil and remove the oil filter (see Chapter 1). If you're working on a 2.4L engine, remove the dipstick and the dipstick tube.
16   Disconnect the exhaust pipe from the exhaust manifold.
17   Attach a chain or an engine lifting fixture to the engine lifting brackets (or to bolts which are securely mounted in the cast iron block or accessory mounting bracket) and hook up the hoist. **Warning:** *Attaching the engine lifting chain to a bolt or stud located in an aluminum component (such as the cylinder head) may not provide the necessary strength to support the weight of the engine/transmission assembly during removal.* Take up the slack until there is tension on the chain to support the engine.
18   Support the engine with a floor jack. Place a block of wood on the jack pad to protect the oil pan. **Warning:** *Do not place any part of your body under the engine when it's supported only by a hoist or other lifting device.*
19   Check for clearance and, if necessary, remove the transaxle mount bracket (see Chapter 7).
20   Remove the mount through-bolts on all of the engine or transaxle mounts (see Chapters 2A through 2D).
21   Confirm that all of the cables, hoses, wires and other items are disconnected from the engine.
22   Carefully lift the engine up to clear obstructions.
23   Lift the engine high enough to clear the front of the vehicle and slowly move the hoist away.
24   Lower the hoist and set the engine on blocks - leave the hoist hooked up.
25   Remove the clutch components, if equipped (see Chapter 8) and flywheel (or driveplate) (see Chapters 2A through 2D) and the engine rear plate. Mount the engine on a stand.

Installation

26   Check the engine/transaxle mounts. If they're worn or damaged, replace them.

27 On manual transaxle equipped models, inspect the clutch components (see Chapter 8) and apply a very small amount of high temperature grease to the transaxle input shaft splines.

28 On automatic transaxle equipped vehicles, inspect the converter seal and bushing.

29 Attach the hoist to the engine and carefully lower the engine into the vehicle.

30 Install the mount bolts and tighten them securely.

31 Reinstall the remaining components and fasteners in the reverse order of removal.

32 Add coolant, oil, power steering and transmission fluid/lubricant as needed (see Chapter 1).

33 Run the engine and check for proper operation and leaks. Shut off the engine and recheck the fluid levels.

7 Engine rebuilding alternatives

The do-it-yourselfer is faced with a number of options when performing an engine overhaul. The decision to replace the engine block, piston/connecting rod assemblies and crankshaft depends on a number of factors, with the number one consideration being the condition of the block. Other considerations are cost, access to machine shop facilities, parts availability, time required to complete the project and the extent of prior mechanical experience on the part of the do-it-yourselfer. Some of the rebuilding alternatives include:

Individual parts - If the inspection procedures reveal that the engine block and most engine components are in reusable condition, purchasing individual parts may be the most economical alternative. The block, crankshaft and piston/connecting rod assemblies should all be inspected carefully. Even if the block shows little wear, the cylinder bores should be surface honed.

Short block - A short block consists of an engine block with a crankshaft and piston/connecting rod assemblies already installed. All new bearings are incorporated and all clearances will be correct. The existing camshaft, valve train components, cylinder head(s) and external parts can be bolted to the short block with little or no machine shop work necessary.

Long block - A long block consists of a short block plus an oil pump, oil pan, cylinder head(s), rocker arm cover(s), camshaft and valve train components, timing sprockets and chain or gears and timing cover. All components are installed with new bearings, seals and gaskets incorporated throughout. The installation of manifolds and external parts is all that's necessary.

Give careful thought to which alternative is best for you and discuss the situation with local automotive machine shops, auto parts dealers and experienced rebuilders before ordering or purchasing replacement parts.

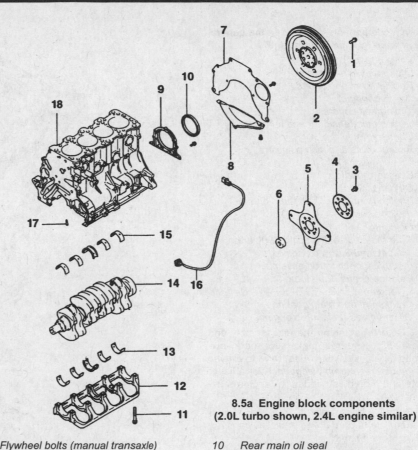

8.5a Engine block components (2.0L turbo shown, 2.4L engine similar)

1	Flywheel bolts (manual transaxle)	10	Rear main oil seal
2	Flywheel (manual transaxle)	11	Main bearing cap bolt
3	Driveplate bolt (automatic transaxle)	12	Main bearing cap assembly
4	Adapter plate	13	Lower main bearing halves
5	Driveplate	14	Crankshaft
6	Crankshaft bushing	15	Upper main bearing halves
7	Engine rear plate	16	Knock sensor
8	Bellhousing cover	17	Oil jet
9	Rear oil seal housing	18	Cylinder block

8 Engine overhaul - disassembly sequence

Refer to illustrations 8.5a and 8.5b

1 It's much easier to disassemble and work on the engine if it's mounted on a portable engine stand. A stand can often be rented quite cheaply from an equipment rental yard. Before the engine is mounted on a stand, the flywheel/driveplate should be removed from the engine.

2 If a stand isn't available, it's possible to disassemble the engine with it blocked up on the floor. Be extra careful not to tip or drop the engine when working without a stand.

3 If you're going to obtain a rebuilt engine, all external components must come off first, to be transferred to the replacement engine, just as they will if you're doing a complete engine overhaul yourself. These include:

Alternator and brackets
Emissions control components
Ignition coils (four-cylinder engines) or distributor (3.0L V6L engine), spark plug wires and spark plugs
Thermostat cover, thermostat and housing
Water pump
Fuel injection components
Intake/exhaust manifolds
Oil filter
Engine mounts
Clutch and flywheel/driveplate
Engine rear plate

Note: *When removing the external components from the engine, pay close attention to details that may be helpful or important during installation. Note the installed position of gaskets, seals, spacers, pins, brackets, washers, bolts and other small items.*

4 If you're obtaining a short block, which consists of the engine block, crankshaft, pistons and connecting rods all assembled, then the cylinder head(s), oil pan and oil pump will have to be removed as well. See *Engine rebuilding alternatives* for additional information regarding the different possibilities to be considered.

5 If you're planning a complete overhaul, the engine must be disassembled and the

internal components removed in the general following order (**see illustrations**):

> Valve cover(s)
> Intake and exhaust manifolds
> Rocker arms and shafts (2.4L and 3.0L V6 engines)
> Timing belt covers
> Timing belt, tensioner and sprockets
> Camshaft(s)
> Rocker arms and lash adjusters (2.0L engines)
> Cylinder head(s)
> Oil pan
> Engine front case (2.0L turbo and 2.4L engines)
> Oil pump
> Rear main oil seal housing (2.0L turbo, 2.4L and 3.0L V6 engines)
> Piston/connecting rod assemblies
> Balance shafts (2.0L turbo and 2.4L engines)
> Crankshaft and main bearings
> Oil jet valves (2.0L turbo engines)

6   Before beginning the disassembly and overhaul procedures, make sure the following items are available. Also, refer to *Engine overhaul - reassembly sequence* for a list of tools and materials needed for engine reassembly.

> Common hand tools
> Small cardboard boxes or plastic bags for storing parts
> Gasket scraper
> Ridge reamer
> Micrometers
> Telescoping gauges
> Dial indicator set
> Valve spring compressor
> Cylinder surfacing hone
> Piston ring groove cleaning tool
> Electric drill motor
> Tap and die set
> Wire brushes
> Oil gallery brushes
> Cleaning solvent

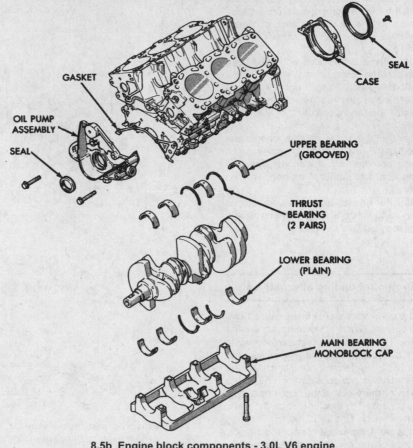

8.5b Engine block components - 3.0L V6 engine

9   Cylinder head - disassembly

Refer to illustrations 9.2, 9.3a, 9.3b, 9.4a and 9.4b

Note: *New and rebuilt cylinder heads are commonly available for most engines at dealerships and auto parts stores. Due to the fact that some specialized tools are necessary for the disassembly and inspection procedures, and replacement parts may not be readily available, it may be more practical and economical for the home mechanic to purchase a replacement head rather than taking the time to disassemble, inspect and recondition the original.*

1   Cylinder head disassembly involves removal of the intake and exhaust valves and

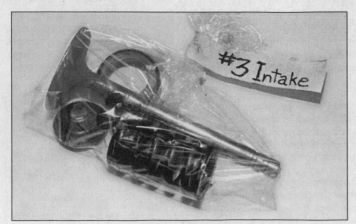

9.2 A small plastic bag, with an appropriate label, can be used to store the valvetrain components so they can be kept together and reinstalled in the correct guide location

9.3a Use a valve spring compressor (and where needed, an adapter like the one shown) to compress the springs, then remove the keepers from the valve stem with a magnet or small needle-nose pliers

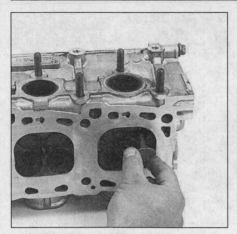

9.3b Remove the valve from the cylinder head . . .

9.4a . . . then use pliers to remove the valve stem seal from the valve guide

9.4b If the valve won't pull through the guide, deburr the edge of the stem end and the area around the top of the keeper groove with a file or whetstone

related components. If they're still in place, remove the rocker arm shafts and camshaft, on the 2.4L and 3.0L V6 engines (see Chapter 2C or 2D) or the bearing caps, camshafts and lash adjusters, on the 2.0L non-turbo and turbo engines (see Chapter 2A or 2B). Label the parts or store them separately so they can be reinstalled in their original locations.

2   Before the valves are removed, arrange to label and store them, along with their related components, so they can be kept separate and reinstalled in the same valve guides they are removed from **(see illustration)**.

3   Compress the springs on the first valve with a spring compressor and remove the keepers **(see illustrations)**. Carefully release the valve spring compressor and remove the retainer, the spring and the spring seat (if used).

4   Pull the valve out of the head, then remove the oil seal from the guide **(see illustration)**. If the valve binds in the guide (won't pull through), push it back into the head and deburr the area around the keeper groove with a fine file or whetstone **(see illustration)**.

5   Repeat the procedure for the remaining valves. Remember to keep all the parts for each valve together so they can be reinstalled in the same locations.

6   Pull off the valve stem seals with pliers and discard them.

7   Once the valves and related components have been removed and stored in an organized manner, the head should be thoroughly cleaned and inspected. If a complete engine overhaul is being done, finish the engine disassembly procedures before beginning the cylinder head cleaning and inspection process.

10   Cylinder head - cleaning and inspection

1   Thorough cleaning of the cylinder head and related valvetrain components, followed by a detailed inspection, will enable you to decide how much valve service work must be done during the engine overhaul. **Note:** *If the*

engine was severely overheated, the cylinder head is probably warped (see Step 11).

Cleaning

2   Scrape all traces of old gasket material and sealing compound off the head gasket, intake manifold and exhaust manifold sealing surfaces. Be very careful not to gouge the cylinder head. Special gasket removal solvents that soften gaskets and make removal much easier are available at auto parts stores.

3   Remove all built-up scale from the coolant passages.

4   Run a stiff wire brush through the various holes to remove deposits that may have formed in them.

5   Run an appropriate size tap into each of the threaded holes to remove corrosion and thread sealant that may be present. If compressed air is available, use it to clear the holes of debris produced by this operation. **Warning:** *Wear eye protection when using compressed air!*

6   Clean the cylinder head with solvent and dry it thoroughly. Compressed air will speed the drying process and ensure that all holes and recessed areas are clean. **Note:** *Decarbonizing chemicals are available and may prove very useful when cleaning cylinder heads and valve train components. They are very caustic and should be used with caution. Be sure to follow the instructions on the container.*

7   Clean the rocker arms and hydraulic lash adjusters (all engines) and the spacers and shafts (2.4L and 3.0L V6 engines) with solvent and dry them thoroughly (don't mix them up during the cleaning process). Compressed air will speed the drying process and can be used to clean out the oil passages.

8   Clean all the valve springs, spring seats, keepers and retainers with solvent and dry them thoroughly. Do the components from one valve at a time to avoid mixing up the parts.

9   Scrape off any heavy deposits that may have formed on the valves, then use a motorized wire brush to remove deposits from the valve heads and stems. **Warning:** *Wear eye protection!* Again, make sure the valves don't get mixed up.

Inspection

Note: *Be sure to perform all of the following inspection procedures before concluding that machine shop work is required. Make a list of the items that need attention.*

Cylinder head
Refer to illustrations 10.10, 10.11 and 10.13

10   Inspect the head very carefully for cracks, evidence of coolant leakage and other damage **(see illustration)**. If cracks are found, check with an automotive machine shop concerning repair. If repair isn't possible, a new cylinder head should be obtained.

10.10 Inspect the cylinder head internal passages for cracks or other defects

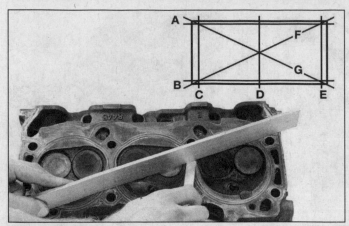

10.11 Measure the cylinder head gasket surfaces for warpage and compare to the limits listed in this Chapter's Specifications

10.13 Checking valve stem-to-guide clearance - remember to divide the measurement by two to obtain the correct dimension

11   Using a straightedge and feeler gauge, check the head gasket mating surface **(see illustration)**. Check the intake and exhaust manifold surfaces on the cylinder head also. If the warpage on any of the surfaces exceeds the limits listed in this Chapter's Specifica-

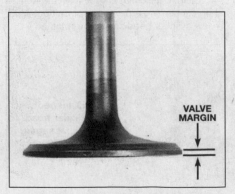

10.15 Check for valve wear at the points shown here

tions, they can be resurfaced at an automotive machine shop.
12   Examine the valve seats in each of the combustion chambers. If they're pitted, cracked or burned, the head will require valve service that's beyond the scope of the home mechanic.
13   Check the valve stem-to-guide clearance, using a clamping dial indicator base attached securely to the head, by measuring the lateral movement of the valve stem inside the valve guide **(see illustration)**. **Note:** *If you only have a magnetic dial indicator base and a steel bench or vise, you can clamp or bolt the head down to the bench and mount the indicator next to the head and extend the dial indicator to the valve stem and measure the side play. The valve must be in the guide and approximately 1/16-inch off the seat. The total valve stem movement indicated by the gauge needle must be divided by two to obtain the actual clearance.*
14   After this is done, if there's still some doubt regarding the condition of the valve guides they should be checked by an automotive machine shop (the cost should be minimal).

Valves

Refer to illustrations 10.15 and 10.16
15   Carefully inspect each valve face for

uneven wear, deformation, cracks, pits and burned areas **(see illustration)**. Check the valve stem for scuffing and galling and the neck for cracks. Rotate the valve and check for any obvious indication that it's bent. Look for pits and excessive wear on the end of the stem. The presence of any of these conditions indicates the need for valve service by an automotive machine shop.
16   Measure the margin width on each valve **(see illustration)**. Any valve with a margin narrower than listed in this Chapter's Specifications will have to be replaced with a new one.

Valve components

Refer to illustrations 10.17 and 10.18
17   Check each valve spring for wear (on the ends) and pits. Measure the free length **(see illustration)** and compare it to the Specifications listed in this Chapter. Any springs that are shorter than specified have sagged and should not be reused. The tension of all springs should be checked with a special fixture before deciding that they're suitable for use in a rebuilt engine (take the springs to an automotive machine shop for this check).
18   Stand each spring on a flat surface and check it for squareness **(see illustration)**. If any of the springs are distorted or sagged,

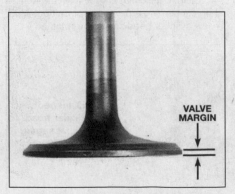

10.16 The margin width on each valve must be as specified (if no margin exists, the valve cannot be reused)

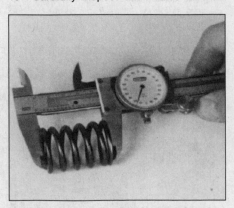

10.17 Measure the free length of each valve spring with a dial or vernier caliper

10.18 Check each valve spring for squareness

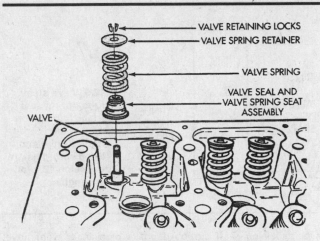

12.4a On 2.0L non-turbo models, the valve seal and spring seat are an assembly

12.4b Install the valve stem seal using an appropriate size socket and hammer

replace all of them with new parts.

19   Check the spring retainers and keepers for obvious wear and cracks. Any questionable parts should be replaced with new ones, as extensive damage will occur if they fail during engine operation.

Rocker arm components

20   Refer to Chapters 2A through 2D for the rocker arm (and shaft, if equipped) inspection procedures.

21   Any damaged or excessively worn parts must be replaced with new ones.

22   If the inspection process indicates that the valve components are in generally poor condition and worn beyond the limits specified, which is usually the case in an engine that's being overhauled, reassemble the valves in the cylinder head and refer to Section 11 for valve servicing recommendations.

11   Valves - servicing

1   Because of the complex nature of the job and the special tools and equipment needed, servicing of the valves, the valve seats and the valve guides, commonly known as a valve job, should be done by a professional.

2   The home mechanic can remove and disassemble the head, do the initial cleaning and inspection, then reassemble and deliver it to a dealer service department or an automotive machine shop for the actual service work. Doing the inspection will enable you to see what condition the head and valvetrain components are in and will ensure that you know what work and new parts are required when dealing with an automotive machine shop.

3   The dealer service department, or automotive machine shop, will remove the valves and springs, recondition or replace the valves and valve seats, recondition the valve guides, check and replace the valve springs, spring retainers and keepers (as necessary), replace the valve seals with new ones, reassemble the valve components and make sure the installed spring height is correct. The cylinder

head gasket surface will also be resurfaced if it's warped.

4   After the valve job has been performed by a professional, the head will be in like-new condition. When the head is returned, be sure to clean it again before installation on the engine to remove any metal particles and abrasive grit that may still be present from the valve service or head resurfacing operations. Use compressed air, if available, to blow out all the oil holes and passages.

12   Cylinder head - reassembly

Refer to illustrations 12.4a, 12.4b, 12.6a, 12.6b, 12.7 and 12.9

1   Regardless of whether or not the head was sent to an automotive repair shop for valve servicing, make sure it's clean before beginning reassembly.

2   If the head was sent out for valve servicing, the valves and related components will already be in place. Begin the reassembly procedure with Step 8.

3   If the valve faces or seats have been ground on a 2.0L non-turbo engine, mea-

sure the valve stem tip-to-spring seat surface height (without spring or seat installed) **(see illustration 12.9 dimension "A")**. If the dimension is greater than the tolerance listed in this Chapter's Specifications, grind the valve stem as required to achieve the correct dimension.

4   Install the combined spring seats/valve stem seal (2.0L non-turbo engine) or separate spring seats and valve stem seals (2.0L turbo, 2.4L and 3.0L V6 engines) onto each of the valve guides **(see illustration)**. **Note:** *On 3.0L V6 engines, install the gray stem seals on the intake valves and the green stem seals on the exhaust valves.* Using a hammer and a deep socket or seal installation tool, gently tap each seal into place until it's completely seated on the guide **(see illustration)**. Don't twist or cock the seals during installation or they won't seal properly on the valve stems.

5   Beginning at one end of the head, apply moly-base grease or clean engine oil to the valve stem and install the first valve.

6   Set the valve spring and retainer in place **(see illustrations)**. **Note:** *On 2.0L turbo, 2.4L and 3.0L V6 engines, install the spring with its enameled end (more widely spaced coils) up.*

12.6a Install the spring over the valve guide and onto the seat . . .

12.6b . . . and place the retainer onto the spring

12.7 Apply a small dab of grease to each keeper as shown here before installation - it'll hold them in place on the valve stem as the spring is released

7   Compress the spring with a valve spring compressor and carefully install the keepers in the upper groove, then slowly release the compressor and make sure the keepers seat properly. Apply a small dab of grease to each keeper to hold it in place if necessary **(see illustration)**.

13.1 A ridge reamer is required to remove the ridge from the top of each cylinder - do this BEFORE removing the pistons!

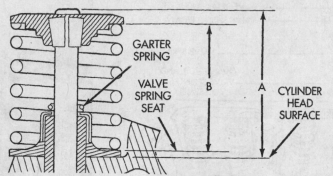

12.9 Valve stem tip-to-spring seat surface (dimension "A" - 2.0L non-turbo engines only) and installed spring height (dimension "B" - all engines)

8   Repeat the procedure for the remaining valves. Be sure to return the components to their original locations - don't mix them up!
9   Check the installed valve spring height (dimension "B") with a vernier or dial caliper. If the head was sent out for service work, the installed height should be correct (but don't automatically assume that it is). The measurement is taken from the spring seat to the top of the valve stem **(see illustration)**. If the height is greater than listed in this Chapter's Specifications, shims can be added under the springs to correct it. **Caution:** *Do not shim the springs to the point where the installed height is less than specified.*
10   Refer to the appropriate Part (2A through 2D) of this Chapter for the procedure to install the camshaft(s) and rocker arms.

13 Pistons and connecting rods - removal

Refer to illustrations 13.1, 13.3, 13.4 and 13.6
Note: *Prior to removing the piston/connecting rod assemblies, remove the cylinder head and the oil pan by referring to the appropriate Sections in Chapter 2A through 2D.*
1   Use your fingernail to feel if a ridge has formed at the upper limit of ring travel (about 1/4-inch down from the top of each cylinder).

If carbon deposits or cylinder wear have produced ridges, they must be completely removed with a special tool **(see illustration)**. Follow the manufacturer's instructions provided with the tool. Failure to remove the ridges before attempting to remove the piston/connecting rod assemblies may result in piston breakage.
2   After the cylinder ridges have been removed, turn the engine upside-down so the crankshaft is facing up.
3   Before the connecting rods are removed, check the endplay with feeler gauges. Slide them between the first connecting rod and the crankshaft throw until the play is removed **(see illustration)**. The endplay is equal to the thickness of the feeler gauge(s). If the endplay exceeds the service limit, new connecting rods will be required. If new rods (or a new crankshaft) are installed, the endplay may fall under the minimum listed in this Chapter's Specifications (if it does, the rods will have to be machined to restore it - consult an automotive machine shop for advice if necessary). Repeat the procedure for the remaining connecting rods.
4   Check the connecting rods and caps for identification marks **(see illustration)**. If they aren't plainly marked, use a small center-punch to make the appropriate number of indentations on each rod and cap (1, 2, 3,

13.3 Check the connecting rod side clearance (endplay) with a feeler gauge

13.4 The connecting rods and caps should be marked to indicate which cylinder they're installed in - if they aren't, mark them with a center-punch to avoid confusion during reassembly

13.6 To prevent damage to the crankshaft journals and cylinder walls, slip sections of hose over the rod bolts before removing the pistons

etc., depending on the cylinder they're associated with).

5 Loosen each of the connecting rod cap nuts or bolts 1/2-turn at a time until they can be removed by hand. Remove the number one connecting rod cap and bearing insert. Don't drop the bearing insert out of the cap.

6 Slip a short length of plastic or rubber hose over each connecting rod cap bolt to protect the crankshaft journal and cylinder wall as the piston is removed (see illustration).

7 Remove the bearing insert and push the connecting rod/piston assembly out through the top of the engine. Use a wooden or plastic hammer handle to push on the upper bearing surface in the connecting rod. If resistance is felt, double-check to make sure that all of the ridge was removed from the cylinder.

8 Repeat the procedure for the remaining cylinders.

9 After removal, reassemble the connecting rod caps and bearing inserts in their respective connecting rods and install the cap nuts or bolts finger tight. Leaving the old bearing inserts in place until reassembly will help prevent the connecting rod bearing surfaces from being accidentally nicked or gouged.

10 Don't separate the pistons from the connecting rods (see Section 19 for additional information).

14 Balance shafts (2.0L turbo and 2.4L engines only) - removal, inspection and installation

1 Remove the engine from the vehicle (Section 6).

2 Remove the timing belt, sprockets and engine front case (see Chapter 2B or 2C).

3 Pull the balance shafts from the cylinder block, rotating them as you go (see illustration 13.6 in Chapter 2B). Be careful not to nick or gouge the balance shaft bearings as you pull the shafts out. **Note:** *Be sure to label the upper and lower balance shafts. They are not interchangeable.*

4 Check the balance shaft bearings in the cylinder block, and the balance shaft bearing journals, for wear or damage. Dimensions and wear tolerances aren't specified by the manufacturer, but if wear or damage can be seen, the worn components should be replaced. The bearings can be replaced with tools and methods similar to those used to replace camshaft bearings in a pushrod engine. Special tools are required, but it should be a simple job for a dealer service department or automotive machine shop.

5 Coat the balance shaft bearing journals with assembly lube. Slip the balance shafts into the engine, making sure they are installed in the correct bores.

6 The remainder of installation is the reverse of the removal steps.

15 Crankshaft - removal

Refer to illustrations 15.1 and 15.3
Note: *The crankshaft can be removed only after the engine has been removed from the vehicle. It's assumed that the flywheel or driveplate, crankshaft pulley, timing belt, oil pan, oil pump and piston/connecting rod assemblies have already been removed. The rear main oil seal housing (all except 2.0L non-turbo engines) must be unbolted and separated from the block before proceeding with crankshaft removal.*

1 Before the crankshaft is removed, check the endplay. Mount a dial indicator with the stem in line with the crankshaft and touching one of the crank throws (see illustration).

2 Push the crankshaft all the way to the rear and zero the dial indicator. Next, pry the crankshaft to the front as far as possible and check the reading on the dial indicator. The distance that it moves is the endplay. If it's greater than listed in this Chapter's Specifications, check the crankshaft thrust surfaces for wear. If no wear is evident, new main bearings should correct the endplay.

3 If a dial indicator isn't available, feeler gauges can be used. Gently pry or push the crankshaft all the way to the front of the engine. Slip feeler gauges between the crankshaft and the front face of the thrust main bearing to determine the clearance (see illustration).

4 Loosen the main bearing cap assembly bolts 1/4-turn at a time each, until they can be removed by hand.

5 Gently tap the main bearing cap assembly with a soft-face hammer around the perimeter of the assembly. Pull the main bearing cap assembly straight up and off the cylinder block. Try not to drop the bearing inserts if they come out with the cap assembly.

6 Carefully lift the crankshaft out of the engine. It may be a good idea to have an assistant available, since the crankshaft is quite heavy and awkward to handle. With the bearing inserts in place in the engine block and main bearing caps, reinstall the main bearing cap assembly onto the engine block and tighten the bolts finger tight. Make sure the directional arrow is facing the front (timing belt end) of the engine.

15.1 Checking crankshaft endplay with a dial indicator

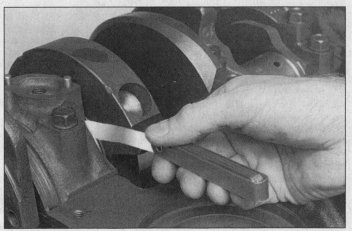

15.3 Checking crankshaft endplay with a feeler gauge at the thrust bearing journal

16.1a Use a hammer and a large punch to knock the core plugs sideways in their bores

16.1b Pull the core plugs from the block with pliers

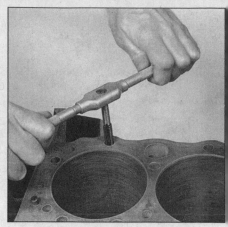

16.9 All bolt holes in the block - particularly the main bearing cap and head bolt holes - should be cleaned and restored with a tap (be sure to remove debris from the holes after this is done)

16 Engine block - cleaning

Refer to illustrations 16.1a, 16.1b, 16.9 and 16.11

1   Remove the core plugs from the engine block. To do this, knock one side of the plugs into the block with a hammer and a punch, then grasp them with large pliers and pull them out **(see illustrations)**.

2   Using a gasket scraper, remove all traces of gasket material from the engine block. Be very careful not to nick or gouge the gasket sealing surfaces.

3   Remove the main bearing caps and separate the bearing inserts from the caps and the engine block. Tag the bearings, indicating which cylinder they were removed from and whether they were in the cap or the block, then set them aside.

4   Remove all of the threaded oil gallery plugs from the block. The plugs are usually very tight - they may have to be drilled out and the holes retapped. Use new plugs when the engine is reassembled.

5   On 2.0L turbo engines, drive out the oil jets located in the block side of each main bearing saddle (insert a punch from above, through the cylinder) and check them for clogged passages. Discard the oil jets; they can't be reused once they're removed.

6   If the engine is extremely dirty it should be taken to an automotive machine shop for cleaning.

7   After the block is returned, clean all oil holes and oil galleries one more time. Brushes specifically designed for this purpose are available at most auto parts stores. Flush the passages with warm water until the water runs clear, dry the block thoroughly and wipe all machined surfaces with a light, rust preventive oil. If you have access to compressed air, use it to speed the drying process and to blow out all the oil holes and galleries. **Warning:** *Wear eye protection when using compressed air!*

8   If the block isn't extremely dirty or sludged up, you can do an adequate clean-

ing job with hot soapy water and a stiff brush. Take plenty of time and do a thorough job. Regardless of the cleaning method used, be sure to clean all oil holes and galleries very thoroughly, dry the block completely and coat all machined surfaces with light oil.

9   The threaded holes in the block must be clean to ensure accurate torque readings during reassembly. Run the proper size tap into each of the holes to remove rust, corrosion, thread sealant or sludge and restore damaged threads **(see illustration)**. If possible, use compressed air to clear the holes of debris produced by this operation. Now is a good time to clean the threads on the head bolts and the main bearing cap bolts as well.

10   Reinstall the main bearing caps and tighten the bolts finger tight.

11   After coating the sealing surfaces of the new core plugs with core plug sealant, install them in the engine block **(see illustration)**. Make sure they're driven in straight and seated properly or leakage could result. Special tools are available for this purpose, but a large socket, with an outside diameter that will just slip into the core plug, an extension and a hammer will work just as well.

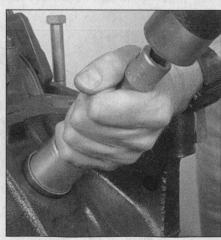

16.11 A large socket on an extension can be used to drive the new core plugs into the bores

12   Apply non-hardening sealant (such as Permatex no. 2 or Teflon pipe sealant) to the new oil gallery plugs and thread them into the holes in the block. Make sure they're tightened securely.

13   If you're working on a 2.0L turbo engine, carefully tap new oil jet valves into their bores from the underside of the engine, using a 0.15 to 0.20-inch diameter punch, until they bottom in the bores.

14   If the engine isn't going to be reassembled right away, cover it with a large plastic trash bag to keep it clean.

17 Engine block - inspection

Refer to illustrations 17.4a, 17.4b, 17.4c, 17.4d and 17.13

1   Before the block is inspected, it should be cleaned as described in Section 16.

2   Visually check the block for cracks, rust and corrosion. Look for stripped threads in the threaded holes. It's also a good idea to have the block checked for hidden cracks by an automotive machine shop that has the special equipment to do this type of work. If defects are found, have the block repaired, if possible, or replaced.

3   Check the cylinder bores for scuffing and scoring.

4   Measure the diameter of each cylinder at the top (just under the ridge area), center and bottom of the cylinder bore, parallel to the crankshaft axis **(see illustrations)**.

5   Next, measure each cylinder's diameter at the same three locations across the crankshaft axis. Compare the results to the Specifications.

6   If the required precision measuring tools aren't available, the piston-to-cylinder clearances can be obtained, though not quite as accurately, using feeler gauge stock. Feeler gauge stock comes in 12-inch lengths and various thicknesses and is generally available at auto parts stores.

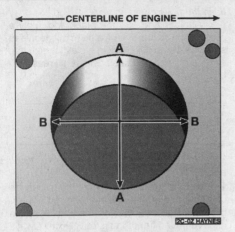

17.4a Measure cylinder diameter at right angles (A) and parallel (B) to the crankshaft centerline - the difference between the measurements is out-of-round

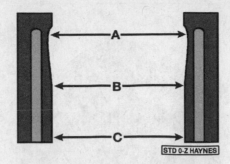

17.4b Measure the diameter of each cylinder just under the wear ridge (A), at the center (B) and at the bottom (C) - the difference between the measurements is taper

7   To check the clearance, select a feeler gauge and slip it into the cylinder along with the matching piston. The piston must be positioned exactly as it normally would be. The feeler gauge must be between the piston and

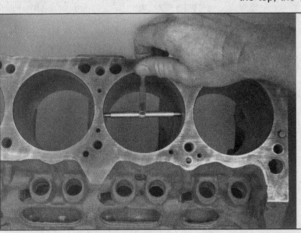

17.4c The ability to "feel" when the telescoping gauge is at the correct point will be developed over time, so work slowly and repeat the check until you're satisfied that the bore measurement is accurate

cylinder on one of the thrust faces (90-degrees to the piston pin bore).
8   The piston should slip through the cylinder (with the feeler gauge in place) with moderate pressure.
9   If it falls through or slides through easily, the clearance is excessive and a new piston will be required. If the piston binds at the lower end of the cylinder and is loose toward the top, the cylinder is tapered. If tight spots

are encountered as the piston/feeler gauge is rotated in the cylinder, the cylinder is out-of-round.
10   Repeat the procedure for the remaining pistons and cylinders.
11   If the cylinder walls are badly scuffed or scored, or if they're out-of-round or tapered beyond the limits given in the Specifications, have the engine block rebored and honed at an automotive machine shop. If a rebore is done, oversize pistons and rings will be required.
12   If the cylinders are in reasonably good condition and not worn to the outside of the limits, and if the piston-to-cylinder clearances can be maintained properly, then they don't have to be rebored. Honing is all that's necessary (see Section 18).
13   Using a precision straightedge and a feeler gauge, check the block deck (the surface that mates with the cylinder head) for distortion **(see illustration)**. If it's distorted beyond the specified limit, it can be resurfaced by an automotive machine shop.

18   Cylinder honing

Refer to illustrations 18.3a and 18.3b
1   Prior to engine reassembly, the cylinder bores must be honed so the new piston rings will seat correctly and provide the best possible combustion chamber seal. **Note:** *If you don't have the tools or don't want to tackle the honing operation, most automotive machine shops will do it for a reasonable fee.*
2   Before honing the cylinders, install the main bearing cap assembly and tighten the bolts to the torque listed in this Chapter's Specifications.
3   Two types of cylinder hones are commonly available - the flex hone or "bottle brush" type and the more traditional surfacing hone with spring-loaded stones. Both will do the job, but for the less experienced mechanic the "bottle brush" hone will probably be easier to use. You'll also need some kerosene or

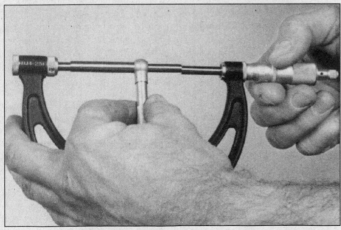

17.4d The gauge is then measured with a micrometer to determine the bore size

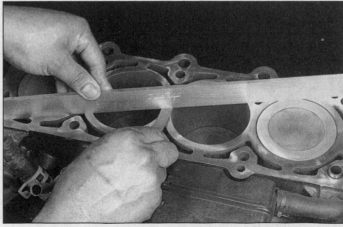

17.13 Check the cylinder block gasket surface for warpage by placing a precision straightedge on the surface and trying to slip a feeler gauge between them

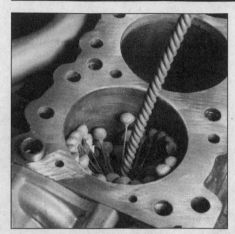

18.3a A "bottle brush" hone is the easiest type of hone to use

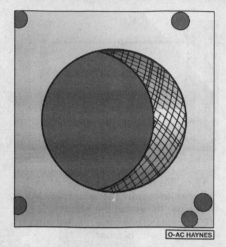

18.3b The cylinder hone should leave a smooth, crosshatch pattern with the lines intersecting at approximately a 60-degree angle

honing oil, rags and an electric drill motor. Proceed as follows:

 a) *Mount the hone in the drill motor, compress the stones and slip it into the first cylinder* **(see illustration)**. *Be sure to wear safety goggles or a face shield!*

 b) *Lubricate the cylinder with plenty of honing oil, turn on the drill and move the hone up-and-down in the cylinder at a pace that will produce a fine crosshatch pattern on the cylinder walls. Ideally, the crosshatch lines should intersect at approximately a 60-degree angle* **(see illustration)**. *Be sure to use plenty of lubricant and don't take off any more material than is absolutely necessary to produce the desired finish.* **Note:** *Piston ring manufacturers may specify a smaller crosshatch angle than the traditional 60-degrees - read and follow any instructions included with the new rings.*

 c) *Don't withdraw the hone from the cylinder while it's running. Instead, shut off the drill and continue moving the hone up-and-down in the cylinder until it comes to a complete stop, then com-*

press the stones and withdraw the hone. If you're using a "bottle brush" type hone, stop the drill motor, then turn the chuck in the normal direction of rotation while withdrawing the hone from the cylinder.

 d) *Wipe the oil out of the cylinder and repeat the procedure for the remaining cylinders.*

4   After the honing job is complete, chamfer the top edges of the cylinder bores with a small file so the rings won't catch when the pistons are installed. Be very careful not to nick the cylinder walls with the end of the file.

5   The entire engine block must be washed again very thoroughly with warm, soapy water to remove all traces of the abrasive grit produced during the honing operation. **Note:** *The bores can be considered clean when a lint-free white cloth - dampened with clean engine oil - used to wipe them out doesn't pick up any more honing residue, which will show up as gray areas on the cloth. Be sure to run a brush through all oil holes and galleries and*

flush them with running water.

6   After rinsing, dry the block and apply a coat of light rust preventive oil to all machined surfaces. Wrap the block in a plastic trash bag to keep it clean and set it aside until reassembly.

19   Pistons/connecting rods - inspection

Refer to illustrations 19.2, 19.4a, 19.4b, 19.10 and 19.11

1   Before the inspection process can be carried out, the piston/connecting rod assemblies must be cleaned and the original piston rings removed from the pistons. **Note:** *Always use new piston rings when the engine is reassembled.*

2   Using a piston ring removal tool **(see illustration)**, carefully remove the rings from the pistons. Be careful not to nick or gouge the pistons in the process.

3   Scrape all traces of carbon from the top of the piston. A hand-held wire brush or a piece of fine emery cloth can be used once the majority of the deposits have been scraped away. Do not, under any circumstances, use a wire brush mounted in a drill motor to remove deposits from the pistons. The piston material is soft and may be eroded away by the wire brush.

4   Use a piston ring groove cleaning tool to remove carbon deposits from the ring grooves. If a tool isn't available, a piece broken off the old ring will do the job. Be very careful to remove only the carbon deposits - don't remove any metal and do not nick or scratch the sides of the ring grooves **(see illustrations)**.

5   Once the deposits have been removed, clean the piston/rod assemblies with solvent and dry them with compressed air (if available). Make sure the oil return holes in the back sides of the ring grooves are clear.

6   If the pistons and cylinder walls aren't damaged or worn excessively, and if the engine block is not rebored, new pistons won't

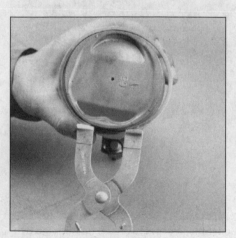

19.2 Use a special tool to remove the piston rings from the piston

19.4a The piston ring grooves can be cleaned with a special tool like this one . . .

19.4b . . . or a section of a broken ring

2E-19

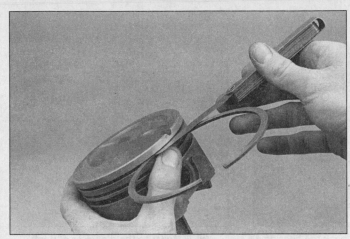

19.10 Check the ring side clearance with a feeler gauge at several points around the groove

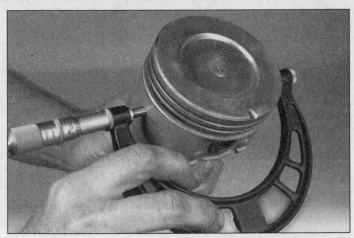

19.11 Measure the piston diameter at a 90-degree angle to the piston pin and the specified distance from the bottom of the skirt

be necessary. Normal piston wear appears as even, vertical wear on the piston thrust surfaces and slight looseness of the top ring in its groove. New piston rings, however, should always be used when an engine is rebuilt.

7   Carefully inspect each piston for cracks around the skirt, at the pin bosses and at the ring lands.

8   Look for scoring and scuffing on the thrust faces of the skirt, holes in the piston crown and burned areas at the edge of the crown. If the skirt is scored or scuffed, the engine may have been suffering from overheating and/or abnormal combustion, which caused excessively high operating temperatures. The cooling and lubrication systems should be checked thoroughly. A hole in the piston crown is an indication that abnormal combustion (preignition) was occurring. Burned areas at the edge of the piston crown are usually evidence of spark knock (detonation). If any of the above problems exist, the causes must be corrected or the damage will occur again. The causes may include intake air leaks, incorrect fuel/air mixture, incorrect ignition timing and EGR system malfunctions.

9   Corrosion of the piston, in the form of small pits, indicates that coolant is leaking into the combustion chamber and/or the crankcase. Again, the cause must be corrected or the problem may persist in the rebuilt engine.

10   Measure the piston ring side clearance by laying a new piston ring in each ring groove and slipping a feeler gauge in beside it **(see illustration)**. Check the clearance at three or four locations around each groove. Be sure to use the correct ring for each groove - they are different. If the side clearance is greater than specified, new pistons will have to be used.

11   Check the piston-to-bore clearance by measuring the bore (see Section 17) and the piston diameter. Make sure the pistons and bores are correctly matched. Measure the piston across the skirt 11/16-inch above the bottom of the piston, at a 90-degree angle to and

in line with the piston pin **(see illustration)**. Subtract the piston diameter from the bore diameter to obtain the clearance. If it's greater than specified, the block will have to be rebored and new pistons and rings installed.

12   Check the piston-to-rod clearance by twisting the piston and rod in opposite directions. Any noticeable play indicates excessive wear, which must be corrected. The piston/connecting rod assemblies should be taken to an automotive machine shop to have the pistons and rods resized and new pins installed.

13   If the pistons must be removed from the connecting rods for any reason, they should be taken to an automotive machine shop. While they are there have the connecting rods checked for bend and twist, since automotive machine shops have special equipment for this purpose. **Note:** *Unless new pistons and/or connecting rods must be installed, do not disassemble the pistons and connecting rods.*

14   Check the connecting rods for cracks and other damage. Temporarily remove the rod caps, lift out the old bearing inserts, wipe

the rod and cap bearing surfaces clean and inspect them for nicks, gouges and scratches. After checking the rods, replace the old bearings, slip the caps into place and tighten the nuts or bolts finger tight. **Note:** *If the engine is being rebuilt because of a connecting rod knock, be sure to install new rods.*

20   Crankshaft - inspection

Refer to illustration 20.1, 20.2, 20.4 and 20.7

1   Remove all burrs from the crankshaft oil holes with a stone, file or scraper **(see illustration)**.

2   Clean the crankshaft with solvent and dry it with compressed air (if available). Be sure to clean the oil holes with a stiff brush and flush them with solvent **(see illustration)**. **Warning:** *If compressed air is used always wear eye protection to prevent solvents or debris from causing and injury to your eyes.*

3   Check the main and connecting rod bearing journals for uneven wear, scoring, pits and cracks.

4   Rub a penny across each journal several

20.1 The oil holes should be chamfered so sharp edges don't gouge or scratch the new bearings

20.2 Use a wire or stiff bristle brush to clean the oil passages in the crankshaft

times. If a journal picks up copper from the penny, it's too rough and must be reground **(see illustration)**.

5   Remove all burrs from the crankshaft oil holes with a stone, file or scraper.

6   Check the rest of the crankshaft for cracks and other damage. It should be magnafluxed to reveal hidden cracks - an automotive machine shop will handle the procedure.

7   Using a micrometer, measure the diameter of the main and connecting rod journals and compare the results to the Specifications **(see illustration)** listed in this Chapter. By measuring the diameter at a number of points around each journal's circumference, you'll be able to determine whether or not the journal is out-of-round. Take the measurement at each end of the journal, near the crank throws, to determine if the journal is tapered.

8   If the crankshaft journals are damaged, tapered, out-of-round or worn beyond the limits given in the Specifications, have the crankshaft reground by an automotive machine shop. Be sure to use the correct size bearing inserts if the crankshaft is reconditioned.

9   Check the oil seal journals at each end of the crankshaft for wear and damage. If the seal has worn a groove in the journal, or if it's nicked or scratched, the new seal may leak when the engine is reassembled. In some cases, an automotive machine shop may be able to repair the journal by pressing on a thin sleeve. If repair isn't feasible, a new or different crankshaft should be installed.

10   Refer to Section 21 and examine the main and rod bearing inserts.

20.4 An easy way to check the bearing journal surface is to rub a penny lengthwise on each journal - if copper rubs off and is embedded in the crankshaft, the journals should be reground

20.7 Measure the diameter of each crankshaft journal at several points to detect wear, taper and out-of-round conditions

tions and normal engine wear are often present. Abrasives are sometimes left in engine components after reconditioning, especially when parts are not thoroughly cleaned using the proper cleaning methods. Whatever the source, these foreign objects often end up embedded in the soft bearing material and are easily recognized. Large particles will not embed in the bearing and will score or gouge the bearing and journal. The best prevention for this cause of bearing failure is to clean all parts thoroughly and keep everything spot-lessly clean during engine assembly. Frequent and regular engine oil and filter changes are also recommended.

5   Lack of lubrication (or lubrication breakdown) has a number of interrelated causes. Excessive heat (which thins the oil), overloading (which squeezes the oil from the bearing face) and oil leakage or throw off (from excessive bearing clearances, worn oil pump or high engine speeds) all contribute to lubrication breakdown. Blocked oil passages, which usually are the result of misaligned oil holes in a bearing shell, will also oil starve a bearing

21   Main and connecting rod bearings - inspection

Refer to illustration 21.1

1   Even though the main and connecting rod bearings should be replaced with new ones during the engine overhaul, the old bearings should be retained for close examination, as they may reveal valuable information about the condition of the engine **(see illustration)**.

2   Bearing failure occurs because of lack of lubrication, the presence of dirt or other foreign particles, overloading the engine and corrosion. Regardless of the cause of bearing failure, it must be corrected before the engine is reassembled to prevent it from happening again.

3   When examining the bearings, remove them from the engine block, the main bearing caps, the connecting rods and the rod caps and lay them out on a clean surface in the same general position as their location in the engine. This will enable you to match any bearing problems with the corresponding crankshaft journal.

4   Dirt and other foreign particles get into the engine in a variety of ways. It may be left in the engine during assembly, or it may pass through filters or the PCV system. It may get into the oil, and from there into the bearings. Metal chips from machining opera-

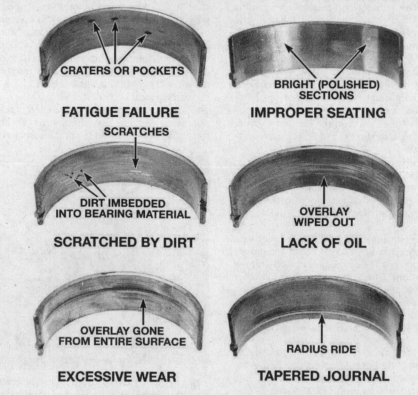

CRATERS OR POCKETS

FATIGUE FAILURE

BRIGHT (POLISHED) SECTIONS

IMPROPER SEATING

SCRATCHES

DIRT IMBEDDED INTO BEARING MATERIAL

SCRATCHED BY DIRT

OVERLAY WIPED OUT

LACK OF OIL

OVERLAY GONE FROM ENTIRE SURFACE

EXCESSIVE WEAR

RADIUS RIDE

TAPERED JOURNAL

21.1 Typical bearing wear patterns and probable causes

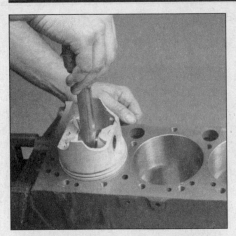

23.3 When checking piston ring end gap, the ring must be square in the cylinder bore (this is done by pushing the ring down with the top of a piston as shown)

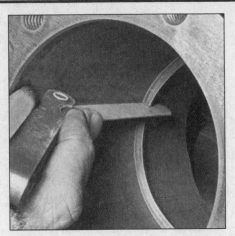

23.4 With the ring square in the cylinder, measure the end gap with a feeler gauge

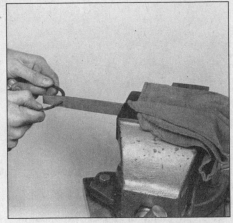

23.5 If the end gap is too small, clamp a file in a vise and file the ring ends (from the outside end of the file in towards the vise only) to enlarge the gap slightly

and destroy it. When lack of lubrication is the cause of bearing failure, the bearing material is wiped or extruded from the steel backing of the bearing. Temperatures may increase to the point where the steel backing turns blue from overheating.

6   Driving habits can have a definite effect on bearing life. Full throttle, low speed operation (lugging the engine) puts very high loads on bearings, which tends to squeeze out the oil film. These loads cause the bearings to flex, which produces fine cracks in the bearing face (fatigue failure). Eventually the bearing material will loosen in pieces and tear away from the steel backing. Short trip driving leads to corrosion of bearings because insufficient engine heat is produced to drive off the condensed water and corrosive gases. These products collect in the engine oil, forming acid and sludge. As the oil is carried to the engine bearings, the acid attacks and corrodes the bearing material.

7   Incorrect bearing installation during engine assembly will lead to bearing failure as well. Tight fitting bearings leave insufficient bearing oil clearance and will result in oil starvation. Dirt or foreign particles trapped behind a bearing insert result in high spots on the bearing which lead to failure.

22   Engine overhaul - reassembly sequence

1   Before beginning engine reassembly, make sure you have all the necessary new parts, gaskets and seals as well as the following items on hand:

  Common hand tools
  A 1/2-inch drive torque wrench
  Piston ring installation tool
  Piston ring compressor
  Short lengths of rubber or plastic hose to fit over connecting rod bolts
  Plastigage

  Feeler gauges
  A fine-tooth file
  New engine oil
  Engine assembly lube or moly-base grease
  Gasket sealant
  Thread locking compound

2   In order to save time and avoid problems, engine reassembly must be done in the following general order:

  Piston rings
  Oil jet valves (2.0L turbo engine)
  Crankshaft and main bearings
  Balance shafts (2.0L turbo and 2.4L engines)
  Piston/connecting rod assemblies
  Rear main oil seal housing (except 2.0L non-turbo engine)
  Front case and oil pump assembly (2.0L turbo and 2.4L engines)
  Oil pump (2.0L non-turbo and 3.0L V6 engines)
  Oil pan
  Cylinder head(s)
  Water pump
  Timing belt and sprockets
  Timing belt covers
  Intake and exhaust manifolds
  Valve cover(s)
  Engine rear plate
  Flywheel/driveplate

23   Piston rings - installation

Refer to illustrations 23.3, 23.4, 23.5, 23.9a, 23.9b, 23.11 and 23.12

1   Before installing the new piston rings, the ring end gaps must be checked. It's assumed that the piston ring side clearance has been checked and verified correct (see Section 19).

2   Lay out the piston/connecting rod assemblies and the new ring sets so the ring sets will be matched with the same piston and cylinder

during the end gap measurement and engine assembly.

3   Insert the top (number one) ring into the first cylinder and square it up with the cylinder walls by pushing it in with the top of the piston **(see illustration)**. The ring should be near the bottom of the cylinder, at the lower limit of ring travel.

4   To measure the end gap, slip feeler gauges between the ends of the ring until a gauge equal to the gap width is found **(see illustration)**. The feeler gauge should slide between the ring ends with a slight amount of drag. Compare the measurement to the Specifications listed in this Chapter. If the gap is larger or smaller than specified, double-check to make sure you have the correct rings before proceeding.

5   If the gap is too small, it must be enlarged or the ring ends may come in contact with each other during engine operation, which can cause serious damage to the engine. The end gap can be increased by filing the ring ends very carefully with a fine file. Mount the file in a vise equipped with soft jaws, slip the ring over the file with the ends contacting the file face and slowly move the ring to remove material from the ends. When performing this operation, file only by pushing the ring from the outside end of the file towards the vise **(see illustration)**.

6   Excess end gap isn't critical unless it's greater than 0.039-inch. Again, double-check to make sure you have the correct rings for your engine.

7   Repeat the procedure for each ring that will be installed in the first cylinder and for each ring in the remaining cylinders. Remember to keep rings, pistons and cylinders matched up.

8   Once the ring end gaps have been checked/corrected, the rings can be installed on the pistons.

9   The oil control ring (lowest one on the piston) is usually installed first. It's composed of three separate components. Slip the

23.9a Installing the spacer/expander in the oil control ring groove

23.9b DO NOT use a piston ring installation tool when installing the oil ring side rails

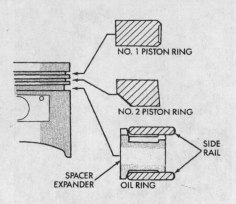

23.11 Piston ring assembly details

spacer/expander into the groove **(see illustration)**. If an anti-rotation tang is used, make sure it's inserted into the drilled hole in the ring groove. Next, install the lower side rail. Don't use a piston ring installation tool on the oil ring side rails, as they may be damaged. Instead, place one end of the side rail into the groove between the spacer/expander and the ring land, hold it firmly in place and slide a finger around the piston while pushing the rail into the groove **(see illustration)**. Next, install the upper side rail in the same manner.

10   After the three oil ring components have been installed, check to make sure that both the upper and lower side rails can be turned smoothly in the ring groove.

11   The number two (middle) ring is installed next. It's usually stamped with a mark which must face up, toward the top of the piston. **Note:** *Always follow the instructions printed on the ring package or box - different manufacturers may require different approaches. Do not mix up the top and middle rings, as they have different cross-sections* **(see illustration)**.

12   Use a piston ring installation tool and make sure the identification mark is facing the top of the piston, then slip the ring into the middle groove on the piston **(see illustra-**

tion). Don't expand the ring any more than necessary to slide it over the piston.

13   Install the number one (top) ring in the same manner. Make sure the mark is facing up. Be careful not to confuse the number one and number two rings.

14   Repeat the procedure for the remaining pistons and rings.

24   Crankshaft - installation and main bearing oil clearance check

1   Crankshaft installation is the first step in engine reassembly. It's assumed at this point that the engine block and crankshaft have been cleaned, inspected and repaired or reconditioned.

2   Position the engine with the bottom facing up.

3   Remove the main bearing cap bolts and lift out the cap assembly. Check the main bearing cap bolts for stretching (refer to the cylinder head bolt inspection procedure in Chapter 2A). If you're working on a 2.0L turbo or 2.4L engine, measure the length of the bolts from the underside of the head to the end of the

threads and compare it with the length listed in this Chapter's Specifications. Replace bolts that are stretched beyond the limit.

4   If they're still in place, remove the original bearing inserts from the block and the main bearing caps. Wipe the bearing surfaces of the block and caps with a clean, lint-free cloth. They must be kept spotlessly clean.

Main bearing oil clearance check

Refer to illustrations 24.6a, 24.6b, 24.11, 24.13a, 24.13b, 24.13c and 24.15

5   Clean the back sides of the new main bearing inserts and lay one in each main bearing saddle in the block. If one of the bearing inserts from each set has a large groove in it, make sure the grooved insert is installed in the block. Lay the other bearing from each set in the corresponding main bearing cap. Make sure the tab on the bearing insert fits into the recess in the block or cap. **Caution:** *The oil holes in the block must line up with the oil holes in the bearing insert. Do not hammer the bearing into place and don't nick or gouge the bearing faces.* No lubrication should be used at this time.

6   Install the thrust bearings as follows:

23.12 Install the compression rings with a ring expander - the mark on the ring must face up

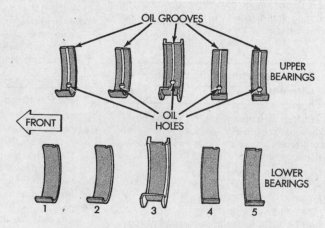

24.6a 2.0L engine main bearing locations

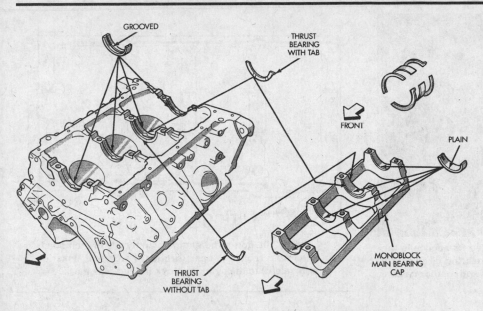

24.6b 3.0L V6 engine main and thrust bearing locations

24.11 Lay the Plastigage strips (arrow) on the main bearing journals, parallel to the crankshaft centerline

a) On 2.0L non-turbo and 2.0L turbo engines, the flanged thrust bearing must be installed in the no. 3 (center) main cap and saddle **(see illustration)**.

b) On 2.4L engines, the flanged thrust bearing half goes in the cap side of the center main bearing. The separate thrust bearing halves go in the block side of the center main bearing, with the oil grooves facing the crankshaft.

c) On 3.0L V6 engines, the separate thrust bearings (four halves total) must be installed in the no. 3 main cap and saddle (counting from the timing belt end of the engine) **(see illustration)**. *Note that two of the thrust bearing halves have tabs that extend from the ends of the bearing. One of these bearing halves goes in the cap, on the side toward the front (timing belt end) of the engine, with the tab facing the left side of the engine. The other goes in the block, on the side of the saddle toward the flywheel/drive-plate end of the engine, with its tab also facing the left side of the engine.*

7   Clean the faces of the bearings in the block and the crankshaft main bearing jour-

nals with a clean, lint-free cloth.

8   Check or clean the oil holes in the crankshaft, as any dirt here can go only one way - straight through the new bearings.

9   Once you're certain the crankshaft is clean, carefully lay it in position in the main bearings.

10   Before the crankshaft can be permanently installed, the main bearing oil clearance must be checked.

11   Cut several pieces of the appropriate size Plastigage (they must be slightly shorter than the width of the main bearings) and place one piece on each crankshaft main bearing journal, parallel with the journal axis **(see illustration)**.

12   Clean the faces of the bearings in the cap assembly and install the cap in the cylinder block with the directional arrow pointing toward the front (timing belt end) of the engine. Don't disturb the Plastigage.

13   Tighten the main bearing cap bolts, in three steps, to the torque listed in this Chap-

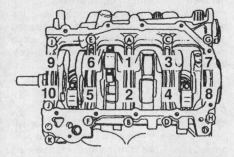

24.13a Main cap bearing tightening sequence (2.0L non-turbo engine)

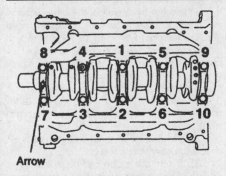

Arrow

24.13b Main bearing cap tightening sequence - 2.0L turbo and 2.4L engines

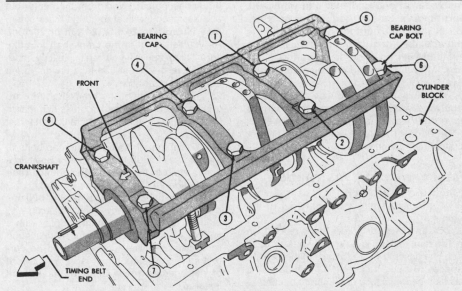

24.13c Main bearing cap tightening sequence - 3.0L V6 engine

24.15 Compare the widest point of the crushed Plastigage to the scale on the envelope to determine the main bearing oil clearance - be sure to use the correct scale; standard and metric scales are included

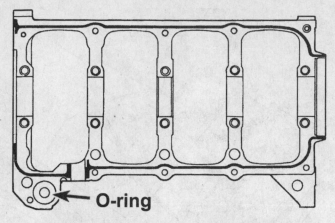

24.22 On 2.0L non-turbo engines, apply a 1/16-inch bead of anaerobic sealant (Mopar Torque Cure Gasket Maker or equivalent) to the cylinder block in the areas marked

ter's Specifications, following the correct sequence for the engine you're working on **(see illustrations)**. Don't rotate the crankshaft at any time during this operation.

14   Remove the bolts and carefully lift off the main bearing cap assembly. Don't disturb the Plastigage or rotate the crankshaft.

15   Compare the width of the crushed Plastigage on each journal to the scale printed on the Plastigage envelope to obtain the main bearing oil clearance **(see illustration)**. Check the Specifications listed in this Chapter to make sure it's correct.

16   If the clearance is not as specified, the bearing inserts may be the wrong size (which means different ones will be required). Before deciding that different inserts are needed, make sure that no dirt or oil was between the bearing inserts and the caps or block when the clearance was measured. If the Plastigage was wider at one end than the other, the journal may be tapered (refer to Section 19). If the clearance still exceeds the limit specified, the bearing will have to be replaced with an undersize bearing. **Caution:** *When installing a new crankshaft always use a standard bearing.*

17   Carefully scrape all traces of the Plastigage material off the main bearing journals and/or the bearing faces. Use your fingernail or the edge of a credit card - don't nick or scratch the bearing faces.

Final crankshaft installation

Refer to illustration 24.22

18   Carefully lift the crankshaft out of the engine.

19   Clean the bearing faces in the block, then apply a thin, uniform layer of moly-base grease or engine assembly lube to each of the bearing surfaces. Be sure to coat the thrust faces as well as the journal face of the thrust bearing.

20   Make sure the crankshaft journals are clean, then lay the crankshaft back in place

in the block. **Caution:** *Be sure to install the thrust bearings in the correct location.*

21   Clean the faces of the bearings in the caps, then apply lubricant to them.

22   Install the cap assembly in the cylinder block with the directional arrow pointing toward the front (timing belt end) of the engine. If you're working on a 2.0L non-turbo engine, lay a 1/16-inch wide bead of anaerobic sealant (Mopar Torque Cure Gasket Maker, part. no. 4773257 or equivalent) on the cylinder block **(see illustration)**. **Caution:** *Don't place the sealant anywhere except where indicated, and don't use any other type of sealant, or the main bearing cap assembly may not seat properly.* **Note:** *Make sure to replace any O-ring seals between the cap assembly and the engine block, if equipped.*

23   Install the bolts.

24   Tighten the bolts to the torque listed in this Chapter's Specifications (start from the thrust bearing cap, work from the center out and approach the final torque in three steps) **(see illustration 24.13a, 24.13b or 24.13c)**. As you tighten, turn the crankshaft to make sure it turns freely. If you can't spin it by hand, make sure the thrust bearings haven't been pushed out of position.

25   Tap the ends of the crankshaft forward and backward with a lead or brass hammer to line up the main bearing and crankshaft thrust surfaces.

26   Retighten all main bearing cap bolts to the torque listed in this Chapter's Specifications, again in the specified sequence **(see illustration 24.13a, 24.13b or 24.13c)**.

27   Rotate the crankshaft a number of times by hand to check for any obvious binding.

28   Recheck the crankshaft endplay with a feeler gauge or a dial indicator as described in Section 20. The endplay should be correct if the crankshaft thrust faces aren't worn or damaged and new bearings have been installed.

29   Install a new rear main oil seal (see Chapters 2A through 2D).

25 Pistons and connecting rods - installation and rod bearing oil clearance check

Refer to illustrations 25.5, 25.11, 25.13, 25.14 and 25.17

1   Before installing the piston/connecting rod assemblies, the cylinder walls must be perfectly clean, the top edge of each cylinder must be chamfered, and the crankshaft must be in place.

2   Remove the cap from the end of the number one connecting rod (refer to the marks made during removal). Remove the original bearing inserts and wipe the bearing surfaces of the connecting rod and cap with a clean, lint-free cloth. They must be kept spotlessly clean.

Connecting rod bearing oil clearance check

3   Clean the back side of the new upper bearing insert, then lay it in place in the connecting rod. Make sure the tab on the bearing fits into the recess in the rod. Don't hammer the bearing insert into place and be very careful not to nick or gouge the bearing face. Don't lubricate the bearing at this time.

4   Clean the back side of the other bearing insert and install it in the rod cap. Again, make sure the tab on the bearing fits into the recess in the cap, and don't apply any lubricant. It's critically important that the mating surfaces of the bearing and connecting rod are perfectly clean and oil free when they're assembled.

5   Position the piston ring gaps at 90-degree intervals around the piston **(see illustration)**.

6   Slip a section of plastic or rubber hose over each connecting rod cap bolt.

7   Lubricate the piston and rings with clean engine oil and attach a piston ring compressor to the piston. Leave the skirt protruding about 1/4-inch to guide the piston into the cylinder.

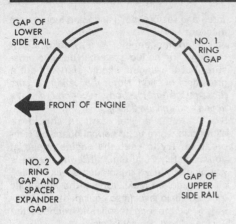

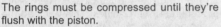

25.5 Position the piston ring end gaps as shown

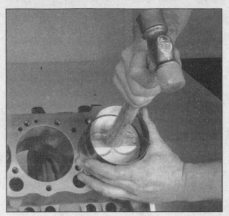

25.11 Use a wooden or plastic hammer handle to tap the piston into the bore

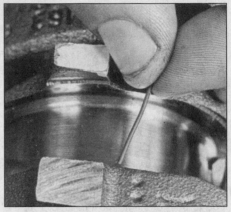

25.13 Lay the Plastigage strips on each rod bearing journal, parallel to the crankshaft centerline

The rings must be compressed until they're flush with the piston.

8   Rotate the crankshaft until the number one connecting rod journal is at BDC (bottom dead center) and apply a coat of engine oil to the cylinder walls.

9   With the mark on top of the piston facing the front (timing belt end) of the engine, gently insert the piston/connecting rod assembly into the number one cylinder bore and rest the bottom edge of the ring compressor on the engine block. **Note:** *The connecting rod also has a mark on it that must face the front of the engine (if it faces the opposite direction, the piston and connecting rod have been assembled improperly.*

10   Tap the top edge of the ring compressor to make sure it's contacting the block around its entire circumference.

11   Gently tap on the top of the piston with the end of a wooden or plastic hammer handle **(see illustration)** while guiding the end of the connecting rod into place on the crankshaft journal. The piston rings may try to pop out of the ring compressor just before entering the cylinder bore, so keep some downward pressure on the ring compressor. Work slowly, and

if any resistance is felt as the piston enters the cylinder, stop immediately. Find out what's hanging up and fix it before proceeding. Do not, for any reason, force the piston into the cylinder - you might break a ring and/or the piston.

12   Once the piston/connecting rod assembly is installed, the connecting rod bearing oil clearance must be checked before the rod cap is permanently bolted in place.

13   Cut a piece of the appropriate size Plastigage slightly shorter than the width of the connecting rod bearing and lay it in place on the number one connecting rod journal, parallel with the journal axis **(see illustration)**.

14   Clean the connecting rod cap bearing face, remove the protective hoses from the connecting rod bolts and install the rod cap. Make sure the mating mark on the cap is on the same side as the mark on the connecting rod **(see illustration)**. **Note:** *Check to make sure the identification mark on the connecting rod faces toward the front (timing belt) end of the engine.*

15   Install the nuts and tighten them to the torque listed in this Chapter's Specifications, working up to it in three steps. **Note:**

Use a thin-wall socket to avoid erroneous torque readings that can result if the socket is wedged between the rod cap and nut. If the socket tends to wedge itself between the nut and the cap, lift up on it slightly until it no longer contacts the cap. Do not rotate the crankshaft at any time during this operation.

16   Remove the nuts and detach the rod cap, being very careful not to disturb the Plastigage.

17   Compare the width of the crushed Plastigage to the scale printed on the Plastigage envelope to obtain the oil clearance **(see illustration)**. Compare it to the Specifications (listed in this Chapter) to make sure the clearance is correct.

18   If the clearance is not as specified, the bearing inserts may be the wrong size (which means different ones will be required). Before deciding that different inserts are needed, make sure that no dirt or oil was between the bearing inserts and the connecting rod or cap when the clearance was measured. Also, recheck the journal diameter. If the Plastigage was wider at one end than the other, the journal may be tapered (see Section 20). If the clearance still exceeds the limit

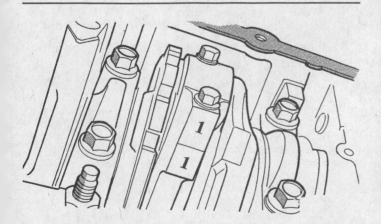

25.14 Install the connecting rod cap, making sure the cap and rod identification marks match (and are on the same side)

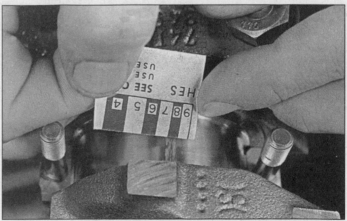

25.17 Compare the widest point of the crushed Plastigage to the scale on the envelope to determine the rod bearing oil clearance - be sure to use the correct scale; standard and metric scales are included

specified, the bearing will have to be replaced with an undersize bearing. **Caution:** *When installing a new crankshaft always use a standard bearing.*

Final connecting rod installation

19   Carefully scrape all traces of the Plastigage material off the rod journal and/or bearing face. Be very careful not to scratch the bearing - use your fingernail or the edge of a credit card.

20   Make sure the bearing faces are perfectly clean, then apply a uniform layer of clean moly-base grease or engine assembly lube to both of them. You'll have to push the piston into the cylinder to expose the face of the bearing insert in the connecting rod - be sure to slip the protective hoses over the rod bolts first.

21   Slide the connecting rod back into place on the journal, remove the protective hoses from the rod cap bolts, install the rod cap and tighten the nuts to the torque listed in this Chapter's Specifications. Again, work up to the torque in three steps.

22   Repeat the entire procedure for the remaining pistons/connecting rods.

23   The important points to remember are:

a) *Keep the back sides of the bearing inserts and the insides of the connecting rods and caps perfectly clean when assembling them.*

b) *Make sure you have the correct piston/ rod assembly for each cylinder.*

c) *The mark on the piston must face the front of the engine.*

d) *Lubricate the cylinder walls with clean oil.*

e) *Lubricate the bearing faces when installing the rod caps after the oil clearance has been checked.*

24   After all the piston/connecting rod assemblies have been properly installed, rotate the crankshaft a number of times by hand to check for any obvious binding.

25   As a final step, the connecting rod endplay must be checked. Refer to Section 13 for this procedure.

26   Compare the measured endplay to the Specifications to make sure it's correct. If it was correct before disassembly and the original crankshaft and rods were reinstalled, it should still be right. If new rods or a new crankshaft were installed, the endplay may be inadequate. If so, the rods will have to be removed and taken to an automotive machine shop for resizing.

26   Initial start-up and break-in after overhaul

Warning: *Have a fire extinguisher handy when starting the engine for the first time.*

1   Once the engine has been installed in the vehicle, double-check the engine oil and coolant levels. Add transaxle fluid as needed.

2   With the spark plugs out of the engine and the ignition system and fuel system disabled (see Section 3, Step 5), crank the engine until the oil pressure light goes out.

3   Install the spark plugs, hook up the plug wires and restore the ignition and fuel system functions.

4   Start the engine. It may take a few moments for the fuel system to build up pressure, but the engine should start without a great deal of effort. **Note:** *If backfiring occurs through the throttle body, recheck the valve timing and ignition timing.*

5   After the engine starts, it should be allowed to warm up to normal operating temperature. Try to keep the engine speed at approximately 2000 rpm. While the engine is warming up, make a thorough check for fuel, oil and coolant leaks. Check the automatic transaxle fluid level (if so equipped).

6   Shut the engine off and recheck the engine oil and coolant levels.

7   Drive the vehicle to an area with minimum traffic, accelerate at full throttle from 30 to 50 mph, then allow the vehicle to slow to 30 mph with the throttle closed. Repeat the procedure 10 or 12 times. This will load the piston rings and cause them to seat properly against the cylinder walls. Check again for oil and coolant leaks.

8   Drive the vehicle gently for the first 500 miles (no sustained high speeds) and keep a constant check on the oil level. It is not unusual for an engine to use oil during the break-in period.

9   At approximately 500 to 600 miles, change the oil and filter.

10   For the next few hundred miles, drive the vehicle normally. Do not pamper it or abuse it.

11   After 2000 miles, change the oil and filter again and consider the engine broken in.

Chapter 3
Cooling, heating and air conditioning systems

Contents

Specifications

General

Radiator cap pressure rating	11 to 15 psi
Thermostat rating (opening temperature)...............................	190-degrees F
Cooling system capacity..	See Chapter 1
Cooling system testing pressure	13 psi
Refrigerant capacity..	Refer to the HVAC specification label under the hood
Refrigerant oil capacity (complete system)	
2.0L non-turbo models	3.4 fl oz
2.0L turbo, 1998 and 1999 2.4L models.............................	5.7 fl oz
2000 and later 2.4L, all 3.0L V6 models.............................	4.1 fl oz

Torque specifications

Ft-lbs (unless otherwise indicated)

Note: *One foot-pound (ft-lb) of torque is equivalent to 12 inch-pounds (in-lbs) of torque. Torque values below approximately 15 ft-lbs are expressed in inch-pounds, since most foot-pound torque wrenches are not accurate at these smaller values.*

Thermostat cover bolts	
2.0L turbo	112 in-lbs
2.0L non-turbo..	16
2.4L	
1999 and earlier..	112 in-lbs
2000 and later...	109 in-lbs
3.0L V6..	156 in-lbs
Thermostat housing-to-engine bolts (V6 engine)	156 in-lbs
Water pump-to-engine block bolts	
2.0L turbo	
All except 2-1/2 inch bolt...	132 in-lbs
2-1/2 inch bolt	17
2.0L non-turbo...	104 in-lbs
2.4L	
1999 and earlier	
All except 2-1/2 inch bolt	132 in-lbs
2-1/2 inch bolt...	17
2000 and later	
All except 2-1/2 inch bolt	117 in-lbs
2-1/2 inch bolt...	17
3.0L V6 **(see illustration 9.18)**	
Bolts A..	17
Bolt B	30
Upper bracket bolts...	17

1   General information

Engine cooling system

All vehicles covered by this manual employ a pressurized engine cooling system with thermostatically controlled coolant circulation. An impeller type water pump mounted on the drivebelt end of the block pumps coolant through the engine. The coolant flows around each cylinder and toward the transaxle end of the engine. Cast-in coolant passages direct coolant around the intake and exhaust ports, near the spark plug areas and in close proximity to the exhaust valve guides.

A wax pellet type thermostat is located in a housing on the timing belt end of the engine (2.0L non-turbo models) or on the other end of the engine (all others). During warm up, the closed thermostat prevents coolant from circulating through the radiator. As the engine nears normal operating temperature, the thermostat opens and allows hot coolant to travel through the radiator, where it's cooled before returning to the engine.

The cooling system is sealed by a pressure type radiator cap, which raises the boiling point of the coolant and increases the cooling efficiency of the radiator. If the system pressure exceeds the cap pressure relief value, the excess pressure in the system forces the spring-loaded valve inside the cap off its seat and allows the coolant to escape through the overflow tube into a coolant reservoir. When the system cools, the excess coolant is automatically drawn from the reservoir back into the radiator.

The coolant reservoir serves as both the point at which fresh coolant is added to the cooling system to maintain the proper fluid level and as a holding tank for overheated coolant.

This type of cooling system is known as a closed design because coolant that escapes past the pressure cap is saved and reused.

Heating system

The heating system consists of a blower fan and heater core located in the heater box, the hoses connecting the heater core to the engine cooling system and the heater/air conditioning control head on the dashboard. Hot engine coolant is circulated through the heater core. When the heater mode is activated, a flap opens to expose the heater box to the passenger compartment. A fan switch on the control head activates the blower motor, which forces air through the core, heating the air.

Air conditioning system

The air conditioning system consists of a condenser mounted in front of the radiator, an evaporator mounted adjacent to the heater core, a compressor mounted on the engine, a receiver-drier which contains a high pressure relief valve and the plumbing connecting all of the above components.

A blower fan forces the warmer air of the passenger compartment through the evaporator core (sort of a radiator-in-reverse), transferring the heat from the air to the refrigerant. The liquid refrigerant boils off into low pressure vapor, taking the heat with it when it leaves the evaporator.

2   Antifreeze - general information

Warning: *Do not allow antifreeze to come in contact with your skin or painted surfaces of the vehicle. Rinse off spills immediately with plenty of water. Antifreeze is highly toxic if ingested. Never leave antifreeze lying around in an open container or in puddles on the floor; children and pets are attracted by it's sweet smell and may drink it. Check with local authorities about disposing of used antifreeze. Many communities have collection centers which will see that antifreeze is disposed of safely.*

The cooling system should be filled with a water/ethylene glycol based antifreeze solution, which will prevent freezing down to at least -20-degrees F, or lower if local climate requires it. It also provides protection against corrosion and increases the coolant boiling point.

The cooling system should be drained, flushed and refilled at the specified intervals (see Chapter 1). Old or contaminated antifreeze solutions are likely to cause damage and encourage the formation of corrosion and scale in the system. Use distilled water with the antifreeze.

Before adding antifreeze, check all hose connections, because antifreeze tends to leak through very minute openings. Engines don't normally consume coolant, so if the level goes down, find the cause and correct it.

The exact mixture of antifreeze-to-water which you should use depends on the relative weather conditions. The mixture should contain at least 50-percent antifreeze, but should never contain more than 70-percent antifreeze. Consult the mixture ratio chart on the antifreeze container before adding coolant. Hydrometers are available at most auto parts stores to test the coolant. Use antifreeze which meets the vehicle manufacturer's specifications.

3   Thermostat - check and replacement

Warning: *Do not remove the radiator cap, drain the coolant or replace the thermostat until the engine has cooled completely. Do not allow antifreeze to come in contact with your skin or painted surfaces of the vehicle. Rinse off spills immediately with plenty of water. Antifreeze is highly toxic if ingested. Never leave antifreeze lying around in an open container or in puddles on the floor; children and pets are attracted by its sweet smell and may drink it. Check with local authorities about disposing of used antifreeze. Many communities have collection centers which will see that antifreeze is disposed of safely.*

Check

1   Before assuming the thermostat is to blame for a cooling system problem, check the coolant level, drivebelt tension (see Chapter 1) and temperature gauge operation.

2   If the engine seems to be taking a long time to warm up (based on heater output or temperature gauge operation), the thermostat is probably stuck open. Replace the thermostat with a new one.

3   If the engine runs hot, use your hand to check the temperature of the upper radiator hose. If the hose isn't hot, but the engine is, the thermostat is probably stuck closed, preventing the coolant inside the engine from escaping to the radiator. Replace the thermostat. **Caution:** *Don't drive the vehicle without a thermostat. The computer may stay in open loop, causing emissions and fuel economy to suffer.*

4   If the upper radiator hose is hot, it means that the coolant is flowing and the thermostat is open. Consult the *Troubleshooting* section at the front of this manual for cooling system diagnosis.

Replacement

Refer to illustrations 3.7a, 3.7b and 3.7c

5   Disconnect the cable from the negative terminal of the battery.

6   Drain the cooling system (see Chapter 1). If the coolant is relatively new or in good condition, save it and reuse it.

7   Follow the upper radiator hose to the

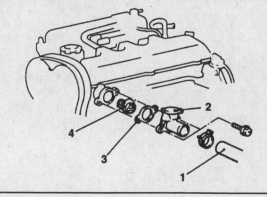

3.7a Thermostat housing (2.0L non-turbo engine) - exploded view

1   *Radiator upper hose*
2   *Water outlet fitting (thermostat housing)*
3   *Gasket*
4   *Thermostat*

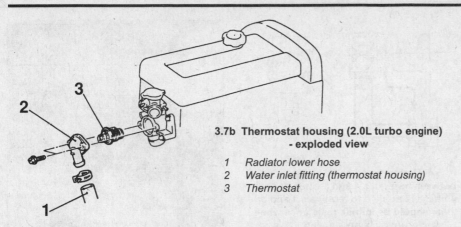

3.7b Thermostat housing (2.0L turbo engine) - exploded view

1 Radiator lower hose
2 Water inlet fitting (thermostat housing)
3 Thermostat

3.7c The 3.0L V6 thermostat cover is mounted horizontally and hidden below the air cleaner duct (arrow)

engine to locate the thermostat cover **(see illustrations)**.

8   Loosen the hose clamp and detach the hose from the fitting. If the hose is stuck, grasp it near the end with a pair of adjustable pliers and twist it to break the seal, then pull it off. If the hose is old or deteriorated, cut it off and install a new one.

9   If the outer surface of the large fitting that mates with the hose is deteriorated (corroded, pitted, etc.) it may be damaged further by hose removal. If it is, the thermostat cover will have to be replaced.

10   Remove the bolts and detach the thermostat cover. If the cover is stuck, tap it with a soft-face hammer to jar it loose. Be prepared for some coolant to spill as the gasket seal is broken.

11   Note the position of the air bleed valve and how the thermostat is installed, then remove the thermostat and all traces of old gasket material and sealant from the housing and cover with a gasket scraper.

12   If you're working on a 2.0L non-turbo engine, apply a thin, uniform layer of RTV sealant to both sides of the new gasket and position it on the housing. On all other models, install the rubber sealing ring around the flange of the thermostat.

13   Install the new thermostat in the housing with the spring end directed into the engine. Turn the thermostat so the air bleed valve (jiggle valve) is straight up.

14   Install the thermostat cover and bolts.

Tighten the bolts to the torque listed in this Chapter's Specifications.

15   Reattach the hose to the fitting and tighten the hose clamp securely.

16   Refill the cooling system (see Chapter 1).

17   Start the engine and allow it to reach normal operating temperature, then check for leaks and proper thermostat operation (as described in Steps 3 and 4).

4   Thermostat housing (3.0L V6 engine models) - removal and installation

Refer to illustration 4.2

1   The thermostat on these models is mounted in a removable housing located on the transaxle end of the engine. The housing also contains the coolant temperature gauge sending unit and the coolant temperature sensor for the engine management system.

2   Drain the cooling system (see Chapter 1). Disconnect the large hoses from the thermostat cover and the water inlet fitting, as well as the small hoses **(see illustration)**.

3   Unbolt the thermostat housing from the cylinder heads. Take the housing off, separating it from the water tube located in the V between the cylinder banks and the two heater tubes.

4   Installation is the reverse of the removal

steps. Lubricate new water tube O-rings with antifreeze and install them on the water tubes. Use new gaskets where the housing joins the cylinder heads. Tighten the housing bolts to the torque listed in this Chapter's Specifications.

5   Engine cooling fan(s) and circuit - check and component replacement

Warning: *To avoid possible injury or damage, DO NOT operate the engine with a damaged fan. Do not attempt to repair fan blades - replace a damaged fan with a new one.*
Note: *Always check for blown fuses or fusible links before attempting to diagnose an electrical circuit problem.*

Check
1995 through 1999 models
Refer to illustrations 5.1a, 5.1b and 5.4

1   If the engine is overheating and the cooling fan is not coming on, disconnect the electrical connector at the motor and use fused jumper wires to connect the fan directly to the battery. If the fan still doesn't work, replace

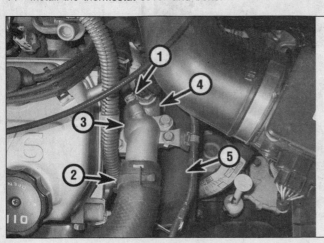

4.2 Thermostat housing details (3.0L V6 engine)

1 Water hose
2 Radiator upper hose
3 Water outlet fitting
4 Thermostat housing (partially hidden)
5 Radiator lower hose

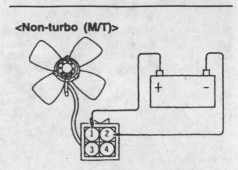

5.1a If the vehicle has a single fan, connect battery voltage as shown to test the fan motor . . .

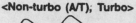

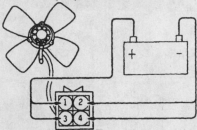

<Non-turbo (A/T); Turbo>

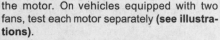

5.1b . . . if the vehicle has two fans, connect the battery between terminals 1 and 2, then between terminals 3 and 4

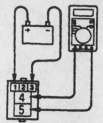

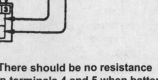

5.4 There should be no resistance between terminals 4 and 5 when battery voltage is applied to terminals 1 and 3; there should be infinite resistance when power is not applied

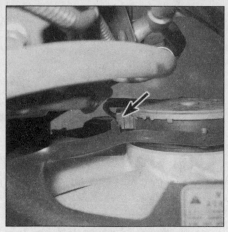

5.7 Disconnect the upper (3-pin) connector from the fan motor

the motor. On vehicles equipped with two fans, test each motor separately **(see illustrations)**.

2   If the motor is OK, but the cooling fan doesn't come on when the engine gets hot, the fault may be in the coolant temperature sensor, the fan relay(s), the engine control computer or the wiring which connects the components.

3   The engine coolant temperature sensor sends temperature signals to the powertrain control module (PCM), which uses them together with other data to regulate fan speed. A test for checking the sensor is located in Chapter 6.

4   Remove the fan relays from the relay box in the engine compartment. Using an ohmmeter, check the resistance between terminals 4 and 5 with and without power applied to terminals 1 and 3 **(see illustration)**. To apply power, connect the vehicle's battery to terminals 1 and 3 with jumper wires.

5   There should be no continuity between terminals 4 and 5 when no power is applied. There should be continuity between terminals 4 and 5 when battery power is applied to terminals 1 and 3. If a relay doesn't perform as described, replace it.

6   If the fan motor, coolant temperature sensor and relays are good, carefully check the wiring and connections (wiring diagrams are included at the end of Chapter 12). If no obvious problems are found, the problem may be in the powertrain control module. Further diagnosis should be done by a dealer service department or repair shop with the proper diagnostic equipment.

2000 and later models
Refer to illustrations 5.7, 5.8 and 5.9

7   Disconnect the three-pin connector at the fan motor **(see illustration)**. Connect an ohmmeter between terminal 1 and ground. It should indicate less than 2 ohms, indicating that the ground circuit is good. If the reading is too high, follow the ground wire to its connections, checking for breaks or poor connections.

8   To test the fan control module, disconnect the two-pin connector from the condenser fan **(see illustration)**. Connect a voltmeter between the terminals. Run the engine at idle with the engine coolant temperature at 176-degrees F or less. The voltmeter reading should vary continuously from zero, to 5.6-to-10.8 volts, to battery voltage +/-2.6

volts. If voltage doesn't change as described, replace the fan motor/control module assembly.

9   Remove the fan relay from the relay box in the engine compartment. Using an ohmmeter, check the resistance between terminals 2 and 5 with and without power applied to terminals 1 and 3 **(see illustration)**. To apply power, connect the vehicle's battery to terminals 1 and 3 with jumper wires. There should be no continuity between terminals 2 and 5 when no power is applied. There should be continuity between terminals 2 and 5 when battery power is applied to terminals 1 and 3. If a relay doesn't perform as described, replace it.

Replacement
Refer to illustration 5.12

10   Disconnect the cable from the negative terminal of the battery.

11   Disconnect the electrical connector from the fan you're removing (condenser fan or cooling fan).

5.8 Unplug the connector from the condenser fan, then connect a voltmeter between the terminals of the connector

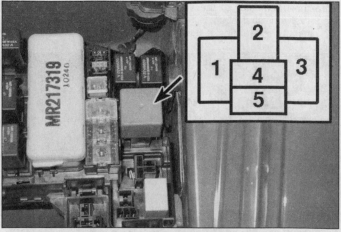

5.9 There should be no resistance between terminals 2 and 5 when battery voltage is applied to terminals 1 and 3; there should be infinite resistance when power is not applied

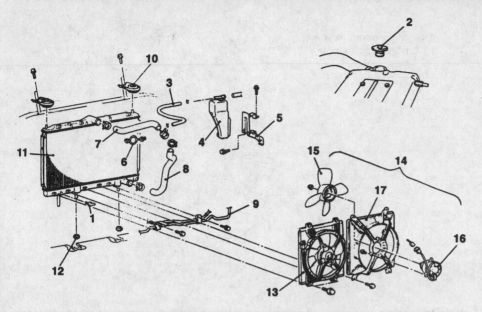

5.12 Radiator and fans (2.0L turbo shown) - exploded view

1	Drain plug	10	Upper insulator
2	Radiator cap	11	Radiator
3	Overflow tube	12	Lower insulator
4	Coolant reservoir	13	Condenser fan
5	Reservoir bracket	14	Radiator fan
6	Clip	15	Fan blades
7	Upper radiator hose	16	Fan motor
8	Lower radiator hose	17	Shroud
9	Automatic transaxle fluid cooler lines		

12 Remove the fan shroud bolts **(see illustration)**.
13 Lift the fan assembly out of the engine compartment, being careful not to damage the radiator.
14 To remove the fan motor, unscrew the nut from the center of the fan and remove the fan from the motor shaft. Unbolt the fan motor (and the control module if you're removing the radiator fan) from the shroud.
15 Installation is the reverse of the removal steps.

6 Radiator - removal and installation

Refer to illustration 6.5
Warning: *Do not start this procedure until the engine is completely cool. Do not allow antifreeze to come in contact with your skin or painted surfaces of the vehicle. Rinse off spills immediately with plenty of water. Antifreeze is highly toxic if ingested. Never leave antifreeze lying around in an open container or in puddles on the floor; children and pets are attracted by its sweet smell and may drink it. Check with local authorities about disposing of used antifreeze. Many communities have collection centers which will see that antifreeze is disposed of safely.*

Removal
1 Disconnect the cable from the negative terminal of the battery.
2 Raise the front of the vehicle and support it securely on jackstands. Remove the lower splash shield.
3 Drain the cooling system (see Chapter 1). If the coolant is relatively new or in good condition, save it and reuse it.
4 Disconnect the coolant reservoir hose from the radiator. Loosen the upper and lower radiator hose clamps, then detach the radiator hoses from the fittings. If they're stuck, grasp

each hose near the end with a pair of adjustable pliers and twist it to break the seal, then pull it off - be careful not to damage the radiator fittings! If the hoses are old or deteriorated, cut them off and install new ones.
5 Remove the radiator upper supports **(see illustration)**.
6 Disconnect the electrical connector(s) from the cooling fan(s).
7 If the vehicle is equipped with an automatic transaxle, disconnect the transmission fluid cooler lines and plug the lines and fittings.
8 Carefully lift out the radiator. Don't spill coolant on the vehicle or scratch the paint. Remove the bolts securing the cooling fan to the radiator and pull it free.
9 With the radiator removed, it can be inspected for leaks and damage. If it needs repair, have a radiator shop or dealer service department perform the work.
10 Bugs and dirt can be removed from the radiator with a garden hose or a soft brush. Don't bend the cooling fins as this is done.

Installation
11 Installation is the reverse of the removal procedure. Be sure the rubber cushions are seated properly at the base of the radiator.
12 After installation, fill the cooling system with the proper mixture of antifreeze and water (see Chapter 1).
13 Start the engine and check for leaks. Allow the engine to reach normal operating temperature, indicated by the upper radiator hose becoming hot. Recheck the coolant level and add more if required.
14 If you're working on an automatic transaxle equipped vehicle, check and add fluid as needed (see Chapter 1).

7 Coolant reservoir - removal and installation

Warning: *Do not start this procedure until the engine is completely cool. Do not allow antifreeze to come in contact with your skin or painted surfaces of the vehicle. Rinse off*

6.5 Remove the radiator upper supports (arrows)

spills immediately with plenty of water. Antifreeze is highly toxic if ingested. Never leave antifreeze lying around in an open container or in puddles on the floor; children and pets are attracted by it's sweet smell and may drink it. Check with local authorities about disposing of used antifreeze. Many communities have collection centers which will see that antifreeze is disposed of safely.

1   Disconnect the hose from the radiator filler neck and inspect the hose for cracks.

2   Follow the hose from the filler neck to the reservoir cap and lift the cap off the coolant reservoir and withdraw the overflow hose.

3   Remove the hold-down bolt.

4   Slide the coolant reservoir straight up from its guides to remove it **(see illustration 5.12)**.

5   Pour the coolant into a container. Wash out and inspect the reservoir for cracks and chafing. Replace it if it's damaged.

6   Installation is the reverse of removal.

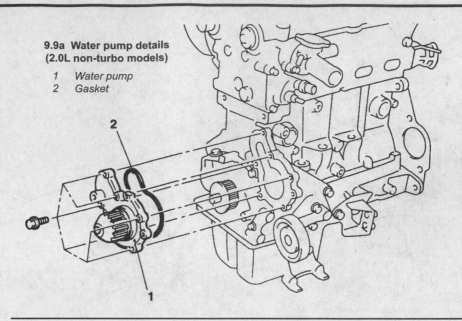

9.9a Water pump details (2.0L non-turbo models)

1   *Water pump*
2   *Gasket*

8   Water pump - check

1   A failure in the water pump can cause serious engine damage due to overheating.

2   There are two ways to check the operation of the water pump while it's installed on the engine. If the pump is defective, it should be replaced with a new or rebuilt unit.

3   Loosen the tension on the water pump belt (see Chapter 1). Grasp the water pump pulley and try to rock it up-and-down. If any play is felt, the shaft bearings are worn out and the pump should be replaced.

4   Remove the timing belt cover(s) (see Chapters 2A through 2D). Water pumps are equipped with weep or vent holes. If a failure occurs in the pump seal, coolant will leak from the hole. In most cases you'll need a flashlight to find the hole on the water pump from underneath to check for leaks.

5   If the water pump shaft bearings fail there may be a howling sound at the drivebelt end of the engine while it's running. Don't mistake drivebelt slippage, which causes a squealing sound, for water pump bearing failure.

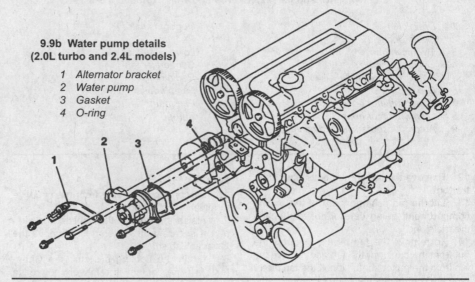

9.9b Water pump details (2.0L turbo and 2.4L models)

1   *Alternator bracket*
2   *Water pump*
3   *Gasket*
4   *O-ring*

9   Water pump - removal and installation

Four-cylinder engines

Refer to illustration 9.9a, 9.9b, 9.10 and 9.11

1   Disconnect the negative battery cable from the battery.

2   Raise the vehicle and support it securely on jackstands.

3   Remove the splash shield.

4   Remove the drivebelts (see Chapter 1).

5   Drain the cooling system (see Chapter 1).

6   Remove the timing belt (see Chapter 2A, 2B or 2C). If you're working on a 2.0L non-

turbo engine, remove the rear timing belt cover.

7   If you're working on a 2.0L turbo or 2.4L engine, remove the alternator and its mounting bracket (see Chapter 5).

8   If you're working on a 2.4L engine, remove the timing belt tensioner pulley (see Chapter 2C).

9   Remove the bolts attaching the water pump to the engine block. Label the bolts so they can be reinstalled in the correct positions (they're different lengths) and remove the pump **(see illustrations)**.

10   If you're working on a 2.0L non-turbo, install a new O-ring in the water pump body groove **(see illustration)**.

11   If you're working on a 2.0L turbo or 2.4L engine, lubricate a new water inlet O-ring with coolant and install it on the water inlet pipe **(see illustration)**. Coat a new gasket on both sides with sealant and install it on the engine.

12   Install the water pump on the engine. If you're working on a 2.0L turbo or 2.4L engine, fit the water pump securely over the inlet pipe and O-ring. Tighten the mounting bolts to the torque listed in this Chapter's specifications.

13   The remainder of installation is the reverse of the removal steps.

14   Check drivebelt tension and refill the cooling system (see Chapter 1). Run the engine and check for leaks.

V6 engine

Refer to illustrations 9.18 and 9.21

15   Disconnect the negative battery cable from the battery.

16   Remove the drivebelts and drain the cooling system (see Chapter 1).

17   Refer to Chapter 2, Part D and remove the crankshaft damper/pulley, timing belt covers and timing belt.

18   Remove the water pump mounting bolts **(see illustration)**. Label the bolts so they can

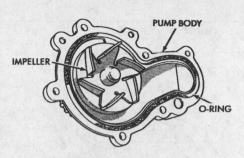

9.10 Install a new O-ring on the water pump (2.0L non-turbo)

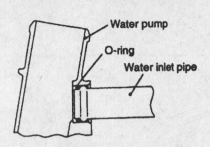

9.11 Lubricate a new O-ring with coolant and install it on the water inlet pipe (2.0L turbo)

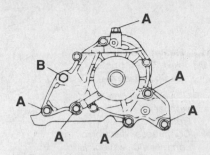

9.18 Remove the water pump bolts (3.0L V6 engine)

be reinstalled in the correct positions (they're different lengths).

19   Separate the pump from the water inlet pipe and remove the pump.

20   Clean all the gasket and O-ring surfaces on the pump and the water pipe inlet tube.

21   Install a new O-ring on the water inlet pipe **(see illustration)**. Wet the O-ring with water or coolant to facilitate assembly.

22   Install a new gasket on the water pump and install the inlet opening over the water pipe. Press the water pipe into the pump housing.

23   Install the water pump mounting bolts and tighten the bolts to the torque listed in this Chapter's Specifications.

24   Install the timing belt (see Chapter 2D).

25   The remainder of installation is the reverse of removal.

26   Refill the cooling system (see Chapter 1) and operate the engine to check for leaks.

10   Coolant temperature sending unit - check and replacement

Refer to illustrations 10.3 and 10.4
Warning: *The engine must be completely cool before removing the sending unit.*

Check

1   If the coolant temperature gauge is inoperative, check the fuses first (see Chapter 12).

2   If the temperature indicator shows excessive temperature after running awhile, see the *Troubleshooting* section in the front of the manual.

3   If the temperature gauge indicates Hot shortly after the engine is started cold, disconnect the wire at the coolant temperature sending unit - it's located on the thermostat housing **(see illustration)**. **Note:** *On some models, the sending units for the gauge and the engine management system are both located on the thermostat housing. You can differentiate between the two by wire color (refer to the wiring diagrams at the end of Chapter 12).* If the gauge reading drops, replace the sending unit. If the reading remains high, the wire to the gauge may be shorted to ground or the gauge is faulty.

4   If the coolant temperature gauge fails to indicate after the engine has been warmed up (approximately 10 minutes) and the fuses checked out okay, shut off the engine. Disconnect the wire at the sending unit and, using a jumper wire equipped with a 12-volt, 3.4-watt bulb, connect the wiring harness to a clean ground on the engine **(see illustration)**.

5   Turn on the ignition without starting the engine. If the test bulb lights up and gauge needle hasn't been moving, replace the gauge. If the bulb lights up and the gauge

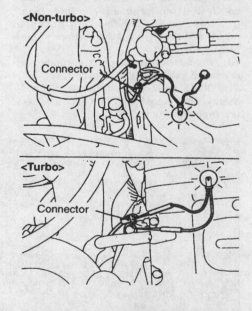

9.21 Lubricate a new O-ring with coolant and install it on the water inlet pipe (3.0L V6)

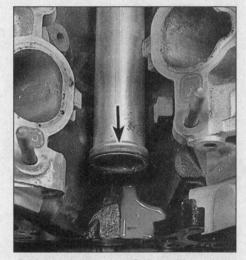

10.4 Connect a 3.4-watt bulb between the connector and ground (bare metal) on the engine

10.3 Here's a typical temperature gauge sending unit - on all models, it's mounted on the thermostat housing

1   Temperature gauge sending unit
2   Engine Coolant Temperature (ECT) sensor

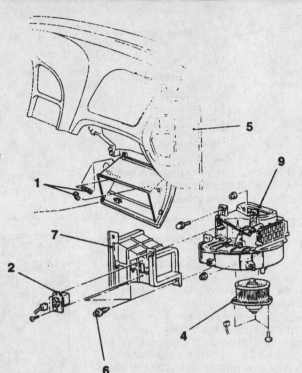

11.2 Heater blower (1995 through 1999 models) - exploded view

1   *Glove compartment stopper*
2   *Resistor*
3   *Compressor electronic control module (vehicles so equipped)*
4   *Blower fan and motor*
5   *Instrument panel*
6   *Clip*
7   *Joint duct (non-air conditioned models)*
8   *Cooling unit nuts and bolts (air conditioned models)*
9   *Blower housing*

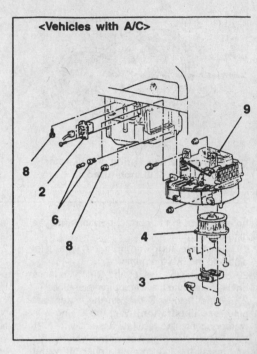

<Vehicles with A/C>

needle has been moving, replace the sending unit.

Replacement

6   With the engine completely cool, remove the cap from the radiator to release any pressure, then reinstall the cap. This reduces coolant loss during sending unit replacement.
7   Disconnect the electrical connector from the sending unit.
8   Prepare the new sending unit for installation by wrapping the threads with Teflon tape.
9   Unscrew the sending unit from the engine and quickly install the new one to prevent coolant loss.
10   Tighten the sending unit securely and connect the electrical connector.
11   Check the coolant level and add, if necessary. Start the engine and check for leaks and proper gauge operation.

11   Blower motor and circuit - check and replacement

Warning: *These models are equipped with airbags. Always disable the airbag system before working in the vicinity of any airbag system component to avoid the possibility of accidental deployment of the airbag, which could cause personal injury (see Chapter 12).*

Check

Refer to illustrations 11.2, 11.3 and 11.4
1   Check the fuse and all connections in the circuit for looseness and corrosion. Make sure the battery is fully charged.
2   If you're working on a 1995 through 1999 model, remove the glove box stay and let the glove box hang down **(see illustration)**.
3   If you're working on a 2000 or later model, remove the glove box (see Chap-

ter 12). Remove the joint duct from the left side of the blower motor housing **(see illustration)**.
4   Remove the resistor screws and take the resistor out of the blower housing or air duct. Connect an ohmmeter between pairs of terminals **(see illustration)** and note the readings as described below and replace the resistor if they aren't correct. **Note:** *Resistance readings are approximate.*
5   If you're working on a 1995 through 1999 model:

a)   *Between terminals 2 and 3: 1.83 ohms.*
b)   *Between terminals 3 and 4: 0.87 ohms.*
c)   *Between terminals 1 and 3: 0.31 ohms.*

6   If you're working on a 2000 or later model:

a)   *Between terminals 2 and 3: 2.3 ohms.*
b)   *Between terminals 3 and 4: 1.1 ohms.*
c)   *Between terminals 1 and 3: 0.4 ohms.*

7   Disconnect the blower motor connector. Using jumper wires, connect one terminal of the connector's motor side to a chassis

11.3 Remove the joint duct (arrow)

11.4 Measure the resistance between specified pairs of resistor terminals (see text)

11.13 Remove the blower motor screws (arrows) and take the motor out

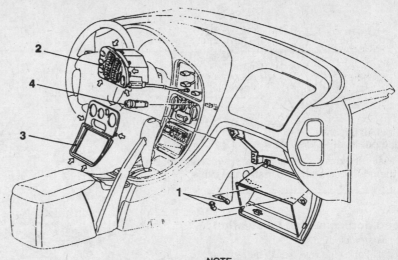

NOTE
⇦ indicates sheet metal clip positions.

12.2 Air conditioning switch and related components (1995 through 1999 models)

1	Glove compartment stopper	3	Center panel
2	Center air outlet	4	Air conditioning switch

ground and the other terminal to the battery positive terminal (install a fuse in the jumper wire running to the battery). If the blower motor doesn't operate, it's faulty.

8   If the resistor and motor tested OK, the problem is in the blower switch in the control panel assembly or the related wiring.

9   To test the blower switch, refer to Section 12 and check for continuity through the switch in each position. Refer to the wiring diagrams at the end of Chapter 12 to determine the correct terminals for testing.

Replacement

Refer to illustration 11.13

10   Disconnect the battery negative cable from the battery.

11   If you're working on a 1995 through 1999 model with air conditioning, remove the compressor control module from the underside of the blower motor **(see illustration 11.2)**.

12   Disconnect the wiring connector at the blower motor resistor.

13   Remove the screws retaining the blower motor to the heater housing **(see illustration)**.

14   Lower the blower motor from the housing.

15   The fan is balanced with the blower motor, and is available only as an assembly. If the fan is damaged, both the fan and blower motor must be replaced.

16   Installation is the reverse of removal.

12   Heater/air conditioner control assembly - removal, check and installation

Warning: *These models are equipped with airbags. Always disable the airbag system before working in the vicinity of any airbag system component to avoid the possibility of accidental deployment of the airbag, which could cause personal injury (see Chapter 12).*
Note: *The air conditioning switch on 1995 through 1999 models can be removed either as a unit with the control assembly or separately. If you're only working on the air conditioning switch, it will be easier to remove it separately.*

1995 through 1999 models

Air conditioning switch removal

Refer to illustration 12.2

1   Disconnect the negative battery cable from the battery.

2   Remove the glove compartment stopper and let the glove compartment hang down **(see illustration)**.

3   Remove the retaining clips from the center air outlet and trim panel. Disconnect the cool air bypass cable from the damper lever on the heater unit to free the center air outlet, then remove the center air outlet and the trim panel.

4   Disconnect the wiring connector from the back of the air conditioning switch, squeeze the tabs on the switch and remove it from the control panel.

Air conditioning switch check

Refer to illustration 12.5a and 12.5b

5   Use an ohmmeter to check continuity between the switch terminals with the switch in each position **(see illustrations)**. If there's continuity when there shouldn't be, or no continuity when there should be, replace the switch.

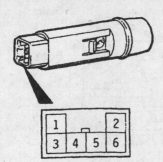

12.5a Air conditioning switch terminal numbers (1995 through 1999 models)

12.5b Air conditioning switch continuity diagram (1995 through 1999 models)

Switch position	Terminal No.						
	1	4	IND	5	3	ILL	6
OFF	○		○▷⚡ ○			○⟲ ○	
ON	○		○▷⚡ ○			○⟲ ○	

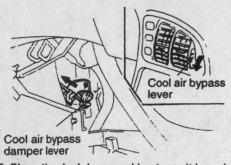

12.6 Place the dash lever and heater unit lever in the positions shown to install the cable

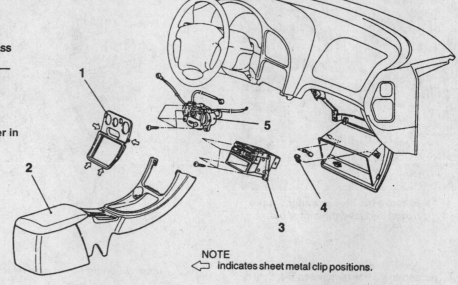

NOTE
◁ indicates sheet metal clip positions.

12.8 Heater control assembly details (1995 through 1999 models)

1	Center trim panel	4	Glove compartment stopper
2	Console	5	Heater control assembly
3	Radio		

Air conditioning switch installation

Refer to illustration 12.6

6   Installation is the reverse of the removal steps. When you install the center air outlet, place the cool air bypass lever in the lowest position **(see illustration)**. Pull the damper lever on the heater unit toward you, push the outer cable in the direction shown to eliminate any slack and tighten the cable clip.

Control assembly removal

Refer to illustrations 12.8, 12.11 and 12.13

7   Disconnect the negative battery cable from the battery.

8   Remove the trim bezel from the instrument panel **(see illustration)**.

9   Remove the center console (see Chapter 11) and the radio (see Chapter 12).

10   Remove the glove compartment stopper and let the glove compartment hang down.

11   Locate the air outlet changeover damper cable under the instrument panel. Squeeze the latch and slide the cable off the lever pin **(see illustration)**.

12   Remove the control assembly screws **(see illustration 12.8)**.

13   Snap off the boss and clamp with a screwdriver or locking pliers **(see illustration)**. These are used on the assembly line when the vehicle is built, but are not needed later.

14   Disconnect the wiring harness from the rear of the control assembly.

15   Disconnect the temperature control, recirculation control and defroster cables.

16   Remove the control assembly.

Control assembly check

Refer to illustrations 12.18a, 12.18b, 12.19a, 12.19b, 12.20 and 12.21

17   Remove the control assembly (see Steps 7 through 16).

18   Using an ohmmeter, measure the resistance between the blower switch terminals at the back of the control assembly **(see illustration)**. Turn the control assembly to each position and check for continuity as indicated **(see illustration)**.

19   Check the defroster switch continuity with the ohmmeter **(see illustrations)**.

20   If there's continuity when there shouldn't be, or no continuity when there should be, replace the defective switch **(see illustration)**.

21   If any of the cables needs to be replaced, disengage the claw with a screwdriver blade and remove the cable **(see illustration)**.

Control assembly installation

Refer to illustrations 12.23, 12.24 and 12.25

22   Installation is the reverse of removal. If you're installing a new control assembly, snap off the boss and clamp first **(see illustration 12.13)**. If necessary, adjust the cables as described below.

23   Temperature control cable:

a) *Turn the control knob to MAX HOT.*

b) *Place the lever on the heater unit in the MAX HOT position and connect the cable to the lever.*

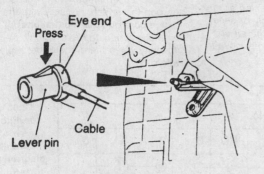

12.11 Press the prong into the pin, then slip the pin out of the cable end

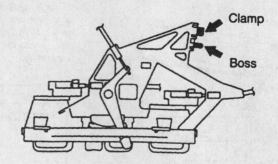

12.13 Snap off the boss and clamp with a screwdriver blade or locking pliers

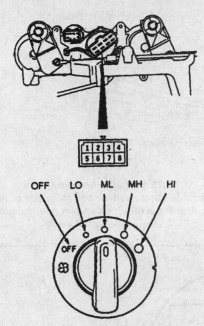

Switch position	Terminal No.							
	1	2	3	4	5	6	7	8
OFF								
● (LO)			○—	—○				
	○							○
● (ML)					○—	—○		
	○							○
● (MH)			○—	—○				
	○			○				○
● (HI)					○—	—○		
	○			○				○

12.18b Blower switch continuity diagram (1995 through 1999 models)

12.18a Blower switch terminal identification (1995 through 1999 models)

Air outlet changeover control knob position	Terminal No.	
	1	2
DEF, DEF/FOOT	○—	—○
Any other position		

12.19a Defroster switch continuity diagram

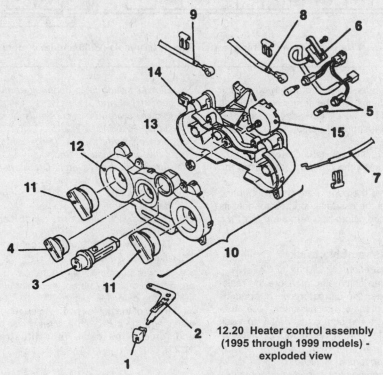

12.20 Heater control assembly (1995 through 1999 models) - exploded view

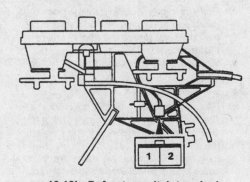

12.19b Defroster switch terminals (1995 through 1999 models)

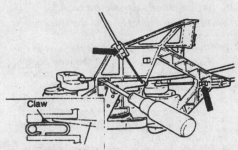

12.21 Press the claw with a flat-tipped screwdriver and disengage the cable

1   Knob
2   Lever assembly
3   Air conditioning switch
4   Knob
5   Bulb and socket
6   Defroster switch
7   Air outlet changeover damper cable
8   Air mix damper cable
9   Inside/outside air changeover damper cable
10 Control base assembly
11 Knob
12 Panel case
13 Nut
14 Control base
15 Blower switch

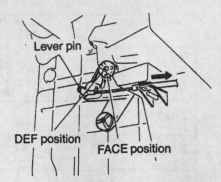

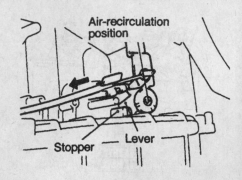

12.23 Place the lever in the MAX HOT position and move the outer cable toward the MAX COOL position, then secure the cable with the clip

12.24 Place the lever in the DEF position and move the outer cable toward the FACE position, then secure the cable with the clip

12.25 Place the lever in the air recirculation position and move the outer cable in the direction shown, then secure the cable with the clip

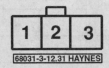

12.31 Defroster switch terminals (2000 and later models)

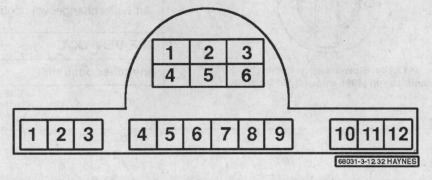

12.32 Blower (upper)/air conditioning switch (lower) terminals (2000 and later models)

c) *Pull the cable housing away from the cable end to remove all freeplay and clip the cable housing to the heater unit* (**see illustration**).
d) *Verify the knob travels through its full range.*

24   Defroster cable:
a) *Place the knob in the DEF position.*
b) *Place the lever on the heater unit in the DEF position and connect the cable to the lever.*
c) *Pull the cable housing away from the cable end to remove all freeplay and clip the cable housing to the heater unit* (**see illustration**).
d) *Verify the knob travels through its full range.*

25   Inside-outside air selector cable:
a) *Place the control lever in the Recirculate position.*
b) *Place the lever on the heater unit in the Recirculate position, all the way against the stopper on the heater case, and connect the cable to the lever.*
c) *Pull the cable housing away from the cable end to remove all freeplay and clip the cable housing to the heater unit* (**see illustration**).
d) *Verify the lever travels through its full range.*

2000 and later models

Control assembly removal

26   Disconnect the negative battery cable from the battery.
27   Remove the instrument panel center trim panel, the under covers from both driver and passenger sides and the center console (see Chapter 11). Where necessary for access, remove the instrument panel center reinforcing bracket.
28   Remove the radio (see Chapter 12).
29   Disconnect the control cables from the heater unit.
30   Remove the control assembly mounting screws. Pull the assembly out, disconnect its electrical connectors and remove it from the vehicle.

Control assembly check

Refer to illustrations 12.31 and 12.32

31   Using an ohmmeter, measure the resistance between the defroster switch terminals at the back of the control assembly (**see illustration**). Turn the control assembly to each position and check for continuity as indicated.
a) *Defroster, defroster/foot: continuity between terminals 2 and 3.*
b) *All other positions: continuity between terminals 1 and 3.*

32   Check the blower, air conditioner and inside/outside air switch continuity with the ohmmeter (**see illustration**).
a) *Blower switch in 0 (Off): no continuity between any terminals.*
b) *Blower switch in 1: continuity between terminals 3 and 5.*
c) *Blower switch in 2: continuity between terminals 1 and 3.*
d) *Blower switch in 3: continuity between terminals 3 and 6.*
e) *Blower switch in 4 (Hi): continuity between terminals 3 and 4.*
f) *Air conditioner switch Off: continuity between terminals 8 and 9.*
g) *Air conditioner switch On: continuity between terminals 5, 6 and 7.*
h) *Recirc switch Off: continuity between terminals 1 and 3.*
i) *Recirc switch On: continuity between terminals 2, 3 and 4.*

33   If there's continuity when there shouldn't be, or no continuity when there should be, replace the defective switch.
34   If any of the cables needs to be replaced, disengage the claw with a screwdriver blade and remove the cable (**see illustration 12.21**).

13   Heater core - replacement

Warning: *These models are equipped with airbags. Always disable the airbag system before working in the vicinity of any airbag system component to avoid the possibility of accidental deployment of the airbag, which could cause personal injury (see Chapter 12).*

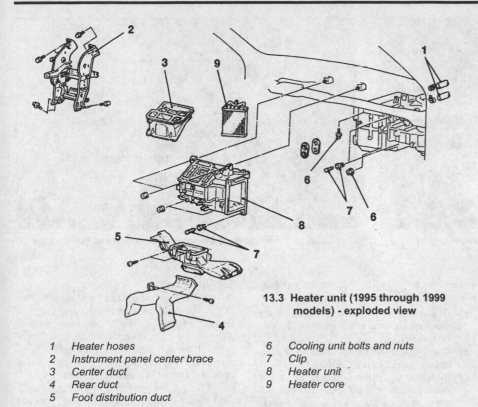

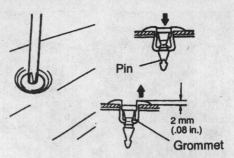

13.8 Push in the center of the pin (but not too far) and pull the pin's grommet out of the hole

13.3 Heater unit (1995 through 1999 models) - exploded view

1	Heater hoses	6	Cooling unit bolts and nuts
2	Instrument panel center brace	7	Clip
3	Center duct	8	Heater unit
4	Rear duct	9	Heater core
5	Foot distribution duct		

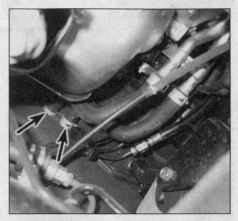

13.19 Disconnect the heater hoses

1995 through 1999 models

Refer to illustrations 13.3 and 13.8

1 Disconnect the cable from the negative terminal of the battery.

2 Drain the cooling system (see Chapter 1).

3 Working in the engine compartment, disconnect the heater hoses where they enter the firewall **(see illustration)**. Plug the heater core tubes to prevent leakage when the core is removed.

4 Remove the instrument panel and its metal center reinforcement structure from the vehicle (see Chapter 11).

5 Disconnect the control cables at the heater case.

6 Remove the center, rear and foot ducts from the vehicle **(see illustration 13.3)**.

7 If the vehicle is equipped with air conditioning, remove the nuts and bolts that secure the cooling unit to the dash.

8 Release the pins that secure the bottom of the heater unit **(see illustration)**, then pull them out.

9 Remove the nuts from the upper portion of the heater unit.

10 On air-conditioned vehicles, slide the cooling unit slightly into the passenger compartment to free the heater unit, then pull the heater unit all the way into the passenger compartment.

11 Take out the old heater core and install the new one **(see illustration 13.3)**.

12 Reassemble the heater unit and check the operation of the control flaps. If any parts bind, correct the problem before installation.

13 Reinstall the remaining parts in the reverse order of removal. To install the heater unit lower retaining pins, pull the center out, place the grommet in the hole and push the center in until it's flush with the grommet.

14 Refer to Section 12 and adjust the heater cables.

15 Refill the cooling system (see Chapter 1), reconnect the battery and start the engine. Check for leaks and proper system operation.

2000 and later models

Refer to illustrations 13.19, 13.22, 13.23a and 13.23b

Warning: *The air conditioning system is under high pressure. DO NOT disassemble any part of the system (hoses, compressor, line fittings, etc.) until after the system has been evacuated and the refrigerant recovered by a dealer service department or air conditioning service station.*

Note: *Some of the following procedures apply to vehicles equipped with air conditioning. If you're working on a non-air conditioned vehicle, ignore the steps which don't apply.*

16 Have the air conditioning system evacuated by a dealer service department or air conditioning service station.

17 Disconnect the negative battery cable from the battery.

18 Drain the cooling system (see Chapter 1).

19 Working in the engine compartment, disconnect the heater hoses where they join the heater unit at the firewall **(see illustration)**.

Note: *On 3.0L V6 models, it may be neces-*

sary to remove the intake manifold plenum for access to the hoses.

20 Remove the glove compartment, center console and instrument panel under covers (see Chapter 11). Plug the heater core tubes to prevent leakage when the core is removed.

21 Remove the joint duct that connects the blower unit to the heater/cooler unit **(see illustration 11.3)**.

22 If the vehicle is equipped with air conditioning, remove the automatic compressor controller **(see illustration)**.

13.22 Remove the automatic compressor controller (arrow)

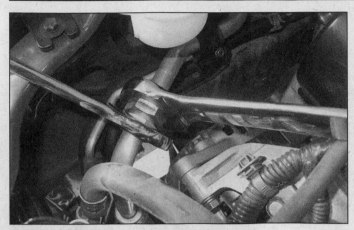

13.23a Disconnect the refrigerant tubes . . .

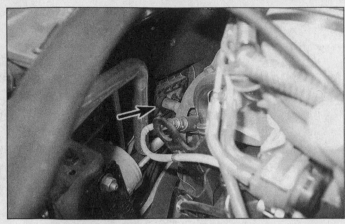

13.23b . . . then remove the expansion valve and the O-rings

23   Disconnect the air conditioning tubes from the expansion valve, then remove the expansion valve and O-rings **(see illustrations)**.
24   Remove the air conditioning evaporator from the heater/cooling unit.
25   Disconnect the electrical connector and remove the thermistor sensor.
26   Remove the evaporator drain hose.
27   Remove the radio (see Chapter 12).
28   Remove the heater control unit (see Section 12).
29   Remove the instrument panel and its center brace (see Chapter 11).
30   Remove the front deck crossmember.
31   Remove the foot ducts.
32   Remove the heater unit fasteners.
33   Remove the heater unit into the passenger compartment.
34   Withdraw the heater core from the unit and install a new one.
35   Check the operation of the heater unit control flaps. If any parts bind, correct the problem before installation.
36   Reinstall the remaining parts in the reverse order of removal.
37   Refer to Section 12 and adjust the heater cables.
38   Refill the cooling system (see Chapter 1), reconnect the battery and start the engine. Check for leaks and proper system operation.
39   Have the air conditioning system evacuated, charged and leak tested by the shop that discharged it.

14   Air conditioning and heating system - check and maintenance

Warning: *The air conditioning system is under high pressure. Do not loosen any hose fittings or remove any components until after the system has been discharged by a dealer service department or air conditioning service station. Always wear eye protection when disconnecting air conditioning system fittings.*

1   The following maintenance checks should be performed on a regular basis to ensure the air conditioner continues to operate at peak efficiency.

a) *Check the compressor drivebelt. If it's worn or deteriorated, replace it (see Chapter 1).*
b) *Check the drivebelt tension and, if necessary, adjust it (see Chapter 1).*
c) *Check the system hoses. Look for cracks, bubbles, hard spots and deterioration. Inspect the hoses and all fittings for oil bubbles and seepage. If there's any evidence of wear, damage or leaks, replace the hose(s).*
d) *Inspect the condenser fins for leaves, bugs and other debris. Use a fin comb or compressed air to clean the condenser.*
e) *Make sure the system has the correct refrigerant charge.*
f) *Check the evaporator housing drain tube for blockage.*

2   It's a good idea to operate the system for about 10 minutes at least once a month, particularly during the winter. Long term non-use can cause hardening, and subsequent failure, of the seals.
3   Because of the complexity of the air conditioning system and the special equipment necessary to service it, in-depth troubleshooting and repairs are not included in this manual (refer to the *Haynes Automotive Heating and Air Conditioning Repair Manual*). However, simple checks and component replacement procedures are provided in this Chapter.
4   The most common cause of poor cooling is simply a low system refrigerant charge. If a noticeable drop in cool air output occurs, the following quick check will help you determine if the refrigerant level is low.

Checking the refrigerant charge

5   Warm the engine up to normal operating temperature.
6   Place the air conditioning temperature selector at the coldest setting and the blower at the highest setting. Open the doors (to make sure the air conditioning system does not cycle off as soon as it cools the passenger compartment).
7   With the compressor engaged - the clutch will make an audible click and the center of the clutch will rotate - note the temperature of the compressor inlet and discharge lines. If the compressor discharge line feels warm and the compressor inlet pipe feels cool, the system is properly charged.
8   Place a thermometer in the dashboard vent nearest the evaporator and operate the system until the indicated temperature is around 40 to 45 degrees F. If the ambient (outside) air temperature is very high, say 110 degrees F, the duct air temperature may be as high as 60 degrees F, but generally the air conditioning is 30-50 degrees F cooler than the ambient air. **Note:** *Humidity of the ambient air also affects the cooling capacity of the system. Higher ambient humidity lowers the effectiveness of the air conditioning system.*

Adding refrigerant

Refer to illustration 14.12
Caution: *There are two types of refrigerant used in automotive systems; R-12 - which has been widely used on earlier models and the more environmentally-friendly R-134a used in all models covered by this manual. These two refrigerants (and their appropriate refrigerant oils) are not compatible and must never be mixed or components will be damaged. Use only R-134a refrigerant in the models covered by this manual.*

9   Buy an R-134a charging kit at an auto parts store. A charging kit includes a 14-ounce can of refrigerant, a tap valve and a short section of hose that can be attached between the tap valve and the system low side service valve. Because one can of refrigerant may not be sufficient to bring the system charge up to the proper level, it's a good idea to buy an additional can. Make sure that one of the cans contains red refrigerant dye. If the system is leaking, the red dye will leak out with the refrigerant and help you pinpoint the location of the leak.
10   Hook up the charging kit by following the manufacturer's instructions. **Warning:** *DO*

14.12 Cans of R-134A refrigerant, available in auto parts stores, can be added to your system with a simple recharging kit

NOT hook the charging kit hose to the system high side! The fittings on the charging kit are designed to fit **only** on the low side of the system.

11   Back off the valve handle on the charging kit and screw the kit onto the refrigerant can, making sure first that the O-ring or rubber seal inside the threaded portion of the kit is in place. **Warning:** *Wear protective eyewear when dealing with pressurized refrigerant cans.*

12   Remove the dust cap from the low-side charging connection and attach the quick-connect fitting on the kit hose **(see illustration)**.

13   Warm up the engine and turn on the air conditioner. Keep the charging kit hose away from the fan and other moving parts. **Note:** *The charging process requires the compressor to be running.*

14   Turn the valve handle on the kit until the stem pierces the can, then back the handle out to release the refrigerant. You should be able to hear the rush of gas. Add refrigerant to the low side of the system until both the receiver-drier surface and the evaporator inlet pipe feel about the same temperature. Allow stabilization time between each addition.

15   If you have an accurate thermometer, you can place it in the center air conditioning duct inside the vehicle and keep track of the "conditioned" air temperature. A charged system that is working properly should cool down to approximately 40 degrees F. If the ambient (outside) air temperature is very high, say 110 degrees F, the duct air temperature may be as high as 60 degrees F, but generally the air conditioning is 30 to 40 degrees F cooler than the ambient air.

16   When the can is empty, turn the valve handle to the closed position and release the connection from the low-side port. Replace the dust cap. **Warning:** *Never add more than two cans of refrigerant to the system.*

17   Remove the charging kit from the can

and store the kit for future use with the piercing valve in the UP position, to prevent inadvertently piercing the can on the next use.

15 Air conditioning receiver/drier - removal and installation

Refer to illustration 15.3
Warning: *The air conditioning system is under high pressure. Do not loosen any fittings or remove any components until after the system has been discharged. Air conditioning refrigerant should be properly discharged into an EPA-approved container at a dealer service department or an automotive air conditioning repair facility. Always wear eye protection when disconnecting air conditioning system fittings.*

1   Have the refrigerant discharged at a dealer service department or an automotive air conditioning repair facility.

2   The receiver/drier, which acts as a reservoir and filter for the refrigerant, is located in front of the air conditioning condenser. The receiver/drier bracket is attached to the side of the air conditioning condenser.

3   Detach the refrigerant lines and electrical connector from the receiver/drier **(see illustration)**. Immediately cap the open fittings to prevent the entry of dirt and moisture.

4   Remove the receiver/drier mounting

bolts and detach it from the condenser.

5   Install new O-rings on the lines and lubricate them with clean refrigerant oil.

6   If a new receiver/drier is being installed, add one fluid ounce of refrigerant oil to the system.

7   Installation is the reverse of removal.
Note: *Do not remove the sealing caps until you are ready to reconnect the lines.*

8   Have the system evacuated, charged and leak tested by the shop that discharged it.

16 Air conditioning compressor - removal and installation

Warning: *The air conditioning system is under high pressure. Do not loosen any fittings or remove any components until after the system has been discharged. Air conditioning refrigerant should be properly discharged into an EPA-approved container at a dealer service department or an automotive air conditioning repair facility. Always wear eye protection when disconnecting air conditioning system fittings.*

1   Have the refrigerant discharged at a dealer service department or an automotive air conditioning repair facility.

2   Disconnect the negative cable from the battery.

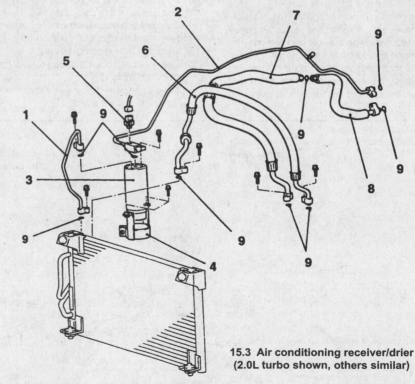

15.3 Air conditioning receiver/drier (2.0L turbo shown, others similar)

1	Liquid tube	4	Bracket	7	Suction hose
2	Liquid tube	5	Dual pressure switch	8	Suction tube
3	Receiver assembly	6	Discharge hose	9	O-ring

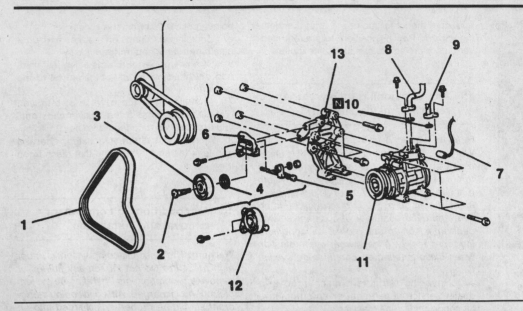

16.5 Air conditioning compressor mounting details (2.0L non-turbo engine)

1   Drivebelt
2   Shaft
3   Tensioner pulley
4   Cover
5   Adjuster plate
6   Tensioner pulley bracket
7   Compressor connector
8   Discharge hose connection
9   Suction hose connection
10 O-ring
11 Compressor
12 Tensioner pulley and bracket
13 Compressor bracket

3   Disconnect the electrical connector from the compressor clutch.

4   Remove the air conditioning drivebelt (see Chapter 1) from the engine compartment.

2.0L non-turbo models

Refer to illustration 16.5

5   Unbolt the suction and discharge hoses from the compressor and remove the O-rings **(see illustration)**. Immediately cap the open fittings to prevent the entry of dirt and moisture.

6   Unbolt the compressor from the bracket.

7   If necessary, remove the tensioner pulley from the compressor bracket and remove the compressor bracket from the engine. **Note:** *Keep the compressor level during handling and storage. If the compressor seized or you find metal particles in the refrigerant lines, the*

system must be flushed out by an air conditioning technician and the receiver/drier must be replaced (see Section 15).

8   Install the compressor in the reverse order of removal.

9   If you are installing a new compressor, follow the manufacturer's instructions for calculating how much refrigerant oil should be used in the new compressor. If instructions are not available (and you're installing an original equipment compressor), calculate the amount as follows:

a) *Pour the oil out of the old compressor and measure it in fluid ounces.*

b) *Subtract the measured amount from 3.4 (the amount of oil, in fluid ounces, that comes in a new compressor).*

c) *The result is how much oil you will need to drain from the new compressor to leave the same amount in it that the old compressor contained.*

10   Have the system evacuated, charged and leak tested by the shop that discharged it.

All 2.0L turbo and 1998 and 1999 2.4L models

Refer to illustration 16.12

11   Remove the brake master cylinder reservoir (see Chapter 9).

12   Unbolt the suction and discharge hoses from the compressor and remove the O-rings **(see illustration)**. Immediately cap the open fittings to prevent the entry of dirt and moisture.

13   Unbolt the compressor from the bracket.

14   If necessary, remove the tensioner pulley from the compressor bracket and remove the compressor bracket from the engine. **Note:** *Keep the compressor level during handling and storage. If the compressor seized or you*

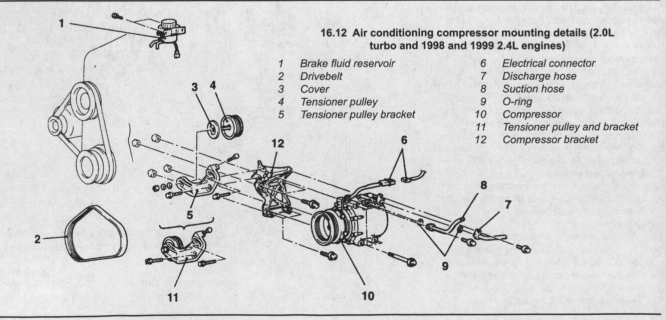

16.12 Air conditioning compressor mounting details (2.0L turbo and 1998 and 1999 2.4L engines)

1 Brake fluid reservoir		6 Electrical connector
2 Drivebelt		7 Discharge hose
3 Cover		8 Suction hose
4 Tensioner pulley		9 O-ring
5 Tensioner pulley bracket		10 Compressor
		11 Tensioner pulley and bracket
		12 Compressor bracket

16.18 Remove the retaining bolts, detach and plug the refrigerant lines at the compressor

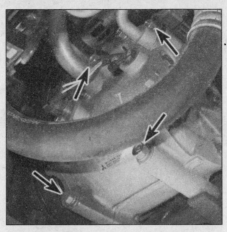

16.19 To detach the compressor from its bracket, remove these bolts (arrows)

find metal particles in the refrigerant lines, the system must be flushed out by an air conditioning technician and the receiver/drier must be replaced (see Section 15).

15   Install the compressor in the reverse order of removal.

16   If you are installing a new compressor, follow the manufacturer's instructions for calculating how much refrigerant oil should be used in the new compressor. If instructions are not available (and you're installing an original equipment compressor), calculate the amount as follows:

a) *Pour the oil out of the old compressor and measure it in fluid ounces.*

b) *Subtract the measured amount from 5.7 (the amount of oil, in fluid ounces, that comes in a new compressor).*

c) *The result is how much oil you will need to drain from the new compressor to leave the same amount in it that the old compressor contained.*

17   Have the system evacuated, charged and leak tested by the shop that discharged it.

2000 and later 2.4L and all 3.0L V6 models

Refer to illustrations 16.18 and 16.19

18   Unbolt the suction and discharge hoses from the compressor and remove the O-rings **(see illustration)**. Immediately cap the open fittings to prevent the entry of dirt and moisture.

19   Unbolt the compressor from the bracket **(see illustration)**.

20   If necessary, remove the tensioner pulley from the compressor bracket and remove the compressor bracket from the engine. **Note:** *Keep the compressor level during handling and storage. If the compressor seized or you find metal particles in the refrigerant lines, the system must be flushed out by an air conditioning technician and the receiver/drier must be replaced (see Section 15).*

21   Install the compressor in the reverse order of removal.

22   If you are installing a new compressor, follow the manufacturer's instructions for calculating how much refrigerant oil should be used in the new compressor. If instructions are not available (and you're installing an

original equipment compressor), calculate the amount as follows:

a) *Pour the oil out of the old compressor and measure it in fluid ounces.*

b) *Subtract the measured amount from 4.1 (the amount of oil, in fluid ounces, that comes in a new compressor).*

c) *The result is how much oil you will need to drain from the new compressor to leave the same amount in it that the old compressor contained.*

23   Have the system evacuated, charged and leak tested by the shop that discharged it.

17   Air conditioning condenser - removal and installation

Refer to illustration 17.4

Warning: *The air conditioning system is under high pressure. Do not loosen any fittings or remove any components until after the system has been discharged. Air conditioning refrigerant should be properly discharged into an EPA-approved container at a dealer service department or an automotive air conditioning repair facility. Always wear eye protection when disconnecting air conditioning system fittings.*

1   Have the refrigerant discharged at a dealer service department or an automotive air conditioning repair facility.

2   If you're working on a 2000 or later model, remove the air cleaner, front bumper, air duct, and left fog lamp bracket (see Chapters 4 and 11).

3   Remove the radiator and condenser fans and remove the radiator mounting bolts (see Section 6). If you're working on a 2.0L turbo model or a 1998 or 1999 2.4L engine model, remove the coolant reservoir tank.

4   Disconnect the compressor discharge line and the liquid line from the condenser and remove the O-rings **(see illustration)**. Immediately cap the open fittings to prevent the entry of dirt and moisture.

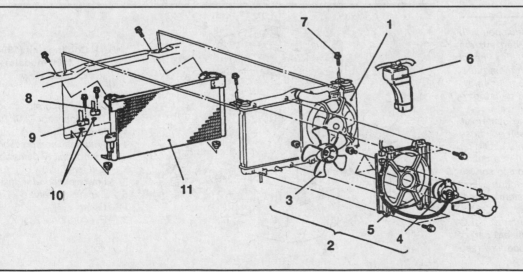

17.4 Air conditioning condenser details (2.0L turbo and 1998 and 1999 2.4L engines shown)

1   Radiator fan
2   Condenser fan assembly
3   Condenser fan
4   Fan motor
5   Shroud
6   Coolant reservoir
7   Upper insulator bolt
8   Liquid tube
9   Discharge hose
10   O-ring
11   Condenser

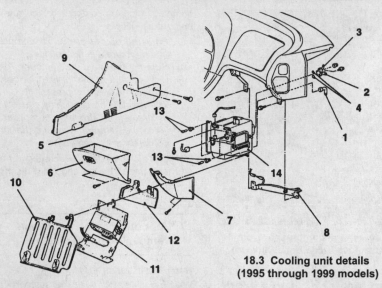

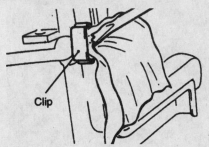

18.10 Pry the clips off with a padded screwdriver

18.3 Cooling unit details (1995 through 1999 models)

1	Drain hose	7	Corner panel	11	Bracket (antilock brake system control unit)
2	Suction tube or hose	8	Glove compartment support frame	12	Harness protector (turbo models)
3	Liquid tube	9	Console side trim	13	Clip
4	O-ring	10	Control unit cover	14	Cooling unit
5	Stopper				
6	Glove compartment				

5   Unbolt the condenser. Lean the radiator back and lift out the condenser. Store the condenser upright to prevent oil loss.

6   If a new condenser is to be installed, add the following amount of new refrigerant oil to the system:

  a) *2.0L non-turbo engine models: 1.35 fl oz*
  b) *2.0L turbo, 2.4L and 3.0L engine models: 0.5 fl oz*

7   Installation is the reverse of removal.

8   Have the system evacuated, charged and leak tested by the shop that discharged it.

18   Air conditioning evaporator and expansion valve (1995 through 1999 models) - removal and installation

Warning 1: *These models are equipped with airbags, always disable the airbag system before working in the vicinity of the impact sensors, steering column or instrument panel to avoid the possibility of accidental deployment of the airbag, which could cause personal injury (see Chapter 12).*

Warning 2: *The air conditioning system is under high pressure. Do not loosen any hose fittings or remove any components until after the system has been discharged by a dealer service department or air conditioning service station. Always wear eye protection when disconnecting air conditioning system components.*

Note: *Evaporator and expansion valve removal on 2000 and later models are part of the heater core replacement procedure (see Section 13).*

Removal

Refer to illustrations 18.3, 18.10 and 18.11

1   Have the system discharged (see the **Warning** at the beginning of this Section).

2   Disconnect the negative battery cable from the battery.

3   Disconnect the evaporator drain hose **(see illustration)**.

4   Disconnect and cap the cooling unit refrigerant lines.

5   Refer to Chapter 11 and remove the glove compartment. Remove the corner trim panel, glove compartment support frame and the console right side trim panel.

6   Remove the bracket that supports the electronic control unit for the antilock brake system.

7   If you're working on a 2.0L turbo model, remove the harness protector.

8   Disconnect any wiring harness connectors attached to the cooling unit housing.

9   Remove the clips securing the housing to the firewall and carefully remove the housing from the vehicle. To remove the clips, push their center pins inward about 3/16-inch, then pull the clips out of the holes.

10   Carefully pry off the clips retaining the housing sections together **(see illustration)**.

11   Separate the upper and lower housings from the heater/distribution housing **(see illustration)**.

12   Withdraw the evaporator core and expansion valve from the housing.

Installation

Note: *When installing a new evaporator, always use new O-rings on the expansion valve and reinstall the temperature sensor from the old core into the new core before installation.*

13   Installation is the reverse of removal. If a new evaporator is being installed, add 1.35 fl oz (non-turbo) or 2.0 fl oz (turbo) of new, R-134a-compatible refrigerant oil into it prior to installation.

14   Take the vehicle back to the shop that discharged it. Have the system evacuated, recharged and leak tested.

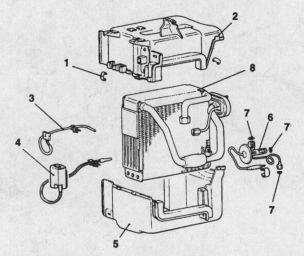

18.11 Cooling unit (1995 through 1999 models) - exploded view

1 *Clip*
2 *Upper evaporator case*
3 *Thermosensor (2.0L non-turbo engine)*
4 *Automatic compressor control unit (2.0L turbo and 2.4L engines)*
5 *Lower evaporator case*
6 *Expansion valve*
7 *O-ring*
8 *Evaporator*

Chapter 4
Fuel and exhaust systems

Contents

Specifications

General

Fuel pressure
  2.0L non-turbo engine
    1995 models .... 46 to 49 psi
    1996 and later models .... 47 to 50 psi
  2.0L turbo engine
    At idle, regulator vacuum hose connected .... 33 psi
    Regulator vacuum hose disconnected .... 42 to 45 psi
  2.4L four-cylinder and 3.0L V6 engines
    At idle, regulator vacuum hose connected .... 38 psi
    Regulator vacuum hose disconnected .... 47 to 50 psi

Fuel injector resistance (approximate)
  2.0L non-turbo engine .... 11 to 15 ohms @ 68-degrees F
  2.0L turbo engine .... 2 to 3 ohms @ 68-degrees F
  2.4L four-cylinder and 3.0L V6 engines .... 13 to 16 ohms @ 68-degrees F

Fuel level sending unit resistance (approximate)
  1995 through 1999 models
    FWD models
      Full position .... 4 ohms (minimum)
      Empty position .... 112 ohms
    4WD models (main unit)
      Full position .... 2 ohms
      Empty position .... 56.9 ohms
    4WD model (sub unit)
      Full position .... 2 ohms
      Empty position .... 50 ohms
  2000 and later models
    Full position .... 3 to 5 ohms
    Empty position .... 110 to 112 ohms

Torque specifications   Ft-lbs (unless otherwise indicated)

Note: *One foot-pound (ft-lb) of torque is equivalent to 12 inch-pounds (in-lbs) of torque. Torque values below approximately 15 ft-lbs are expressed in inch-pounds, since most foot-pound torque wrenches are not accurate at these smaller values.*

Fuel rail mounting bolts	
2.0L non-turbo engine	Not specified
2.0L turbo, 2.4L engines...	104 inch-lbs
3.0L V6 engine	100 inch-lbs
Fuel tank mounting nuts/bolts..	19
Throttle body mounting bolts	
2.0L non-turbo engine	Not specified
2.0L turbo engine	11 to 16
2.4L four-cylinder and 3.0L V6 engines.....................................	12 to 16
Exhaust pipe fitting-to-turbocharger nuts/bolts.............................	45
Turbocharger-to-exhaust manifold nuts/bolts	
Step 1	23
Step 2	Tighten an additional 65-degrees

1   General information

The vehicles covered by this manual are equipped with a sequential Multi-Port Fuel Injection (MPFI) system. This system uses timed impulses to sequentially inject the fuel directly into the intake ports of each cylinder. The injectors are controlled by the Powertrain Control Module (PCM). The PCM monitors various engine parameters and delivers the exact amount of fuel, in the correct sequence, to the intake ports. It also controls the engine idle speed via the idle air control motor which is mounted to the throttle body.

All models are equipped with an electric fuel pump which is located inside the fuel tank. Fuel pressure is controlled by a regulator mounted on the fuel rail, on all models except 1996 and later 2.0L non-turbo models (on these it's mounted to the fuel filter).

The exhaust system consists of the exhaust manifold(s), a catalytic converter, an exhaust pipe and a muffler. Each of these components is replaceable. For further information regarding the catalytic converter, refer to Chapter 6.

2   Fuel pressure relief procedure

Refer to illustrations 2.2 and 2.3

Warning: *Gasoline is extremely flammable, so take extra precautions when you work on any part of the fuel system. Don't smoke or allow open flames or bare light bulbs near the work area, and don't work in a garage where a gas-type appliance (such as a water heater or a clothes dryer) is present. Since gasoline is carcinogenic, wear latex gloves when there's a possibility of being exposed to fuel, and if you spill any on your skin, rinse it off immediately with soap and water. Mop up any spills immediately and do not store fuel-soaked rags where they could ignite. The fuel system is under constant pressure, so, if any fuel lines are to be disconnected, the pressure must be relieved first. When you perform any kind of work on the fuel system, wear safety glasses and have a Class B type fire extinguisher on hand.*

1   Remove the fuel filler cap to relieve the fuel tank pressure.
2   If you're working on a 1995 through 1999 model, remove the rear seat cushion (see Chapter 11) and disconnect the fuel pump electrical connector **(see illustration)**.
3   If you're working on a 2000 or later model, remove the fuel pump relay from the relay box in the engine compartment **(see illustration)**.
4   Next, start the engine and allow it to run until it stops. This should only take a few seconds. Crank the engine again, to ensure the fuel pressure is completely relieved. Before working on any part of the fuel system, disconnect the negative battery cable from the battery.
5   Even after the fuel pressure has been relieved, always lay a shop towel over any fuel connection that is to be separated to absorb the residual fuel that will leak out.
6   When you are finished working on the fuel system, reconnect the fuel pump electrical connector to the wiring harness. Turn the ignition key to the ON position a few times to pressurize the system and check the serviced area for leaks.
7   Install the fuel filler cap and tighten it securely. **Note:** *If the fuel filler cap seal allows the fuel tank pressure to escape because of a damaged seal or it has not been tightened sufficiently, the CHECK ENGINE light will illuminate on the instrument panel.*

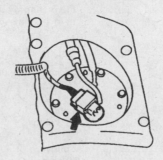

2.2 Remove the cover from the floorpan and disconnect the fuel pump connector (arrow)

3   Fuel pump/fuel pressure - check

Warning: *Gasoline is extremely flammable, so take extra precautions when you work on any part of the fuel system (see the **Warning** in Section 2).*

Note: *To perform the fuel pressure check, you will need to obtain a fuel pressure gauge and adapter set (fuel line fittings). The fuel supply line on 2.0L turbo, 2.4L four-cylinder and 3.0L V6 engines is not equipped with a fuel pressure test port (Schrader valve fitting). A special fuel pressure test adapter (factory tool nos. MD998742 and MD998709 or equivalent) must be installed between the fuel supply line and the fuel rail.*

Preliminary check

Note: *On all models, the fuel pump is located inside the fuel tank (see Section 5).*

1   If you suspect insufficient fuel delivery, first inspect all fuel lines to ensure that the problem is not simply a leak in a line.
2   Set the parking brake and remove the fuel filler cap. Have an assistant turn the ignition switch to the ON position while you listen at the fuel filler neck opening. You should hear a "whirring" sound, lasting for a couple of seconds. Start the engine. The whirring sound should now be continuous (although harder to hear with the engine running). If there is no

2.3 The fuel pump relay on 2000 and later models is in the engine compartment (arrow)

sound, either the fuel pump fuses, fuel pump, fuel pump relay, automatic shutdown (ASD) relay or related circuits are defective (proceed to Step 13).

System pressure check

Refer to illustrations 3.4 and 3.5

3   Perform the fuel pressure relief procedure (see Section 2).

4   On 2.0L non-turbo engines, connect a fuel pressure gauge to the fuel pressure test port (Schrader valve) on the fuel rail **(see illustration)**.

5   On 2.0L turbo, 2.4L four-cylinder and 3.0L V6 engines, the fuel supply line is not equipped with a fuel pressure test port (Schrader valve fitting). A special fuel pressure test adapter must be installed between the fuel supply line and the fuel rail **(see illustration)**. Unbolt the fuel supply line from the fuel rail (see Section 4) and install the fuel pressure test adapter between the supply line and the fuel rail. Attach a fuel pressure gauge to the test adapter fitting.

6   Start the engine and let it idle. Observe the pressure reading on the gauge. Compare it with the pressure listed in this Chapter's Specifications.

7   If the fuel pressure is higher than specified, check for a kinked or restricted fuel return line (all models except 1996 and later 2.0L non-turbo engines). If the line is OK, replace the fuel pressure regulator (all models) (see Section 15).

8   If the fuel pressure is lower than specified, replace the fuel filter (see Section 6) and perform the pressure check again. If it's still low, remove the fuel pump module (see Section 5) and inspect the fuel inlet strainer for obstructions. If it's clogged, replace the strainer. If the strainer is OK, replace the fuel pump.

9   If there is no fuel pressure, check the fuel pump, ASD (MPI) and fuel pump relays as outlined below.

10   If you're working on a 2.0L turbo, 2.4L four-cylinder or 3.0L V6 engine, disconnect the vacuum hose from the pressure regulator. Fuel pressure should increase to the unregulated value listed in this Chapter's Specifications. If it stays the same, check for a plugged vacuum line or replace the pressure regulator.

11   Next, verify that the system holds pressure. Note the fuel pressure with the engine running, then turn off the engine and observe the reading on the fuel pressure gauge. The fuel pressure should remain constant for a minimum of one minute. A drop of more than 5 psi in one minute indicates an unacceptable leak in the system. If the pressure drop is unacceptable, first visually inspect the system for obvious leaks, especially at the fittings. **Note:** *A sudden drop in pressure with no visible leak indicates a stuck-open check valve in the fuel pump. Replace the fuel pump.*

12   If there's a gradual pressure drop, and there aren't any obvious leaks, the fuel is escaping either from one or more of the fuel injectors (into the engine) or through the fuel pressure regulator. See Section 16 for the injector leak checking procedure.

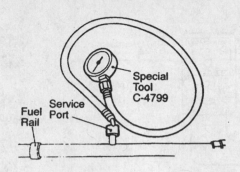

3.4 On 2.0L non-turbo models, connect the pressure gauge to the test fitting (Schrader valve) on the fuel rail

Fuel pump check

Refer to illustration 3.15

Note: *The fuel pressure regulator check is part of the system pressure check.*

13   If you cannot hear the fuel pump operate when energized (refer to preliminary check above), connect it directly to battery voltage with a pair of jumper wires.

14   Remove the rear seat cushion (see Chapter 11). Locate the fuel pump 2-pin electrical connector and disconnect it **(see illustration 2.2)**.

15   Connect the positive terminal of a 12-volt battery (the vehicle's battery will work if it's fully charged) to the fuel pump positive terminal and the negative terminal to the ground terminal of the electrical connector **(see illustration)**.

16   The fuel pump should run. If you can't hear it running, squeeze the fuel line coming from the pump and check for pressure. If there's no pressure, replace the pump.

MFI and fuel pump relay check

Note: *The multiport fuel injection (MFI) relay (also called the automatic shutdown relay) and the fuel pump relay must both be tested to insure proper fuel pump operation. The relays are identical and the same test procedure is used for both.*

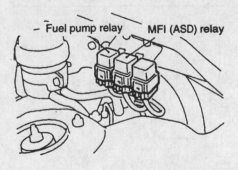

3.17 The fuel pump and MFI relays on 2.0L non-turbo models are located next to each other near the brake fluid reservoir

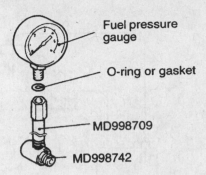

3.5 On 2.0L turbo, 2.4L four-cylinder and 3.0L V6 engines, use adapters like these to connect the fuel pressure gauge into the line where it attaches to the fuel rail

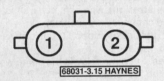

3.15 Connect the voltmeter to the fuel pump terminals (1, positive; 2, ground)

2.0L non-turbo models

Refer to illustrations 3.17, 3.19 and 3.20

17   If you're working on a 2.0L non-turbo model, locate the relays near the master cylinder reservoir **(see illustration)**.

18   Remove the relay being tested from the bracket.

19   Connect an ohmmeter between terminals 4 and 6 **(see illustration)**. It should indicate between 35 and 75 ohms. If not, replace the relay.

20   Connect the ohmmeter between terminals 2 and 8. There should be no continuity (infinite resistance). Leave the ohmmeter connected like this and connect a 12-volt battery between relay terminals 4 and 6 (use the

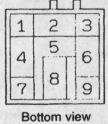

3.19 Terminal numbers of the 2.0L non-turbo MFI and fuel pump relays

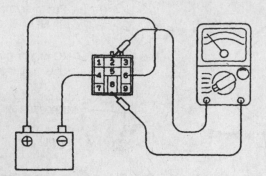

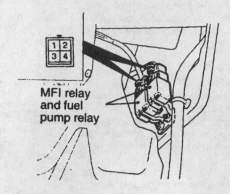

3.20 Connect a battery and an ohmmeter to the relay as shown and measure continuity

3.23 The fuel pump and MFI relays on 2.0L turbo models are located next to each other to the right of the console

vehicle's battery and a pair of jumper wires) **(see illustration)**. The ohmmeter should now indicate continuity (zero ohms).

21   If the relay doesn't perform as described, replace it.

22   Test the other relay in the same way you tested the first one.

All 2.0L turbo models, 1998 and 1999 2.4L models

Refer to illustrations 3.23 and 3.25

23   Locate the relays in the passenger compartment **(see illustration)**.

24   Remove the relay being tested from the bracket.

25   Connect an ohmmeter between terminals 2 and 4 **(see illustration)**. It should indicate approximately 70 ohms. If not, replace the relay.

26   Connect the ohmmeter between terminals 1 and 3. There should be no continuity (infinite resistance). Leave the ohmmeter connected like this and connect a 12-volt battery between relay terminals 2 and 4 (use the vehicle's battery and a pair of jumper wires) **(see illustration 3.25)**. The ohmmeter should now indicate continuity (zero ohms).

27   If the relay doesn't perform as described, replace it.

28   Test the other relay in the same way you tested the first one.

2000 and later models

Refer to illustration 3.29

29   Locate the relays in the engine compartment **(see illustration)**.

30   Remove the relay being tested from the relay box.

31   Connect an ohmmeter between terminals 1 and 3. There should be no continuity (infinite resistance). Leave the ohmmeter connected like this and connect a 12-volt battery between relay terminals 2 and 4 (use the vehicle's battery and a pair of jumper wires) **(see illustration 3.25)**. The ohmmeter should now indicate continuity (zero ohms).

32   If the relay doesn't perform as described, replace it.

33   Test the other relay in the same way you tested the first one.

---

4   Quick-connect fittings and fuel lines - disassembly, assembly and replacement

Warning: *Gasoline is extremely flammable, so take extra precautions when you work on any part of the fuel system (see the* **Warning** *in Section 2).*

General information

1   Always perform the fuel pressure relief procedure (see Section 2) before servicing fuel lines or fittings.

2   The fuel supply and vapor lines extend from the fuel tank to the engine compartment. The lines are constructed of steel, plastic and rubber. They are secured to the underbody with clips and brackets. These lines should be inspected for leaks, kinks and dents anytime the vehicle is raised for service.

3   If evidence of dirt is found in the fuel system or fuel filter during service, the affected line should be disconnected and blown out. Check the fuel inlet strainer on the fuel pump module for blockage or contamination (see Section 5).

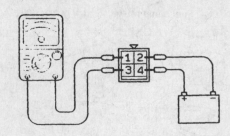

3.25 Connect a battery and ohmmeter to the relay as shown and measure continuity

Quick-connect fittings

4   In addition to the bolted, threaded or clamped connections used on most of these vehicles' fuel lines, there are three different types of quick-connect fittings to join various fuel lines and components. The first type uses a single-tab retainer, the second type a two-tab retainer and the third type incorporates a plastic retainer ring (usually black in color) which connects/disconnects much like a common compressed air hose fitting. Some are equipped with safety latch clips. The fittings are equipped with non-serviceable O-ring seals located in the female part of the fitting. In the event the fitting or tubing becomes damaged or develops a leak, replace the entire fuel line/quick-connect fitting as an assembly. Always use original equipment parts, or parts that meet or exceed the original equipment standards.

Single and two-tab retainer fittings

Disassembly

Refer to illustrations 4.5a, 4.5b, 4.9a and 4.9b

5   These quick-connect fittings have one or 2 windows (depending on type) located in

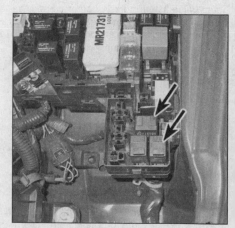

3.29 2000 and later 2.4L four-cylinder and 3.0L V6 MFI and fuel pump relays (arrows) are on this bracket in the engine compartment

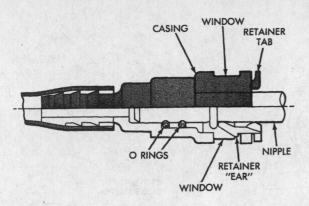

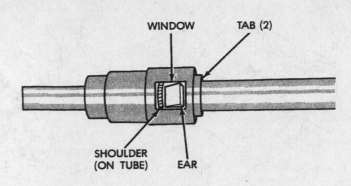

4.5a   Cross-sectional view of a two-tab quick-connect fuel line fitting

4.5b   When properly assembled, the tab ear and shoulder on the male fitting should be visible in the window

the side(s) of the female fitting. When the male fitting is inserted into the female, the tab(s) on the male engage in the window(s) and lock the fitting together **(see illustrations)**.

6   Perform the fuel pressure relief procedure (see Section 2).

7   Remove all fasteners, brackets or clips securing the lines as applicable.

8   Clean the area around the fitting to remove dirt and foreign debris.

9   Depress the retaining tab(s) on the quick-connect fitting and pull it apart **(see illustrations)**. **Note:** *The retaining tabs and shoulder should remain on the metal fuel line after separation.*

Assembly

10   Clean the male part of the fitting and lightly lubricate it with clean engine oil.

11   Position the retaining tab ears on the tube so they align with the windows in the female fitting and push them together. You should hear the fitting snap into place as the retaining tab ears lock into the windows.

12   Verify the fitting is properly fastened by trying to pull the lines apart.

13   Secure the fuel line using any clips or brackets as applicable.

14   Pressurize the system and check for leaks.

Plastic retainer ring fittings

Disassembly

Refer to illustration 4.18

15   Perform the fuel pressure relief procedure (see Section 2).

16   Remove all fasteners, brackets or clips securing the lines as applicable.

17   Clean the area around the fitting to remove dirt and foreign debris.

18   Grasp the male line and push it in (towards the fitting). While applying pressure on the male line, press the plastic retainer ring into the female fitting and then pull the male line from the female fitting **(see illustration)**. **Note:** *The plastic retainer ring must be pushed into the female fitting squarely! If it gets cocked, the fitting will be difficult to sepa-*

rate. If necessary, use an open-end wrench applied to the plastic retainer to assist in evenly pressing it into the female fitting. The plastic retainer ring should remain attached to the female fitting after separation.

Assembly

19   Clean the male part of the fitting and lightly lubricate it with clean engine oil.

20   Insert the male end into the female and push them together **(see illustration 4.18)**. You should hear the retainer ring snap into

4.9a   Depress the plastic tabs on the male fitting . . .

place as it locks the fitting together. Make sure the retainer ring is fully extended after assembly.

21   Verify the fitting is properly fastened by trying to pull the lines apart.

22   Secure the fuel line using any clips or brackets as applicable.

23   Pressurize the system and check for leaks.

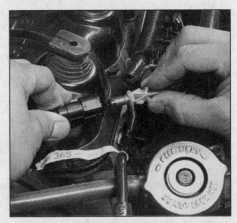

4.9b . . . and separate the fitting - to assemble it, lubricate the male end with a small amount of clean engine oil, then push the fitting together until it locks into place - tug on it to ensure the connection is secure

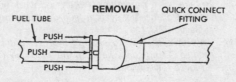

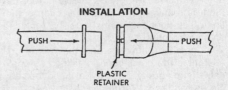

4.18   Plastic retainer ring type quick-connect fitting removal and installation

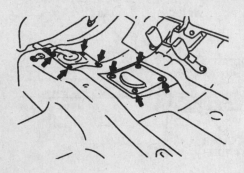

5.4 Remove the covers from the floorpan (arrows) for access to the fuel pump and fuel level sending unit

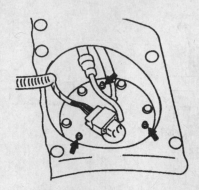

5.6a On FWD models, disconnect the connector and lines and remove the screws (arrows)

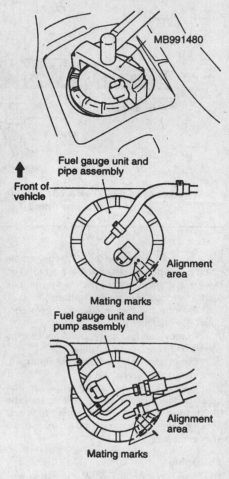

5.6b On 1995 through 1999 4WD models and all 2000 and later models, disconnect the connector and lines and unscrew the ring nut with the special tool or equivalent

Fuel lines - replacement

Steel tubing

24   If replacement of a metal line is required, disassemble the applicable quick-connect fittings as described above and remove the line from the vehicle. If the quick-connect fitting is damaged or leaks, replace the affected section of fuel line/quick-connect fittings as an assembly.

25   If the quick-connect fittings are acceptable, a new piece of steel tubing may be spliced-in to replace a damaged section by flaring the tubing ends and joining them with a union. Use tubing that meets or exceeds original equipment standards. Do not use copper or aluminum tubing to replace steel tubing. These materials cannot withstand normal vehicle vibration. Do not use a rubber hose to replace a damaged section of steel tubing!

26   When installing the replacement section into the line, assemble the quick-connect fittings first, then tighten the unions. **Warning:** *Metal lines must never be allowed to rub against other components or each other. A minimum of 1/4-inch clearance must be maintained to prevent contact unless it is properly secured.*

27   After replacing the line or section, pressurize the system and check for leaks.

Plastic lines

28   If replacement of a plastic line is required, disassemble the applicable quick-connect fittings as described above and remove the line from the vehicle. The plastic lines used on these vehicles are not serviceable. If replacement is required, the affected section of fuel line/quick-connect fittings must be replaced as an assembly.

29   Install the new line onto the vehicle and assemble the quick-connect fittings as applicable (see above). Secure the line to the vehicle as required. **Warning:** *Plastic lines must never be allowed to rub against other components or each other. A minimum of 1/4-inch clearance must be maintained to prevent contact unless it is properly secured. Do not route*

plastic fuel lines within four inches of any part of the exhaust system or within ten inches of the catalytic converter.

30   After replacing the line, pressurize the system and check for leaks.

Rubber hoses

Warning: *Fuel-injected vehicles use specially constructed hoses. Only use hoses marked EFM/EFI. Replace with only original equipment hoses, or hoses that meet or exceed original equipment standards. Others may have a lower fatigue threshold.*

31   Perform the fuel pressure relief procedure (see Section 2).

32   Loosen the clamps securing the hose and remove the hose from the vehicle.

33   Installation is the reverse of removal. **Warning:** *Do not route rubber fuel hoses within four inches of any part of the exhaust system or within ten inches of the catalytic converter. Rubber hoses must never be allowed to rub against other components or each other. A minimum of 1/4-inch clearance must be maintained to prevent contact with other components unless it is properly secured.*

34   After replacing the hose, pressurize the system and check for leaks.

---

5   Fuel pump - removal and installation

Warning: *Gasoline is extremely flammable, so take extra precautions when you work on any part of the fuel system (see the* **Warning** *in Section 2).*

Caution: *Be sure to change the fuel pump module O-ring seal whenever the assembly is removed for service.*

Removal

Refer to illustrations 5.4, 5.6a and 5.6b

1   Perform the fuel pressure relief procedure (see Section 2).

2   Disconnect the negative cable from the battery.

3   Remove the rear seat cushion (see Chapter 11).

4   Remove the protective cover from above the fuel pump **(see illustration)**.

5   Clean the top of the fuel tank around the fuel pump cover to remove any dirt or debris.

6   Disconnect the fuel pump electrical connector and fuel lines. If you're working on a FWD model, remove the screws that secure the fuel pump to the tank **(see illustration)**. On 4WD models, unscrew the fuel pump ring nut with special tool MB991480 or equivalent **(see illustration)**. **Caution:** *Do not apply too much pressure on the ring nut during removal or damage may result.*

7   Lift the fuel pump out of the tank. Remove and discard the O-ring seal.

8   If you're working on a 2000 or later model, release the locking bracket and remove the fuel pump from the module.

9   The electric fuel pump is not serviceable. In the event of failure, the pump must be replaced. On 1995 through 1999 models, the

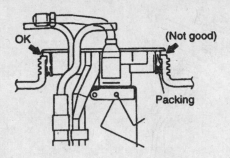

5.16 Make sure the packing (O-ring) is seated properly

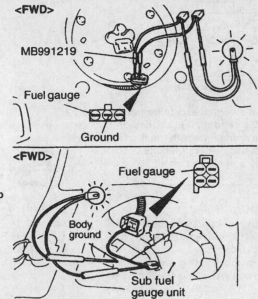

7.3 Connect a 3.4-watt bulb like this to test the gauge unit

fuel pump is a separate unit from the filter and the fuel level sending unit. On 2000 and later models, the pump is part of a module that includes the fuel filter and fuel level sending unit.

10   For service procedures on the fuel filter refer to Section 6.

11   For service procedures on the fuel level sending unit refer to Section 7.

Installation
Refer to illustration 5.16

12   If you're working on a 2000 or later model, install the new fuel pump on the module and secure it with the locking bracket.

13   Clean the sealing area on the fuel tank.

FWD models

14   Install the fuel pump in the tank and secure it with the screws.

4WD models

15   Lightly lubricate a new O-ring seal with clean engine oil and install it on the fuel tank opening.

16   Carefully insert the fuel pump into the fuel tank, making sure the O-ring stays in alignment **(see illustration)**. Align the tab on the fuel pump with the notch in the fuel tank.

17   While holding the fuel pump in place, install the ring nut, tightening it securely. **Caution:** *Over-tightening the ring nut may result in a leak.*

All models

18   The remaining installation steps are the reverse of removal. Run the engine and check for fuel leaks.

---

6   Fuel filter - replacement

2.0L four-cylinder models

1   Fuel filter replacement is described in Chapter 1.

2.4L four-cylinder and V6 models

2   Remove the fuel pump module from the tank (see Section 5).

3   Detach the fuel filter from the module and install a new one.

4   Install the fuel pump module in the tank (see Section 5).

---

7   Fuel level sending unit - check and replacement

Warning: *Gasoline is extremely flammable, so take extra precautions when you work on any part of the fuel system (see the **Warning** in Section 2).*

1   On all models, the fuel level sending unit is mounted in the fuel tank. On 1995 through 1999 FWD models, the unit is separate from the fuel pump. On 1995 through 1999 4WD models, the main sending unit is part of the fuel pump and the sub-gauge sending unit is separate. On 2000 and later models, the sending unit is part of the fuel pump module.

1995 through 1999 models
Check (sending unit installed)
Refer to illustration 7.3

2   Remove the rear seat cushion and remove the protective cover from the sending unit (see Chapter 11 and Section 5).

3   Disconnect the sending unit electrical connector. Connect a 3.4-watt bulb to the connector using two jumper wires **(see illustration)**.

4   Turn the ignition key to ON but don't start the engine. If the bulb lights but the gauge needle hasn't been moving, replace the gauge (see Chapter 12). If the bulb lights and the gauge needle has been moving, replace the sending unit (see below). If the bulb doesn't light, check the gauge wiring harness for a break or bad connection.

Check (sending unit removed)
Refer to illustration 7.6

5   Remove the unit from the tank (see Steps 7 through 9).

6   Connect an ohmmeter to the sending unit terminals **(see illustration)**. Slowly move the sending unit arm up and down through the full range of its travel. The ohmmeter reading should change smoothly from high resistance at the bottom to low resistance at the top (resistance values are listed in this Chapter's Specifications). If the reading doesn't change smoothly or is not within the Specifications, replace the sending unit.

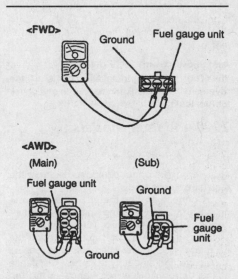

7.6 Connect an ohmmeter to the sending unit and measure resistance with the float in the full and empty positions (1995 through 1999 models)

7.17 Connect an ohmmeter to terminals 1 and 2 of the sending unit connector and measure resistance with the float in the full and empty positions (2000 and later models)

Replacement

7   Perform the fuel pressure relief procedure (see Section 2) and remove the rear seat cushion (see Chapter 11).

8   Disconnect the sending unit electrical connector. Remove the screws (FWD models) or locking ring (4WD models). This is basically the same as for fuel pump removal, described in Section 5.

9   Remove the sending unit from the fuel tank.

10   Installation is the reverse of the removal steps, with the following additions:

FWD models

11   Install the fuel pump in the tank and secure it with the screws.

4WD models

12   Lightly lubricate a new O-ring seal with clean engine oil and install it on the fuel tank opening.

13   Carefully insert the sending unit into the fuel tank, making sure the O-ring stays in alignment **(see illustration 5.16)**. Align the tab on the sending unit with the notch in the fuel tank.

14   While holding the sending unit in place, install the ring nut, tightening it securely. **Caution:** *Over-tightening the ring nut may result in a leak.*

All 1995 through 1999 models

15   The remaining installation steps are the reverse of removal. Run the engine and check for fuel leaks.

2000 and later models

Check

Refer to illustration 7.17

16   Remove the fuel pump module from the tank (see Section 5).

17   Connect an ohmmeter between terminals 1 and 2 the sending unit electrical connector **(see illustration)**. Slowly move the sending unit arm up and down through the full range of its travel. The ohmmeter reading should change smoothly from high resistance at the bottom to low resistance at the top (resistance values are listed in this Chapter's Specifications). If the reading doesn't change smoothly or is not within the Specifications, replace the sending unit.

18   Install the fuel pump module in the tank.

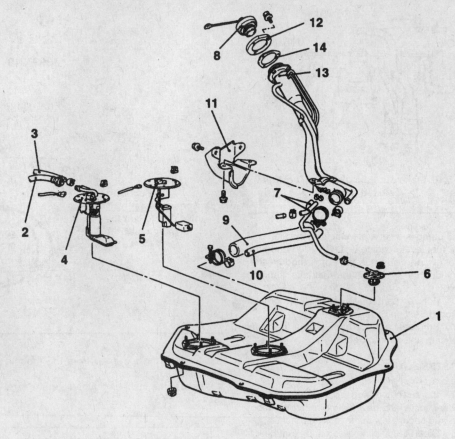

8.10a Fuel tank details (1995 through 1999 FWD models with 2.0L non-turbo engine)

1	Fuel tank	5	Fuel level sending unit	10	Vapor hose
2	High pressure fuel hose	6	Fuel cut-off valve	11	Filler neck shield
3	Return hose	7	Vapor hose	12	Reinforcing plate
4	Fuel pump	8	Fuel filler cap	13	Filler neck
		9	Filler hose	14	Gasket

Replacement

19   Remove the fuel pump module from the tank (see Section 5).

20   Detach the sending unit from the fuel pump module.

21   Install the fuel pump module in the tank.

22   The remaining installation steps are the reverse of removal.

8   Fuel tank - removal and installation

Warning: *Gasoline is extremely flammable, so take extra precautions when you work on any part of the fuel system (see the* **Warning** *in Section 2).*

Removal

Refer to illustrations 8.10a and 8.10b

1   Remove the fuel tank filler cap to relieve fuel tank pressure.

2   Perform the fuel pressure relief procedure (see Section 2).

3   Disconnect the negative battery cable from the battery.

4   Remove the rear seat cushion (see Chapter 11). Remove the protective shield(s) over the fuel pump (and the separate fuel level sending unit on 1995 through 1999 models). Disconnect the electrical connectors and fuel lines.

5   Raise the vehicle and support it securely on jackstands.

6   If you're working on a 1995 through 1999 4WD model, remove the center exhaust pipe and the driveshaft (see Section 22 and Chapter 8).

7   Loosen the clamp and detach the filler neck hose from the fuel tank. **Warning:** *There may be fuel inside the filler neck and hose. Protect yourself accordingly.*

8   At the rear of the fuel tank, detach the vapor hose from the rollover valve.

9   Support the fuel tank with a floor jack. Place a piece of wood between the jack head and the fuel tank to protect the tank.

10   Remove the fuel tank mounting nuts (1995 through 1999 FWD models) or strap bolts and nuts and straps (1995 through 1999 4WD models and all 2000 and later models) **(see illustrations)**.

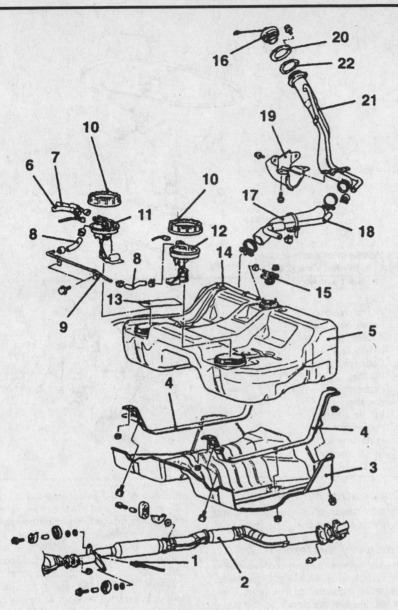

10.1 Loosen the clamp and disconnect the air cleaner intake duct

8.10b Fuel tank details (1995 through 1999 4WD models; all 2000 and later models similar)

1	Oxygen sensor connector	8	Suction hose	15	Fuel cutoff valve
2	Center exhaust pipe	9	Pipe	16	Fuel filler cap
3	Protector	10	Ring nut	17	Filler hose
4	Tank mounting strap	11	Fuel pump and level sending unit	18	Vapor hose
5	Fuel tank	12	Fuel level sending unit	19	Filler neck shield
6	High pressure fuel hose	13	Tape	20	Reinforcing plate
7	Return hose	14	Vapor hose	21	Filler neck
				22	Gasket

11   Lower the fuel tank and remove it from the vehicle.

Installation

12   Installation is the reverse of removal. However, before installing the fuel tank, tie a length of string or wire to the fuel pump and sending unit wiring harness(es) and route it through the hole(s) in the floorpan. Once the fuel tank is securely in position, pull the string to access the wiring harness.

13   Tighten the fuel tank mounting nuts or strap bolts and nuts to the torque listed in this Chapter's Specifications.

9   Fuel tank cleaning and repair - general information

Warning: *Gasoline is extremely flammable, so take extra precautions when you work on any part of the fuel system* (see the **Warning** in Section 2).

1   The fuel tank on some models is made of plastic and is not repairable.

2   All repairs on metal fuel tanks should be carried out by a professional who has experience in this critical and potentially dangerous work. Even after cleaning and flushing of the fuel system, explosive fumes can remain and ignite during repair of the tank.

3   If the fuel tank is removed from the vehicle, do not place it in an area where sparks or open flames could ignite the fuel vapors escaping from the tank. Be especially careful inside a garage where a gas-type appliance is located, because it could cause an explosion.

10   Air cleaner assembly - removal and installation

Refer to illustration 10.1

1   Loosen the air duct clamp at the air cleaner housing and remove the air intake duct **(see illustration)**.

2   Remove the housing cover and take out the air filter element (see Chapter 1).

3   Unbolt the housing from the vehicle and lift it out.

4   Installation is the reverse of removal. Make sure the lower housing is free of dirt and contamination prior to installation.

11   Accelerator cable - replacement

Refer to illustrations 11.1 and 11.6

1   Rotate the throttle valve cam to the full throttle position and disconnect the accelera-

tor cable from the slot in the throttle valve cam **(see illustration)**.

2   Unbolt the cable adjusting bracket from the intake manifold plenum and unbolt the cable retainer from the firewall.

3   At the accelerator pedal arm inside the vehicle, slide the cable out of the slot in the accelerator pedal arm.

4   Push the cable through the firewall into the engine compartment and remove it from the vehicle.

5   Installation is the reverse of removal.

6   Check the cable freeplay. It should be 0.040 to 0.080 inch, and the throttle should close fully when the pedal is released. If not, loosen the adjusting bolts and reposition the cable housing **(see illustration)**.

12   Fuel injection system - general information

The sequential Multi-Port Fuel Injection (MPFI) system consists of three sub-systems: air intake, engine control and fuel delivery. The MPFI system is controlled by the Powertrain Control Module (PCM) which uses the information from various sensors to determine the proper air/fuel ratio under all operating conditions.

The fuel injection, emissions and engine control systems work together to provide maximum performance, fuel economy and the lowest exhaust emissions. For complete information on the emissions and engine control systems, refer to Chapter 6.

Air intake system

The air intake system consists of the air filter, the air ducts, air inlet resonator, the throttle body, the idle control system and the intake manifold.

The engine idle speed is controlled by the PCM via the Idle Air Control (IAC) motor. The IAC motor regulates the flow of air allowed to bypass the throttle valve in the throttle body, thereby increasing engine speed. The PCM uses information from various sensors to determine the correct amount of airflow required to maintain the proper engine speed during engine warm-up and when a load is placed on the engine, such as engaging the air conditioning compressor, low speed steering or when an automatic transaxle is placed in gear.

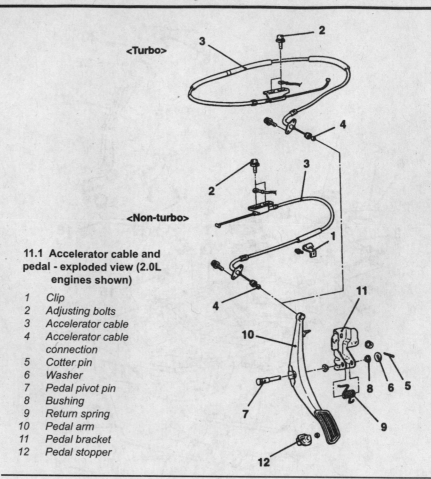

11.1 Accelerator cable and pedal - exploded view (2.0L engines shown)

1   Clip
2   Adjusting bolts
3   Accelerator cable
4   Accelerator cable connection
5   Cotter pin
6   Washer
7   Pedal pivot pin
8   Bushing
9   Return spring
10 Pedal arm
11 Pedal bracket
12 Pedal stopper

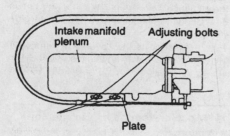

11.6 Cable freeplay is adjusted by loosening these bolts and repositioning the outer cable

Engine control system

For information on the engine control system, refer to Chapter 6.

Fuel delivery system

The fuel delivery system consists of the following components: an electric fuel pump, a fuel pressure regulator, an in-line fuel filter, the fuel rail, the fuel injectors, various metal and plastic lines, the Automatic Shutdown (ASD) relay and the fuel pump relay.

The fuel pump is located inside the fuel tank. Fuel is drawn through the fuel inlet strainer into the pump, then through the fuel filter and delivered to the injectors.

The fuel pressure regulator maintains a constant fuel pressure to the injectors. Excess fuel is released back into the fuel tank through the fuel pressure regulator, which is mounted on the fuel rail on all except 1996 and later 2.0L non-turbo models. On these models it's mounted in the line leading from the fuel tank.

The fuel rail supplies the regulated fuel to each electronically controlled fuel injector. The injectors are solenoid types consisting of a solenoid, plunger, needle valve and housing. When the PCM sends a voltage signal to the fuel injector, the needle valve raises off its seat and lets metered fuel enter the intake manifold. The injection quantity is determined by the length of time which current is supplied to the injector.

The MFI relay (also known as the auto-

shutdown or ASD relay) and the fuel pump relay are located next to each other, in the passenger compartment or engine compartment depending on model. The MFI relay connects battery voltage to the fuel injectors and the ignition coil while the fuel pump relay connects battery voltage only to the fuel pump. If the PCM senses there is NO signal from the camshaft or crankshaft sensors while the ignition key is RUN or cranking, the PCM will de-energize both relays in approximately one second.

13   Fuel injection system - general check

Refer to illustration 13.6

Warning: *Gasoline is extremely flammable, so take extra precautions when you work on any part of the fuel system (see the* **Warning** *in Section 2).*

Note: *The following procedure is based on the assumption that the fuel pump/pressure is acceptable (see Section 3).*

1   Visually check all electrical connectors that are related to the system. Check ground wire connections on the intake manifold and engine for tightness. Loose connectors and poor grounds can cause many problems that resemble more serious component malfunctions.

2   Check to see that the battery is fully charged, as the PCM and information sensors

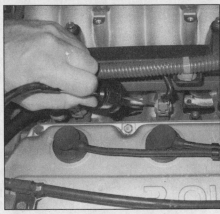

13.6 Use a stethoscope to determine if the injectors are working properly - they should make a steady clicking sound that rises and falls with engine speed changes

depend on proper battery voltage in order to operate correctly.

3   Check the air filter element - a dirty or partially blocked filter will severely impede performance and economy (see Chapter 1).

4   Check the air intake ducts for cracks or loose connections. Also check the condition of all vacuum hoses connected to the intake manifold. Make sure they fit tightly on the vacuum ports and are free from cracks or other defects.

5   Remove the air intake duct from the throttle body and inspect for dirt, carbon or other residue build-up around the throttle valve and Idle Air Control bypass port. If the throttle body is dirty, clean it with a spray-type carburetor cleaner and a toothbrush or clean rag. **Note:** *If the throttle body cannot be cleaned properly while installed on the vehicle, remove it* (see Section 14).

6   With the engine running, place an automotive stethoscope against each injector, one at a time, and listen for a clicking sound, indicating operation **(see illustration)**. If you don't have a stethoscope, place the tip of a screwdriver against the injector and listen through the handle. **Note:** *On V6 engines, the right (rear, closest to the firewall) bank of fuel injectors CANNOT be checked using this procedure, as they are covered by the upper intake manifold.*

7   If an injector is not making a clicking sound, stop the engine, unplug its electrical connector and measure the resistance of the injector with an ohmmeter (see Section 16). If the resistance doesn't fall within the range listed in this Chapter's Specifications, replace the injector.

8   Individual component checks can be found in their appropriate Sections.

14 Throttle body - check, removal and installation

Check

1   Remove the air cleaner assembly (see Section 10).

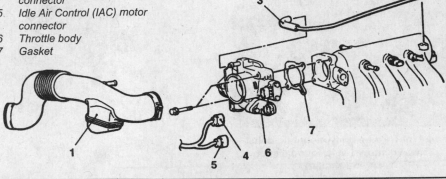

14.6 Throttle body details (2.0L non-turbo engine)

1   Air intake hose
2   Accelerator cable
3   Vacuum hose
4   Throttle Position Sensor (TPS) connector
5   Idle Air Control (IAC) motor connector
6   Throttle body
7   Gasket

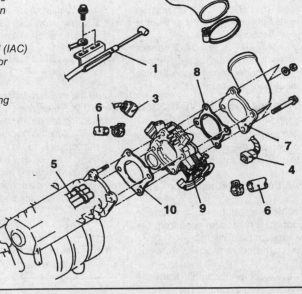

14.11 Throttle body details (2.0L turbo engine)

1   Accelerator cable
2   Intercooler hose
3   Throttle position sensor (TPS) connector
4   Idle Air Control (IAC) motor connector
5   Vacuum ports
6   Coolant hose
7   Intercooler fitting
8   Gasket
9   Throttle body
10   Gasket

2   Verify the accelerator cable, cruise control cable (if equipped) and throttle valve operate smoothly without binding or sticking.

3   Inspect the throttle bore, throttle valve, IAC bypass port and canister purge vacuum port for carbon deposits. If carbon build-up is present, remove the throttle body from the vehicle and remove the IAC motor (see Section 17). Clean the throttle body and IAC motor pintle with a spray-type carburetor cleaner and a toothbrush.

4   If the throttle valve does not operate freely after cleaning, replace the throttle body.

Removal

2.0L non-turbo models

Refer to illustration 14.6

Warning: *Wait until the engine is completely cool before beginning this procedure.*

5   Remove the battery (see Chapter 5).

6   Remove the air intake hose **(see illustration)**.

7   Disconnect the canister purge vacuum hose from the throttle body.

8   Detach the accelerator cable and cruise control cable (if equipped), from the throttle valve lever (see Section 11).

9   Disconnect the TPS and IAC sensor connectors from the throttle body, remove the mounting bolts and then withdraw the throttle body and gasket from the manifold.

2.0L turbo models

Refer to illustration 14.11

Warning: *Wait until the engine is completely cool before beginning this procedure.*

10   Drain the cooling system (see Chapter 1).

11   Remove the intercooler hose **(see illustration)**.

14.21a Throttle body mounting bolts (3.0L V6 shown, 2.4L four-cylinder engine similar)

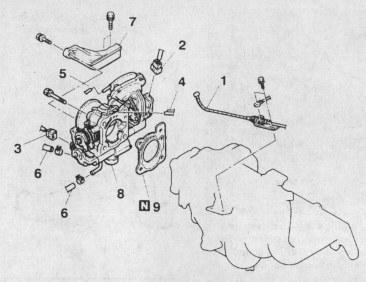

14.21b Throttle body details (2.4L engine)

1 Accelerator cable connection	6 Water hose connection
2 Throttle position sensor connector	7 Throttle body stay
3 Idle air control motor connector	8 Throttle body
4 Vacuum hose connection	9 Throttle body gasket
5 Vacuum hose connection - vehicles with auto-cruise control system	

12   Label and disconnect the vacuum hoses from the throttle body.

13   Disconnect the coolant hoses from the throttle body

14   Detach the accelerator cable and cruise control cable (if equipped), from the throttle valve lever (see Section 11).

15   Disconnect the TPS and IAC sensor connectors from the throttle body, remove the mounting bolts, then withdraw the throttle body and gasket from the manifold.

2.4L four-cylinder and 3.0L V6 models

Refer to illustrations 14.21a and 14.21b
Warning: *Wait until the engine is completely cool before beginning this procedure.*

16   Drain the cooling system (see Chapter 1).

17   Remove the air cleaner (see Section 10).

18   If the vehicle is equipped with cruise control, disconnect the vacuum hose from the throttle body vacuum diaphragm.

19   Disconnect the coolant hoses from the throttle body.

20   Detach the accelerator cable from the throttle valve lever (see Section 11).

21   Disconnect the TPS and IAC sensor connectors from the throttle body and remove the mounting bolts **(see illustrations)**, then withdraw the throttle body, mounting stay (2.4L), vacuum hose bracket (3.0L) and gasket from the manifold. **Note:** *On 2.4L four-cylinder and 3.0L V6 engine models, note the position of the projecting tab on the gasket (it projects upward from one of the upper bolt holes). Be sure to install the new gasket with its tab in the same location.*

All models

22   Remove all traces of gasket material from the throttle body and manifold.

23   If necessary, clean the throttle body as described in Step 3.

Installation

24   Install the throttle body with a new gasket

onto the intake manifold. On 2.4L four cylinder and 3.0L V6 engines, place the gasket with its projecting tab upward.

25   Tighten the throttle body mounting bolts to the torque listed in this Chapter's Specifications.

26   The remaining installation steps are the reverse of removal. After installation, check to see that the throttle body operates freely.

---

15   Fuel pressure regulator - replacement

Warning: *Gasoline is extremely flammable, so take extra precautions when you work on any part of the fuel system (see the **Warning** in Section 2).*

1996 and later 2.0L non-turbo models

Note: *The fuel pressure regulator on 1995 2.0L non-turbo models is an integral part of the fuel rail and is replaced as a unit with it (see Section 16).*

1   Perform the fuel pressure relief procedure (see Section 2).

2   Locate the pressure regulator at the fuel filter **(see illustration 33.1 in Chapter 1)**.

3   Disconnect the hose from the regulator and unscrew the regulator from the fitting at the fuel filter.

4   Installation is the reverse of the removal steps.

2.0L turbo, 2.4L four-cylinder and 3.0L V6 models

Refer to illustrations 15.6a and 15.6b

5   Perform the fuel pressure relief procedure (see Section 2).

6   Locate the pressure regulator on the fuel rail **(see illustrations)**.

7   Disconnect the regulator vacuum hose. Remove the regulator mounting bolts and take it off the fuel rail.

8   Installation is the reverse of the removal steps. Lubricate the O-ring with a drop of engine oil, but don't let any oil get into the fuel rail.

---

16   Fuel rail and injectors - check, removal and installation

Warning: *Gasoline is extremely flammable, so take extra precautions when you work on any part of the fuel system (see the **Warning** in Section 2).*

Fuel injector operation check

Refer to illustrations 16.5 and 16.6

1   Start the engine and allow it warm up to normal operating temperature.

2   If the vehicle is not equipped with a tachometer, connect one to the engine in accordance with the tool manufacturer's instructions.

3   Make sure all test equipment is positioned away from the drivebelts and cooling

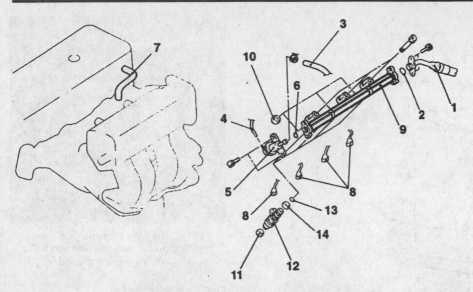

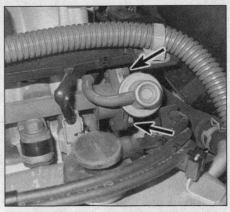

15.6b After relieving fuel system pressure, unbolt the fuel pressure regulator from the fuel rail (3.0L V6 engine shown)

15.6a Fuel rail and injector details (2.0L turbo models)

1	High pressure fuel hose	8	Injector connectors
2	O-ring	9	Fuel rail
3	Fuel return hose	10	Insulators
4	Vacuum hose	11	Insulator
5	Fuel pressure regulator	12	Injector
6	O-ring	13	O-ring
7	PCV hose	14	Grommet

fans, then start the engine. With the engine idling, detach each fuel injector electrical connector one-at-a-time, and note the rpm change on the tachometer, then reconnect the injector. **Note:** *On V6 engines, this test can only be applied to the left front bank of fuel injectors.* If the rpm change is approximately the same for each cylinder, the injectors are operating correctly. If disconnecting a particular injector fails to change the engine rpm, proceed to Step 5. If the fuel injectors are operating properly, check the ignition system (see Chapter 5), condition of the spark plugs and wires (see Chapter 1) and, if necessary, perform a com-

pression check (see Chapter 2E) to determine the cause of the dead cylinder.
4   On V6 engines, remove the upper intake manifold (see Chapter 2D).
5   Disconnect the injector electrical connectors and using an ohmmeter, measure the resistance of each injector **(see illustration)**. Compare the measured resistance to the value given this Chapter's Specifications. If the resistance is not within specifications, replace the injector.
6   If the resistance is as specified, connect a special injector harness test light (commonly known as a "noid light" which is avail-

able at most auto parts stores) to the injector electrical connector **(see illustration)**. If the light flashes, the injector is receiving voltage. If there is no voltage, check the MFI relay operation (see Section 3). If the MFI relay is OK, check the injector wiring circuit for a short, a break in the wire or a bad connection (see Chapter 12 if necessary).
7   With the electrical connector removed from the injector, use a fused jumper wire to connect one terminal of the injector to the positive terminal of the battery. Attach another jumper wire to the other terminal on the fuel injector. Make sure the jumper wires are properly insulated from each other! Quickly connect and disconnect the end of the second jumper wire to a solid ground on the engine. **Note:** *Do not subject the fuel injector to battery voltage any longer than necessary.* Each time the injector is energized and de-energized, the injector should make an audible "clicking" sound. If no sound is heard, replace the injector. Repeat the test for each injector.
8   If the fuel injectors are operating properly, install all removed components in the reverse order of removal.

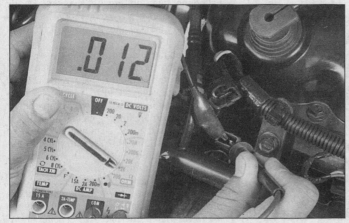

16.5 Measure the resistance between the injector terminals with an ohmmeter

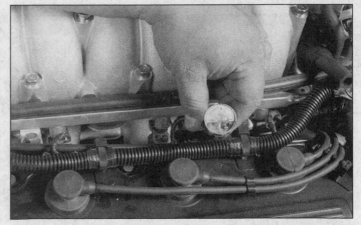

16.6 Connect a "noid" light (available at most auto parts stores) to each injector electrical connector and confirm that it flashes when the engine is cranking or running

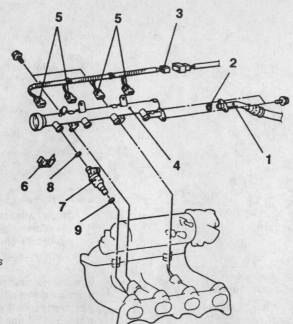

16.26a Fuel rail and injector details (2.0L non-turbo engine)

1   High pressure fuel hose
2   O-ring
3   Injector harness connector
4   Fuel rail
5   Injector connectors
6   Injector retainer
7   Injector
8   O-ring
9   O-ring

16.26b The high pressure fuel line is attached to the fuel rail with two bolts (3.0L V6 engine shown)

Fuel injector leak check

Warning: *Wear eye protection during this check.*

Note: *After identifying that a fuel injector is leaking (see Section 3), use the following procedure to determine which one (or more) of the fuel injectors is defective.*

9   Perform the fuel pressure relief procedure (see Section 2).

10   Remove the fuel rail and injector assembly from the intake manifold as described below, however, do not disconnect the fuel supply line or the fuel injectors from the fuel rail.

11   With the fuel rail resting on the intake manifold (injectors nozzles exposed), place some clean shop rags under the fuel injectors to catch the fuel that will leak out of the defective injector(s).

12   Attach the fuel pump module electrical connector to the wiring harness and the battery negative cable to the battery.

13   Turn the ignition key to the ON position (engine OFF) several times to pressurize the fuel system. **Warning:** *Do not crank the engine over.* With the system under pressure, inspect each injector for fuel leaking out of the nozzle. Label the faulty injector(s).

14   Next, relieve the fuel pressure via a faulty fuel injector by using a small Phillips head screwdriver (or equivalent) to push the injector pintle off its seat to release the fuel pressure through the injector nozzle. Wrap a dry shop rag around the faulty injector to catch the fuel as it escapes.

15   Once the fuel pressure has been relieved, detach the fuel supply line from the fuel rail (see Section 4 if necessary) and replace the faulty fuel injector(s) (see below).

Removal

16   Perform the fuel pressure relief procedure (see Section 2).

17   Disconnect the negative battery cable

from the battery.

2.0L non-turbo engine

18   Remove the battery (see Chapter 5).
19   Remove the air cleaner intake hose.

2.0L turbo engine

20   Remove the spark plug wires (see Chapter 1).

2.4L engine

21   Drain the cooling system (see Chapter 1).
22   Remove the air cleaner (see Section 10).
23   Remove the throttle body (see Section 14).

3.0L V6 engine

24   Drain the cooling system (see Chapter 1).
25   Remove the upper intake manifold (see Chapter 2D).

All engines

Refer to illustrations 16.26a, 16.26b, 16.29, 16.30, 16.31a, 16.31b and 16.31c

26   Detach the fuel supply line from the fuel rail **(see illustration 15.6a or the accompanying illustrations)**.

27   Disconnect the wiring harness electrical connectors from the fuel injectors. Clearly label and remove any vacuum hoses or electrical wiring that will interfere with the fuel rail removal.

28   Clean the injector-to-manifold area using compressed air (a can of compressed-gas duster like those used to blow out electrical components will work just as well) or spray-type carburetor cleaner to remove any dirt or debris from around the injectors.

29   Remove the fuel rail mounting bolts **(see illustration 15.6a, 16.26a or the accompanying illustration)**.

30   Remove the fuel rail assembly (with the fuel injectors attached) from the engine. **Note:** *On all except 2.0L non-turbo models, there are spacers located between the fuel rail and the lower intake manifold. If they become dislodged, make sure you reinstall them (see illustration).*

31   Remove the retaining clips and withdraw

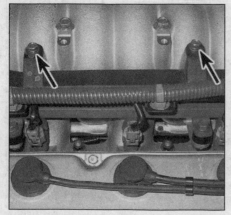

16.29 Typical fuel rail mounting bolts (arrows) (3.0L V6 engine, left [front] side shown)

16.30 On most engines, these plastic spacers must be installed between the fuel rail and the lower intake manifold

16.31a Using a screwdriver or pliers, remove the injector retaining clip securing the injector to the fuel rail . . .

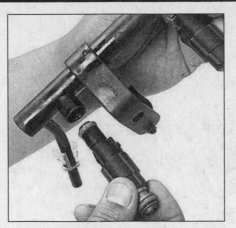

16.31b . . . then withdraw the injector from the fuel rail

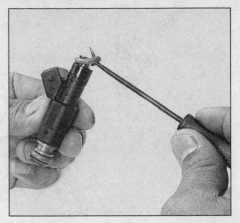

16.31c Remove the old O-ring seals from the fuel injector and discard them

the injectors from the fuel rail **(see illustrations)**. Remove the O-ring seals and discard them **(see illustration)**. **Note:** *Whether you're replacing an injector or a bad O-ring seal, it's standard practice to replace all O-ring seals at this time.*

32   On V6 engines, clean and inspect the upper-to-lower manifold gasket surfaces (see Chapter 2D).

Installation

33   Apply a light coating of clean engine oil to the new O-ring seals and carefully install them onto the injectors.

34   Insert each injector into its corresponding bore in the fuel rail. Position the electrical terminals appropriately and secure the fuel injectors to the fuel rail with the retaining clips.

35   On all except 2.0L non-turbo engines, make sure the fuel rail spacers are installed **(see illustration 16.30)**.

36   Apply a light coating of clean engine oil to the injector-to-manifold O-ring seals and install the injector/fuel rail assembly onto the intake manifold. Make sure the injectors are fully seated, then tighten the fuel rail mounting bolts to the torque listed in this Chapter's Specifications.

37   Connect the fuel supply line to the fuel rail.

38   Attach the fuel pump electrical connector to the wiring harness and the battery negative cable to the battery.

39   Disable the ignition system (see Chapter 2E, Section 3, Step 5).Turn the ignition key to the ON position (engine OFF) several times to pressurize the fuel system. Inspect the fuel rail and injectors for leaks. If leakage is evident, perform the fuel pressure relief procedure (see Section 2) and rectify the problem. **Warning:** *On 3.0L V6 engines, before performing the fuel pressure relief procedure, make sure all loose objects or rags have been removed from inside or around the lower intake manifold ports. Since the ignition system has been disabled - simply crank the engine over with the fuel pump relay unplugged to relieve the fuel pressure.*

40   The remaining installation steps are the reverse of removal. On 3.0L V6 engines,

make sure to install a new upper intake manifold gasket and tighten the upper intake manifold bolts to the torque listed in the Chapter 2D Specifications.

17   Idle Air Control (IAC) motor - check and replacement

General description

The engine idle speed is controlled by the PCM via the Idle Air Control motor, which is mounted on the throttle body. The IAC motor regulates the flow of air allowed to bypass the throttle valve in the throttle body thereby increasing engine speed. The PCM uses information from various sensors to determine the correct amount of airflow required to maintain the proper engine speed during engine warm-up and when a load is placed on the engine, such as engaging the air conditioning compressor, low speed steering or when an automatic transaxle is placed in gear.

Check

1   Make sure the coolant temperature sensor is below 68-degrees F (chill it with ice if necessary).

2   Listen to the idle air control motor while an assistant turns the key to ON and back to

off (without starting the engine). There should be a clicking sound. If not, check the wiring harness to the motor (see Chapter 12 if necessary). If the harness is good, test the motor as described below.

2.0L non-turbo models
Refer to illustration 17.4

3   Disconnect the idle air control motor electrical connector **(see illustration 14.6)**.

4   Connect an ohmmeter between terminals 1 and 4, then between terminals 2 and 3 **(see illustration)**. The ohmmeter should read 38 to 52 ohms in each case. If not, replace the IAC motor.

All other models
Refer to illustration 17.6

5   Disconnect the idle air control motor electrical connector **(see illustration 14.11)**.

6   Connect one probe of an ohmmeter to terminal 2, then connect the other probe to terminals 1 and 3 in turn **(see illustration)**. The ohmmeter should read 28 to 33 ohms in

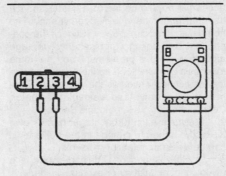

17.4 On 2.0L non-turbo engines, connect an ohmmeter between terminals 1 and 4, then between terminals 2 and 3 to check the IAC motor resistance

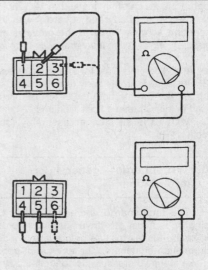

17.6 IAC motor test connections and terminals (all except 2.0L non-turbo engines)

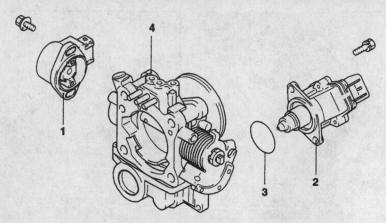

**17.10 The IAC motor is attached to the throttle body with two or three screws
(2.0L turbo shown)**

1	Throttle position sensor	3	O-ring
2	Idle air control motor	4	Throttle body

each case. If not, replace the IAC motor.

7   Connect one probe of an ohmmeter to terminal 5, then connect the other probe to terminals 4 and 6 in turn **(see illustration 17.6)**. Again, the ohmmeter should read 28 to 33 ohms in each case. If not, replace the IAC motor.

Removal
Refer to illustration 17.10

8   Remove the air cleaner assembly (see Section 10).

9   Remove the throttle body (see Section 14).

10   Remove the IAC motor from the throttle body **(see illustration)**. Make sure the O-ring seal is removed with the IAC motor. If not, retrieve it from the throttle body orifice.

Installation
11   With the pintle retracted and the O-ring seal in place, carefully install the IAC motor into the throttle body and secure it with the mounting screws. **Note:** *If the pintle is not retracted, slowly push it inward while wiggling it from side-to-side.* Tighten the screws to the torque given in this Chapter's Specifications.

12   Install the throttle body (see Section 14). Tighten the throttle body bolts to the torque listed in this Chapter's Specifications.

13   Install the air cleaner assembly (see Section 10).

---

18   Turbocharger - general information

The turbocharger increases power by using an exhaust gas-driven turbine to pressurize the fuel/air mixture before it enters the combustion chambers. The amount of boost (intake manifold pressure) is controlled by the wastegate (exhaust bypass valve). The wastegate is operated by a spring-loaded actuator assembly which controls the maximum boost level by allowing some of the exhaust gas to

bypass the turbine. The wastegate is controlled by the computer.

Only the 2.0L engine is equipped with the turbocharger option. The turbocharger system is equipped with an intercooler, which cools the compressed air and makes it even more dense (denser air can absorb more gasoline molecules for a given volume).

The computerized fuel injection and emission control system is equipped with self-diagnosis capabilities that can access certain turbocharging system components. Refer to Chapter 6 for information pertaining to trouble codes and diagnosis.

---

19   Turbocharger - check

General checks

1   While it is a relatively simple device, the turbocharger is also a precision component which can be severely damaged by an interrupted oil or coolant supply or loose or damaged ducts.

2   Due to the special techniques and equipment required, checking and diagnosis of suspected problems dealing with the turbocharger should be left to a dealer service department or other qualified repair shop. The home mechanic can, however, check the connections and linkages for security, damage and other obvious problems. Also, the home mechanic can check components that govern the turbocharger such as the wastegate solenoid, bypass valve and wastegate actuator. Refer to the checks later in this Section.

3   Because each turbocharger has its own distinctive sound, a change in the noise level can be a sign of potential problems.

4   A high-pitched or whistling sound is a symptom of an inlet air or exhaust gas leak.

5   If an unusual sound comes from the vicinity of the turbine, the turbocharger can be removed and the turbine wheel inspected. **Caution:** *All checks must be made with the engine off and cool to the touch and the tur-*

bocharger stopped or personal injury could result. Operating the engine without all the turbocharger ducts and filters installed is also dangerous and can result in damage to the turbine wheel blades.

6   With the engine turned off and completely cool, reach inside the housing and turn the turbine wheel to make sure it spins freely. If it doesn't, it's possible the cooling oil has sludged or coked from overheating. Push in on the turbine wheel and check for binding. The turbine should rotate freely with no binding or rubbing on the housing. If it does, the turbine bearing is worn out.

7   Check the exhaust manifold for cracks and loose connections.

8   Because the turbine wheel rotates at speeds up to 140,000 rpm, severe damage can result from the interruption of coolant or contamination of the oil supply to the turbine bearings. Check for leaks in the coolant and oil inlet lines and obstructions in the oil drain-back line, as this can cause severe oil loss through the turbocharger seals. Burned oil on the turbine housing is a sign of this. **Caution:** *Whenever a major engine bearing such as a main or connecting rod bearing is replaced, the turbocharger should be flushed with clean engine oil.*

Component checks
Refer to illustrations 19.9 and 19.12

Wastegate solenoid
9   Disconnect and plug the black vacuum hose at the wastegate solenoid **(see illustration)**. Connect a hand-held vacuum pump to the valve port.

10   Start the engine and let it idle.

11   Apply vacuum to the port with the vacuum pump. The solenoid should hold vacuum while the engine is idling, and release it when the engine is shut off. If not, replace the solenoid.

Bypass valve
12   Connect a hand-held vacuum pump to the port on the bypass valve **(see illustration)**. Apply vacuum.

13   At approximately 16.0 in-Hg, the valve

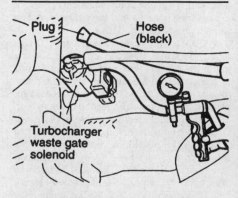

**19.9 Disconnect and plug the black hose
and attach a vacuum pump in its place**

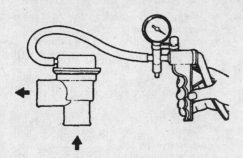

19.12 Use a vacuum pump to check the turbocharger bypass valve

should start opening and allowing air to flow.
14   If the test results are incorrect, replace the bypass valve with a new part.

20   Turbocharger - removal and installation

Refer to illustration 20.2

Removal

1   Remove the exhaust manifold together with the turbocharger (see Chapter 2B).
2   Separate the turbocharger from the exhaust manifold, together with the exhaust fitting, coolant tube, oil tube and oil return tube **(see illustration)**.

Installation

3   Carefully clean the mating surfaces of the turbocharger and exhaust manifold.
4   Place the turbocharger in position on the manifold.
5   Apply anti-seize compound to the stud/bolts and install the nuts/bolts. Tighten the fasteners to the torque listed in this Chapter's Specifications.
6   Install new sealing washers on the lower inlet coolant line fitting and install the fitting into the turbocharger housing.
7   Install the upper coolant line, again using new sealing washers.
8   Install the oil return tube and fitting, along with a new gasket, to the turbocharger housing.
9   Install the exhaust pipe fitting, using a new gasket, and tighten the fasteners to the torque listed in this Chapter's Specifications.
10   The remainder of installation is the reverse of the removal steps.
11   Refill the cooling system (see Chapter 1).
12   Change the engine oil (see Chapter 1).

21   Intercooler - removal and installation

Refer to illustration 21.3

1   Remove the front bumper (see Chapter 11).

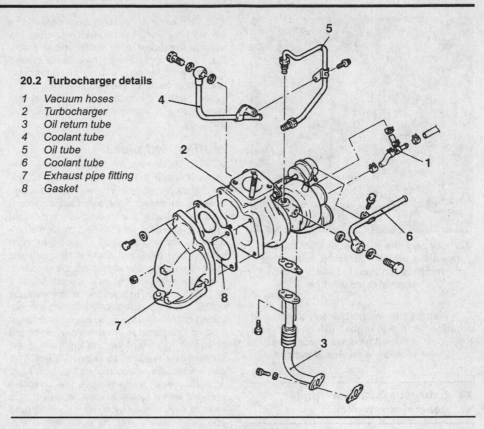

20.2 Turbocharger details

1	*Vacuum hoses*
2	*Turbocharger*
3	*Oil return tube*
4	*Coolant tube*
5	*Oil tube*
6	*Coolant tube*
7	*Exhaust pipe fitting*
8	*Gasket*

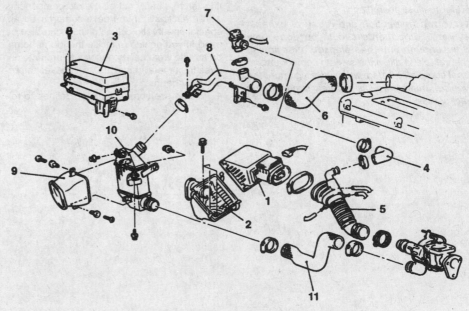

21.3 Intercooler details (2.0L turbo models)

1	*Air cleaner upper housing*	4	*Air bypass hose*	8	*Air hose B*
2	*Air cleaner lower housing*	5	*Air intake hose*	9	*Intercooler duct*
3	*Relay box*	6	*Air hose C*	10	*Intercooler*
		7	*Turbocharger bypass valve*	11	*Air hose A*

2   Remove the air cleaner (see Section 10).
3   Remove the relay box **(see illustration)**.
4   Disconnect the vacuum line from the turbocharger bypass valve.

5   Loosen the hose clamps, then remove the air bypass hose, air intake hose, air hoses A, B and C and the intercooler duct **(see illustration 21.3)**.
6   Unbolt and remove the intercooler.

22.1 Inspect the exhaust system gaskets, mounting brackets, clamps and rubber hangers (arrows) for damage or improper installation

7   Inspect the intercooler for cracks and damage to the flanges, tubes and fins. Replace it or have it repaired if necessary.
8   Installation is the reverse of removal.

---

22 Exhaust system servicing - general information

Refer to illustration 22.1
Warning: *Inspection and repair of exhaust system components should be done only after enough time has elapsed after driving the vehicle to allow the system components to cool completely. Also, when working under the vehicle, make sure it is securely supported on jackstands.*

1   The exhaust system consists of the exhaust manifold, the catalytic converter, the resonator, exhaust pipe, muffler and all brackets, hangers and clamps. The exhaust system is attached to the body with mounting brackets and rubber hangers **(see illustration)**. If any of the parts are improperly installed, excessive noise and vibration will be transmitted to the body.

Muffler and pipes

2   Conduct regular inspections of the exhaust system to keep it safe and quiet. Look for any damaged or bent parts, open seams, holes, loose connections, excessive corrosion or other defects which could allow exhaust fumes to enter the vehicle. Also check the catalytic converter when you inspect the exhaust system (see following). Deteriorated exhaust system components should not be repaired; they should be replaced with new parts.
3   Before trying to disassemble any exhaust components, spray the fasteners with a penetrating oil to help ease removal. If the exhaust system components are extremely corroded or rusted together, welding equipment will probably be required to remove them. The convenient way to accomplish this is to have a muffler repair shop remove the corroded sections with a cutting torch. If, however, you want to save money by doing it yourself (and you don't have a welding outfit with a cutting torch), simply cut off the old components with a hacksaw. If you have compressed air, special pneumatic cutting chisels can also be used. If you decide to tackle the job at home, be sure to wear safety goggles to protect your eyes from metal chips and work gloves to protect your hands.
4   Here are some simple guidelines to fol-

low when repairing the exhaust system:
a) *Work from the back to the front when removing exhaust system components.*
b) *Apply penetrating oil to the exhaust system component fasteners to make them easier to remove.*
c) *Use new gaskets, hangers and clamps when installing exhaust systems components.*
d) *Apply anti-seize compound to the threads of all exhaust system fasteners at reassembly.*
e) *Be sure to allow sufficient clearance between newly installed parts and all points on the underbody to avoid overheating the floor pan and possibly damaging the interior carpet and insulation. Pay particularly close attention to the catalytic converter and heat shield.*

Catalytic converter

Warning: *The converter gets extremely hot during operation, and can remain very hot for hours after the engine has been turned off. Make sure it has cooled down before you touch it.*
Note: *See Chapter 6 for more information on the catalytic converter.*

5   Periodically inspect the heat shield for cracks, dents and loose or missing fasteners.
6   Remove the heat shield and inspect the converter for cracks or other damage.
7   If the converter must be replaced, detach the exhaust system from the exhaust manifold. Loosen the rear band clamp at the resonator and separate the converter from the exhaust system.
8   Installation is the reverse of removal. Be sure to use new gaskets and tighten the fasteners securely.

Chapter 5
Engine electrical systems

Contents

Specifications

General

Battery voltage	12 volts (approximate)
Engine firing order	
Four-cylinder engines	1-3-4-2
V6 engine	1-2-3-4-5-6
Ignition timing	Not adjustable

Ignition system

Ignition coil resistance (approximate, at 70 to 80-degrees F)	
2.0L non-turbo engine	
Primary resistance	0.51 to 0.61 ohms
Secondary resistance	11,500 to 13,500 ohms
2.0L turbo engine	
Primary resistance	0.70 to 0.86 ohms
Secondary resistance	11,300 to 15,300 ohms
2.4L engine	
Primary resistance	Not specified
Secondary resistance	8500 to 11,500 ohms
3.0L V6 engine	
Primary resistance	0.56 to 0.68 ohms
Secondary resistance	9400 to 12,800 ohms
Spark plug wire resistance (approximate)	
2.0L non-turbo engine	8,000 ohms maximum
All others	22,000 ohms maximum

Torque specifications

Note: *One foot-pound (ft-lb) of torque is equivalent to 12 inch-pounds (in-lbs) of torque. Torque values below approximately 15 ft-lbs are expressed in inch-pounds, since most foot-pound torque wrenches are not accurate at these smaller values.*

Distributor hold-down nuts (3.0L V6 engine)	109 inch-lbs
Starter motor mounting bolts	
2.0L non-turbo engines	40 ft-lbs
All others	22 ft-lbs

1   General information

The engine electrical systems include all ignition, charging and starting components. Because of their engine-related functions, these components are considered separately from chassis electrical devices like the lights, instruments, etc.

Be very careful when working on the engine electrical components. They are easily damaged if checked, connected or handled improperly. The alternator is driven by an engine drivebelt which could cause serious injury if your hands, hair or clothes become entangled in it with the engine running. Both the starter and alternator are connected directly to the battery and could arc or even cause a fire if mishandled, overloaded or shorted out.

Never leave the ignition switch on for long periods of time with the engine off. Don't disconnect the battery cables while the engine is running. Correct polarity must be maintained when connecting battery cables

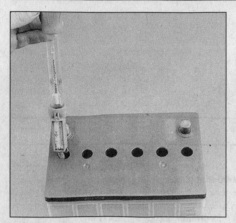

3.1a Use a battery hydrometer to draw electrolyte from the battery cell - this hydrometer is equipped with a thermometer to make temperature corrections

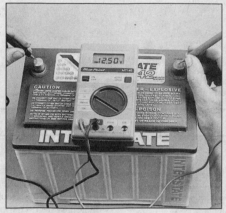

3.1b To test the open circuit voltage of the battery, connect the black probe of the voltmeter to the battery negative terminal and the red probe to the positive terminal of the battery - a fully charged battery should indicate approximately 12.5 volts depending on the outside air temperature

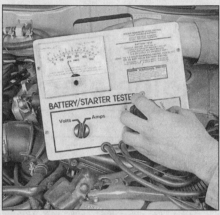

3.1c Battery load testers are equipped with an ammeter which enables the battery load to be precisely dialed in, as shown - less expensive testers have a load switch and voltmeter only

from another source, such as another vehicle, during jump starting. Always disconnect the negative cable first and hook it up last or the battery may be shorted by the tool being used to loosen the cable clamps.

Additional safety related information on the engine electrical systems can be found in *Safety first* near the front of this manual. It should be referred to before beginning any operation included in this Chapter.

2   Battery - emergency jump starting

Refer to the *Booster battery (jump) starting* procedure at the front of this manual.

3   Battery - check and replacement

Note: *Anytime the battery is disconnected, stored operating parameters may be lost from*

3.1d To find out whether there's a drain on the battery, detach the negative cable and connect a test light between the battery post and the cable clamp

the PCM causing the engine to run rough for a period of time while the PCM relearns the information.

Check

Refer to illustrations 3.1a, 3.1b, 3.1c and 3.1d
1   A battery cannot be accurately tested until it is at or near a fully charged state. Disconnect the negative battery cable, then the positive cable from the battery and perform the following tests:

  a)   ***Battery state of charge test*** - *Visually inspect the indicator eye (if equipped) on the top of the battery. If the indicator eye is dark in color, charge the battery as described in Chapter 1. If the battery is equipped with removable caps, check the battery electrolyte. The electrolyte level should be above the upper edge of the plates. If the level is low, add distilled water. DO NOT OVERFILL. The excess electrolyte may spill over during periods of heavy charging. Test the specific gravity of the electrolyte using a hydrometer* **(see illustration)**. *Remove the caps and extract a sample of the electrolyte and observe the float inside the barrel of the hydrometer. Follow the instructions from the tool manufacturer and determine the specific gravity of the electrolyte for each cell. A fully charged battery will indicate approximately 1.270 (green zone). If the specific gravity of the electrolyte is low (red zone), charge the battery as described in Chapter 1.*

  b)   ***Open voltage circuit test*** - *Using a digital voltmeter, perform an open voltage circuit test* **(see illustration)**. **Note:** *The battery's surface charge must be removed before accurate voltage measurements can be made. Turn On the high beams for ten seconds, then turn them Off, let the vehicle stand for two*

minutes. With the engine and all accessories Off, connect the negative probe of the voltmeter to the negative terminal of the battery and the positive probe to the positive terminal of the battery. The battery voltage should be approximately 12.5 volts. If the battery is less than the specified voltage, charge the battery before proceeding to the next test. Do not proceed with the battery load test until the battery is fully charged.

  c)   ***Battery load test*** - *An accurate check of the battery condition can only be performed with a load tester (available at most auto parts stores). This test evaluates the ability of the battery to operate the starter and other accessories during periods of heavy amperage draw (load). Install a special battery load testing tool onto the battery terminals* **(see illustration)**. *Load test the battery according to the tool manufacturer's instructions. This tool utilizes a carbon pile to increase the load demand (amperage draw) on the battery. Maintain the load on the battery for 15 seconds and observe that the battery voltage does not drop below 9.6 volts. If the battery condition is weak or defective, the tool will indicate this condition immediately.* **Note:** *Cold temperatures will cause the minimum voltage requirements to drop slightly. Follow the chart given in the tool manufacturer's instructions to compensate for cold climates. Minimum load voltage for freezing temperatures (32 degrees F) should be approximately 9.1 volts.*

  d)   ***Battery drain test*** - *This test will indicate whether there's a constant drain on the vehicle's electrical system that can cause the battery to discharge. Make sure all accessories are turned Off. If the vehicle has an underhood light, verify it's working properly, then disconnect it. Disconnect the cable from the negative terminal of the battery and attach one lead of a test light to the negative battery*

3.3 Remove the nuts (arrows) from the battery hold-down clamp

cable and the other end to the negative battery terminal **(see illustration)**. *The test light should not glow. If the test light glows, it indicates a constant drain on the battery which could cause the battery to discharge.* **Note:** *On vehicles equipped with engine control computers, clocks, digital radios, power seats with memory and/or other components which normally cause a key-off battery drain, it's normal for the test light to glow dimly. If you suspect the drain is excessive, install an ammeter in place of the test light. The reading should not exceed 0.05 amps (50 milliamps).*

Replacement

Refer to illustration 3.3

Caution: *Always disconnect the negative cable first and hook it up last or the battery may be shorted by the tool being used to loosen the cable clamps.*

2   Disconnect the negative battery cable, then the positive cable from the battery.

3   Remove the battery hold-down clamp

(see illustration). Note: *On some models, one of the clamp nuts also secures a throttle cable clamp.*

4   Remove the battery cover (if equipped) and lift out the battery. Be careful - it's heavy. **Note:** *Battery straps and handlers are available at most auto parts stores for a reasonable price. They make it easier to remove and carry the battery.*

5   While the battery is out, inspect the battery tray for corrosion.

6   If corrosion exists on the battery tray, detach the bolts and remove the tray from the engine compartment. Clean the deposits from the metal underneath the tray to prevent further corrosion.

7   If you are replacing the battery, make sure you replace it with a battery with the identical dimensions, amperage rating, cold cranking rating, etc.

8   Installation is the reverse of removal.

4   Battery cables - check and replacement

Refer to illustrations 4.2, 4.4a, 4.4b and 4.4c

1   Periodically inspect the entire length of each battery cable for damage, cracked or burned insulation and corrosion. Poor battery cable connections can cause starting problems and decreased engine performance.

2   Check the cable-to-terminal connections at the ends of the cables for cracks, loose wire strands and corrosion **(see illustration)**. The presence of white, fluffy deposits under the insulation at the cable terminal connection is a sign that the cable is corroded and should be replaced. Check the terminals for distortion, missing mounting bolts and corrosion.

3   When replacing the cables, always disconnect the negative cable first and hook it up last or the battery may be shorted by the tool used to loosen the cable clamps. Even if only

Terminal end corrosion or damage.

Insulation cracks.

Chafed insulation or exposed wires.

Burned or melted insulation.

4.2 Typical battery cable problems

the positive cable is being replaced, be sure to disconnect the negative cable from the battery first.

4   Disconnect and remove the cable **(see illustrations)**. Make sure the replacement cable is the same length and diameter.

4.4a Disconnect the negative cable from the battery first and connect it last

4.4b The positive terminal is larger than the negative terminal and labeled with a +

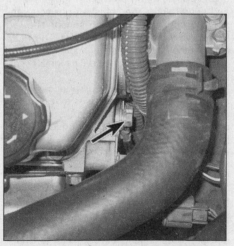

4.4c Follow the cables, removing any retainers and disconnecting the other end (arrow)

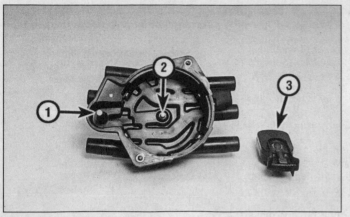

6.4 Distributor cap and rotor (3.0L V6 engine only)

1   *Coil terminal*   3   *Rotor*
2   *Rotor button*

6.6 Using a calibrated ignition tester to verify that spark is reaching the spark plugs - if the engine starts during this check, do not let it run for more than one minute or the catalytic converter may be damaged

5   Clean the threads of the relay or ground connection with a wire brush to remove rust and corrosion. Apply a light coat of petroleum jelly to the threads to prevent future corrosion.

6   Attach the cable to the relay or ground connection and tighten the mounting nut/bolt securely.

7   Before connecting the new cable to the battery, make sure that it reaches the battery post without having to be stretched. Clean the battery posts thoroughly and apply a light coat of petroleum jelly to prevent corrosion (see Chapter 1).

8   Connect the positive cable first, followed by the negative cable.

5   Ignition system - general information

All models are equipped with an electronic ignition system. The ignition system consists of the ignition switch, the battery, the coil, the primary (low voltage) and secondary (high voltage) wiring circuits, the ignition wires and spark plugs, the camshaft position sensor, the crankshaft position sensor and the Powertrain Control Module (PCM). The PCM controls the ignition timing and spark advance characteristics for the engine. The ignition timing is not adjustable.

The crankshaft sensor and camshaft sensor generate voltage pulses that are sent to the PCM. The PCM then determines the crankshaft position, injector sequence and ignition timing. The PCM supplies battery voltage to the ignition coil through the Automatic Shutdown Relay (ASD). The PCM also controls the ground circuit for the coil.

If the PCM does not receive a signal from the crankshaft or camshaft position sensors, the PCM signals the ASD relay and fuel pump relay to shut down the ignition and fuel delivery systems respectively. Refer to Chapter 6 for testing and replacement procedures for the crankshaft and camshaft sensors.

On all four-cylinder engines covered in this manual, the secondary ignition system is controlled by energizing the coil drivers in the proper firing order. On 3.0L V6 engines, a conventional type distributor with a rotor is used to send the ignition voltage to the proper cylinder in the firing order. On 3.0L V6 engines, the ignition coil and camshaft position sensor are part of the distributor, which is located on the rear of the engine on the right side (rear) cylinder head and driven by the camshaft (see Section 9).

6   Ignition system - check

Refer to illustrations 6.4, 6.6 and 6.9
Warning: *Because of the very high voltage generated by the ignition system (approximately 40,000 volts), extreme care should be taken whenever an operation is performed involving ignition components. This not only includes the coil and spark plug wires, but related items connected to the system as well, such as the electrical connectors, tachometer and any test equipment.*

1   With the ignition switch turned to the "ON" position, a glowing instrument panel "Battery" light or "Oil Pressure" light is a basic check for battery voltage supply to the ignition system and PCM.

2   First, check all ignition wiring connections for tightness, cuts, corrosion or any other signs of a bad connection.

3   Check the condition of the spark plug wires (see Chapter 1). Using an ohmmeter, measure the resistance of each spark plug wire and compare the measured value to the resistance value listed in this Chapter's Specifications. A bad spark plug wire or poor connection at the spark plug or coil (four-cylinder engines) or distributor cap (V6 engine) could also result in a misfire.

4   On 3.0L V6 engines, remove the distributor cap and rotor (see Section 9). Inspect the cap and rotor for moisture, cracks, erosion, carbon tracks, worn rotor button or other damage **(see illustration)**. Remove one spark

plug wire at a time from the cap (so they don't get mixed up) and check the terminals inside the cap for corrosion, which will appear as a white crusty powder (slight corrosion can be removed with a screwdriver or round wire brush). On the distributor cap, use an ohmmeter to measure the resistance between the rotor button and the coil terminal. The resistance should be approximately 5,000 ohms. On the distributor, inspect the coil high-tension tower for cracks, carbon tracks or corrosion. If the coil is found to be defective, the entire distributor must be replaced. If the cap or rotor is defective and the ignition components (including spark plugs) have been in service for more than 60,000 miles, the manufacturer recommends replacing all ignition components at the same time.

5   If the engine turns over but won't start, disconnect the number 1 spark plug wire (four-cylinder engines) or the number 2 spark plug wire (3.0L V6 engines) (see Chapter 1 if necessary) and install a calibrated ignition tester (available at most auto parts stores). Make sure the tester is designed for electronic ignition systems if a universal tester is not available.

6   Connect the clip of the tester to a bolt or metal bracket located on the engine **(see illustration)**. Ground the threaded portion of the spark plug to the engine. Crank the engine while observing the ignition tester - if bright blue, well defined sparks occur, sufficient voltage is reaching the spark plug to fire it. **Caution:** *If the engine starts, do not run the engine for longer than one minute during this test - the raw fuel escaping from the cylinder being tested may cause damage to the catalytic converter.*

7   On four-cylinder engines, perform this check at the number 2 spark plug location also. This will check the other ignition coil inside the coil pack. **Note:** *It is not necessary to perform this check at another location on V6 engines because that system uses a single coil.*

8   If spark is present, the coil is firing. However, the spark plugs themselves may

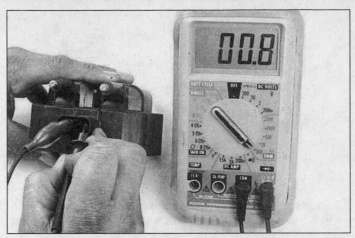

6.9 On four-cylinder engines, connect a test light between the coil electrical connector center terminal and one of the outer terminals and crank the engine - the light should blink on-and-off

7.5a Connect an ohmmeter to the center terminal, then to each of the side terminals in turn to test individual coils (2.0L non-turbo shown; 1998 and 1999 2.4L similar)

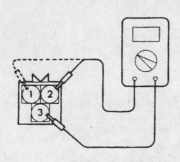

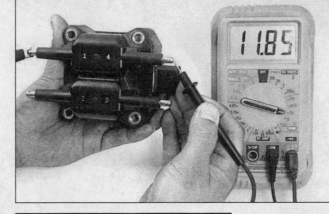

7.5b On 2.0L turbo models, connect an ohmmeter to terminal 3, then to terminals 1 and 2 in turn

7.6a Checking the secondary resistance of the 1-4 cylinder coil (2.0L non-turbo models) - test the 2-3 cylinder coil in the same way

be fouled or damaged, so remove and check them (see Chapter 1) or install new ones.

9   If no spark or intermittent sparks occur, disconnect the coil electrical connector **(see illustration)** and connect a test light to the center terminal of the coil electrical connector and one of the outer terminals (four-cylinder engines only).

10   With the test light placed where you can see it from the driver's seat, crank the engine and watch the test light. It should flash on-and-off while the engine is cranking. If the test light does not blink, check the wiring harness for damage or a short. If the wiring is OK, check the operation of the MFI or ASD relay (see Chapter 4). If necessary, check the operation of the camshaft and crankshaft position sensors (see Chapter 6). If the MFI relay and cam/crank sensors check out OK, have the PCM diagnosed by a dealer service department or other qualified repair shop.

11   If voltage is present (light blinks), check the ignition coil (see Section 7) and replace it if necessary.

12   If these checks do not identify the problem, further diagnosis should be performed by a dealer service department or other qualified repair shop.

7   Ignition coil - check and replacement

Check
Four-cylinder engines
Refer to illustrations 7.5a, 7.5b, 7.6a and 7.6b

1   2.0L non-turbo, 2.0L turbo and 1998 and 1999 2.4L engines use two individual ignition coils, combined into a single unit (coil pack). Coil "1" supplies voltage for cylinders 1 and 4, while coil "2" supplies voltage for cylinders 2 and 3. 2000 and later 2.4L engines use a coil-on-plug design, with two coils fitting directly onto the no. 2 and no. 4 spark plugs and connected to the no. 1 and no. 3 spark plugs by cables.

2   The coil pack on 2.0L non-turbo, 2.0L turbo and 2000 and later 2.4L engines is mounted on top of the engine. The coil pack on 1998 and 1999 2.4L engines is on a bracket at the front (timing belt end) of the engine.

3   Clearly label the spark plug wires and detach them from the coil pack.

4   Disconnect the primary wiring electrical connector(s) from the coil pack.

5   Measure the primary resistance of each coil.

a) *All except 1998 and 1999 2.4L models: Connect an ohmmeter between the center terminal (B+) and one of the outer terminals and note the resistance* **(see illustrations)**. *Repeat the check with the probe connected to the other outer terminal. Compare the measured resistances with the coil primary resistance value listed in this Chapter's Specifications. Replace the coil if the primary resistance is out of tolerance.*

b) *1998 and 1999 2.4L models: Connect an ohmmeter between the two primary (small) terminals on each ignition coil and note the resistance. Compare the measured resistances with the coil primary resistance value listed in this Chapter's Specifications. Replace the coil if the primary resistance is out of tolerance.*

6   Next, measure the secondary resistance of each coil.

a) *2.0L non-turbo engine: Connect an ohmmeter between spark plug wire terminals 1 and 4 and note the resistance* **(see illustration)**. *Repeat the check on terminals 2 and 3. Compare the measured resistances with the secondary resistance value listed in this Chapter's Specifications. Replace the coil if the secondary resistance is out of tolerance.*

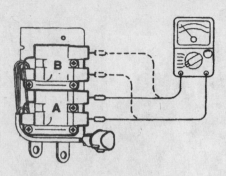

7.6b Measure secondary resistance between both terminals of coil A, then between both terminals of coil B (2.0L turbo shown; 1998 and 1999 2.4L similar)

7.11 Distributor connector terminal identification (3.0L V6 engine)

7.17a Disconnect the electrical connector from the coil pack, then remove the mounting nuts to detach the coil (2.0L non-turbo)

b) *2.0L turbo, 1998 and 1999 2.4L engines: Connect an ohmmeter between both secondary terminals on each coil and note the resistance* **(see illustration).** *Compare the measured resistances with the secondary resistance value listed in this Chapter's Specifications. Replace the coil if the secondary resistance is out of tolerance.*

c) *2000 and later 2.4L engines: Connect the ohmmeter between the secondary terminal that fits over the spark plug and the secondary terminal that connects to the spark plug wire and note the resistance. Compare the measured resistances with the secondary resistance value listed in this Chapter's Specifications. Replace the coil if the secondary resistance is out of tolerance.*

7   Install the spark plug wires in their proper locations and connect the primary wiring electrical connector.

V6 engine
Refer to illustration 7.11

8   Remove the air cleaner assembly (see Chapter 4).

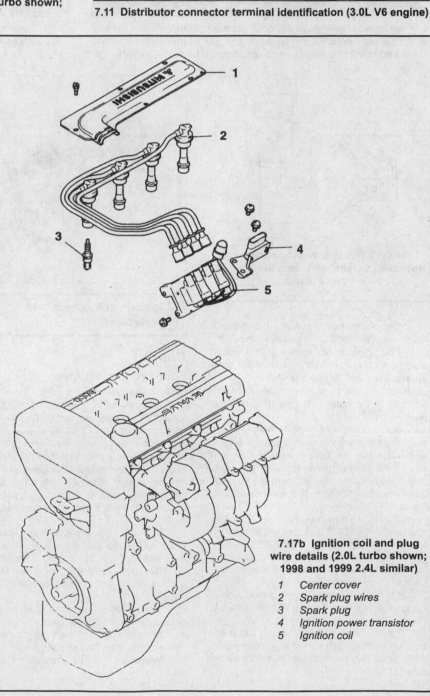

7.17b Ignition coil and plug wire details (2.0L turbo shown; 1998 and 1999 2.4L similar)

1   *Center cover*
2   *Spark plug wires*
3   *Spark plug*
4   *Ignition power transistor*
5   *Ignition coil*

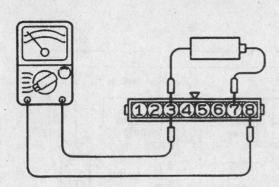

8.3 Connect an ohmmeter and a 1.5-volt battery (no higher voltage) to the connectors to test the power transistor

9.6 Distributor cap mounting screws (3.0L V6 engine)

9   Label each spark plug wire with its location in the distributor cap and then disconnect them.

10   Loosen the 2 screws and remove the distributor cap.

11   Disconnect the primary wiring electrical connector from the distributor **(see illustration)**.

12   Measure the coil primary resistance. Connect an ohmmeter between terminals 1 and 2 of the seven-pin connector on the distributor and note the resistance. Compare the measured resistance with the coil primary resistance value listed in this Chapter's Specifications. If the coil primary resistance is out of tolerance, the entire distributor must be replaced - the coil is not serviceable.

13   Measure the coil secondary resistance. Using an ohmmeter, measure the resistance between the coil high-tension tower terminal and terminal 1 of the seven-pin connector. Compare the measured resistances with the secondary resistance value listed in this Chapter's Specifications. If the coil secondary resistance is out of tolerance, the entire distributor must be replaced - the coil is not serviceable.

14   Install the distributor cap and related components in the reverse order of removal.

Replacement

Four-cylinder engines

Refer to illustrations 7.17a and 17.7b

15   Label the spark plug wires and detach them from the coils.

16   Disconnect the primary wiring electrical connector from the coil pack.

17   Remove the coil mounting nuts **(see illustrations)** and lift the coils from the mounting bracket on the valve cover.

18   Installation is the reverse of removal.

V6 engine

19   The ignition coil on V6 engines is not serviceable. If the coil is defective, replace the distributor assembly (see Section 9).

8   Power transistor - check and replacement

1   A power transistor is used on the 2.0L turbo, 1998 and 1999 2.4L models and 3.0L models **(see illustration 7.17b)**.

Check

Refer to illustration 8.3

2   Disconnect the power transistor's electrical connector.

Four-cylinder engines

3   To check the side of the power transistor that affects cylinders 1 and 4, connect an ohmmeter between terminals 3 and 8 **(see illustration)**. There should be no continuity. When a 1.5-volt battery is connected between terminals 3 and 7, there should be continuity. **Caution:** *Don't use the vehicle's battery for this test and don't connect the battery for more than 10 seconds or the power transistor may be burned out.*

4   To check the side of the power transistor that affects cylinders 2 and 3, connect the ohmmeter between terminals 1 and 3. There should be no continuity. When a 1.5-volt battery is connected between terminals 2 and 3, there should be continuity.

5   If the power transistor fails either test, replace it.

3.0L V6 engine

6   The test is the same as described above, but the connections are made to the seven-pin terminal on the side of the distributor. When the battery is connected to terminals 3 and 4 **(see illustration 7.11)**, there should be continuity between terminals 2 and 3. When the battery is disconnected, there should be no continuity between terminals 2 and 3.

Replacement

7   If you're working on a 2.0L turbo engine, remove the center cover from the valve cover **(see illustration 7.17b)**.

8   Disconnect the power transistor's electrical connector, remove the mounting screws and take it off the engine.

9   Installation is the reverse of the removal steps.

9   Distributor (3.0L V6 engine) - removal and installation

Removal

Refer to illustration 9.6

1   Position the engine with cylinder no. 1 set at Top Dead Center (TDC) on the compression stroke (see Chapter 2D). Disconnect the negative battery cable from the battery.

2   Remove the air cleaner assembly (see Chapter 4).

3   Disconnect the electrical connectors from the distributor.

4   Label each spark plug wire with its location in the distributor cap and then disconnect the wires.

5   Remove the spark plug wire routing bracket from the distributor.

6   Loosen the three screws and remove the distributor cap **(see illustration)**.

7   Using a felt tip pen and/or a piece of tape, match-mark the rotor tip to the distributor body.

8   Remove the two nuts and washers securing the distributor and withdraw it from the cylinder head.

Installation

9   Inspect the distributor O-ring seal for hardness, cracks, swelling or other damage and replace it if necessary.

10   Install the rotor onto the distributor shaft.

11   Apply a light coat of clean engine oil to the distributor O-ring seal and carefully insert the distributor into the cylinder head with the rotor aligned with the previously applied match-mark. Make sure the distributor is fully

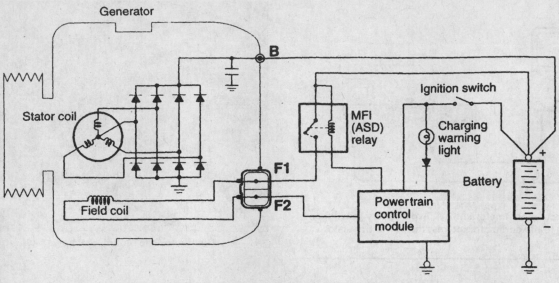

12.1a Charging system circuit (2.0L non-turbo engine)

seated in the cylinder head and secure with the two nuts and washers. Tighten the distributor hold-down nuts to the torque given in this Chapter's Specifications.

12   If the engine was rotated while the distributor was removed, rotate the engine to Top Dead Center (TDC) for the number 1 piston (see Chapter 2D), then align the rotor with the match-mark made in Step 7. Install the distributor as described in Step 11.

13   The remaining installation steps are the reverse of removal.

10   Ignition failure sensor (2000 and later 2.4L engines) - check and replacement

1   Locate the ignition failure sensor on the upper intake manifold.

2   Disconnect the electrical connector from the sensor. Connect an ohmmeter between terminals 3 and 4 (counting from the left). It should indicate 0.1 ohms or less.

3   If the ohmmeter reading is incorrect, remove the sensor mounting screws and install a new one. Connect the connector.

11   Charging system - general information and precautions

The charging system includes the alternator (with integral voltage regulator on all except 2.0L non-turbo models), a charge indicator light, the battery, the Powertrain Control Module (PCM), the MFI (ASD) relay, a fusible link and the wiring between all the components. The charging system supplies electrical power to maintain the battery at its full

charge capacity. The alternator is driven by a drivebelt on the front of the engine.

On 2.0L non-turbo models, the Electronic Voltage Regulator (EVR) within the PCM varies the battery charge rate in accordance with driving conditions. Depending on electric load, vehicle speed, engine coolant temperature, battery temperature sensor, accessories (air conditioning system, radio, cruise control etc.) and the intake air temperature, the PCM will adjust the amount of voltage generated, creating less load on the engine.

On all except 2.0L non-turbo models, the voltage regulator performs the same function, but is built into the alternator rather than the PCM.

The purpose of the voltage regulator is to limit the alternator's voltage to a preset value. This prevents power surges, circuit overloads, etc., during peak voltage output. Since the EVR on 2.0L non-turbo models is contained within the PCM, the PCM must be replaced in the event of EVR failure.

The alternator has a rating of 75 or 90 amperes, depending on model. The alternator is not serviceable and therefore must be replaced as a unit in the event of failure.

The charging system doesn't ordinarily require periodic maintenance. However, the drivebelt, battery, wires and connections should be inspected at the intervals outlined in Chapter 1.

The dashboard warning light should illuminate when the ignition key is turned to ON, but it should go off immediately after the engine is started. If it remains on, there is a malfunction in the charging system which must be diagnosed (see Section 11).

Be very careful when making electrical circuit connections to a vehicle equipped with an alternator and note the following:

a) *When reconnecting wires to the alternator from the battery, be sure to note the polarity.*

b) *Never start the engine with a battery charger connected.*

c) *Before using arc welding equipment to repair any part of the vehicle, disconnect the wiring from the alternator and the cables from the battery.*

d) *Always disconnect both battery cables before using a battery charger.*

e) *The alternator is turned by an engine drivebelt which could cause serious injury if your hands, hair or clothes become entangled in it with the engine running.*

f) *Because the alternator is connected directly to the battery, it could arc or cause a fire if overloaded or shorted out.*

g) *Wrap a plastic bag over the alternator and secure it with rubber bands before steam cleaning the engine.*

12   Charging system - check

Refer to illustrations 12.1a and 12.1b

Note: *These vehicles are equipped with an On Board Diagnostic (OBD-II) system that is useful for detecting charging system problems. Refer to Chapter 6 for the trouble code extracting procedures.*

1   If a malfunction occurs in the charging circuit **(see illustrations)**, do not immediately assume that the alternator is causing the problem. First check the following items:

a) *The battery cables where they connect to the battery and at the remote terminals. Make sure the connections are clean and tight (see Section 4).*

b) *Check the alternator wiring connections; make sure they are clean and tight.*

c) *Check the battery voltage. If it's less than 12 volts, charge the battery (see Chapter 1).*

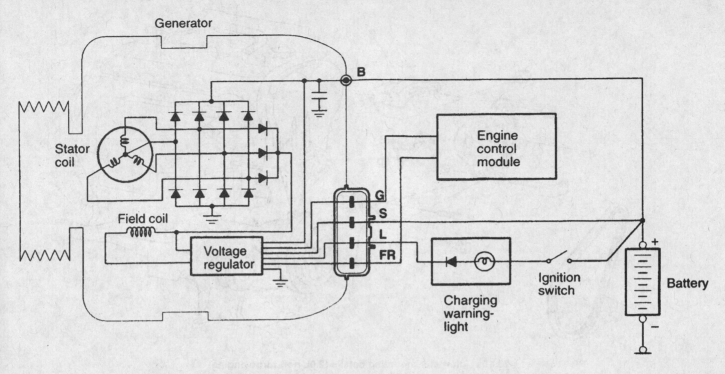

12.1b Charging system circuit (2.0L turbo; 2.4L four-cylinder and 3.0L V6 similar)

d) *Check the drivebelt condition and·tension (see Chapter 1).*

e) *Check the alternator mounting bolts for tightness.*

f) *Run the engine and check the alternator for abnormal noise.*

2   Using a voltmeter, check the battery voltage with the engine off. It should be approximately 12 volts.

3   Start the engine and check the battery voltage again. If the system is operating properly, the voltage should increase to a value between 13 to 15 volts.

4   If the indicated voltage reading is less or more than the specified charging voltage, have the voltage regulator diagnosed at a dealer service department or other qualified repair shop. The voltage regulator on these models is contained within the PCM (2.0L non-turbo) or alternator (all others) and it cannot be removed or serviced in any way.

5   Due to the special equipment necessary to test the PCM and alternator, it is recommended that if a fault is suspected, the vehicle be taken to a dealer service department or other qualified repair shop with the proper equipment. **Note:** *Some auto parts stores will test the alternator for free.* Because of this, the home mechanic should limit maintenance to checking connections and the inspection and replacement of the alternator itself. As a general rule, when the battery is in good condition and all electrical connections are clean and tight, if the charging voltage is low, the alternator is faulty. If the charging voltage is high, the voltage regulator is the problem.

13   Alternator - removal and installation

General information

1   If you are replacing the alternator, take the old one with you when purchasing a replacement unit. Make sure the new/rebuilt unit looks identical to the old alternator. Look at the terminals - they should be the same in number, size and location as the terminals on the old alternator. Finally, look at the identification numbers - they will be stamped into the housing or printed on a tag attached to the housing. Make sure the numbers are the same on both the old and new alternators.

2   Many new/rebuilt alternators do not have a pulley installed, so you may have to switch the pulley from the old unit to the new/rebuilt one. When buying an alternator, find out the shop's policy regarding pulleys; some shops will perform this service free of charge.

Removal

Refer to illustrations 13.8, 13.10a and 13.10b

3   Disconnect the negative battery cable from the battery.

4   Remove the splash panel from under the front of the vehicle (see Chapter 11).

5   If you're working on a 2.0L non-turbo model or a 1998 or 1999 2.4L engine model, remove the cruise control unit (see Chapter 12). On 1998 and 1999 2.4L engines, unscrew the oil pressure switch near the oil filter.

6   If you're working on a 2.0L turbo model, remove the power steering pump and place it out of the way without disconnecting the hoses (see Chapter 10).

7   If you're working on a 2000 or later model, remove the front engine mount (see Chapter 2C or 2D). Unbolt the engine oil dipstick tube and pull it out of the engine.

8   Disconnect the electrical connector and B+ cable from the alternator **(see illustration)**.

13.8 Disconnect the wiring connector(s) from the alternator

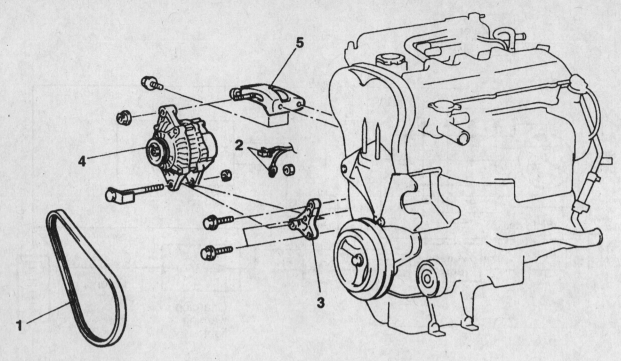

13.10a Alternator mounting details (2.0L non-turbo engine)

1	Drivebelt	3	Mounting bracket	5	Brace
2	Electrical connectors	4	Alternator		

9   Remove the alternator drivebelt (see Chapter 1).
10   Remove the pivot bolt, bracket(s) and mounting bolts and nuts **(see illustrations)**.
11   Support the alternator and remove it from the engine compartment. On 1998 and 1999 2.4L engines, lower it out of the engine compartment.

Installation

12   Installation is the reverse of removal.

13   After the alternator is installed, adjust the drivebelt tension (see Chapter 1).
14   Check the charging voltage to verify proper operation of the alternator (see Section 13).

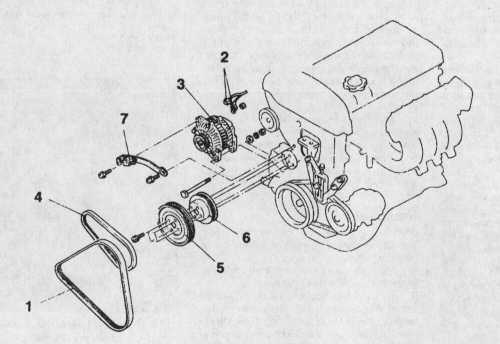

13.10b Alternator mounting details (2.0L turbo and 2.4L four-cylinder engines)

1   Alternator drivebelt
2   Electrical connectors
3   Alternator
4   Power steering drivebelt
5   Water pump pulley
6   Power steering pulley
7   Brace

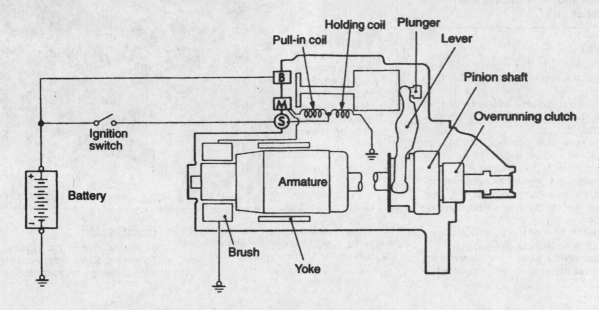

14.2 Typical starter motor circuit

14   Starting system - general information and precautions

Refer to illustration 14.2

1   The starter motor used on 2.0L non-turbo engines is a direct drive type. On all other engines, the starter uses a planetary gear reduction system.

2   The starting system consists of the battery, the starter motor, the starter solenoid, the starter relay, clutch start switch (manual transaxles), PARK/NEUTRAL switch (automatic transaxles), ignition switch and the wires that connect the components. The solenoid is located on the starter motor **(see illustration)**.

3   When the ignition key is turned to the Start position, the starter solenoid is actuated through the starter control circuit, which includes a starter relay located in the engine compartment. The starter solenoid then connects the battery to the starter. The battery supplies the electrical energy to the starter motor, which does the actual work of cranking the engine.

4   Always observe the following precautions when working on the starting system:

a) Excessive cranking of the starter motor can overheat it and cause serious damage. Never operate the starter motor for more than 15 seconds at a time without pausing for at least two minutes to allow it to cool.

b) The starter is connected directly to the battery and could arc or cause a fire if mishandled, overloaded or shorted out.

c) Always detach the negative battery cable from the battery before working on the starting system.

15   Starter motor - in-vehicle check

1   Make sure the battery is fully charged and all cable connections - at the battery and starter solenoid terminals - are clean and secure.

2   If the starter motor does not function at all when the switch is operated, make sure the shift lever is in Neutral or Park (automatic transaxles) and check the operation of the PARK/NEUTRAL switch (see Chapter 7B). On vehicles equipped with manual transaxles, check the operation of the clutch start switch (see Chapter 8).

3   If the starter motor spins but the engine is not cranking, the overrunning clutch in the starter motor is slipping and the starter motor must be replaced. Also, the ring gear on the driveplate may be worn or have broken teeth (this is especially likely if the starter works properly most of the time and spins only occasionally). Inspect it after removing the starter.

4   If, when the switch is actuated, the starter motor does not operate at all but the solenoid clicks, the problem lies with the battery, the main solenoid contacts or the starter motor itself (or, possible but less likely, the engine is seized).

5   If the solenoid plunger cannot be heard when the switch is actuated, the battery may be faulty, the fusible link may be burned (the circuit is open), the starter relay may be faulty or the solenoid itself is defective.

6   To check the solenoid, connect a remote starter switch (available at auto parts stores) between the positive battery terminal and the ignition switch wire terminal (the small terminal) on the solenoid. If the starter motor operates when the remote switch is activated, the solenoid is OK and the problem is elsewhere in the circuit.

7   Locate the starter relay in the engine compartment (see Chapter 12). Remove the relay and test it. Replace the relay if it does not function correctly.

8   If the starter motor still does not operate, remove the starter/solenoid assembly for replacement as a complete unit (see Section 16).

9   If the starter motor cranks the engine at an abnormally slow speed, first make sure that the battery is fully charged and that all electrical connections are clean and tight. If the engine is partially seized, or has the wrong viscosity oil in it, it will crank slowly.

10   If the engine starts, warm up the engine to normal operating temperature, then turn off the engine. Remove the fuel pump relay to keep the engine from starting (see Chapter 4 if necessary).

11   Connect a voltmeter positive lead to the positive battery terminal and the negative lead to the negative battery terminal.

12   Crank the engine and take the voltmeter reading as soon as a steady figure is indicated. Do not allow the starter motor to turn for more than 15 seconds at a time. A reading of 9 volts or more, with the starter motor turning at normal cranking speed, is normal. If the reading is 9 volts or more but the cranking speed is slow, the motor, solenoid contacts or circuit connections are faulty. If the reading is less than 9 volts and the cranking speed is slow, the battery is probably bad.

16   Starter motor - removal and installation

Removal

Refer to illustration 16.6

1   Detach the negative battery cable from the battery.

2   If you're working on a 2.0L turbo or 1998 or 1999 2.4L model, remove the air cleaner (see Chapter 4).

3   If you're working on a 2000 or later model (2.4L or 3.0L V6 engine), remove the air cleaner assembly (see Chapter 4).

4   Remove the starter motor upper mounting bolt. If you're working on a 2000 or later 2.4L model, unbolt the heat shield from the starter motor.

5   Raise the front of the vehicle and support it securely on jackstands.

6   Disconnect the wires from the terminals on the starter motor solenoid **(see illustration)**.

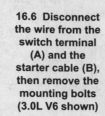

16.6 Disconnect the wire from the switch terminal (A) and the starter cable (B), then remove the mounting bolts (3.0L V6 shown)

7   While supporting the starter motor, remove the lower mounting bolt and withdraw the starter motor from the vehicle.

Installation

8   Installation is the reverse of removal. Tighten the starter motor mounting bolts to the torque listed in this Chapter's Specifications.

Chapter 6
Emissions and engine control systems

Contents

Specifications

General

Throttle position sensor resistance (all models)	3.5 to 6.5 k-ohms
Intake air temperature sensor resistance	
2.0L non-turbo	
77-degrees F	9000 to 11,000 ohms
212-degrees F	600 to 800 ohms
All others	
32-degrees F	5300 to 6700 ohms
68-degrees F	2300 to 3000 ohms
104-degrees F	1000 to 1500 ohms
176-degrees F	300 to 420 ohms
Engine coolant temperature resistance reading	
32-degrees F	5100 to 6500 ohms
86-degrees F	2100 to 2700 ohms
104-degrees F	900 to 1300 ohms
140-degrees F	480 to 680 ohms
176-degrees F	260 to 36 ohms

Torque specifications

Ft-lbs (unless otherwise indicated)

Note: *One foot-pound (ft-lb) of torque is equivalent to 12 inch-pounds (in-lbs) of torque. Torque values below approximately 15 ft-lbs are expressed in inch-pounds, since most foot-pound torque wrenches are not accurate at these smaller values.*

Camshaft position sensor	
2.0L non-turbo engine	
Sensor bolts	84 inch-lbs
Target magnet bolt	24 inch-lbs
2.0L turbo and 2.4L engines	78 inch-lbs
3.0L engine	Integral with distributor
Crankshaft position sensor retaining bolt	
2.0L non-turbo engine	Not specified
2.0L turbo, 2.4L, 3.0L V6 engines	78 inch-lbs
Engine Coolant Temperature sensor	
2.0L non-turbo	60 in-lbs
2.0L turbo, 2.4L four-cylinder and V6 engines	22
EGR valve bolts (all engines)	16
Intake Air Temperature sensor (2.0L non-turbo only)	60 in-lbs
Knock sensor	
2.0L non-turbo engine	89 in-lbs
2.0L turbo, 2.4L, 3.0L V6 engines	14 to 18
Oxygen sensor	33

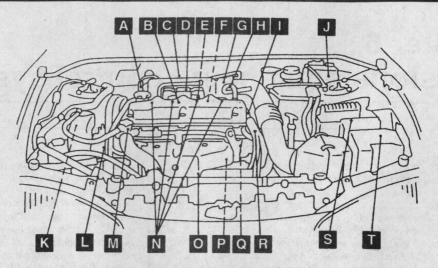

1.1a Typical emission and engine control system components - 2.0L non-turbo models

A   Manifold Absolute Pressure (MAP) sensor
B   Crankshaft position sensor
C   Intake air temperature sensor
D   Ignition coil
E   Rear oxygen sensor
F   Knock sensor
G   Idle air control motor
H   Throttle Position Sensor
I   Camshaft position sensor
J   Fuel pump and MFI (ASD) relays
K   EVAP system purge and vent solenoids
L   Power steering pressure switch
M   Engine coolant temperature (ECT) sensor
N   Injector
O   Front oxygen sensor
P   Vehicle Speed Sensor
Q   Park/neutral switch
R   EGR transducer solenoid
S   Powertrain Control Module (PCM)
T   Air conditioning compressor clutch relay
U   CHECK ENGINE light
V   Data link connector
W   Air conditioning switch

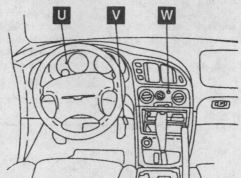

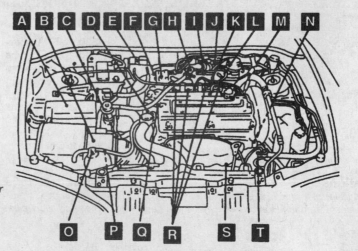

1.1b Typical emission and engine control system components - 2.0L turbo models

A   Air conditioning compressor clutch relay
B   Volume Airflow (VAF) sensor
C   Vehicle speed sensor
D   Engine coolant temperature (ECT) sensor
E   Fuel pump check terminal
F   Idle air control motor
G   Throttle position sensor
H   Manifold Differential Pressure (MDP) sensor
I   Resistor
J   EGR solenoid
K   Ignition coil and power transistor
L   Knock sensor
M   Fuel pressure solenoid
N   Crankshaft position sensor
O   Park/neutral switch
P   Turbocharger wastegate solenoid
Q   Camshaft position sensor
R   Injectors
S   Front oxygen sensor
T   Power steering pressure switch
U   CHECK ENGINE light
V   Data link connector
W   Air conditioning switch
X   Powertrain Control Module (PCM)
Y   Fuel pump relay

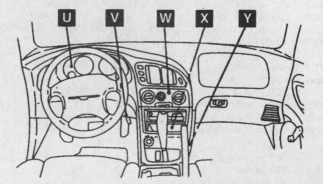

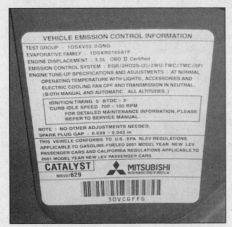

1.5a The Vehicle Emission Control Information (VECI) decal in the engine compartment contains information about the emission devices on your vehicle

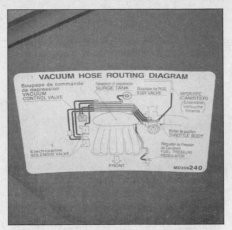

1.5b A vacuum hose routing diagram provides the specific vacuum hose routing information for the vehicle

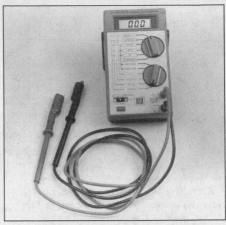

2.1 Digital multi-meters can be used for testing all types of circuits; because of their high impedance, they are much more accurate than analog type meters for measuring low voltage computer circuits

1 General information

Refer to illustrations 1.1a, 1.1b, 1.5a and 1.5b

1   To prevent pollution of the atmosphere from incompletely burned and evaporating fuel gases and to maintain good driveability and fuel economy, a number of emission control systems are incorporated **(see illustrations)**. The major systems incorporated on the vehicles with which this manual is concerned include the:

Evaporative Emission Control (EVAP) system
Exhaust Gas Recirculation (EGR) system
Oxygen sensor (O2) system
Positive Crankcase Ventilation (PCV) system
Powertrain Control Module (PCM) (computer) and information sensors
Catalytic converter
Pulse secondary air injection (1995 2.0L non-turbo with manual transaxle only)

2   The Sections in this Chapter include general descriptions, checking procedures within the scope of the home mechanic and component replacement procedures (when possible) for each of the systems listed above.

3   Before assuming an emissions control system is malfunctioning, check the fuel and ignition systems carefully. The diagnosis of some emission control devices requires specialized tools, equipment and training. If checking and servicing become too difficult or if a procedure is beyond your ability, consult a dealer service department or other qualified service facility. Remember, the most frequent cause of emissions problems is simply a loose or broken vacuum hose or wire, so always check the hose and electrical connections that interconnect the components within each system first.

4   This doesn't mean, however, that emission control systems are particularly difficult to maintain and repair. You can quickly and easily perform many checks and do most of the regular maintenance at home with common tune-up and hand tools. **Note:** *Because of a Federally mandated extended warranty which covers the emission control system components, check with your dealer about warranty coverage before working on any emissions-related systems. Once the warranty has expired, you may wish to perform some of the component checks and/or replacement procedures in this Chapter to save money.*

5   Pay close attention to any special precautions outlined in this Chapter. A Vehicle Emissions Control Information (VECI) label is located in the engine compartment **(see illustrations)**. This label contains important emissions specifications and adjustment information. When servicing the engine or emissions systems, check the VECI label for information on your particular vehicle.

2 On Board Diagnosis (OBD-II) system - description and trouble code access

Diagnostic tool information

Refer to illustrations 2.1 and 2.2

1   A digital multi-meter is necessary for checking fuel injection and emission related components **(see illustration)**. A digital volt-ohmmeter is preferred over the older style analog multi-meter for several reasons. The analog multi-meter cannot display the volt, ohms or amps measurement in hundredths and thousandths increments. When working with electronic circuits which are often very low voltage, this accurate reading is most important. Another good reason for the digital multi-meter is the high impedance circuit. The digital multi-meter is equipped with a high resistance internal circuitry (10 million ohms). Because a voltmeter is hooked up in parallel with the circuit when testing, it is vital that none of the voltage being measured should be allowed to travel the parallel path set up by the meter itself. This dilemma does not show itself when measuring larger amounts of voltage (9 to 12 volt circuits) but if you are measuring a low voltage circuit such as the oxygen sensor signal voltage, a fraction of a volt may be a significant amount when diagnosing a problem.

2   Hand-held scanners are the most powerful and versatile tools for analyzing engine management systems used on later model vehicles **(see illustration)**. Each brand scan tool must be examined carefully to match the year, make and model of the vehicle you are working on. Often interchangeable cartridges are available to access the particular manufacturer (Chrysler, Ford, GM, etc.). Some manufacturers will even specify by continent (Asia, Europe, USA, etc.).

2.2 Scanners like these from Actron and AutoXray are powerful diagnostic aids - they can tell you just about anything you want to know about your electronic engine management system

2.11 The OBD-II diagnostic connector (arrow) is located under the left (driver's) side of the instrument panel

OBD-II system general description

3   The OBD-II system consists of an on-board computer, known as the Powertrain Control Module (PCM) and information sensors which monitor various functions of the engine and then relay the data to the PCM. Based on the data received and the information programmed into the computer's memory, the PCM then generates output signals to control various engine functions via control relays, solenoids and other output actuators.

4   The PCM, in different locations depending on model, is the "brain" of the OBD-II system. The PCM is specifically calibrated to optimize the emissions, fuel economy and driveability of the vehicle.

5   Because of a Federally mandated extended warranty which covers the OBD-II system components and because any owner-induced damage to the PCM, the sensors and/or the control devices may void the warranty, it is not recommended to attempt diagnosis of, or replace the PCM at home while the vehicle is under warranty. Take the vehicle to your local dealer service department if the PCM or a system component malfunctions.

Information sensors

6   The following is a list of the OBD-II system information sensors. For complete information and service procedures, refer to the Chapter or Section specified.

Camshaft Position sensor
Crankshaft Position sensor
Engine Coolant Temperature (ECT) sensor
Intake Air Temperature (IAT) sensor
Knock sensor
Manifold Absolute Pressure (MAP) sensor
Oxygen sensors
PARK/NEUTRAL switch (see Chapter 7B)
Power steering pressure switch
Throttle Position Sensor (TPS)
Vehicle Speed Sensor (VSS)

Output actuators

7   The following is a list of the OBD-II system output actuators. For complete information and service procedures, refer to the Chapter or Section as specified.

MFI (ASD) relay (see Chapter 4)

Canister purge control solenoid
  (see Section 7)
EGR solenoid (see Section 17)
Fuel injectors (see Chapter 4)
Fuel pump relay (see Chapter 4)
Idle Air Control (IAC) motor (see Chapter 4)
CHECK ENGINE light or Malfunction
  Indicator Light (MIL)

General description

8   The CHECK ENGINE light or Malfunction Indicator Light (MIL), is located in the instrument panel and should illuminate for three seconds as a bulb test each time the engine is started. When the Powertrain Control Module (PCM) detects a fault in the emissions or engine control system it sets a trouble code in the PCM's memory. If the PCM detects a fault related to vehicle emissions, it illuminates the CHECK ENGINE light which means an emissions component or system is in need of immediate service. In the event the PCM detects an active engine misfire, the CHECK ENGINE light will flash continuously. If this occurs, turn off the engine as soon as possible and diagnose/correct the problem or severe catalytic converter damage may occur.

9   The EVAP system (see Section 18) will cause the PCM to store the appropriate fault code and illuminate the CHECK ENGINE light on the instrument panel in the event of a pressure leak. The most common cause of CHECK ENGINE light illumination is EVAP system pressure loss due to a loose or poor sealing fuel filler cap. Before accessing the trouble codes and trying to determine the faulty component, make sure your gas cap seal is free from defects and is tightened securely. **Caution:** *Over-tightening the gas cap may cause the fuel tank filler neck to crack.*

10   In addition to notifying the driver when an emissions fault has occurred, the CHECK ENGINE light can be used to display the stored trouble codes from the PCM's memory (see below).

Trouble code access

Refer to illustration 2.11

Note: *All models covered by this manual are equipped with the OBD-II system. Generic trouble codes on 1997 and earlier models can be accessed using the ignition key method, but it is necessary to use a SCAN tool to read and interpret manufacturer-specific trouble codes (or any trouble codes on 1998 and later models). Before outputting the trouble codes, thoroughly inspect ALL electrical connectors and hoses. Make sure all electrical connections are tight, clean and free of corrosion; make sure all hoses are properly connected, fit tightly and are in good condition (no cracks or tears).*

11   The self-diagnosis information contained in the PCM (computer) can be accessed either by the ignition key (1995 through 1997 only) or by using a scan tool. This tool is attached to the diagnostic connector **(see illustration)** located under the dash to the left of the console and reads the codes and parameters on the digital display screen. Most problems can be solved or diagnosed quite easily and if the

information cannot be obtained readily, have the vehicle's self-diagnosis system analyzed by a dealer service department or other qualified repair shop.

12   To obtain the codes using the ignition key method, first set the parking brake and put the shift lever in Park. Raise the engine speed to approximately 2,500 rpm and slowly let the speed down to idle. Also, if equipped, cycle the air conditioning system (on briefly, then off). Next, on models equipped with an automatic transaxle, apply the brakes and select each position on the transmission (Reverse, Drive, Low etc.), finally bring the shifter back to Park and turn off the engine. This will allow the computer to obtain any fault codes that might be linked to any of the sensors controlled by the transmission, engine speed or air conditioning system.

13   To display the codes on the instrument panel (CHECK ENGINE light or Malfunction Indicator Light), with the engine NOT running, turn the ignition key ON, OFF, ON, OFF and finally ON (must be done within 5 seconds). The codes will begin to flash. The light will blink the number of the first digit then pause and blink the number of the second digit. For example: Code 23, air temperature sensor circuit, would be indicated by two flashes, pause, three flashes.

14   Certain criteria must be met for a fault code to be entered into the PCM's memory. The criteria might be a specific range of engine rpm, engine temperature or input voltage to the PCM. It's possible that a fault code for a particular monitored circuit may not be entered into the memory despite a malfunction. This may happen because one of the fault code criteria has not been met. For example, the engine must be operating between 750 and 2,000 rpm in order to monitor the MAP sensor circuit correctly. If the engine speed is raised above 2,400 rpm, the MAP sensor output circuit shorts to ground and will not allow a fault code to be entered into the memory. Then again, the exact opposite could occur: A code is entered into the memory that suggests a malfunction within another component that is not monitored by the computer. For example, a fuel pressure problem cannot register a fault directly but instead, it will cause a rich or lean fuel mixture problem. Consequently, this will cause an oxygen sensor malfunction resulting in a stored code in the computer for the oxygen sensor. Be aware of the interrelationship of the sensors and circuits and the overall relationship of the emissions control and fuel injection systems. A trouble code does not identify which component in a circuit is faulty, therefore the code should be treated as a symptom, not the direct cause of the problem.

15   The accompanying table is a list of the typical trouble codes which may be encountered while diagnosing the system. Also included are simplified troubleshooting procedures. If the problem persists after these checks have been made, more detailed service procedures will have to be performed by a dealer service department or other qualified repair shop.

Trouble codes - 1995 through 1997 models (using CHECK ENGINE light)

Note: *Not all trouble codes apply to all models.*

Code	Probable cause
Code 11	Intermittent loss of crankshaft and/or camshaft position sensor signals to PCM, complete loss of crankshaft position sensor signal to PCM, or timing belt skipped one or more teeth
Code 13	Problem with the MAP sensor circuit.
Code 14	MAP sensor voltage out of normal range.
Code 15	A problem with the Vehicle Speed Sensor signal. No Vehicle Speed Sensor signal detected during road load conditions.
Code 16	No input signal from knock sensor.
Code 17	Engine is cold too long. Engine coolant temperature remains below normal operating temperatures during initial operation (check the thermostat).
Code 21	Problem with upstream oxygen sensor signal circuit. Sensor voltage to computer not fluctuating.
Code 22	Engine coolant temperature sensor voltage out of normal range.
Code 24	Throttle position sensor voltage high or low. Test the throttle position sensor.
Code 25	Idle Air Control (IAC) motor circuits. A shorted condition is detected in one or more of the IAC motor circuits.
Code 27	One of the injector control circuit output drivers does not respond properly to the control signal. Check the circuits.
Code 31	EVAP system fault.
Code 32	An open or shorted condition detected in the EGR solenoid circuit. Possible air/fuel ratio imbalance not detected during diagnosis.
Code 35	Open or shorted condition detected in the radiator fan high or low speed relay circuits.
Code 36	Pulsed secondary air injection system problem (1995 manual transaxle only)
Code 37	Transaxle PARK/NEUTRAL switch failure.
Code 42	Fuel pump relay or MFI (ASD) relay control circuit indicates an open or shorted circuit condition.
Code 43	Misfire on one or more cylinders detected. Spark plug, injector, cylinder compression or air intake problem; primary circuit problem in one or both ignition coils.
Code 45	Transaxle fault present in transmission control module - automatic transaxles.
Code 46	Charging system voltage too high. Computer indicates that the battery voltage is not properly regulated.
Code 47	Charging system voltage too low. Battery voltage sensor input below target charging voltage during engine operation and no significant change in voltage detected during active test of alternator output.
Code 51	Oxygen sensor signal input indicates lean fuel/air ratio condition during engine operation.
Code 52	Oxygen sensor signal input indicates rich fuel/air ratio condition during engine operation.
Code 53	Internal PCM failure detected.
Code 54	No camshaft position sensor signal. Problem with the sensor or circuit.
Code 62	Unsuccessful attempt to update EMR mileage in the PCM EEPROM. PCM failure.
Code 63	Controller failure. EEPROM write denied. Check the PCM.
Code 64	Catalytic converter efficiency below required level.
Code 65	Power steering switch failure detected.
Code 66	Transmission control module (TCM) not sensed by PCM.

Trouble codes - using scan tool

Note: *These are "generic" trouble codes and pertain to all models covered by this manual.*

Code	Probable cause
P0102	Mass Airflow (MAF) sensor circuit low input
P0103	Mass Airflow (MAF) sensor circuit high input
P0106	Barometric pressure out of range
P0107	Manifold Absolute Pressure (MAP) sensor voltage too low
P0108	Manifold Absolute Pressure (MAP) sensor voltage too high
P0112	Intake Air Temperature (IAT) sensor circuit low input
P0113	Intake Air Temperature (IAT) sensor circuit high input
P0117	Electronic Coolant Temperature (ECT) sensor circuit low input
P0118	Electronic Coolant Temperature (ECT) sensor circuit high input
P0121	In range Throttle Position Sensor (TPS) fault
P0122	Throttle Position Sensor (TPS) circuit low input
P0123	Throttle Position Sensor (TPS) circuit high input
P0131	Upstream heated O2 sensor circuit low voltage (Bank 1)
P0132	Upstream heated O2 sensor shorted to voltage

Trouble codes - using scan tool (continued)

Note: *These are "generic" trouble codes and pertain to all models covered by this manual.*

Code	Probable cause
P0133	Upstream heated O2 sensor circuit slow response (Bank 1)
P0135	Upstream heated O2 sensor heater circuit fault (Bank 1)
P0136	Downstream heated O2 sensor fault (Bank 1)
P0138	Downstream heated 02 sensor shorted to voltage
P0140	Downstream heated 02 sensor - neither rich nor lean condition detected
P0141	Downstream heated O2 sensor heater circuit fault (Bank 1)
P0151	Upstream heated O2 sensor circuit low voltage (Bank 2)
P0153	Upstream heated O2 sensor circuit slow response (Bank 2)
P0155	Upstream heated O2 sensor heater circuit fault (Bank 2)
P0156	Downstream heated O2 sensor fault (Bank 2)
P0161	Downstream heated O2 sensor heater circuit fault (Bank 2)
P0171	System Adaptive fuel too lean (Bank 1)
P0172	System Adaptive fuel too rich (Bank 1)
P0174	System Adaptive fuel too lean (Bank 2)
P0172	System Adaptive fuel too rich (Bank 2)
P0191	Injector Pressure sensor system performance
P0192	Injector Pressure sensor circuit low input
P0193	Injector Pressure sensor circuit high input
P0201	Injector no. 1 output driver not responding properly
P0202	Injector no. 2 output driver not responding properly
P0203	Injector no. 3 output driver not responding properly
P0204	Injector no. 4 output driver not responding properly
P0205	Injector no. 5 output driver not responding properly
P0206	Injector no. 6 output driver not responding properly
P0300	Multiple cylinder misfiring detected
P0301	Cylinder no. 1 misfire detected
P0302	Cylinder no. 2 misfire detected
P0303	Cylinder no. 3 misfire detected
P0304	Cylinder no. 4 misfire detected
P0305	Cylinder no. 5 misfire detected
P0306	Cylinder no. 6 misfire detected
P0325	Knock sensor circuit fault
P0326	Knock sensor circuit performance
P0335	Crankshaft Position sensor circuit
P0340	Camshaft Position sensor circuit
P0351	Ignition coil no. 1 primary circuit fault
P0352	Ignition coil no. 2 primary circuit fault
P0353	Ignition coil no. 3 primary circuit fault
P0354	Ignition coil no. 4 primary circuit fault
P0355	Ignition coil no. 5 primary circuit fault
P0356	Ignition coil no. 6 primary circuit fault
P0400	EGR flow fault
P0401	EGR insufficient flow detected
P0402	EGR excessive flow detected
P0403	EGR transducer circuit open or shorted
P0420	Catalyst system efficiency below threshold (Bank 1)
P0421	Catalyst system efficiency below threshold (Bank 1)
P0430	Catalyst system efficiency below threshold (Bank 2)
P0431	Catalyst system efficiency below threshold (Bank 2)
P0441	EVAP incorrect purge flow

Code	Probable cause
P0442	EVAP small leak detected
P0443	EVAP VMV circuit fault
P0450	EVAP pressure sensor malfunction
P0451	EVAP pressure sensor range/performance
P0452	EVAP fuel tank pressure sensor low input
P0453	EVAP fuel tank pressure sensor high input
P0455	Leak in EVAP system detected
P0462	Fuel level sending unit - low voltage indicated
P0463	Fuel level sending unit - high voltage indicated
P0460	Fuel level sending unit - no movement detected
P0500	VSS fault
P0505	IAC valve system fault
P0600	PCM internal fault
P0601	PCM internal fault
P0603	PCM Keep Alive Memory test error
P0605	PCM Read Only Memory test error
P0622	Alternator field circuit open or shorted
P0645	A/C clutch relay circuit open or shorted
P0700	Automatic transmission fault detected
P0703	Brake switch stuck open or closed

3   Powertrain Control Module (PCM) - check and replacement

Caution: *The PCM is an Electro-Static Discharge (ESD) sensitive electronic device, meaning a static electricity discharge from your body could possibly damage internal electrical components. Make sure to properly ground yourself and the PCM before handling it. Avoid touching the electrical terminals of the PCM unless absolutely necessary.*

Check

Note: *Because of a Federally mandated extended warranty which covers the OBD-II*
system components and because any owner-induced damage to the PCM, the sensors and/or the control devices may void the warranty, it is not recommended to attempt diagnosis of, or replace the PCM at home while the vehicle is under warranty.*

1   The PCM requires special test equipment to verify its integrity. Therefore, if the PCM is suspected to be faulty, the vehicle should be taken to your local dealer service department or other qualified repair shop for testing or repair.

Replacement

Refer to illustrations 3.3, 3.4 and 3.5
2   Disconnect the negative battery cable
from the battery.
3   The PCM on 2.0L non-turbo models is mounted to a bracket in the engine compartment behind the relay box **(see illustration)**.
4   The PCM on 2.0L turbo models and 1998 and 1999 2.4L models is located under the dash to the left of the instrument panel center bracket **(see illustration)**.
5   The PCM on 2000 and later models is behind the right side of the dash **(see illustration)**.
6   Disconnect the PCM electrical connector(s), remove the mounting screws and withdraw it from the vehicle.
7   Installation is the reverse of removal.

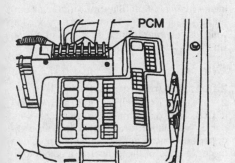

3.3 The PCM on 2.0L non-turbo models is in the engine compartment behind the relay box

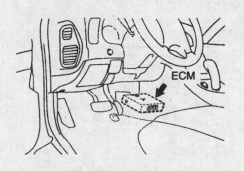

3.4 The PCM on 2.0L turbo and 1998 and 1999 2.4L engine models is under the driver's side of the dash

3.5 The PCM on 2000 and later models is under the passenger side of the dash

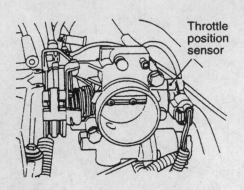

4.2a Throttle position sensor location (2.0L non-turbo shown; other four-cylinder models similar)

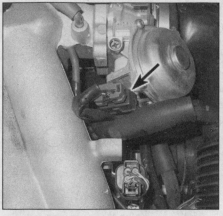

4.2b Throttle position sensor location (3.0L V6 engine)

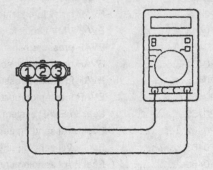

4.3a Throttle position sensor connector terminals (2.0L non-turbo engine)

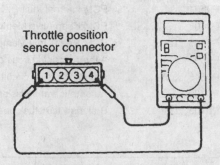

4.3b Throttle position sensor connector terminals (2.0L turbo, 2.4L and 3.0L V6 engine models)

4   Throttle Position Sensor (TPS) - check, replacement and adjustment

General description

1   The Throttle Position Sensor (TPS) is located on the end of the throttle shaft on the throttle body. By monitoring the output voltage from the TPS, the PCM can determine fuel delivery based on throttle valve angle (driver demand). A broken or loose TPS can cause intermittent bursts of fuel from the injectors and an unstable idle because the PCM senses the throttle is moving.

Check

Refer to illustration 4.2a, 4.2b, 4.3a and 4.3b

2   Disconnect the electrical connector from the throttle position sensor, mounted on the throttle body **(see illustrations)**.
3   Connect an ohmmeter between TPS terminals 1 and 3 (2.0L non-turbo) or 1 and 4 (all others) **(see illustrations)**. Compare the reading to the value listed in this Chapter's Specifications.

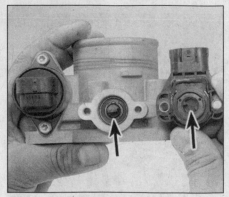

4.10 When installing the TPS onto the throttle body, make sure the socket tangs are on the proper side of the throttle valve shaft blade (arrows), then rotate the TPS clockwise or counterclockwise (see text) to align the screw holes

4   If you're working on a 2.0L non-turbo model, connect the ohmmeter probes to terminals 2 and 3.
5   If you're working on a 2.0L turbo or a 1998 or 1999 2.4L model, connect the ohmmeter between terminals 2 and 4.
6   If you're working on a 2000 or later model, connect the ohmmeter between terminals 1 and 3.
7   Slowly move the throttle from fully closed to fully open. The ohmmeter reading should change smoothly as the throttle valve is moved, and stay within the specified limits the entire time. If not, replace it.

Replacement

Refer to illustration 4.10

8   Remove the throttle body from the intake manifold (see Chapter 4).
9   Unscrew the mounting screws and remove the TPS from the throttle body.
10   When installing the TPS, be sure to align the socket locating tangs on the TPS with the throttle shaft in the throttle body **(see illustration)**. When the TPS is installed correctly, it must be rotated slightly clockwise (1995 through 1999) or counterclockwise (2000 and later) to align the screw holes. After installing the screws, the throttle valve should be fully closed. If it's open, remove the TPS and reposition it on the shaft tangs.

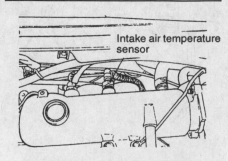

5.1 The intake air temperature sensor on 2.0L non-turbo models is a separate unit mounted in the intake manifold

11   Tighten the TPS screws securely. Repeat Step 7 above to make sure the TPS is positioned properly.
12   The remaining installation steps are the reverse of removal.

5   Intake Air Temperature (IAT) sensor - check and replacement

General information

Refer to illustration 5.1

1   The Intake Air Temperature (IAT) sensor on 2.0L non-turbo models is located in the intake manifold **(see illustration)**. On all others, it's built into the volume air flow sensor, which is mounted on the air cleaner housing where the intake hose joins it.

Check

2.0L non-turbo models

2   To check the sensor, release the locking tab and disconnect the electrical connector **(see illustration 5.1)**. Using an ohmmeter across the sensor terminals, measure the resistance of the sensor at ambient temperature (approximately 70-degrees F). The resistance should be as listed in this Chapter's Specifications. Next, start the engine and allow it to reach operating temperature (approximately 200-degrees F). Measure the resistance again and compare it with the value listed in the Specifications.

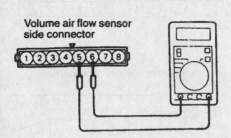

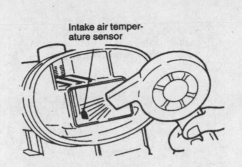

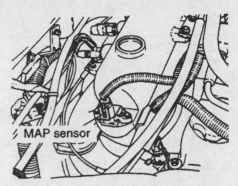

5.3 Connect an ohmmeter to the VAF sensor connector terminals (2.0L turbo engine shown)

5.5 Cool the sensor with ice and heat it with a hair dryer to achieve the specified test temperatures

6.1 The manifold absolute pressure sensor on 2.0L non-turbo models is mounted on the end of the upper intake manifold

2.0L turbo, 2.4L and 3.0L V6 models

Refer to illustrations 5.3 and 5.5

3   Disconnect the air intake temperature sensor connector **(see illustration)**. Connect an ohmmeter to terminals 5 and 6.

4   Disconnect the air intake hose from the air cleaner housing to gain access to the air intake temperature sensor.

5   Cool, then heat, the IAT sensor, using ice and a hair dryer **(see illustration)**. The ohmmeter readings at different temperatures should be as listed in this Chapter's Specifications. If not, replace the volume air flow sensor (the IAT sensor isn't available separately).

Replacement

6   On 2.0L non-turbo engines, unscrew the sensor from the intake manifold **(see illustration 5.1)**. Screw in a new one, using thread sealant on the threads, and tighten it to the torque listed in this Chapter's Specifications.

7   On 2.0L turbo, 2.4L and 3.0L V6 engines, remove the volume air flow sensor from the air cleaner assembly (see Section 8) and install a new one. Reconnect the intake hose to the air cleaner.

6   Manifold Absolute Pressure (MAP) sensor (2.0L non-turbo models) - check and replacement

General description

Refer to illustration 6.1

1   The MAP sensor monitors the intake manifold pressure changes resulting from changes in engine load and speed and converts the information into a voltage output. The PCM uses the MAP sensor to control fuel delivery and ignition timing. The MAP sensor is located on the intake manifold **(see illustration)**.

Check

Refer to illustration 6.2

2   Check the MAP sensor supply voltage. Disconnect the electrical connector and turn the ignition key ON (engine OFF). Using a voltmeter, check for voltage between terminal 2 and ground **(see illustration)**. There should be 4.7 to 5.2 volts present. If no voltage is indicated, check for a blown fuse and examine the wires for obvious damage. If the circuit looks OK, have the PCM checked out at a dealer service department or other qualified repair shop.

3   Check the ground side of the circuit. Connect an ohmmeter between terminal 1 and ground. It should show continuity. If not, check the circuit for a break or bad connection, referring to the wiring diagrams in Chapter 12. If the circuit is good, the MAP sensor may be defective. Have it checked by a dealer service department or other qualified repair shop.

Replacement

4   Disconnect the electrical connector from the MAP sensor.

6.2 MAP sensor terminals (2.0L non-turbo models)

5   Remove the MAP sensor mounting bolts and detach the sensor from the intake manifold.

6   Installation is the reverse of removal. Tighten the sensor bolts securely, but don't overtighten them.

7   Manifold Differential Pressure (MDP) sensor (2.0L turbo, 2.4L and 3.0L V6 models) - check and replacement

General description

Refer to illustration 7.1

1   The MDP sensor produces a voltage signal that varies according to the intake manifold vacuum and sends it to the PCM. The MDP sensor is located on the intake manifold **(see illustration)**.

Check

Refer to illustration 7.2

2   Disconnect the electrical connector from the MDP sensor. Connect a voltmeter

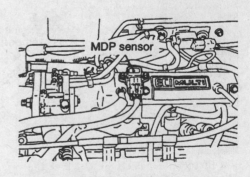

7.1 The manifold differential pressure sensor is mounted on top of the engine (2.0L turbo shown)

68031-6-7.2 HAYNES

7.2 MDP sensor terminals

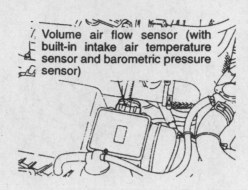

8.1 The VAF sensor is mounted on the air cleaner housing where the intake hose joins it (2.0L turbo shown)

8.2 VAF sensor terminals

between sensor terminal 1 and ground **(see illustration)**.

3   Start the engine and let it idle. The voltmeter should indicate 0.8 volts. When the accelerator is depressed and released suddenly, voltage should jump from 0.8 to 2.4 volts. If not, replace the MDP sensor.

Replacement

4   Disconnect the electrical connector from the MDP sensor.
5   Remove the MDP sensor mounting bolts and detach the sensor from the intake manifold.
6   Installation is the reverse of removal. Tighten the sensor bolts securely, but don't overtighten them.

8   Volume airflow sensor (2.0L turbo, 2.4L and 3.0L V6 models) - check and replacement

General description

Refer to illustration 8.1

1   The volume airflow (VAF) sensor is mounted on the air cleaner where the intake hose joins it **(see illustration)**. It produces a voltage signal that tells the PCM how much air is entering the engine.

Check

Refer to illustration 8.2

2   Backprobe terminal 4 of the connector with the positive probe of a voltmeter **(see illustration)**. Connect the negative probe to ground. Turn the key to ON, but don't start the engine If the voltmeter doesn't indicate approximately 12 volts (battery voltage), check the circuit back to the MFI relay and fusible link (see Chapters 4 and 12).
3   Backprobe terminal 3 of the connector and measure voltage between terminal 3 and ground. It should be 4.8 to 5.2 volts with the key ON (engine not running). If not, check the circuit back to the PCM.
4   Backprobe terminal 5 with an ohmmeter and measure resistance between terminal 5 and ground. It should be less than 2 ohms. If not, check the circuit from terminal 5 back to the chassis ground.
5   If the preceding checks didn't locate the problem, the VAF or PCM is at fault. Have the system checked further by a dealer service department or other qualified repair shop.

Replacement

6   Disconnect the air intake hose from the VAF sensor (if not already done). Remove the mounting screws and take the sensor off the air cleaner housing.
7   Installation is the reverse of the removal steps.

9   Engine Coolant Temperature (ECT) sensor

General description

Refer to illustrations 9.1a and 9.1b

1   The ECT sensor is a thermistor (a resistor which varies the value of its resistance in accordance with temperature changes) **(see illustrations)**. The change in the resistance values will directly affect the voltage signal from the coolant thermosensor. As the sensor temperature DECREASES, the resistance values will INCREASE. As the sensor temperature INCREASES, the resistance values will DECREASE.

Check

Refer to illustration 9.4

2   To quickly check the ECT sensor, release the locking tab and disconnect the electrical connector. Using an ohmmeter across the sensor terminals, measure the resistance of the ECT sensor with the engine cold (approximately 70-degrees F). Next, start the engine and allow it to reach operating temperature

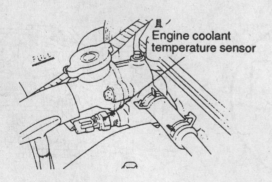

9.1a The engine coolant temperature (ECT) sensor on four-cylinder engines is in the thermostat housing (2.0L non-turbo shown)

9.1b The 3.0L V6 engine coolant temperature sensor is in the crossover portion of the thermostat housing on the driver's side of the engine

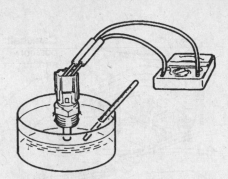

9.4 Immerse the sensor probe in water with a thermometer and test its resistance as the water is heated

9.7 If the sensor isn't already coated with sealant, wrap the sensor threads with Teflon tape

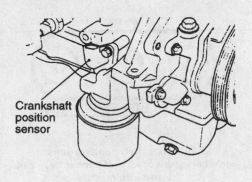

10.1a Crankshaft position sensor (2.0L non-turbo models)

(approximately 200-degrees F), then turn off the engine. Measure the ECT resistance again. Use the values listed in this Chapter's Specifications to get an idea of whether the ECT is changing resistance values at approximately the correct rate.

3   If the quick check doesn't give a definite answer about the condition of the ECT sensor, remove it from the engine (see Steps 5 and 6 below).

4   Place the sensor probe in a pan of water with a thermometer and connect an ohmmeter between its terminals **(see illustration)**. Heat the water and compare the resistance readings on the ohmmeter with the values listed in this Chapter's Specifications. If the readings are incorrect, replace the sensor.

Replacement

Refer to illustration 9.7

Warning: *Wait until the engine is completely cool before beginning this procedure.*

5   Drain the cooling system until the coolant level is below the sensor (see Chapter 1).

6   Release the locking tab and disconnect the electrical connector, then carefully unscrew the sensor. **Caution:** *Handle the coolant sensor with care. Damage to this sensor will affect the operation of the entire fuel injection system.*

7   If you are re-installing the old sensor, clean the threads and then wrap them with Teflon tape to prevent leakage and thread corrosion **(see illustration)**. **Note:** *New ECT sensors have sealant already applied to the threads.*

8   Installation is the reverse of removal. Tighten the ECT sensor to the torque listed in this Chapter's Specifications. Refill the cooling system after installation (see Chapter 1).

10   Crankshaft position sensor - check and replacement

General description

Refer to illustrations 10.1a and 10.1b

1   The PCM uses the crankshaft position sensor to determine fuel injector sequence,

ignition timing and engine rpm. The crankshaft position sensor is a Hall-Effect device which sends voltage pulses to the PCM. The fuel injection and ignition systems will not operate if the PCM does not receive a signal from the crankshaft position sensor. On 2.0L non-turbo engines, the crankshaft position sensor is located on the side of the engine block above the oil filter **(see illustration)**. On 2.0L turbo, 2.4L and 3.0L V6 engines, the crankshaft position sensor is located on the

front of the engine inside the timing belt cover **(see illustration)**.

Check

Refer to illustrations 10.2a and 10.2b

Note: *To backprobe an electrical connector, use pins or paper clips inserted into the rear of the connector (or wire) to facilitate meter attachment. Be careful not to short the probes during this process.*

2   To start, identify the three terminals in the crankshaft position sensor's harness con-

10.1b Crankshaft and camshaft position sensors (2.0L turbo shown)

1   *Camshaft position sensor*
2   *O-ring*
3   *Crankshaft position sensor*

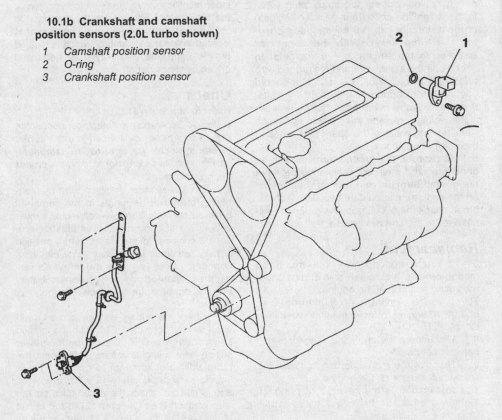

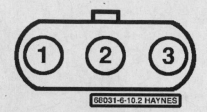

10.2a Crankshaft position sensor terminals (sensor side of connector) - 2.0L non-turbo models

1　Signal output
2　Power supply
3　Ground

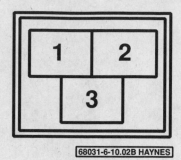

10.2b Crankshaft position sensor terminals (sensor side of connector) - 2.0L turbo, 2.4L and 3.0L V6 models

1　Signal output
2　Power supply
3　Ground

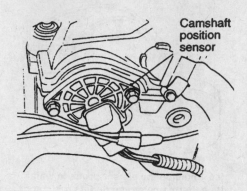

11.1 Camshaft position sensor (2.0L non-turbo engine)

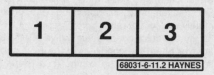

11.2 Camshaft position sensor terminals (sensor side of connector) - four-cylinder engines

1　Power supply
2　Ground
3　Signal output

nector: power supply, signal and ground **(see illustrations)**.

3　Check the supply voltage to the crankshaft sensor from the PCM. With the ignition key ON (engine OFF) backprobe the power supply wire using a voltmeter (connect the other voltmeter terminal to ground). There should be approximately 9.0 volts present on 2.0L non-turbo models and approximately 12 volts on all others. If no voltage is present, check the circuit for a broken wire or short (see Chapter 12). If the circuit checks out OK, have the PCM checked out by your local dealer service department or other qualified repair shop.

4　Next, disconnect the spark plug wires from the ignition coils (four-cylinder engines) or the distributor cap (V6 engine) (see Chapter 1 if necessary). With the connector attached to the sensor, use a voltmeter to backprobe the signal wire and the ground wire and crank the engine. The voltmeter should fluctuate from approximately 0.4 to 4 volts. If supply voltage is detected but there is no signal voltage, replace the crankshaft sensor. After testing, replace the spark plug wires in their proper positions.

5　Backprobe the ground terminal with an ohmmeter and measure resistance between the ground terminal and ground (bare metal on the engine). It should be less than 2 ohms. If not, check the circuit from the ground terminal back to the chassis ground.

Replacement

6　If you're working on a 2.0L non-turbo model, remove the splash shield from under the timing belt end of the engine.

7　If you're working on a 2.0L turbo, 2.4L or 3.0L V6 engine, remove the timing belt (see Chapter 2B, 2C or 2D).

8　Disconnect the crankshaft sensor wiring harness connector.

9　Remove the mounting bolt and take the crankshaft sensor off the engine.

10　Installation is the reverse of removal. Tighten the bolt to the torque listed in this Chapter's Specifications.

11　The remainder of installation is the reverse of the removal steps.

11　Camshaft position sensor - check and replacement

General description

Refer to illustration 11.1

1　On four-cylinder engines, the camshaft position sensor is located at the rear of the cylinder head **(see illustration 10.1b and the accompanying illustration)**. It provides cylinder identification to the PCM to synchronize the fuel system with the ignition system. On V6 engines the camshaft position sensor is located inside the distributor which is located on the right side (rear) cylinder head and driven by the camshaft.

Check

Refer to illustration 11.2

Note: *To backprobe an electrical connector, use pins or paper clips inserted into the rear of the connector (or wire) to facilitate meter attachment. Be careful not to short the probes during this process.*

2　On four-cylinder engines, start by identifying the three terminals in the camshaft position sensor's harness connector: power supply, signal and ground **(see illustration)**. On V6 engines, locate the camshaft position sensor terminals in the distributor electrical connector. Counting from the left while facing the distributor side of the connector, they are: 5, signal output; 6, power supply; 7, ground.

3　Check the supply voltage to the crankshaft sensor from the PCM. With the ignition key ON (engine OFF) backprobe the power supply wire using a voltmeter (connect the other voltmeter terminal to ground). There should be approximately 12 volts. If no voltage is present, check the circuit for a broken wire or short (see Chapter 12). If the circuit checks out OK, have the PCM checked out by your local dealer service department or other qualified repair shop.

4　Next, disconnect the spark plug wires from the ignition coils (four-cylinder engines) or the distributor cap (V6 engine) (see Chapter 1 if necessary). With the connector attached to the sensor, use a voltmeter to backprobe the signal wire and the ground wire and crank the engine. The voltmeter should fluctuate from approximately 0.4 to 3 volts. If supply voltage is detected but there is no signal voltage, replace the crankshaft sensor. After testing, replace the spark plug wires in their proper positions.

5　Backprobe the ground terminal with an ohmmeter and measure resistance between the ground terminal and ground (bare metal on the engine). It should be less than 2 ohms. If not, check the circuit from the ground terminal back to the chassis ground.

Replacement

Four-cylinder engines

6　On 2.0L non-turbo engines, remove the air cleaner assembly intake hose (see Chapter 4).

7　Remove the bolt(s) from the camshaft sensor and withdraw the sensor from the rear of the cylinder head.

8　If necessary, remove the target magnet mounting screw and remove the magnet.

13.1a Typical front (upstream) oxygen sensor

13.1b Typical rear (downstream) oxygen sensor

9   Installation is the reverse of removal. If removed, align the locating pins on the back-side of the target magnet with the locating holes in the rear of the camshaft. Tighten the fasteners to the torques listed in this Chapter's Specifications.

3.0L V6 engines
10   If the camshaft position sensor is determined to be defective, replace the distributor as an assembly (see Chapter 5).

12 Power steering pressure switch - general description

1   Turning the steering wheel increases the power steering fluid pressure and the load placed upon the engine by the power steering pump. The pressure switch will close before the load causes an idle problem.
2   A pressure switch that will not open or an open circuit from the PCM will cause the ignition timing to retard at idle and this will affect idle quality.
3   A pressure switch that will not close or an open circuit may cause the engine to die when the power steering system is used heavily.
4   Any problems with the power steering pressure switch or circuit should be diagnosed and repaired by a dealer service department or other qualified repair shop.

13 Oxygen sensor - check and replacement

General description
Refer to illustrations 13.1a and 13.1b
1   All models are equipped with two oxygen sensors, an upstream oxygen sensor, which is located upstream of the catalytic converter and a downstream oxygen sensor, which is

located at the outlet pipe of the catalytic converter **(see illustrations)**. **Note:** *On models with two catalytic converters, the oxygen sensors are located upstream and downstream of the converter closest to the engine.* The upstream oxygen sensor(s) act as a rich/lean switch indicating the air/fuel mixture to the PCM which then adjusts the injector pulse width to obtain the ideal mixture ratio of 14.7 parts of air to 1 part fuel. The downstream oxygen sensor provides the PCM with the same information as the upstream sensor, but by comparing the data from both sensors, the PCM can monitor catalytic converter efficiency. The oxygen content in the exhaust reacts with the oxygen sensor to produce a voltage output which varies from 0.1 volt (high oxygen, lean mixture) to 1.0 volts (low oxygen, rich mixture). The sensors are equipped with a heating element that keeps them at proper operating temperature during all operating modes.
2   The oxygen sensor produces no voltage when it is below its normal operating temperature of about 600 degrees F. During this initial period before warm-up, the PCM operates in the OPEN LOOP mode.
3   When there is a problem with the oxygen sensor or its circuit, the PCM operates in the open loop mode - that is, it controls fuel delivery in accordance with a programmed default value instead of feedback information from the oxygen sensors.
4   The proper operation of the oxygen sensors depends on four conditions:
  a) *Electrical - The low voltages generated by the sensors depend upon good, clean connections which should be checked whenever a malfunction of the sensor(s) is suspected or indicated.*
  b) *Outside air supply - The sensors are designed to allow air circulation to the internal portion of the sensor. Whenever the sensor is removed and installed or replaced, make sure the air passages are not restricted.*

  c) *Proper operating temperature - The PCM will not react to the sensor signal until the sensor reaches approximately 600-degrees F. This factor must be taken into consideration when evaluating the performance of the sensor.*
  d) *Unleaded fuel - The use of unleaded fuel is essential for proper operation of the sensors. Make sure the fuel you are using is of this type.*
5   In addition to observing the above conditions, special care must be taken whenever the sensor(s) is serviced.
  a) *The oxygen sensors have a permanently attached pigtail and electrical connector which should not be removed from the sensor. Damage or removal of the pigtail or electrical connector can adversely affect operation of the sensor(s) and engine.*
  b) *Grease, dirt and other contaminants should be kept away from the electrical connector and the louvered end of the sensor(s).*
  c) *Do not use cleaning solvents of any kind on the oxygen sensors.*
  d) *Do not drop or roughly handle the sensors.*

Check
6   Raise the vehicle and support it securely on jackstands.
7   Locate the oxygen sensor electrical connector and disconnect it.
8   Using an ohmmeter, measure the resistance between the heater terminals of the sensor electrical connector (refer to the wiring diagrams in Chapter 12 if necessary). There should be continuity. If not, replace the sensor.
9   Locate the output terminals of the oxygen sensor (refer to the wiring diagrams in Chapter 12 if necessary). Connect a digital voltmeter to the terminals.
10   Start the engine and warm it up to normal operating temperature. Check the oxygen

13.13 Special sockets like this one are available for oxygen sensor removal, but a flare-nut wrench or crow's foot socket will also work

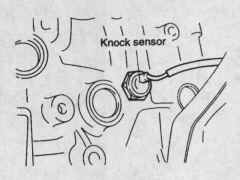

14.2 Typical knock sensor (2.0L turbo shown)

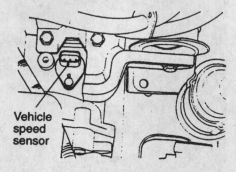

15.1 The vehicle speed sensor is on top of the transaxle (2.0L non-turbo shown)

sensor signal voltage.

  a) *Voltage from an upstream sensor should range from 100 to 900 millivolts (0.1 to 0.9 volt) and switch actively between high and low readings.*

  b) *Voltage from a downstream sensor should also read between 100 and 900 millivolts (0.9 to 1.0 volt) but it should not switch actively. The downstream oxygen sensor voltage may stay toward the center of the range or stay for relatively longer periods of time at the upper and lower limits of the range.*

11   If the oxygen sensor tests good, follow the oxygen sensor circuits back to the PCM and check for breaks or poor connections. If the wiring is good, have the vehicle checked by a dealer service department or other qualified repair shop.

Replacement

Refer to illustration 13.13

Note: *Because they are installed in the exhaust manifold and catalytic converter, which contracts when cool, the oxygen sensors may be very difficult to loosen when the engine is cold. Rather than risk damage to the sensor (assuming you are planning to reuse it in another manifold or pipe), start and run the engine for a minute or two, then shut it off. Be careful not to burn yourself during the following procedure.*

12   Raise the vehicle and place it securely on jackstands.

13   Carefully disconnect the electrical connector from the sensor and unscrew the sensor from the exhaust manifold or catalytic converter **(see illustration)**.

14   If the sensor is to be re-installed, apply an anti-seize compound to the threads to facilitate future removal. The threads of new sensors are already coated with this compound.

15   Install the sensor and tighten it to the torque given in this Chapter's Specifications.

16   Reconnect the electrical connector of the sensor lead to the engine wiring harness and lower the vehicle.

14   Knock sensor - removal and installation

Refer to illustration 14.2

1   All models are equipped with a knock sensor. The knock sensor is a piezoelectric crystal that oscillates with engine vibration. When knock is detected, the PCM retards the ignition timing until the knocking stops. **Caution:** *Do not drop or strike the knock sensor or it may be damaged.*

2   The knock sensor on four-cylinder engines is located in the engine block beneath the intake manifold **(see illustration)**. On 3.0L V6 engines, the knock sensor is in the "V" between the cylinder banks, also beneath the intake manifold.

3   On 2.0L non-turbo models, remove the splash shield from under the front of the vehicle.

4   On 2.0L turbo models, remove the intake manifold stay.

5   On 3.0L V6 models, remove the intake manifold (see Chapter 2D).

6   Disconnect the electrical connector and unscrew the knock sensor from the engine block.

7   Installation is the reverse of removal. Tighten the knock sensor to the torque listed in this Chapter's Specifications.

15   Vehicle Speed Sensor (VSS) - check and replacement

Refer to illustration 15.1

1   The Vehicle Speed Sensor (VSS) is located on the transaxle **(see illustration)**.

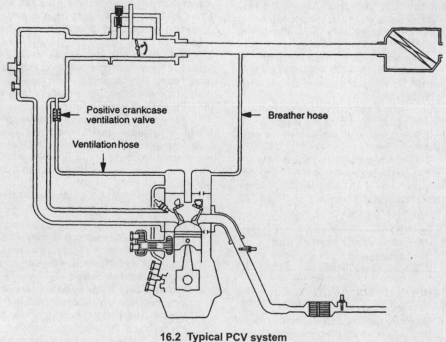

16.2 Typical PCV system

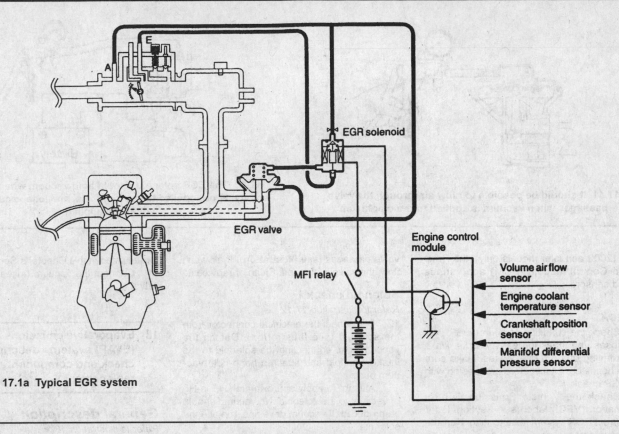

17.1a Typical EGR system

This sensor is a permanent magnetic variable reluctance sensor that produces a pulsing voltage. These pulses are translated by the PCM to determine vehicle speed.

Check

Note: *To backprobe an electrical connector, use pins or paper clips inserted into the rear of the connector (or wire) to facilitate meter attachment. Be careful not to short the probes during this process.*

2   Locate the VSS output terminal (refer to the wiring diagrams in Chapter 12). Back-probe the connector with the positive probe of a voltmeter and connect the other probe to ground. Place the voltmeter where you can see it from the driver's seat.

3   In a driveway or on an unoccupied road, slowly drive the vehicle forward. The voltage should fluctuate between 0 and 8-to-12 volts. If there is no signal voltage, replace the VSS.

Replacement

4   Clean the area around the VSS to prevent contaminating the transaxle.

5   Disconnect the electrical connector from the VSS.

6   Remove the retaining bolt(s) and lift the VSS from the transaxle. **Note:** *When removing the VSS make sure the drive gear comes out along with the VSS. Should the drive gear fall into the transaxle, retrieve it and install it back onto the VSS.*

7   Installation is the reverse of removal. Tighten the VSS retaining bolt securely.

16   Positive Crankcase Ventilation (PCV) system - general description

Refer to illustration 16.2

1   The Positive Crankcase Ventilation (PCV) system reduces hydrocarbon exhaust emissions by scavenging crankcase vapors. This is accomplished by circulating fresh air from the air cleaner through the crankcase, where it mixes with blow-by gases and is then re-routed through the PCV valve to the intake manifold to be burned in the combustion process.

2   The main components of the PCV system are the PCV valve and the vacuum hoses that connect it to the manifold **(see illustration)**.

3   To maintain idle quality, the PCV valve restricts the flow when the intake manifold vacuum is high. If abnormal operating conditions (such as piston ring problems) arise, the system is designed to allow excessive amounts of blow-by gases to flow back through the crankcase vent tube into the air cleaner to be consumed by normal combustion.

4   Check and replacement of the PCV valve is performed in Chapter 1.

17   Exhaust Gas Recirculation (EGR) system - description, check and component replacement

Note: *If the EGR valve control solenoid becomes disconnected or damaged, the elec-*

trical signal will be lost and the EGR valve will be open at all times during warm-up and driving conditions. The symptoms will be poor performance, rough idle and driveability problems.

General description

Refer to illustration 17.1a and 17.1b

1   The EGR system reduces oxides of nitrogen (NOx) by recirculating exhaust gases from the exhaust ports through the EGR valve and back into the intake manifold for ingestion into the engine, which lowers the peak combustion temperature **(see illustrations)**.

2   The EGR system consists of the EGR valve, the EGR solenoid, vacuum control

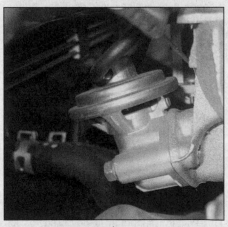

17.1b EGR valve (3.0L V6 engine shown)

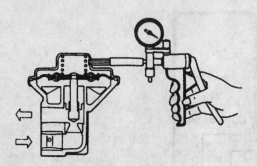

17.11 It should be possible to blow air through the valve passages when vacuum is applied to the diaphragm

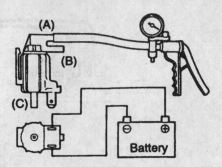

17.12 The EGR solenoid should hold vacuum when battery voltage is not applied to the terminals, and lose vacuum when voltage is applied

valve (2000 and later models only), the Powertrain Control Module (PCM) and various related sensors.

Check

3   Check the condition of all the EGR system hoses and tubes for leaks, cracks, kinks or hardening of the rubber hoses. Make sure all the hoses are intact before proceeding with the EGR check.
4   Check the Vehicle Emission Control Information (VECI) label (see Section 1) for the correct EGR system hose routing. Reroute the hoses if necessary.
5   With the engine cold, detach the vacuum hose from the top of the EGR valve and connect a vacuum gauge into the hose using a T-fitting.
6   Start the engine and let it idle. Rev the engine (not over 3000 rpm) and note the reading on the gauge. It shouldn't change.
7   Start the engine and warm it to its normal operating temperature. Rev the engine again. This time, the vacuum gauge should indicate 4 psi or more. If not, test the individual system components.
8   Apply approximately 5-to-10 in-Hg of vacuum to the EGR valve with the engine at idle. The engine speed should drop considerably or even stall as vacuum is applied. This indicates that the EGR system is operating properly. If the engine speed does not change, this indicates a possible faulty EGR valve, blocked or plugged EGR tube or passages in the intake and exhaust manifolds that may be plugged with carbon build-up. **Note:** *If the EGR valve is severely plugged with carbon deposits, do not attempt to scrape them out, replace it with a new one.*

EGR valve check
Refer to illustration 17.11
9   Unbolt the EGR valve and lift it off the engine.
10   Apply approximately 15 in-Hg of vacuum to the EGR valve and see if the stem on the EGR valve moves. If the stem moves, the valve diaphragm is good. If not, replace the valve.
11   With the diaphragm in the raised position (vacuum applied), try to blow air through the

valve passages **(see illustration)**. If air won't flow, the valve is clogged. Clean or replace it.

Solenoid check
Refer to illustration 17.12
12   Disconnect the electrical connector from the solenoid **(see illustration)**. Detach the vacuum hose connecting the solenoid to the intake manifold and attach a hand-held vacuum pump.
13   Attempt to apply approximately 15 in-Hg of vacuum to the solenoid. No vacuum should be produced. If vacuum develops, replace the solenoid.
14   Next, connect one of the solenoid electrical terminals to the positive battery terminal using a fused jumper wire. Using another jumper wire, connect the other terminal to a good ground (this will energize the solenoid - be careful not to short them together). With battery voltage applied to the solenoid, try to pull approximately 15 in-Hg of vacuum on the solenoid. Vacuum should develop and hold steady. If vacuum is not produced or the pressure does not remain constant, replace the solenoid. Re-attach the vacuum hose and the electrical connector.

Vacuum control valve check (2000 and later models)
15   Disconnect and plug the white-striped hose from the vacuum control valve.
16   Connect a vacuum gauge to the disconnected fitting on the vacuum control valve.
17   Start the engine and let it idle. The gauge should indicate 6.3 to 7.1 in-Hg. If not, replace the valve.

EGR valve replacement
18   Remove the EGR valve mounting bolts and then remove the EGR valve and tube.
19   Clean the gasket surfaces of the EGR valve, tube and intake manifold. If the EGR valve is to be re-installed, clean the gasket surfaces and, if necessary, remove any carbon build-up that may be present. If carbon build-up is excessive, replace the EGR valve.
20   Loosely assemble the EGR valve and tube, using new gaskets. Then hand tighten all the bolts. Next, tighten the tube bolts. Finish by tightening the EGR valve bolts to the

torque listed in this Chapter's Specifications.
21   Connect the vacuum hoses to the EGR valve.

---

18   Evaporative emissions control (EVAP) system - description, check and component replacement

---

General description
Refer to illustration 18.1
1   The Evaporative Emissions Control (EVAP) system absorbs fuel vapors, and during engine operation releases them into the engine intake where they mix with the incoming air/fuel mixture. The EVAP system consists of a charcoal-filled canister, the lines connecting the canister to the fuel tank and engine, and related solenoids and valve **(see illustration)**.
2   When the engine is not operating, fuel vapors are transferred from the fuel tank, throttle body and intake manifold to the charcoal canister where they are stored. When the engine is running, the fuel vapors are purged from the canister by the purge control solenoid. The gases are consumed in the normal combustion process.
3   On 2000 and later models, a ventilation control solenoid is used to monitor fuel tank pressure for the On-Board Diagnostic (OBD-II) system.

Check
Note: *The evaporative control system, like all emission control systems, is protected by a Federally mandated extended warranty. The EVAP system probably won't fail during the service life of the vehicle; however, if it does, the hoses, gas cap or charcoal canister are usually to blame.*
4   If the CHECK ENGINE light is illuminated, check the gas cap. A loose or poorly sealing gas cap will cause the PCM to register a leak in the system.
5   Poor idle, stalling or poor driveability can be caused by a defective canister purge solenoid, a damaged canister, split or cracked

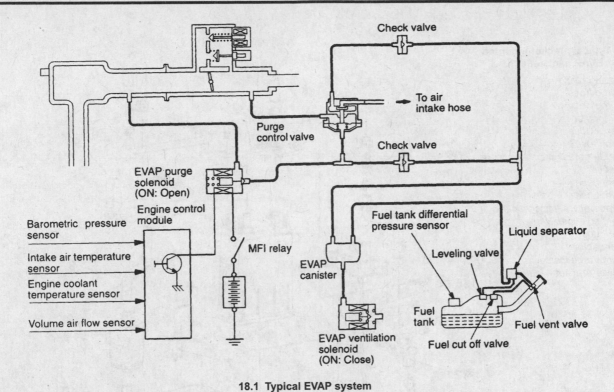

18.1 Typical EVAP system

hoses or hoses connected to the wrong tubes.
6   Evidence of fuel loss or fuel odor can
be caused by the following items: fuel leaking from fuel lines or a cracked or damaged
canister, an inoperative fuel tank check valve,
an inoperative purge solenoid, disconnected,
misrouted, kinked, deteriorated or damaged
vapor or control hoses or an improperly
seated air filter or air filter gasket.
7   Inspect each hose attached to the canister for kinks, leaks or breaks along its entire
length. Repair or replace as necessary.
8   Inspect the canister. If it's cracked or
damaged, replace it.
9   Look for fuel leaking from the bottom of
the canister. If fuel is leaking, replace the canister and check the hoses and hose routing.

Canister replacement

Refer to illustrations 18.14a and 18.14b

10   The canister is mounted in the engine
compartment on early models and at the
rear of the vehicle on later models. Canisters
mounted at the rear are either on top of the
fuel tank or on a bracket.
11   Remove the fuel filler cap to relieve the
pressure inside the fuel tank.
12   If you're working on a 1995 through 1997
2.0L non-turbo model, remove the splash
shield from under the engine.
13   If you're working on a 1995 through 1997
2.0L turbo model, remove the battery (see
Chapter 5).
14   Clearly label, then disconnect the vacuum hoses, remove the nuts/bolts securing
the canister and withdraw it from the vehicle
(see illustrations).
15   Installation is the reverse of removal.

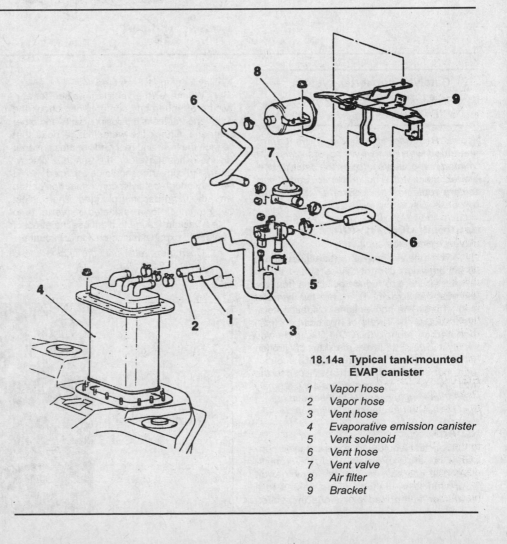

18.14a Typical tank-mounted
EVAP canister

1   *Vapor hose*
2   *Vapor hose*
3   *Vent hose*
4   *Evaporative emission canister*
5   *Vent solenoid*
6   *Vent hose*
7   *Vent valve*
8   *Air filter*
9   *Bracket*

18.14b Typical bracket-mounted EVAP canister

1   Upper bracket
2   Purge hose
3   Purge hose
4   Connector
5   Vapor hose
6   Vent hose
7   Air filter bracket
8   Air filter
9   Vent hose
10   Vent hose
11   Evaporative emission canister
12   Vent solenoid
13   Vent hose
14   Connector
15   Vapor tube clamp
16   Lower bracket

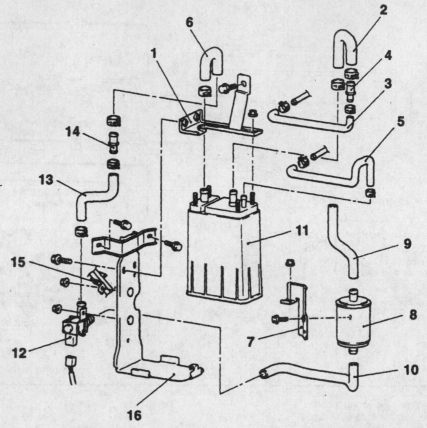

19 Catalytic converter system - description, check and replacement

Note: *Because of a Federally mandated extended warranty which covers emissions related components such as the catalytic converter, check with a dealer service department before replacing the converter at your own expense.*

General description

Refer to illustration 19.1

1   The catalytic converter **(see illustration)** is an emission control device added to the exhaust system to reduce pollutants from the exhaust gas stream. There are two types of converters. The conventional oxidation catalyst reduces the levels of hydrocarbon (HC) and carbon monoxide (CO). The three-way catalyst lowers the levels of oxides of nitrogen (NOx) as well as hydrocarbons (HC) and carbon monoxide (CO). **Caution:** *Because the two types of catalytic converters are extremely similar looking, make sure you are purchasing the correct part for your particular vehicle.*

Check

2   The test equipment for a catalytic converter is very expensive and highly sophisticated. If you suspect that the converter on your vehicle is malfunctioning, take it to a dealer or authorized emissions inspection facility for diagnosis and repair.

3   Whenever the vehicle is raised for servicing of underbody components, check the converter for leaks, corrosion, dents and other damage. Check the welds/flange bolts that attach the front and rear ends of the converter to the exhaust system. If damage is discovered, the converter should be replaced.

4   Although catalytic converters don't often fail, they can become plugged. The easiest way to check for a restricted converter is to use a vacuum gauge to diagnose the effect of a blocked exhaust based on intake vacuum.

a) *Open the throttle until the engine speed is about 2000 rpm.*
b) *Release the throttle quickly.*

c) *If there is no restriction, the gauge will quickly drop to not more than 2 in-Hg or more above its normal reading.*
d) *If the gauge does not show 5 in-Hg or more above its normal reading, or seems to momentarily hover around its highest reading for a moment before it returns, the exhaust system, or the converter, is plugged (or an exhaust pipe is bent or dented, or the core inside the muffler has shifted).*

Replacement

5   Refer to the exhaust system removal and installation Section in Chapter 4.

19.1 Typical catalytic converter

Chapter 7 Part A
Manual transaxle

Contents

Specifications

Transaxle fluid type.. See Chapter 1

Torque specifications **Ft-lbs** (unless otherwise indicated)

Note: *One foot-pound (ft-lb) of torque is equivalent to 12 inch-pounds (in-lbs) of torque. Torque values below approximately 15 ft-lbs are expressed in inch-pounds, since most foot-pound torque wrenches are not accurate at these smaller values.*

Engine-to-transaxle bolts
  2.0L non-turbo models 70
  2.0L turbo, 1998 and 1999 2.4L engine models
    Upper two bolts 35
    Ground cable bolt 22
    Lower (beneath starter motor, threaded into transaxle) .... 22 to 25
  2000 and later 2.4L engine 36
  3.0L V6 engine 52
Bellhousing inspection cover bolts
  2.0L non-turbo engine .... 104 inch-lbs
  2.0L turbo, 1998 and 1999 2.4L engines
    Vertical bolts .... 104 to 132 inch-lbs
    Horizontal bolts .... 78 inch-lbs
  2000 and later 2.4L, all 3.0L V6 engines
    To engine .... 78 inch-lbs
    To transaxle 19

1   General information

The vehicles covered by this manual are equipped with either a 5-speed manual transaxle or a 4-speed automatic transaxle. Information on the manual transaxle is included in this Part of Chapter 7. Service procedures for the automatic transaxle are contained in Chapter 7, Part B.

The manual transaxle is a compact, two-piece, lightweight aluminum alloy housing containing both the transmission and differential assemblies.

Because of the complexity of the transaxle and the special tools needed to work on it, internal repair procedures for the manual transaxle are beyond the scope of this manual. The information in this Chapter is devoted to removal and installation procedures.

2   Oil seal replacement

1   Oil leaks can occur as a result of worn seals or O-rings. Replacement of these seals or O-rings is relatively easy, since the repairs can usually be performed without removing the transaxle from the vehicle.

Driveaxle oil seals
Refer to illustrations 2.4 and 2.5
2   The driveaxle oil seals are located on the sides of the transaxle, where the inner ends of the driveaxles are splined into the differential side gears. If you suspect that a driveaxle oil seal is leaking, raise the vehicle and support it securely on jackstands. If the seal is leaking, you'll see lubricant on the side of the transaxle, below the seal.

2.4 Pry the oil seal out of the transaxle with a large screwdriver or pry bar; if that doesn't work, try a seal removal tool (available from auto parts stores)

2.5 Drive the new seal squarely into the bore with a seal driver or a large socket - make sure it's fully seated

3   Remove the driveaxle(s) (see Chapter 8).

4   Using a seal removal tool, screwdriver or prybar, carefully pry the seal out of the transaxle bore (**see illustration**).

5   Using a seal driver or a large deep socket as a drift, install the new oil seal. Drive it into the bore squarely and make sure it's fully seated (**see illustration**).

6   Lubricate the lip of the new seal with multi-purpose grease.

7   Install the driveaxle(s). Be careful not to damage the lip(s) of the new seal(s).

Vehicle speed sensor (speedometer drive) O-ring

8   The vehicle speed sensor is located on the transaxle housing. Look for lubricant around the housing to determine if the O-ring is leaking.

9   Disconnect the electrical connector, remove the hold-down bolt and remove the pinion assembly and vehicle speed sensor from the transaxle (see Chapter 6).

10   Using a scribe or a small screwdriver, remove the O-ring seal.

11   Install a new O-ring on the pinion gear housing. Smear some transmission lubricant on the O-ring before installing the sensor.

12   Installation is the reverse of removal.

---

3   Shift cables - removal and installation

Removal

Refer to illustration 3.6

Warning: *Some models covered by this manual are equipped with a Supplemental Restraint System, more commonly known as airbags. Always disable the airbag system before working in the vicinity of any airbag system components (see Chapter 12).*

1   Disconnect the cable from the negative terminal of the battery. On airbag-equipped models also disconnect the positive cable, then wait three minutes before proceeding.

2   Remove the battery from the vehicle (see Chapter 5).

3   Remove the air cleaner and air intake hose (see Chapter 4).

4   Remove the center console (see Chapter 11).

3.6 Shift cable details (1995-1999 shown; later models similar)

1   Air filter housing/intake duct
2   Battery tray and bracket
3   Shift lever and knob
4   Center panel
5   Cup holder assembly
6   Center console
7   Shift lever boot
8   Console side cover
9   Nut
10   Clips
11   Clips
12   Shift cables (passenger compartment side)
13   Shift cables (transaxle side)
14   Grommet
15   Shift lever assembly
16   Spacer
17   Bushing

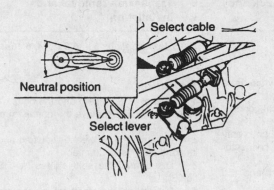

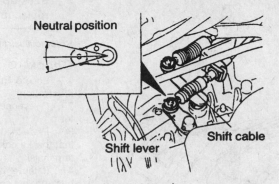

3.9a Place the select lever on the transaxle in the Neutral position

3.9b Place the shift lever on the transaxle in the Neutral position

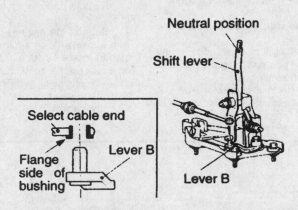

3.10 The flanged side of the select cable bushing faces downward

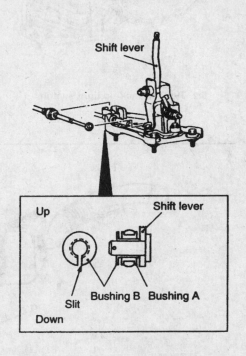

3.11 The slit in the shift cable bushing goes straight up or straight down

5   On 2000 and later models, remove the heater core/evaporator housing assembly (see Chapter 3).

6   On 1995 through 1999 models, remove the cotter pins and retaining washers from both ends of each cable. Remove the fasteners and separate the grommet from the firewall, then withdraw the cables from the vehicle **(see illustration)**.

7   On 2000 and later models, remove the cotter pins and retaining washers from both ends of the select cable and the transaxle end of the shift cable. At the passenger compartment end of the shift cable, carefully spread the fingers of the wire retainer clip and pivot it upward to free the cable end from the shift lever, then slide the cable end up off the lever. Remove the fasteners and separate the grommet from the firewall, then withdraw the cables from the vehicle.

Installation

Refer to illustrations 3.9a, 3.9b, 3.10 and 3.11

8   Installation is the reverse of the removal steps, with the following additions.

1995 through 1999 models

9   Place the transaxle levers in the neu-tral position (if they're not already there) **(see illustrations)**. Also place the shift lever in the passenger compartment in the neutral position.

10   Connect the shift cable to the lever in the passenger compartment so the flange side of the bushing is downward **(see illustration)**.

11   When connecting the select cable to the shift lever in the passenger compartment, make sure the slit in the bushing is straight up or straight down **(see illustration)**.

2000 and later models

12   Measure the gap between the fingers on the wire retainer shift cable retainer clip. If it's more than 3/8-inch, squeeze the ends together until the gap narrows to 3/16 to 5/16 inch.

13   Place the transaxle levers in the neutral position (if they're not already there). Also place the shift lever in the passenger compartment in the neutral position.

14   When connecting the transaxle ends of the cables to the levers, make sure the paint marks (white and yellow) on the ends of the cables face the cotter pins.

15   Refill the cooling system and check the operation of the heater and air conditioner.

All models

16   Move the shift lever through the gear positions and check for smooth operation.

4   Shift lever - removal and installation

1   Remove the center console (see Chapter 11).

2   Disconnect the cables from the shift lever (see Section 3).

3   Remove the shift lever mounting bolts and lift it out.

4   Installation is the reverse of the removal steps.

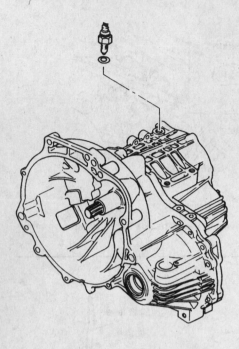

5.1 Typical back-up light switch

5　Back-up light switch - check and replacement

Refer to illustration 5.1

Check

1　Locate the back-up light switch **(see illustration)**.
2　Disconnect the switch electrical connector.
3　Place the transaxle in Reverse and verify that there's continuity between the connector terminals.
4　If there is no continuity, replace the back-up light switch.

Replacement

5　Clean the transaxle case around the switch.
6　Disconnect the switch electrical connector.
7　Unscrew the switch and pull it out of the transaxle.
8　Apply a light coat of clean oil to a new O-ring, install the new switch and O-ring, and tighten the switch securely.
9　Plug in the electrical connector.
10　Check the switch as described above to ensure it's working properly.

6　Transaxle - removal and installation

Refer to illustrations 6.4, 6.8, 6.14, 6.16a and 6.16b

Removal

1　Remove the battery and the battery tray (see Chapter 5). Remove the battery support stay.
2　Remove the air cleaner housing and air intake duct(s) (see Chapter 4).
3　Disconnect the shift cables (see Section 3).
4　Disconnect the electrical connectors for the back-up light switch and speed sensor **(see illustration)**.
5　Jack up the front end of the vehicle and support it securely on jackstands.
6　Remove the starter motor (see Chapter 5).
7　Support the engine. This can be done from above with an engine hoist or engine support fixture, or from underneath by placing a jack (with a wood block as an insulator) under the engine oil pan. The engine must be supported at all times while the transaxle is out of the vehicle.

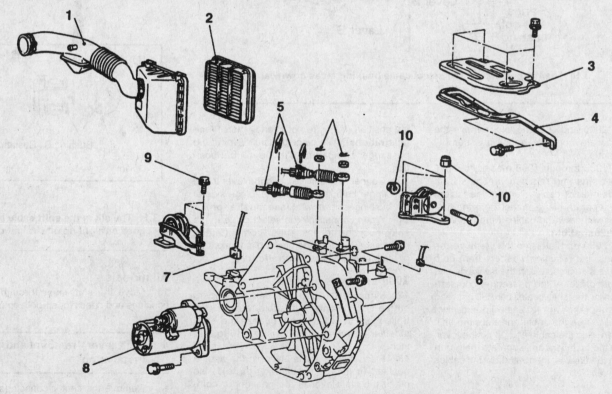

6.4 Typical transaxle removal details (part 1 of 2)

1　Air cleaner cover and intake hose	5　Shift and select cables	9　Rear roll stopper bolt
2　Air cleaner element	6　Back-up light switch connector	10　Transaxle mount nuts
3　Battery tray	7　Vehicle speed sensor connector	
4　Battery tray support stay	8　Starter motor	

8   Remove the front and rear roll stoppers and crossmember and remove the upper transaxle mount (see Chapters 2A through 2D and the accompanying illustration) **(see illustration)**.

9   Remove the transaxle upper mounting bolts.

10   Remove the clutch release cylinder from the transaxle (see Chapter 8). Don't disconnect the fluid line unless you have to; just set the cylinder aside and tie it up out of the way.
Caution: *Don't depress the clutch pedal while the release cylinder is removed.*

11   Disconnect all ground wires.

12   Drain the transaxle fluid (see Chapter 1).

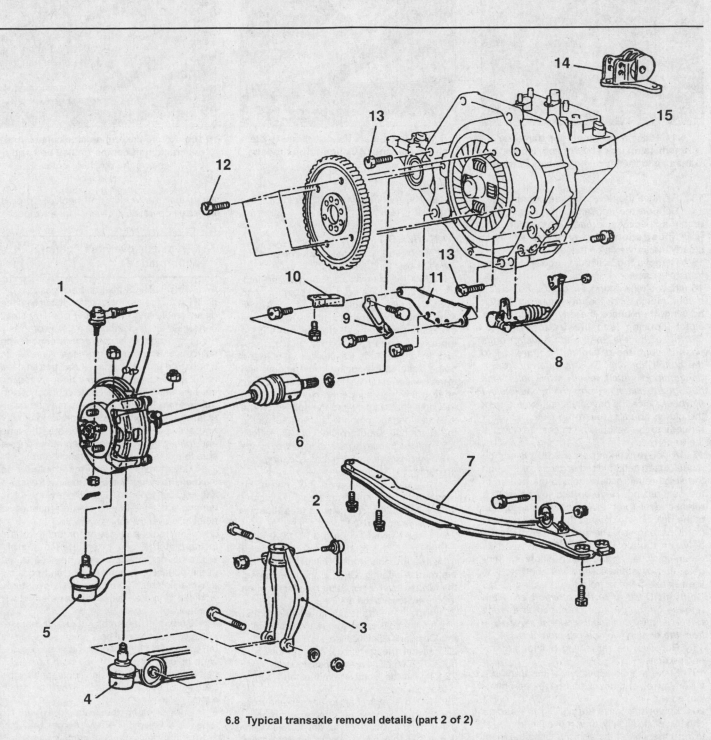

6.8 Typical transaxle removal details (part 2 of 2)

1	Tie-rod end	7	Crossmember	12	Flywheel-to-clutch housing bolts
2	Stabilizer bar link	8	Clutch release cylinder		(2.0L non-turbo engine)
3	Damper fork	9	Front plate	13	Transaxle mounting bolts
4	Lateral lower arm ball-joint	10	Rear plate	14	Transaxle mount
5	Compression lower arm ball-joint	11	Bellhousing cover	15	Transaxle
6	Driveaxle				

6.14 Place a jack under the transaxle (transmission jack shown) and secure the transaxle to the jack using chains or straps

6.16a Match-mark the driveplate to the clutch housing (2.0L non-turbo models)

6.16b Rotate the engine clockwise using the crankshaft damper/pulley bolt and remove the flywheel bolts

13   Remove the driveaxles (see Chapter 8).

14   Support the transaxle with a jack (preferably a special jack made for this purpose) **(see illustration)**. Safety chains will help steady the transaxle on the jack.

15   Remove the bellhousing cover from the transaxle case.

16   If you're working on a 2.0L non-turbo model, match-mark the driveplate and clutch housing, then unbolt the driveplate from the clutch housing **(see illustrations)**. **Note:** *On these models, the clutch housing bolts pass through the driveplate and thread into the clutch housing. This is different from a conventional clutch, in which the bolts pass through the clutch housing and thread into the flywheel.* Once the driveplate is unbolted from the clutch housing, push the clutch housing farther into the bellhousing to ease removal of the transaxle.

17   If you're working on a 3.0L V6 engine model, insert a flat-bladed screwdriver through the small round access hole in the bottom of the bellhousing. Have an assistant push the release lever (protruding from its hole on top of the bellhousing) toward the transaxle (away from the engine). Place the screwdriver tip between the clutch release bearing and its retaining collar on the clutch diaphragm fingers, then twist the screwdriver gently to free the release bearing from the retaining collar. **Caution:** *Don't force the screwdriver or the release bearing will be damaged. If it won't twist easily, try pushing the release lever away from the engine two or three more times.*

18   Remove the remaining bellhousing-to-engine bolts.

19   Make a final inspection of the transaxle for any wires and hoses that have been overlooked.

20   Lower the jacks supporting the engine and transaxle slightly, then move the transaxle toward the side of the vehicle. Once the input shaft is clear, lower the transaxle and remove it from under the vehicle. Try to keep the transaxle as level as possible.

21   While the transaxle is removed, be sure to inspect the clutch components (see Chapter 8). In most cases, new clutch components

should be routinely installed whenever the transaxle is removed.

Installation

22   If removed, install the clutch components (see Chapter 8).

23   With the transaxle secured to the jack as on removal, raise it into position and then carefully engage the input shaft with the splines in the clutch hub. Do not use excessive force to install the transaxle. If the input shaft does not slide into place, readjust the angle of the transaxle so it is in the same plane as the engine. If the engine and transaxle are in the same plane, but the input shaft still won't engage the clutch hub, turn the input shaft slightly and the splines on the shaft will engage properly with the splines in the clutch hub. **Caution:** *On 3.0L V6 models, don't roll the transaxle in relation to the engine while you install it, or the release bearing may be damaged.*

24   If you're working on a 2.0L non-turbo model, align the match marks and bolt the driveplate to the clutch housing **(see illustrations 6.16a and 6.16b)**.

25   If you're working on a 3.0L V6 engine model, push the release lever toward the transaxle to engage the retaining collar with the release bearing. Once properly engaged, the release lever should offer resistance when it's moved toward the engine.

26   Install the transaxle-to-engine bolts. Tighten the bolts to the torque values listed in this Chapter's Specifications.

27   Install the transaxle mount nuts and bolts. Tighten all nuts and bolts securely.

28   Install the transaxle mount and center crossmember.

29   Remove all transaxle and engine supports. Install the various items removed previously. Refer to Chapter 8 for driveaxle installation and Chapter 5 for starter motor installation.

30   Make a final check that all electrical wiring has been connected and that the transaxle has been filled with the specified lubricant to the proper level (see Chapter 1). Lower the vehicle.

31   Connect the negative battery cable.

Road test the vehicle to check for proper transaxle operation and check for leakage.

7   Transaxle overhaul - general information

1   Overhauling a manual transaxle is a difficult job for the do-it-yourselfer. It involves the disassembly and reassembly of many small parts. Numerous clearances must be precisely measured and, if necessary, changed with select fit spacers and snap-rings. As a result, if transaxle problems arise, it can be removed and installed by a competent do-it-yourselfer, but overhaul should be left to a transmission repair shop. Rebuilt transaxles may be available, check with your dealer parts department and auto parts stores. At any rate, the time and money involved in an overhaul is almost sure to exceed the cost of a rebuilt unit.

2   Nevertheless, it's not impossible for an inexperienced mechanic to rebuild a transaxle if the special tools are available and the job is done in a deliberate step-by-step manner so nothing is overlooked.

3   The tools necessary for an overhaul include internal and external snap-ring pliers, a bearing puller, a slide hammer, a set of pin punches, a dial indicator and possibly a hydraulic press. In addition, a large, sturdy workbench and a vise or transaxle stand will be required.

4   During disassembly of the transaxle, make careful notes of how each piece comes off, where it fits in relation to other pieces and what holds it in place. If you note how each part is installed before removing it, getting the transaxle back together again will be much easier.

5   Before taking the transaxle apart for repair, it will help if you have some idea what area of the transaxle is malfunctioning. Certain problems can be closely tied to specific areas in the transaxle, which can make component examination and replacement easier. Refer to the *Troubleshooting* section at the front of this manual for information regarding possible sources of trouble.

Chapter 7 Part B
Automatic transaxle

Contents

Specifications

Transaxle fluid type and capacity .... See Chapter 1

Torque specifications
Ft-lbs (unless otherwise indicated)

Driveplate-to-torque converter bolts
2.0L non-turbo	55
2.0L turbo, 1998 and 1999 2.4L	33 to 38
2000-on 2.4L, 3.0L V6	37

Transaxle-to-engine bolts
2.0L non-turbo	70

2.0L turbo, 1998 and 1999 2.4L
Into engine	35
Into transaxle	22 to 25
2000 and later 2.4L	36

3.0L V6
Lower	52

Upper
Flange bolt	52
Bolt with washer	65

1 General information

All models covered by this manual are equipped with either a 5-speed manual transaxle or a 4-speed automatic transaxle. All information on the automatic transaxle is included in this Part of Chapter 7. Information for the manual transaxle can be found in Part A of this Chapter.

Because of the complexity of the automatic transaxle and the specialized equipment needed to service it, this Chapter contains only those procedures related to general diagnosis, routine maintenance, adjustment, and removal and installation.

If the transaxle requires major repair work, it should be taken to a dealer service department or an automotive or transmission repair shop. You can, however, save money by removing and installing the transaxle yourself, even if the repair work is done by a shop.

2 Diagnosis and trouble codes

Note: *Automatic transaxle malfunctions may be caused by five general conditions: poor engine performance, improper adjustments, hydraulic malfunctions, mechanical malfunctions or malfunctions in the computer or its signal network. Diagnosis of these problems should always begin with a check of the easily repaired items: fluid level and condition (see Chapter 1), shift linkage adjustment and throttle linkage adjustment. Next, perform a road test to determine if the problem has been corrected or if more diagnosis is necessary. If the problem persists after the preliminary tests and corrections are completed, additional diagnosis should be done by a dealer service department or transmission repair shop. Refer to the Troubleshooting section at the front of this manual for information on symptoms of transaxle problems.*

Preliminary checks

1 Drive the vehicle to warm the transaxle to normal operating temperature.

2 Check the fluid level as described in Chapter 1:

a) *If the fluid level is unusually low, add enough fluid to bring the level within the designated area of the dipstick, then check for external leaks (see below).*

b) *If the fluid level is abnormally high, drain off the excess, then check the drained fluid for contamination by coolant. The presence of engine coolant in the automatic transmission fluid indicates that a failure has occurred in the internal radiator walls that separate the coolant from the transmission fluid (see Chapter 3).*

c) *If the fluid is foaming, drain it and refill the transaxle, then check for coolant in the fluid, or a high fluid level.*

3 Make sure the engine idle speed is correct. If the idle speed is incorrect, have it

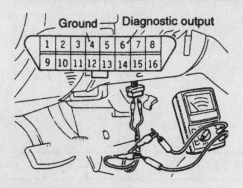

2.20a Transaxle diagnostic codes can be accessed with an analog voltmeter . . .

adjusted by a dealer service department or other qualified repair shop before proceeding.

4   Inspect the shift cable (see Section 3). Make sure that it's properly adjusted and operates smoothly.

Fluid leak diagnosis

5   Most fluid leaks are easy to locate visually. Repair usually consists of replacing a seal or gasket. If a leak is difficult to find, the following procedure may help.

6   Identify the fluid. Make sure it's transmission fluid and not engine oil or brake fluid (automatic transmission fluid is a deep red color).

7   Try to pinpoint the source of the leak. Drive the vehicle several miles, then park it over a large sheet of cardboard. After a minute or two, you should be able to locate the leak by determining the source of the fluid dripping onto the cardboard.

8   Make a careful visual inspection of the suspected component and the area immediately around it. Pay particular attention to gasket mating surfaces. A mirror is often helpful for finding leaks in areas that are hard to see.

9   If the leak still cannot be found, clean the suspected area thoroughly with a degreaser or solvent, then dry it.

10   Drive the vehicle for several miles at normal operating temperature and varying

speeds. After driving the vehicle, visually inspect the suspected component again.

11   Once the leak has been located, the cause must be determined before it can be properly repaired. If a gasket is replaced but the sealing flange is bent, the new gasket will not stop the leak. The bent flange must be straightened.

12   Before attempting to repair a leak, check to make sure that the following conditions are corrected or they may cause another leak. **Note:** *Some of the following conditions cannot be fixed without highly specialized tools and expertise. Such problems must be referred to a transmission shop or a dealer service department.*

Gasket leaks

13   Check the pan periodically. Make sure the bolts are tight, no bolts are missing, the gasket is in good condition and the pan is flat (dents in the pan may indicate damage to the valve body inside).

14   If the pan gasket is leaking, the fluid level or the fluid pressure may be too high, the vent may be plugged, the pan bolts may be too tight, the pan sealing flange may be warped, the sealing surface of the transaxle housing may be damaged, the gasket may be damaged or the transaxle casting may be cracked or porous. If sealant instead of gasket material has been used to form a seal between the pan and the transaxle housing, it may be the wrong sealant.

Seal leaks

15   If a transaxle seal is leaking, the fluid level or pressure may be too high, the vent may be plugged, the seal bore may be damaged, the seal itself may be damaged or improperly installed, the surface of the shaft protruding through the seal may be damaged or a loose bearing may be causing excessive shaft movement.

16   Make sure the dipstick tube seal is in good condition and the tube is properly seated. Periodically check the area around the speedometer gear or sensor for leakage. If transmission fluid is evident, check the O-ring for damage.

Case leaks

17   If the case itself appears to be leaking, the casting is porous and will have to be repaired or replaced.

18   Make sure the oil cooler hose fittings are tight and in good condition.

Fluid comes out vent pipe or fill tube

19   If this condition occurs, the transaxle is overfilled, there is coolant in the fluid, the case is porous, the dipstick is incorrect, the vent is plugged or the drain-back holes are plugged.

Diagnostic trouble codes

Refer to illustrations 2.20a and 2.20b

20   The computer for the automatic transaxle has a self-diagnostic capability; it continually monitors important information sensor and output actuator circuits for malfunctions. When a monitored circuit is damaged, shorted or disconnected, a diagnostic trouble code is stored in the computer's memory. At a dealer service department, stored trouble codes are extracted from computer memory with a scanner. There are several other methods of extracting codes, depending on model and year of the vehicle. On 1995 through 1999 models, codes can be read by connecting a voltmeter between terminals 4 and 6 of the data link connector (the same connector that's used for scan tool hookups) **(see illustration)**. You can also cause the Check Engine light to flash the codes, with a pattern of long and short flashes indicating the code number **(see illustration)**. On 2000 and later models (those equipped with Sport Mode only), you can cause the neutral indicator light in the instrument cluster to flash the codes by shorting terminal 1 of the data link connector to ground.

Erasing a diagnostic trouble code

21   If you have the transaxle repaired at a dealer service department or transmission shop, they will erase the trouble codes when they're done making the repair. If you make a repair yourself, either erase the codes with

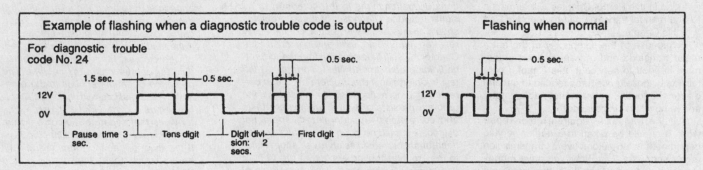

2.20b . . . or with flashes of the Check Engine light

a scanner, or turn the ignition Off and disconnect the battery negative cable for 10 seconds. Reconnect the cable and turn the ignition On; a normal code should now be indicated.

3 Shift cable - check, adjustment and replacement

Check

1   Move the shift lever from the "P" position to the "1" position. You should be able to feel the detents in each range. If you can't feel the detents, or if the pointer indicating the ranges is incorrectly aligned, adjust the shift cable.

Adjustment
Refer to illustration 3.3

2   Place the shift lever inside the vehicle in the N position.

3   Locate the shift lever on the transaxle case. Loosen the adjusting nut and make sure the transaxle lever is in the N position **(see illustration)**.

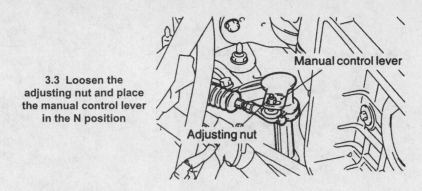

3.3 Loosen the adjusting nut and place the manual control lever in the N position

Manual control lever

Adjusting nut

4   Gently tug the cable to remove any slack, then tighten the nut.

Replacement
Refer to illustration 3.7

Warning: *Some models covered by this manual are equipped with airbags. Always disable the airbag system when working in the vicinity of airbag system components (see Chapter 12).*

5   Remove the air cleaner (see Chapter 4).

6   Remove the center console and the center dash trim bezel (see Chapter 11).

7   If you're working on a 1995 through 1999 model, remove the transmission control module bracket and the module **(see illustration)**.

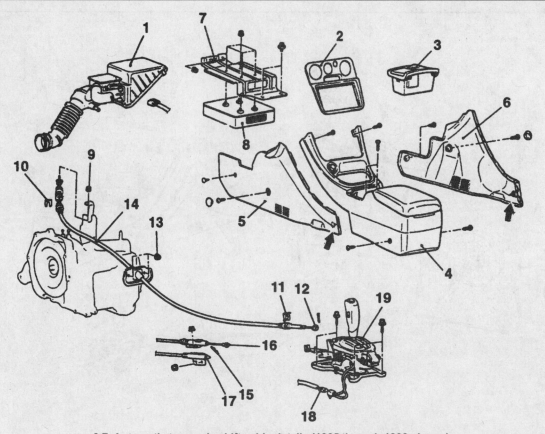

3.7 Automatic transaxle shift cable details (1995 through 1999 shown)

1	Air cleaner housing	8	Transaxle control module	15 Snap pin
2	Cluster center trim	9	Nut	16 Key interlock cable fitting
3	Ashtray	10	Clip	17 Shift lock cable fitting
4	Console	11	Clip	18 Overdrive switch/PRNDL light
5	Console side trim	12	Transaxle cable fitting	electrical connector
6	Console side trim	13	Nut	19 Shift lever
7	Transaxle control module bracket	14	Shift cable	

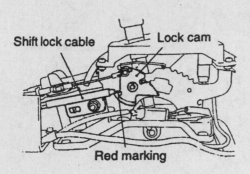

5.3 Position the end of the cable directly over the red mark on the cam

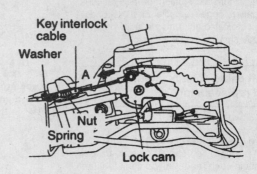

5.4 Loosen the nut, gently push the cable in direction "A" and tighten the nut

8   If you're working on a 2000 or later model, remove the splash shield from under the front of the vehicle (see Chapter 11).

9   On 1995 through 1999 models, remove the clips at each end of the cable and the cotter pin at the transaxle end. On all models, remove the nut at the transaxle end of the cable and disconnect the cable from the transaxle shift lever.

10   Disconnect the cable from the shift lever in the passenger compartment and remove it from the vehicle.

11   Remove the fasteners and separate the grommet from the firewall, then remove the cable from the vehicle.

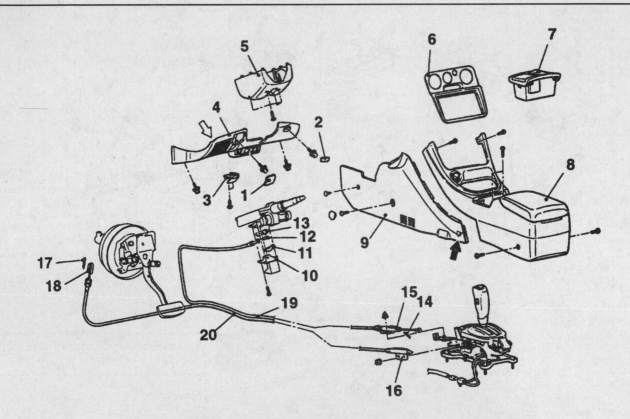

5.6 Typical key interlock and shift lock cable details (2.0L turbo shown)

1	Cover plug	8	Center console	15	Key interlock cable
2	Cover plug	9	Console trim cover	16	Shift lock cable
3	Hood latch lever	10	Cover	17	Cotter pin
4	Instrument panel under cover	11	Cam and lever	18	Shift lock cable
5	Steering column lower cover	12	Key interlock cable	19	Key interlock cable
6	Center trim panel	13	Slide lever	20	Shift lock cable
7	Cup holder	14	Snap pin		

12   Installation is the reverse of removal. Be sure to adjust the cable when you're done.

4   Shift lever - removal and installation

Warning: *Some models covered by this manual are equipped with airbags. Always disable the airbag system when working in the vicinity of airbag system components (see Chapter 12).*
1   Remove the center console and the center dash trim bezel (see Chapter 11).
2   Disconnect the shift cable, key interlock cable and shift lock cable (see Sections 3 and 5).
3   Disconnect the shift lever electrical connector(s).
4   Remove the shift lever assembly mounting bolts and lift the assembly off the vehicle floor.
5   Installation is the reverse of removal. Be sure to adjust the shift cable, key interlock cable and shift lock cable (see Sections 3 and 5).

5   Shift interlock system - description, adjustment and cable replacement

Warning: *Some models covered by this manual are equipped with airbags. Always disable the airbag system when working in the vicinity of airbag system components (see Chapter 12).*

Description

1   The shift lock system prevents the shift lever from being shifted out of Park or Neutral until the brake pedal is applied. Other than the following simple component checks, diagnosis of the shift lock system should be left to a dealer service department or other qualified repair shop.

Adjustment
Refer to illustrations 5.3 and 5.4
2   Remove the center console (see Chapter 11).
3   With the shift lever in the P position, the end of the shift lock cable should be directly over the red mark on the lock cam **(see illustration)**. If not, loosen the cable locknut, reposition the cable as necessary and tighten the locknut.
4   Loosen the nut on the key interlock cable **(see illustration)**. Gently push the cable fitting on the lock cam in the direction shown and tighten the nut.

Cable replacement
Refer to illustration 5.6
5   If the key interlock cable breaks, you'll have to remove the steering column cover and

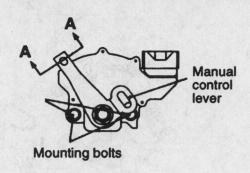

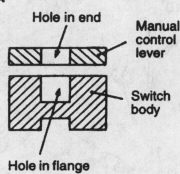

Section A-A

6.5 Align the holes in the lever and switch body, then tighten the bolts

the center console to replace it (see Chapter 11).
6   Remove the locknuts and disconnect the shift lever ends of the cables **(see illustration)**. Remove the cotter pin and disconnect the transaxle end of the shift lock cable. Remove the cover and disconnect the steering column end of the key interlock cable.
7   Installation is the reverse of removal. Adjust the cables as described above.

6   Park/Neutral position switch - adjustment and replacement

1   If the engine will start with the shift lever in any position other than Park or Neutral, adjust the Park/Neutral position switch.

Adjustment
Refer to illustration 6.5
2   Place the shift lever in the Neutral position.
3   Loosen the adjusting nut on the shift cable (see Section 3).
4   Make sure the shift lever on the transaxle is in the Neutral position.
5   Loosen the switch mounting bolts **(see illustration)**.
6   Align the hole in the end of the manual control lever with the hole in the switch body, then tighten the switch body mounting bolts to

the torque listed in this Chapter's Specifications.
7   Adjust the shift cable (see Section 3).

Replacement
8   Disconnect the negative cable from the battery.
9   Unplug the switch electrical connectors.
10   Remove the switch mounting bolts **(see illustration 6.5)** and remove the switch.
11   Installation is the reverse of removal. Don't tighten the retaining screws until you have adjusted the switch as described in Step 6.

7   Automatic transaxle - removal and installation

Removal
Refer to illustrations 7.3a, 7.3b and 7.16
Note: *When removing the transaxle mounting bolts, record the position and length of each bolt so they can be returned to their original locations.*
1   Detach the cable from the negative battery terminal. Remove the battery, tray and support stay.
2   Remove the air cleaner and air intake duct assembly (see Chapter 4). If the vehicle is equipped with cruise control, remove the

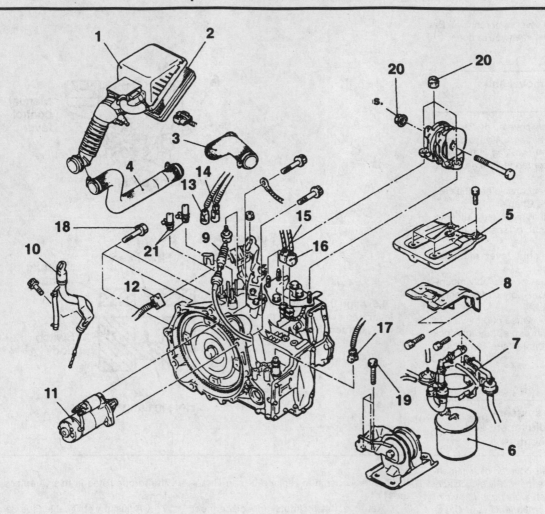

7.3a Typical automatic transaxle removal and installation details (2.0L turbo 4WD shown) (part 1 of 2)

1	Air cleaner assembly	8	Battery tray support stay	15	Solenoid connector
2	Air cleaner element	9	Shift cable	16	Pulse generator connector
3	Air hose	10	Fluid dipstick	17	Speedometer connector
4	Air hose	11	Starter motor	18	Transaxle mounting bolts
5	Battery tray	12	Park/Neutral switch connector	19	Rear roll stopper bolts
6	Evaporative emission canister	13	Oil temperature sensor connector	20	Transaxle mounting bracket nuts
7	Canister bracket	14	Kickdown servo switch connector	21	Oil cooler hoses

cruise control actuator.

3   Clearly label, then disconnect, all electrical connectors **(see illustrations)**.

4   Disconnect the shift cable from the lever on the transaxle (see Section 3).

5   Disconnect the key interlock cable (see Section 5).

6   Loosen the hose clamps and disconnect the oil cooler hoses. Plug the hoses to prevent contamination and leaks.

7   Remove the starter motor (see Chapter 5).

8   Remove the upper transaxle-to-engine bolts.

9   Remove the transaxle mounting bracket.

10   Loosen the wheel lug nuts, raise the vehicle and support it securely on jackstands. Remove the wheels.

11   Remove any exhaust components which will interfere with transaxle removal (see Chapter 4). If you're working on a 2.0L turbo model, remove the evaporative emission canister (see Chapter 6).

12   Remove the splash shield from under the front of the vehicle.

13   Drain the transaxle fluid (see Chapter 1).

14   Remove both driveaxles (see Chapter 8). If the vehicle is a 4WD model, remove the driveshaft (see Chapter 8). On 4WD models, it's also a good idea to remove the transfer case now (see Chapter 8). You can, however, leave the transfer case attached to the transaxle and remove it after you've removed the transaxle, but it's easier to unbolt the transfer case while the transaxle is still bolted to the engine.

15   Remove the torque converter cover.

16   Mark the relationship of the torque converter to the driveplate so they can be installed in the same position **(see illustration)**.

17   Remove the torque converter-to-driveplate bolts. Turn the crankshaft 90-degrees at a time for access to each bolt. After all three bolts are removed, push the torque converter into the bellhousing so it doesn't stay with the engine when the transaxle is removed.

18   Support the engine from above with a hoist, or place a jack and a block of wood under the oil pan to spread the load.

19   Support the transaxle with a transmission jack (a special jack made for this purpose), if available, or with a floor jack. Safety chains will help steady the transaxle on the jack.

20   Remove any remaining chassis or sus-

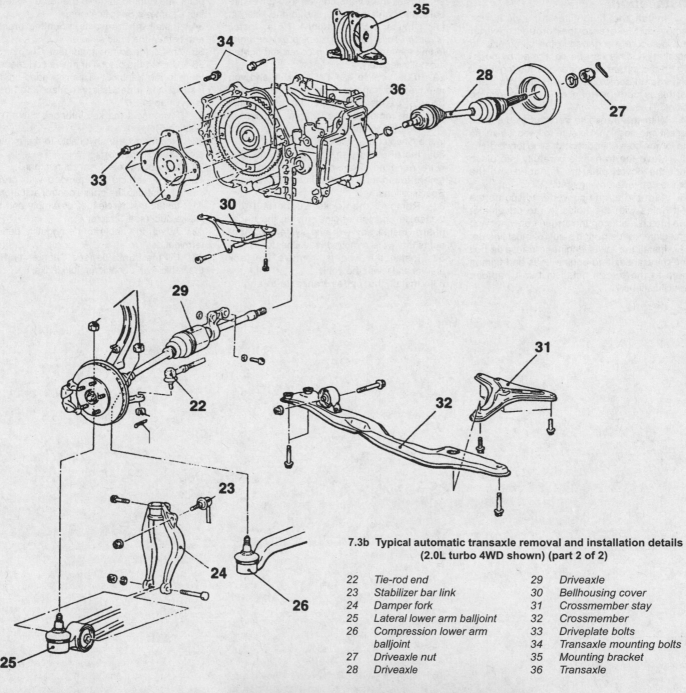

7.3b Typical automatic transaxle removal and installation details (2.0L turbo 4WD shown) (part 2 of 2)

22	Tie-rod end	29	Driveaxle
23	Stabilizer bar link	30	Bellhousing cover
24	Damper fork	31	Crossmember stay
25	Lateral lower arm balljoint	32	Crossmember
26	Compression lower arm balljoint	33	Driveplate bolts
		34	Transaxle mounting bolts
27	Driveaxle nut	35	Mounting bracket
28	Driveaxle	36	Transaxle

pension components which will interfere with transaxle removal.

21   Remove the lower engine-to-transaxle bolt and the transaxle-to-engine bolts.

22   Move the transaxle to the side to disengage it from the engine block dowel pins. Make sure the torque converter is detached from the driveplate. Secure the torque converter to the transaxle so that it will not fall out during removal. Lower the transaxle from the vehicle. If you're swapping transaxles, remove the transaxle fluid filler tube. If the vehicle is a 4WD model, remove the transfer case (see Chapter 8).

7.16 Mark the relationship of the torque converter to the driveplate so they can be reassembled in the same relative position

Installation

23   Install the fluid filler tube, if it was removed. Make sure the torque converter hub is securely engaged in the pump prior to installation. This can be confirmed by pushing on the torque converter and turning it (if it isn't seated completely, it will drop into place as this is done, evidenced by one or more "clunks").

24   With the transaxle secured to the jack, raise it into position. Be sure to keep it level so the torque converter does not slide forward.

25   Move the transaxle carefully into place until the dowel pins are engaged and the torque converter is engaged.

26   Turn the torque converter to line up the bolt holes with the holes in the driveplate. The match marks on the torque converter and driveplate, made during step 16, must line up.

27   Install the lower engine-to-transaxle bolt and the transaxle-to-engine bolts and tighten them to the torque listed in this Chapter's Specifications.

28   Install the torque converter-to-driveplate bolts and tighten them to the torque listed in this Chapter's Specifications. **Note:** *Install all of the bolts before tightening any of them*. Install the torque converter cover and tighten the bolts securely.

29   If the vehicle is a 4WD model, and you removed the transfer case, install it now (see Chapter 8). Install all drivetrain components that were removed (see Chapter 8). Tighten all drivetrain components to the torque listed in the Chapter 8 Specifications.

30   Install all suspension components that were removed. Tighten all suspension fasteners to the torque listed in the Chapter 10 Specifications.

31   Remove the jacks supporting the transaxle and the engine. Install the under guard. Install any exhaust system components that were removed (see Chapter 4).

32   Install the wheels, remove the jack stands and lower the vehicle.

33   Install the upper transaxle-to-engine bolts and tighten them to the torque listed in this Chapter's Specifications.

34   Install the transaxle mounting bracket and tighten the bolts securely.

35   Install the starter motor (see Chapter 5).

36   Unplug the oil cooler hoses and reattach them to the transaxle. This is a good time to inspect and if necessary, replace the hoses (see Chapter 3).

37   Reconnect the key interlock cable (see Section 5).

38   Reconnect the shift cable to the manual lever (see Section 3).

39   Connect all electrical connectors.

40   If the vehicle is equipped with cruise control, reattach the cruise control actuator.

41   Install the air cleaner assembly and the intake duct (see Chapter 4).

42   Attach the cable to the negative battery terminal.

43   Fill the transaxle (see Chapter 1). Run the vehicle and check for fluid leaks.

Chapter 8 Clutch and driveline

Contents

Specifications

Clutch

Fluid type	See Chapter 1
Type	Single dry plate, diaphragm spring
Four-cylinder engines	Push type
3.0L V6 engine	Pull type
Actuation	Hydraulic

CV joint boot dimensions

Front driveaxles (tripod joint)	
1995 through 1999	3-5/32 inches
2000 through 2002	3-15/16 inches
2003 and later	
2.4L engine	3-/12 inches
3.0L engine	3-3/8 inches
Rear driveaxles (tripod joint)	
Conventional differential	3-7/64 inches
Limited slip differential	3-5/16 inches

Universal joint (4WD models)

Clearance between snap-ring and spider bearing cap (standard)	0.0004 to 0.0012 inch

Torque specifications

Ft-lbs

Note: *One foot-pound (ft-lb) of torque is equivalent to 12 inch-pounds (in-lbs) of torque. Torque values below approximately 15 ft-lbs are expressed in inch-pounds, since most foot-pound torque wrenches are not accurate at these smaller values.*

Pressure plate-to-flywheel bolts	
2.0L non-turbo engine	55
All other engines	168 inch-lbs
Intermediate shaft bearing bracket bolts	30
Driveaxle hub nut (front and rear, all models)	146 to 188*
Rear hub-to-knuckle bolts	60
Driveshaft (4WD models)	
Support bearing assembly mounting nuts	22
Differential companion flange-to-rear U-joint yoke nuts and bolts	22 to 25
Center yoke-to-center driveshaft nut	137
Companion flange-to-rear driveshaft nut	137
Rear differential (4WD models)	
Support member-to-differential bolts	65
Differential support member nuts/bolts	72
Differential rear mounting bolts	53
Driveshaft-to-differential bolts	22 to 25

*Start with the lower torque. Tighten as necessary, up to the maximum listed torque, to align the cotter pin holes.

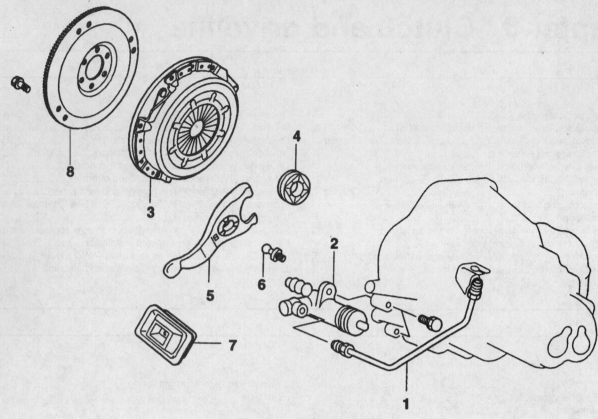

2.1a Clutch (2.0L non-turbo models) - exploded view

1	*Fluid line*	4	*Clutch release bearing*	6	*Ball stud (fulcrum)*
2	*Release cylinder*	5	*Clutch release lever*	7	*Release fork boot*
3	*Modular clutch/flywheel assembly*			8	*Driveplate*

1   General information

The information in this Chapter deals with the components that transmit power to the wheels, except for the transaxle, which is in Chapter 7. The components covered in this Chapter are grouped into four categories - clutch, driveaxles, driveshaft and transfer case. You'll find general descriptions, inspection and overhaul procedures for all of these components in this Chapter (those Sections covering the driveshaft, the rear differential and the rear driveaxles apply only to 4WD models).

Warning: *Since nearly all the procedures covered in this Chapter involve working under the vehicle, make sure it's securely supported on sturdy jackstands or on a hoist where the vehicle can be easily raised and lowered.*

2   Clutch - description and check

Refer to illustration 2.1a and 2.1b

1   All vehicles with a manual transaxle use a single dry plate, diaphragm spring type clutch **(see illustrations)**. The clutch disc has a splined hub which allows it to slide along the splines of the transaxle input shaft. The clutch and pressure plate are held in contact by spring pressure exerted by the diaphragm in the pressure plate.

2   The clutch release system is operated by hydraulic pressure. The hydraulic release system consists of the clutch pedal, a master cylinder and fluid reservoir, the hydraulic line, a slave cylinder which actuates the clutch release lever and the clutch release (or throw-out) bearing.

3   When pressure is applied to the clutch pedal to release the clutch, hydraulic pressure is exerted against the outer end of the clutch release lever. As the lever pivots, the shaft fingers push against the release bearing. On all except 3.0L V6 models, the bearing pushes against the fingers of the diaphragm spring of the pressure plate assembly, which in turn releases the clutch plate. On 3.0L V6 models, the bearing pulls the fingers rather than pushing them.

4   Terminology can be a problem regarding the clutch components because common names have in some cases changed from that used by the manufacturer. For example, the driven plate is also called the clutch

plate or disc, the pressure plate assembly is sometimes referred to as the clutch cover, the clutch release bearing is sometimes called a throw-out bearing, and the release cylinder is sometimes called the operating or slave cylinder.

5   Other than replacing components that have obvious damage, some preliminary checks should be performed to diagnose a clutch system failure.

a) *The first check should be of the fluid level in the clutch master cylinder (see Chapter 1). If the fluid level is low, add fluid as necessary and inspect the hydraulic clutch system for leaks. If the master cylinder reservoir has run dry, bleed the system (see Section 7) and retest the clutch operation.*

b) *To check "clutch spin down time," run the engine at normal idle speed with the transaxle in Neutral (clutch pedal up - engaged). Disengage the clutch (pedal down), wait several seconds and shift the transaxle into Reverse. No grinding noise should be heard. A grinding noise would most likely indicate a problem in the pressure plate or the clutch disc.*

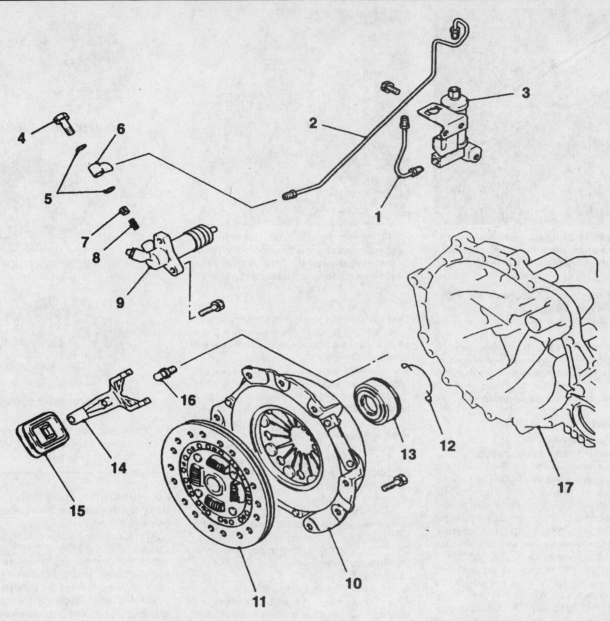

2.1b Clutch (2.0L turbo models, 2.4L four-cylinder similar) - exploded view

1	Fluid line	7	Valve plate	13	Clutch release bearing
2	Fluid line	8	Valve plate spring	14	Clutch release lever
3	Clutch damper	9	Release cylinder	15	Release fork boot
4	Union bolt	10	Pressure plate assembly	16	Ball stud (fulcrum)
5	Sealing washers	11	Clutch disc	17	Transaxle
6	Banjo fitting	12	Release bearing clip		

c) To check for complete clutch release, run the engine (with the parking brake applied to prevent movement) and hold the clutch pedal approximately 1/2-inch from the floor. Shift the transaxle between 1st gear and Reverse several times. If the shift is not smooth, component failure is indicated. Check the release cylinder pushrod travel. With the clutch pedal depressed completely the release cylinder pushrod should extend substantially. If it doesn't, check the fluid level in the clutch master cylinder.

d) Visually inspect the clutch pedal bushing at the top of the clutch pedal to make sure there is no sticking or excessive wear.

e) Under the vehicle, check that the clutch release lever is solidly mounted on the ball stud.

3 Clutch components - removal, inspection and installation

Warning: Dust produced by clutch wear and deposited on clutch components is hazardous to your health. DO NOT blow it out with compressed air and DO NOT inhale it. DO NOT use gasoline or petroleum based solvents to remove the dust. Brake system cleaner should be used to flush the dust into a drain

3.6 If you're going to re-use the same pressure plate, mark the relationship of the pressure plate to the flywheel

3.10 Inspect the clutch disc for signs of excessive wear such as smeared friction material, chewed-up rivets, worn hub splines and distorted damper cushions or springs

NORMAL FINGER WEAR

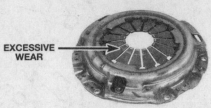

EXCESSIVE WEAR

EXCESSIVE FINGER WEAR

BROKEN OR BENT FINGERS

3.12a Replace the pressure plate if excessive wear or damaged fingers are noted

pan. After the clutch components are wiped clean with a rag, dispose of the contaminated rags and cleaner in a labeled, covered container.

Note: The clutch on 2.0L non-turbo models is a modular-type unit and must be replaced as an assembly (clutch disc, pressure plate and flywheel); therefore, many of the steps in this section will not apply to those models.

Removal

Refer to illustration 3.6

1   Access to the clutch components is normally accomplished by removing the transaxle, leaving the engine in the vehicle. If, of course, the engine is being removed for major overhaul, then the opportunity should always be taken to check the clutch for wear and replace worn components as necessary. However, the relatively low cost of the clutch components compared to the time and labor involved in gaining access to them warrants their replacement any time the engine or transaxle is removed, unless they are new or in near-perfect condition. The following procedures assume that the engine will stay in place.

3.12b Examine the pressure plate friction surface for score marks, cracks and evidence of overheating

2   Remove the release cylinder (see Section 6). Hang it out of the way with a piece of wire - it's not necessary to disconnect the hose.
3   Remove the transaxle from the vehicle (see Chapter 7A). Support the engine while the transaxle is out. Preferably, an engine hoist should be used to support it from above. However, if a jack is used underneath the engine, make sure a piece of wood is used between the jack and oil pan to spread the load. **Caution:** The pick-up for the oil pump is very close to the bottom of the oil pan. If the pan is bent or distorted in any way, engine oil starvation could occur.
4   The release fork and release bearing can remain attached to the transaxle for the time being.
5   To support the clutch disc during removal, install a clutch alignment tool through the clutch disc hub.
6   Carefully inspect the flywheel and pressure plate for indexing marks. The marks are usually an X, an O or a white letter. If they cannot be found, scribe marks yourself so the pressure plate and the flywheel will be in the same alignment during installation **(see illustration)**.
7   Slowly loosen the pressure plate-to-flywheel bolts. Work in a diagonal pattern and loosen each bolt a little at a time until all spring pressure is relieved. Then hold the pressure plate securely and completely remove the bolts, followed by the pressure plate and clutch disc.

Inspection

Refer to illustrations 3.10, 3.12a and 3.12b

8   Ordinarily, when a problem occurs in the clutch, it can be attributed to wear of the clutch driven plate assembly (clutch disc). However, all components should be inspected at this time.
9   Inspect the flywheel for cracks, heat checking, score marks and other damage. If the imperfections are slight, a machine shop

can resurface it to make it flat and smooth. Refer to Chapter 2 for the flywheel removal procedure.
10   Inspect the lining on the clutch disc. There should be at least 1/16-inch of lining above the rivet heads. Check for loose rivets, distortion, cracks, broken springs and other obvious damage **(see illustration)**. As mentioned above, ordinarily the clutch disc is replaced as a matter of course, so if in doubt about the condition, replace it with a new one.
11   The release bearing should be replaced along with the clutch disc (see Section 4).
12   Check the machined surface and the diaphragm spring fingers of the pressure plate **(see illustrations)**. If the surface is grooved or otherwise damaged, replace the pressure plate assembly. Also check for obvious damage, distortion, cracking, etc. Light glazing can be removed with emery cloth or sandpaper. If a new pressure plate is indicated, new or factory rebuilt units are available.

Installation

Refer to illustration 3.14

13   Before installation, carefully wipe the flywheel and pressure plate machined surfaces clean. It's important that no oil or grease is on these surfaces or the lining of the clutch disc. Handle these parts only with clean hands.
14   Position the clutch disc and pressure plate with the clutch held in place with an

3.14 Center the clutch disc in the pressure plate with a clutch alignment tool or a wooden dowel of the appropriate diameter

4.5 To check the operation of the release bearing, hold it by the outer race and rotate the inner race while applying pressure - the bearing should turn smoothly - if it doesn't replace it

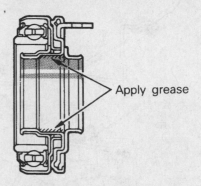

4.7 Fill the groove of the release bearing with high-temperature grease in the indicated area; also apply a light coat of the same grease to the transaxle input shaft splines and bearing retainer sleeve

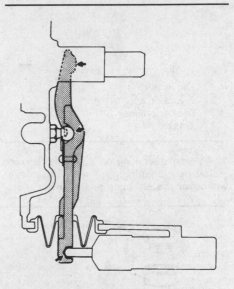

4.8 Using high-temperature grease, lubricate the release lever ball socket (where the ball stud seats into the underside of the lever), the ball stud itself, the contact surfaces on the lever tips that push against the release bearing and the release cylinder pushrod socket

alignment tool **(see illustration)**. Make sure it's installed properly (most replacement clutch plates will be marked "flywheel side" or something similar - if not marked, install the clutch disc with the damper springs or cushion toward the transaxle).

15   Install the pressure plate-to-flywheel bolts only finger tight, working around the pressure plate.

16   Center the clutch disc by ensuring the alignment tool is through the splined hub and into the recess in the crankshaft. Wiggle the tool up, down or side-to-side as needed to bottom the tool. Tighten the pressure plate-to-flywheel bolts a little at a time, working in a criss-cross pattern to prevent distortion of the cover. After all of the bolts are snug, tighten them to the torque listed in this Chapter's Specifications. Remove the alignment tool.

17   Using high-temperature grease, lubricate the inner groove of the release bearing (see Section 4). Also place grease on the release lever contact areas and the transaxle input shaft bearing retainer.

18   Install the clutch release bearing (see Section 4).

19   Install the transaxle, release cylinder and all components removed previously, tightening all fasteners to the proper torque specifications.

4   Clutch release bearing and lever - removal, inspection and installation

Warning: *Dust produced by clutch wear and deposited on clutch components is hazardous to your health. DO NOT blow it out with compressed air and DO NOT inhale it. DO NOT use gasoline or petroleum-based solvents to remove the dust. Brake system cleaner should be used to flush it into a drain pan.*

After the clutch components are wiped clean with a rag, dispose of the contaminated rags and cleaner in a labeled, covered container.

Removal

1   Disconnect the negative cable from the battery.

2   Remove the transaxle (see Chapter 7).

3   If you're working on a four-cylinder engine, pull the clutch release lever toward the release cylinder end to separate it from the ball stud, then remove the bearing from the lever.

4   If you're working on a 3.0L V6 engine, separate the release bearing from the lever. If you need to remove the lever from the bell housing, unscrew the pivot shaft lockbolt and remove the release fork pivot shaft. Remove the shaft springs, seals and the shaft.

Inspection

Refer to illustration 4.5

5   Hold the bearing by the outer race and rotate the inner race while applying pressure **(see illustration)**. If the bearing doesn't turn smoothly or if it's noisy, replace the bearing with a new one. Wipe the bearing with a clean rag and inspect it for damage, wear and cracks. Don't immerse the bearing in solvent - it's sealed for life and to do so would ruin it. Also check the release lever for cracks and bends.

6   If you're working on a 3.0L V6 engine, inspect the pivot bushings in the release lever for wear or damage. If necessary, press the old bushings out and press new ones in. Install new bushings whenever the old ones are removed.

Installation

Refer to illustrations 4.7 and 4.8

7   Fill the inner groove of the release bearing with high-temperature grease. Also apply a light coat of the same grease to the

transaxle input shaft splines and the front bearing retainer **(see illustration)**.

8   If you're working on a four-cylinder engine, lubricate the release lever ball socket, lever ends and release cylinder pushrod socket with high-temperature grease **(see illustration)**.

9   Attach the release bearing to the release lever.

10   Slide the release bearing onto the transaxle input shaft front bearing retainer while passing the end of the release lever through the opening in the clutch housing.

11   If you're working on a four-cylinder engine, push the clutch release lever onto the ball stud until it's firmly seated.

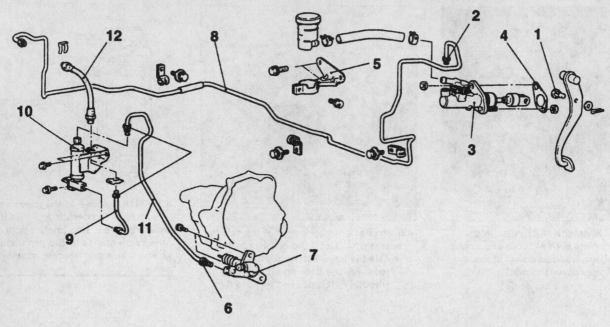

5.2 Typical clutch hydraulic release system (2.0L turbo shown)

1	Clevis pin	5	Reservoir bracket	9	Hydraulic line
2	Hydraulic line flare nut	6	Hydraulic line flare nut	10	Clutch damper
3	Master cylinder	7	Release cylinder	11	Hydraulic line
4	Gasket	8	Hydraulic line	12	Hydraulic hose

12   If you're working on a 3.0L V6 engine, install new bushings in the release lever whenever the old ones are removed. Position the release lever in the bell housing, then install the pivot shaft, seals and springs.

13   Apply a light coat of high-temperature grease to the face of the release bearing where it contacts the pressure plate diaphragm fingers.

14   The remainder of installation is the reverse of the removal procedure.

5   Clutch master cylinder - removal, overhaul and installation

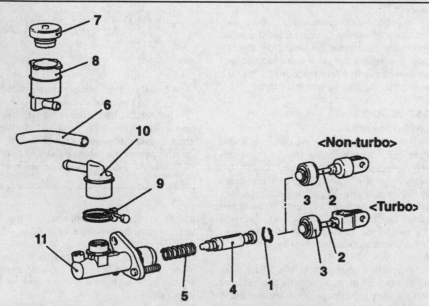

5.5 Typical clutch master cylinder - exploded view

1	Piston stop ring	6	Reservoir hose
2	Pushrod	7	Reservoir cap
3	Boot	8	Reservoir
4	Piston assembly (DO NOT disassemble)	9	Clamp
5	Return spring	10	Fluid hose fitting
		11	Master cylinder body

Note: *Before beginning this procedure, contact local parts stores and dealer service departments concerning the purchase of a rebuild kit or a new master cylinder. Availability and cost of the necessary parts may dictate whether the cylinder is rebuilt or replaced with a new one. If it's decided to rebuild the cylinder, inspect the bore as described in Step 9 before purchasing parts.*

Removal
Refer to illustration 5.2

1   Disconnect the negative cable from the battery.

2   Under the dashboard, remove the cotter pin and clevis pin and disconnect the pushrod clevis from the clutch pedal arm **(see illustration)**. Also remove the lower mounting nut from the cylinder.

3   Working in the engine compartment, disconnect the hydraulic line at the clutch master cylinder. If available, use a flare-nut wrench on the fitting to prevent the fitting from being rounded off. Have some rags handy to absorb any fluid lost as the line is removed. **Caution:**

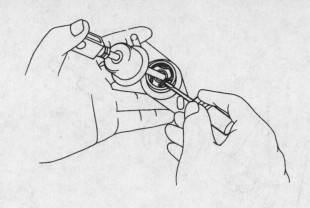

5.6 Pull back the dust cover on the pushrod and pry the snap-ring from its groove

5.8 To remove the piston assembly from the clutch master cylinder, grasp the cylinder with its open end facing down and tap it against a block of wood

Don't allow brake fluid to come into contact with paint, as it will damage the finish.

4   Remove the other nut that secures the master cylinder to the firewall. Remove the master cylinder, again being careful not to spill any of the fluid.

Overhaul

Refer to illustrations 5.5, 5.6, 5.8 and 5.13
Caution: *Do not attempt to disassemble the piston/spring/seal assembly. If any part is defective, you must replace the entire assembly; separate pieces aren't available.*

5   Remove the reservoir cap and drain all fluid from the master cylinder. Loosen the clamp that secures the reservoir to the master cylinder body **(see illustration)** and separate the reservoir from the body.

6   Pull back the dust cover on the pushrod and remove the snap-ring **(see illustration)**.

7   Remove the pushrod and boot from the cylinder.

8   Tap the master cylinder on a block of wood to eject the piston assembly from inside the bore **(see illustration)**.

9   Inspect the bore of the master cylinder for deep scratches, score marks and ridges. The surface must be smooth to the touch. If the bore isn't perfectly smooth, the master cylinder must be replaced with a new or factory rebuilt unit.

10   If you're rebuilding the master cylinder, use the new parts contained in the rebuild kit and follow any specific instructions which may have accompanied the rebuild kit. Wash all parts to be re-used with brake cleaner, denatured alcohol or clean brake fluid. DO NOT use petroleum-based solvents.

11   Lubricate the bore of the cylinder and the seals with plenty of fresh brake fluid.

12   Carefully guide the new piston assembly into the bore, being careful not to damage the seals. Make sure the spring end is installed first, with the pushrod end of the piston closest to the opening.

13   Apply a liberal amount of rubber grease to the contact surfaces between the push-

rod and the piston and between the pushrod and the boot **(see illustration)**. Position the pushrod in the bore, compress the spring and install a new snap-ring.

14   Install the fluid reservoir and tighten the reservoir clamp (the clamp screw should be positioned across the master cylinder body, not parallel with it).

Installation

15   Position the master cylinder on the firewall and install the upper mounting nut finger-tight.

16   Connect the hydraulic line to the master cylinder, moving the cylinder slightly as necessary to thread the fitting properly into the bore. Don't cross-thread the fitting.

17   Apply a light film of grease to the clevis pin and washer, then connect the pushrod to the clutch pedal lever with the clevis pin, washer and a new cotter pin.

18   Install the lower mounting nut, then tighten both mounting nuts and the hydraulic line fitting securely.

19   Fill the clutch master cylinder reservoir with the brake fluid listed in the Chapter 1 Specifications and bleed the clutch system (see Section 7).

20   Check and, if necessary, adjust the

clutch pedal height and freeplay (see Chapter 1). Connect the negative battery cable.

6   Clutch release cylinder - removal, overhaul and installation

Note: *Before beginning this procedure, contact local parts stores and dealer service departments concerning the purchase of a rebuild kit or a new release cylinder. Availability and cost of the necessary parts may dictate whether the cylinder is rebuilt or replaced with a new one. If it's decided to rebuild the cylinder, inspect the bore as described in Step 8 before purchasing parts.*

Removal

1   Disconnect the negative cable from the battery.

2   Raise the vehicle and support it securely on jackstands.

3   Disconnect the hydraulic line **(see illustration 5.2)** from the release cylinder. Plug the open fitting to prevent fluid loss and contamination. Have a small can and rags handy, as some fluid will be spilled as the line is removed. On models that use a banjo fitting,

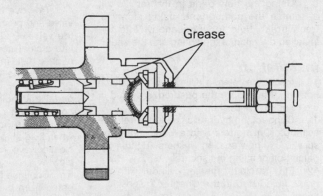

5.13 Apply a liberal amount of rubber grease to the contact surfaces between the pushrod and the piston assembly, and between the pushrod and the boot as shown

Grease

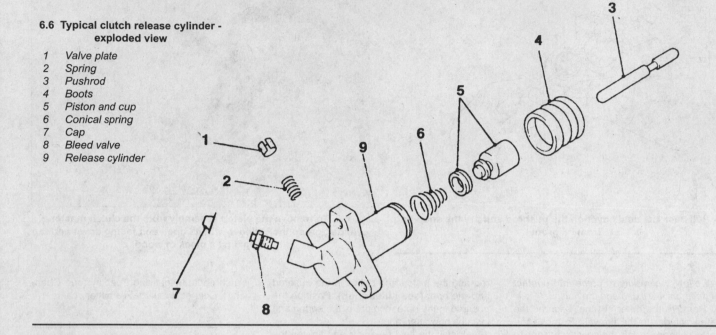

6.6 Typical clutch release cylinder - exploded view

1   Valve plate
2   Spring
3   Pushrod
4   Boots
5   Piston and cup
6   Conical spring
7   Cap
8   Bleed valve
9   Release cylinder

discard the sealing washers and be sure to use new ones upon installation.
4   Remove the release cylinder mounting bolts.
5   Remove the release cylinder.

Overhaul

Refer to illustration 6.6

6   Remove the pushrod and the boot **(see illustration)**.
7   Tap the cylinder on a block of wood to eject the piston and seal. Remove the spring from inside the cylinder. If the piston is stuck in the bore, you may have to use compressed air to pop it out. If you do so, wear goggles to protect your eyes and place a rag over the end of the release cylinder to prevent the piston from shooting out of the cylinder. Use only enough compressed air to ease the piston out of the bore.
8   Carefully inspect the bore of the cylinder. Check for deep scratches, score marks and ridges. The bore must be smooth to the touch. If any imperfections are found, the release cylinder must be replaced with a new one.
9   Using the new parts in the rebuild kit, assemble the components using plenty of fresh brake fluid for lubrication. Note the installed direction of the spring and the seal.

Installation

10   Install the release cylinder on the clutch housing. Make sure the pushrod is seated in the release fork pocket.
11   Connect the hydraulic line to the release cylinder. On models with a banjo fitting be sure to use new sealing washers. Tighten the banjo bolt or fitting nut securely.
12   Fill the clutch master cylinder with the brake fluid listed in the Chapter 1 Specifications.

13   Bleed the system (see Section 7).
14   Lower the vehicle and connect the negative battery cable.

7   Clutch hydraulic system - bleeding

1   The hydraulic system should be bled of all air whenever any part of the system has been removed or if the fluid level has been allowed to fall so low that air has been drawn into the master cylinder. The procedure is very similar to bleeding a brake system.
2   Fill the master cylinder with new brake fluid of the type listed in the Chapter 1 Specifications. **Caution:** *Do not re-use any of the fluid coming from the system during the bleeding operation or use fluid which has been inside an open container for an extended period of time.*
3   Raise the vehicle and place it securely on jackstands to gain access to the release cylinder, which is located on the front side of the clutch housing.
4   Remove the dust cap from the bleeder valve and push a length of plastic hose over the valve. Place the other end of the hose into a clear container with about two inches of brake fluid in it. The hose end must be submerged in the fluid.
5   Have an assistant depress the clutch pedal and hold it. Open the bleeder valve on the release cylinder, allowing fluid to flow through the hose. Close the bleeder valve when fluid stops flowing from the hose. Once closed, have your assistant release the pedal slowly.
6   Continue this process until all air is evacuated from the system, indicated by a full, solid stream of fluid being ejected from the

bleeder valve each time and no air bubbles in the hose or container. Keep a close watch on the fluid level inside the clutch master cylinder reservoir; if the level drops too low, air will be sucked back into the system and the process will have to be started all over again.
7   Install the dust cap and lower the vehicle. Check carefully for proper operation before placing the vehicle in normal service.

8   Clutch start switch - check and replacement

Refer to illustration 8.5

Check

1   Check the clutch pedal height and freeplay (see Chapter 1).
2   Verify that the engine will not start when the clutch pedal is released. Verify that the engine will start when the clutch pedal is depressed all the way.
3   If the clutch start switch doesn't perform as described, adjust and, if necessary, replace it.
4   Locate the switch and unplug the electrical connector.
5   Connect an ohmmeter to the terminals of the switch **(see illustration)**.
6   Depress and release the clutch pedal and watch the meter; it should alternate between continuity and no continuity.
7   If there is no change in the meter reading as the pedal is actuated, replace the switch.

Replacement

8   Unplug the electrical connector, loosen the locknut and unscrew the switch.
9   Installation is the reverse of removal. To

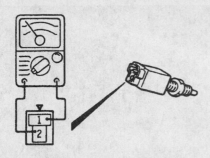

8.5 Connect an ohmmeter between the terminals to test continuity of the clutch switch

adjust the switch, fully depress the clutch pedal and screw the switch in or out of its bracket so there is 9/64-inch clearance between the pedal and the switch body. Tighten the lock-nut.

10   Verify again that the engine doesn't start when the clutch pedal is released, and does start when the pedal is depressed.

9   Driveaxles - general information and inspection

1   Power is transmitted from the transaxle to the front wheels and also (on 4WD models only) from the rear differential to the rear wheels through a pair of driveaxles. The inner end of each driveaxle is splined to the (front or rear) differential side gears. The outer ends of the driveaxles are splined to the axle hubs and locked in place by a large nut.

2   The inner ends of the driveaxles are equipped with sliding constant velocity joints which are capable of both angular and axial motion. Each inner joint assembly consists of a tripod-type bearing and a joint tulip (housing).

3   The outer joints are the ball-and-cage type capable of angular but not axial movement.

4   The boots should be inspected periodically for damage and leaking lubricant. Torn CV joint boots must be replaced immediately or the joints can be damaged. Boot replacement involves removal of the driveaxle (front driveaxle, see Section 10; rear driveaxle, see Section 12). **Note:** *Some auto parts stores carry "split" type replacement boots, which can be installed without removing the driveaxle from the vehicle. This may seem like a convenient alternative, but the CV joint(s) should be disassembled and cleaned to ensure the joint is free from contaminants such as moisture and dirt which will accelerate CV joint wear.* The most common symptom of worn or damaged CV joints, besides lubricant leaks, is a clicking noise in turns, a clunk when accelerating after coasting and vibration at highway speeds. To check for wear in the CV joints and driveaxle shafts, grasp each axle (one at a time) and rotate it in both directions while

10.4 Remove the cotter pin from the driveaxle/hub nut

10.6 Tap the driveaxle out of the hub with a hammer and soft metal punch; if the driveaxle is stuck, remove the brake disc and push the driveaxle out with a puller

holding the CV joint housings, feeling for play indicating worn splines or sloppy CV joints. Also check the driveaxle shafts for cracks, dents and distortion.

10   Driveaxle (front) - removal and installation

Removal
Refer to illustrations 10.4, 10.5, 10.6, 10.9, 10.10 and 10.11

1   Disconnect the cable from the negative terminal of the battery.

2   Set the parking brake. Loosen the front wheel lug nuts, raise the vehicle and support it securely on jackstands. Remove the wheel.

3   If the vehicle is equipped with ABS, unbolt the wheel speed sensor and remove it from the steering knuckle.

4   Remove the cotter pin from the driveaxle/hub nut **(see illustration)**.

5   Remove the driveaxle/hub nut and washer. To prevent the hub from turning,

10.5 To prevent the hub from turning when you're breaking loose the driveaxle/hub nut, wedge a prybar between two of the wheel studs and allow the prybar to rest against the ground or the floorpan of the vehicle

10.9 Pull out on the steering knuckle and detach the driveaxle from the hub

wedge a prybar between two of the wheel studs and allow the prybar to rest against the ground or the floor pan of the vehicle **(see illustration)**.

6   To loosen the driveaxle from the hub splines, tap the end of the driveaxle with a soft-faced hammer or a hammer and a soft metal drift **(see illustration)**. If the driveaxle is stuck in the hub splines and won't move, it may be necessary to remove the brake disc (see Chapter 9) and push it from the hub with a two-jaw puller.

7   Place a drain pan underneath the transaxle to catch any lubricant that leaks out when the driveaxle is removed.

8   Separate the suspension control arm(s) from the steering knuckle (see Chapter 10). Disconnect the steering tie-rod end from the steering knuckle. If you're working on a 1995 through 1999 model, remove the damper fork.

9   Pull out on the steering knuckle and detach the driveaxle from the hub **(see illustration)**.

10.10 If you're removing the right driveaxle from any model, or the left driveaxle from a 2WD model, carefully pry the inner CV joint out of the transaxle (if you're removing the left driveaxle on a 2000 or later 4WD model, refer to Section 11)

10   If you're removing the right driveaxle on any model, or the left driveaxle on a 2WD model, carefully pry the inner CV joint out of the transaxle **(see illustration)**. If you're removing the left driveaxle on a 2000 or later 4WD model, refer to the next Section; the driveaxle and the intermediate shaft must be removed as a single assembly, then separated.

11   Should it become necessary to move the vehicle while the driveaxle is out, place a large bolt with two large washers (one on each side of the hub) through the hub and tighten the nut securely **(see illustration)**.

Installation

12   Installation is the reverse of the removal procedure, but with the following additional points:

  a) *When installing the splined inner end of the driveaxle, push the driveaxle sharply inward to seat the retaining ring on the splined inner end of the CV joint into the groove in the bore of the differential side gear.*
  b) *Tighten the driveaxle/hub nut to the torque listed in this Chapter's Specifications, then install a new cotter pin.*
  c) *Install the wheel and lug nuts, lower the vehicle and tighten the lug nuts to the torque listed in the Chapter 1 Specifications.*
  d) *Check the transaxle lubricant and add, if necessary, to bring it to the proper level (see Chapter 1).*

11   Intermediate shaft - removal and installation

Refer to illustrations 11.2 and 11.4

1   Set the parking brake. Loosen the left front wheel lug nuts, raise the vehicle, place it securely on jackstands and remove the left

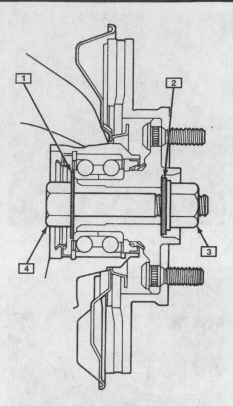

10.11 Moving the vehicle with a driveaxle removed may damage the hub bearings - if you must do so, first install a bolt and a pair of washers as shown here, and tighten them securely

1	Washer	3	Nut
2	Washer	4	Bolt

front wheel. Detach the outer end of the driveaxle from the hub following the procedure described in Section 10.

2   Remove the intermediate shaft bearing bracket bolts **(see illustration)**.

3   Before removing the shaft, position a drain pan underneath the transaxle and inspect the differential seal for evidence of leakage. If the seal is leaking, refer to Chapter 7A for the seal replacement procedure. Lightly tap the bearing bracket with a plastic hammer to free the intermediate shaft splines from the differential side gear and pull the shaft straight out of the side gear.

4   Check the intermediate shaft bearing for smooth operation. If it feels rough or sticky it should be replaced **(see illustration)**. Special tools are needed for disassembling the intermediate shaft/bearing bracket/CV joint housing assembly. Take it to a dealer service department or an automotive machine shop to have the bearing bracket, axleshaft and the left inner CV joint housing separated. You can, however, replace a CV joint boot without removing the CV joint housing from the bearing bracket (see Section 14).

5   Installation is the reverse of removal. Make sure you tighten the bearing bracket bolts to the torque listed in this Chapter's Specifications.

11.2 The intermediate shaft bearing bracket is fastened to the engine block with two bolts (arrows)

12   Driveaxle (rear) - removal and installation

Refer to illustration 12.2

1   Block the front wheels, loosen the rear wheel lug nuts, raise the vehicle and support it securely on jackstands. Remove the rear wheel.

2   If the vehicle is equipped with ABS, remove the wheel speed sensor **(see illustration)**. Remove the brake caliper, disc and parking brake assembly (rear disc brakes) or brake drum and shoes (rear drum brakes). On drum brake models, disconnect the brake hydraulic line (see Chapter 9).

3   Remove the cotter pin from the driveaxle/hub nut **(see illustration 10.4)**.

4   Remove the driveaxle/hub nut and washer. To prevent the hub from turning, wedge a prybar between two of the wheel studs and allow the prybar to rest against the ground or the floor pan of the vehicle **(see illustration 10.5)**.

5   Unbolt the shock absorber lower end, the trailing arm rear end and the lower arm outer end. Remove the nut and separate the toe control arm balljoint (see Chapter 10).

6   To loosen the driveaxle from the hub splines, tap the end of the driveaxle with a soft-faced hammer or a hammer and a soft metal drift **(see illustration 10.6)**. If the driveaxle is stuck in the hub splines and won't move, it may be necessary to push it from the hub with a two-jaw puller.

7   Place a drain pan under the rear differential to catch any lubricant that might spill over the seal lip when the driveaxle is removed. Inspect the seal for evidence of lubricant leaking past the side gear seal. If you see any signs of leakage, replace the seal (see Section 17) after removing the driveaxle.

8   Using a large screwdriver or prybar, pry the inner CV joint out of the differential side gear **(see illustration 10.10)**.

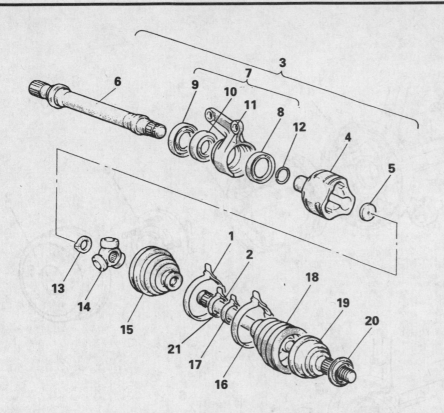

11.4 Intermediate shaft and left
front driveaxle (2000 and later
4WD models) - exploded view

1   Inner CV joint large boot clamp
2   Inner CV joint small boot clamp
3   Inner CV joint, bearing
    bracket and intermediate shaft
    assembly
4   Inner CV joint housing
5   Seal plate
6   Intermediate shaft
7   Bearing bracket assembly
8   Outer dust seal
9   Inner dust seal
10 Support bearing
11 Bearing bracket
12 Circlip
13 Snap-ring
14 Spider (tripod) assembly
15 Inner CV joint boot
16 Outer CV joint large boot clamp
17 Outer CV joint small boot clamp
18 Outer CV joint boot
19 Outer CV joint assembly
20 Dust cover
21 Axleshaft (available only as an
    integral part of outer CV joint
    assembly)

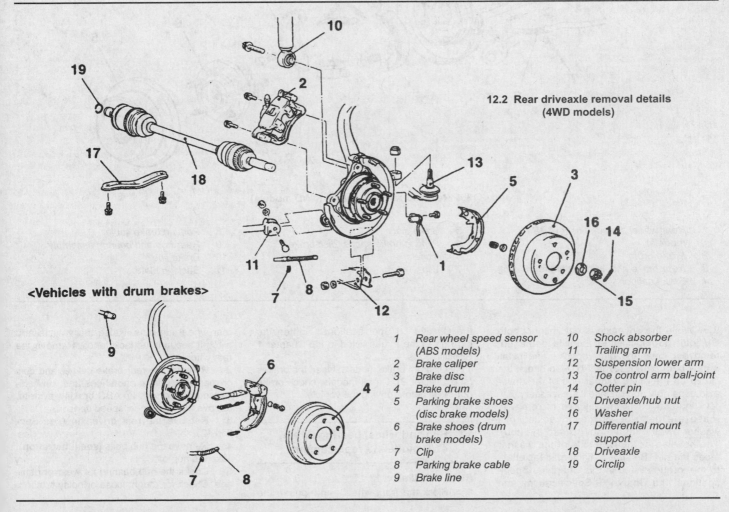

12.2 Rear driveaxle removal details
(4WD models)

<Vehicles with drum brakes>

1	Rear wheel speed sensor	10	Shock absorber
	(ABS models)	11	Trailing arm
2	Brake caliper	12	Suspension lower arm
3	Brake disc	13	Toe control arm ball-joint
4	Brake drum	14	Cotter pin
5	Parking brake shoes	15	Driveaxle/hub nut
	(disc brake models)	16	Washer
6	Brake shoes (drum	17	Differential mount
	brake models)		support
7	Clip	18	Driveaxle
8	Parking brake cable	19	Circlip
9	Brake line		

<Vehicles with drum brakes>

<Vehicles with disc brakes>

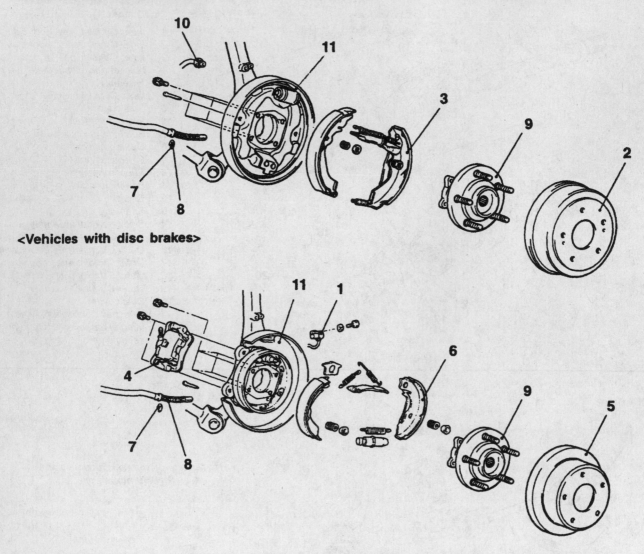

13.4 Rear hub removal details (4WD models)

1	Rear wheel speed sensor (ABS models)	
2	Brake drum	
3	Rear brake shoes (drum brake models)	
4	Brake caliper	
5	Brake disc	
6	Parking brake shoes (disc brake models)	
7	Clip	
8	Parking brake cable	
9	Rear hub and bearing assembly	
10	Brake line	
11	Backing plate	

9   While the driveaxle is out, inspect both CV joint boots; if either boot is damaged, remove it, clean the joint, repack it and install a new boot (see Section 14). Also check the circlip on the splined inner end of the drive-axle assembly and replace it if necessary.

10   Installation is the reverse of removal. Place the flat side of the driveaxle nut's washer away from the nut (toward the hub). The beveled or rounded side of the washer faces the nut. Be sure to tighten all fasteners to the torques listed in this Chapter's Speci-fications, the Chapter 9 Specifications and

the Chapter 10 Specifications. Tighten the lug nuts to the torque listed in the Chapter 1 Specifications.

11   On drum brake models, bleed the brakes (see Chapter 9). On all models, check brake operation before driving the vehicle.

13   Hub and wheel bearings (rear, 4WD models) - replacement

Refer to illustration 13.4

1   Block the front wheels and loosen the

rear wheel lug nuts. Raise the vehicle and place it securely on jackstands. Remove the rear wheel.

2   Remove the rear brake caliper and disc or rear brake drum and shoes and, on vehi-cles equipped with an ABS braking system, remove the rear wheel speed sensor.

3   Remove the rear driveaxle (see Sec-tion 12).

4   Remove the hub bolts **(see illustration)**. Take the hub off.

5   Check the hub bearing for wear or dam-age. Check for rough, loose or noisy rotation.

14.3a Lift the tabs on all the boot clamps with a screwdriver, then open the clamps

14.3b Remove the boot from the inner CV joint and slide the tripod from the joint housing

14.4 Use a center-punch to place marks (arrows) on the tripod and the driveaxle to ensure that they are reassembled properly

14.5 Remove the snap-ring with a pair of snap-ring pliers

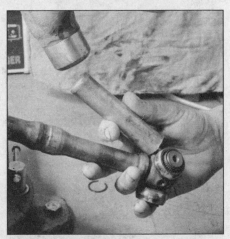

14.6 Drive the tripod joint from the driveaxle with a brass punch and hammer (be careful not to damage the bearing surfaces or the splines on the shaft)

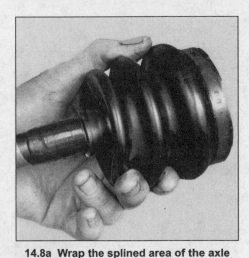

14.8a Wrap the splined area of the axle with tape to prevent damage to the boot when installing it

The bearing can't be replaced separately, so if the bearing is bad or any other problems are found, replace the hub as an assembly. **Note:** *Bearing rotation starting torque and bearing end play can be measured using special tools if the hub's condition is uncertain. If the hub is not obviously bad, have it checked by a dealer service department or machine shop before replacing the hub.*

6   Installation is the reverse of removal. Tighten the hub bolts to the torque listed in this Chapter's Specifications. Tighten the lug nuts to the torque listed in the Chapter 1 Specifications.

14   Driveaxle boot replacement

Note: *If the CV joint boots must be replaced, explore all options before beginning the job. Complete rebuilt driveaxles are available on an exchange basis, which eliminates much time and work. Whichever route you choose*

to take, check on the cost and availability of parts before disassembling the vehicle.
1   Remove the driveaxle from the vehicle, referring to the appropriate Section.
2   Mount the driveaxle in a vise with wood lined jaws (to prevent damage to the axle-shaft). Check for smooth operation throughout the full range of motion for each CV joint. If a boot is torn, the recommended procedure is to disassemble the joint, clean the components and inspect for damage due to loss of lubrication and possible contamination by foreign matter. **Note:** *Outer joints can't be disassembled, but they can be cleaned, checked and packed with new grease.*

Inner CV joint
Disassembly
Refer to illustrations 14.3a, 14.3b, 14.4, 14.5 and 14.6
3   After removing the boot clamps **(see illustration)**, pull the boot back from the inner

joint and slide the tulip from the tripod **(see illustration)**.
4   Use a center punch to mark the tripod and driveaxle to ensure that they are reassembled properly **(see illustration)**.
5   Remove the tripod joint snap-ring with a pair of snap-ring pliers **(see illustration)**.
6   Use a hammer and a brass punch to drive the tripod joint from the driveaxle **(see illustration)**.

Check
7   Clean all components with solvent to remove the grease, and check for cracks, pitting, scoring and other signs of wear.

Reassembly
Refer to illustrations 14.8a through 14.8e, 14.9, 14.10a, 14.10b and 14.10c
8   Wrap the splines on the axleshaft with tape to prevent damaging the boot **(see illustration)**. Slide the clamps and boot onto the axleshaft, then place the tripod on the shaft

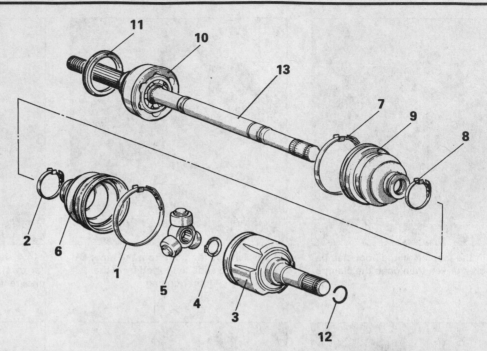

14.8b An exploded view of the front driveaxle assembly (left and right driveaxles on 2WD models; right driveaxle only on 4WD models)

1   Boot clamp
2   Boot clamp
3   Inner CV joint housing
4   Snap-ring
5   Spider (tripod) assembly
6   Inner CV joint boot
7   Boot clamp
8   Boot clamp
9   Outer CV joint boot
10 Outer CV joint assembly
11 Dust cover
12 Circlip
13 Axleshaft (available only as an integral part of outer CV joint)

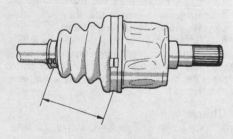

14.8c Install the tripod with the recessed portion of the splines facing the axleshaft

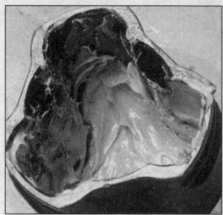

14.8d Place grease at the bottom of the CV joint housing

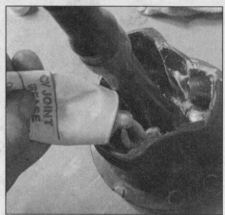

14.8e Insert the tripod into the tulip, followed by the rest of the grease

14.9 Before tightening down the boot clamps, make sure you adjust the inner driveaxle boot dimension as shown in accordance with the dimensions listed in this Chapter's Specifications (this dimension is critical for maintaining the correct pressure inside sliding CV joints)

(see illustrations). Apply grease to the tripod assembly and inside the tulip (see illustrations).

9   Slide the boot into place, making sure both ends seat in their grooves. Adjust the length of the CV joint (see illustration) to the dimension listed in this Chapter's Specifications.

10   Equalize the pressure in the boot, then tighten and secure the boot clamps (see illustrations).

Outer CV joint

Disassembly

11   Remove the inner CV joint following Steps 3 through 6.

12   Remove the CV joint boot clamps, using the technique described in Step 3. Slide the boot off the axleshaft.

Inspection

Refer to illustration 14.14

13   Thoroughly wash the inner and outer CV joints in clean solvent and blow them dry with compressed air, if available. **Warning:** *Wear eye protection.* **Note:** *Because the outer joint can't be disassembled, it is difficult to wash away all the old grease and to rid the bearing of solvent once it's clean. But it's imperative the job be done thoroughly, so take your time and do it right.*

14   Bend the CV joint housing at an angle to the driveaxle to expose the bearings, inner race and cage (see illustration). Inspect the bearing surfaces for signs of wear. If the bearings are damaged or worn, replace the drive-axle/CV joint assembly.

Reassembly

15   Slide the new outer boot and boot clamps. Be sure to wrap the splines on the axleshaft with tape so the boot isn't damaged (see illustration 14.8a). Fill the joint with the specified amount of CV joint grease (usually included with the boot kit), then slide the boot into position. **Note:** *Pack the joint with as*

14.10a Equalize the pressure inside the boot by inserting a small, dull screwdriver between the boot and the outer race

14.10b To install the new boot clamps, bend the tang down . . .

14.10c . . . then bend the tabs over to hold it in place

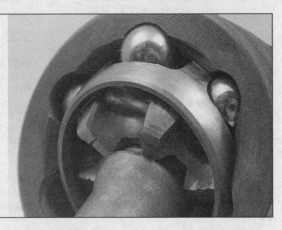

14.14 After the old grease has been rinsed away and the solvent blown out with compressed air, rotate the joint housing through its full range of motion and inspect the bearing surfaces for wear and damage - if any of the balls, the race or the cage look damaged, replace the driveaxle and joint assembly

much grease as it will hold and put the rest into the boot.

16   Install the boot clamps and tighten them **(see illustrations 14.10a, 14.10b and 14.10c)**.

17   Install the inner CV joint and boot following Steps 8 through 10.

15   Driveshaft (4WD models) - removal and installation

Refer to illustrations 15.2, 15.3, 15.4 and 15.5
Caution: *It would be a good idea to have a helper for this procedure. Trying to support the driveshaft and remove the support bearing bolts and yoke-to-flange bolts by yourself could result in damage to the driveshaft components.*

1   Raise the rear of the vehicle and support it securely on jackstands. Block the front tires to keep the vehicle from rolling.

2   The driveshaft is composed of three pieces: A front shaft from the transmission to the forward support bearing, a middle section from the forward support bearing to the rear support bearing; and a rear shaft from the support bearing to the rear differential **(see illustration)**.

1	Self-locking nut
2	Insulator
3	Spacer
4	Rear part of driveshaft
5	Rear U-joint and companion flange yoke
6	Rear differential companion flange
7	Rear support bearing assembly
8	Löbro joint and boot
9	Center part of driveshaft
10	Forward support bearing assembly
11	Front part of driveshaft
12	Forward U-joint and slip-yoke

15.2 Driveshaft (4WD models) - exploded view

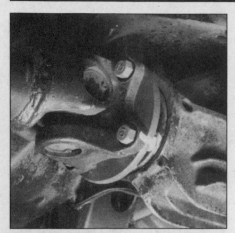

15.3 Start driveshaft removal by marking the U-joint companion flange yoke (at the rear end of the driveshaft) to the differential companion flange, then remove the nuts and bolts

15.4 With an assistant supporting the driveshaft, remove the mounting nuts (arrows) from the forward support bearing assemblies

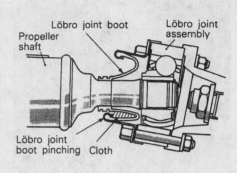

15.5 When removing the driveshaft, keep it straight! If the driveshaft sections hinge at the "Löbro" joint (in front of the rear support bearing assembly), the joint boot could be torn

3   Start by marking the relationship of the flange yoke (at the rear end of the driveshaft) to the differential companion flange with paint or a center punch **(see illustration)**, then remove the nuts and bolts from the flanges.

4   Next, with an assistant supporting the driveshaft, remove the mounting nuts, insulators and spacers from the support bearing assemblies **(see illustration)**. The number of spacers used with each nut varies, so draw a sketch of each support bearing assembly and write down the number of spacers used at each location for reference during reassembly. The spacers must be returned to their original locations when the support bearings are installed.

5   Lower the rear end of the driveshaft assembly and carefully withdraw the front end of the driveshaft from the transfer extension housing. Try to keep the three driveshaft sections straight as you lower the driveshaft to

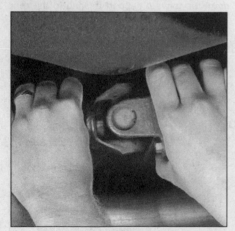

16.2 To check a U-joint for excessive freeplay, hold the yoke with one hand and try to turn the driveshaft with the other like this; there shouldn't be any play in the joint - if there is, you need to rebuild or replace it

the ground. **Caution:** *Allowing the rear end of the driveshaft to droop in relation to the center section could pinch and possibly tear the boot protecting the "Löbro" joint at the rear support bearing assembly* **(see illustration)**. Plug the extension housing to prevent fluid loss (as long as the rear end of the vehicle is level with, or higher than, the front end, fluid shouldn't leak from the transfer case).

6   Check the support bearing assemblies, the Löbro joint and boot, and the U-joints for wear (see Section 16) and repair as necessary.

7   Installation of the driveshaft is basically the reverse of removal. However, the following points should be noted: Return all spacers to their original locations at each support bearing. Hand tighten the support bearing nuts initially, then, after the flange yoke joint-to-companion flange bolts and nuts are installed, verify that the support bearing brackets are at a right angle to the driveshaft. Once they're correctly aligned, tighten the support bearing mounting nuts to the torque listed in this Chapter's Specifications. Check the transfer case oil level and add oil if necessary (see Chapter 1).

---

16   Driveshaft (4WD models) - check and overhaul

Universal joints
Check
Refer to illustration 16.2

1   Wear in the universal joints is characterized by vibration in the transmission, noise during acceleration, and in extreme cases of lack of lubrication, metallic squeaking and grating sounds as the bearings disintegrate.

2   It's unnecessary to remove the driveshaft to determine whether the needle bearings are worn: Try to turn each section of the drive-

shaft with one hand while holding the U-joint yoke with the other hand **(see illustration)**. Any relative play or movement between any of the three sections of the driveshaft assembly and their respective U-joints is evidence of considerable wear. If you find signs of wear, you'll have to remove the driveshaft (see Section 15) to replace the U-joint(s).

3   With the driveshaft assembly removed, you can check the U-joints by holding each part of the driveshaft in one hand and turning the yoke or flange with the other. If there's axial freeplay at any U-joint, rebuild or replace it.

Replacement
Refer to illustrations 16.6a, 16.6b, 16.8a and 16.8b

4   Remove the driveshaft, if you haven't already done so (see Section 15). Mark the relationship of the corresponding yokes of each U-joint you're planning to disassemble.

5   Using a socket extension or similar tool and hammer, tap lightly on the bearing outer races of the universal joint to relieve pressure on the snap-rings.

6   Using snap-ring pliers, remove the snap-rings from their grooves **(see illustrations)**.

7   To remove the bearings from the yokes, you will need two sockets. One should be large enough to fit into the yoke where the snap-rings were installed and the other should have an inside diameter just large enough for the bearings to fit into when they are forced out of the yoke.

8   Mount the universal joint in a vise with the large socket on one side of the yoke and the small socket on the other side, pushing against the bearing. Carefully tighten the vise until the bearing is pushed out of the yoke and into the large socket **(see illustration)**. If it cannot be pushed all the way out, remove the universal joint from the vise and use pliers to finish removing the bearing **(see illustration)**.

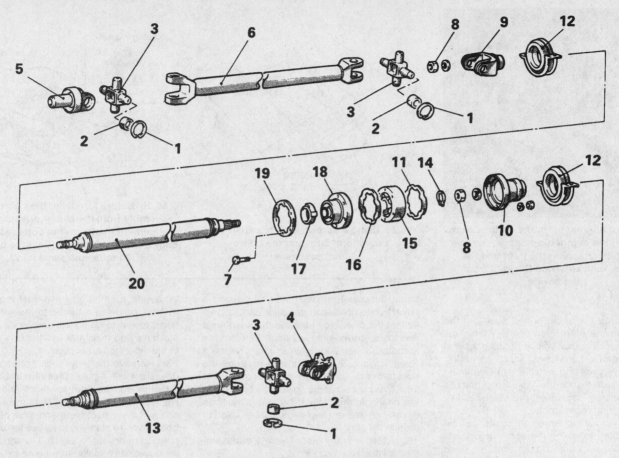

16.6a An exploded view of the driveshaft assembly

1	U-joint spider snap-ring	11	Löbro joint rubber gasket
2	U-joint spider bearing	12	Support bearing assembly
3	U-joint spider	13	Rear driveshaft
4	Flange yoke	14	Löbro joint-to-center driveshaft snap-ring
5	Sleeve yoke	15	Löbro joint assembly
6	Front driveshaft	16	Löbro joint rubber gasket
7	Boot-to-Löbro joint bolt	17	Löbro joint boot clamp
8	Companion flange-to-rear driveshaft nut	18	Löbro joint boot
9	Center yoke	19	Löbro joint washer
10	Companion flange	20	Center driveshaft

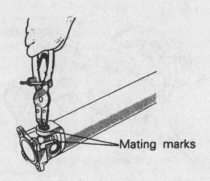

16.6b Remove the snap-rings from their grooves with snap-ring pliers

16.8a Use a vise, a large socket (left) and a small socket (right) to press the bearing out of the U-joint

16.8b You may need to use pliers to finish removing the bearing

16.22 Put alignment marks on the Löbro joint and the companion flange, remove the bolts attaching the joint and the flange, then separate the joint from the flange

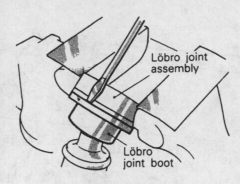

16.25 Using a screwdriver, pry apart the Löbro joint boot and the Löbro joint assembly

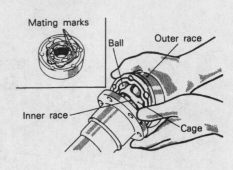

16.26 Before removing the Löbro joint assembly from the center driveshaft, put alignment marks on the outer race, the cage and the inner race (if you're planning to reuse the same joint)

9   Reverse the sockets and push out the bearing on the other side of the yoke. This time, the small socket will be pushing against the cross-shaped universal joint spider end.

10   Before pressing out the two remaining bearings, make sure the yokes are marked so they can be installed in the same relative position during reassembly.

11   The remaining universal joints can be disassembled following the same procedure. Be sure to mark all components for each universal joint so they can be kept together and reassembled in the proper position. It's a good idea to replace one U-joint at a time so you don't mix up any parts.

12   Check the spider journals for scoring, needle roller impressions, rust and pitting. Replace it if any of the above conditions exist.

13   Check the sleeve yoke, center yoke and flange yoke for wear, damage and cracks; if damage or wear are evident, replace that yoke. Check the yokes on both ends of the front driveshaft and on the rear end of the rear driveshaft for wear, damage and cracks; if any of them are damaged or worn, replace that part of the driveshaft.

14   When reassembling the universal joints, use a new spider, new needle bearings, new dust seals and new snap-rings (the U-joint kit includes these parts).

15   Before reassembly, pack each grease cavity in the spiders with a small amount of grease. Also, apply a thin coat of grease to the new needle bearing rollers and the roller contact areas on the spiders.

16   Apply a thin coat of grease to the dust seal lips and install the bearings and spider into the yoke using the vise and sockets that were used to remove the old bearings. Work slowly and be very careful not to damage the bearings as they are being pressed into the yokes.

17   Press in the new bearings until they're flush with or below the snap-ring grooves in the bore of the yoke. Install snap-rings of the same thickness on each side and, using a feeler gauge of the appropriate thickness, verify that the clearance between the snap-rings and the spider/bearing assembly is within the standard dimension listed in this Chapter's Specifications. If the clearance exceeds the standard limit, use thicker snap-rings.

18   Make sure that the spider moves freely in the bearings, then check the axial play. If it's excessive, thicker snap-rings must be used to reduce the play.

19   Assemble any other U-joints disassembled as described above.

20   Install the driveshaft (see Section 15).

Löbro joint

Disassembly and inspection

Refer to illustrations 16.22, 16.25, 16.26 and 16.28

21   Remove the driveshaft, if you haven't already done so (see Section 15).

22   Put mating marks on the Löbro joint and the companion flange **(see illustration)**.

23   Remove the bolts and nuts that attach the Löbro joint boot to the companion flange **(see illustration 16.22)**.

24   Separate the Löbro joint from the companion flange.

25   Using a screwdriver, pry apart the Löbro joint boot and the Löbro joint assembly **(see illustration)**.

26   Before removing the Löbro joint assembly from the center driveshaft, place alignment marks on the outer race, the cage and the inner race **(see illustration)**.

27   Remove the outer race and balls. If you're planning to reuse the same Löbro joint, the balls must be returned to the same locations from which they're removed during disassembly. The easiest way to do this is to put each ball in a plastic sandwich bag or other small container and label it. For example, you could number the bags one through six and label the first ball removed as "Ball No. 1, first ball to right of alignment mark," then simply remove the balls in a clockwise fashion, putting the second ball in the No. 2 bag, etc.

Whatever method you use, just make sure that the balls are returned to the same locations; failure to do so will accelerate wear on the balls and their grooved bearing surfaces in the inner and outer races.

28   Remove the inner race from the center driveshaft with a puller **(see illustration)**.

29   Inspect the boot for tears and cracks. Replace it if it's damaged (a boot kit is available): Cut the boot band and slide off the old boot. If you're planning to re-use the boot - but need to remove it to switch it to another center driveshaft - make sure you don't damage the boot when removing the old boot clamp (you'll have to use a new boot clamp when you install the old boot on the new driveshaft section).

30   Inspect the splines on the driveshaft for wear or damage. Inspect the ball grooves in the inner and outer races, the cage and the balls themselves, for uneven wear, damage and rust. If anything is worn or damaged, replace the Löbro joint (a joint kit, which includes the boot kit mentioned above, is available).

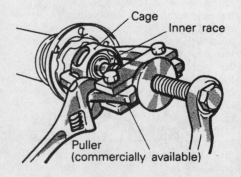

16.28 You'll probably need a small puller to remove the inner race from the center driveshaft splines

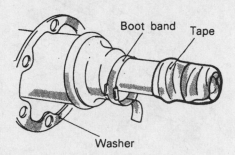

16.31 Slide the washer and new boot band onto the center driveshaft and wrap the splined end of the shaft with tape to protect the new boot from damage during installation

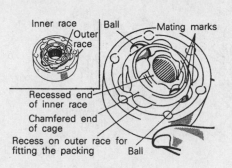

16.34 Put the inner race inside the cage and align the mating marks you made prior to disassembly, then insert two of the balls into the grooves at 12 o'clock and 6 o'clock

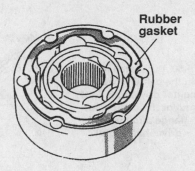

16.37 Apply a thin coating of repair kit grease to the new rubber gasket and install the gasket as shown

Reassembly

Refer to illustrations 16.31, 16.34, 16.37, 16.41 and 16.43

31   Slide the washer and new boot band onto the center driveshaft and wrap the splined end of the shaft with tape to protect the new boot from damage during installation **(see illustration)**.

32   Slide the Löbro joint boot onto the end of the shaft and remove the adhesive tape.

33   Apply a thin coat of the grease included with the repair kit to the grooves of the inner and outer races.

34   Put the inner race inside the cage and align the mating marks you made prior to disassembly **(see illustration)**. Insert two of the balls into the grooves at 12 o'clock and 6 o'clock (grooves directly opposite each other) to hold this alignment. Make sure the balls are returned to the same grooves from which they were removed in Step 27.

35   Install the inner race, cage and two balls into the outer race. Make sure the recessed end of the inner race (where the snap-ring fits), the recessed end of the outer race (where the rubber gasket fits) and the chamfered end of the cage are all on the same side. Now install the rest of the balls in the same positions from which they were removed. Verify that the outer race rotates smoothly on the inner race.

36   Apply about two ounces of the grease from the repair kit to the Löbro joint assembly. Make sure you work the grease down into the joint so that it coats all the bearing surfaces.

37   Apply a thin coating of repair kit grease to the new rubber gasket and install the gasket as shown **(see illustration)**.

38   Make sure that the concave side of the outer race is facing toward the boot and the holes in the outer race are aligned with the holes in the boot flange, then drive the Löbro assembly onto the center shaft splines with a hammer and a socket about the same size as the inner race.

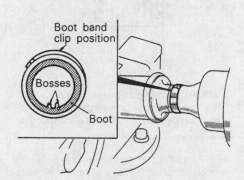

16.41 Position the boot clamp so that the clip is opposite the bosses in the boot provided for ventilation; if there's any excess grease on the bosses, be sure to wipe it off - grease obstructs the vent passages

39   Secure the inner race with a new snap-ring.

40   Insert the bolts through the boot flange and rotate the boot until the bolts are aligned with the holes in the outer race. Install the bolts but don't install the nuts yet.

41   Install a new boot clamp. Position the clamp so that the clip is opposite the bosses in the boot provided for ventilation **(see illustration)**. If there's any excess grease on the bosses, be sure to wipe it off - grease obstructs the vent passages.

42   Verify that the Löbro joint operates smoothly.

43   Apply a thin coat of repair kit grease and install the other rubber gasket to the other face of the outer race **(see illustration)**.

44   Align the mating marks you made on the outer race and the companion flange, install the nuts and tighten them securely.

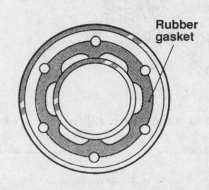

16.43 Apply a thin coat of repair kit grease and install the other rubber gasket to the other face of the outer race

Support bearing assemblies

Refer to illustrations 16.50, 16.52, 16.53 and 16.54

45   Raise the vehicle and support it on jackstands.

46   To check either support bearing, rotate the driveshaft and listen carefully to the bearing. It should rotate smoothly and silently. If you hear a grating, grinding metallic sound from either support bearing, replace it. Also inspect the rubber bushing around each bearing for cracks or other deterioration. If the bushing is damaged or worn, replace the bearing.

47   Remove the driveshaft, if you haven't already done so (see Section 15).

48   If you're replacing the forward support bearing assembly, you'll need to disconnect the front and center parts of the driveshaft by disassembling the U-joint that connects them (see Steps 4 through 9); if you're replacing the rear support bearing assembly, disconnect the center and rear parts of the driveshaft by disassembling the Löbro joint that connects them.

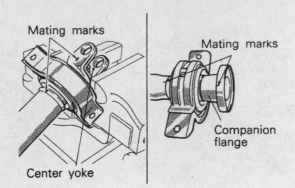

16.50 Put match marks on the center yoke and center driveshaft (left) and/or the companion flange and the rear driveshaft (right)

16.52 Put alignment marks on the forward support bearing assembly and the center driveshaft, or on the rear support bearing assembly and the rear driveshaft, then remove the support bearing bracket assembly

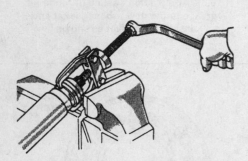

16.53 Remove either support bearing with a small puller

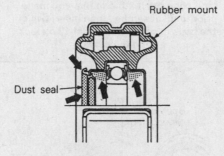

16.54 Apply multi-purpose grease to the front and rear grease grooves in the support bearing and to the dust seal lip

17   Rear differential oil seals - replacement (4WD models)

Pinion seal

1   Replacing the pinion oil seal affects the drive pinion turning torque. Setting this specification requires changing the drive pinion shims or spacers and can cause the pinion gear to break if it's done wrong. For this reason, replacement of the pinion seal should be done by a dealer service department or other qualified repair shop.

Differential side gear seals
Refer to illustrations 17.4 and 17.5
2   Raise the rear of the vehicle and support it on jackstands.
3   Remove the driveaxle (see Section 12).
4   Use a large screwdriver or prybar to pry the seal out **(see illustration)**.
5   Use a seal driver, a large socket or section of pipe and a hammer to install the new seal **(see illustration)**.

49   To remove the forward support bearing, place the center yoke in a vise and break the nut loose; to remove the rear support bearing, place the rear driveshaft in a vise and break the nut loose (don't vise up the companion flange - tightening the vise enough to hold the shaft will damage the flange). **Caution**: *Tightening the vise too much will damage the driveshaft tube.*
50   Before pulling the center yoke or the companion flange off the driveshaft, be sure to put alignment marks on the yoke and shaft or on the companion flange and shaft **(see illustration)**.
51   Pull off the yoke or flange. If the yoke/flange sticks, use a small puller to get it off.
52   Put alignment marks on the forward support bearing assembly and the center driveshaft, or on the rear support bearing assembly and the rear driveshaft, then remove the support bearing bracket assembly **(see illustration)**.
53   Remove either support bearing with a small puller **(see illustration)**.
54   Apply multi-purpose grease to the front and rear grease grooves in the support bearing and to the dust seal lip **(see illustration)**.
55   Install the bearing into the rubber mounting groove on the support bearing bracket. The bearing dust seal should face toward the side of the support bearing bracket mating mark you made before removing the bearing bracket.

56   Press the bearing onto the center and/or rear driveshaft(s). If you're using the old bearing bracket, make sure it's oriented the same as it was when you took it off - the mating mark on the bracket should face toward the mating mark on the shaft.
57   Reassemble the driveshaft by reattaching the U-joint (center driveshaft) or the companion flange (rear driveshaft).
58   Install the driveshaft (see Section 15).
59   Remove the jackstands and lower the vehicle.

17.4 Pry the side gear seal out of the rear differential . . .

17.5 . . . and use a large socket or section of pipe and a hammer to install the new side gear seal into the rear differential

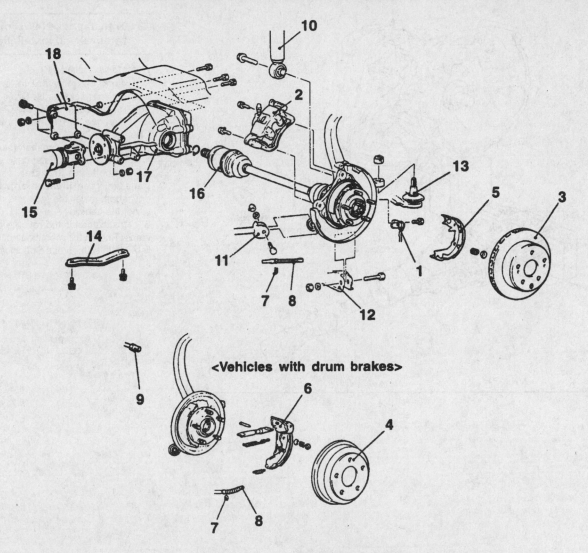

18.5 Differential removal details (4WD models)

1	Rear wheel speed sensor (ABS models)	10	Shock absorber
2	Brake caliper	11	Trailing arm
3	Brake disc	12	Suspension lower arm
4	Brake drum	13	Toe control arm balljoint
5	Parking brake shoes (disc brake models)	14	Differential mount support
6	Brake shoes (drum brake models)	15	Driveshaft
7	Clip	16	Driveaxle
8	Parking brake cable	17	Differential
9	Brake line	18	Differential mounting bracket

6   The rest of installation is the reverse of removal. Be sure to apply grease to the lip of the seal before installing the driveaxle.

18   Differential carrier (4WD models) - removal and installation

Refer to illustration 18.5

1   Loosen the rear wheel lug nuts. Raise the rear of the vehicle and support it securely on jackstands. Remove the rear wheels.

2   Drain the differential lubricant (see Chapter 1).

3   Remove the rear driveaxles (see Section 12).

3   Disconnect the rear end of the driveshaft from the differential carrier (see Section 15) and hang the driveshaft from the exhaust pipe with a piece of wire to prevent it from bending.

4   Place a transaxle jack or a large floor jack directly underneath the differential carrier and raise the jack head until it's supporting the carrier.

5   Remove the differential mounting bolts **(see illustration)**.

6   Carefully lower the differential carrier and support member as a single assembly and slide them out from underneath the vehicle.

7   Remove the two bolts that attach the differential support member to the rear differential.

8   Installation is the reverse of removal. Tighten the differential nuts and bolts to the torques listed in this Chapter's Specifications. Tighten the lug nuts to the torque listed in the Chapter 1 Specifications.

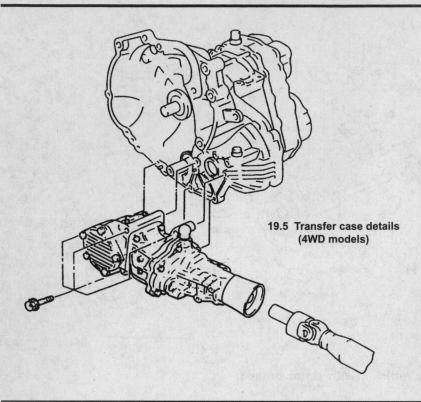

19 Transfer case (4WD models) - removal and installation

Refer to illustration 19.5

1   Jack up the vehicle and support it securely on jackstands. Drain the transaxle and transfer case fluids (see Chapter 1).

2   Remove the front exhaust pipe (see Chapter 4).

3   Remove the driveshaft (see Section 15).

4   Support the transfer case with a jack.

5   Unbolt the transfer case from the transaxle **(see illustration)**. Slip it off the driveshaft, lower the jack and remove it from under the vehicle.

6   Installation is the reverse of the removal steps. Tighten the mounting bolts to the torque listed in this Chapter's Specifications.

19.5 Transfer case details (4WD models)

Chapter 9   Brakes

Contents

Specifications

General

Brake fluid type	See Chapter 1
Brake pedal	
Height (between pedal and floorboard)	6-57/64 to 7 inches
Freeplay (amount of pedal movement	
before resistance is met)	1/8 to 5/16 inch
Reserve distance (between depressed pedal	
and floorboard)	3-1/2 inches
Brake light switch-to-brake pedal stopper	0.020 to 0.040 inch
Power brake booster pushrod-to-master cylinder piston clearance	0.0 to 0.010 inch

Disc brakes

Minimum pad lining thickness	See Chapter 1
Disc minimum thickness	Cast into disc
Disc runout limit	
1999 and earlier	0.0031 inch
2000 and later	
Front	0.002 inch
Rear	0.003 inch
Maximum disc thickness variation (parallelism)	0.0006 inch

Drum brakes

Shoe lining minimum thickness	See Chapter 1
Maximum drum diameter	Cast into drum

Torque specifications

Ft-lbs (unless otherwise indicated)

Caliper mounting bolts (guide pin/lock pin)	
Front	
2000 and earlier	54
2001 and later	
Four-cylinder engines	54
V6 engine	28
Rear	
1999 and earlier	54
2000 and later	32

Torque specifications (continued)

Ft-lbs (unless otherwise indicated)

Note: *One foot-pound (ft-lb) of torque is equivalent to 12 inch-pounds (in-lbs) of torque. Torque values below approximately 15 ft-lbs are expressed in inch-pounds, since most foot-pound torque wrenches are not accurate at these smaller values.*

Caliper mounting bracket bolts	
Front	
1999 and earlier	65
2000 and later	74
Rear	
1999 and earlier	36 to 43
2000	45
2001 and later	
Bolts with washers	41
Flange-head bolts	44
Front brake hose banjo fitting bolts	
1995 through 1999	11
2000 and later	22
Master cylinder-to-brake booster nuts	
1995 through 1999	84 inch-lbs
2000 and later	
With traction control	87 inch-lbs
Without traction control	113 inch-lbs
Power brake booster mounting nuts	
1995 through 1999	120 inch-lbs
2000 and later	122 inch-lbs

1   General information

The vehicles covered by this manual are equipped with hydraulically operated front disc brakes, either of two-piston caliper or single-piston caliper design. Single-piston rear disc brakes are used on some models, while others are equipped with rear drum brakes. Both the front and rear disc brakes automatically compensate for disc and pad wear: As the pads wear down, the pistons gradually protrude farther from the calipers, but don't retract as far, automatically compensating for the thinner pads. Rear drum brakes have automatic adjusters which compensate for wear of the brake shoes.

Hydraulic system

The hydraulic system consists of two separate circuits that are diagonally split (one circuit operates the left front and right rear brakes, while the other circuit operates the right front and left rear brakes). The master cylinder has separate reservoirs for the two circuits, and, in the event of a leak or failure in one hydraulic circuit, the other circuit will remain operative. A dual proportioning valve on the firewall provides brake balance between the front and rear brakes.

Power brake booster

The power brake booster, which is mounted on the firewall, utilizes engine manifold vacuum and atmospheric pressure to provide assistance to the hydraulically operated brakes.

Parking brake

The parking brake operates the rear brakes only, through cable actuation. It's activated by a lever mounted in the center console. The parking brake on rear disc brake models uses brake shoes and small brake drums integral with the rear brake discs.

Service

After completing any operation involving disassembly of any part of the brake system, always test drive the vehicle to check for proper braking performance before resuming normal driving. When testing the brakes, perform the tests on a clean, dry, flat surface. Conditions other than these can lead to inaccurate test results.

Test the brakes at various speeds with both light and heavy pedal pressure. The vehicle should stop evenly without pulling to one side or the other. Avoid locking the brakes, because this slides the tires and diminishes braking efficiency and control of the vehicle.

Tires, vehicle load and wheel alignment are factors which also affect braking performance.

2   Anti-lock Brake System (ABS) - general information

The anti-lock brake system is designed to maintain vehicle steerability, directional stability and optimum deceleration under severe braking conditions on most road surfaces. It does so by monitoring the rotational speed of each wheel and controlling the brake line pressure to each wheel during braking. This prevents the wheels from locking up.

The ABS system has three main components - the wheel speed sensors, the electronic control unit (ECU) and the hydraulic unit. Four wheel speed sensors - one at each wheel - send a variable voltage signal to the control unit, which monitors these signals, compares them to its program and determines whether a wheel is about to lock up. When a wheel is about to lock up, the control unit signals the hydraulic unit to reduce hydraulic pressure (or not increase it further) at that wheel's brake caliper. Pressure modulation is handled by electrically-operated solenoid valves.

If a problem develops within the system, an "ABS" warning light will glow on the dashboard. Sometimes, a visual inspection of the ABS system can help you locate the problem. Carefully inspect the ABS wiring harness. Pay particularly close attention to the harness and connections near each wheel. Look for signs of chafing and other damage caused by incorrectly routed wires. If a wheel sensor harness is damaged, the sensor must be replaced. **Warning:** *Do NOT try to repair an ABS wiring harness. The ABS system is sensitive to even the smallest changes in resistance. Repairing the harness could alter resistance values and cause the system to malfunction. If the ABS wiring harness is damaged in any way, it must be replaced.* **Caution:** *Make sure the ignition is turned off before unplugging or reattaching any electrical connections.*

Diagnosis and repair

If a dashboard warning light comes on and stays on while the vehicle is in operation, the ABS system requires attention. Although special electronic ABS diagnostic testing tools are necessary to properly diagnose the system, you can perform a few preliminary checks before taking the vehicle to a dealer service department.

a) *Check the brake fluid level in the reservoir.*

b) *Verify that the computer electrical connectors are securely connected.*

c) *Check the electrical connectors at the hydraulic control unit.*

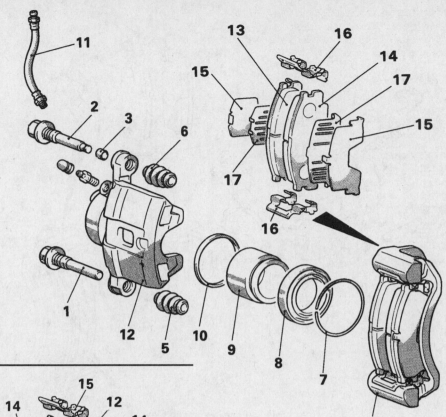

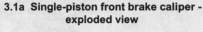

3.1a Single-piston front brake caliper - exploded view

1. Guide pin
2. Lock pin
3. Bushing
4. Torque plate (caliper mounting bracket)
5. Guide pin boot
6. Lock pin boot
7. Boot ring
8. Piston boot
9. Piston
10. Piston seal
11. Brake hose
12. Caliper body
13. Inner brake pad
14. Outer brake pad
15. Pad shim (if applicable)
16. Anti-rattle clip
17. Inner pad shim

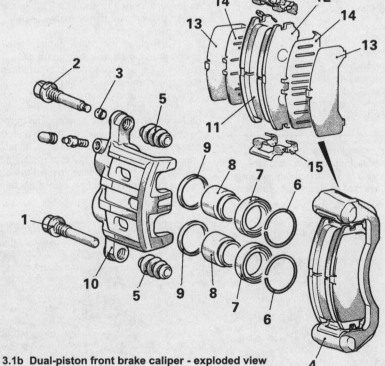

3.1b Dual-piston front brake caliper - exploded view

1	Guide pin	8	Piston
2	Lock pin	9	Piston seal
3	Bushing	10	Caliper body
4	Torque plate (caliper mounting bracket)	11	Inner brake pad
5	Guide pin boot (below); lock pin boot (above)	12	Outer brake pad
		13	Pad shim
6	Boot ring	14	Inner pad shim
7	Piston boot	15	Anti-rattle clip

d) Check the fuses.

e) Follow the wiring harness to each wheel and verify that all connections are secure and that the wiring is undamaged.

If the above preliminary checks do not rectify the problem, the vehicle should be diagnosed by a dealer service department. Due to the complex nature of this system, all actual repair work must be done by a dealer service department.

3   Disc brake pads - replacement

Refer to illustrations 3.1a, 3.1b, 3.1c, 3.5, 3.6, 3.7a through 3.7o and 3.10

Warning: *Disc brake pads must be replaced on both front or rear wheels at the same time - never replace the pads on only one wheel. Also, the dust created by the brake system is harmful to your health. Never blow it out with compressed air and don't inhale any of it. An approved filtering mask should be worn when working on the brakes. Do not, under any circumstances, use petroleum-based solvents to clean brake parts. Use brake system cleaner only!*

1   All disc brake calipers - front or rear, dual-piston or single-piston - are of basically the same design and pad replacement is the same for all. Pad shims differ in location and number **(see illustrations)**.

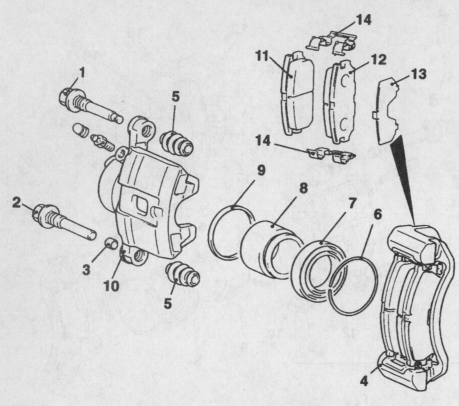

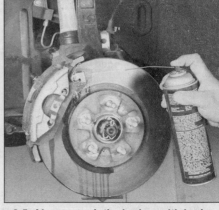

3.5 Always wash the brakes with brake system cleaner before working on them

3.1c Rear brake caliper - exploded view

1	Guide pin	7	Piston boot
2	Lock pin	8	Piston
3	Bushing	9	Piston seal
4	Torque plate (caliper mounting bracket)	10	Caliper body
5	Guide pin boot (below); lock pin boot (above)	11	Inner brake pad
		12	Outer brake pad
6	Boot ring	13	Pad shim
		14	Anti-rattle clip

4   Remove the wheels. Work on one brake assembly at a time, using the assembled brake for reference if necessary.

5   Position a drain pan under the brake assembly and clean the caliper and surrounding area with brake system cleaner **(see illustration)**.

6   Push the piston back into its bore using a C-clamp **(see illustration)**. As the piston(s) is depressed to the bottom of the caliper bore, the fluid level in the master cylinder will rise as the brake fluid is displaced. Make sure it doesn't overflow. If necessary, siphon off some more of the fluid.

7   To replace the brake pads, follow the accompanying photos, beginning with **illustration 3.7a**. Be sure to stay in order and read the caption under each illustration.

8   While the pads are removed, inspect the caliper for brake fluid leaks and ruptures of the piston dust boot. Replace the caliper if necessary (see Section 4). Also inspect the brake disc carefully (see Section 5). If machining is necessary, follow the information in that Section to remove the disc. Inspect the brake hoses for damage and replace if necessary (see Section 11).

2   Remove the cap from the brake fluid reservoir. Unless the reservoir is near empty, use a syringe or equivalent to siphon approximately two-thirds of the fluid from the master cylinder reservoir and discard it. **Warning:** *Never siphon brake fluid by mouth!*

3   Loosen the wheel lug nuts, raise the end of the vehicle you're working on and support it securely on jackstands. Block the wheels that remain on the ground.

3.6 Push the piston(s) back into the caliper bore with a large C-clamp

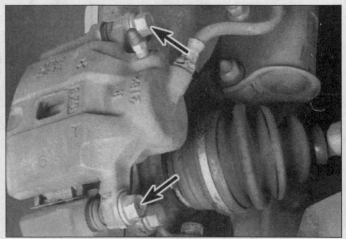

3.7a Remove the caliper guide pin (lower arrow) - it's only necessary to remove the lock pin (upper arrow) if you're removing the caliper

3.7b Swing the caliper up like this . . .

3.7c . . . and support it in this position with a piece of wire

3.7d Remove the inner pad and shim(s)

3.7e Remove the outer pad . . .

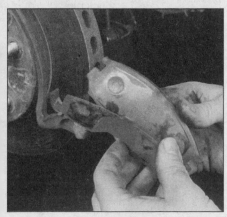

3.7f . . . and pull off the anti-squeal shim(s)

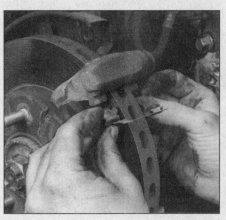

3.7g Remove the upper anti-rattle clip . . .

3.7h . . . and the lower anti-rattle clip, paying close attention to how they're installed in the torque plate

3.7i Remove the dust boots from the torque plate (removed for clarity), inspect them for cracks and tears, and replace as necessary

3.7j Install the upper anti-rattle clip . . .

3.7k . . . and the lower anti-rattle clip in the torque plate - make sure both are fully seated

3.7l Apply anti-squeal compound (available at auto parts stores - follow label instructions) to the back of the brake pad and install the anti-squeal shim(s)

3.7m Lubricate the guide pin with multi-purpose grease before installing it

3.7n Install the inner pad . . .

9   Before installing the caliper guide pin boots, clean and check them for corrosion and damage. If they're significantly corroded or damaged, replace them.

10   If you removed both the guide pin and the lock pin (all except 2001 and later 3.0L V6 engine models), be sure to reinstall them in the correct locations **(see illustration)**.

Tighten the guide pin and lock pin (all except 2001 and later 3.0L V6 engine models) or the caliper guide pin bolt (2001 and later 3.0L V6 engine models) to the torque listed in this Chapter's Specifications.

11   Repeat the procedure on the opposite wheel, then install the wheels and lug nuts, lower the vehicle and tighten the lug nuts.

12   Add the appropriate brake fluid to the reservoir until it's full (see Chapter 1).

13   Pump the brake pedal a few times to bring the pads into contact with the disc. Check the level of the brake fluid, adding some if necessary.

14   Check the operation of the brakes carefully before placing the vehicle into normal

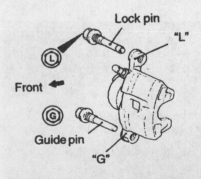

3.7o . . . and the outer pad into the torque plate - make sure both pads are fully seated, then swing the caliper down into place, install the guide pin and tighten it to the torque listed in this Chapter's Specifications

3.10 If you removed the guide pin and lock pin (all except 2001 and later 3.0L V6 engines), install them in the correct locations by referring to the letters stamped in the ends of the pins. Note: *On rear calipers the guide pin is at the top and the lock pin is at the bottom*

5.3 The brake pads on this vehicle were obviously neglected - they wore down to the rivets and cut deep grooves into the disc (wear this severe means the disc must be replaced)

5.4a Use a dial indicator to measure disc runout - if the reading exceeds the maximum allowable runout limit, the disc will have to be machined or replaced

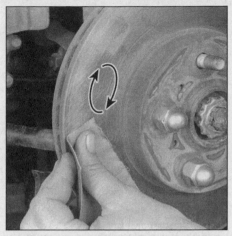

5.4b Using a swirling motion, remove the glaze from the disc surface with sandpaper or emery cloth

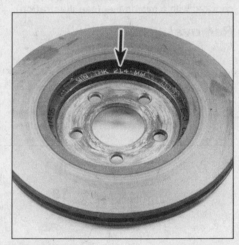

5.5a The minimum wear dimension is cast into the back side of the disc (typical)

service. Try to avoid heavy brake application until the brakes have been applied lightly several times to seat the pads.

4 Disc brake caliper - removal and installation

Warning: *Dust created by the brake system is harmful to your health. Never blow it out with compressed air and don't inhale any of it. An approved filtering mask should be worn when working on the brakes. Do not, under any circumstances, use petroleum-based solvents to clean brake parts. Use brake system cleaner only!*
Note: *If caliper replacement is required (usually because of fluid leakage), explore all options before beginning the job. New and factory rebuilt calipers are available on an exchange basis, which makes this job quite easy. Always replace the calipers in pairs - never replace just one of them.*

Removal

1   Loosen the wheel lug nuts, raise the end of the vehicle you're working on and support it securely on jackstands. Block the wheels that remain on the ground.
2   Remove the wheels.
3   On front calipers, unscrew the banjo bolt from the caliper and detach the hose. On rear calipers, disconnect the metal line from the hose, then unscrew the hose from the caliper (see Section 11). Place the end of the hose in a plastic bag and secure it with a rubber band to reduce brake fluid loss and prevent the entry of dirt. **Note:** *If you're removing the caliper just for access to other components, don't disconnect the hose.*
4   Remove the caliper (see Section 3 - it's part of the brake pad replacement procedure). Clean the caliper assembly with brake system cleaner.

5   Be sure to check the pads and replace them if necessary (see Section 3).

Installation

6   Install the brake pads and caliper (see Section 3). Tighten the guide pin and the lock pin to the torque listed in this Chapter's Specifications.
7   If you disconnected the brake hose, reconnect it, using new sealing washers on each side of the banjo bolt.
8   Bleed the brake system (see Section 12). Make sure there are no leaks from the hose connections. Test the brakes carefully before returning the vehicle to normal service.

5 Brake disc - inspection, removal and installation

Note: *This procedure applies to both front and rear brake discs.*

Inspection

Refer to illustrations 5.3, 5.4a, 5.4b, 5.5a and 5.5b

1   Loosen the wheel lug nuts, raise the vehicle and support it securely on jackstands. Remove the wheel and reinstall the lug nuts to hold the disc in place (washers may be required). If the rear brake disc is being worked on, release the parking brake.
2   Remove the brake caliper (see Section 3) but don't disconnect the brake hose from the caliper, or you'll have to bleed the brakes when everything is reassembled. After removing the caliper bolts, suspend the caliper out of the way with a piece of wire **(see illustration 3.7c)**.
3   Visually inspect the disc surface for score marks and other damage. Light scratches and shallow grooves are normal after use and may not always be detrimental to brake operation, but deep scoring requires disc removal and

refinishing by an automotive machine shop. Be sure to check both sides of the disc **(see illustration)**. If pulsating has been noticed during application of the brakes, suspect disc runout.
4   To check disc runout, place a dial indicator at a point about 1/2-inch from the outer edge of the disc **(see illustration)**. Set the indicator to zero and turn the disc. The indicator reading should not exceed the specified allowable runout limit. If it does, the disc should be refinished by an automotive machine shop. **Note:** *The discs should be resurfaced regardless of the dial indicator reading, as this will impart a smooth finish and ensure a perfectly flat surface, eliminating any brake pedal pulsation or other undesirable symptoms related to questionable discs. At the very least, if you elect not to have the discs resurfaced, remove the glaze from the surface with emery cloth using a swirling motion* **(see illustration)**.
5   It's absolutely critical that the disc not be machined to a thickness under the specified minimum allowable thickness. The minimum thickness is cast into the inside of the disc

5.5b Use a micrometer to measure disc thickness

5.6a Caliper (torque plate) mounting bracket bolts (front shown, rear similar)

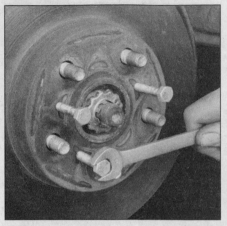

5.6b To free a stuck disc, thread bolts of the appropriate size into the holes provided in the disc, then tighten them alternately a little at a time until the disc is free

(see illustration). The disc thickness can be checked with a micrometer (see illustration).

Removal

Refer to illustrations 5.6a and 5.6b

6   Remove the caliper mounting bracket (see illustration). Remove the lug nuts which were put on to hold the disc in place and remove the disc from the hub. If the disc is stuck to the hub and won't come off, thread bolts into the holes provided and tighten them.

Alternate between the bolts, turning them 1/4-turn at a time, until the disc is free (see illustration).

Installation

7   Place the disc in position over the wheel studs.
8   Install the caliper and pads (see Section 3). Tighten the torque plate bolts to the torque listed in this Chapter's Specifications.
9   Install the wheel, lower the vehicle to the

ground and tighten the lug nuts.
10   Pump the brake pedal a few times to bring the brake pads into contact with the disc. Bleeding won't be necessary unless the brake hose was disconnected from the caliper. Check the operation of the brakes carefully before driving the vehicle.

---

6   Drum brake shoes - replacement

Refer to illustrations 6.2, 6.9, 6.11, 6.12a and 6.12b
Warning: *Drum brake shoes must be replaced on both wheels at the same time - never replace the shoes on only one wheel. Also, the dust created by the brake system is*

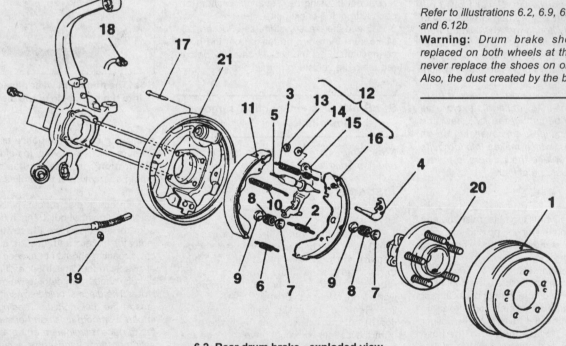

6.2 Rear drum brake - exploded view

1	Brake drum	8	Hold-down spring	15	Parking brake lever
2	Lever return spring	9	Hold-down cup	16	Brake shoe
3	Shoe-to-lever spring	10	Shoe-to-shoe spring	17	Hold-down pin
4	Adjuster lever	11	Brake shoe	18	Brake line
5	Automatic adjuster	12	Brake shoe and adjuster components	19	Snap-ring
6	Anchor spring	13	Retainer	20	Rear hub and bearing
7	Hold-down cup	14	Wave washer	21	Brake backing plate

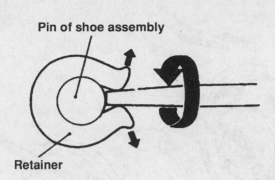

6.9 Spread the retainer ends just far enough to slip it off the pin

6.11 The maximum allowable diameter is stamped into the drum (typical)

harmful to your health. Never blow it out with compressed air and don't inhale any of it. An approved filtering mask should be worn when working on the brakes. Do not, under any circumstances, use petroleum-based solvents to clean brake parts. Use brake system cleaner only!

1   Loosen the rear wheel lug nuts, raise the rear end of the vehicle and support it securely on jackstands. Block the front wheels to keep the vehicle from rolling. Release the parking brake and remove the rear wheels.

2   Remove the brake drum. If the drum won't come off, the brake shoes must be retracted from their fully adjusted position. Insert a screwdriver through the adjuster hole in the brake backing plate and turn the adjuster wheel to retract the shoes (see illustration).

3   Once the drum is removed, clean the brake assembly with brake system cleaner.

4   Using locking pliers, unhook the lever return spring from the parking brake lever and brake shoe (see illustration 6.2).

5   Unhook and remove the shoe-to-lever spring.

6   Disengage the adjuster lever and remove the adjuster assembly from between the brake shoes.

7   Grasp one of the shoe hold-down cups with pliers and push it toward the brake backing plate to compress the hold-down spring. Twist the cup 1/4-turn to align the slot in the hold-down pin with the cup, then release the spring pressure (the pin will pass through the cup slot) and take off the cup, spring and second cup. Repeat this with the cup and spring on the other brake shoe.

8   Take the shoes off the backing plate. Disengage the parking brake lever from the cable.

9   Pry the retainer on the parking brake lever open just far enough to remove it, then remove the wave washer and parking brake lever from the brake shoe (see illustration).

10   Check all parts for wear and damage, paying special attention to metal-to-metal contact points. Replace worn or damaged

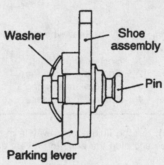

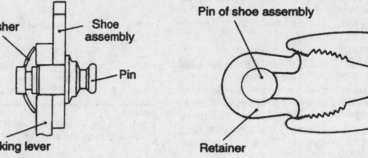

6.12a Install the parking brake lever and wave washer on the brake shoe . . .

6.12b . . . and secure them with the retainer

parts. **Note:** *If the vehicle has high mileage, it's a good idea to replace all of the springs as well as any parts that have visible problems.*

11   Check the brake drum for score marks, cracks, deep scratches and hard spots, which will appear as small discolored areas. If the hard spots cannot be removed with emery cloth or if any of the other conditions are seen, the drum must be resurfaced by an automotive machine shop. **Note:** *Professionals recommend resurfacing the drum whenever a brake job is performed. Resurfacing will correct out-of-roundness in the drums as well as removing visible problems. If the drums are so worn that they can't be resurfaced without exceeding the maximum allowable diameter stamped into the drum* (see illustration), *then new ones will be required. At the very least, if you don't have the drums resurfaced, remove the glazing from the surface with emery cloth or sandpaper using a swirling motion.*

12   Attach the parking brake lever to the new brake shoe and install the wave washer (see illustration). Place the retainer in the pin groove and secure it with pliers (see illustration).

13   Apply a small amount of high-temperature brake grease to the friction points of the backing plate, adjuster assembly and brake shoes (see illustration 6.2).

14   Reverse the removal steps to install the brake shoes. Expand the shoes, using the adjuster screw, until the drum will just fit over them.

15   Now, working through the backing plate, turn the adjuster screw wheel until the shoes drag on the drum when the drum is turned. Finally, back off the adjuster screw wheel so the shoes don't drag. Depress the brake pedal firmly several times, then rotate the drum to ensure that the brakes are not dragging. If they are, back off the star wheel a little more.

16   Install the wheel and lug nuts. Lower the vehicle and tighten the lug nuts.

17   Start the engine, pump the brake pedal and operate the parking brake lever several times to actuate the automatic adjusters.

18   Carefully test brake operation before driving the vehicle in traffic.

7   Drum brake wheel cylinder - inspection, removal and installation

Inspection

Refer to illustrations 7.2a and 7.2b

1   Remove the brake drum (see Section 6).

2   Carefully pull back the lip of the rubber

7.2a To check for wheel cylinder leakage, use a small screwdriver to pry the boot away from the cylinder

cup on each end of the wheel cylinder **(see illustrations)**. If brake fluid runs out, the wheel cylinder must be replaced.

Removal

3   Remove the brake shoes (see Section 6).
4   Disconnect the brake line from the wheel cylinder with a flare nut wrench **(see illustration 7.2b)**. Don't bend the brake line away from the wheel cylinder; just unscrew the flare nut until it's completely disengaged from the wheel cylinder.
5   Unbolt the wheel cylinder from the backing plate, take it off and remove the gasket.

Installation

6   Installation is the reverse of the removal steps. Use a new gasket and tighten the bolts to the torque listed in this Chapter's Specifications.
7   Bleed the brakes (see Section 12).

8   Master cylinder - removal and installation

Removal

Refer to illustration 8.3

1   The master cylinder, which is located in the engine compartment, is mounted on the power brake booster. On 1995 through 1999 models the remote reservoir is mounted on the firewall, next to the booster. On 2000 and later models the reservoir is mounted directly on the master cylinder.
2   Remove as much fluid as possible from the reservoir with a syringe.
3   If the vehicle has a remote reservoir, place rags under the fittings and prepare caps or plastic bags to cover the ends of the lines once they're disconnected. **Caution:** *Brake fluid will damage paint. Cover all body parts and be careful not to spill fluid during this procedure.* Loosen the clamps that attach the brake hoses to the reservoir **(see illustra-**

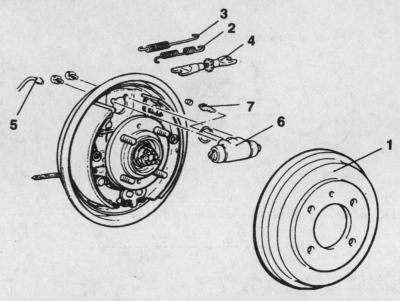

7.2b Rear wheel cylinder installation details (drum brake models)

1	Brake drum	5	Brake line
2	Shoe-to-lever spring	6	Wheel cylinder
3	Shoe-to-shoe spring	7	Bleed valve
4	Automatic adjuster		

tion). Pull the fluid hoses away from the reservoir and plug the ends to prevent contamination.
4   Disconnect the fluid lines from the master cylinder with a flare nut wrench.

5   Remove the nuts attaching the master cylinder to the power booster **(see illustration 8.3)** and pull the master cylinder off the studs. Again, be careful not to spill the fluid as this is done.

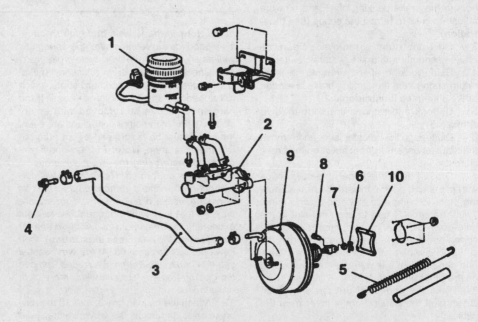

8.3 Typical master cylinder and brake booster mounting details

1	Reservoir (remote reservoir models)	6	Clevis pin clip
2	Master cylinder	7	Washer
3	Vacuum hose and check valve	8	Clevis pin
4	Hose fitting	9	Brake booster
5	Brake pedal return spring	10	Gasket

8.7 The best way to bleed air from the master cylinder before installing it on the vehicle is with a pair of bleeder tubes that direct brake fluid into the reservoir during bleeding

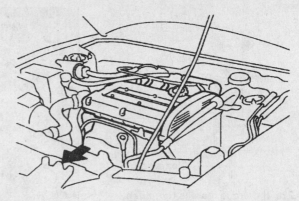

9.14 On 2.0L turbo models, the engine must be shifted forward to remove the brake booster

Installation

Refer to illustration 8.7

6   Bench bleed the master cylinder before installing it. Mount the master cylinder in a vise, with the jaws of the vise clamping on the mounting flange.

7   Attach a pair of master cylinder bleeder tubes to the outlet ports of the master cylinder **(see illustration)**.

8   Fill the reservoir with brake fluid of the recommended type (see Chapter 1).

9   Slowly push the pistons into the master cylinder (a large Phillips screwdriver can be used for this) - air will be expelled from the pressure chambers and into the reservoir. Because the tubes are submerged in fluid, air can't be drawn back into the master cylinder when you release the pistons.

10   Repeat the procedure until no more air bubbles are present.

11   Remove the bleed tubes, one at a time, and install plugs in the open ports to prevent fluid leakage and air from entering. Install the reservoir cap.

12   Install the master cylinder over the studs on the power brake booster and tighten the nuts only finger-tight at this time. Connect the reservoir hoses to the inlet fittings and install the clamps.

13   Thread the brake line fittings into the master cylinder. Since the master cylinder is still a bit loose, it can be moved slightly so the fittings thread in easily. Don't strip the threads as the fittings are tightened.

14   Tighten the mounting nuts and the brake line fittings.

15   Fill the master cylinder reservoir with fluid, then bleed the master cylinder and the brake system (see Section 12). To bleed the master cylinder on the vehicle, have an assistant depress the brake pedal and hold it down. Loosen the fitting to allow air and fluid to escape. Tighten the fitting, then allow your assistant to return the pedal to its rest position. Repeat this procedure on both fittings until the fluid is free of air bubbles.

16   Re-check the brake fluid level, then check the operation of the brake system carefully before driving the vehicle.

9   Power brake booster - check, removal and installation

Operating check

1   Depress the brake pedal several times with the engine off and make sure there's no change in the pedal reserve distance.

2   Depress the pedal and start the engine. If the pedal goes down slightly, operation is normal.

Airtightness check

3   Start the engine and turn it off after one or two minutes. Depress the brake pedal slowly several times. If the pedal depresses less each time, the booster is airtight.

4   Depress the brake pedal while the engine is running, then stop the engine with the pedal depressed. If there's no change in the pedal reserve travel after holding the pedal for 30 seconds, the booster is airtight.

Removal

5   Power brake booster units shouldn't be disassembled. They require special tools not normally found in most automotive repair stations or shops. They're fairly complex and, because of their critical relationship to brake performance, should be replaced with a new or rebuilt one.

6   Due to limited access, booster removal on 2.0L turbo models is a complicated procedure that requires shifting the engine forward. Read the procedure through before starting.

2.0L non-turbo models

7   Remove the clutch fluid reservoir bracket (see Chapter 8).

8   Remove the battery (see Chapter 5).

9   Unbolt the engine compartment relay box (see Chapter 12).

10   Unbolt the windshield washer tank. Proceed to Step 15.

2.0L turbo models

Refer to illustration 9.14

11   Support the engine with a hoist or jack.

Remove the engine mounting bracket and lower crossmember (see Chapter 2B).

12   Unbolt the air conditioning compressor and its high pressure hose clamp (see Chapter 3). Place the compressor out of the way without disconnecting any refrigerant lines.

13   Unbolt the power steering pressure hose, tube and return tube (see Chapter 10).

14   Shift the engine forward to provide removal access for the brake booster **(see illustration)**.

All models

Refer to illustration 9.17

15   Remove the brake master cylinder (see Section 8).

16   Locate the pushrod clevis connecting the booster to the brake pedal **(see illustration 8.3)**. It's accessible from inside the vehicle, under the dash on the driver's side.

17   Remove the clevis pin retaining clip with pliers and pull out the pin **(see illustration 8.3)**.

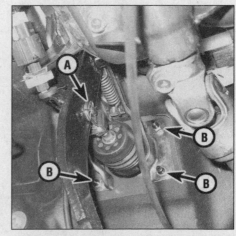

9.17 Remove the clevis pin retaining clip (A) and pull out the pin, then remove the booster-to-firewall nuts (B, fourth nut not visible)

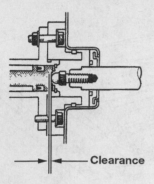

9.22a If there is there is too much clearance between the booster pushrod and the master cylinder piston, there will be excessive brake pedal travel, if there is interference between the two, the brakes may drag

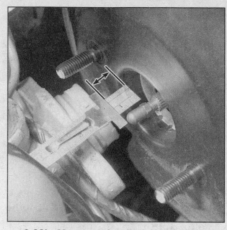

9.22b Measure the distance that the pushrod protrudes from the brake booster at the master cylinder mounting surface (including the gasket, *if* one is used)

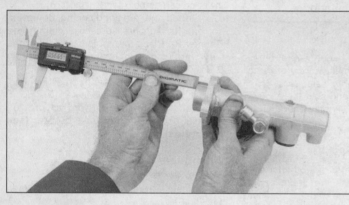

9.22c Measure the distance from the mounting flange to the end of the master cylinder

18   Disconnect the hose leading from the engine to the booster. Be careful not to damage the hose when removing it from the booster fitting.

19   Remove the four nuts holding the brake booster to the firewall **(see illustration 9.17)**. You may need a light to see them.

20   Slide the booster straight out from the firewall until the studs clear the holes.

Installation

Refer to illustrations 9.22a, 9.22b, 9.22c, 9.22d and 9.22e

21   Installation procedures are basically the reverse of removal. Tighten the clevis locknut securely (if loosened) and the booster mounting nuts to the torque listed in this Chapter's Specifications. **Note:** *Apply a film of multi-purpose grease to the clevis pin before installing it.*

22   If a new power brake booster unit is being installed, check the pushrod clearance **(see illustration)** as follows:

a)   *Measure the distance that the pushrod protrudes from the master cylinder mounting surface on the front of the power brake booster, including the gasket, if one is used. Write down this measurement* **(see illustration)**. *This is "dimension A."*

b)   *Measure the distance from the mounting flange to the end of the master cylinder* **(see illustration)**. *Write down this measurement. This is "dimension B."*

c)   *Measure the distance from the end of the master cylinder to the bottom of the pocket in the piston* **(see illustration)**. *Write down this measurement. This is "dimension C."*

d)   *Subtract measurement B from measurement C, then subtract measurement A from the difference between B and C. This is the pushrod clearance.*

e)   *Compare your calculated pushrod clearance to the pushrod clearance listed in this Chapter's Specifications. If necessary, adjust the pushrod length to achieve the correct clearance* **(see illustration)**.

23   After the final installation of the master cylinder and brake hoses and lines, the brake pedal height and freeplay must be adjusted and the system must be bled. See the appropriate Sections of this Chapter for the procedures.

10   Proportioning valve - removal and installation

Refer to illustration 10.1

1   All models have a proportioning valve that balances hydraulic pressure between the front and rear brakes. It's mounted in the engine compartment **(see illustration)**.

2   If either rear wheel skids prematurely under hard braking, it could mean a defective proportioning valve. If this occurs, have the system checked by a dealer service department or other qualified brake shop. A pair of special pressure gauges and fittings are required for proper diagnosis of the proportioning valve.

3   If you're working on a 2.0L non-turbo model, remove the intake manifold (see Chapter 2A).

4   If you're working on a 2.0L turbo model, remove the cruise control link assembly (it's mounted midway in the throttle cable).

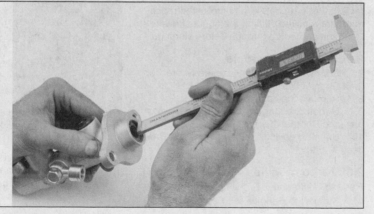

9.22d Measure the distance from the piston pocket to the end of the master cylinder

9.22e To adjust the length of the booster pushrod, hold the serrated portion of the rod with a pair of pliers and turn the adjusting screw in or out, as necessary, to achieve the desired setting

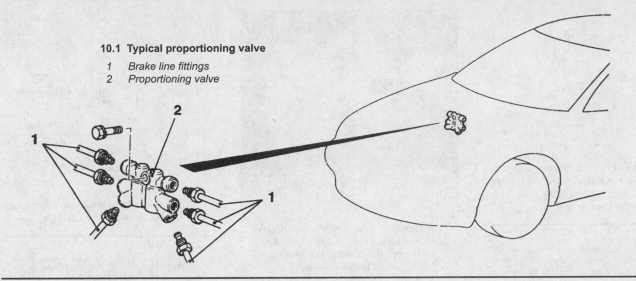

10.1 Typical proportioning valve

1   *Brake line fittings*
2   *Proportioning valve*

5   Disconnect the brake lines from the proportioning valve with a flare nut wrench **(see
illustration 10.1)**.
6   Installation is the reverse of the removal
steps. Tighten the brake line flare nuts securely, then bleed the brakes (see Section
12).

11   Brake hoses and lines - inspection and replacement

Inspection
1   About every six months, with the vehicle raised and supported securely on jackstands, the rubber hoses which connect the
steel brake lines with the front and rear brake
assemblies should be inspected for cracks,
chafing of the outer cover, leaks, blisters and
other damage. These are important and vulnerable parts of the brake system and inspection should be complete. A light and mirror
will be helpful for a thorough check. If a hose
exhibits any of the above conditions, replace
it with a new one.

Replacement
Front brake hose
Refer to illustration 11.3
2   Loosen the wheel lug nuts, raise the
vehicle and support it securely on jackstands.
Remove the wheel.
3   At the strut or frame bracket, hold the
hose fitting with an open-end wrench and
unscrew the brake line fitting from the hose
(see illustration). Use a flare-nut wrench to
prevent rounding off the corners.
4   Remove the U-clip from the female fitting
at the bracket with a pair of pliers, then pass
the hose through the bracket.
5   Unscrew the banjo fitting bolt and detach
the hose from the caliper (if you're replacing
the hose between the strut and the metal line
on the frame, ignore this step). Discard the

sealing washers (new ones should be used
during installation).
6   To install the hose, connect it to the caliper (using new sealing washers) and tighten
the banjo fitting bolt to the torque listed in this
Chapter's Specifications (if you're replacing
the hose between the strut and the metal line
on the frame, ignore this step).
7   Insert the female end of the hose into the
strut bracket and install the U-clip. Make sure
the hose isn't twisted. If you're replacing the
hose between the strut and the frame, do this
at the other end too.
8   Connect the brake line fitting, starting the
threads by hand. Tighten the fitting securely.
9   Bleed the caliper (see Section 12).
10   Install the wheel and lug nuts, lower the
vehicle and tighten the lug nuts.

Rear brake hose
11   Perform Steps 2, 3 and 4, then repeat
Steps 3 and 4 at the other end of the hose.
Be sure to bleed the caliper or wheel cylinder
(see Section 12).

Metal brake lines
12   When replacing brake lines, be sure to
use the correct parts. Don't use copper tubing

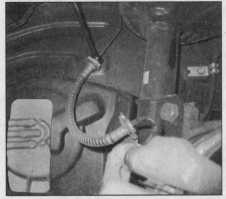

**11.3 Disconnect the front brake hose from
the metal line with a flare nut wrench**

for any brake system components. Purchase
steel brake lines from a dealer or auto parts
store.
13   Prefabricated brake line, with the tube
ends already flared and fittings installed, is
available at auto parts stores and dealer parts
departments. These lines can be bent to the
proper shapes using a tubing bender.
14   When installing the new line, make sure
it's securely supported in the brackets and
has plenty of clearance between moving or
hot components.
15   After installation, check the master cylinder fluid level and add fluid as necessary.
Bleed the brake system (see Section 12) and
test the brakes carefully before driving the
vehicle in traffic.

12   Brake hydraulic system - bleeding

Refer to illustrations 12.7 and 12.9
Warning: *Wear eye protection when bleeding
the brake system. If the fluid comes in contact
with your eyes, immediately rinse them with
water and seek medical attention.*
Note: *Bleeding the hydraulic system is necessary to remove any air that manages to find
its way into the system when it's been opened
during removal and installation of a hose, line,
caliper, drum brake wheel cylinder or master
cylinder.*
1   You'll probably have to bleed the system
at all four brakes if air has entered it due to
low fluid level, or if the brake lines have been
disconnected at the master cylinder. **Caution:** *If the vehicle is equipped with anti-lock
brakes (ABS), pass the brake fluid through a
fine strainer before adding it to the master cylinder reservoir to prevent damage to the ABS
hydraulic unit form any particles that may be
in the fluid.*
2   If a brake line was disconnected only at
a wheel, then only that caliper or wheel cylinder must be bled.

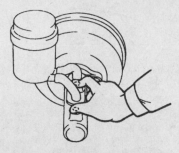

12.7 With the brake pedal down, cover the master cylinder outlet(s) with fingers and release the pedal to draw fluid into the master cylinder

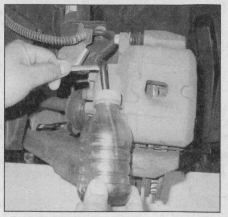

12.9 Connect a hose to the bleed valve and place the other end in a container of brake fluid (disc brake shown; drum brake similar)

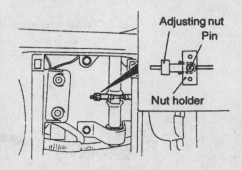

13.3 The parking brake lever adjusting nut is beneath the console

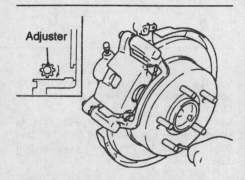

13.5 Insert a screwdriver into the hole and turn the adjuster (rear disc brakes)

3   If a brake line is disconnected at a fitting located between the master cylinder and any of the brakes, that part of the system served by the disconnected line must be bled.

4   Remove any residual vacuum from the brake power booster by applying the brake several times with the engine off.

5   Remove the master cylinder reservoir cover and fill the reservoir with brake fluid. Reinstall the cover. **Note:** *Check the fluid level often during the bleeding operation and add fluid as necessary to prevent the fluid level from falling low enough to allow air bubbles into the master cylinder.*

6   Have an assistant on hand, as well as a supply of new brake fluid, a clear plastic container partially filled with clean brake fluid, a length of 3/16-inch plastic, rubber or vinyl tubing to fit over the bleeder valve and a wrench to open and close the bleeder valve.

Master cylinder

7   If bleeding is necessary because of a low fluid level in the master cylinder, bleed the master cylinder first. Fill the reservoir with brake fluid. Disconnect the fluid outlet line(s) from the side of the master cylinder. Have an assistant hold the brake pedal down, place your fingers over the outlets and have the assistant let the pedal up **(see illustration)**. Repeat this three or four times, then reconnect the fluid lines to the outlets.

Wheels

Warning: *The manufacturer recommends bleeding the brakes with the engine running. Ideally, the vehicle should be on the ground with the wheels securely blocked so it can't roll. If you must jack it up for access, block the wheels that remain on the ground and be sure the vehicle is very securely positioned so it can't fall.*

8   Beginning at the right rear wheel, loosen the bleeder valve slightly, then tighten it to a point where it's snug but can still be loosened quickly and easily.

9   Place one end of the tubing over the bleeder valve and submerge the other end in brake fluid in the container **(see illustration)**.

10   Have the assistant slowly depress the brake pedal and hold the pedal down firmly.

11   While the pedal is held down, open the bleeder valve just enough to allow a flow of fluid to leave the valve. Watch for air bubbles to exit the submerged end of the tube. When the fluid flow slows after a couple of seconds, close the valve and have your assistant release the pedal.

12   Repeat Steps 10 and 11 until no more air is seen leaving the tube, then tighten the bleeder valve and proceed to the left front wheel, the left rear wheel and the right front wheel, in that order, and perform the same procedure. Be sure to check the fluid in the master cylinder reservoir frequently.

13   Never use old brake fluid. It contains moisture which can boil, rendering the brakes useless.

14   Refill the master cylinder with fluid at the end of the operation.

15   Check the operation of the brakes. The pedal should feel solid when depressed, with no sponginess. If necessary, repeat the entire process. **Warning:** *Do not operate the vehicle if you're in doubt about the effectiveness of the brake system.*

13   Parking brake - adjustment

Refer to illustrations 13.3 and 13.5

1   The parking brake lever, when properly adjusted, should travel five to seven clicks (rear disc brakes) or three to five clicks (rear drum brakes) when a moderate pulling force is applied. If it travels less than specified, there's a chance the parking brake might not be releasing completely and might be dragging on the drum. If the lever can be pulled up more than eight clicks, the parking brake may not hold adequately on an incline, allowing the car to roll.

2   To gain access to the parking brake cable adjuster, remove the center console (see Chapter 11).

3   Turn the adjusting nut on the parking brake cable all the way to the end of the cable **(see illustration)**.

4   If you're working on a vehicle with rear drum brakes, press the brake pedal firmly several times to operate the rear brake adjusters. The pedal stroke should change, then stop changing, as the pedal is pumped.

5   If you're working on a vehicle with rear disc brakes, loosen the rear wheel lug nuts, jack up the rear end and remove the rear wheels. Insert a screwdriver into the parking brake adjustment hole and turn the adjuster to lock the brake disc **(see illustration)**. Turn the adjuster back five notches. Install the rear wheels and leave the rear end jacked up.

6   Loosen or tighten the adjusting nut **(see illustration 13.3)** until the desired travel is attained. Tighten the nut. Make sure there's no play between the adjusting nut and the pin in the nut holder **(see illustration 13.3)**.

7   On drum brake models, jack up the rear end and support the vehicle on jackstands.

8   Spin the rear wheels by hand and make sure the rear brakes don't drag.

9   Lower the vehicle. On rear disc brake models, install the wheel and lug nuts, then lower the vehicle and tighten the lug nuts.

10   Install the console.

14   Parking brake shoes (rear disc brake models) - replacement

Refer to illustrations 14.5 and 14.12
Warning: *Parking brake shoes must be replaced on both wheels at the same time - never replace the shoes on only one wheel.*

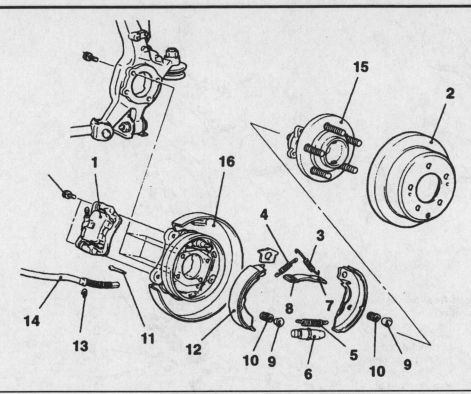

14.5 Parking brake shoes (rear disc brake models) - exploded view

1   Brake caliper
2   Brake disc
3   Rear shoe-to-anchor spring
4   Front shoe-to-anchor spring
5   Adjusting wheel spring
6   Adjuster
7   Strut
8   Strut return spring
9   Hold-down cup
10 Hold-down spring
11 Hold-down pin
12 Parking brake shoe
13 Clip
14 Parking brake cable
15 Rear hub and bearing
16 Brake backing plate

Also, the dust created by the brake system is harmful to your health. Never blow it out with compressed air and don't inhale any of it. An approved filtering mask should be worn when working on the brakes. Do not, under any circumstances, use petroleum-basic solvents to clean brake parts. Use brake system cleaner only!

1   Loosen the rear wheel lug nuts, raise the rear end of the vehicle and support it securely on jackstands. Block the front wheels to keep the vehicle from rolling. Release the parking brake and remove the rear wheels.

2   Remove the caliper (see Section 4) and support it with wire. Leave the brake hose connected.

3   Remove the brake disc. If the disc won't come off, the parking brake shoes must be retracted from their fully adjusted position. Insert a screwdriver through the adjuster hole in the brake backing plate and turn the adjuster wheel to retract the shoes **(see illustration 13.5)**.

4   Once the drum is removed, clean the brake assembly with brake system cleaner.

5   Using locking pliers, unhook and remove the springs **(see illustration)**.

6   Remove the adjuster assembly and strut from between the brake shoes.

7   Grasp one of the shoe hold-down cups with pliers and push it toward the brake backing plate to compress the hold-down spring. Twist the cup 1/4-turn to align the slot in the hold-down pin with the cup, then release the spring pressure (the pin will pass through the cup slot) and take off the cup, spring and second cup. Repeat this with the cup and spring on the other parking brake shoe.

8   Take the shoes off the backing plate.

Disengage the parking brake lever from the cable.

9   Check all parts for wear and damage, paying special attention to metal-to-metal contact points. Replace worn or damaged parts. The parking brake lever is integral with the shoe it's attached to. **Note:** *If the vehicle has high mileage, it's a good idea to replace all of the springs as well as any parts that have visible problems.*

10 Check the parking brake drum surface inside the brake disc for score marks, cracks, deep scratches and hard spots, which will appear as small discolored areas. If the hard spots cannot be removed with emery cloth or if any of the other conditions are seen, the drum must be resurfaced by an automotive machine shop. **Note:** *Professionals recommend resurfacing the parking brake drum surface whenever a brake job is performed. Resurfacing will correct out-of-roundness in the drums as well as removing visible problems. If the drum surfaces are so worn that they can't be resurfaced without exceeding the maximum allowable diameter, then new ones will be required. At the very least, if you don't have the drums resurfaced, remove the glazing from the surface with emery cloth or sandpaper using a swirling motion.*

11 Apply a small amount of high-temperature brake grease to the friction points of the backing plate, adjuster assembly and brake shoes **(see illustration 14.5)**.

12 Reverse the removal steps to install the brake shoes. The bolt portion of the left adjuster goes toward the front of the vehicle. The bolt portion of the right adjuster goes toward the rear of the vehicle. The shoe-to-anchor spring with the paint mark is installed

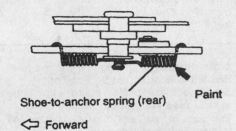

Shoe-to-anchor spring (rear)   Paint
⬅ Forward

14.12 Position the springs with the paint marks toward the rear of the vehicle

with the paint mark toward the rear of the vehicle (for both left and right sides) **(see illustration)**. Expand the shoes, using the automatic adjuster, until the drum will just fit over them.

13 Install the brake disc and caliper. Adjust the parking brake (see Section 13).

14 Install the wheel and lug nuts. Lower the vehicle and tighten the lug nuts.

15 Carefully test brake operation before driving the vehicle on traffic.

15   Parking brake cables - replacement

Refer to illustration 15.5

1   Remove the console (see Chapter 11).

2   Loosen the rear wheel lug nuts, raise the rear of the vehicle and support it securely on jackstands. Block the front wheels. Remove the rear wheels.

3   Make sure the parking brake is completely released.

4   Remove the rear brake shoes (rear drum

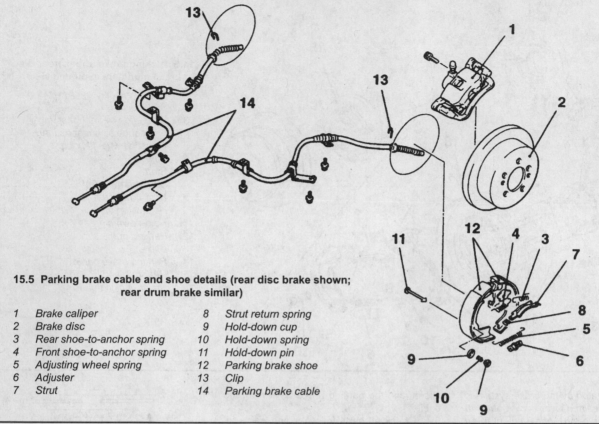

15.5 Parking brake cable and shoe details (rear disc brake shown; rear drum brake similar)

1	Brake caliper	8	Strut return spring
2	Brake disc	9	Hold-down cup
3	Rear shoe-to-anchor spring	10	Hold-down spring
4	Front shoe-to-anchor spring	11	Hold-down pin
5	Adjusting wheel spring	12	Parking brake shoe
6	Adjuster	13	Clip
7	Strut	14	Parking brake cable

brake models) or parking brake shoes (rear disc brake models) (see Section 6 or 14).

5   Unbolt the cable retainers from the vehicle **(see illustration)**. Rotate the cable end plugs to free them from the equalizer and remove them from the vehicle.

6   Installation is the reverse of the removal procedure. Apply a light coat of grease to the portion of the cable end that contacts the equalizer. Adjust the parking brake lever as outlined previously (see Section 13).

16   Brake light switch - removal, installation and adjustment

Refer to illustration 16.1

1   The brake light switch is located on a bracket near the top of the brake pedal **(see illustration)**.

Models with a locknut
Removal and installation

2   Disconnect the wiring harness at the brake light switch.

3   Loosen the locknut and unscrew the switch from the pedal bracket.

4   Installation is the reverse of removal.

Adjustment
Refer to illustration 16.5

5   Loosen the locknut, adjust the switch so the threaded portion lightly contacts the tab on the pedal, then unscrew the switch 1/2 to one

turn and tighten the locknut. There should be a clearance of 0.020 to 0.040-inch (0.5 to 1.0 mm) between the threaded part of the switch and the tab on the pedal **(see illustration)**.

6   Reconnect the electrical connector, then make sure the brake lights are functioning properly.

Models without a locknut

7   Disconnect the electrical connector from the brake light switch **(see illustration 16.1)**.

8   Rotate the switch counterclockwise

slightly, so it unlocks from its holder, then pull it out of the holder.

9   To install the switch, insert it into its holder (canted slightly counterclockwise as during removal) and push it in until the switch body contacts the tab on the brake pedal, then pull it back so there is approximately 3/64-inch (1 mm) clearance between the switch body and the tab on the pedal. Rotate the switch clockwise to lock it into place.

10   Plug the electrical connector into the switch, then verify proper operation.

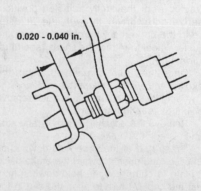

16.1 Location of the brake light switch (model without a locknut shown, models with a locknut similar)

16.5 To adjust the brake light switch on models with a locknut, adjust the position of the switch in its bracket until the gap between the switch body and the tab on the pedal is as specified

Chapter 10
Suspension and steering systems

Contents

Specifications

Torque specifications

Ft-lbs (unless otherwise indicated)

Front suspension (1995 through 1999)

Shock absorber
Upper mounting nuts	44
Lower mounting bolt-to-damper fork	65 to 87
Damper rod nut	14 to 18
Damper fork-to-lateral arm bolt/nut	65

Stabilizer bar
Bracket bolts	28
Link nuts	28

Compression lower arm
Balljoint nut	43 to 52
Pivot bolt	65

Lateral lower arm
Balljoint nut	43 to 52
To damper fork bolt	65
Mounting bolts	60

Upper control arm
Shaft-to-body nuts	62
Pivot bolt nuts	41
Balljoint nut	20

Driveaxle/hub nut .... See Chapter 8

Torque specifications (continued)

Ft-lbs (unless otherwise indicated)

Front suspension (2000 and later)
Note: *One foot-pound (ft-lb) of torque is equivalent to 12 inch-pounds (in-lbs) of torque. Torque values below approximately 15 ft-lbs are expressed in inch-pounds, since most foot-pound torque wrenches are not accurate at these smaller values.*

Strut
Upper mounting nuts	33
Damper rod nut	47
Strut-to-steering knuckle bolts/nuts	221

Stabilizer bar
Bracket bolts	33
Link nuts	33

Control arm
Clamp-to-body bolts	60
Arm-to-clamp bushing nut	73
Pivot bolt nut	80
Control arm-to-steering knuckle pinch bolt/nut	80

Driveaxle/hub nut	See Chapter 8
Front hub-to-knuckle bolts	65

Rear suspension
Rear stabilizer bar

Clamp bolts
1995 through 1999	84 to 120 in-lbs
2000 and later	33
Link nuts	28

Shock absorber
To body nuts	32
Lower mounting bolt/nut	71
Damper rod nut	16

Trailing arm-to-body bolt	109
Trailing arm-to-knuckle bolt	94
Upper control arm-to-knuckle bolt/nut	72
Upper control arm-to-bracket pivot bolts/nuts	41
Upper control arm bracket-to-body bolts	28
Lower arm-to-crossmember bolt	71

Lower arm-to-knuckle bolt
1995 through 1999	71
2000 and later	80

Toe control arm-to-crossmember bolt
1995 through 1999	71
2000 and later	55

Toe control arm balljoint nut
1995 through 1999	20
2000 and later	80
Rear hub-to-knuckle bolts	58

Steering system
Steering wheel nut
1995 through 1999	25
2000 and later	31
Steering gear mounting bracket bolts	51
Steering column mounting bolts	108 in-lbs
Intermediate shaft pinch bolt	156 in-lbs
Tie-rod end-to-steering knuckle nut	21

Power steering pressure line banjo fitting
Nut (2.0L turbo)	156 in-lbs
Bolt	42

1   General information

Refer to illustrations 1.2, 1.3a, and 1.3b

The front suspension on 1995 through 1999 models uses a single upper and two lower control arms connected by a knuckle. Damping is provided by a coil spring/shock absorber unit, which is attached to the body at the top and through a damper fork to the compression lower control arm at the bottom.

The front suspension on 2000 and later models is a MacPherson strut design. The upper end of each strut is attached to the vehicle body. The lower end of the strut is connected to the upper end of the steering knuckle. The steering knuckle is attached to a balljoint in the outer end of the control arm **(see illustration)**. On all models, a front stabilizer bar is attached to the lower control arms to minimize body roll during cornering.

The rear suspension on all models also uses shock absorber/coil spring assemblies. The upper end of each shock is attached to the vehicle body. The lower end of the shock is attached to the rear knuckle. The knuckle is located by an upper control arm at the top, and two lateral links and a trailing arm at the bottom. The basic design of the rear suspension is the same for all model years covered in this manual. The shapes of some components differ between 1995 through 1999 and 2000 and later models, but the overall design is the same for all years **(see illustrations)**.

The rack-and-pinion steering gear is located below and behind the engine/transaxle assembly on the crossmember and

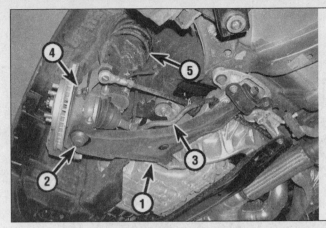

1.2 An underside view of the front suspension components (2000 and later models)

1   Control arm
2   Balljoint
3   Stabilizer bar
4   Knuckle
5   Strut

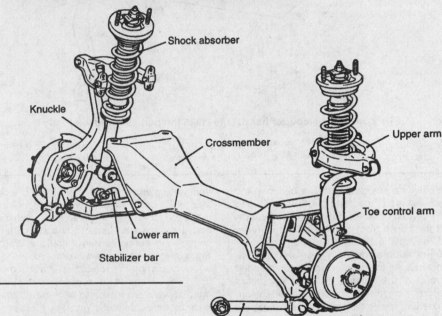

Shock absorber

Knuckle

Crossmember

Upper arm

Toe control arm

Lower arm

Stabilizer bar

Trailing arm

1.3a An underside view of the rear suspension components (1995 through 1999 2WD models; all 2000 and later models similar)

actuates the tie-rods, which are attached to the steering knuckles. The steering column is designed to collapse in the event of an accident.

Frequently, when working on the suspension or steering system components, you may come across fasteners which seem impossible to loosen. These fasteners on the underside of the vehicle are continually subjected to water, road grime, mud, etc., and can become rusted or "frozen," making them extremely difficult to remove. In order to unscrew these stubborn fasteners without damaging them (or other components), be sure to use lots of penetrating oil and allow it to soak in for a while. Using a wire brush to clean exposed threads will also ease removal of the nut or bolt and prevent damage to the threads.

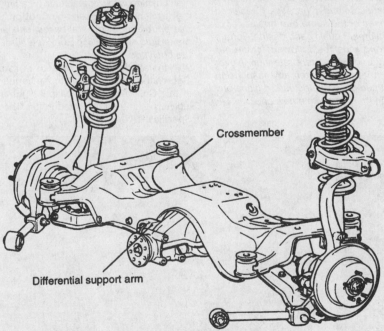

Crossmember

Differential support arm

1.3b An underside view of the rear suspension components (1995 through 1999 4WD models)

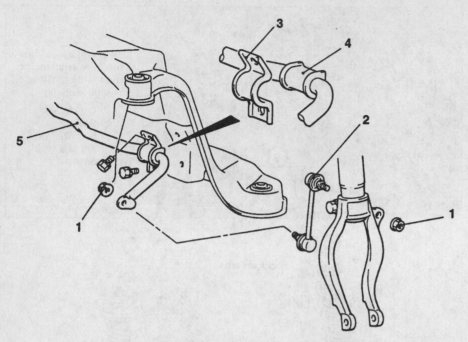

2.3a Front stabilizer bar details (1995 through 1999 models)

1	Stabilizer bar-to-link nut	2	Link	4	Stabilizer bar bushing
		3	Stabilizer bar clamp	5	Stabilizer bar

Sometimes a sharp blow with a hammer and punch will break the bond between a nut and bolt threads, but care must be taken to prevent the punch from slipping off the fastener and ruining the threads. Heating the stuck fastener and surrounding area with a torch sometimes helps too, but isn't recommended because of the obvious dangers associated with fire. Long breaker bars and extension, or "cheater," pipes will increase leverage, but never use an extension pipe on a ratchet - the ratcheting mechanism could be damaged. Sometimes tightening the nut or bolt first will help to break it loose. Fasteners that require drastic measures to remove should always be replaced with new ones.

Since most of the procedures dealt with in this Chapter involve jacking up the vehicle and working underneath it, a good pair of jackstands will be needed. A hydraulic floor jack is the preferred type of jack to lift the vehicle, and it can also be used to support certain components during various operations. **Warning:** *Never, under any circumstances, rely on a jack to support the vehicle while working on it. Whenever any of the suspension or steering fasteners are loosened or removed they must be inspected and, if necessary, replaced with new ones of the same part number or of original equipment quality and design. Torque specifications must be followed for proper reassembly and component retention. Never attempt to heat or straighten any suspension or steering components. Instead, replace any bent or damaged part with a new one.*

2   Stabilizer bar and bushings (front) - removal, inspection and installation

Removal

Refer to illustrations 2.3a, 2.3b and 2.4

1   Loosen the front wheel lug nuts. Raise the front of the vehicle and support it securely on jackstands. Apply the parking brake and block the rear wheels to keep the vehicle from rolling off the stands. Remove the front wheels.

2   If you're working on a 2000 or later 2.4L engine model, remove the front exhaust pipe, engine support crossmember and roll stoppers. On all 2000 or later models, remove the lower control arm (see Chapters 4 and 2C and Section 8).

3   Detach the stabilizer bar links from the damper forks (1995 through 1999 models) or the brackets on the MacPherson struts (2000 and later models) **(see illustrations)**.

4   Detach both stabilizer bar brackets from the crossmember **(see illustration 2.3a and the accompanying illustration)**.

5   Remove the stabilizer bar.

Inspection

6   While the stabilizer bar is off the vehicle, slide the bracket bushings off and inspect them. If they're cracked, worn or deteriorated, replace them.

7   Clean the bushing area of the stabilizer bar with a stiff wire brush to remove any rust or dirt.

Installation

8   Lubricate the inside and outside of the new bushing with vegetable oil (used in cooking) to simplify reassembly. **Caution:** *Don't use petroleum or mineral-based lubricants or brake fluid - they will lead to deterioration of the bushings.*

9   Installation is the reverse of removal. Tighten the nuts and bolts to the torque listed in this Chapter's Specifications. Tighten the lug nuts to the torque listed in the Chapter 1 Specifications.

2.3b Remove the link-to-strut nut (2000 and later models)

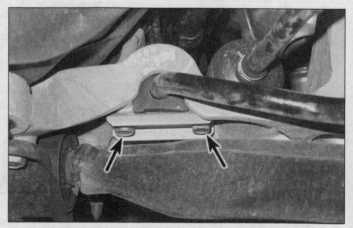

2.4 Stabilizer bar clamp bolts (2000 and later models)

3   Shock absorber/spring assembly (front) (1995 through 1999 models) - removal, inspection and installation

Removal

Refer to illustration 3.3

1   Loosen the wheel lug nuts, raise the front of the vehicle, support it securely on jackstands and remove the front wheels.

2   Mark the shock absorbers as to left and right sides if they're both removed at the same time.

3   Remove the nut and detach the stabilizer bar link from the damper fork (see illustration).

4   Remove the upper mounting nuts that secure the shock absorber to the body (see illustration 3.3). **Warning:** *Do not remove the shock absorber damper rod nut (the nut in the center of the upper mount).*

5   Remove the pinch bolt that secures the lower end of the shock absorber to the damper fork. Remove the through-bolt that secures the lower end of the damper fork to the suspension arm. Separate the damper fork from the shock absorber, using a brass hammer if necessary, and remove them both from the vehicle.

Inspection

6   Check the shock absorber/coil spring assembly for leaking fluid, dents, cracks and other obvious damage which would warrant replacement.

7   Check the coil spring for chips and corrosion. Replace it if any undesirable symptoms are found. See Section 5 for the shock absorber or coil spring replacement procedure.

Installation

8   Installation is the reverse of the removal steps. Tighten the nuts and bolts to the torques listed in this Chapter's Specifications. Tighten the lug nuts to the torque listed in the Chapter 1 Specifications.

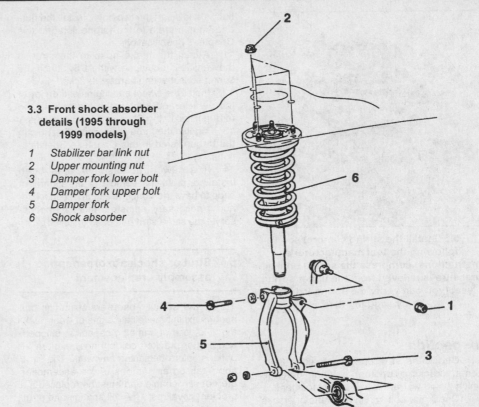

3.3 Front shock absorber details (1995 through 1999 models)

1   *Stabilizer bar link nut*
2   *Upper mounting nut*
3   *Damper fork lower bolt*
4   *Damper fork upper bolt*
5   *Damper fork*
6   *Shock absorber*

4   Strut assembly (front) (2000 and later models) - removal, inspection and installation

Removal

Refer to illustrations 4.2 and 4.5

1   Loosen the wheel lug nuts, raise the vehicle and support it securely on jackstands. Remove the wheel.

2   Detach the brake hose from the strut. If the vehicle is equipped with ABS, detach the speed sensor wiring harness from the strut by removing the clamp bracket bolt **(see illustration).**

3   Remove the strut-to-knuckle nuts and knock the bolts out with a hammer and punch **(see illustration 4.2).**

4   Separate the strut from the steering knuckle. Be careful not to overextend the inner CV joint. And make sure you don't push down too far on the control arm or you could overextend - and damage - the ABS speed sensor wiring harness and the brake hose. **Caution:** *Don't allow the steering knuckle and hub assembly to swing outward, as this could strain the brake hose.*

5   Support the strut and spring assembly with one hand and remove the three strut upper mounting nuts **(see illustration).** Remove the assembly from the fenderwell.

4.2 On ABS models, unbolt the sensor harness clamp (left arrow); on all models, remove the strut nuts and bolts (right arrows)

4.5 Remove the strut upper mounting nuts

5.3 Install the spring compressor following the tool manufacturer's instructions; compress the spring until all pressure is relieved from the upper spring seat (you can verify the spring is loose by wiggling it)

Inspection

6   Check the strut body for leaking fluid, dents, cracks and other obvious damage which would warrant repair or replacement.

7   Check the coil spring for chips or cracks in the spring coating (this will cause premature spring failure due to corrosion). Inspect the spring seat for cuts, hardness and general deterioration.

8   If any undesirable conditions exist, proceed to the strut disassembly procedure (see Section 5).

Installation

9   Guide the strut assembly up into the fenderwell and insert the three mounting studs through the holes in the strut tower. Once the three studs protrude from the shock tower, install the nuts so the strut won't fall back through. This is most easily accomplished with the help of an assistant, as the strut is quite heavy and awkward.

10   Slide the steering knuckle into the strut

flange and insert the two bolts. Install the nuts and tighten them to the torque listed in this Chapter's Specifications.

11   Attach the brake hose to the strut. If the vehicle is equipped with ABS, attach the speed sensor wiring harness bracket.

12   Install the wheel and lug nuts, then lower the vehicle and tighten the lug nuts to the torque listed in the Chapter 1 Specifications.

13   Tighten the three upper mounting nuts to the torque listed in this Chapter's Specifications.

14   If a new strut assembly has been installed, drive the vehicle to an alignment shop to have the front end alignment checked, and if necessary, adjusted (this isn't necessary if the same strut has been installed).

---

5   Strut or shock absorber/spring assembly - replacement

1   If the shock absorbers/struts or coil springs exhibit the telltale signs of wear (leaking fluid, loss of damping capability, chipped, sagging or cracked coil springs) explore all options before beginning any work. The strut/shock absorber portions of the assemblies are not serviceable and must be replaced if a problem develops. The coil springs and strut/shock absorber assemblies can be replaced separately, using the procedures in this Section. In the case of 2000 and later models, you'll need a special tool or equivalent to hold the damper rod while you unscrew the nut. Strut/shock absorber assemblies complete with springs may be available on an exchange basis, which eliminates much time and work. Whichever route you choose to take, check on the cost and availability of parts before disassembling your vehicle. **Warning:** *Disassembling a strut/shock absorber assembly is a potentially dangerous undertaking and utmost attention must be directed to the job, or serious injury may result. Use only a high quality spring compressor and carefully follow the manufacturer's instructions furnished with the tool. After removing the coil spring, set it aside in a safe, isolated area.*

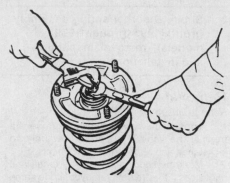

5.4 On 1995 through 1999 models, hold the damper shaft with one wrench while you loosen the nut with another wrench

Disassembly

Refer to illustrations 5.3, 5.4, 5.5, 5.6a, 5.6b, 5.7 and 5.8

2   Remove the front shock absorber/coil spring assembly (see Section 3), the strut and spring assembly (see Section 4) or the rear shock absorber/coil spring assembly (see Section 13). Mount the assembly in a vise. Line the vise jaws with wood or rags to prevent damage to the unit and don't tighten the vise excessively.

3   Following the tool manufacturer's instructions, install the spring compressor (which can be obtained at most auto parts stores or equipment yards on a daily rental basis) on the spring and compress it sufficiently to relieve all pressure from the spring seats insulator **(see illustration)**. This can be verified by wiggling the spring.

4   If you're working on a 1995 through 1999 model, hold the flat on the strut with a wrench and unscrew the nut with another wrench **(see illustration)**.

5   If you're working on a 2000 or later model, hold the damper rod with special tool MB991176, or prevent it from turning by some other means. Loosen the damper rod nut with a socket wrench **(see illustration)**.

6   Remove the nut and the upper mount **(see illustrations)**. Inspect the bearing in the

5.5 On 2000 and later models, remove the damper rod nut with a socket (if the damper rod turns, you'll have to immobilize it)

5.6a Lift the upper mount off the rod

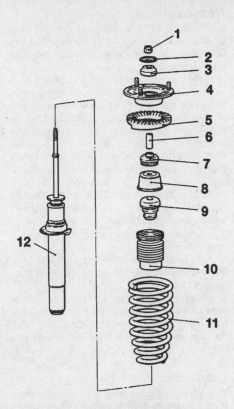

5.6b Shock absorber/coil spring details (1995 through 1999 shown)

1	Self-locking	7	Bushing
	nut	8	Cup
2	Washer	9	Bump rubber
3	Bushing	10	Dust cover
4	Mount	11	Coil spring
5	Upper pad	12	Shock
6	Collar		absorber

mount for smooth operation. If it doesn't turn smoothly, replace the mount. Inspect the rubber portion of the mount for cracking and general deterioration. If there is any separation of the rubber, replace it.

5.7 Remove the upper spring seat and the upper pad from the damper rod

7   Lift the upper spring seat and upper pad from the damper rod **(see illustration)**. Check the spring seat for cracking and hardness, replacing it if necessary.

8   Carefully lift the compressed spring from the assembly **(see illustration)** and set it in a safe place. **Warning:** *Never place your head near the end of the spring!*

9   Slide the rubber bumper and dust cover off the damper rod.

10 **Warning:** *This step may cause metal chips to fly. Wear eye protection.* 2000 and later models use gas struts, from which the gas must be released before the strut is discarded. If you're purchasing exchange units, the supplier can take care of this. If you're discarding the struts yourself, lay them on a bench with the lower mounting bolt holes upward. Wear eye protection and drill a 1/8-inch hole in the cylinder body, halfway between the lower mounting bolt holes and the lower spring seat.

Reassembly

Refer to illustrations 5.12, 5.14a and 5.14b

11   If the lower insulator is being replaced, set it into position with the dropped portion

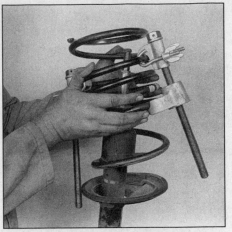

5.8 Remove the compressed spring from the strut/shock absorber assembly - keep the ends of the spring pointed away from your body

seated in the lowest part of the seat. Extend the damper rod to its full length and install the rubber bumper and dust cover.

12   Carefully place the coil spring onto the lower insulator, with the end of the spring resting in the lowest part of the insulator **(see illustration)**.

13   Install the upper pad and, on 2000 and later models, upper spring seat.

14   Install the upper mount onto the damper shaft. If you're working on a front shock absorber of a 1995 through 1999 model, make sure the studs of the upper mount are aligned correctly with the pinch bolt that secures the damper fork to the shock absorber body **(see illustration)**. If you're working on a rear shock absorber assembly (any year), make sure the upper mount bracket is properly aligned with the lower mounting bushing of the shock absorber **(see illustration)**.

15   Install the damper rod nut and tighten it to the torque listed in this Chapter's Specifications.

16   Install the strut/shock absorber and coil spring assembly following the procedure in Section 3, 4 or 13.

5.12 When installing the spring, make sure the end fits into the recessed portion of the lower seat

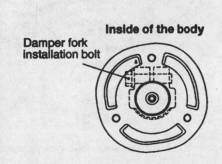

5.14a On 1995 through 1999 front shock absorbers, the damper fork bolt must align with the three upper mounting studs as shown

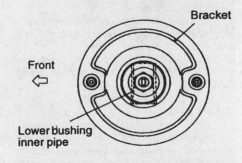

5.14b On rear shock absorbers align the lower bushing with the upper bracket like this before tightening the damper rod nut

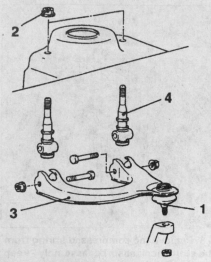

6.3a   Upper control arm details (1995 through 1999 models)

1	Balljoint	3	Control arm
2	Shaft mounting nut	4	Shaft

6   Upper control arm (front) (1995 through 1999 models) - removal, inspection and installation

Removal

Refer to illustrations 6.3a and 6.3b

1   Loosen the wheel lug nuts on the side to be disassembled, raise the front of the vehicle, support it securely on jackstands and remove the wheel.

2   Support the suspension from below with a jack.

3   Remove the nut from the balljoint stud that's connected to the control arm (see illustration). Using a large ball peen hammer (and wearing goggles to protect your eyes), give the steering knuckle a few good whacks in the vicinity of the balljoint stud to break the stud loose from the knuckle. Use a prybar to disconnect the control arm from the steering knuckle. If that doesn't work, use a tie-rod or balljoint separator (see illustration). Similar tools can be rented from rental outlets and some auto parts stores.

4   Loosen the nuts on the control arm pivot bolts now, while the control arm is still attached to the vehicle.

5   Remove the nuts from the control arm shafts (see illustration 6.3a) and remove the control arm.

Inspection

6   Check the control arm for distortion and the pivot bolts and shafts for wear. If the arm is bent or the pivot shafts are worn, replace them. Don't try to straighten a bent control arm. Also check the balljoint (see Section 9). If a balljoint is worn out, you'll have to replace the control arm; the balljoint is not available separately.

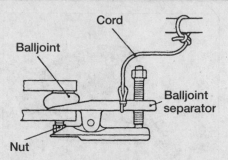

6.3b   Separate the balljoint with a tool like this one

Installation

7   Installation is the reverse of removal. Do NOT reuse self-locking nuts. Replace them with new ones. Tighten all of the fasteners to the torque values listed in this Chapter's Specifications.

8   Install the wheel and lug nuts, lower the vehicle and tighten the lug nuts to the torque listed in the Chapter 1 Specifications.

9   It's a good idea to have the front wheel alignment checked, and if necessary, adjusted after this job has been performed.

7   Lower control arms (front) (1995 through 1999 models) - removal, inspection and installation

Refer to illustration 7.1

1   These vehicles have two lower control arms, a lateral lower arm and a compression lower arm (see illustration).

Removal

2   Loosen the wheel lug nuts on the side to be disassembled, raise the front of the vehicle, support it securely on jackstands and remove the wheel.

3   Remove the nut from the balljoint stud on the arm you're removing. Using a large ball peen hammer (and wearing goggles to protect your eyes), give the steering knuckle a few good whacks in the vicinity of the balljoint stud to break the stud loose from the knuckle. Use a prybar to disconnect the control arm from the steering knuckle. If that doesn't work, use a tie-rod or balljoint separator (see illustration 6.3b). Similar tools can be rented from rental outlets and some auto parts stores.

4   Unbolt the support stay and remove it from the vehicle.

5   To remove the compression lower arm, remove its bushing bolts and separate it from the vehicle.

6   To remove the lateral lower arm, remove the bolt and nut that secure it to the damper fork, then remove the pivot bolt and nut. Work the arm free of its pivot point in the body and take it out of the vehicle.

Inspection

7   Check the control arms for distortion and the bushings for wear. If the arm is bent or any of the bushings are cracked, torn or worn out, replace the control arm. These parts are not replaceable and you can't straighten a bent control arm. Also check the balljoint (see Section 9). If a balljoint is worn out, you'll have to replace the control arm; the balljoint is not available separately.

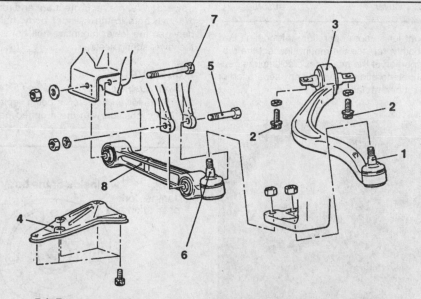

7.1   Front suspension lower arm details (1995 through 1999 models)

1	Balljoint	5	Lower arm-to-damper fork bolt
2	Bolt	6	Balljoint
3	Compression lower arm	7	Lateral arm pivot bolt
4	Stay	8	Lateral arm

8.3 Unscrew the nut and remove the balljoint pinch bolt completely (arrow)

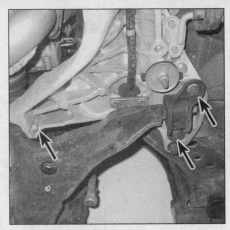

8.4 Control arm pivot bolt (left) and clamp bolts (right) (2000 and later models)

Installation

8   Installation is the reverse of removal. Do NOT reuse self-locking nuts. Replace them with new ones. Tighten all of the fasteners to the torque values listed in this Chapter's Specifications.

9   Install the wheel and lug nuts, lower the vehicle and tighten the lug nuts to the torque listed in the Chapter 1 Specifications.

10   It's a good idea to have the front wheel alignment checked, and if necessary, adjusted after this job has been performed.

8   Control arm (front) (2000 and later models) - removal, inspection and installation

1   These models have a single control arm on each side.

Removal

Refer to illustrations 8.3 and 8.4

2   Loosen the wheel lug nuts on the side to be disassembled, raise the front of the vehicle, support it securely on jackstands and remove the wheel.

3   Completely remove the nut and pinch bolt from the balljoint stud that's connected to the steering knuckle **(see illustration)**. Use a prybar to disconnect the control arm from the steering knuckle.

4   Remove the nut and washer from the control arm forward pivot bolt **(see illustration)**. Pull out the pivot bolt.

5   Remove the two nuts and two bolts from the clamp for the rear control arm bushing **(see illustration 8.4)**.

6   Remove the control arm and rear clamp from the vehicle.

Inspection

7   Remove the nut that secures the rear clamp and bushing to the control arm. Slide the bushing off the control arm stud.

8   Check the control arm for distortion and the bushings for wear. If the arm is bent or the

forward bushing is cracked, torn or worn out, replace the control arm. These parts are not replaceable and you can't straighten a bent control arm.

9   If the bushing in the clamp is worn or damaged, have it pressed out and a new one pressed in by a dealer service department or machine shop.

10   Also check the balljoint (see Section 9). If a balljoint is worn out, you'll have to replace the control arm; the balljoint is not available separately.

Installation

11   Installation is the reverse of removal. Do NOT reuse self-locking nuts. Replace them with new ones. Tighten all of the fasteners to the torque values listed in this Chapter's Specifications.

12   Install the wheel and lug nuts, lower the vehicle and tighten the lug nuts to the torque listed in the Chapter 1 Specifications.

13   Have the front wheel alignment checked, and if necessary, adjusted after this job has been performed.

9   Balljoints - check and replacement

Refer to illustration 9.10

Check

Lower balljoint(s)

1   Raise the front of the vehicle and support it securely on jackstands. Apply the parking brake and block the rear wheels to keep the vehicle from rolling off the jackstands.

2   If you're working on a 1999 or earlier model, remove the damper fork-to-lateral arm nut and bolt.

3   Place a large prybar under the balljoint and resting on the wheel, then try to pry the balljoint up while feeling for movement between the balljoint and steering knuckle. Now, pry between the control arm and the steering knuckle and try to lever the con-

trol arm down while feeling for movement between the balljoint and steering knuckle. If any movement is evident in either check, the balljoint is worn.

4   Have an assistant grasp the tire at the top and bottom and move the top of the tire in-and-out. Touch the balljoint stud nut. If any looseness is felt, suspect a worn balljoint stud or a widened hole in the steering knuckle boss. If the latter problem exists, the steering knuckle should be replaced as well as the balljoint/control arm.

Upper balljoint (1999 and earlier models only)

5   Loosen the wheel lug nuts, raise the front of the vehicle and support it securely on jackstands. Remove the wheel.

6   Place a floor jack under the lower balljoints and raise it slightly.

7   Using a prybar, attempt to pry the upper control arm up and down while feeling for play in the balljoint. If any play is felt, replace the control arm.

All balljoints

8   Separate the control arm from the steering knuckle (see Section 7 or 8). Using your fingers (don't use pliers), try to twist the stud in the socket. If the stud turns, replace the balljoint.

Replacement

9   The balljoints are not replaceable separately (the entire control arm must be replaced).

10   The balljoint dust boot can be replaced separately. This should not be done if the dust boot has cracked or been damaged while the vehicle is in use, since dirt has probably gotten into the balljoint. However, if the dust boot was damaged during removal of the control arm, the dust boot can be replaced. To do this, pry off the old dust boot. Grease the balljoint stud and the upper lip of the dust boot. Push the dust boot onto the balljoint with a special tool or a socket the same diameter as the dust boot **(see illustration)**. If you're working on a 2000 or later model, push the dust boot upper lip down with a smaller socket until it locks into the groove in the bottom of the balljoint stud.

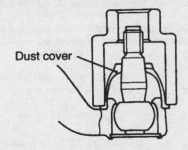

Dust cover

9.10 Push the dust boot onto the balljoint with a tool like this one

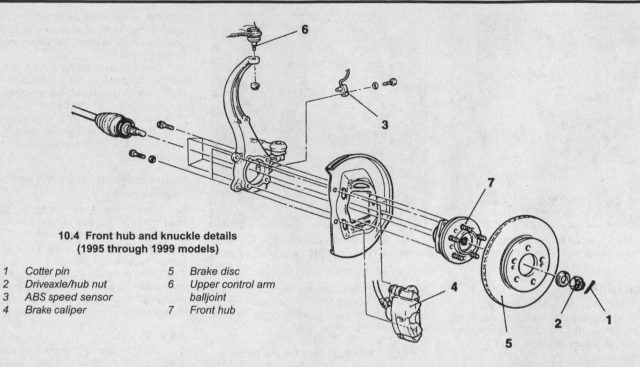

**10.4 Front hub and knuckle details
(1995 through 1999 models)**

1	Cotter pin	5	Brake disc
2	Driveaxle/hub nut	6	Upper control arm
3	ABS speed sensor		balljoint
4	Brake caliper	7	Front hub

11   Install the wheel and lug nuts (if removed) and lower the vehicle. Tighten the lug nuts to the torque listed in the Chapter 1 Specifications.

10   Hub and bearing assembly (front) - removal and installation

Refer to illustration 10.4
Warning: *Dust created by the brake system is harmful to your health. Never blow it out with compressed air and don't inhale any of it. Do not, under any circumstances, use petroleum-based solvents to clean brake parts. Use brake system cleaner only.*
1   Loosen the wheel lug nuts, raise the vehicle and support it securely on jackstands. Remove the wheel.
2   Remove the brake caliper and support it with a piece of wire as described in Chapter 9. Remove the caliper torque plate, separate the brake disc from the hub, then remove the driveaxle/hub nut (see Chapter 8).
3   Separate the lower balljoint(s) from the steering knuckle (see Section 7 or 8). Pivot the knuckle outward and push the driveaxle from the hub to provide removal access for the hub mounting bolts. Support the end of the driveaxle with a piece of wire.
4   Unbolt the hub from the knuckle **(see illustration)**. Remove the hub from the vehicle.
5   If necessary, remove the brake caliper shield from the knuckle.
6   Check the hub bearing for wear or damage. Spin it with your fingers and check for rough, loose or noisy rotation. The bearing can't be replaced separately, so if the bearing is bad or any other problems are found,

replace the hub as an assembly. **Note:** *Bearing rotation starting torque and bearing end play can be measured using special tools if the hub's condition is uncertain. If the hub is not obviously bad, have it checked by a dealer service department or machine shop before replacing the hub.*
7   Installation is the reverse of removal. Tighten the hub bolts and balljoint fasteners to the torque listed in this Chapter's Specifications. Tighten the driveaxle/hub nut to the torque listed in the Chapter 8 Specifications (and be sure to use a new cotter pin), the brake fasteners to the torque listed in Chapter 9 and the wheel lug nuts to the torque listed in Chapter 1.

11   Steering knuckle - removal and installation

Warning: *Dust created by the brake system is harmful to your health. Never blow it out with compressed air and don't inhale any of it. Do not, under any circumstances, use petroleum-based solvents to clean brake parts. Use brake system cleaner only.*

Removal
1   Loosen the wheel lug nuts, raise the vehicle and support it securely on jackstands. Remove the wheel.
2   Remove the brake caliper and support it with a piece of wire as described in Chapter 9. If the vehicle is equipped with ABS, unbolt and remove the wheel speed sensor from the knuckle. Remove the caliper torque plate, separate the brake disc from the hub, then remove the driveaxle/hub nut (see Chapter 8).

3   Separate the tie-rod end from the steering knuckle arm (see Section 21).
4   Separate the control arm(s) from the knuckle (see Sections 6 and 7 [1999 and earlier models] or Section 8 [2000 and later models]).
5   Push the driveaxle from the hub as described in Chapter 8. Support the end of the driveaxle with a piece of wire.
6   If you're working on a 2000 or later model, remove the bolts and carefully separate the steering knuckle from the strut **(see illustration 4.2)**.
7   If necessary, unbolt the hub from the knuckle.

Installation
8   Installation is the reverse of the removal steps. Tighten all suspension and steering fasteners to the torque listed in this Chapter's Specifications. Tighten the driveaxle/hub nut to the torque listed in the Chapter 8 Specifications (and be sure to use a new cotter pin), the brake fasteners to the torque listed in Chapter 9 and the wheel lug nuts to the torque listed in Chapter 1.

12   Stabilizer bar and bushings (rear) - removal, inspection and installation

Removal
Refer to illustrations 12.2 and 12.3
1   Loosen the wheel lug nuts, raise the vehicle and support it securely on jackstands. Remove the wheels.
2   Remove the nuts attaching the stabilizer

12.2 Detach the rear stabilizer link from the stabilizer and lower control arm (arrows)

12.3 Unbolt the rear stabilizer clamp on each side of the stabilizer

links to the stabilizer and lower control arm **(see illustration)**.

3   Unbolt the stabilizer bar clamps from the crossmember **(see illustration)**. Remove the stabilizer bar from the vehicle.

Inspection

4   Inspect the stabilizer bushings for cracks and tears. If the bushings are damaged, distorted or excessively worn, replace them. Also, inspect the link balljoints for damage or excessive looseness.

Installation

Refer to illustration 12.5

5   Installation is the reverse of the removal steps. Position the stabilizer bar in the brackets so its alignment mark is within the specified distance of the bracket **(see illustration)**. Tighten all fasteners to the torque listed in this Chapter's Specifications.

---

13   Shock absorber/spring assembly (rear) - removal, inspection and installation

---

Removal

Refer to illustrations 13.2 and 13.4

1   Loosen the wheel lug nuts, raise the vehicle and support it securely on jackstands.

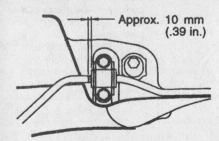

12.5 Position the stabilizer alignment mark at the specified distance from the bracket

Remove the wheel.

2   On hard-top models, raise the hatch and remove the small plastic access cover from the rear side trim panel. If you're working on a convertible model, fully close the top and unhook the trim panel near the rear glass for access to the shock upper mount. Inside, you'll find a small protective cap over the shock damper nut. Remove this cap **(see illustration)**.

3   Support the trailing arm with a floor jack. Raise the jack just enough to take the load off the shock absorber, then remove the two

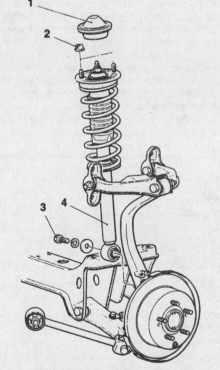

13.2 Rear shock absorber/spring details

1   Cap
2   Mounting nut
3   Lower mounting bolt
4   Shock absorber

shock absorber upper mounting nuts **(see illustration 13.2)**. **Warning:** *Don't remove the nut from the damper rod (the center nut).*

4   Remove the shock absorber lower mounting bolt and remove the shock **(see illustration)**.

Inspection

5   Follow the inspection procedures described in Section 3. If the shock absorber assembly must be disassembled for replacement of the shock or the coil spring, refer to Section 5.

Installation

6   Maneuver the shock absorber assembly up into the fenderwell and insert the mounting studs through the holes in the body. Install the nuts, but don't tighten them yet.

7   If you're working on a 2000 or later model, position the lower end of the shock so the flanged portion of the bushing is toward the outside of the vehicle. On all models, push the lower end of the shock into its bracket on the knuckle, install the bolt and nut and tighten them to the torque listed in this Chapter's Specifications.

8   Install the wheel and lug nuts, lower the vehicle and tighten the lug nuts to the torque

13.4 Unscrew the lower mounting bolt

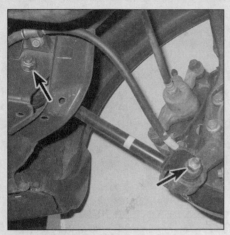

14.2 Trailing arm attachment points (arrows)

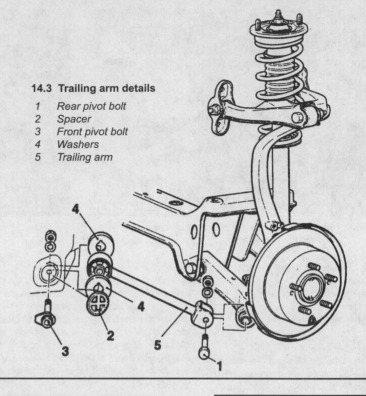

14.3 Trailing arm details

1   Rear pivot bolt
2   Spacer
3   Front pivot bolt
4   Washers
5   Trailing arm

listed in the Chapter 1 Specifications.
9   Tighten the two upper mounting nuts to the torque listed in this Chapter's Specifications.

14   Trailing arm (rear) - removal, inspection and installation

Refer to illustrations 14.2 and 14.3
1   Loosen the wheel lug nuts, raise the vehicle and support it securely on jackstands. Remove the wheels.
2   Remove the nut, washer and bolt that attach the rear end of the trailing arm to the rear knuckle **(see illustration)**.
3   Remove the grommet at the front end of the trailing arm. Remove the nut, washer and bolt that attach the front end of the trailing arm to the body, then remove the stopper and trailing arm **(see illustration)**.
4   Inspect the bushings in the front end of the trailing arm and in the knuckle for cracks

and deterioration. If the front bushing is worn, replace the trailing arm. If the rear bushing is worn, replace the knuckle (see Section 18).
5   Installation is the reverse of removal. Make sure you install the bolts with the heads facing outward. Tighten the nuts and bolts slightly with the vehicle jacked up, then tighten the bolts/nuts to the torque listed in this Chapter's Specifications with the vehicle's weight resting on the wheels. As an alternative, you can raise the suspension with a floor jack to simulate normal ride height, then tighten the fasteners to the specified torque.
6   Tighten the lug nuts to the torque listed in the Chapter 1 Specifications.

15   Lower and toe control arms (rear) - removal, inspection and installation

Removal

Refer to illustrations 15.2 and 15.5
1   Loosen the wheel lug nuts, raise the vehicle and support it securely on jackstands. Remove the wheels.

Lower control arm
2   Remove the nut that connects the stabilizer bar link to the lower control arm **(see illustration)**.

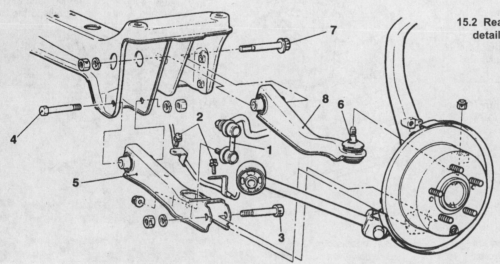

15.2 Rear lower arm and toe control arm details (1995 through 1999 shown)

1   Stabilizer bar link
2   ABS speed sensor harness bolts
3   Lower arm-to-knuckle bolt
4   Lower arm pivot bolt
5   Lower arm
6   Toe control arm balljoint
7   Toe control arm pivot bolt
8   Toe control arm

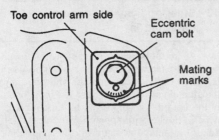

15.5 Line up the eccentric mating marks when installing the toe control arm

3   If you're working on a vehicle equipped with ABS, unbolt the clamp that secures the wheel speed sensor wiring harness.

4   Remove the nut, lockwasher and bolt that secure the outer end of the lower control arm to the knuckle. Do the same thing at the inner end, then remove the control arm from the vehicle.

Toe control arm

5   Mark the position of the eccentric at the inner end of the toe control arm before removing it **(see illustration)**.

6   Loosen the nut on the toe control arm balljoint. Strike the knuckle in the vicinity of the balljoint several times with a hammer to free the balljoint stud, then pry it loose with a pry bar. If that doesn't work, use a tie-rod or balljoint separator **(see illustration 6.3b)**. Similar tools can be rented from rental outlets and some auto parts stores.

7   Remove the toe control arm pivot bolt, lockwasher and nut and take the arm out.

Inspection

8   Check the bushing in the inner end of each arm, and the lower control arm bushing in the knuckle, for wear or damage. If the inner bushings are bad, replace the affected arm. If the lower control arm outer bushing is bad, replace the knuckle (see Section 18).

9   Refer to Section 9 to inspect the balljoint in the outer end of the toe control arm.

Installation

10   Installation is the reverse of the removal steps. Tighten all fasteners slightly with the vehicle jacked up, then tighten them to the specified torque with the vehicle's weight resting on the wheels. As an alternative, you can raise the suspension with a floor jack to simulate normal ride height, then tighten the fasteners to the specified torque.

11   Tighten the lug nuts to the torque listed in the Chapter 1 Specifications.

12   Have rear wheel alignment checked and adjusted if necessary by a dealer service department or other qualified shop.

---

16   Hub and bearing assembly (rear) (2WD models) - removal and installation

---

This procedure is basically the same as for 4WD models, described in Chapter 8, but

there's no rear driveaxle. Refer to this Chapter's Specifications for torque settings.

---

17   Upper control arm (rear) - removal, inspection and installation

---

Removal

Refer to illustrations 17.2 and 17.4

1   Loosen the wheel lug nuts, raise the vehicle and support it securely on jackstands. Remove the wheels.

2   Unscrew the bolts that attach the upper control arm pivots to the body **(see illustration)**.

3   Remove the bolt, nut and washer that attach the upper control arm to the knuckle. Remove the upper control arm from the vehicle. Don't allow the knuckle to fall outward - the brake hose or CV joint (4WD models) could be damaged.

4   Remove the pivot bolts and nuts and separate the pivots from the control arm **(see illustration)**.

Inspection

Refer to illustration 17.6

5   Check the control arm for cracks or bending and check the bushings for wear or damage. Replace the control arm and bushings as an assembly if any problems are found.

6   When you reinstall the pivots to the control arm, place them at the correct angle **(see illustration)**. The vertical distance between

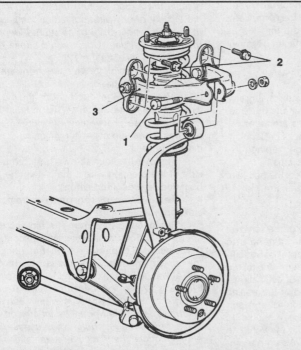

17.2 Rear upper control arm details (1995 through 1999 shown)

    1   Control arm-to-knuckle bolt
    2   Control arm mounting bolts
    3   Control arm

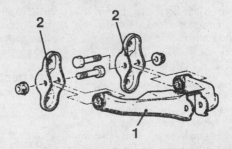

17.4 Rear upper control arm mounting details (1995 through 1999 shown)

    1   Control arm   *2   Mounting bracket*

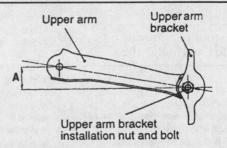

17.6 With the upper arm at the correct installed angle, the vertical distance between pivots (dimension A) should be 1.46 +/-0.080 inch

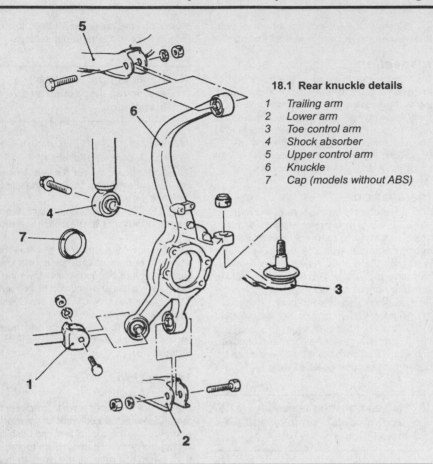

18.1 Rear knuckle details

1 Trailing arm
2 Lower arm
3 Toe control arm
4 Shock absorber
5 Upper control arm
6 Knuckle
7 Cap (models without ABS)

the outer control arm pivot point and the inner pivot point should be 1.46 +/-0.080 inch. With this distance set correctly, tighten the pivot bolts and nuts to the torque listed in this Chapter's Specifications.

Installation

7   Installation is the reverse of the removal steps. Tighten the outer pivot bolt and nut slightly, then tighten them to the specified torque with the vehicle's weight resting on the wheels. As an alternative, you can raise the suspension with a floor jack to simulate normal ride height, then tighten the fasteners to the specified torque.
8   Tighten the lug nuts to the torque listed in the Chapter 1 Specifications.

18   Knuckle (rear) - removal, inspection and installation

Removal
Refer to illustration 18.1
1   If the vehicle is equipped with ABS, remove the rear wheel speed sensor ring. If not, remove the cap from inside the knuckle **(see illustration)**.
2   Remove the rear brake caliper, bracket and disc (disc brakes) or brake drum and shoes (drum brakes) (see Chapter 9).

3   Remove the rear hub (see Section 16).
4   Disconnect the lower shock absorber, trailing arm, lower control arm, toe control arm and upper control arm from the knuckle as described elsewhere in this Chapter. Remove the knuckle from the vehicle.

Inspection
5   Check the control arm and trailing arm bushings in the knuckle for wear and damage. Replace the knuckle if problems are found.
6   Check the knuckle for cracks or bending. Don't try to repair any damage; replace the knuckle if there are visible problems.
7   Refer to Section 9 to inspect the ball-joint at the outer end of the toe control arm.

Installation
8   Installation is the reverse of the removal steps. Tighten all suspension fasteners to the torque listed in this Chapter's Specifications. Tighten the brake fasteners to the torque listed in the Chapter 9 Specifications. The pivot bolts at the rear end of the trailing arm, outer end of the lower control arm and outer end of the upper control arm should be tightened to the final torque with the vehicle's weight resting on the wheels. As an alternative, you can raise the suspension with a floor jack to simulate normal ride height, then tighten the fasteners to the specified torque.
9   Tighten the lug nuts to the torque listed in the Chapter 1 Specifications.

19   Steering system - general information

All models are equipped with power rack-and-pinion steering. The steering gear is bolted to the crossmember and operates the steering arms via tie-rods. The inner ends of the tie-rods are protected by rubber boots which should be inspected periodically for secure attachment, tears and leaking lubricant.

The power assist system consists of a belt-driven pump and associated lines and hoses. The fluid level in the power steering pump reservoir should be checked periodically (see Chapter 1).

The steering wheel operates the steering shaft, which actuates the steering gear through universal joints. Looseness in the steering can be caused by wear in the steering shaft universal joints, the steering gear, the tie-rod ends and loose retaining bolts.

The power assist system consists of a belt-driven pump and associated lines and hoses. The fluid level in the power steering pump reservoir should be checked periodically (see Chapter 1).

20   Steering wheel - removal and installation

Removal
Refer to illustrations 20.3 and 20.5
Warning: *These models have airbags. Always disable the airbag system before working in the vicinity of any airbag system component to avoid the possibility of accidental deployment of the airbag, which could cause personal injury (see Chapter 12).*
1   Park the vehicle with the front wheel pointing straight ahead.
2   Disconnect the cable from the negative terminal of the battery. Wait at least two minutes before proceeding (the airbag system has a back-up capacitor which must fully discharge).
3   Remove the four screws from the back side of the steering wheel that retain the airbag module **(see illustration)**.
4   Remove the airbag module from the steering wheel.
5   Remove the lock from the airbag clock spring electrical connector and disconnect the electrical connector from the back of the airbag module **(see illustration)**. Set the airbag aside in a safe, isolated area.
Warning: *When handling the airbag module, make sure that at no time any source of electricity is allowed near the inflator on the back of the airbag module; when carrying the airbag module, the trim cover must be pointed away from your body or any other person; if the airbag module is placed on a workbench or any other surface, the trim cover must face upwards. When removing the airbag module, tag or mark all fasteners, screws, bolts and*

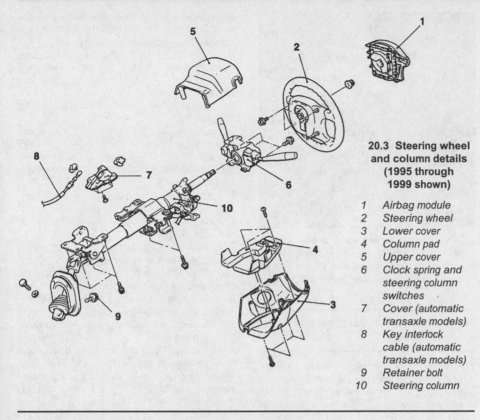

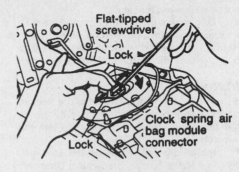

20.3 Steering wheel and column details (1995 through 1999 shown)

1   Airbag module
2   Steering wheel
3   Lower cover
4   Column pad
5   Upper cover
6   Clock spring and steering column switches
7   Cover (automatic transaxle models)
8   Key interlock cable (automatic transaxle models)
9   Retainer bolt
10 Steering column

20.5 Unlock the connector with a flat-tipped screwdriver, then disconnect it

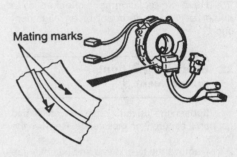

20.10 After centering the clock spring, align the mating marks (see text)

other parts for the airbag module with their location as removed, for correct installation later.

6   Remove the steering wheel retaining nut, then mark the relationship of the steering shaft to the hub (if marks don't already exist or don't line up) to simplify installation and ensure steering wheel alignment.

7   Use a puller to disconnect the steering wheel from the shaft. Do NOT pound on the steering wheel or shaft in an attempt to remove the wheel.

8   Remove the clock spring only if the steering column switches must be checked or replaced **Caution:** *Regardless of whether the clock spring will be removed or not, tape the center hub of the clock spring to the outer ring so the center hub cannot rotate. This will retain the clock spring in the centered position.* **Warning:** *Don't allow the steering shaft to rotate with the steering wheel removed.*

9   If necessary, remove the screws, disconnect the remaining connectors and remove the clock spring from the steering column.

Installation

Refer to illustration 20.10

10   Verify that the front wheels are pointing straight ahead. Turn the clock spring for the airbag clockwise by hand until it stops (don't apply too much force), then rotate the clock spring counterclockwise approximately 3 to 3-1/8 turns, as necessary, until the marks align **(see illustration)**.

11   Pull the electrical leads for the airbag

module through the steering wheel.

12   Install the steering wheel on the shaft, taking care not to snag the wiring. Make sure the clock spring pin guides and pins are properly engaged.

13   Install the steering wheel retaining nut and tighten it to the torque listed in this Chapter's Specifications.

14   Connect the wiring and install the airbag module.

15   Reconnect the negative cable to the battery.

16   Verify that the airbag circuit is operational by turning the ignition key to the On position. The airbag warning light should illuminate for about seven seconds, then turn off.

21   Tie-rod ends - removal and installation

Removal

Refer to illustrations 21.2a, 21.2b and 21.4

1   Loosen the wheel lug nuts. Raise the front of the vehicle, support it securely on jackstands, block the rear wheels and set the parking brake. Remove the front wheel.

2   Hold the tie-rod with a pair of locking pliers or wrench and loosen the jam nut enough to mark the position of the tie-rod end in relation to the threads **(see illustrations)**.

3   Remove the cotter pin and loosen the

21.2a Loosen the tie-rod end jam nut . . .

21.2b . . . and mark the relationship of the tie-rod end to the tie-rod (arrow)

nut on the tie-rod end stud.

4   Disconnect the tie-rod from the steering knuckle arm with a puller **(see illustration)**. Remove the nut and separate the tie-rod end.

5   Unscrew the tie-rod end from the tie-rod.

Installation

6   Thread the tie-rod end on to the marked position and insert the tie-rod stud into the steering knuckle arm. Tighten the jam nut securely.

7   Install the castle nut on the stud and tighten it to the torque listed in this Chapter's Specifications. Install a new cotter pin.

8   Install the wheel and lug nuts. Lower the vehicle and tighten the lug nuts to the torque listed in the Chapter 1 Specifications.

9   Have wheel alignment checked by a dealer service department or an alignment shop.

22   Steering gear boots - replacement

1   Loosen the lug nuts, raise the vehicle and support it securely on jackstands. Remove the wheel.

2   Remove the tie-rod end and jam nut (see Section 21).

3   Remove the steering gear boot clamps and slide the boot off.

4   Before installing the new boot, wrap the threads and serrations on the end of the steering rod with a layer of tape so the small end of the new boot isn't damaged.

5   Slide the new boot into position on the steering gear until it seats in the grooves, then install new clamps.

6   Remove the tape and install the tie-rod end (see Section 21).

7   Install the wheel and lug nuts. Lower the vehicle and tighten the lug nuts to the torque listed in the Chapter 1 Specifications.

8   Have wheel alignment checked by a dealer service department or an alignment shop.

21.4 A tie-rod end separator is being used here to detach the tie-rod end from the steering knuckle - if you don't have one of these tools, a two-jaw puller will work

23   Steering gear - removal and installation

Warning: *These models are equipped with airbags. Always disable the airbag system before working in the vicinity of the any airbag system component to avoid the possibility of accidental deployment of the airbag, which could cause personal injury (see Chapter 12). Also, don't allow the steering wheel to turn after the steering gear has been removed. To prevent this, pass the seat belt through the steering wheel and plug it into its latch.*

Removal

Refer to illustrations 23.5 and 23.6

1   Disconnect the cable from the negative terminal of the battery.

2   If you're working on a 2.0L turbo model, unbolt the brake fluid reservoir and set it aside without disconnecting the fluid hoses (see Chapter 9). Unbolt the air conditioning compressor and set it aside without disconnecting

any refrigerant lines (see Chapter 3). If you're working on a 1995 through 1999 model, remove the windshield washer reservoir.

3   Loosen the front wheel lug nuts, raise the front of the vehicle and support it securely on jackstands. Apply the parking brake and remove the wheels.

4   Remove the front exhaust pipe (see Chapter 4).

5   On all models, remove the support stay(s) from under the steering gear. On 1995 through 1999 models, remove the transaxle rear roll stopper and crossmember **(see illustration)**.

6   Mark the relationship of the lower universal joint to the steering gear input shaft. Remove the lower intermediate shaft pinch bolt **(see illustration)**.

7   Place a drain pan under the steering gear. Detach the power steering pressure and return lines and cap the ends to prevent excessive fluid loss and contamination.

8   Separate the tie-rod ends from the steering knuckle arms (see Section 21).

9   Support the steering gear and remove the steering gear bracket-to-crossmember mounting bolts and clamps **(see illustration 23.6)**. Separate the intermediate shaft from the steering gear input shaft, move the steering gear unit to the right as far as it will go, then lower the left end down and pull it out to the left.

10   Check the steering gear mounting grommets for excessive wear or deterioration, replacing them if necessary.

Installation

Note: *Be sure to center the steering gear before installing it. To do this, turn the steering gear input shaft counterclockwise until it stops, then count the number of turns as you turn the shaft clockwise until it stops. Divide that number by two, then turn the shaft counterclockwise that amount.*

11   Raise the steering gear into position and connect the U-joint, aligning the marks.

12   Install the mounting brackets and bolts

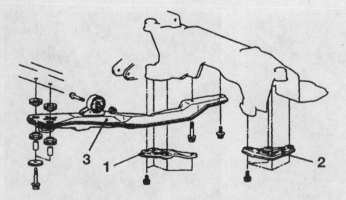

23.5 Crossmember details (1995 through 1999 models)

1	Stay	3	Crossmember and rear
2	Stay		roll stopper

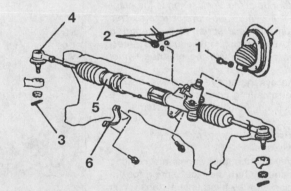

23.6 Steering gear mounting details (1995 through 1999 shown)

1	Pinch bolt	4	Tie-rod end
2	Power steering line fittings	5	Steering gear
3	Cotter pin	6	Steering gear clamp

and tighten them to the torque listed in this Chapter's Specifications.

13   Connect the tie-rod ends to the steering knuckle arms (see Section 21).

14   Install the U-joint pinch bolt and tighten it to the torque listed in this Chapter's Specifications.

15   Connect the power steering pressure and return hoses to the steering gear and fill the power steering pump reservoir with the recommended fluid (see Chapter 1).

16   The remainder of installation is the reverse of the removal steps.

17   Lower the vehicle and bleed the steering system (see Section 25).

18   Tighten the lug nuts to the torque listed in the Chapter 1 Specifications.

24   Power steering pump - removal and installation

Removal

Refer to illustration 24.4

1   Disconnect the cable from the negative battery terminal.

2   Using a large syringe or suction gun, suck as much fluid out of the power steering fluid reservoir as possible. Place a drain pan under the vehicle to catch any fluid that spills out when the hoses are disconnected.

3   Raise the vehicle and support it securely on jackstands.

4   Disconnect the pressure switch connector **(see illustration)**.

5   Loosen the clamp and disconnect the fluid suction hose from the power steering pump.

6   Remove the pressure line-to-pump banjo bolt (all except 2.0L turbo models) or nut (2.0L turbo models) and separate the line from the pump. Remove the sealing washers or O-rings on each side of the fitting; these should be replaced when installing the pump.

7   Remove the pivot, adjuster and mounting bolts, detach the drivebelt from the pulley and lower the pump from the vehicle.

Installation

8   To install the pump, reverse the removal procedure. Tighten the banjo bolt or nut to the torque listed in this Chapter's Specifications. Adjust the drivebelt tension following the procedure described in Chapter 1.

9   Top up the fluid level in the reservoir (see Chapter 1) and bleed the system (see Section 25).

25   Power steering system - bleeding

1   Following any operation in which the power steering fluid lines have been disconnected, the power steering system must be bled to remove all air and obtain proper steering performance.

2   With the front wheels in the straight ahead position, check the power steering fluid

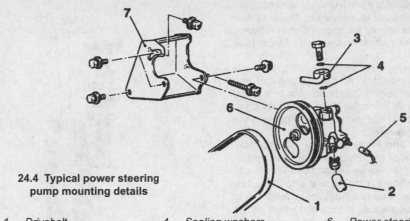

24.4 Typical power steering pump mounting details

1	Drivebelt	4	Sealing washers	6	Power steering pump
2	Return hose	5	Pressure switch	7	Mounting bracket
3	Pressure hose		connector		

level and, if low, add fluid until it reaches the Cold mark on the dipstick.

3   Start the engine and allow it to run at fast idle. Recheck the fluid level and add more if necessary to reach the Cold mark on the dipstick.

4   Bleed the system by turning the wheels from side to side, without hitting the stops. This will work the air out of the system. Keep the reservoir full of fluid as this is done.

5   When the air is worked out of the system, return the wheels to the straight ahead position and leave the vehicle running for several more minutes before shutting it off.

6   Road test the vehicle to be sure the steering system is functioning normally and noise free.

7   Recheck the fluid level to be sure it is up to the Hot mark on the dipstick while the engine is at normal operating temperature. Add fluid if necessary (see Chapter 1).

26   Wheels and tires - general information

Refer to illustration 26.1

1   Vehicles covered by this manual are equipped with metric-sized radial tires **(see illustration)**. Use of other size or type of tires may affect the ride and handling of the vehicle. Don't mix different types of tires, such as radials and bias belted, on the same vehicle as handling may be seriously affected. It's recommended that tires be replaced in pairs on the same axle, but if only one tire is being replaced, be sure it's the same size, structure and tread design as the other.

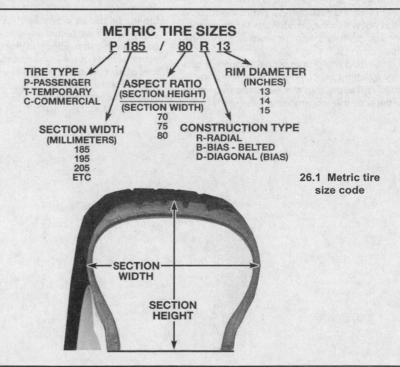

26.1 Metric tire size code

2   Because tire pressure has a substantial effect on handling and wear, the pressure on all tires should be checked at least once a month or before any extended trips (see Chapter 1).

3   Wheels must be replaced if they are bent, dented, leak air, have elongated bolt holes, are heavily corroded, out of vertical symmetry or if the lug nuts won't stay tight. Wheel repairs that use welding or peening are not recommended.

4   Tire and wheel balance is important in the overall handling, braking and performance of the vehicle. Unbalanced wheels can adversely affect handling and ride characteristics as well as tire life. Whenever a tire is installed on a wheel, the tire and wheel should be balanced by a shop with the proper equipment.

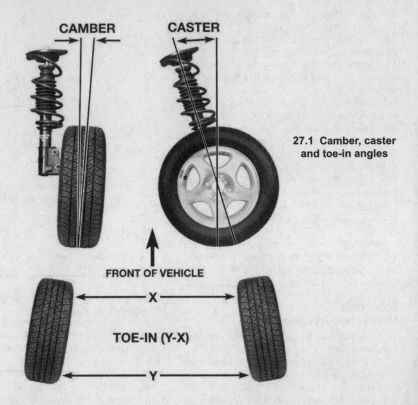

27.1 Camber, caster and toe-in angles

27   Wheel alignment - general information

Refer to illustration 27.1

A wheel alignment refers to the adjustments made to the wheels so they are in proper angular relationship to the suspension and the ground. Wheels that are out of proper alignment not only affect vehicle control, but also increase tire wear. The front end should be measured for camber, caster and toe-in **(see illustration)**; toe-in can be adjusted by turning the tie-rods in or out but camber and caster are pre-set at the factory and cannot be adjusted. If camber and caster aren't within the specified dimensions, suspension parts are bent or worn and must be replaced. The rear should be measured for camber and toe-in. Toe-in is adjusted by an eccentric cam at the inner end of the toe control arm. Rear camber isn't adjustable; it's set at the factory. If it is not within the standard dimensions, suspension parts are bent or worn and must be replaced.

Getting the proper wheel alignment is a very exacting process, one in which complicated and expensive machines are necessary to perform the job properly. Because of this, you should have a technician with the proper equipment perform these tasks. We will, however, use this space to give you a basic idea of what is involved with a wheel alignment so you can better understand the process and deal intelligently with the shop that does the work.

Toe-in is the turning in of the wheels. The purpose of a toe specification is to ensure parallel rolling of the wheels. In a vehicle with zero toe-in, the distance between the front edges of the wheels will be the same as the distance between the rear edges of the wheels. The actual amount of toe-in is normally only a fraction of an inch. Incorrect toe-in will cause the tires to wear improperly by making them scrub against the road surface.

Camber is the tilting of the wheels from vertical when viewed from one end of the vehicle. When the wheels tilt out at the top, the camber is said to be positive (+). When the wheels tilt in at the top the camber is negative (-). The amount of tilt is measured in degrees from vertical and this measurement is called the camber angle. This angle affects the amount of tire tread which contacts the road and compensates for changes in the suspension geometry when the vehicle is cornering or traveling over an undulating surface.

Caster is the tilting of the front steering axis from the vertical. A tilt toward the rear is positive caster and a tilt toward the front is negative caster.

Chapter 11 Body

Contents

1 General information

These models feature a "unibody" layout, using a floor pan with front and rear frame side rails which support the body components, front and rear suspension systems and other mechanical components. Certain components are particularly vulnerable to accident damage and can be unbolted and repaired or replaced. Among these parts are the body moldings, bumpers, hood, liftgate and some glass.

Only general body maintenance practices and body panel repair procedures within the scope of the do-it-yourselfer are included in this Chapter.

2 Body - maintenance

1   The condition of your vehicle's body is very important, because the resale value depends a great deal on it. It's much more difficult to repair a neglected or damaged body than it is to repair mechanical components. The hidden areas of the body, such as the wheel wells, the frame and the engine compartment, are equally important, although they don't require as frequent attention as the rest of the body.
2   Once a year, or every 12,000 miles, it's a good idea to have the underside of the body steam cleaned. All traces of dirt and oil will be removed and the area can then be inspected carefully for rust, damaged brake lines, frayed electrical wires, damaged cables and other problems.
3   At the same time, clean the engine and the engine compartment with a steam cleaner or water soluble degreaser.
4   The wheel wells should be given close attention, since undercoating can peel away and stones and dirt thrown up by the tires can cause the paint to chip and flake, allowing rust to set in. If rust is found, clean down to the bare metal and apply an anti-rust paint.
5   The body should be washed about once a week. Wet the vehicle thoroughly to soften the dirt, then wash it down with a soft sponge and plenty of clean soapy water. If the surplus dirt is not washed off very carefully, it can wear down the paint.
6   Spots of tar or asphalt thrown up from the road should be removed with a cloth soaked in solvent.
7   Once every six months, wax the body and chrome trim. If a chrome cleaner is used to remove rust from any of the vehicle's plated parts, remember that the cleaner also removes part of the chrome, so use it sparingly.

3 Vinyl trim - maintenance

Don't clean vinyl trim with detergents, caustic soap or petroleum-based cleaners. Plain soap and water works just fine, with a soft brush to clean dirt that may be ingrained. Wash the vinyl as frequently as the rest of the vehicle.

After cleaning, application of a high quality rubber and vinyl protectant will help prevent oxidation and cracks. The protectant can also be applied to weatherstripping, vacuum lines and rubber hoses, which often fail as a result of chemical degradation, and to the tires.

4 Upholstery and carpets - maintenance

1   Every three months remove the carpets or mats and clean the interior of the vehicle (more frequently if necessary). Vacuum the upholstery and carpets to remove loose dirt and dust.
2   Leather upholstery requires special care. Stains should be removed with warm water and a very mild soap solution. Use a clean, damp cloth to remove the soap, then wipe again with a dry cloth. Never use alcohol, gasoline, nail polish remover or thinner to clean leather upholstery.
3   After cleaning, regularly treat leather upholstery with a leather wax. Never use car wax on leather upholstery.
4   In areas where the interior of the vehicle is subject to bright sunlight, cover leather seats with a sheet if the vehicle is to be left out for any length of time.

These photos illustrate a method of repairing simple dents. They are intended to supplement *Body repair - minor damage* in this Chapter and should not be used as the sole instructions for body repair on these vehicles.

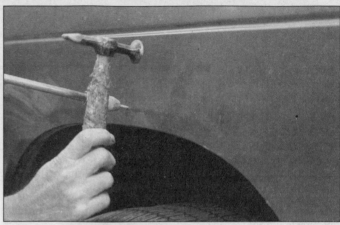

1 If you can't access the backside of the body panel to hammer out the dent, pull it out with a slide-hammer-type dent puller. In the deepest portion of the dent or along the crease line, drill or punch hole(s) at least one inch apart . . .

2 . . . then screw the slide-hammer into the hole and operate it. Tap with a hammer near the edge of the dent to help 'pop' the metal back to its original shape. When you're finished, the dent area should be close to its original contour and about 1/8-inch below the surface of the surrounding metal

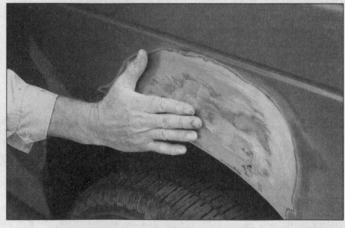

3 Using coarse-grit sandpaper, remove the paint down to the bare metal. Hand sanding works fine, but the disc sander shown here makes the job faster. Use finer (about 320-grit) sandpaper to feather-edge the paint at least one inch around the dent area

4 When the paint is removed, touch will probably be more helpful than sight for telling if the metal is straight. Hammer down the high spots or raise the low spots as necessary. Clean the repair area with wax/silicone remover

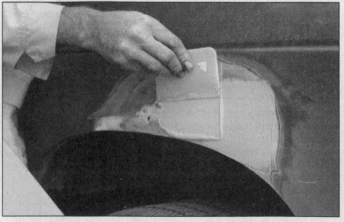

5 Following label instructions, mix up a batch of plastic filler and hardener. The ratio of filler to hardener is critical, and, if you mix it incorrectly, it will either not cure properly or cure too quickly (you won't have time to file and sand it into shape)

6 Working quickly so the filler doesn't harden, use a plastic applicator to press the body filler firmly into the metal, assuring it bonds completely. Work the filler until it matches the original contour and is slightly above the surrounding metal

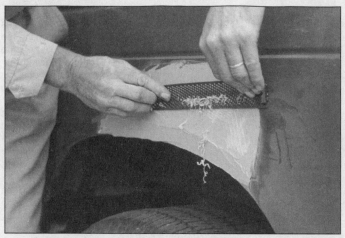

7 Let the filler harden until you can just dent it with your fingernail. Use a body file or Surform tool (shown here) to rough-shape the filler

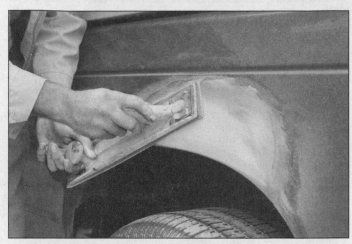

8 Use coarse-grit sandpaper and a sanding board or block to work the filler down until it's smooth and even. Work down to finer grits of sandpaper - always using a board or block - ending up with 360 or 400 grit

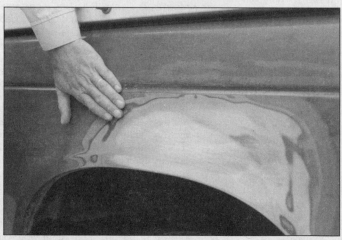

9 You shouldn't be able to feel any ridge at the transition from the filler to the bare metal or from the bare metal to the old paint. As soon as the repair is flat and uniform, remove the dust and mask off the adjacent panels or trim pieces

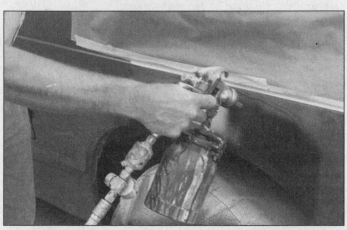

10 Apply several layers of primer to the area. Don't spray the primer on too heavy, so it sags or runs, and make sure each coat is dry before you spray on the next one. A professional-type spray gun is being used here, but aerosol spray primer is available inexpensively from auto parts stores

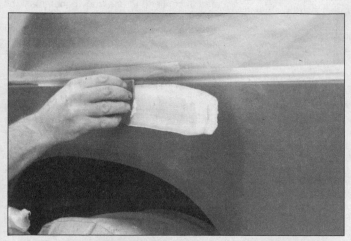

11 The primer will help reveal imperfections or scratches. Fill these with glazing compound. Follow the label instructions and sand it with 360 or 400-grit sandpaper until it's smooth. Repeat the glazing, sanding and respraying until the primer reveals a perfectly smooth surface

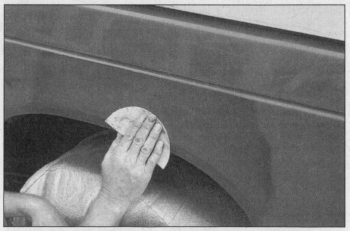

12 Finish sand the primer with very fine sandpaper (400 or 600-grit) to remove the primer overspray. Clean the area with water and allow it to dry. Use a tack rag to remove any dust, then apply the finish coat. Don't attempt to rub out or wax the repair area until the paint has dried completely (at least two weeks)

5   Body repair - minor damage

See photo sequence

Repair of minor scratches

1   If the scratch is superficial and does not penetrate to the metal of the body, repair is very simple. Lightly rub the scratched area with a fine rubbing compound to remove loose paint and built-up wax. Rinse the area with clean water.

2   Apply touch-up paint to the scratch, using a small brush. Continue to apply thin layers of paint until the surface of the paint in the scratch is level with the surrounding paint. Allow the new paint at least two weeks to harden, then blend it into the surrounding paint by rubbing with a very fine rubbing compound. Finally, apply a coat of wax to the scratch area.

3   If the scratch has penetrated the paint and exposed the metal of the body, causing the metal to rust, a different repair technique is required. Remove all loose rust from the bottom of the scratch with a pocket knife, then apply rust inhibiting paint to prevent the formation of rust in the future. Using a rubber or nylon applicator, coat the scratched area with glaze-type filler. If required, the filler can be mixed with thinner to provide a very thin paste, which is ideal for filling narrow scratches. Before the glaze filler in the scratch hardens, wrap a piece of smooth cotton cloth around the tip of a finger. Dip the cloth in thinner and then quickly wipe it along the surface of the scratch. This will ensure that the surface of the filler is slightly hollow. The scratch can now be painted over as described earlier in this section.

Repair of dents

4   When repairing dents, the first job is to pull the dent out until the affected area is as close as possible to its original shape. There is no point in trying to restore the original shape completely as the metal in the damaged area will have stretched on impact and cannot be restored to its original contours. It is better to bring the level of the dent up to a point which is about 1/8-inch below the level of the surrounding metal. In cases where the dent is very shallow, it is not worth trying to pull it out at all.

5   If the back side of the dent is accessible, it can be hammered out gently from behind using a soft-face hammer. While doing this, hold a block of wood firmly against the opposite side of the metal to absorb the hammer blows and prevent the metal from being stretched.

6   If the dent is in a section of the body which has double layers, or some other factor makes it inaccessible from behind, a different technique is required. Drill several small holes through the metal inside the damaged area, particularly in the deeper sections. Screw long, self-tapping screws into the holes just enough for them to get a good grip in the metal. Now the dent can be pulled out by pulling on the protruding heads of the screws with locking pliers.

7   The next stage of repair is the removal of paint from the damaged area and from an inch or so of the surrounding metal. This is done with a wire brush or sanding disk in a drill motor, although it can be done just as effectively by hand with sandpaper. To complete the preparation for filling, score the surface of the bare metal with a screwdriver or the tang of a file, or drill small holes in the affected area. This will provide a good grip for the filler material. To complete the repair, see the subsection on filling and painting later in this Section.

Repair of rust holes or gashes

8   Remove all paint from the affected area and from an inch or so of the surrounding metal using a sanding disk or wire brush mounted in a drill motor. If these are not available, a few sheets of sandpaper will do the job just as effectively.

9   With the paint removed, you will be able to determine the severity of the corrosion and decide whether to replace the whole panel, if possible, or repair the affected area. New body panels are not as expensive as most people think and it is often quicker to install a new panel than to repair large areas of rust.

10   Remove all trim pieces from the affected area except those which will act as a guide to the original shape of the damaged body, such as headlight shells, etc. Using metal snips or a hacksaw blade, remove all loose metal and any other metal that is badly affected by rust. Hammer the edges of the hole in to create a slight depression for the filler material.

11   Wire brush the affected area to remove the powdery rust from the surface of the metal. If the back of the rusted area is accessible, treat it with rust inhibiting paint.

12   Before filling is done, block the hole in some way. This can be done with sheet metal riveted or screwed into place, or by stuffing the hole with wire mesh.

13   Once the hole is blocked off, the affected area can be filled and painted. See the following subsection on filling and painting.

Filling and painting

14   Many types of body fillers are available, but generally speaking, body repair kits which contain filler paste and a tube of resin hardener are best for this type of repair work. A wide, flexible plastic or nylon applicator will be necessary for imparting a smooth and contoured finish to the surface of the filler material. Mix up a small amount of filler on a clean piece of wood or cardboard (use the hardener sparingly). Follow the manufacturer's instructions on the package, otherwise the filler will set incorrectly.

15   Using the applicator, apply the filler paste to the prepared area. Draw the applicator across the surface of the filler to achieve the desired contour and to level the filler sur-
face. As soon as a contour that approximates the original one is achieved, stop working the paste. If you continue, the paste will begin to stick to the applicator. Continue to add thin layers of paste at 20-minute intervals until the level of the filler is just above the surrounding metal.

16   Once the filler has hardened, the excess can be removed with a body file. From then on, progressively finer grades of sandpaper should be used, starting with a 180-grit paper and finishing with 600-grit wet-or-dry paper. Always wrap the sandpaper around a flat rubber or wooden block, otherwise the surface of the filler will not be completely flat. During the sanding of the filler surface, the wet-or-dry paper should be periodically rinsed in water. This will ensure that a very smooth finish is produced in the final stage.

17   At this point, the repair area should be surrounded by a ring of bare metal, which in turn should be encircled by the finely feathered edge of good paint. Rinse the repair area with clean water until all of the dust produced by the sanding operation is gone.

18   Spray the entire area with a light coat of primer. This will reveal any imperfections in the surface of the filler. Repair the imperfections with fresh filler paste or glaze filler and once more smooth the surface with sandpaper. Repeat this spray-and-repair procedure until you are satisfied that the surface of the filler and the feathered edge of the paint are perfect. Rinse the area with clean water and allow it to dry completely.

19   The repair area is now ready for painting. Spray painting must be carried out in a warm, dry, windless and dust free atmosphere. These conditions can be created if you have access to a large indoor work area, but if you are forced to work in the open, you will have to pick the day very carefully. If you are working indoors, dousing the floor in the work area with water will help settle the dust which would otherwise be in the air. If the repair area is confined to one body panel, mask off the surrounding panels. This will help minimize the effects of a slight mismatch in paint color. Trim pieces such as chrome strips, door handles, etc., will also need to be masked off or removed. Use masking tape and several thicknesses of newspaper for the masking operations.

20   Before spraying, shake the paint can thoroughly, then spray a test area until the spray painting technique is mastered. Cover the repair area with a thick coat of primer. The thickness should be built up using several thin layers of primer rather than one thick one. Using 600-grit wet-or-dry sandpaper, rub down the surface of the primer until it is very smooth. While doing this, the work area should be thoroughly rinsed with water and the wet-or-dry sandpaper periodically rinsed as well. Allow the primer to dry before spraying additional coats.

21   Spray on the top coat, again building up the thickness by using several thin layers of paint. Begin spraying in the center of the

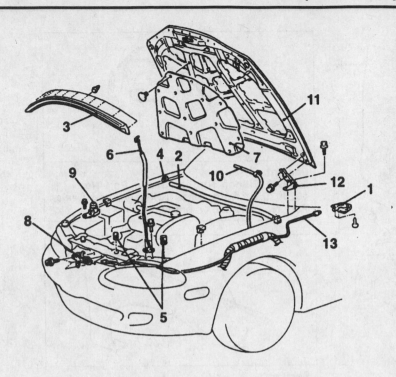

Adjustment of clearance around hood and height

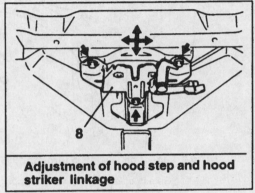

Adjustment of hood step and hood striker linkage

9.4 Hood details (1995 through 1999 shown)

1	Hood latch release handle	6	Support rod	10	Windshield washer hose
2	Weatherstrip	7	Silencer	11	Hood
3	Front weatherstrip	8	Latch	12	Hinge
4	Hood damper	9	Anti-theft switch	13	Latch release cable
5	Bumper				

repair area and then, using a circular motion, work out until the whole repair area and about two inches of the surrounding original paint is covered. Remove all masking material 10 to 15 minutes after spraying on the final coat of paint. Allow the new paint at least two weeks to harden, then use a very fine rubbing compound to blend the edges of the new paint into the existing paint. Finally, apply a coat of wax.

6   Body repair - major damage

1   Major damage must be repaired by an auto body shop specifically equipped to perform unibody repairs. These shops have the specialized equipment required to do the job properly.

2   If the damage is extensive, the body must be checked for proper alignment or the vehicle's handling characteristics may be adversely affected and other components may wear at an accelerated rate.

3   Due to the fact that all of the major body components (hood, fenders, etc.) are separate and replaceable units, any seriously damaged components should be replaced rather than

repaired. Sometimes the components can be found in a wrecking yard that specializes in used vehicle components, often at considerable savings over the cost of new parts.

7   Hinges and locks - maintenance

Once every 3000 miles, or every three months, the hinges and latch assemblies on the doors, hood and liftgate should be given a few drops of light oil or lock lubricant. The door latch strikers should also be lubricated with a thin coat of grease to reduce wear and ensure free movement. Lubricate the door and trunk locks with spray-on graphite lubricant.

8   Windshield and fixed glass - replacement

Replacement of the windshield and fixed glass requires the use of special fast-setting adhesive/caulk materials and some specialized tools. It is recommended that these operations be left to a dealer or a shop specializing in glass work.

9   Hood - removal, installation and adjustment

Refer to illustration 9.4
Note: *The hood is heavy and somewhat awkward to remove and install - at least two people should perform this procedure.*

Removal and installation

1   Make marks around the bolt heads to ensure proper alignment during installation.

2   Use blankets or pads to cover the cowl area of the body and fenders. This will protect the body and paint as the hood is lifted off.

3   Disconnect any cables or wires that will interfere with removal.

4   Have an assistant support the hood. Remove the hinge-to-hood bolts **(see illustration)**.

5   Lift off the hood.

6   Installation is the reverse of removal.

Adjustment

7   Fore-and-aft and side-to-side adjustment of the hood is done by moving the hinge plate slot after loosening the bolts or nuts.

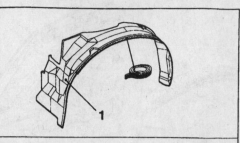

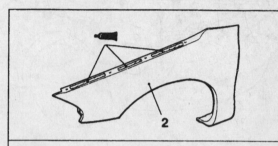

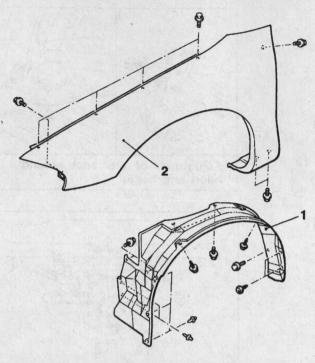

10.2 Fender details (1995 through 1999 shown)

1   Splash shield   2   Fender panel

Sealant:
MOPAR Silicon Rubber Sealer Part No.
4026070 or Auto Glass Adhesive and Sealer
Part No.2298825 or equivalent

Sealant:
MOPAR Silicon Rubber Sealer Part No.
4026070 or equivalent

8   Scribe or draw a line around the bolt heads and the entire hinge plate so you can judge the amount of movement.

9   Loosen the bolts or nuts and move the hood into correct alignment. Move it only a little at a time. Tighten the hinge bolts or nuts and carefully lower the hood to check the position.

10   If necessary after installation, the entire hood latch assembly can be adjusted up-and-down as well as from side-to-side on the radiator support so the hood closes securely, flush with the fenders. To make the adjustment, scribe a line around the hood latch mounting bolts to provide a reference point, then loosen them and reposition the latch assembly, as necessary **(see illustration 9.4)**. Following adjustment, retighten the mounting bolts.

11   Finally, adjust the hood bumpers on the radiator support so the hood, when closed, is flush with the fenders.

12   The hood latch assembly, as well as the hinges, should be periodically lubricated with lithium-base grease to prevent binding and wear.

10   Front fender - removal and installation

Refer to illustration 10.2

Warning: These models have airbags. Always disable the airbag system before working in the vicinity of the impact sensors, steering column or instrument panel to avoid the possibility of accidental deployment of the airbag, which could cause personal injury (see Chapter 12) (1995 models).

1   Remove the headlight, turn signal light and front bumper (see Chapter 12 and Section 18).

2   Remove the screws and detach the splash shield **(see illustration)**.

3   Remove the bolts and detach the fender.

4   Prior to installation, apply silicone sealant to the contact surfaces of the fender and body **(see illustration 10.2)**. Installation is the reverse of removal.

11   Liftgate - removal, installation and adjustment

Refer to illustration 11.3

Note: The liftgate is heavy and somewhat awkward to remove and install - at least two people should perform this procedure.

1   Open the liftgate and cover the edges of the rear compartment with pads or cloths to protect the painted surfaces when the lid is removed.

2   Disconnect any cables or electrical connectors attached to the liftgate that would interfere with removal.

3   Make alignment marks around the hinge bolts **(see illustration)**.

4   Have an assistant support the liftgate and detach the support struts (see Section 12).

5   While an assistant supports the liftgate, remove the lid-to-hinge bolts on both sides and lift it off.

6   Installation is the reverse of removal. **Note:** When reinstalling the liftgate, align the lid-to-hinge bolts with the marks made during removal.

7   After installation, close the liftgate and make sure it's in proper alignment with the surrounding body.

8   Forward-or-backward and side-to-side adjustments are made by detaching the headliner, loosening the hinge-to-liftgate nuts and gently moving the liftgate into correct alignment **(see illustration 11.3)**.

9   The liftgate latch striker can be adjusted up-and-down as well as from side-to-side. To make the adjustment, scribe a line around the mounting bolts to provide a reference point, then loosen them and reposition the latch assembly, as necessary **(see illustration 11.3)**. Following adjustment, retighten the mounting bolts.

12   Liftgate support struts - replacement

Warning: The support strut is filled with pressurized gas - do not disassemble this component (if it is faulty replace it with a new one).

Note: The trunk lid/rear liftgate is heavy and somewhat awkward to hold securely while replacing the struts - at least two people should perform this procedure.

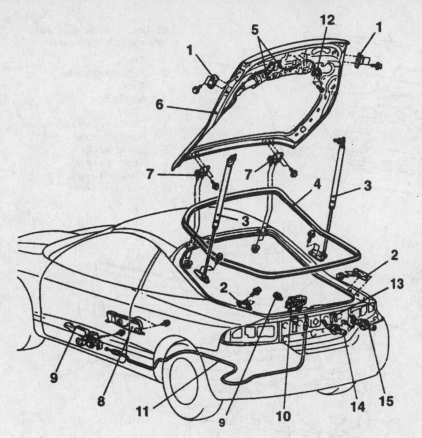

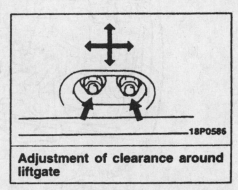

Adjustment of clearance around liftgate

Adjustment of liftgate step and liftgate striker linkage

11.3 Liftgate details (1995 through 1999 shown)

1	Upper damper	7	Hinge	12	Striker	
2	Lower damper	8	Release handle cover	13	Retainer	
3	Strut	9	Release handle	14	Lock cylinder (without anti-theft system)	
4	Weatherstrip	10	Latch			
5	Wiring harness	11	Latch release cable	15	Lock cylinder (with anti-theft system)	
6	Liftgate					

1   Remove the weatherstrip from the liftgate opening for access to the strut fasteners.

2   With the liftgate supported in the open position, remove the nuts or bolts **(see illustration 11.3)**. **Warning:** *Guide the end of the strut away from the liftgate glass, because it will extend suddenly when released.*

3   Detach the trim panel, remove the nut or bolts securing the lower end, and lift the strut from the vehicle.

4   Installation is the reverse of the removal procedure.

---

13   Door trim panel - removal and installation

Refer to illustrations 13.2, 13.3 and 13.5

1   Disconnect the negative cable from the battery.

2   Remove the window crank on manual regulator equipped models by working a cloth back-and-forth behind the handle to dislodge the clip **(see illustration)**.

3   Remove any door trim panel retaining screws and door pull/armrest assemblies **(see illustration)**.

4   Insert a wide putty knife or screwdriver between the trim panel and door to disengage the retaining clips. Work around the outer edge until the panel is free.

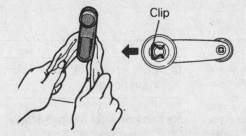

13.2 On models with manual window regulators, work a cloth back and forth behind the window crank until the clip is dislodged

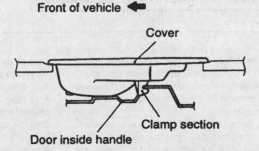

13.3 Door handle cross-section view (1995 through 1999 models)

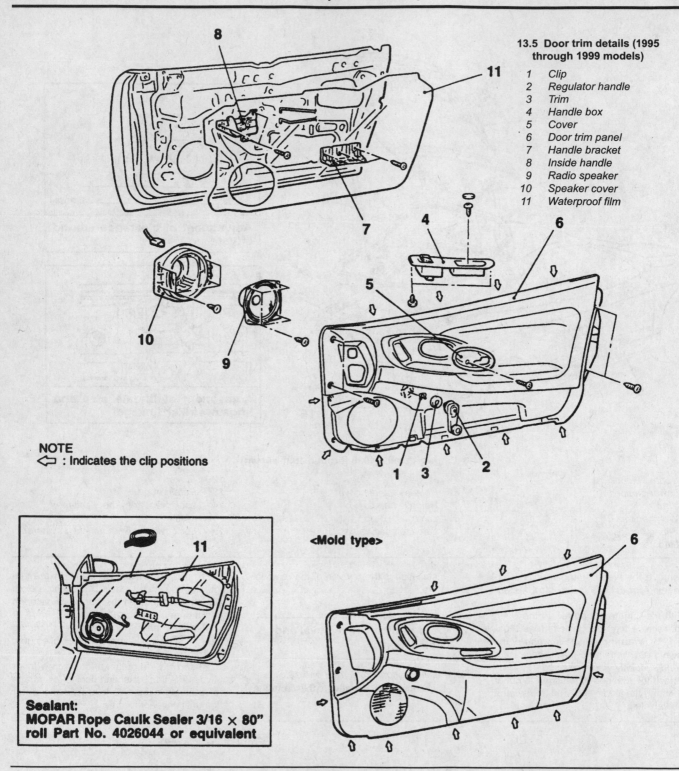

13.5 Door trim details (1995 through 1999 models)

1. Clip
2. Regulator handle
3. Trim
4. Handle box
5. Cover
6. Door trim panel
7. Handle bracket
8. Inside handle
9. Radio speaker
10. Speaker cover
11. Waterproof film

NOTE
⇦ : Indicates the clip positions

<Mold type>

Sealant:
MOPAR Rope Caulk Sealer 3/16 × 80"
roll Part No. 4026044 or equivalent

5   Once all of the clips are disengaged, detach the trim panel, disconnect any electrical connectors and remove the trim panel from the vehicle by gently pulling it up and out **(see illustration)**.

6   For access to the inner door, peel back the plastic waterproof film, taking care not to tear it. To install the trim panel, first press the waterproof film into place.

7   Prior to installation of the door panel, be sure to reinstall any clips in the panel which may have come out during the removal procedure and stayed in the door.

8   Plug in any electrical connectors and place the panel in position. Press it into place until the clips are seated and install any retaining screws and armrest/door pulls. Install the manual regulator window crank.

14   Door - removal, installation and adjustment

Removal and installation
Refer to illustrations 14.3 and 14.6

1   Remove the door trim panel (see Section 13), disconnect any electrical connectors and push them through the door opening so they

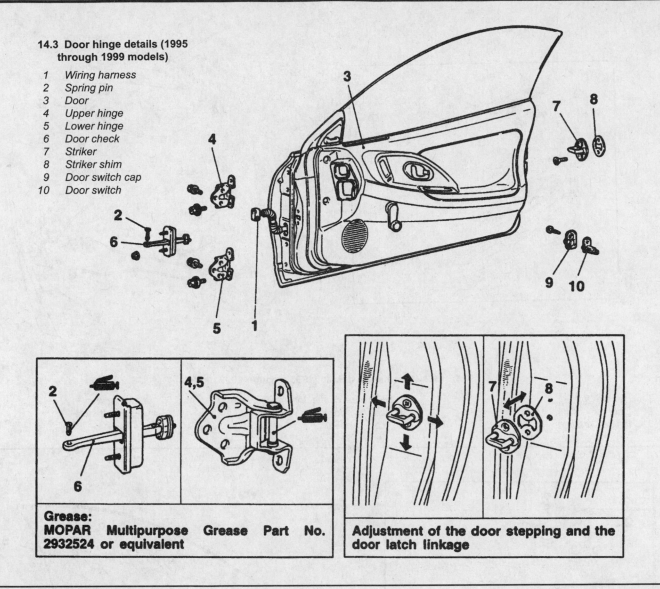

14.3 Door hinge details (1995 through 1999 models)

1   Wiring harness
2   Spring pin
3   Door
4   Upper hinge
5   Lower hinge
6   Door check
7   Striker
8   Striker shim
9   Door switch cap
10 Door switch

Grease:
MOPAR   Multipurpose   Grease   Part   No. 2932524 or equivalent

Adjustment of the door stepping and the door latch linkage

won't interfere with removal.

2   Position a floor jack under the door or have an assistant on hand to support the door when the hinge bolts are removed. **Note:** *If a jack is used, place a rag between it and the door to protect the door's paint.*

3   Remove the center pin from the door stop strut **(see illustration)**.

4   Scribe around the door bolts.

5   Remove the hinge-to-door bolts and carefully detach the door. Installation is the reverse of removal.

Adjustment

6   Following installation, make sure the door is aligned properly. Adjust it if necessary as follows:

a) *Up-and-down and forward-and-backward*

adjustments are made by loosening the hinge-to-body bolts and moving the door, as necessary. A special offset tool may be required to reach some of the bolts **(see illustration)**.

b) *In-and-out and up-and-down adjustments are made by loosening the door side hinge bolts and moving the door, as necessary.*

c) *The door lock striker can also be adjusted both up-and-down and sideways to provide a positive engagement with the locking mechanism. This is done by loosening the screws and moving the striker, as necessary.*

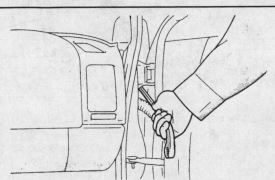

14.6 A cranked wrench such as this one may be required to reach the hinge-to-body bolts when adjusting the doors

15 Door latch, lock cylinder and handle - removal and installation

Refer to illustration 15.2

1   Remove the door trim panel and water deflector (see Section 13).

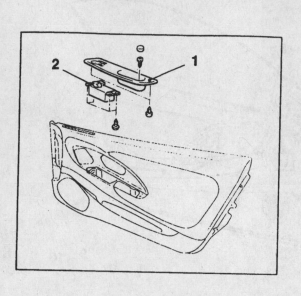

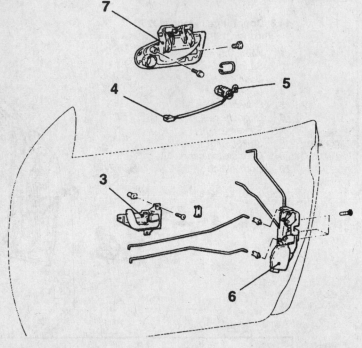

15.2 Door handle details (1995 through 1999 models)

1   Handle box
2   Door lock switch
3   Inside handle

4   Electrical connector (models with
    central door locking system)
5   Lock cylinder

6   Latch
7   Outside handle

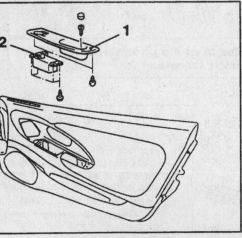

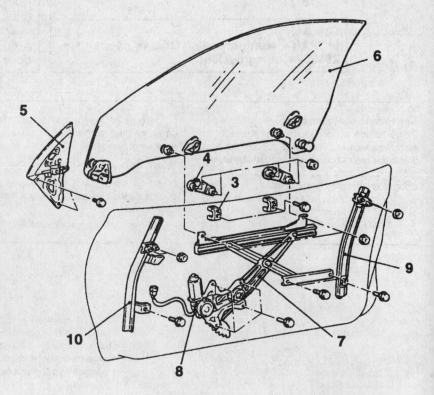

**16.3 Door glass and regulator details
(1995 through 1999 models)**

1   Handle box
2   Power window switch
3   Up-stop
4   Inner stabilizer
5   Delta sash
6   Window glass
7   Window regulator
8   Power window motor
9   Glass guide rear track
10 Glass guide front track

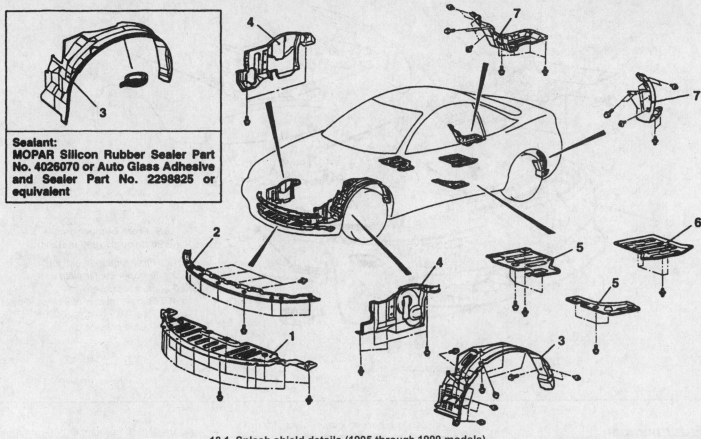

**Sealant:
MOPAR Silicon Rubber Sealer Part
No. 4026070 or Auto Glass Adhesive
and Sealer Part No. 2298825 or
equivalent**

18.1 Splash shield details (1995 through 1999 models)

1	Front center under cover panel	4	Under cover side panel	6	Rear crossmember under cover panel
2	Lower front bumper plate	5	Rear seat under cover panel	7	Rear floor under cover panel
3	Front splash shield				

Door latch

2   Disconnect the rods from the outside handle, the latch and the lock cylinder (see illustration).
3   Remove the latch retaining screws from the end of the door.
4   Remove the door latch.
5   Installation is the reverse of removal.

Lock cylinder and outside handle

6   Disconnect the control link and electrical connector (if equipped) from the lock cylinder and outside handle.
7   Remove the outside handle retention screws and detach the handle (see illustration 15.2) and lock cylinder from the door.
8   Use a screwdriver to pry the retaining clip off and remove the lock cylinder from the door.
9   Installation is the reverse of removal.

Inside handle

10   Disconnect the control rods, remove the handle-to-door screws and lift the handle off the door (see illustration 15.2).
11   Installation is the reverse of removal.

16   Door window glass - removal, installation and adjustment

Refer to illustration 16.3
1   Remove the door trim panel and waterproof film (see Section 13).
2   Raise the window until the retaining bolts are accessible through the access hole.
3   Remove the two bolts and the glass holder, then detach the glass from the regulator and lift it up and out of the door (see illustration).
4   Adjust the glass position by loosening the regulator bolts and move the regulator assembly forward-and-back to achieve the desired angle.
5   Installation is the reverse of the removal procedure.

17   Window regulator - removal and installation

1   Remove the door trim panel and water deflector (see Section 13).
2   Remove the door window glass (see Section 16). If the vehicle you are working on has power windows, unplug the electrical connector from the motor.
3   Remove the bolts, then detach the regulator from the door (see illustration 16.3).
4   Pull the regulator through the access hole in the door hole to remove it.
5   Installation is the reverse of removal.

18   Splash shields and bumpers - removal and installation

Splash shields

Refer to illustration 18.1
1   1995 through 1999 models use a number of panels under the vehicle (see illustration).
2   Where necessary for access, jack up the vehicle, support it securely on jackstands and remove the wheel(s).
3   To remove the panels, remove the bolts and lower the panel clear of the vehicle.
4   Installation is the reverse of the removal steps. If the inner fender panel was removed, coat its outer edge with silicone sealant where it meets the fender.

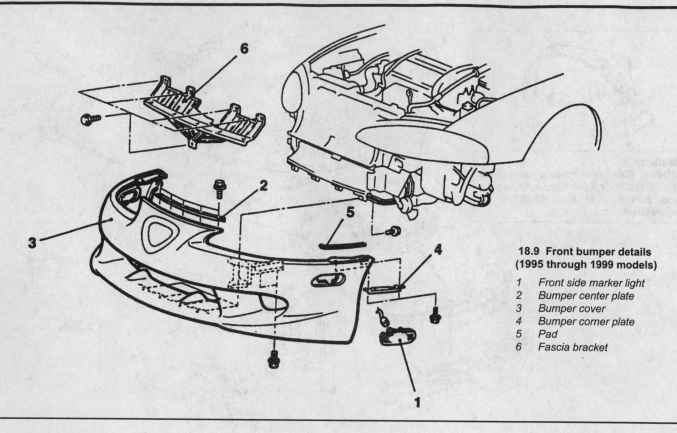

18.9 Front bumper details (1995 through 1999 models)

1   Front side marker light
2   Bumper center plate
3   Bumper cover
4   Bumper corner plate
5   Pad
6   Fascia bracket

Front bumper

Refer to illustrations 18.9 and 18.10

Warning: *These models have airbags. Always disable the airbag system before working in the vicinity of the impact sensors, steering column or instrument panel to avoid the possibility of accidental deployment of the airbag, which could cause personal injury (see Chapter 12).*

5   Apply the parking brake, block the rear wheels, lift the front of the vehicle and support it securely on jackstands.

6   Disconnect any wiring that would interfere with bumper removal.

7   Remove the splash shield **(see illustration 18.1)**.

8   Remove the front trim (some models). Remove the turn signal, fog and parking light assemblies.

9   Remove the bolts and nuts. On some models, the top of the bumper is secured by plastic pins. Pry up the center of each pin with a flat-bladed screwdriver or similar tool, then pull the pin out with your fingers. Detach the bumper assembly **(see illustration)**.

10   Pull the bumper assembly from the vehicle. To remove the bumper cover from the bumper unit, remove the cover nuts/bolts **(see illustration)**.

11   Installation is the reverse of removal.

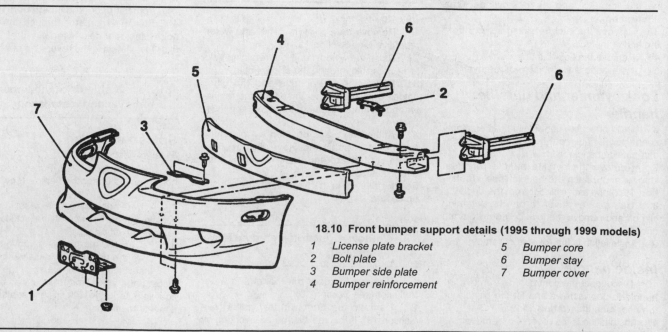

18.10 Front bumper support details (1995 through 1999 models)

1   License plate bracket
2   Bolt plate
3   Bumper side plate
4   Bumper reinforcement
5   Bumper core
6   Bumper stay
7   Bumper cover

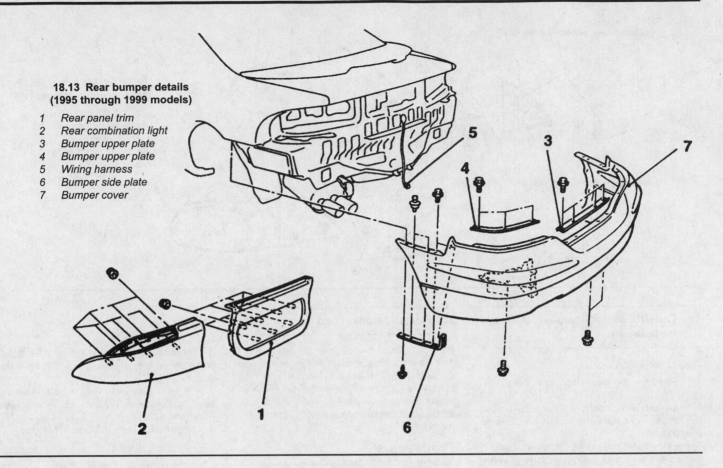

18.13 Rear bumper details (1995 through 1999 models)

1   Rear panel trim
2   Rear combination light
3   Bumper upper plate
4   Bumper upper plate
5   Wiring harness
6   Bumper side plate
7   Bumper cover

Rear bumper

Refer to illustrations 18.13 and 18.14

12   Remove the tail light assemblies and disconnect any wiring that would interfere with bumper removal.

13   Remove the clips, nuts and bolts and detach the rear bumper assembly from the vehicle **(see illustration)**.

14   To remove the bumper cover from the bumper unit, remove the cover nuts/bolts **(see illustration)**.

15   Installation is the reverse of removal.

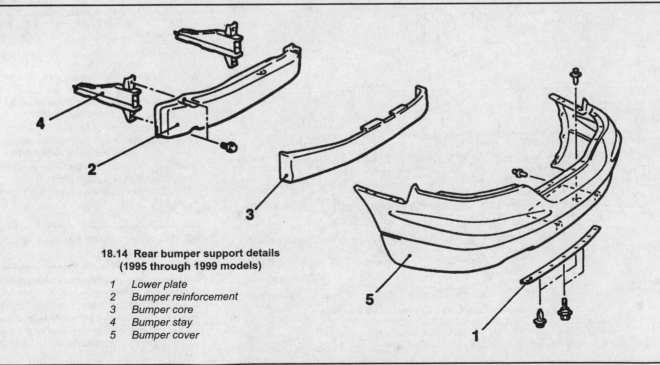

18.14 Rear bumper support details (1995 through 1999 models)

1   Lower plate
2   Bumper reinforcement
3   Bumper core
4   Bumper stay
5   Bumper cover

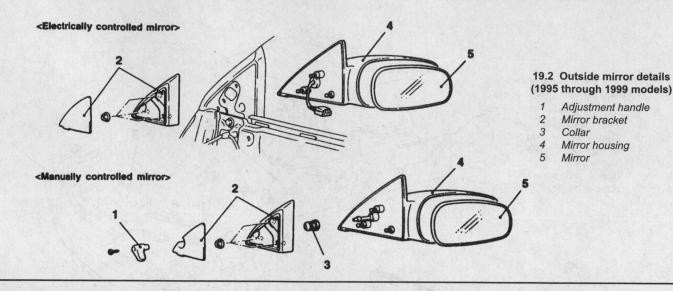

19.2 Outside mirror details (1995 through 1999 models)

1   Adjustment handle
2   Mirror bracket
3   Collar
4   Mirror housing
5   Mirror

19 Outside mirror - removal and installation

Refer to illustration 19.2

1   Remove the door trim panel (see Section 13).
2   On manually controlled models, remove the screw and detach the control handle **(see illustration)**.
3   Pry off the trim cover. On power mirrors, detach the electrical connector **(see illustration 19.2)**.
4   Remove the retaining nuts and detach the mirror **(see illustration 19.2)**.
5   Installation is the reverse of removal.

20 Seats - removal and installation

Warning: *These models have airbags. Always disable the airbag system before working in the vicinity of the impact sensors, steering column or instrument panel to avoid the possibility of accidental deployment of the airbag, which could cause personal injury (see Chapter 12).*

Front seats

Refer to illustration 20.1

1   Remove the retaining nuts and bolts, disconnect any electrical connectors and lift the seat from the vehicle **(see illustration)**.
2   Installation is the reverse of removal.

Rear seats

Refer to illustration 20.4

3   Reach under the lower seat cushion, lifting up on the release levers, then pull the cushion out.
4   Remove the mounting bolts and lift the seat back assembly out of the vehicle **(see illustration)**.
5   Installation is the reverse of removal.

21 Instrument cluster bezel - removal and installation

Refer to illustration 21.1

Warning: *These models have airbags. Always disable the airbag system before working in the vicinity of the impact sensors, steering column or instrument panel to avoid the possibility of accidental deployment of the airbag, which could cause personal injury (see Chapter 12).*

1   If you're working on a 1995 through 1999 model, remove the screws from the top underside of the bezel and withdraw it from the instrument panel **(see illustration 21.1)**.
2   If you're working on a 2000 or later model, remove the instrument cluster under cover (see Section 21). Disengage the two lower clips (one on each side of the trim panel) and two upper clips, then remove the panel from the instrument panel.
3   Installation is the reverse of the removal procedure.

22 Dashboard trim panels - removal and installation

Warning: *These models have airbags. Always disable the airbag system before working in the vicinity of the impact sensors, steering column or instrument panel to avoid the possibility of accidental deployment of the airbag, which could cause personal injury (see Chapter 12).*

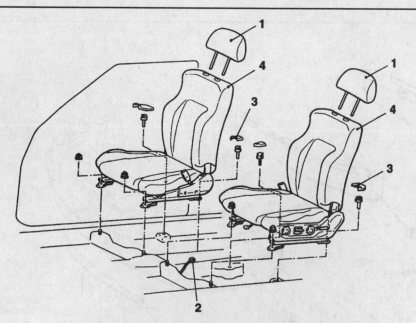

20.1 Front seat details (1995 through 1999 models)

1   Headrest
2   Electrical connector
3   Cover
4   Seat

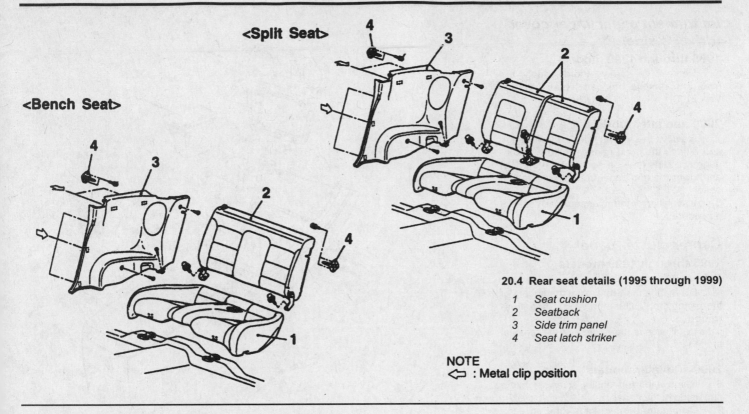

<Split Seat>

<Bench Seat>

20.4 Rear seat details (1995 through 1999)

1   Seat cushion
2   Seatback
3   Side trim panel
4   Seat latch striker

NOTE
⇦ : Metal clip position

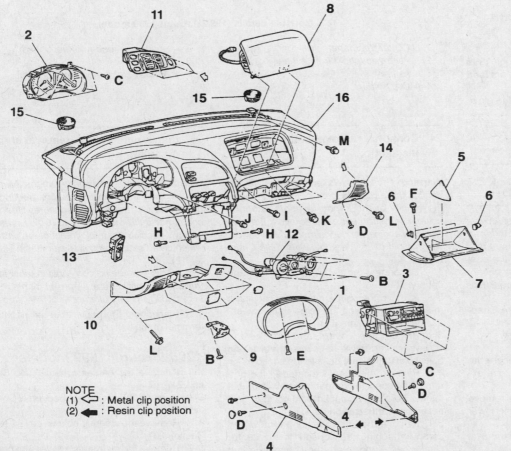

**21.1 Instrument panel details
(1995 through 1999 models)**

1   Meter bezel
2   Combination meter
3   Radio
4   Console side cover
5   Sunglasses holder
6   Stopper
7   Glove box
8   Passenger airbag module
9   Hood latch release handle
10 Instrument panel under cover
11 Center air outlet
12 Heater control
13 Instrument panel switch
14 Instrument panel under cover
15 Front speaker
16 Instrument panel
A   5X16 self-tapping blunt-ended
    screw
B   5X12 self-tapping screw
C   5X16 self-tapping point-ended
    screw
D   5X16 black self-tapping point-
    ended screw
E   5X20 black self-tapping
    flathead screw
F   5X16 screw with washer
G   5X16 black screw with washer
H   6X16 bolt with washer
I   6X16 black bolt with washer
J   6X20 bolt with washer
K   6X20 bolt with wide washer
L   6X25 black bolt with wide
    washer
M   6X16 point-ended bolt with
    washer

NOTE
(1) ⇦ : Metal clip position
(2) ◄ : Resin clip position

Instrument panel under cover (driver's side)

1995 through 1999 models

1   Remove the screws and disengage the clips and remove the panel **(see illustration 21.1)**.

2000 and later models

2   Remove the screws from the lower edge and detach the hood release handle. Disengage two clips (one on each side at the top) and lower the trim panel from the instrument panel.

3   Installation is the reverse of the removal procedure.

Center cluster panel

1995 through 1999 models

Refer to illustration 22.4

4   Disengage the two clips at the bottom of the panel, then pull the panel out **(see illustration)**.

5   Installation is the reverse of the removal procedure.

2000 and later models

6   Remove the self-tapping screws from the underside of the panel.

7   Disengage the two clips (one on each side at the top), then pull the panel out.

8   Installation is the reverse of the removal procedure.

Glove box

9   Open the glove box.

10   If you're working on a 1995 through 1999 model, disengage the glove box stoppers **(see illustration 21.1)**.

11   Remove the screws and lower the glove box from the instrument panel.

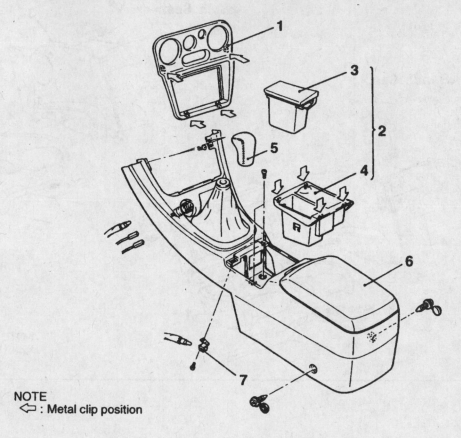

NOTE
◁ : Metal clip position

22.4 Console details (1995 through 1999 models)

1   Center trim panel
2   Ashtray/cupholder assembly
3   Ashtray
4   Cup holder
5   Shift lever knob (manual transaxle)
6   Console
7   Ashtray illumination light bracket

---

23   Steering column covers - removal and installation

Warning: *These models have airbags. Always disable the airbag system before working in the vicinity of the impact sensors, steering column or instrument panel to avoid the possibility of accidental deployment of the airbag, which could cause personal injury (see Chapter 12).*

1   Remove the steering wheel (see Chapter 10).

2   Remove the column cover screws from the underside of the cover.

3   Unhook the plastic tabs that secure the lower cover to the upper cover. Remove the lower cover, then the upper cover.

4   On 1995 through 1999 models, remove the screws and take the pad out of the lower cover if necessary.

5   Installation is the reverse of the removal procedure.

24   Console - removal and installation

Warning: *These models have airbags. Always disable the airbag system before working in the vicinity of the impact sensors, steering column or instrument panel to avoid the possibility of accidental deployment of the airbag, which could cause personal injury (see Chapter 12).*

1   Disconnect the negative cable from the battery.

2   Remove the shift knob by unscrewing it (manual) or removing the screws and detaching the handle (automatic).

3   Pry out the covers and remove the screws holding the side covers in place and bolts holding the seat belts to the console.

4   Remove the screws located in the bottom of the console compartment by lifting out the cup holder (if equipped) and cover to gain access **(see illustration 22.4)**.

5   Remove the trim cover and remove the screws attaching the console to the center cluster panel and rotate the console up and out of the vehicle.

25   Instrument panel - removal and installation

Warning: *These models have airbags. Always disable the airbag system before working in the vicinity of the impact sensors, steering column or instrument panel to avoid the possibility of accidental deployment of the airbag, which could cause personal injury (see Chapter 12).*

Note: *This is a major, complicated job. Read through the procedure before beginning. Be sure to allow plenty of time.*

1   Disconnect the cable from the negative terminal of the battery.

1995 through 1999 models

2   Remove the center console (see Section 24).

3   Remove the steering wheel (see Chapter 10).

4   Remove the steering column covers (see Section 23).

5   Remove the instrument cluster trim panel (see Section 21).

6   Remove the instrument cluster and radio (see Chapter 12).
7   Remove the glove compartment (see Section 22).
8   Remove the passenger airbag module (see Chapter 12).
9   Remove the instrument cluster driver's side under cover (see Section 21).
10   Remove the center air outlet **(see illustration 21.1)**.
11   Remove the heater control assembly (see Chapter 3).
12   Reach behind the switch unit at the left end of the instrument panel. Remove the screws, carefully pull the unit from the panel and disconnect its electrical connectors.
13   Remove the screws, disengage the clips and remove the trim piece from under the passenger side of the dash.
14   Remove the radio speakers from the top of the dash.
15   Unbolt the instrument panel from the vehicle and take it out.
16   Installation is the reverse of the removal steps. Adjust the heater controls as described in Chapter 3.

2000 and later models

17   Remove the steering wheel (see Chapter 10).
18   Remove the steering column covers (see Section 23).
19   Disengage the clips at the top and bottom of the instrument panel end covers and remove the covers.
20   Carefully pull the switch unit from the left end of the instrument panel. Disconnect its electrical connectors.
21   Remove the instrument cluster driver's side under cover (see Section 21).
22   Remove the instrument cluster trim panel (see Section 21).
23   Remove the instrument cluster and radio (see Chapter 12).
24   Remove the instrument cluster center trim panel and its two air outlets (see Section 21).
25   Remove the heater control assembly (see Chapter 3).
26   Remove the center air outlet from the top of the dash.
27   Remove the screw that secures the multi-center display to the dash and remove it.
28   Remove the glove box and striker (see Section 22).
29   Remove the passenger air bag module (see Chapter 12).
30   Unbolt the instrument panel from the vehicle and take it out.
31   If necessary, remove the cruise control and anti-theft electronic control units from the center dash reinforcement. Unbolt the reinforcement from the vehicle and take it out.
32   Installation is the reverse of the removal steps. Adjust the heater controls as described in Chapter 3.

26   Seat belt check

1   Check the seat belts, buckles, latch plates and guide loops for any obvious damage or signs of wear.
2   Make sure the seat belt reminder light comes on when the key is turned on.
3   The seat belts are designed to lock up during a sudden stop or impact, yet allow free movement during normal driving. The retractors should hold the belt against your chest while driving and rewind the belt when the buckle is unlatched.
4   If any of the above checks reveal problems with the seat-belt system, replace parts as necessary.

27   Convertible top service information

Note: *This information is general in nature, as it is intended to apply to all vehicle types, years and models.*

Adjustments
Note: *The following are typical adjustments. Some of these adjustments may not be provided for on your vehicle.*

Latches
The latches secure the convertible top frame to the upper edge of the windshield frame. If the latches are too loose, the top will rattle and move side to side. If the latches are too tight, they will be difficult or impossible to secure. The hooks on some latches are threaded so they can be screwed in or out to tighten or loosen the latch; pliers are often necessary, so make sure you protect the finish of the hook with a rag. Other latches have set-screws that lock the hooks in place - loosen the set-screws (usually with an Allen wrench), position the hooks as desired, then tighten the set-screws.
Also keep in mind that weatherstrip is attached to the front edge of the top. As this weatherstrip deteriorates over time, it will cause the latches and the front edge of the convertible top to become loose. The proper fix for this problem is to replace the deteriorated weatherstrip, which will also reduce wind noise.

Assist springs
Assist springs are attached between the rear of the top framework and the vehicle body. The springs allow the top to be raised and lowered slowly and evenly, without excessive effort in either direction. If the springs are too loose or too tight, they can cause the top to move very quickly in one direction and very slowly in the other direction. Often, the springs can be loosened or tightened by turning threaded adjusters. The springs are sometimes difficult to locate, especially when they travel into the trunk area or are covered by fabric. Search along the rear portion of the framework and remove any access covers.
Some newer vehicles use gas-filled assist struts in place of springs. These struts are similar in design to the gas-filled support struts used to raise and support the hood on many newer vehicles. While these struts are not adjustable, they do lose their gas charge over time and become less effective. Replace the struts if they are not doing their job.

Center joint
On most vehicles, the center joints of the top framework can be adjusted to align the top weatherstrip with the side windows. This adjustment also slightly affects the forward "reach" of the top. The center-joint adjustment changes the angle between the forward and rear sections of the top framework at each side.
To visualize this adjustment, imagine a standard, flat door hinge lying flat on a table top. If you grasp the hinge on each side at its center pivot and lift slightly, the hinge will flex and appear as an arch, with only its ends touching the table - this also shortens the overall length of the hinge. In this analogy, the hinge plates are the front and rear framework sections and the lifting of the center pivot is the center-joint adjustment.
To make this adjustment, it is usually necessary to position the top at approximately its mid-point between raised and lowered. The adjustment mechanism is located at the joint between the front and rear frame sections on each side. The adjuster usually looks like a notched wheel with a set-screw that secures it in position, although some adjusters are a simple screw-and-locknut setup. Mark the position of the adjuster (in case you have to return to the original setting), then loosen or remove the set-screw or locknut. Rotate the wheel or screw, which will sometimes require an Allen wrench. Usually, you'll make the adjustments in the same small increments, side-to-side, until the correct adjustment is achieved. Raise and lower the top after each small adjustment to check alignment.
If the top alignment is not equal side-to-side (compare the alignment of the top to the upper edges of the side windows on each side), adjust one side more than the other to get the proper adjustment.
Adjusting the center joints also changes the height of the top's front edge, so it is usually necessary to adjust the control link after making a center-joint adjustment.

Control link
This adjustment affects both the forward "reach" of the top and the height of the front edge of the top (how high it sits above the windshield frame before the latches are secured). The control link is located at the rear of the top assembly, usually near the main pivot point. Various methods are used to provide adjustment at the control link, such as slotted mounting screw holes and wheel-type adjusters.

With the top down, locate the adjusters, mark their positions, then remove the set-screws or loosen the mounting bolts. Raise the top, then move the adjusters to provide a slight gap between the front edge of the top and the window frame. Walk all around the vehicle to make sure the adjustment is even from side to side. If it is not even, adjust the low side up until it is even. When adjustment is complete, tighten the set-screws or mounting bolts.

Front frame

Some models have separate framework at the forward end of the top assembly that is adjustable by virtue of slotted mounting bolt holes. If, after all other adjustments are carried out, the alignment pins on the top are too far forward or backward to properly engage the holes in the windshield frame, adjust the frame as follows:

Retract the top part-way, loosen the bolts, slide the framework evenly forward or backward, tighten the bolts, then raise the top and check alignment again. Repeat this process until correct alignment is achieved.

Power-top troubleshooting

The power top is operated by a pair of electric motors mounted on each side of the vehicle between the vehicle body (at the rear) and the convertible-top framework. Each motor has a drive gear on one end that operates a driven gear connected to the convertible top mechanism. When the switch is pressed to raise the top, the motor turns the driven gear in a direction that raises the top. When the switch is pressed to lower the top, the motor turns in the opposite direction, driving the gear in the opposite direction and lowering the top.

As a first step in troubleshooting, listen for the whirring sound of the motor as the switch is pressed. If there is no sound from the motor, proceed to *Electrical Troubleshooting*. If you can hear the motor running but the top does not raise, proceed to *Mechanical troubleshooting*.

Mechanical troubleshooting

Mechanical problems will cause the top to not open (or close) or to get stuck part-way through the process. If the motor is operating normally, the cause for these problems is generally a mechanical binding in the top framework.

Checking for binding

If the motor seems to be operating properly, disconnect the motor from the top framework and operate the top by hand. The top should go up and down smoothly, without excessive effort.

If the top binds during manual operation, make sure all adjustments are correct and spray penetrating lubricant on all framework joints.

If the top is operating smoothly during manual operation but will not raise properly with the motor connected, suspect a motor assembly that is not providing adequate power.

Electrical troubleshooting

If you cannot hear the motor running when the switch is pressed, first check for blown fuses and fusible links. If the fuses and fusible links are all OK, disconnect the electrical connector at the motor. Connect a 12-volt test-light to ground and probe each terminal of the disconnected wiring harness connector while an assistant operates the switch. There should be power at one terminal with the switch in the TOP UP position and power at the other terminal with the switch in the TOP DOWN position.

If there is power, but the motor does not operate, check the ground circuit. On most models, there is a third wire from the motor that is attached to ground somewhere near the motor. It is common for this ground connection to become loose or corroded, causing the motor to stop functioning. If the motor is receiving power and has a good ground, but it is still not functioning, the motor itself is the problem. **Note:** *On some models, there is no separate ground connection. A relay in the system alternately grounds one wire and powers the other, depending on switch position. On models with this system, check for a solid ground at the relay.*

If there is no power at the motor, check for power at the three switch terminals by backprobing with the electrical connector still attached. There should be power at one of the switch terminals with the switch in the neutral position, and power at two of the terminals with the switch in either the TOP UP or TOP DOWN position. If there is no power at the switch, the problem lies in the wiring between the battery and the switch. If there is power at only one terminal in the TOP UP or TOP DOWN position, the switch is bad. If the switch tests are OK, the problem lies in the relay(s) (if equipped) or the wiring.

Chapter 12
Chassis electrical system

Contents

1   General information

Warning: *The models covered by this manual are equipped with Supplemental Restraint Systems (SRS), more commonly known as airbags. Always disable the airbag system before working in the vicinity of any airbag system components to avoid the possibility of accidental deployment of the airbags, which could cause personal injury (see Section 27).*

The electrical system is a 12-volt, negative ground type. Power for the lights and all electrical accessories is supplied by a lead/acid-type battery that is charged by the alternator.

This Chapter covers the various electrical components not associated with the engine. Information on the battery, alternator, distributor and starter motor can be found in Chapter 5.

It should be noted that when portions of the electrical system are serviced, the cable should be disconnected from the negative battery terminal to prevent electrical shorts and/or fires.

2   Electrical troubleshooting - general information

Refer to illustrations 2.5a, 2.5b, 2.6, 2.9 and 2.15

A typical electrical circuit consists of an electrical component, any switches, relays, motors, fuses, fusible links or circuit breakers related to that component and the wiring and connectors that link the component to both the battery and the chassis. To help you pinpoint an electrical circuit problem, wiring diagrams are included at the end of this Chapter.

Before tackling any troublesome electrical circuit, first study the appropriate wiring diagrams to get a complete understanding of what makes up that individual circuit. Trouble spots, for instance, can often be narrowed down by noting if other components related to the circuit are operating properly. If several components or circuits fail at one time, chances are the problem is in a fuse or ground connection, because several circuits are often routed through the same fuse and ground connections.

Electrical problems usually stem from simple causes, such as loose or corroded connections, a blown fuse, a melted fusible link or a failed relay. Visually inspect the condition of all fuses, wires and connections in a problem circuit before troubleshooting the circuit.

If test equipment and instruments are going to be utilized, use the diagrams to plan ahead of time where you will make the necessary connections in order to accurately pinpoint the trouble spot.

The basic tools needed for electrical troubleshooting include a circuit tester or voltmeter (a 12-volt bulb with a set of test leads can also be used), a continuity tester, which includes a bulb, battery and set of test leads, and a jumper wire, preferably with a circuit breaker incorporated, which can be used to bypass electrical components **(see illustrations)**. Before attempting to locate a problem with test instruments, use the wiring diagram(s) to decide where to make the connections.

Voltage checks

Voltage checks should be performed if a circuit is not functioning properly. Connect one lead of a circuit tester to either the negative battery terminal or a known good ground. Connect the other lead to a connector in the circuit being tested, preferably nearest to the battery or fuse **(see illustration)**. If the bulb of the tester lights, voltage is present, which means that the part of the circuit between the connector and the battery is problem free. Continue checking the rest of the circuit in the same fashion. When you reach a point at which no voltage is present, the problem lies between that point and the last test point with voltage. Most of the time the problem can be traced to a loose connection. **Note:** *Keep in mind that some circuits receive voltage only when the ignition key is in the Accessory or Run position.*

Finding a short

One method of finding shorts in a circuit is to remove the fuse and connect a test light or voltmeter in place of the fuse terminals. There should be no voltage present in the circuit. Move the wiring harness from side-to-side while watching the test light. If the bulb goes on, there is a short to ground somewhere in that area, probably where the insulation has rubbed through. The same test can be performed on each component in the circuit, even a switch.

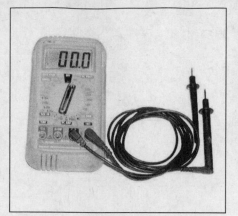

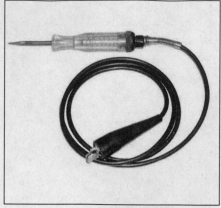

2.5a The most useful tool for electrical troubleshooting is a digital multimeter that can check volts, amps, and test continuity

2.5b A test light is a very handy tool for testing voltage

Ground check

Perform a ground test to check whether a component is properly grounded. Disconnect the battery and connect one lead of a continuity tester or multimeter (set to the ohms scale), to a known good ground. Connect the other lead to the wire or ground connection being tested. If the resistance is low (less than 5 ohms), the ground is good. If the bulb on a self-powered test light does not go on, the ground is not good.

Continuity check

A continuity check is done to determine if there are any breaks in a circuit - if it is passing electricity properly. With the circuit off (no power in the circuit), a self-powered continuity tester or multimeter can be used to check the circuit. Connect the test leads to both ends of the circuit (or to the "power" end and a good ground), and if the test light comes on the circuit is passing current properly **(see illustration)**. If the resistance is low (less than 5

ohms), there is continuity; if the reading is 10,000 ohms or higher, there is a break somewhere in the circuit. The same procedure can be used to test a switch, by connecting the continuity tester to the switch terminals. With the switch turned On, the test light should come on (or low resistance should be indicated on a meter).

Finding an open circuit

When diagnosing for possible open circuits, it is often difficult to locate them by sight because the connectors hide oxidation or terminal misalignment. Merely wiggling a connector on a sensor or in the wiring harness may correct the open circuit condition. Remember this when an open circuit is indicated when troubleshooting a circuit. Intermittent problems may also be caused by oxidized or loose connections.

Electrical troubleshooting is simple if you keep in mind that all electrical circuits are basically electricity running from the battery, through the wires, switches, relays, fuses and fusible links to each electrical component (light bulb, motor, etc.) and to ground, from

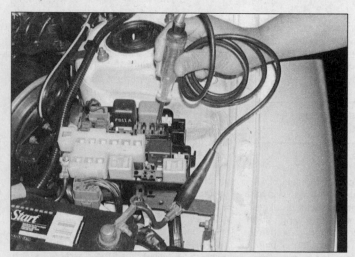

2.6 In use, a basic test light's lead is clipped to a known good ground, then the pointed probe can test connectors, wires or electrical sockets - if the bulb lights, the part being tested has battery voltage

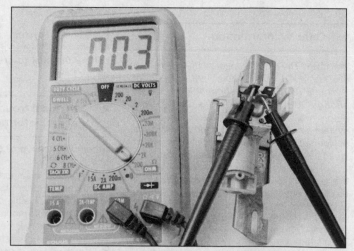

2.9 With a multimeter set to the ohms scale, resistance can be checked across two terminals - when checking for continuity, a low reading indicates continuity, a high reading indicates lack of continuity

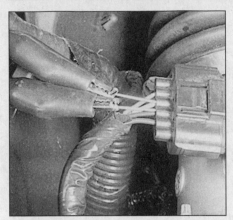

2.15 To backprobe a connector, insert a small, sharp probe (such as a straight-pin) into the back of the connector alongside the desired wire until it contacts the metal terminal inside; connect your meter leads to the probes - this allows you to test a functioning circuit

which it is passed back to the battery. Any electrical problem is an interruption in the flow of electricity to and from the battery.

Connectors

Most electrical connections on these vehicles are made with multiwire plastic connectors. The mating halves of many connectors are secured with locking clips molded into the plastic connector shells. The mating halves of large connectors, such as some of those under the instrument panel, are held together by a bolt through the center of the connector.

To separate a connector with locking clips, use a small screwdriver to pry the clips apart carefully, then separate the connector halves. Pull only on the shell, never pull on the wiring harness as you may damage the individual wires and terminals inside the connectors. Look at the connector closely before trying to separate the halves. Often the locking clips are engaged in a way that is not immediately clear. Additionally, many connectors have more than one set of clips.

Each pair of connector terminals has a male half and a female half. When you look at the end view of a connector in a diagram, be sure to understand whether the view shows the harness side or the component side of the connector. Connector halves are mirror images of each other, and a terminal shown on the right side end-view of one half will be on the left side end view of the other half.

It is often necessary to take circuit voltage measurements with a connector connected. Whenever possible, carefully insert a small straight pin (not your meter probe) into the rear of the connector shell to contact the terminal inside, then clip your meter lead to the pin. This kind of connection is called "backprobing" **(see illustration)**. When inserting a test probe into a male terminal, be careful not to distort the terminal opening. Doing so can lead to a poor connection and corrosion at that terminal

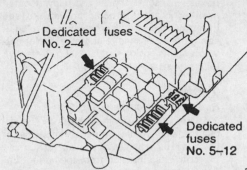
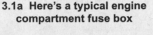

Dedicated fuses No. 2-4

Dedicated fuses No. 5-12

3.1a Here's a typical engine compartment fuse box

later. Using the small straight pin instead of a meter probe results in less chance of deforming the terminal connector.

3 Fuses and fusible links - general information

Fuses

Refer to illustrations 3.1a and 3.1b and 3.3

The electrical circuits of the vehicle are protected by a combination of fuses, circuit breakers and fusible links. The fuse blocks are located under the instrument panel on the left side of the dashboard and in the engine compartment **(see illustrations)**.

Each of the fuses is designed to protect a specific circuit, and the various circuits are identified on the fuse panel itself.

Miniaturized fuses are employed in the fuse blocks. These compact fuses, with blade terminal design, allow fingertip removal and replacement. If an electrical component fails, always check the fuse first. The best way to check the fuses is with a test light. Check for power at the exposed terminal tips of each fuse. If power is present at one side of the fuse but not the other, the fuse is blown. A blown fuse can also be identified by visually inspecting it **(see illustration)**.

Be sure to replace blown fuses with the correct type. Fuses of different ratings are physically interchangeable, but only fuses of the proper rating should be used. Replacing a fuse with one of a higher or lower value than

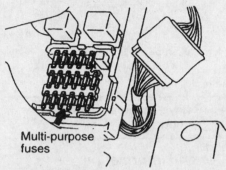

Multi-purpose fuses

3.1b Here's a typical interior fuse box

specified is not recommended. Each electrical circuit needs a specific amount of protection. The amperage value of each fuse is molded into the fuse body.

If the replacement fuse immediately fails, don't replace it again until the cause of the problem is isolated and corrected. In most cases, this will be a short circuit in the wiring caused by a broken or deteriorated wire.

Fusible links

Some circuits are protected by fusible links. The links are used in circuits that are not ordinarily fused, such as the ignition circuit.

The fusible links on these models are located in the engine compartment fuse block and are similar to fuses, but larger.

To replace a fusible link, first disconnect the negative cable from the battery. Unplug the burned-out link and replace it with a new one (available from your dealer or auto parts store). Always determine the cause for the overload that melted the fusible link before installing a new one.

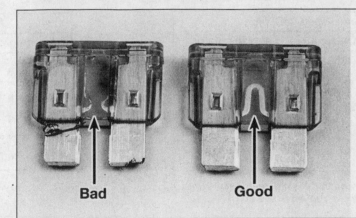

Bad　　Good

3.3 When a fuse blows, the element between the terminals melts - the fuse on the left is blown, the fuse on the right is good

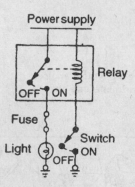

4.1a When power is supplied to the relay coil, it opens or closes a circuit to another component

4 Relays - general information and testing

General information

Refer to illustrations 4.1a and 4.1b

1   Several electrical accessories in the vehicle, such as the fuel injection system, horns, starter, and fog lamps use relays to transmit the electrical signal to the component. Relays use a low-current circuit (the control circuit) to open and close a high-current circuit (the power circuit) **(see illustration)**. If the relay is defective, that component will not operate properly. Most relays are mounted in the engine compartment and interior fuse/relay

boxes, with some specialized relays located in other locations around the vehicle **(see illustration)**. If a faulty relay is suspected, it can be removed and tested by a dealer service department or a repair shop. Defective relays must be replaced as a unit.

Testing

Refer to illustrations 4.3a and 4.3b

2   Refer to the wiring diagrams for the circuit to determine the proper connections for the relay you're testing. If you can't determine the correct connection from the wiring diagrams, however, you may be able to determine the test connections from the information that follows.

3   There are two basic types of relays used on these models **(see illustrations)**. Some are normally open type and some normally closed, while others include a circuit of each type.

4   On most relays, two of the terminals are the relay control circuit (they connect to the relay coil which, when energized, closes the large contacts to complete the circuit). The other terminals are the power circuit (they are connected together within the relay when the control-circuit coil is energized).

5   Some relays may be marked as an aid to help you determine which terminals are the control circuit and which are the power circuit. If the relay is not marked, refer to the wiring diagrams at the end of this Chapter to determine the proper hook-ups for the relay you're testing.

6   To test a relay connect an ohmmeter across the two terminals of the power circuit, continuity should not be indicated. Now connect a fused jumper wire between one of the two control circuit terminals and the positive battery terminal. Connect another jumper wire between the other control circuit terminal and ground. When the connections are made, the relay should click and continuity should be indicated on the meter. On some relays, polarity may be critical, so, if the relay doesn't click, try swapping the jumper wires on the control circuit terminals.

7   If the relay fails the above test, replace it.

5 Turn signal/hazard flasher unit (1995 through 1999 models) - check and replacement

Refer to illustration 5.4

Warning: *The models covered by this manual are equipped with Supplemental Restraint Systems (SRS), more commonly known as airbags. Always disable the airbag system before working in the vicinity of any airbag system components to avoid the possibility of accidental deployment of the airbags, which could cause personal injury (see Section 27).*

1   The turn signal and hazard flasher on these models is a single combination unit (on 2000 and later models, the flasher unit function is handled by the ETACS-ECU, which should be diagnosed by a dealer service

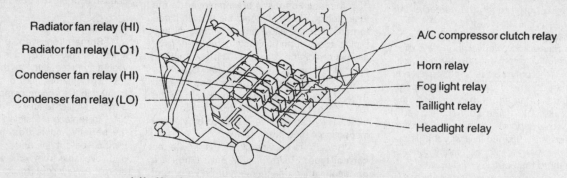

4.1b Here's a typical engine compartment relay box

Normal open (NO) type	
Deenergized state	Energized state
Current does not flow	Current flows

4.3a A normally open relay closes a circuit when power is applied to the coil

Normal close (NC) type	
Deenergized state	Energized state
Current flows	Current does not flow

4.3b A normally closed relay opens a circuit when power is applied to a coil

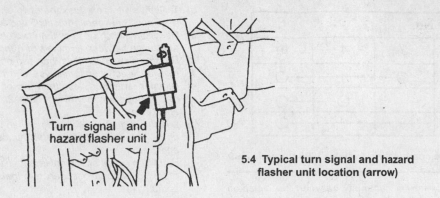

5.4 Typical turn signal and hazard flasher unit location (arrow)

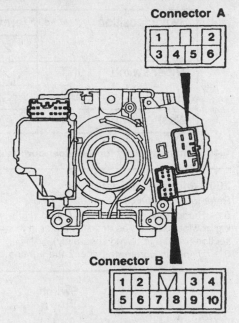

6.4a Terminal identification for the lighting portion of the combination switch - 1995 through 1999

department or other qualified shop).

2   When the flasher unit is functioning properly, an audible click can be heard during its operation. If the turn signals fail on one side or the other and the flasher unit does not make its characteristic clicking sound, or if a bulb on one side of the vehicle flashes much faster than normal but the bulb at the other end of the vehicle (on the same side) doesn't light at all, a faulty turn signal bulb may be indicated.

3   If both turn signals fail to blink, the problem may be due to a blown fuse, a faulty flasher unit, a broken switch or a loose or open connection. If a quick check of the fuse box indicates that the turn signal fuse has blown, check the wiring for a short before installing a new fuse.

4   To replace the flasher, disconnect the electrical connector and remove the flasher unit from its mounting bracket located under

the instrument panel to the right of the steering column (see illustration).

5   Make sure that the replacement unit is identical to the original. Compare the old one to the new one before installing it.

6   Installation is the reverse of removal.

6   Steering column switches - check and replacement

Warning: *The models covered by this manual are equipped with Supplemental Restraint Systems (SRS), more commonly known as airbags. Always disable the airbag system before working in the vicinity of any airbag system components to avoid the possibility of accidental deployment of the airbags, which could cause personal injury (see Section 27).*

Check

1995 through 1999 models

Refer to illustrations 6.4a, 6.4b, 6.4c and 6.4d

1   Disconnect the cable from the negative terminal of the battery.

2   Refer to the replacement procedure later in this Section to remove the combination switch for testing.

3   Using an ohmmeter, check for continuity between the indicated terminals with the various switches in each of the indicated positions.

4   If the continuity is not as specified, replace the defective switch (see illustrations).

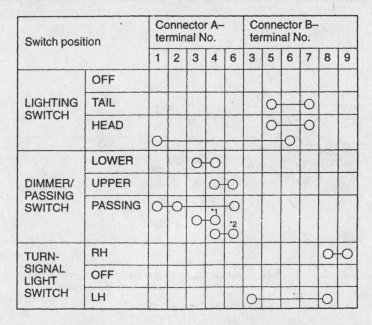

Switch position		Connector A—terminal No.					Connector B—terminal No.					
		1	2	3	4	6	3	5	6	7	8	9
LIGHTING SWITCH	OFF											
	TAIL							○—	—○			
	HEAD	○—	—	—	—	—	—	—○					
DIMMER/ PASSING SWITCH	LOWER			○—○								
	UPPER				○—○							
	PASSING	○—○		○—*1	○ *2 ○—○							
TURN-SIGNAL LIGHT SWITCH	RH									○—○		
	OFF											
	LH						○—|—|—|—○				

6.4b Continuity chart for the lighting portion of the combination switch - 1995 through 1999

6.4c Terminal identification for the wiper portion of the combination switch - 1995 through 1999

Switch position		Terminal No.			
		2	3	4	10
Wiper switch	INT		◯——————◯		◯
	ON			◯————◯	◯
Washer switch	ON	◯——————————————◯			◯

6.4d Continuity chart for the wiper portion of the combination switch - 1995 through 1999

2000 and later models

Refer to illustrations 6.6 and 6.7

5   Remove the switch being tested (lighting or wiper/washer) as described later in this section (they're removed separately).

6   Using an ohmmeter, check the lighting switch for continuity between the indicated terminals with the various switches in each of the indicated positions as follows **(see illustration)**.

a) *Lighting switch off: no continuity between any terminals.*

b) *Taillight switch on: less than two ohms resistance between terminals 5 and 9.*
c) *Headlight switch on: less than two ohms resistance between terminals 5, 7 and 9.*
d) *Passing switch on: less than two ohms resistance between terminals 2 and 12.*
e) *Dimmer switch on: less than two ohms resistance between terminals 2, 11 and 12.*
f) *Left turn signal switch on: less than two ohms resistance between terminals 1 and 2.*
g) *Right turn signal switch on: less than two ohms resistance between terminals 2 and 3.*

7   Using an ohmmeter, check the wiper/washer switch for continuity between the indicated terminals with the various switches in each of the indicated positions as follows **(see illustration)**.

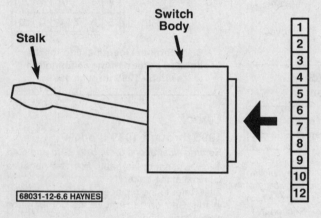

6.6 Terminal identification for the turn signal/lighting portion of the combination switch - 2000 and later

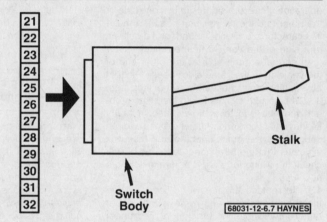

6.7 Terminal identification for the wiper portion of the combination switch - 2000 and later

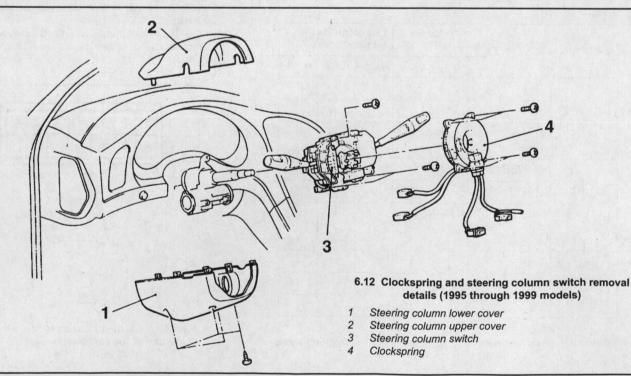

6.12 Clockspring and steering column switch removal details (1995 through 1999 models)

1   *Steering column lower cover*
2   *Steering column upper cover*
3   *Steering column switch*
4   *Clockspring*

a) *Wiper/washer switch off: no continuity between any terminals.*

b) *Wiper mist switch on: less than two ohms resistance between terminals 23 and 32.*

c) *Intermittent wiper switch on: less than two ohms resistance between terminals 23 and 31.*

d) *Low speed wiper switch on: less than two ohms resistance between terminals 23 and 30.*

e) *High speed wiper switch on: less than two ohms resistance between terminals 21 and 23.*

f) *Washer switch on: less than two ohms resistance between terminals 22 and 32.*

g) *Rear intermittent wiper switch on (hardtop only): less than two ohms resistance between terminals 25 and 26.*

h) *Rear washer switch on (hardtop only): less than two ohms resistance between terminals 25 and 29.*

8   If the continuity is not as specified, replace the defective switch.

Replacement
1995 through 1999 models
Refer to illustration 6.12

9   Disconnect the cable from the negative terminal of the battery.

10   Remove the steering wheel (see Chapter 10).

11   Remove the steering column covers (see Chapter 11).

12   Remove the four screws retaining the air-bag clockspring and remove the clockspring from the combination switch (see Chapter 10). Remove the combination switch retaining screws **(see illustration)**.

13   Remove the combination switch. Slide the switch up off the column and disconnect the connectors.

14   Remove the retaining screws from the switch being replaced and remove the defective switch from the switch body.

15   Insert the terminals from the new switch into the connector, pushing in until they are securely locked in place.

16   The remainder or installation is the reverse of removal. Refer to Chapter 10 and center the clockspring before installing the steering wheel.

2000 and later models
17   Disconnect the cable from the negative terminal of the battery.

18   Remove the steering column covers (see Chapter 10).

19   Remove the screws that secure the affected switch to the steering column. Work the switch free of the terminals and take it off.

20   Installation is the reverse of the removal steps.

7   Ignition switch and key lock cylinder - check and replacement

Warning: *The models covered by this manual are equipped with Supplemental Restraint Systems (SRS), more commonly known as airbags. Always disable the airbag system before working in the vicinity of any airbag system components to avoid the possibility of accidental deployment of the airbags, which could cause personal injury (see Section 27).*

Check
Refer to illustrations 7.3, 7.4a, 7.4b, 7.5 and 7.6

1   Disable the airbag system (see Section 27).

2   Remove the instrument panel under cover (1995 through 1999 models) and steering column covers (all models) (see Chapter 11).

3   Disconnect the ignition switch electrical connector below the steering column **(see illustration)**.

4   Check the connector for continuity between the indicated terminals with the key in each position **(see illustrations)**.

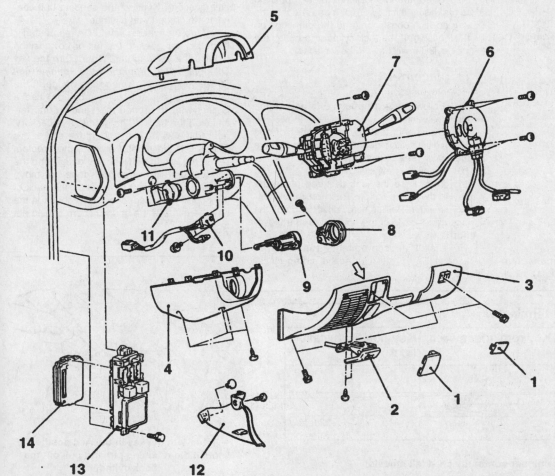

7.3 Ignition switch removal details (1995 through 1999 models)

1   Trim plug
2   Hood latch release handle
3   Instrument panel under cover
4   Steering column lower cover
5   Steering column upper cover
6   Clockspring
7   Combination switch
8   Ignition key illumination ring or cover
9   Lock cylinder
10   Key reminder switch or key light
11   Ignition switch
12   Cowl side trim panel
13   Junction block
14   ETACS ECU

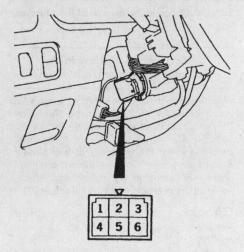

7.4a Ignition switch terminal identification (1995 through 1999 models)

1995 through 1999 models

5   To check the key reminder and key illumination light, disconnect the electrical connector (**see illustration**).
6   Check the connector for continuity between the indicated terminals with the key in each position (**see illustration**).

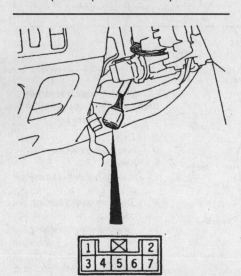

7.5 Key reminder terminal identification (1995 through 1999 models)

Ignition key position	Terminal No					
	1	2	3	4	5	6
LOCK						
ACC	O━━━━━━━━━━━━━━━━━━━━━━━━O				
ON	O━━━━O		O━━━━━O	
START	O━━━O━━━O━━━━O		

7.4b Ignition switch continuity diagram (1995 through 1999 models)

2000 and later models

7   To check the key reminder switch and key ring antenna, disconnect the electrical connector.
8   Check the connector for continuity between the indicated terminals with the key in each position (**see illustration 7.6**).

   a) Key in lock cylinder: no continuity between any terminals.
   b) Key removed from lock cylinder: less than two ohms between terminals 4 and 6.

All models

9   If the continuity is not as specified, replace the switch.
10   Check the lock cylinder in each position to make sure it isn't worn or loose and that the key position corresponds to the markings on the housing. If the lock cylinder is faulty, the lock cylinder will have to be replaced.

Replacement

Refer to illustration 7.14

11   Follow Steps 1 through 3 to access the ignition switch.
12   Disconnect the electrical connector and remove the switch mounting screws to remove the switch (**see illustration 7.3**).
13   Install the new switch.
14   To replace the lock cylinder, place the key in the Acc position. Push on the retaining pin with a Phillips screwdriver and pull the lock cylinder out of the housing (**see illustration**).
15   Install all components removed for access. Be sure to center the airbag clock-

spring before installing the steering wheel (see Chapter 10).

8   Instrument panel gauges - check

Fuel and temperature gauges

1   All tests below require the ignition switch to be turned to Off position before testing.
2   If the gauge pointer does not move from the empty or cold positions, check the fuse. If the fuse is OK, locate the particular sending unit for the circuit you're working on (see Chapter 4 for fuel sending unit location or Chapter 3 for the temperature gauge sending unit location). Connect the sending unit connector to ground with a jumper wire.
3   Turn the ignition key to On momentarily. If the pointer goes to the full or hot position replace the sending unit. **Note:** *Turn the key Off right away; grounding the sending unit for too long could damage the gauge.* If the pointer stays in the same position, use a jumper wire to ground the sending unit terminal on the back of the gauge. If necessary, refer to the wiring diagrams at the end of this Chapter. If the pointer moves, the problem lies in the wiring between the gauge and the sending unit. If the pointer does not move with the sending unit terminal on the back of the gauge grounded, check for voltage at the other terminal of the gauge. There should not be voltage.

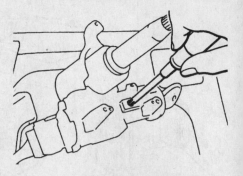

7.14 With the key in the Acc position, push the retaining pin and pull out the lock cylinder

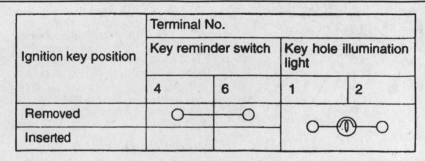

Ignition key position	Terminal No.			
	Key reminder switch		Key hole illumination light	
	4	6	1	2
Removed	O━━━━━━━O		
Inserted			O━━⊗━━O

7.6 Key reminder continuity chart (all models)

9.3 Instrument cluster removal details (1995 through 1999 models)

1 *Cluster bezel*
2 *Instrument cluster*

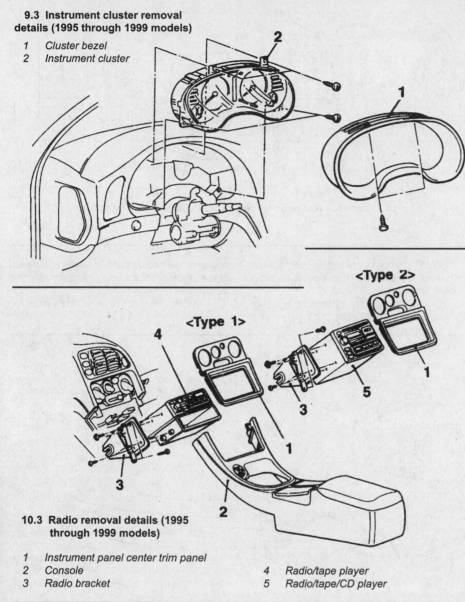

10.3 Radio removal details (1995 through 1999 models)

1 *Instrument panel center trim panel*
2 *Console*
3 *Radio bracket*
4 *Radio/tape player*
5 *Radio/tape/CD player*

<Type 1>
<Type 2>

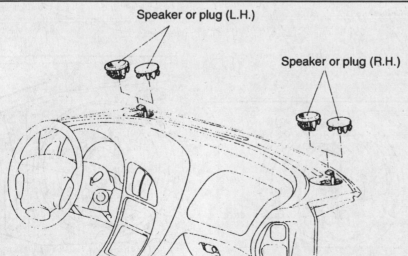

Speaker or plug (L.H.)

Speaker or plug (R.H.)

10.6 Carefully pry the front speaker out and disconnect the electrical connector

9 Instrument cluster - removal and installation

Refer to illustration 9.3

Warning: *The models covered by this manual are equipped with Supplemental Restraint Systems (SRS), more commonly known as airbags. Always disable the airbag system before working in the vicinity of any airbag system components to avoid the possibility of accidental deployment of the airbags, which could cause personal injury (see Section 27).*

1 Disable the airbag system (see Section 27).
2 Remove the instrument cluster bezel (see Chapter 11).
3 Remove the retaining screws and pull the cluster forward **(see illustration)**.
4 Unplug the electrical connectors and remove the cluster from the vehicle.
5 Installation is the reverse of the removal procedure.

10 Radio and speakers - removal and installation

Warning: *The models covered by this manual are equipped with Supplemental Restraint Systems (SRS), more commonly known as airbags. Always disable the airbag system before working in the vicinity of any airbag system components to avoid the possibility of accidental deployment of the airbags, which could cause personal injury (see Section 27).*

Radio/CD player

Refer to illustration 10.3

1 Disable the airbag system (see Section 27).
2 Remove the center bezel panel from the dash. If you're working on a 1995 through 1999 model, remove the console (see Chapter 11).
3 Remove the screws and pull the air conditioning controls/radio/CD player assembly away from the dash **(see illustration)**.
4 Disconnect the antenna lead and the electrical connectors, then remove the screws at each side bracket to remove the radio or CD player from the air conditioning controls/radio/CD player assembly.
5 Installation is the reverse of removal.

Speakers

Dash top

Refer to illustration 10.6

6 Carefully pry the speaker out of the dash **(see illustration)**. Lift the speaker up, disconnect the electrical connector and remove it.
7 Installation is the reverse of removal.

Door

Refer to illustration 10.9

8 Remove the front door trim panel (see Chapter 11).

9   Remove the speaker retaining screws. Disconnect the electrical connector and remove the speaker **(see illustration)**.
10   Installation is the reverse of removal.

Rear
11   Remove the rear quarter trim panel.
12   Remove the rear speaker mounting screws.
13   Installation is the reverse of removal.

11   Antenna - removal and installation

Refer to illustration 11.1
Note: *This procedure applies to whip-type antennas. The antenna on some models is integral with the rear windshield.*
1   If you're working on a non-motorized antenna, remove the antenna mast from the body **(see illustration)**.
2   Remove the antenna retaining nut. Apply masking tape around the antenna mount to avoid scratching the paint.

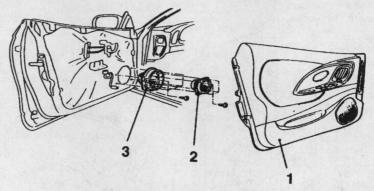

10.9 Door speaker removal details (1995 through 1999 models)

| 1 | *Door trim panel* | 2 | *Speaker* | 3 | *Speaker bracket* |

3   Working in the trunk or rear cargo area, remove the passenger trim panels to allow access to the antenna motor.
4   Detach the motor or antenna body retaining screws **(see illustration 11.1)**. Disconnect the antenna cable (and the electrical connector on motorized antennas) and remove the antenna from the vehicle.
5   Installation is the reverse of removal.

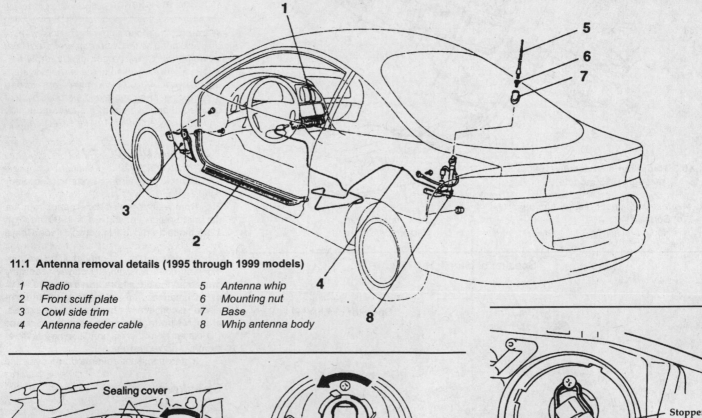

11.1 Antenna removal details (1995 through 1999 models)

1	*Radio*	5	*Antenna whip*
2	*Front scuff plate*	6	*Mounting nut*
3	*Cowl side trim*	7	*Base*
4	*Antenna feeder cable*	8	*Whip antenna body*

12.3 Turn the headlight sealing covers in the direction shown to detach them

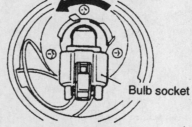

12.4 On early models, unscrew the retaining ring

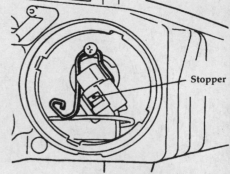

12.5 On later models, unhook the spring clip

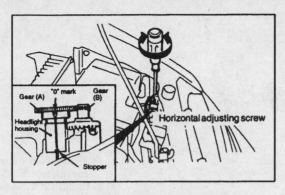

13.1a Typical headlight horizontal adjusting screw

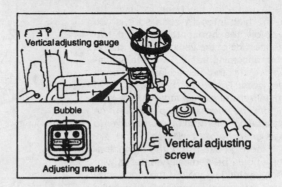

13.1b Typical headlight vertical adjusting screw

12   Headlight bulb - replacement

Refer to illustrations 12.3, 12.4 and 12.5
Warning: *These models are equipped with halogen gas-filled bulbs, which are under pressure and may shatter if the surface is scratched or the bulb is dropped. Wear eye protection and handle the bulbs carefully, grasping only the base whenever possible. Do not touch the surface of the bulb with your fingers because the oil from your skin could cause it to overheat and fail prematurely. If you do touch the bulb surface, clean it with rubbing alcohol.*

1   Open the hood and locate the bulb assembly on the back of the headlight housing.
2   If you're working on a 2.0L turbo model, remove the coolant reservoir and the air cleaner (see Chapters 3 and 4).

3   Disconnect the electrical connector and detach the sealing cover **(see illustration)**.
4   On early models, turn the bulb socket counterclockwise, remove the socket and take out the bulb **(see illustration)**.
5   On later models, release the spring clip and remove the bulb from the headlight housing **(see illustration)**.
6   Without touching the glass with your bare fingers, insert the new bulb into the headlight housing and secure it with the retaining ring.
7   Plug in the electrical connector. Test the headlight operation, then close the hood.

13   Headlights - adjustment

Refer to illustrations 13.1a, 13.1b and 13.2
Note: *It is important that the headlights are aimed correctly. If adjusted incorrectly they could blind the driver of an oncoming vehicle and cause a serious accident or seriously reduce your ability to see the road. The headlights should be checked for proper aim every 12 months and any time a new headlight is installed or front end body work is performed. It should be emphasized that the following procedure is only an interim step that will provide temporary adjustment until the headlights can be adjusted by a properly equipped shop.*
1   These models are equipped with composite headlights with two adjustment screws, one controlling left-and-right movement and one for up-and-down movement **(see illustrations)**.
2   There are several methods of adjusting the headlights. The simplest method requires a blank wall 25 feet in front of the vehicle and a level floor **(see illustration)**.
3   Position masking tape vertically on the wall in reference to the vehicle centerline and the centerlines of both headlights.
4   Position a horizontal tape line in reference to the centerline of all the headlights. **Note:** *It may be easier to position the tape on the wall with the vehicle parked only a few inches away.*
5   Adjustment should be made with the vehicle sitting level, the gas tank half-full and no unusually heavy load in the vehicle.

13.2 Headlight adjustment details

6   Starting with the low beam adjustment, position the high intensity zone so it is two inches below the horizontal line and two inches to the side of the vertical headlight line away from oncoming traffic. Twist the adjustment screws until the desired level has been achieved. **Note:** *The vertical adjuster on 1995 through 1999 models is equipped with a level gauge. It may be necessary to press down on the horizontal adjuster with the screwdriver to engage its gears before it will work.*
7   With the high beams on, the high intensity zone should be vertically centered with the exact center just below the horizontal line. **Note:** *It may not be possible to position the headlight aim exactly for both high and low beams. If a compromise must be made, keep in mind that the low beams are the most used and have the greatest effect on driver safety.*
8   Have the headlights adjusted by a dealer service department or service station at the earliest opportunity.

14 Headlight housing - replacement

Refer to illustration 14.4
1   Disconnect the cable from the negative battery terminal.
2   Remove the headlight bulb (Section 12).
3   Remove the front bumper (Chapter 11).
4   Remove the retaining bolts, detach the housing and withdraw it from the vehicle **(see illustration)**.
5   Installation is the reverse of removal.

15 Bulb replacement

Front turn signal lights
1995 through 1999 models
1   If you're replacing the right-side bulb on a 2.0L non-turbo model, lift the power steering hose for access.
2   If you're replacing the right-side bulb on a 2.0L turbo model, remove the air cleaner (see Chapter 4).
3   Remove the bulb cover (2.0L non-turbo left side only or 2.0L turbo right side only).
4   Remove the socket with the bulb. Push in and rotate the bulb counterclockwise to remove it from the socket.

2000 and later models
5   Remove the screw from the corner of the lens. Slide the light assembly forward out of the bumper.
6   Turn the bulb socket counterclockwise, remove it from the lamp body and remove the bulb.
7   Installation is the reverse of the removal steps.

Front side marker lights
1995 through 1999 models
8   Pad a flat-bladed screwdriver with tape

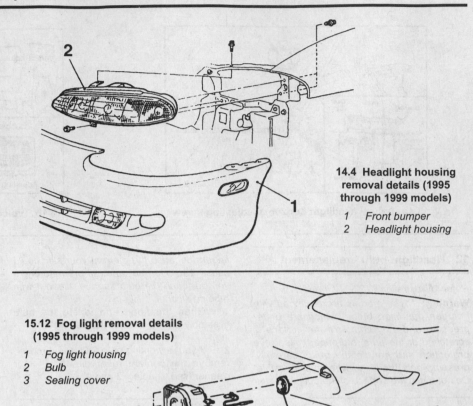

14.4 Headlight housing removal details (1995 through 1999 models)

1   Front bumper
2   Headlight housing

15.12 Fog light removal details (1995 through 1999 models)

1   Fog light housing
2   Bulb
3   Sealing cover

and carefully pry the lamp body out of the bumper.
9   Remove the bulb from the holder, install a new one and carefully push the lamp body back into the bumper.

2000 and later models
10   The front side marker light bulbs are contained in the same housing as the front turn signal bulbs. Refer to Steps 5 through 7 for replacement procedures.

Front fog lights
Refer to illustrations 15.12, 15.14 and 15.15
11   These lights are optional.
12   Remove the screws and pull the lamp body out of the bumper **(see illustration)**.

13   Unscrew the cover mounting screws and take the cover off the back of the lamp.
14   Release the spring clip **(see illustration)**. Pull out the bulb and disconnect its connector.
15   Installation is the reverse of the removal steps. Be sure the mating marks on the sealing cover are lined up correctly or water may leak into the lamp body **(see illustration)**.

Rear combination lights
16   The rear combination lights on 1995 through 1999 models include the back-up lights, rear turn signals, tail/brake lights and rear side marker lights. On 2000 and later models, they include the tail/brake lights and rear turn signals (the rear side marker and back-up lights are in a separate housing).

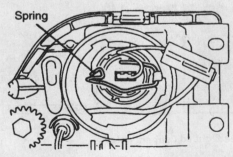

Spring

15.14 Unhook the retaining ring to release the bulb

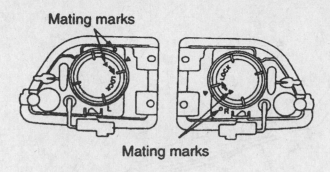

15.15 Align the sealing cover mating marks to prevent water intrusion

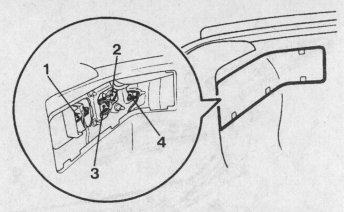

15.17 Rear combination light details (1995 through 1999 models)

1 Back-up light
2 Rear turn signal
3 Stop/taillight

4 Stop/tail/rear side marker light

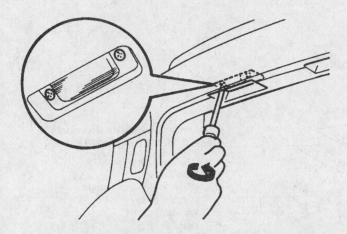

15.32 Remove the screws and pull down the bulb holder to change the license plate bulb

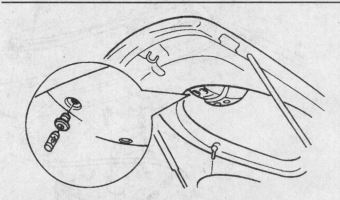

15.35 Remove the trim retainer pin and take off the bulb cover for access to the shelf-mounted brake light bulb

1995 through 1999 models

Refer to illustration 15.17

17   Open the tailgate or trunk and remove the trim cover for access to the taillight housing **(see illustration)**.
18   Turn the bulb sockets counterclockwise and remove them from the lamp body.
19   Push in on the bulbs and rotate them counterclockwise to remove them from the holder.
20   Installation is the reverse of the removal steps.

2000 and later models

21   Open the trunk lid or tailgate.
22   If you're working on a hardtop, swing open the lamp body access cover inside the cargo area.
23   If you're working on a convertible, remove the trim cover clips and remove the trim cover enough for access to the lamp body.
24   Remove the lamp body retaining nuts and pull it away from the vehicle (don't strain the wiring harnesses, which remain connected).
25   Turn the bulb sockets counterclockwise

and remove them from the lamp body.
26   Push in on the bulbs and rotate them counterclockwise to remove them from the holder.
27   Installation is the reverse of the removal steps.

Back-up and rear side marker lights (2000 and later models)

28   Remove the screw from the rearward corner of the lamp body.
29   Swing the lamp body out and disengage its front end from the bumper.
30   Turn the bulb socket counterclockwise and remove it from the lamp body. Replace the bulb with a new one and install the bulb socket in the lamp body.
31   Engage the lamp body hook with the hole in the bumper, swing the lamp body into the bumper and secure it with the screw.

License plate light

Refer to illustration 15.32

32   Remove the screws, detach the lens and pull the bulb holder down for access to the bulb **(see illustration)**.
33   Pull the bulb straight out to replace it.

High-mounted brake light

1995 through 1999 shelf-mounted light

Refer to illustration 15.35

34   Open the tailgate.
35   Remove the trim retainer pin and take off the bulb cover **(see illustration)**. Press the bulb into its socket and turn it counterclockwise to remove.
36   Installation is the reverse of the removal steps.

1995 through 1999 spoiler-mounted light

37   Remove the mounting screws and take the lamp body out of the spoiler. Pull out the bulb, push in a new one and reinstall the lamp body.

2000 and later models

38   Open the tailgate or trunk lid.
39   Twist the bulb socket counterclockwise and pull it out. Pull out the bulb, push in a new one and reinstall the bulb socket.

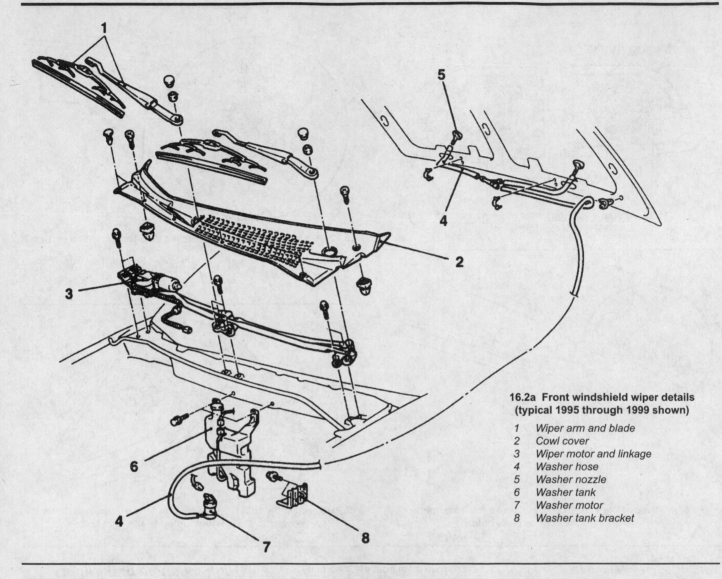

**16.2a Front windshield wiper details
(typical 1995 through 1999 shown)**

1   Wiper arm and blade
2   Cowl cover
3   Wiper motor and linkage
4   Washer hose
5   Washer nozzle
6   Washer tank
7   Washer motor
8   Washer tank bracket

Instrument cluster illumination

40   To gain access to the instrument cluster illumination lights, the instrument cluster will have to be removed (see Section 9). The bulbs can then be removed and replaced from the rear of the cluster.

Interior lights

41   Remove the lenses for the map lights or dome light by prying the cover off with a small screwdriver. Remove the bulb (pry it if necessary with a padded screwdriver).
42   Install the new bulb and push the lens back into position.

16   Wiper motor - removal and installation

Check

Refer to illustrations 16.2a and 16.2b
Note: *Refer to the wiring diagrams for wire colors and locations in the following checks. When checking for voltage, probe a grounded*

12-volt test light to each terminal at a connector until it lights; this verifies voltage (power) at the terminal. If the following checks fail to locate the problem, have the system diagnosed by a dealer service department or other properly equipped repair facility.
1   If the wipers work slowly, make sure the battery is in good condition and has a strong charge (see Chapter 1). If the battery is in good condition, remove the wiper motor (see below) and operate the wiper arms by hand. Check for binding linkage and pivots. Lubricate or repair the linkage or pivots as necessary. Reinstall the wiper motor. If the wipers still operate slowly, check for loose or corroded connections, especially the ground connection. If all connections look OK, replace the motor.
2   If the wipers fail to operate when activated, check the fuse. If the fuse is OK, connect a jumper wire between the wiper motor and ground, then retest. If the motor works now, repair the ground connection. If the motor still doesn't work, turn the wiper switch to the HI position and check for voltage at the motor **(see illustration)**. **Note:** *The cowl cover will*

have to be removed. If there's voltage at the connector, remove the motor and check it off the vehicle with fused jumper wires from the battery. If the motor now works, check for binding linkage (see Step 1 above). If the motor still doesn't work, replace it. If there's no voltage to the motor, check for voltage at the wiper control relays. If there's voltage at the wiper control relays and no voltage at the wiper motor, check the switch for continuity (see Section 6).
3   If the interval (delay) function is inoperative, check the continuity of all the wiring between the switch and wiper control module. If the wiring is OK, check the resistance of the delay control knob of the multi-function switch.
4   If the wipers stop at the position they're in when the switch is turned off (fail to park), check for a good ground on the connector side at the motor. With an ohmmeter connected between any of the black wire terminals and a known ground, resistance should be less than 5 ohms.
5   If the wipers won't shut off unless the ignition is OFF, disconnect the wiring from

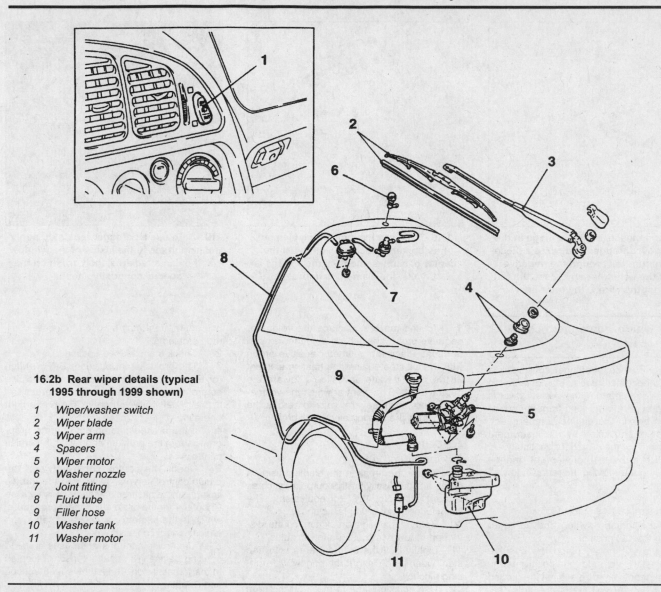

16.2b Rear wiper details (typical 1995 through 1999 shown)

1   Wiper/washer switch
2   Wiper blade
3   Wiper arm
4   Spacers
5   Wiper motor
6   Washer nozzle
7   Joint fitting
8   Fluid tube
9   Filler hose
10 Washer tank
11 Washer motor

the wiper control switch. If the wipers stop, replace the switch. If the wipers keep running, there's a defective limit switch in the motor; replace the motor.

6   If the wipers won't retract below the hood line, check for mechanical obstructions in the wiper linkage or on the vehicle's body that would prevent the wipers from parking. If there are no obstructions, check the wiring between the switch and motor for continuity. If the wiring is OK, replace the wiper motor.

Front wiper motor replacement

7   Remove the windshield wiper arms **(see illustration 16.2a)**.
8   Remove the cowl cover (see Chapter 11).
9   Disconnect the electrical connector from the wiper motor.
10   Detach the wiper motor/linkage assembly from the cowl.
11   Remove the wiper motor retaining bolts and remove the motor.
12   Installation is the reverse of removal.

Rear wiper motor replacement (hardtop only)

13   Remove the windshield wiper arm and spacer **(see illustration 16.2b)**.
14   Remove the trim panel on the inside of the liftgate.
15   Disconnect the electrical connector from the wiper motor.
16   Remove the wiper motor retaining bolts and remove the motor.
17   Installation is the reverse of removal.

17   Horn - check and replacement

Note: *Check the fuses before beginning electrical diagnosis.*
1   Disconnect the electrical connector from the horn.
2   To test the horn, refer to the wiring diagrams and connect battery voltage and ground to the two terminals with a pair of jumper wires. If the horn doesn't sound, replace it. If

it does sound, the problem lies in the switch, relay or the wiring between the components.
3   To replace the horn, disconnect the electrical connector and remove the mounting bolt.
4   Installation is the reverse of removal.

18   Daytime Running Lights (DRL) - general information

The Daytime Running Lights (DRL) system used on Canadian models turns the headlights on whenever the engine is started. The only exception is when the engine is turned on when the parking brake is engaged. Once the parking brake is released, the lights will remain on as long as the ignition switch is on, even if the parking brake is later applied.

The DRL system supplies reduced power to the headlights so they won't be too bright for daytime use while prolonging headlight life.

19.5 When measuring the voltage at the rear window defogger grid, wrap a piece of aluminum foil around the negative probe of the voltmeter and press the foil against the wire with your finger

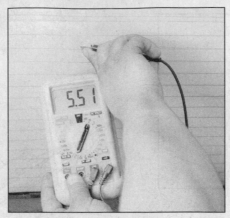

19.6 To determine if a heating element has broken, check the voltage at the center of each element - if the voltage is 6-volts, the element is unbroken

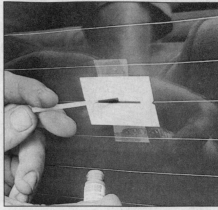

19.14 To use a defogger repair kit, apply masking tape to the inside of the window at the damaged area, then brush on the special conductive coating

19 Rear window defogger - check and repair

1 The rear window defogger consists of a number of horizontal heating elements baked onto the inside surface of the glass. Power is supplied through a large fuse from the power distribution box in the engine compartment. The heater is controlled by the instrument panel switch. Test the switch for continuity.
2 Small breaks in the element can be repaired without removing the rear window.

Check

Refer to illustrations 19.5 and 19.6

3 Turn the ignition switch and defogger switches to the ON position.
4 Using a voltmeter, place the positive probe against the defogger grid positive terminal and the negative probe against the ground terminal. If battery voltage is not indicated, check the fuse, defogger switch and related wiring. If voltage is indicated, but all or part of the defogger doesn't heat, proceed with the following tests.
5 When measuring voltage during the next two tests, wrap a piece of aluminum foil around the tip of the voltmeter positive probe and press the foil against the heating element with your finger **(see illustration)**. Place the negative probe on the defogger grid ground terminal.
6 Check the voltage at the center of each heating element **(see illustration)**. If the voltage is 5 to 6 volts, the element is okay (there is no break). If the voltage is 0 volts, the element is broken between the center of the element and the positive end. If the voltage is 10 to 12 volts the element is broken between the center of the element and the ground side. Check each heating element.
7 If none of the elements are broken, connect the negative probe to a good chassis ground. The voltage reading should stay the same, if it doesn't the ground connection is bad.

8 To find the break, place the voltmeter negative probe against the defogger ground terminal. Place the voltmeter positive probe with the foil strip against the heating element at the positive side and slide it toward the negative side. The point at which the voltmeter deflects from several volts to zero is the point where the heating element is broken.

Repair

Refer to illustration 19.14

9 Repair the break in the element using a repair kit specifically for this purpose, such as Dupont paste No. 4817 (or equivalent). The kit includes conductive plastic epoxy.
10 Before repairing a break, turn off the system and allow it to cool for a few minutes.
11 Lightly buff the element area with fine steel wool; then clean it thoroughly with rubbing alcohol.
12 Use masking tape to mask off the area being repaired.
13 Thoroughly mix the epoxy, following the kit instructions.
14 Apply the epoxy material to the slit in the masking tape, overlapping the undamaged area about 3/4-inch on either end **(see illustration)**.
15 Allow the repair to cure for 24 hours before removing the tape and using the system.

20 Cruise control system - description and check

1 The cruise control system maintains vehicle speed with a vacuum-actuated servo motor located on the firewall in the engine compartment, which is connected to the throttle linkage by a cable. The system consists of the servo motor, brake switch, vacuum pump, control switches, a relay and associated vacuum hoses. Some features of the system require special testers and diagnostic procedures that are beyond the scope of the home mechanic. Listed below are some general

procedures that may be used to locate common problems.
2 Check the fuse (see Section 3).
3 The brake pedal position (BPP) switch (or brake light switch) deactivates the cruise control system. Have an assistant press the brake pedal while you check the brake light operation.
4 If the brake lights do not operate properly, correct the problem and retest the cruise control.
5 Check the control cable between the cruise control servo/amplifier and the throttle linkage and adjust/replace as necessary. See Chapter 4 for the cable adjustment procedure, which is the same for accelerator cable and cruise control cable.
6 The cruise control system uses a speed sensing device. The speed sensor is located in the transmission. To test the speed sensor, see Chapter 6.

21 Power window system - description and check

1 The power window system operates the electric motors mounted in the doors which lower and raise the windows. The system consists of the control switches, the motors (regulators), glass mechanisms and associated wiring.
2 Power windows are wired so they can be lowered and raised from the master control switch by the driver or by remote switches located at the individual windows. Each window has a separate motor that is reversible. The position of the control switch determines the polarity and therefore the direction of operation. Some systems are equipped with relays that control current flow to the motors.
3 Some vehicles are equipped with a separate circuit breaker for each motor in addition to the fuse or circuit breaker protecting the whole circuit. This prevents one stuck window from disabling the whole system.

4   The power window system will only operate when the ignition switch is ON. In addition, many models have a window lock-out switch at the master control switch which, when activated, disables the switches at the rear windows and, sometimes, the switch at the passenger's window also. Always check these items before troubleshooting a window problem.

5   These procedures are general in nature, so if you can't find the problem using them, take the vehicle to a dealer service department or other qualified repair shop.

6   If the power windows don't work at all, check the fuse or circuit breaker.

7   If only the rear windows are inoperative, or if the windows only operate from the master control switch, check the rear window lockout switch for continuity in the unlocked position. Replace it if it doesn't have continuity.

8   Check the wiring between the switches and fuse panel for continuity. Repair the wiring, if necessary.

9   If only one window is inoperative from the master control switch, try the other control switch at the window. **Note:** *This doesn't apply to the driver's door window.*

10   If the same window works from one switch, but not the other, check the switch for continuity.

11   If the switch tests OK, check for a short or open in the wiring between the affected switch and the window motor.

12   If one window is inoperative from both switches, remove the trim panel from the affected door and check for voltage at the switch and at the motor while the switch is operated.

13   If voltage is reaching the motor, disconnect the glass from the regulator (see Chapter 11). Move the window up and down by hand while checking for binding and damage. Also check for binding and damage to the regulator. If the regulator is not damaged and the window moves up and down smoothly, replace the motor. If there's binding or damage, lubricate, repair or replace parts, as necessary.

14   If voltage isn't reaching the motor, check the wiring in the circuit for continuity between the switches and motors. You'll need to consult the wiring diagram for the vehicle. Some power window circuits are equipped with relays. If equipped, check that the relays are grounded properly and receiving voltage from the switches. Also check that each relay sends voltage to the motor when the switch is turned on. If it doesn't, replace the relay.

15   Test the windows after you are done to confirm proper repairs.

22   Power door lock system - description and check

1   The power door lock system operates the door lock actuators mounted in each door. The system consists of the switches, actuators and associated wiring. Diagnosis can usually be limited to simple checks of the wir-ing connections and actuators for minor faults that can be easily repaired.

2   Power door lock systems are operated by bi-directional solenoids located in the doors. The lock switches have two operating positions: Lock and Unlock. These switches activate a relay, which in turn connects voltage to the door lock solenoids. Depending on which way the relay is activated, it reverses polarity, allowing the two sides of the circuit to be used alternately as the feed (positive) and ground side.

3   Some vehicles may have keyless entry, electronic control modules and anti-theft systems incorporated into the power locks. If you are unable to locate the trouble using the following general steps, consult your dealer service department. **Note:** *Some vehicles also have control switches connected to the key locks in the doors, which unlock all the doors when one is unlocked.*

4   Always check the circuit protection first. Some vehicles use a combination of circuit breakers and fuses.

5   Operate the door lock switches in both directions (Lock and Unlock) with the engine off. Listen for the faint click of the relay operating.

6   If there's no click, check for voltage at the switches. If no voltage is present, check the wiring between the fuse panel and the switches for shorts and opens.

7   If voltage is present but no click is heard, test the switch for continuity. Replace it if there's not continuity in both switch positions.

8   If the switch has continuity but the relay doesn't click, check the wiring between the switch and relay for continuity. Repair the wiring if there's no continuity.

9   If the relay is receiving voltage from the switch but is not sending voltage to the sole-noids, check for a bad ground at the relay case. If the relay case is grounding properly, replace the relay.

10   If all but one lock solenoids operate, remove the trim panel from the affected door (see Chapter 11) and check for voltage at the solenoid while the lock switch is operated. One of the wires should have voltage in the Lock position; the other should have voltage in the Unlock position.

11   If the inoperative solenoid is receiving voltage, replace the solenoid.

12   If the inoperative solenoid isn't receiv-ing voltage, check for an open or short in the wire between the lock solenoid and the relay. **Note:** *It's common for wires to break in the portion of the harness between the body and door (opening and closing the door fatigues and eventually breaks the wires).*

23   Electric side view mirrors - description and check

1   Most electric side view mirrors use two motors to move the glass; one for up and down adjustments and one for left-right adjustments.

2   The control switch has a selector portion that sends voltage to the left or right side mir-ror. With the ignition ON but the engine OFF, roll down the windows and operate the mirror control switch through all functions (left-right and up-down) for both the left and right side mirrors.

3   Listen carefully for the sound of the elec-tric motors running in the mirrors.

4   If the motors can be heard but the mir-ror glass doesn't move, there's probably a problem with the drive mechanism inside the mirror. Remove and disassemble the mirror to locate the problem.

5   If the mirrors don't operate and no sound comes from the mirrors, check the fuse (see Chapter 1).

6   If the fuse is OK, remove the mirror con-trol switch from its mounting without discon-necting the wires attached to it. Turn the igni-tion ON and check for voltage at the switch. There should be voltage at one terminal. If there's no voltage at the switch, check for an open or short in the wiring between the fuse panel and the switch.

7   If there's voltage at the switch, discon-nect it. Check the switch for continuity in all its operating positions (see Section 9). If the switch does not have continuity, replace it.

8   Re-connect the switch. Locate the wire going from the switch to ground. Leaving the switch connected, connect a jumper wire between this wire and ground. If the mirror works normally with this wire in place, repair the faulty ground connection.

9   If the mirror still doesn't work, remove the mirror and check the wires at the mirror for voltage. Check with ignition ON and the mirror selector switch on the appropriate side. Operate the mirror switch in all its positions. There should be voltage at one of the switch-to-mirror wires in each switch position (except the neutral "off" position).

10   If voltage isn't present in each switch position, check the wiring between the mirror and control switch for opens and shorts.

11   If there's voltage, remove the mirror and test it off the vehicle with jumper wires. Replace the mirror if it fails this test.

24   Electric sunroof - description and check

1   The electric sunroof is powered by a single motor located in the roof. The motor is protected by a circuit breaker. When sunlight isn't desired, an interior sliding panel can be closed.

2   The control switches (tilt and slide) send a ground signal to the sunroof motor when the switches are pressed. Power is supplied to the motor from the sunroof relay. With the ignition On but the engine Off, operate the sunroof control switch through the tilt and slide func-tions.

3   Listen carefully for the sound of the sun-roof motor running in the roof.

4   If the motor can be heard but the sunroof

glass doesn't move, there's probably a problem with the drive mechanism or drive cables.

5   If the sunroof does not operate and no sound comes from the motor, check the fuses and fusible link.

6   If the fuses and fusible link are OK, pull down the overhead interior light/switch panel. Turn the ignition On and check for voltage at the power wire at the motor. If there's voltage at the motor, check for power and ground at the switch. If power and ground exist at the motor and there's still no voltage at the switch, replace the switch.

7   Connect the vehicle's battery to the sunroof motor, using fused jumper wires. With the positive terminal connected to terminal 1 and the negative terminal connected to terminal 2, the motor should turn counterclockwise. When the jumper wires are swapped, the motor should turn clockwise.

8   If there's voltage at the switch, disconnect it. Check the switch for continuity in all its operating positions. If the switch does not have continuity, replace it.

9   If the switch has continuity re-connect the switch. Locate the wire going from the switch to ground. Leaving the switch connected, connect a jumper wire between this wire and ground. If the motor works normally with this wire in place, repair the faulty ground connection.

10   The sunroof can be closed manually if the motor doesn't work. Remove the motor shaft cover from the rear of the sunroof switch panel, insert the sunroof wrench into the motor shaft and rotate it counterclockwise. If your vehicle is equipped with a factory sunroof, the wrench comes in the factory toolbag in the trunk.

25   Power seats - description and check

1   The optional power seats on these models adjust forward and backward, up and down and tilt forward and backward.

2   The power seat system consists of three motors (front height, rear height, and front-rear slide), a switch on the seat and a fusible link.

3   Look under the seat for any objects which may be preventing the seat from moving.

4   If the seat won't work at all, check the fusible link (see Section 3).

5   With the engine off to reduce the noise level, operate the seat controls in all directions and listen for sound coming from the seat motor(s).

6   If the motor runs or clicks but the seat doesn't move, the integral seat drive mechanism is damaged and the motor assembly must be replaced.

7   If the motor doesn't work or make noise, check for voltage at the motor while an assistant operates the switch.

8   If the motor is getting voltage but doesn't run, test it off the vehicle with jumper wires. If

it still doesn't work, replace it.

9   If the motor isn't getting voltage, check for voltage at the switch. If there's no voltage at the switch, check the wiring between the fuse panel and the switch. If there's voltage at the switch, check the switch for continuity in all its operating positions. Replace the switch if there's no continuity.

10   If the switch is OK, check for a short or open in the wiring between the switch and motor.

11   Test the completed repairs.

26   Simplified Wiring System (2000 and later models) - description

1   The vehicles covered by this manual have a complex electrical system, encompassing many power accessories. To reduce the amount of hard wiring going back and forth throughout the vehicle, the designers have incorporated the Simplified Wiring System (SWS) on 2000 and later models.

2   The main components of the system are the several electronic control units (ECU's) located around the vehicle. Multiplex lines connect the components, and are able to carry large amounts of data back and forth.

3   The various ECU's control the On/Off function of different devices when directed by the computer in the ETACS-ECU. Among the systems controlled by the SWS are the power windows, power door locks, interior lighting, warning lights, theft warning systems (if applicable), and various other components.

4   The ETACS-ECU also has diagnostic capability for the SWS. If you suspect any electrical problem you have is traceable to the SWS, bring your vehicle to a dealer or other qualified repair shop with the diagnostic tools to extract the trouble codes.

27   Airbag system - general information

1   These models are equipped with a Supplemental Restraint System (SRS), more commonly known as airbags, designed to protect the driver and front seat passenger from serious injury in the event of a head-on or frontal collision. All models have a driver's airbag, located in the center of the steering wheel, and a passenger airbag module in the right side of the dash. All models have a diagnostic/control unit located inside the passenger compartment. 1995 models have two impact sensors mounted on the unibody frame members, behind the front fender splash shields. Later models are controlled solely by the diagnostic/control unit.

2   The 2000 and later models have additional occupant protection with supplemental side airbags in the outside rear corners of the driver and passenger front seats. These airbags are designed to operate primarily in side-impact collisions, though they may also activate in some other types of collisions.

Airbag modules

3   The airbag modules consist of a housing incorporating the cushion (airbag) and inflator unit. The inflator assembly is mounted on the back of the housing over a hole through which gas is expelled, inflating the bag almost instantaneously when an electrical signal is sent from the system. The specially wound wire on the driver's side that carries this signal to the module is called a clockspring. The clockspring is a flat, ribbon-like electrically conductive tape that is wound many times so that it can transmit an electrical signal regardless of steering wheel position.

Diagnostic/control unit and tunnel/safing sensors

Refer to illustration 27.4

4   The diagnostic/control unit contains an on-board microprocessor which monitors the operation of the system, and also contains a crash sensor. It checks this system every time the vehicle is started, causing the "AIRBAG" light to go on then off, if the system is operating properly. If there is a fault in the system, the light will go on and stay on and the unit will store fault codes indicating the nature of the fault. If the AIRBAG light goes on and stays on, the vehicle should be taken to your dealer immediately for service. Models with side airbags also have a "satellite" crash sensor in each door "B" pillar. The diagnostic control unit is located under the rear of the floor console on 1995 through 1999 models, and is under the center of the instrument panel on 2000 and later models **(see illustration)**.

Operation

5   For the airbag(s) to deploy, one or both impact sensors and the safing sensor (1995 models) or the crash sensor in the diagnostic/control unit must be activated. When this condition occurs, the circuit to the airbag inflator is closed and the airbag inflates. If the battery is destroyed by the impact, or is too low to power the inflator, a back-up power unit inside the control unit provides power.

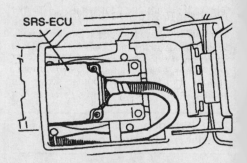

27.4 The diagnostic/control unit is located under the rear of the floor console (1995 through 1999, shown) or under the center of the dash (2000 and later)

Self-diagnosis system

6   A self-diagnosis circuit in the control unit displays a light on the instrument panel when the ignition switch is turned to the On position. If the system is operating normally, the light should go out after about seven seconds. If the light doesn't come on, or doesn't go out after seven seconds, or if it comes on while you're driving the vehicle, or if it blinks at any time, there's a malfunction in the SRS system. Have it inspected and repaired as soon as possible. Do not attempt to troubleshoot or service the SRS system yourself. Even a small mistake could cause the SRS system to malfunction when you need it.

Servicing components near the SRS system

7   Nevertheless, there are times when you need to remove the steering wheel, radio or service other components on or near the dashboard. At these times, you'll be working around components and wire harnesses for the SRS system. The SRS wiring harnesses are easy to identify: The electrical connectors are all bright yellow. Do not use electrical test equipment on airbag system components or wiring harnesses; it could cause the airbag(s) to deploy. *ALWAYS DISABLE THE SRS SYSTEM BEFORE WORKING NEAR THE SRS SYSTEM COMPONENTS OR RELATED WIRING.*
8   Never dispose of a live airbag module. Return it to a dealer service department or other qualified repair shop for safe deployment and disposal.

Disabling the SRS system

Warning: *Any time you are working in the vicinity of airbag wiring or components, DISABLE THE SRS SYSTEM.*
9   Disconnect the battery negative and positive cables, then wait two minutes before proceeding with any work.

Enabling the system

10   After you've disabled the airbag and performed the necessary service, turn the ignition switch to the Off position, then reconnect the battery cables (negative first, positive last).

Removal and installation

Warning: *Whenever handling an airbag module, always keep the airbag opening (the trim side) pointed away from your body. Never place the airbag module on a bench or other surface with the airbag opening facing the surface. Always place the airbag module in a*

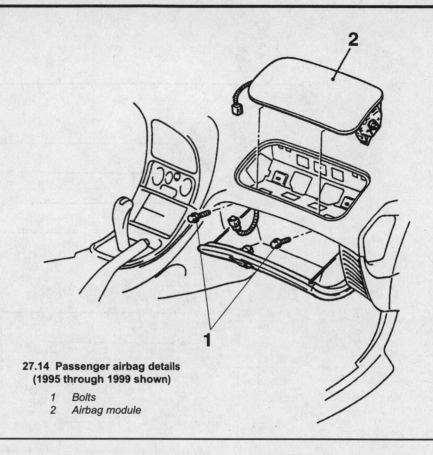

27.14 Passenger airbag details (1995 through 1999 shown)

1   Bolts
2   Airbag module

safe location with the airbag opening facing up.

Driver's side airbag

11   Refer to Chapter 10, *Steering wheel - removal and installation* for removal and installation of the driver's side airbag.

Passenger side airbag

Refer to illustration 27.14
12   Disable the airbag system.
13   Refer to Chapter 11 and remove the passenger-side lower dash panel and the glove box.
14   Disconnect the two-pin connector. Remove the bolts and gently pry the airbag unit from the top of the dashboard with a screwdriver **(see illustration). Caution:** *The airbag assembly is heavier than it looks; use both hands when removing it from the dash.*
15   Installation is the reverse of the removal procedure.

Side-impact airbags

16   The side impact airbags are replaced as

a complete unit with the seatback.

28   Wiring diagrams - general information

Since it isn't possible to include all wiring diagrams for every year covered by this manual, the following diagrams are those that are typical and most commonly needed.

Prior to troubleshooting any circuits, check the fuse and circuit breakers (if equipped) to make sure they are in good condition. Make sure the battery is properly charged and has clean, tight cable connections (see Chapter 1).

When checking the wiring system, make sure that all electrical connectors are clean, with no broken or loose pins. When unplugging an electrical connector, do not pull on the wires, only on the connector housings themselves.

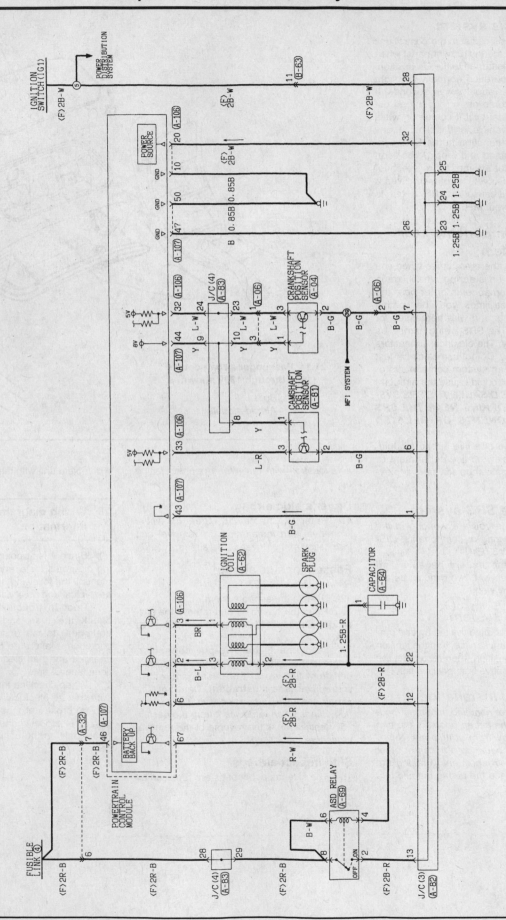

Typical ignition system wiring diagram

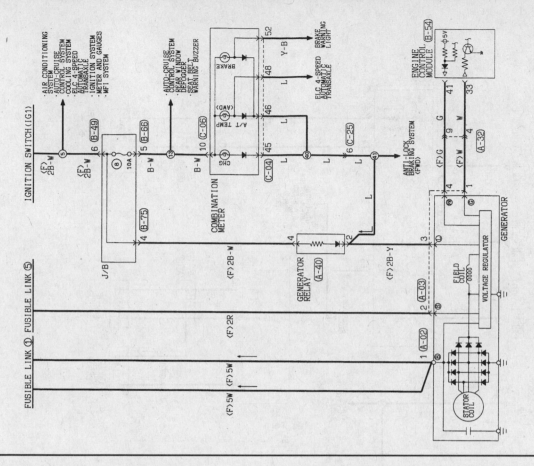

Typical charging system wiring diagram

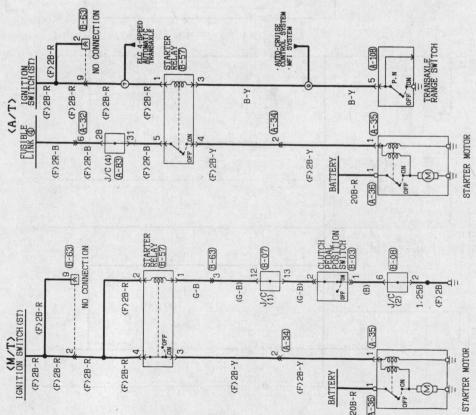

Typical starting system wiring diagram

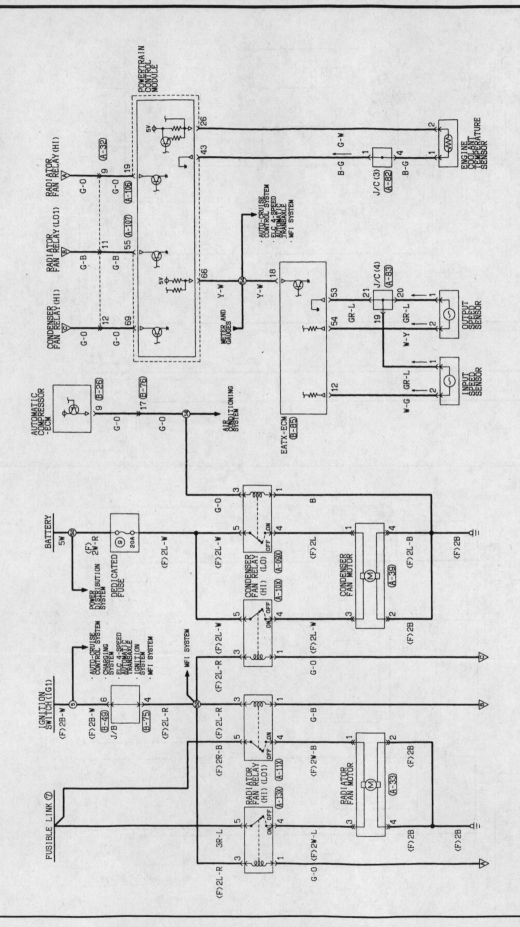

Typical engine cooling fan wiring diagram

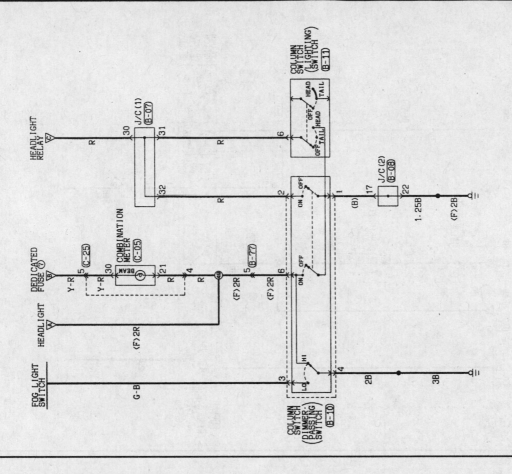

Typical headlight system wiring diagram for US vehicles (2 of 2)

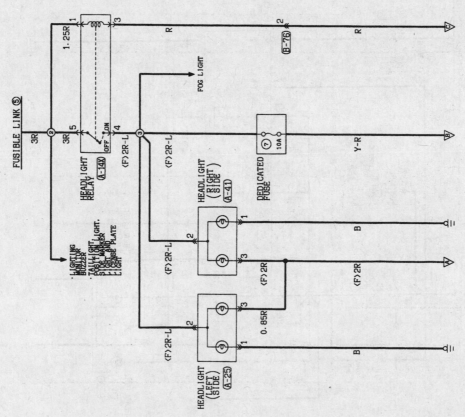

Typical headlight system wiring diagram for US vehicles (1 of 2)

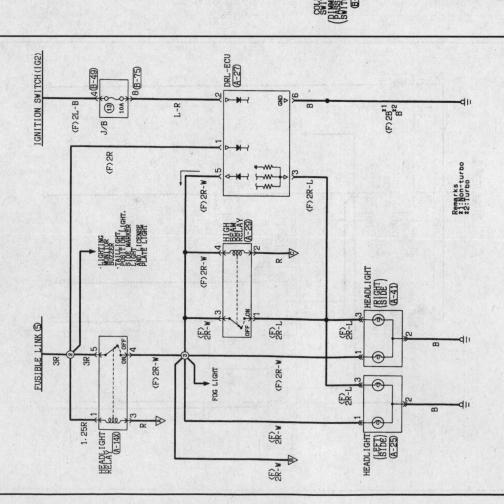

Typical headlight system wiring diagram for Canadian vehicles (2 of 2)

Typical headlight system wiring diagram for Canadian vehicles (1 of 2)

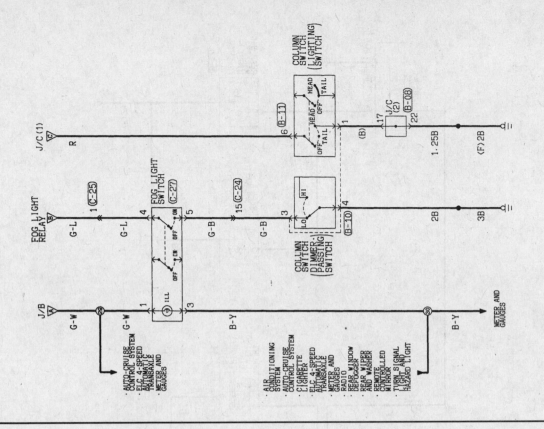

Typical fog light wiring diagram (2 of 2)

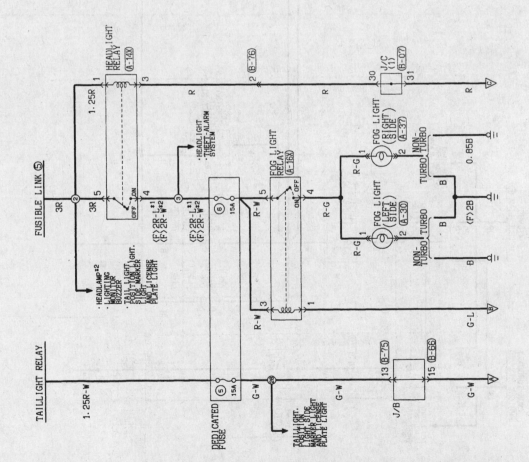

Typical fog light wiring diagram (1 of 2)

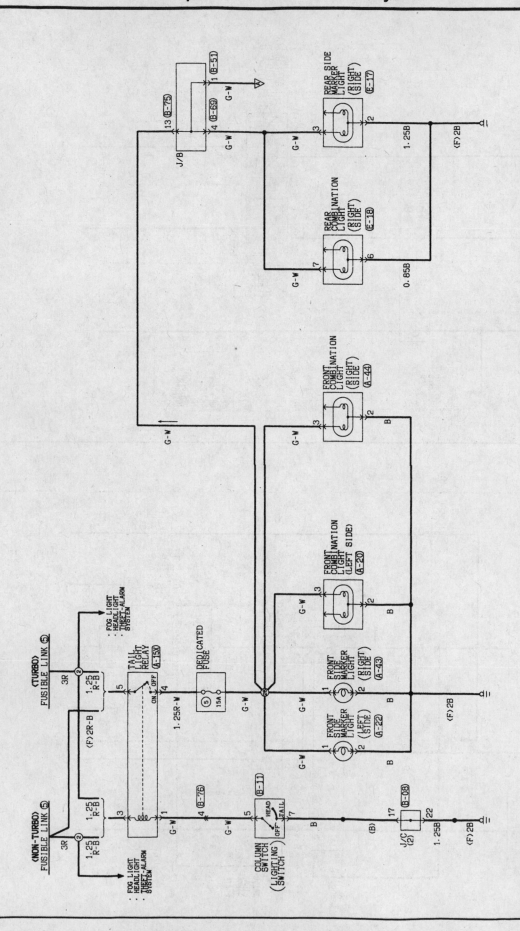

Typical taillight, position light and side marker light wiring diagram (1 of 2)

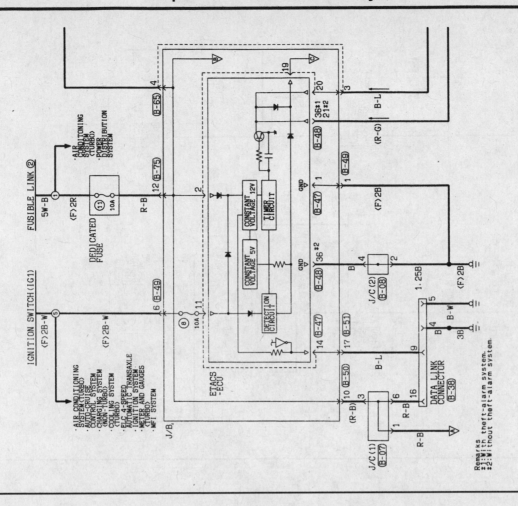

Typical interior light wiring diagram - 1 of 3

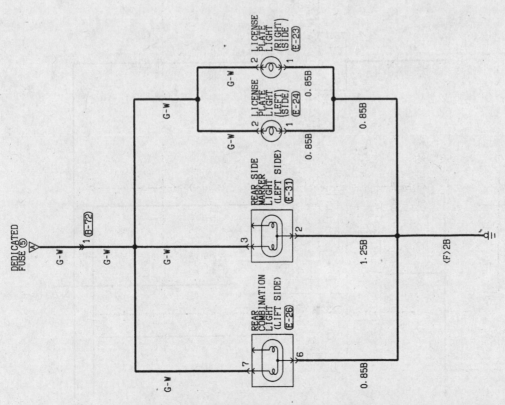

Typical taillight, position light, side marker light and license plate light wiring diagram (2 of 2)

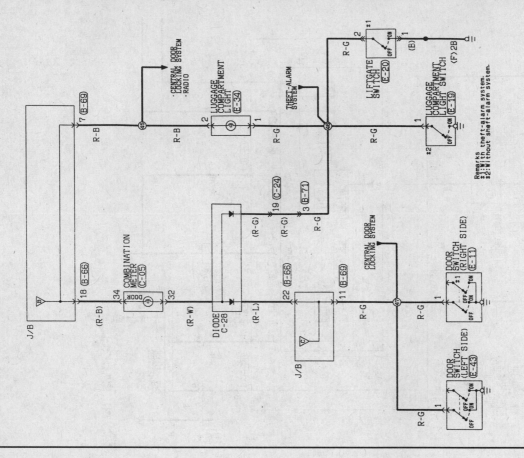

Typical interior light wiring diagram - 3 of 3

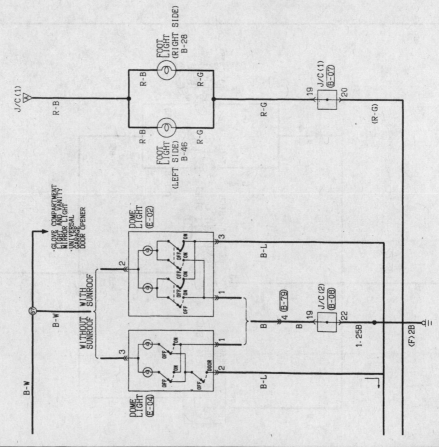

Typical interior light wiring diagram - 2 of 3

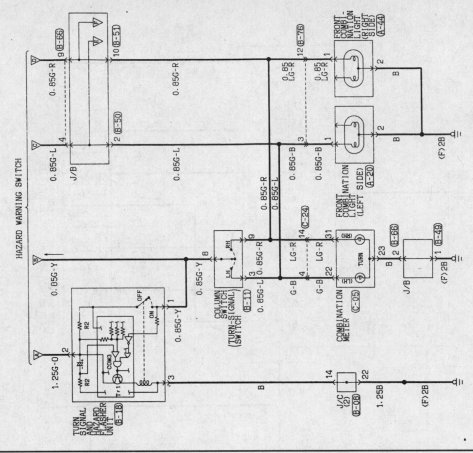

Typical turn signal and hazard warning light wiring diagram - 2 of 3

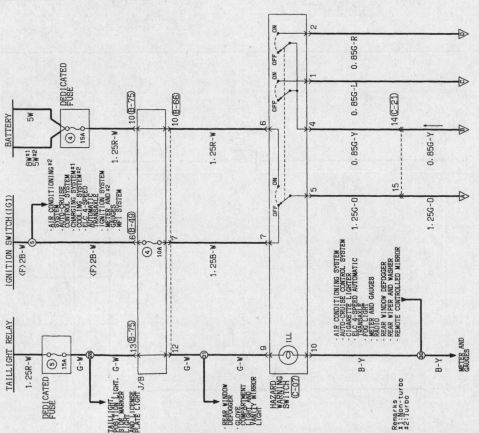

Typical turn signal and hazard warning light wiring diagram - 1 of 3

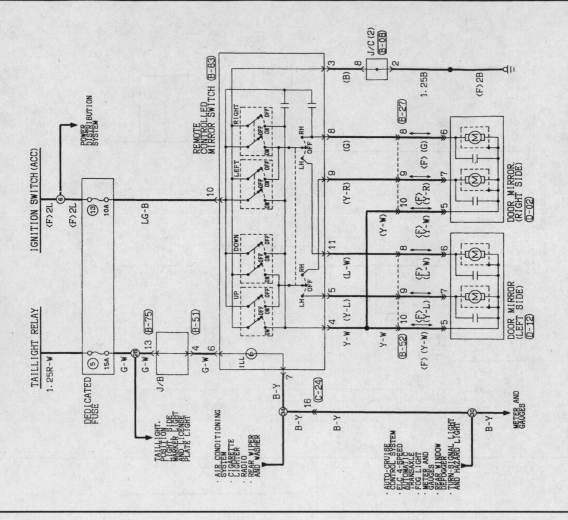

Typical electric mirror wiring diagram

Typical turn signal and hazard warning light wiring diagram - 3 of 3

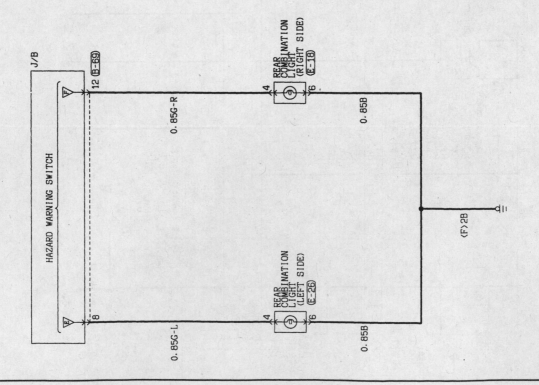

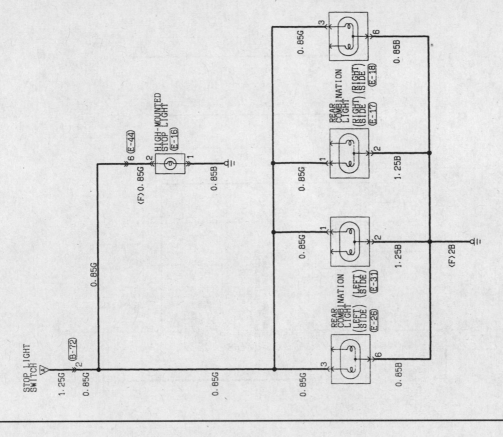

Typical brake light wiring diagram - 2 of 2

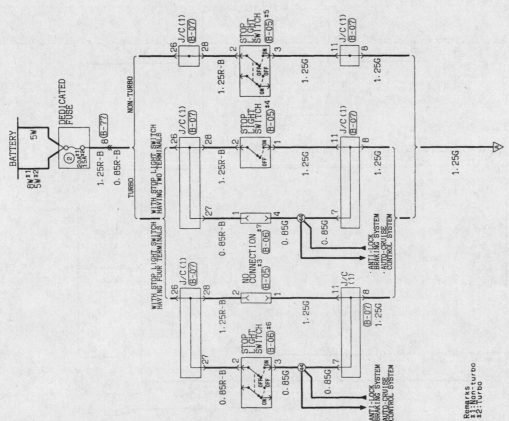

Typical brake light wiring diagram - 1 of 2

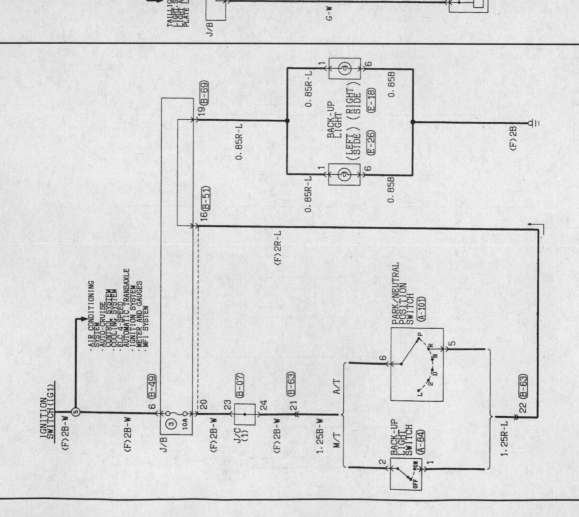

Typical instrument cluster wiring diagram (1 of 2)

Typical back-up light wiring diagram

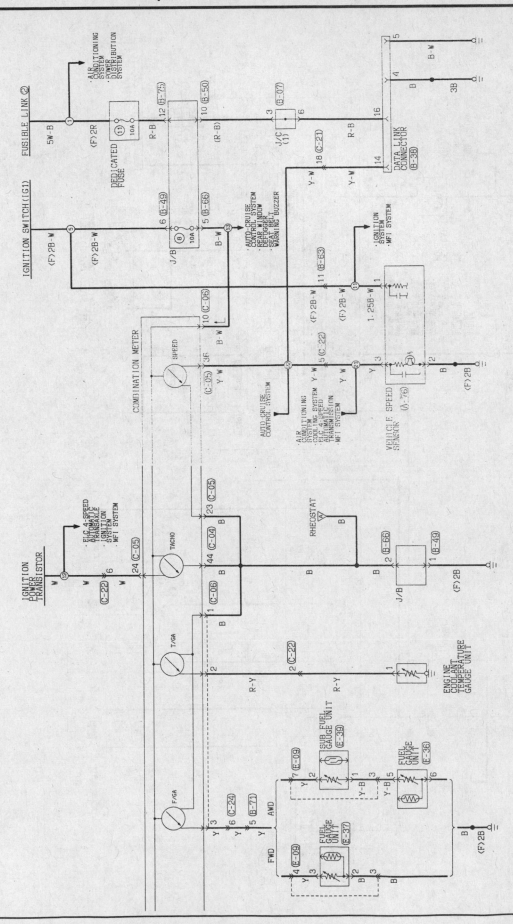

Typical instrument cluster wiring diagram (2 of 2)

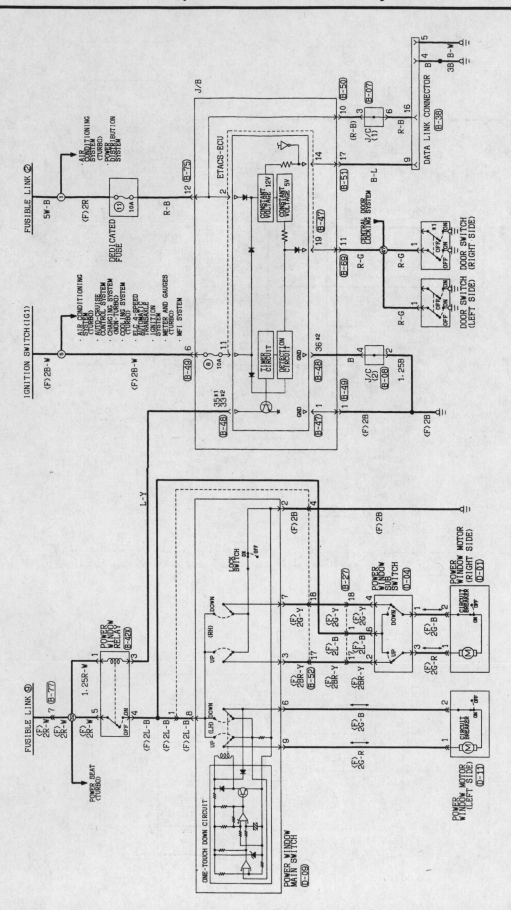

Typical power window wiring diagram

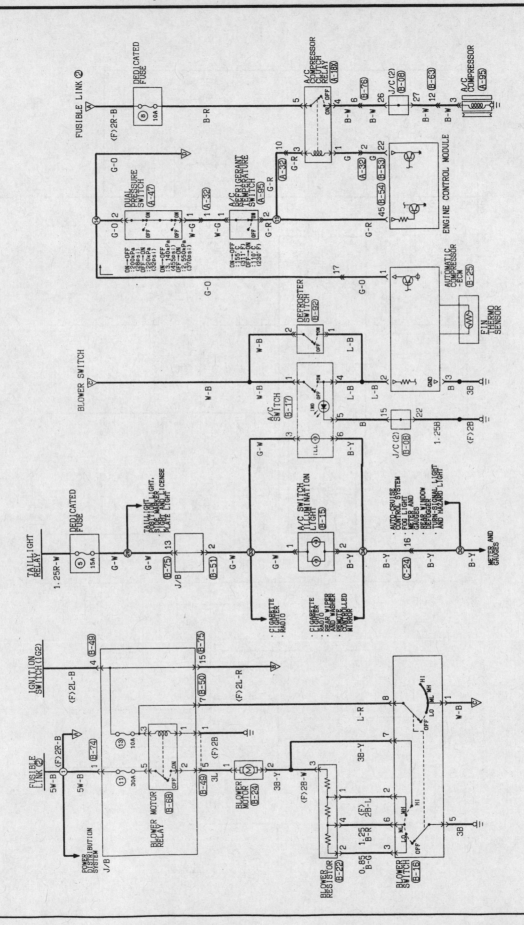

Typical air conditioning wiring diagram (1 of 2)

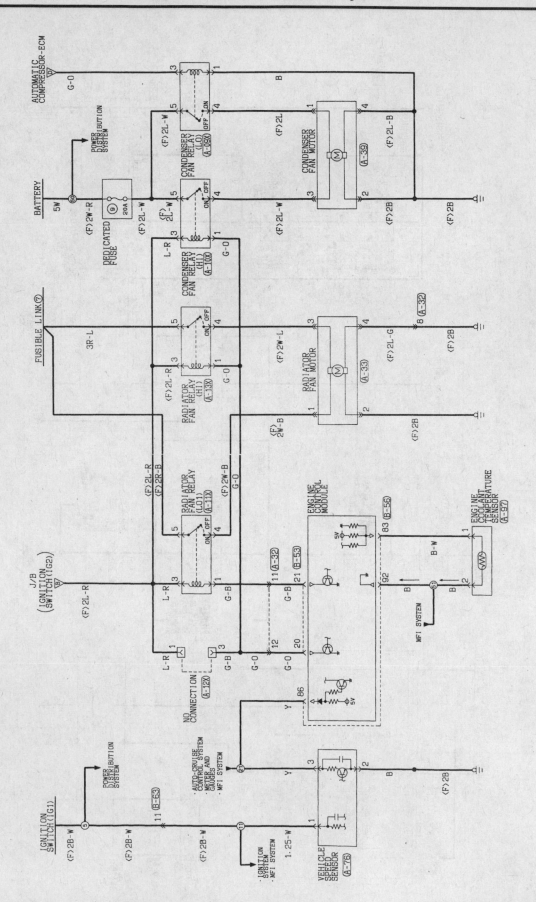

Typical air conditioning wiring diagram (2 of 2)

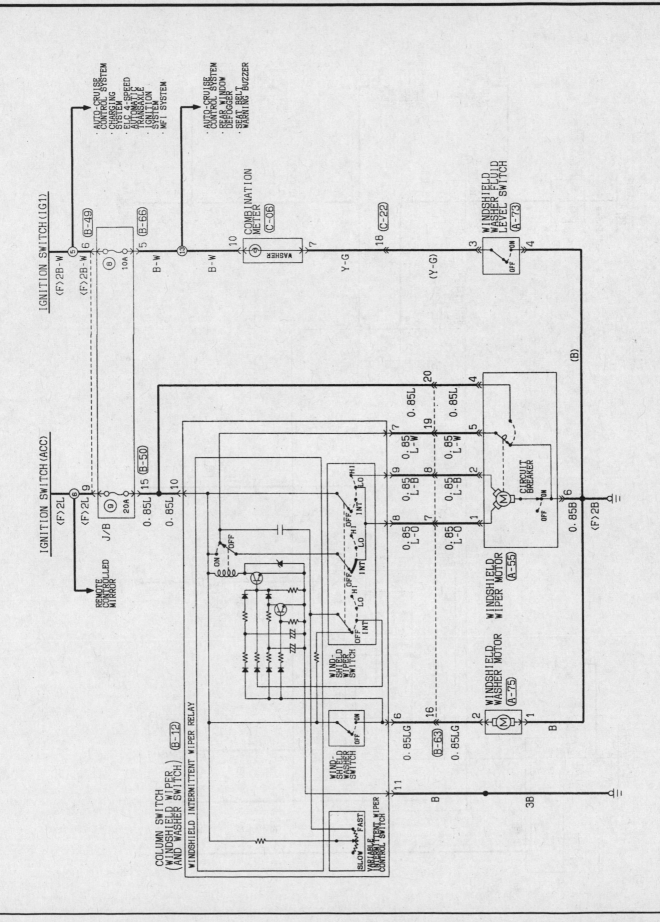

Typical front windshield wiper and washer wiring diagram

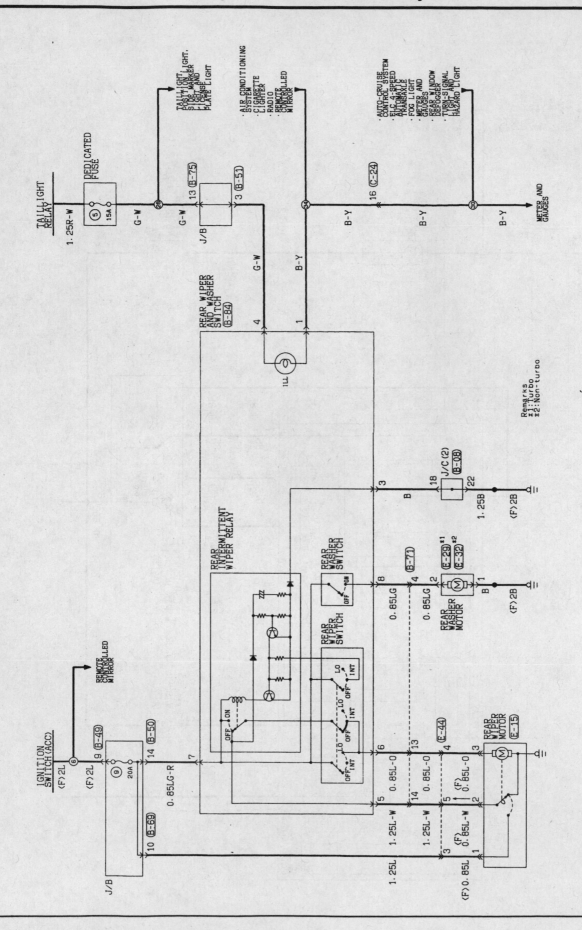

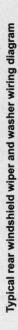

Typical rear windshield wiper and washer wiring diagram

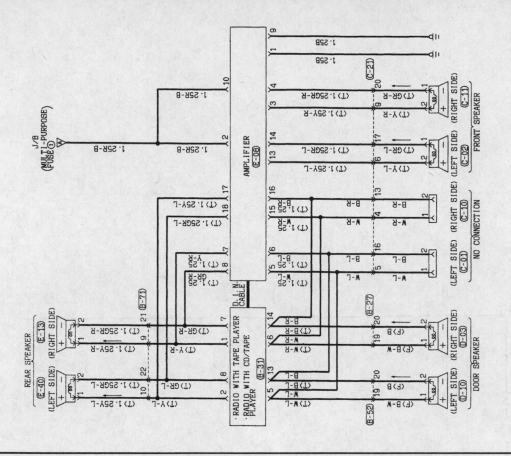

Typical audio system wiring diagram (2 of 2)

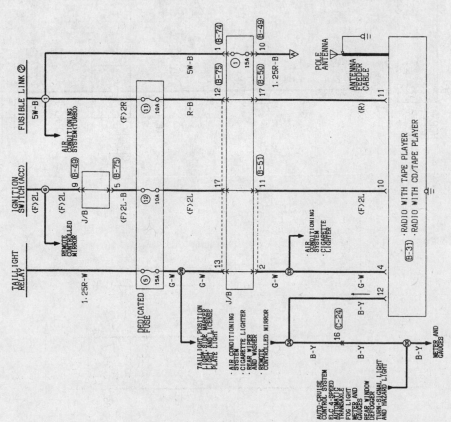

Typical audio system wiring diagram (1 of 2)

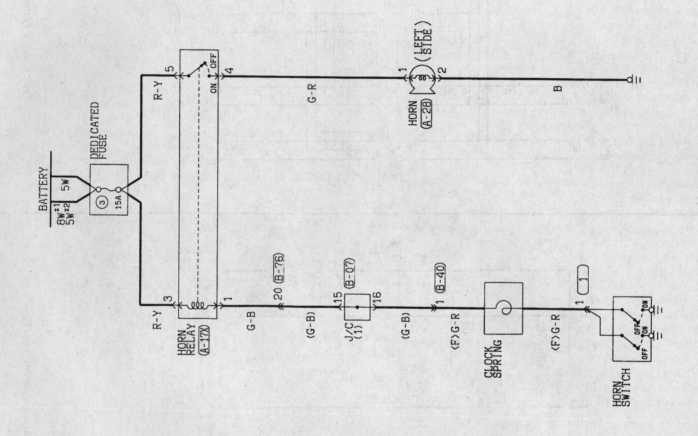

Typical horn wiring diagram

Index

Haynes Automotive Manuals

NOTE: If you do not see a listing for your vehicle, consult your local Haynes dealer for the latest product information.

ACURA
12020 Integra '86 thru '89 & Legend '86 thru '90
12021 Integra '90 thru '93 & Legend '91 thru '95
12050 Acura TL all models '99 thru '08

AMC
Jeep CJ - see JEEP (50020)
14020 Concord/Hornet/Gremlin/Spirit '70 thru '83
14025 (Renault) Alliance & Encore '83 thru '87

AUDI
15020 4000 all models '80 thru '87
15025 5000 all models '77 thru '83
15026 5000 all models '84 thru '88
15030 Audi A4 '02 thru '08

AUSTIN
Healey Sprite - see MG Midget (66015)

BMW
18020 3/5 Series '82 thru '92
18021 3 Series including Z3 models '92 thru '98
18022 3-Series '99 thru '05, including Z4 models
18025 320i all 4 cyl models '75 thru '83
18050 1500 thru 2002 except Turbo '59 thru '77

BUICK
19010 Buick Century '97 thru '05
Century (front-wheel drive) - see GM (38005)
19020 Buick, Oldsmobile & Pontiac Full-size
(Front wheel drive) '85 thru '05
19025 Buick, Oldsmobile & Pontiac Full-size
(Rear wheel drive) '70 thru '90
19030 Mid-size Regal & Century '74 thru '87
Regal - see GENERAL MOTORS (38010)
Skyhawk - see GM (38030)
Skylark - see GM (38020, 38025)
Somerset - see GENERAL MOTORS (38025)

CADILLAC
21030 Cadillac Rear Wheel Drive '70 thru '93
Cimarron, Eldorado & Seville - see
GM (38015, 38030, 38031)

CHEVROLET
10305 Chevrolet Engine Overhaul Manual
24010 Astro & GMC Safari Mini-vans '85 thru '05
24015 Camaro V8 all models '70 thru '81
24016 Camaro all models '82 thru '92, Cavalier -
see GM (38015), Celebrity - see GM (38005)
24017 Camaro & Firebird '93 thru '02
24020 Chevelle, Malibu, El Camino '69 thru '87
24024 Chevette & Pontiac T1000 '76 thru '87
Citation - see GENERAL MOTORS (38020)
24027 Colorado & GMC Canyon '04 thru '08
24032 Corsica/Beretta all models '87 thru '96
24040 Corvette all V8 models '68 thru '82
24041 Corvette all models '84 thru '96
24045 Full-size Sedans Caprice, Impala,
Biscayne, Bel Air & Wagons '69 thru '90
24046 Impala SS & Caprice and
Buick Roadmaster '91 thru '96
Lumina '90 thru '94 - see GM (38010)
24047 Impala & Monte Carlo all models '06 thru '08
24048 Lumina & Monte Carlo '95 thru '05
Lumina APV - see GM (38035)
24050 Luv Pick-up all 2WD & 4WD '72 thru '82
Malibu - see GM (38026)
24055 Monte Carlo all models '70 thru '88
Monte Carlo '95 thru '01 - see LUMINA
24059 Nova all V8 models '69 thru '79
24060 Nova/Geo Prizm '85 thru '92
24064 Pick-ups '67 thru '87 - Chevrolet & GMC,
all V8 & in-line 6 cyl, 2WD & 4WD '67 thru '87;
Suburbans, Blazers & Jimmys '67 thru '91
24065 Pick-ups '88 thru '98 - Chevrolet & GMC,
all full-size models '88 thru '98; C/K Classic
'99 & '00; Blazer & Jimmy '92 thru '94; Suburban
'92 thru '99; Tahoe & Yukon '95 thru '99
24066 Pick-ups '99 thru '06 - Chevrolet
Silverado & GMC Sierra '99 thru '06;
Suburban/Tahoe/Yukon/Yukon XL/Avalanche
'00 thru '06
24067 Chevrolet Silverado & GMC Sierra
'07 thru '09
24070 S-10 & GMC S-15 Pick-ups '82 thru '93
24071 S-10, Sonoma & Jimmy '94 thru '04
24072 Chevrolet TrailBlazer, GMC Envoy &
Oldsmobile Bravada '02 thru '09
24075 Sprint '85 thru '88, Geo Metro '89 thru '01
24080 Vans - Chevrolet & GMC '68 thru '96
24081 Chevrolet Express & GMC Savana
Full-size Vans '96 thru '07

CHRYSLER
10310 Chrysler Engine Overhaul Manual
25015 Chrysler Cirrus, Dodge Stratus,
Plymouth Breeze, '95 thru '00
25020 Full-size Front-Wheel Drive '88 thru '93
K-Cars - see DODGE Aries (30008)
Laser - see DODGE Daytona (30030)
25025 Chrysler LHS, Concorde & New Yorker,
Dodge Intrepid, Eagle Vision, '93 thru '97
25026 Chrysler LHS, Concorde, 300M,
Dodge Intrepid '98 thru '04
25027 Chrysler 300, Dodge Charger &
Magnum '05 thru '09
25030 Chrysler/Plym. Mid-size '82 thru '95
Rear-wheel Drive - see DODGE (30050)
25035 PT Cruiser all models '01 thru '09
25040 Chrysler Sebring/Dodge Avenger '95 thru '05,
Dodge Stratus '01 thru '05

DATSUN
28005 200SX all models '80 thru '83
28007 B-210 all models '73 thru '78
28009 210 all models '79 thru '82
28012 240Z, 260Z & 280Z Coupe '70 thru '78
28014 280ZX Coupe & 2+2 '79 thru '83
300ZX - see NISSAN (72010)
28018 510 & PL521 Pick-up '68 thru '73
28020 510 all models '78 thru '81
28022 620 Series Pick-up all models '73 thru '79
720 Series Pick-up - NISSAN (72030)
28025 810/Maxima all gas models, '77 thru '84

DODGE
400 & 600 - see CHRYSLER (25030)
30008 Aries & Plymouth Reliant '81 thru '89
30010 Caravan & Ply. Voyager '84 thru '95
30011 Caravan & Ply. Voyager '96 thru '02

30012 Challenger/Plymouth Sapporo '78 thru '83
Challenger '67-'76 - see DART (30025)
30013 Caravan, Chrysler Voyager, Town &
Country '03 thru '07
30016 Colt/Plymouth Champ '78 thru '87
30020 Dakota Pick-ups all models '87 thru '96
30021 Durango '98 & '99, Dakota '97 thru '99
30022 Durango '00 thru '03, Dakota '00 thru '04
30023 Durango '04 thru '06, Dakota '05 and '06
30025 Dart, Challenger/Plymouth Barracuda
& Valiant 6 cyl models '67 thru '76
30030 Daytona & Chrysler Laser '84 thru '89
Intrepid - see Chrysler (25025, 25026)
30034 Dodge & Plymouth Neon '95 thru '99
30035 Omni & Plymouth Horizon '78 thru '90
30036 Dodge and Plymouth Neon '00 thru'05
30040 Pick-ups all full-size models '74 thru '93
30041 Pick-ups all full-size models '94 thru '01
30042 Pick-ups full-size models '02 thru '08
30045 Ram 50/D50 Pick-ups & Raider and
Plymouth Arrow Pick-ups '79 thru '93
30050 Dodge/Ply./Chrysler RWD '71 thru '89
30055 Shadow/Plymouth Sundance '87 thru '94
30060 Spirit & Plymouth Acclaim '89 thru '95
30065 Vans - Dodge & Plymouth '71 thru '03

EAGLE
Talon - see MITSUBISHI (68030, 68031)
Vision - see CHRYSLER (25025)

FIAT
34010 124 Sport Coupe & Spider '68 thru '78
34025 X1/9 all models '74 thru '80

FORD
10320 Ford Engine Overhaul Manual
10355 Ford Automatic Transmission Overhaul
36004 Aerostar Mini-vans '86 thru '97
Aspire - see FORD Festiva (36030)
36006 Contour/Mercury Mystique '95 thru '00
36008 Courier Pick-up all models '72 thru '82
36012 Crown Victoria & Mercury
Grand Marquis '88 thru '10
36016 Escort/Mercury Lynx '81 thru '90
36020 Escort/Mercury Tracer '91 thru '02
36022 Expedition - see FORD Pick-up (36059)
36024 Escape & Mazda Tribute '01 thru '07
36025 Explorer & Mazda Navajo '91 thru '01
36028 Explorer/Mercury Mountaineer '02 thru '10
36028 Fairmont & Mercury Zephyr '78 thru '83
36030 Festiva & Aspire '88 thru '97
36032 Fiesta all models '77 thru '80
36034 Focus all models '00 thru '07
36036 Ford & Mercury Full-size '75 thru '87
36044 Ford & Mercury Mid-size '75 thru '86
36048 Mustang V8 all models '64-1/2 thru '73
36049 Mustang II 4 cyl, V6 & V8 '74 thru '78
36050 Mustang & Mercury Capri '79 thru '86
36051 Mustang all models '94 thru '04
36052 Mustang '05 thru '07
36054 Pick-ups and Bronco '73 thru '79
36058 Pick-ups and Bronco '80 thru '96
36059 F-150 & Expedition '97 thru '09, F-250
'97 thru '99 & Lincoln Navigator '98 thru '09
36060 Super Duty Pick-up, Excursion '99 thru '10
36061 F-150 full-size '04 thru '09
36062 Pinto & Mercury Bobcat '75 thru '80
36066 Probe all models '89 thru '92
36070 Ranger/Bronco II gas models '83 thru '92
36071 Ford Ranger '93 thru '10 &
Mazda Pick-ups '94 thru '09
36074 Taurus & Mercury Sable '86 thru '95
36075 Taurus & Mercury Sable '96 thru '01
36078 Tempo & Mercury Topaz '84 thru '94
36082 Thunderbird/Mercury Cougar '83 thru '88
36086 Thunderbird/Mercury Cougar '89 thru '97
36090 Vans all V8 Econoline models '69 thru '91
36094 Vans full size '92 thru '05
36097 Windstar Mini-van '95 thru '07

GENERAL MOTORS
10360 GM Automatic Transmission Overhaul
38005 Buick Century, Chevrolet Celebrity,
Olds Cutlass Ciera & Pontiac 6000 '82 thru '96
38010 Buick Regal, Chevrolet Lumina,
Oldsmobile Cutlass Supreme & Pontiac
Grand Prix front wheel drive '88 thru '07
38015 Buick Skyhawk, Cadillac Cimarron,
Chevrolet Cavalier, Oldsmobile Firenza
Pontiac J-2000 & Sunbird '82 thru '94
38016 Chevrolet Cavalier/Pontiac Sunfire '95 thru '05
38017 Chevrolet Cobalt & Pontiac G5 '05 thru '09
38020 Buick Skylark, Chevrolet Citation,
Olds Omega, Pontiac Phoenix '80 thru '85
38025 Buick Skylark & Somerset, Olds Achieva,
Calais & Pontiac Grand Am '85 thru '98
38026 Chevrolet Malibu, Olds Alero & Cutlass,
Pontiac Grand Am '97 thru '07
38027 Chevrolet Malibu '04 thru '07
38030 Cadillac Eldorado & Oldsmobile
Toronado '71 thru '85, Seville '80 thru '85,
Buick Riviera '79 thru '85
38031 Cadillac Eldorado & Seville '86 thru '91,
DeVille & Buick Riviera '86 thru '93,
Fleetwood & Olds Toronado '86 thru '92
38032 DeVille '94 thru '05, Seville '92 thru '04
Cadillac DTS '06 thru '10
38035 Chevrolet Lumina APV, Oldsmobile
Silhouette & Pontiac Trans Sport '90 thru '96
38036 Chevrolet Venture, Olds Silhouette,
Pontiac Trans Sport & Montana '97 thru '05
General Motors Full-size
Rear-wheel Drive - see BUICK (19025)
38040 Chevrolet Equinox '05 thru '09
Pontiac Torrent '06 thru '09

GEO
Metro - see CHEVROLET Sprint (24075)
Prizm - see CHEVROLET (24060) or
TOYOTA (92036)
40030 Storm all models '90 thru '93
Tracker - see SUZUKI Samurai (90010)

GMC
Vans & Pick-ups - see CHEVROLET

HONDA
42010 Accord CVCC all models '76 thru '83
42011 Accord all models '84 thru '89
42012 Accord all models '90 thru '93
42013 Accord all models '94 thru '97
42014 Accord all models '98 thru '02

42015 Accord models '03 thru '07
42020 Civic 1200 all models '73 thru '79
42021 Civic 1300 & 1500 CVCC '80 thru '83
42022 Civic 1500 CVCC all models '75 thru '79
42023 Civic all models '84 thru '91
42024 Civic & del Sol '92 thru '95
42025 Civic '96 thru '00, CR-V '97 thru '01,
Acura Integra '94 thru '00
Passport - see ISUZU Rodeo (47017)
42026 Civic '01 thru '10, CR-V '02 thru '09
42035 Odyssey models '99 thru '04
42037 Honda Pilot '03 thru '07, Acura MDX '01 thru '07
42040 Prelude CVCC all models '79 thru '89

HYUNDAI
43010 Elantra all models '96 thru '06
43015 Excel & Accent all models '86 thru '09
43050 Santa Fe all models '01 thru '06
43055 Sonata all models '99 thru '08

ISUZU
Hombre - see CHEVROLET S-10 (24071)
47017 Rodeo, Amigo & Honda Passport '89 thru '02
47020 Trooper '84 thru '91, Pick-up '81 thru '93

JAGUAR
49010 XJ6 all 6 cyl models '68 thru '86
49011 XJ6 all models '88 thru '94
49015 XJ12 & XJS all 12 cyl models '72 thru '85

JEEP
50010 Cherokee, Comanche & Wagoneer
Limited all models '84 thru '01
50020 CJ all models '49 thru '86
50025 Grand Cherokee all models '93 thru '04
50026 Grand Cherokee '05 thru '09
50029 Grand Wagoneer & Pick-up '72 thru '91
50030 Wrangler all models '87 thru '08
50035 Liberty '02 thru '07

KIA
54070 Sephia '94 thru '01, Spectra '00 thru '09

LEXUS
ES 300 - see TOYOTA Camry (92007)

LINCOLN
Navigator - see FORD Pick-up (36059)
59010 Rear Wheel Drive all models '70 thru '10

MAZDA
61010 GLC (rear wheel drive) '77 thru '83
61011 GLC (front wheel drive) '81 thru '85
61015 323 & Protegé '90 thru '03
61016 MX-5 Miata '90 thru '09
61020 MPV all models '89 thru '98
Navajo - see Ford Explorer (36024)
61030 Pick-ups '72 thru '93
Pick-up '94 on - see Ford (36071)
61035 RX-7 all models '79 thru '85
61036 RX-7 all models '86 thru '91
61040 626 (rear wheel drive) '79 thru '82
61041 626 & MX-6 (front wheel drive) '83 thru '92
61042 626 '93 thru '01, & MX-6/Ford Probe '93 thru '01

MERCEDES-BENZ
63012 123 Series Diesel '76 thru '85
63015 190 Series 4-cyl gas models, '84 thru '88
63020 230, 250 & 280 6 cyl sohc '68 thru '72
63025 280 123 Series gas models '77 thru '81
63030 350 & 450 all models '71 thru '80
63040 C-Class: C230/C240/C280/C320/C350 '01 thru '07

MERCURY
64200 Villager & Nissan Quest '93 thru '01
All other titles, see FORD listing.

MG
66010 MGB Roadster & GT Coupe '62 thru '80
66015 MG Midget & Austin Healey Sprite
Roadster '58 thru '80

MITSUBISHI
68020 Cordia, Tredia, Galant, Precis &
Mirage '83 thru '93
68030 Eclipse, Eagle Talon &
Plymouth Laser '90 thru '94
68031 Eclipse '95 thru '05, Eagle Talon '95 thru '98
68035 Galant '94 thru '03
68040 Pick-up '83 thru '96, Montero '83 thru '93

NISSAN
72010 300ZX all models incl. Turbo '84 thru '89
72011 350Z & Infiniti G35 all models '03 thru '08
72015 Altima all models '93 thru '06
72020 Maxima all models '85 thru '92
72021 Maxima all models '93 thru '01
72030 Pick-ups '80 thru '97, Pathfinder '87 thru '95
72031 Frontier Pick-up, Xterra, Pathfinder '96 thru '04
72032 Frontier & Xterra '05 thru '08
72040 Pulsar all models '83 thru '86
72050 Sentra all models '82 thru '94
72051 Sentra & 200SX all models '95 thru '06
72060 Stanza all models '82 thru '90
72070 Titan pick-ups '04 thru '09, Armada '05
thru '10

OLDSMOBILE
73015 Cutlass '74 thru '88
For other OLDSMOBILE titles, see
BUICK, CHEVROLET or GM listings.

PLYMOUTH
For PLYMOUTH titles, see DODGE.

PONTIAC
79008 Fiero all models '84 thru '88
79018 Firebird V8 models except Turbo '70 thru '81
79019 Firebird all models '82 thru '92
79025 G6 models '05 thru '09
79040 Mid-size Rear-wheel Drive '70 thru '87
For other PONTIAC titles, see
BUICK, CHEVROLET or GM listings.

PORSCHE
80020 911 Coupe & Targa models '65 thru '89
80025 914 all 4 cyl models '69 thru '76
80030 924 all models incl. Turbo '76 thru '82
80035 944 all models incl. Turbo '83 thru '89

RENAULT
Alliance, Encore - see AMC (14020)

SAAB
84010 900 including Turbo '79 thru '88

SATURN
87010 Saturn all S-series models '91 thru '02
87011 Saturn Ion '03 thru '07
87020 Saturn all L-series models '00 thru '04
87040 Saturn VUE '02 thru '07

SUBARU
89002 1100, 1300, 1400 & 1600 '71 thru '79
89003 1600 & 1800 2WD & 4WD '80 thru '94
89100 Legacy '90 thru '99
89101 Legacy & Forester '00 thru '06

SUZUKI
90010 Samurai/Sidekick/Geo Tracker '86 thru '01

TOYOTA
92005 Camry all models '83 thru '91
92006 Camry all models '92 thru '96
92007 Camry/Avalon/Solara/Lexus ES 300 '97 thru '01
92008 Toyota Camry, Avalon and Solara &
Lexus ES 300/330 all models '02 thru '06
92015 Celica Rear Wheel Drive '71 thru '85
92020 Celica Front Wheel Drive '86 thru '99
92025 Celica Supra all models '79 thru '92
92030 Corolla all models '75 thru '79
92032 Corolla rear wheel drive models '80 thru '87
92035 Corolla front wheel drive models '84 thru '92
92036 Corolla & Geo Prizm '93 thru '02
92037 Corolla models '03 thru '08
92040 Corolla Tercel all models '80 thru '82
92045 Corona all models '74 thru '82
92050 Cressida all models '78 thru '82
92055 Land Cruiser FJ40/43/45/55 '68 thru '82
92056 Land Cruiser FJ60/62/80/FZJ80 '80 thru '96
92060 Matrix & Pontiac Vibe '03 thru '08
92065 MR2 all models '85 thru '87
92070 Pick-up all models '69 thru '78
92075 Pick-up all models '79 thru '95
92076 Tacoma, 4Runner & T100 '93 thru '04
92077 Tacoma '05 thru '09
92078 Tundra '00 thru '06, Sequoia '01 thru '07
92079 4Runner all models '03 thru '09
92080 Previa all models '91 thru '95
92081 Prius '01 thru '08
92082 RAV4 all models '96 thru '05
92085 Tercel all models '87 thru '94
92090 Sienna all models '98 thru '09
92095 Highlander & Lexus RX-330 '99 thru '06

TRIUMPH
94007 Spitfire all models '62 thru '81
94010 TR7 all models '75 thru '81

VW
96008 Beetle & Karmann Ghia '54 thru '79
96009 New Beetle '98 thru '05
96016 Rabbit, Jetta, Scirocco, & Pick-up gas
models '75 thru '92 & Convertible '80 thru '02
96017 Golf, GTI & Jetta '93 thru '98, Cabrio '95 thru '02
96018 Golf, GTI & Jetta '99 thru '05
96020 Rabbit, Jetta, Pick-up diesel '77 thru '84
96023 Passat '98 thru '05, Audi A4 '96 thru '01
96030 Transporter 1600 all models '68 thru '79
96035 Transporter 1700, 1800, 2000 '72 thru '79
96040 Type 3 1500 & 1600 '63 thru '73
96045 Vanagon air-cooled models '80 thru '83

VOLVO
97010 120, 130 Series & 1800 Sports '61 thru '73
97015 140 Series all models '66 thru '74
97020 240 Series all models '76 thru '93
97040 740 & 760 Series all models '82 thru '88

TECHBOOK MANUALS
10205 Automotive Computer Codes
10206 OBD-II & Electronic Engine Management
10210 Automotive Emissions Control Manual
10215 Fuel Injection Manual, 1978 thru 1985
10220 Fuel Injection Manual, 1986 thru 1999
10225 Holley Carburetor Manual
10230 Rochester Carburetor Manual
10240 Weber/Zenith/Stromberg/SU Carburetor
10305 Chevrolet Engine Overhaul Manual
10310 Chrysler Engine Overhaul Manual
10320 Ford Engine Overhaul Manual
10330 GM and Ford Diesel Engine Repair
10333 Engine Performance Manual
10340 Small Engine Repair Manual
10345 Suspension, Steering & Driveline
10355 Ford Automatic Transmission Overhaul
10360 GM Automatic Transmission Overhaul
10405 Automotive Body Repair & Painting
10410 Automotive Brake Manual
10415 Automotive Detailing Manual
10420 Automotive Electrical Manual
10425 Automotive Heating & Air Conditioning
10430 Automotive Reference Dictionary
10435 Automotive Tools Manual
10440 Used Car Buying Guide
10445 Welding Manual
10450 ATV Basics
10452 Scooters 50cc to 250cc

SPANISH MANUALS
98903 Reparación de Carrocería & Pintura
98904 Carburadores para los modelos Holley
& Rochester
98905 Códigos Automotrices de la Computadora
98910 Frenos Automotriz
98913 Electricidad Automotriz
98915 Inyección de Combustible 1986 al 1999
99040 Chevrolet & GMC Camionetas '67 al '87
99041 Chevrolet & GMC Camionetas '88 al '98
99042 Chevrolet Camionetas Cerradas '68 al '95
99043 Chevrolet/GMC Camionetas '94 al '04
99055 Dodge Caravan/Ply. Voyager '84 al '95
99075 Ford Camionetas y Bronco '80 al '94
99077 Ford Camionetas Cerradas '69 al '91
99088 Ford Modelos de Tamaño Mediano '75 al '86
99091 Ford Taurus & Mercury Sable '86 al '95
99095 GM Modelos de Tamaño Grande '70 al '90
99100 GM Modelos de Tamaño Mediano '70 al '88
99106 Jeep Cherokee, Wagoneer & Comanche '84 al '00
99110 Nissan Camionetas & Pathfinder '80 al '96
99118 Nissan Sentra '82 al '94
99125 Toyota Camionetas y 4-Runner '79 al '95

Over 100 Haynes
motorcycle manuals
also available   8-10

Haynes North America, Inc., 861 Lawrence Drive, Newbury Park, CA 91320 • (805) 498-6703 • http://www.haynes.com